P9-AGE-526

Natural Disasters

Natural Disasters

Volume II

Famines — Hurricanes, Typhoons, and Cyclones

Editors

Marlene Bradford, Ph.D.
Texas A&M University

Robert S. Carmichael, Ph.D.
University of Iowa

Project Editor
Tracy Irons-Georges

SALEM PRESS, INC.
Pasadena, California   Hackensack, New Jersey

∞ The paper used in these volumes conforms to the American National Standard for Permanence of Paper for Printed Library Materials, Z39.48-1992(R1997).

Library of Congress Cataloging-in-Publication Data

Natural disasters / editors, Marlene Bradford, Robert S. Carmichael.
p. cm.
Includes bibliographical references.
ISBN 0-89356-071-5 (set : alk. paper) — ISBN 0-89356-072-3 (vol. 1 : alk. paper) — ISBN 0-89356-073-1 (vol. 2 : alk. paper) — ISBN 0-89356-082-0 (vol. 3 : alk. paper)
1. Natural disasters. I. Bradford, Marlene. II. Carmichael, Robert S.
GB5014 .N373 2000
363.34—dc21

00-058763

First Printing

PRINTED IN THE UNITED STATES OF AMERICA

Contents

Natural Disasters

Famines

(AP/Wide World Photos)

Famines recur periodically in many parts of the world, most devastatingly in heavily populated arid and semiarid regions that rely heavily on rainfall for the production of food. Famines are less deadly in modern times because of transportation improvements and international relief capacities.

Factors involved: Geography, human activity, rain, temperature, weather conditions
Regions affected: All

Science

The most common cause of famine is drought, although other weather conditions can cause famine conditions by inhibiting production of food. Severe cold late into a planting season, for instance, can reduce harvests substantially, as can excessive rains during the planting, growing, and harvesting seasons. Excessive rain tends to stimulate the growth of molds and blights, which can severely damage food crops. The Irish potato famine of 1845-1849 is an example of this kind of phenomenon. More often than not, however, weather-induced famines are a function of lack of precipitation, whether in the form of snow or rain, in nonirrigated areas that rely on seasonal precipitation for cultivation.

Research has shown that regional and global weather patterns are responsible for cyclical periods of drought in many parts of the world. The El Niño and La Niña phenomena, for instance, are known to affect weather patterns throughout the world. When the Pacific Ocean heats up, as it does in fairly regular cycles along the equator several hundred miles off the western coast of South America, moisture evaporates into the atmosphere and surges to the east in the Northern Hemisphere, bringing moisture-laden storms in its wake. Moisture in the Southern Hemisphere tends to head away from South America. In 1997, flooding related to El Niño struck as far away as the horn of Africa, where unseasonably heavy rains caused considerable damage in Somalia. El Niño periods are followed by La Niña. The waters of the equatorial Pacific cool down, and, where once moisture-laden storms coursed across the land, sunbaked days follow.

Although drought is a natural phenomenon that lies beyond the control of human science and policy, the activities of human beings combine with natural conditions to worsen droughts. For instance, deforestation reduces the capacity of foliage and land to absorb water, which leads to silting of rivers. The wind and water erosion brought about by deforestation deplete topsoil needed for cultivation. The loss of land for agriculture inhibits growth of the food supply, placing populations at risk, especially during prolonged droughts. Similarly, when land is overcultivated or overgrazed, it becomes less productive. In Bangladesh, where extensive deforestation has occurred, especially in the Himalayas, large-scale death occurs because of both floods and drought, whereas in the Philippines, where deforestation has been less extensive, mortality is not nearly as great, although the frequency of monsoons is about the same for both countries.

Apart from patterns of cultivation and deforestation, which are human-made contributing factors to drought, other human-made factors sometimes operating alone or in concert with drought conditions can cause famine. International and civil wars, for example, can inhibit production of food. A prolonged war can wreak havoc on agricultural production, inducing a largely human-made famine. Government policies that increase food prices can cause localized famine in regions where people have too little money to buy food. Governmental export of food crops is known to have caused famines by reducing domestic food resources.

Geography

Almost any part of the globe can be subject to famine, but some areas are more prone than others. Famines rarely occur, despite periodic drought, in the Western Hemisphere. Centuries ago, the populations of North and South America were predominantly nomadic. When faced with localized drought, nomads responded by migration. When widespread and prolonged drought occurred in the American Southwest, the thriving Anasazi people eventually migrated elsewhere. Generally, peoples in the Americas relied on a variety of crops, some fairly resistant to drought, for food. Moreover, the Americas were sparsely populated, so that widespread famine was less likely. Many areas were well watered, and rivers rising from mountain ranges provided water resources to the widely scattered populations, even in arid regions.

Historically, the continents most susceptible to drought include Europe, Asia, and Africa, where larger concentrations of population often subsisted on arid or semiarid lands more prone to drought. With larger populations, overcultivation of land and deforestation are more common, and these regions became even more susceptible to drought. Several consecutive years of poor rains could provoke widespread and devastating famine. Today, Europe, though still liable to drought, rarely experiences famine. Owing to its highly developed economies with agriculturally diverse production and extensive transportation capacities, famine has been eliminated as a major concern in Europe. Asia and Africa, however, remain highly susceptible to both drought and famine. Asia is heavily populated, and successive years of drought can severely limit food production. North Korea in the late 1990's experienced severe drought and famine. Africa, though less heavily populated than Asia, has seen dramatic population growth for several decades, and in semiarid zones, such as the Sahel region, overcultivation and overgrazing has placed extensive areas of land into highly fragile, drought-prone zones. Coupled with this, Africa, like parts of Asia, has experienced widespread political instability and civil war, which have exacerbated drought-related conditions and contributed to famine.

Prevention and Preparations

Although it is not yet possible for humans to prevent drought or to manipulate weather conditions that lead to drought, it is possible to predict droughts, to prepare for them, and to prevent famine. Because famine is normally a function of prolonged drought, there is usually plenty of warning before famines begin. The same satellite technology that allows meteorologists to predict weather can be used to prepare long-term forecasts. Remote-sensing satellite imagery can document the progress of deforestation and predict crop production.

Social science also comes to humanity's aid. When drought has existed for a year, farmers and livestock owners tend to sell off herds in order to buy food. Similarly, the next year's seed may be consumed in the first year of a drought by farmers who then sell livestock for the purchase of more seed. Yet another year of drought can put producers at immediate risk of starvation.

Migration patterns also suggest where the effects of drought are being felt most acutely. By paying close attention to these indicators, governments and international agencies are in a good position to know when famine is likely to make an appearance. If a country is further troubled by civil wars or regional violence, then famine is likely to be more acute and possibly highly localized.

Given the well-documented factors that contribute to famine and the attention the international community has given to early warning in the past several decades, there is no reason for famine to break out unannounced. However, predicting the localities of famine is one thing, and taking steps to prepare for a famine is quite another. Often, local governments or neighboring governments are reluctant to ask for food and other emergency supplies for fear of precipitating population movements that might be forestalled with good rains. Sometimes, governments are quite willing to overlook famine conditions in areas of their countries controlled by opposition rebel groups. In addition, well-meaning international food aid can actually depress prices for homegrown foods, thereby giving local farmers even less incentive to produce much beyond their subsistence needs. While governments take the primary responsibility for prevention of famine, international agencies have been established within the United Nations system to monitor famine emergencies. The United Nations Disaster Relief Organization did so until the early 1990's, and it was succeeded by the U.N. Department for Humanitarian Affairs and later by the U.N. Office for the Coordination of Humanitarian Affairs (UNOCHA), which coordinates a variety of intergovernmental, governmental, and nongovernmental agencies dedicated to provision of disaster aid. There is increasing awareness, however, that all such measures are highly remedial and that the most significant factor in preventing famine is the broader development of national economies.

Rescue and Relief Efforts

The existence of U.N. organizations for the prevention and mitigation of humanitarian disasters such as famine, when coupled with the phenomenal growth of private humanitarian agencies and the resources of wealthier donor nations, has substantially reduced mortality in modern droughts and famines. In the latter half of the twentieth century, despite the fact that global population more than doubled, mortality during famines rarely exceeded a few hundred thousand, whereas in previous decades and centuries famine often claimed millions of lives. This decline in famine-related deaths is due in large part to the global nature of modern communication and transportation systems, wider public awareness of famine emergencies, the existence of agencies dedicated to the prevention of famine, and to the emergence of disaster mitigation agencies within and among governments.

Within the U.N. system, apart from UNOCHA, the United Nations High Commissioner for Refugees (UNHCR) often provides assistance to people who have fled persecution and natural disasters such as drought and famine. The United Nations Children's Fund (UNICEF) is also very active in famine situations, providing food and medical attention to children who are victims of famine; the United Nations Development Program (UNDP) is similarly involved in famine detection and prevention programs. The World Food Program (WFP) provides food aid to areas experiencing food deficits, and a private agency, the International Committee of the Red Cross (ICRC) often provides relief in famine areas, especially those where civil war is a factor.

Nongovernmental organizations such as Oxford Committee for Famine Relief (Oxfam), Cooperative for American Relief to Everywhere (CARE), Catholic Relief Services, World Vision, Save the Children, and countless other agencies are heavily engaged in the provision of both long-term development and humanitarian aid. The U.S. government's Office of Foreign Disaster Assistance (OFDA) and its parent organization, the U.S. Agency for International Development, are engaged in the provision of emergency famine aid and prolonged development assistance. Likewise, the U.S. Department of States Bureau for Population, Refugees, and Migration provides emergency assistance to populations in distress. Most governments have similar kinds of agencies to provide managerial capacity for response to famine emergencies. Sometimes the military establishments of countries are in a position to bring their logistical capabilities to bear when famines rage out of control and demand immediate and extensive food-delivery capabilities. With a truly global famine mitigation system now in existence, there is little reason, other than political neglect, for famine to cause extensive starvation and death.

Impact

Famines affect more people than any other form of disaster. Although fewer people die from famine today than in previous centuries, it is still not unusual for a famine in a very poor country or in a country experiencing civil war to affect millions and kill hundreds of thousands. Famines can wipe out whole villages and destroy regions. The impact of prolonged famines and civil discontent is felt much more strongly in poor countries than in wealthy ones, where capacities and infrastructure to respond to localized drought is far more developed. Famine kills people in poor countries, not rich ones, which leads most scholars to conclude that long-term economic development is the single most effective way to prevent famine and mitigate its effects.

Robert F. Gorman

Bibliography

Aptekar, Lewis. *Environmental Disasters in Global Perspective.* New York: G. K. Hall, 1994. This is a trim and useful volume concerning the definition of natural disasters and their prevention and mitigation.

Curtis, Donald, Michael Hubbard, and Andrew Shepherd. *Preventing Famine: Policies and Prospects for Africa.* London: Routledge, 1988. An anthology of case studies, this book draws largely from African settings concerning the early detection and prevention of famine.

Field, John Osgood, ed. *The Challenge of Famine: Recent Experience, Lessons Learned.* West Hartford, Conn.: Kumarian Press, 1993. This is a fine collection of critiques of famine responses in several African cases.

Varnis, Stephen. *Reluctant Aid or Aiding the Reluctant: U.S. Food Aid Policy and Ethiopian Famine Relief.* New Brunswick, N.J.: Transaction, 1990. This volume combines balance and careful documentation of the political obstacles preventing timely famine relief.

Notable Events

Historical Overview

Famine has occurred with great regularity and deadliness throughout history. Even in ancient times, it was greatly feared. Along with death, war, and pestilence, famine is portrayed in the Bible as one of the Four Horsemen of the Apocalypse in the New Testament Book of Revelation, where the rider on the black horse carries scales to indicate the scarcity of grain and the need for it to be carefully weighed. References to famine are also frequently found in the Old Testament. Genesis describes famine as reasons for Abraham, Isaac, and Jacob at different times to migrate from Canaan to Egypt, and the story of Jacob's son, Joseph, indicates that famine had also struck Egypt. Ancient Egyptian records and art indicate that famine was a noteworthy reality of the land along the Nile. It is common even today, when famines attain great magnitude, to speak of a famine of "biblical proportions."

Famines occur when a widespread shortage of food causes malnutrition, starvation, and death. Famines are commonly associated with civil wars and conflicts in which food supplies are interrupted, as well as with prolonged droughts that limit food production. A population facing famine and malnutrition is often highly susceptible to disease. Thus, the biblical association of famine with war, pestilence, and death is based on empirical reality. The historical record testifies to this association.

The earliest known reference to famine was in Egypt around 3500 B.C.E. Egypt is situated in a very arid zone, and it depends on the regular flow of the Nile and the seasonal flooding that permits regular planting and harvesting, which in turn depends upon monsoonal rains in the highlands of East Africa. When the rains fail, so does the regular flow of the Nile, thus threatening agriculture. Parts of China, India, the great steppes of Russia, and the Sahel region of Africa are likewise prone to periodic droughts, and thus to famine. Even areas that are normally well watered can be subject to occasional drought, however, and they may put local populations at risk of famine. A traditional means of coping with localized drought and famine is migration to areas where food is more plentiful. This, in turn, has provoked conflict among migrants, however.

The consistently largest and most frequent fam-

Milestones

c. 3500 B.C.E.:	The first known references of famine are recorded in Egypt.
436 B.C.E.:	Thousands of Romans prefer drowning in the Tiber to starvation.
917-918 C.E.:	Famine strikes northern India as uncounted thousands die.
1064-1072:	Egypt faces starvation as the Nile fails to flood for seven consecutive years.
1235:	An estimated 20,000 inhabitants of London die of starvation.
1315-1317:	Central Europe, struck by excessive rains, experiences crop failures and famine.
1320-1352:	Europe is stricken by the bubonic plague, which induces famine, claiming over 40 million lives.
1333-1337:	Famine strikes China, and millions die of starvation.
1557:	Severe cold and excessive rain causes famine in the Volga region of Russia.
1769:	Drought-induced famine kills millions in the Bengal region of India.
1845-1849:	Ireland's potato famine leads to death of over 1 million and the emigration of over 1 million Irish.
1876-1878:	Drought strikes India, leaving about 5 million dead.
1876-1879:	China experiences a drought that leaves 10 million or more dead.
1921-1922:	Famine strikes the Soviet Union, which pleads for international aid; Western assistance saves millions, but several million die.
1932-1934:	Communist collectivization schemes in the Soviet Union precipitate famine; an estimated 5 million die.
1959-1962:	As many as 30 million die of famine in Communist China.
1967-1969:	The Biafran civil war in Nigeria leads to death of 1.5 million Biafrans because of starvation.
1968-1974:	The Sahel drought leads to famine; international aid limits deaths to about a half million.
1975-1979:	Khmer Rouge policies of genocide provoke famine in Cambodia; more than 1 million die of starvation.
1984-1985:	Drought in Ethiopia, the Sahel, and southern Africa endangers more than 20 million Africans, but extensive international aid helps to mitigate the suffering.
1992-1994:	Civil war sparks famine in Somalia, where hundreds of thousands die before international efforts restore food supplies.

ines have occurred in China and India, countries that have always had very large populations. Areas with large populations that rely heavily on monsoonal rains for agricultural production are particularly vulnerable to large-scale famine when several successive years of drought occur. The most devastating famines in modern times have occurred in China. As many as 13 million people perished in the great famine of

1876-1879, during which people sold their children or resorted to cannibalism. During about the same time span, an estimated 5 million people died in India from famine, as drought affected much of Asia. In the twentieth century, famine related to Communist China's Great Leap Forward occurred between 1959 and 1962, when it is estimated by some that as many as 30 million died. The largest death toll owing to famine in history occurred during the Black Death of 1320-1352, in which over 40 million are estimated to have perished either from disease or from starvation resulting from disrupted agriculture.

While drought is a major cause of famine, sometimes too much rain can lead to famine by interrupting harvests or destroying crops. This was the case in Europe from 1315 to 1317; bad weather in Ireland from 1845 to 1847 contributed to the blight of the potato crop, the death of 1 million Irish, and the migration of more than 1 million. The Great Irish Famine was also a function of British economic policy, because wheat exports continued from Ireland to Great Britain during the potato famine, and little was done to divert such food stocks to the starving.

Famine rarely occurs in modern times in wealthy, industrialized countries. Rather, it tends to be associated with poverty in the Third World, where subsistence farming is still the means of livelihood for millions. Thus, Africa and Asia still experience much famine, which is also a result of their being prone to political instability and civil war. Diverse food sources and less extensive population in much of South America and the Western Hemisphere generally prevent these regions from being prone to famine. Moreover, the emergence of international assistance agencies and foreign food aid have mitigated famine emergencies even in the more drought-prone areas of Africa and Asia in modern times, thus substantially reducing mortality.

Robert F. Gorman

1064: Egypt

Date: 1064-1072
Place: Across Egypt
Result: 25,000-40,000 dead

A combination of war, destruction of irrigation infrastructure, drought, and pillaging of Egypt's wealth and storehouses led to nationwide famine there in 1064. The Turks, victorious after two decades of warfare between Berber tribesmen, Turks, and Sudanese for control of Egypt, forced tribute from the Egyptian caliph and looted Cairo and most of Egypt. The Berbers overran the Delta region, destroying the Nile dams and canals. Beginning in 1065, a seven-year failure of the Nile River to stage its annual flood caused crops to wither from lack of water and from lack of nutrients deposited by the annual silting of the Nile flood plain. The starvation resulting from the combination of these three events was accompanied by eventual widespread cannibalism and plague. A good harvest in 1073 and the assassination of the Turk leader brought the crisis to an end.

Gordon Neal Diem

For Further Information:

Oliver, Roland, ed. *Cambridge History of Africa.* Cambridge, England: Cambridge University Press, 1977.

1200: Egypt

Date: 1200-1202
Place: Across Egypt
Result: More than 100,000 dead

From the earliest beginnings of agriculture until the building of modern dams in the twentieth century, the people of Egypt depended on the annual flooding of the Nile for survival. In a typical year, the Nile began to rise in late June and reached its highest level in the middle of September. The water then receded, leaving behind a thick layer of silt that allowed crops to be grown. Without this flooding, the land surrounding the Nile would become a barren desert.

Two months before the flooding of the Nile began in the year 1200, the water in the river turned green and acquired an unpleasant taste and odor. Boiling the water did not improve it, and Egyptians began drinking well water instead. Abd al-Latif, an Arab scholar who left an eyewitness account of the famine, determined that the water was full of plant matter and correctly surmised that this was caused by a lack of rain at the source of the Nile. Although the water eventually returned to normal, the annual flooding failed to reach its usual level.

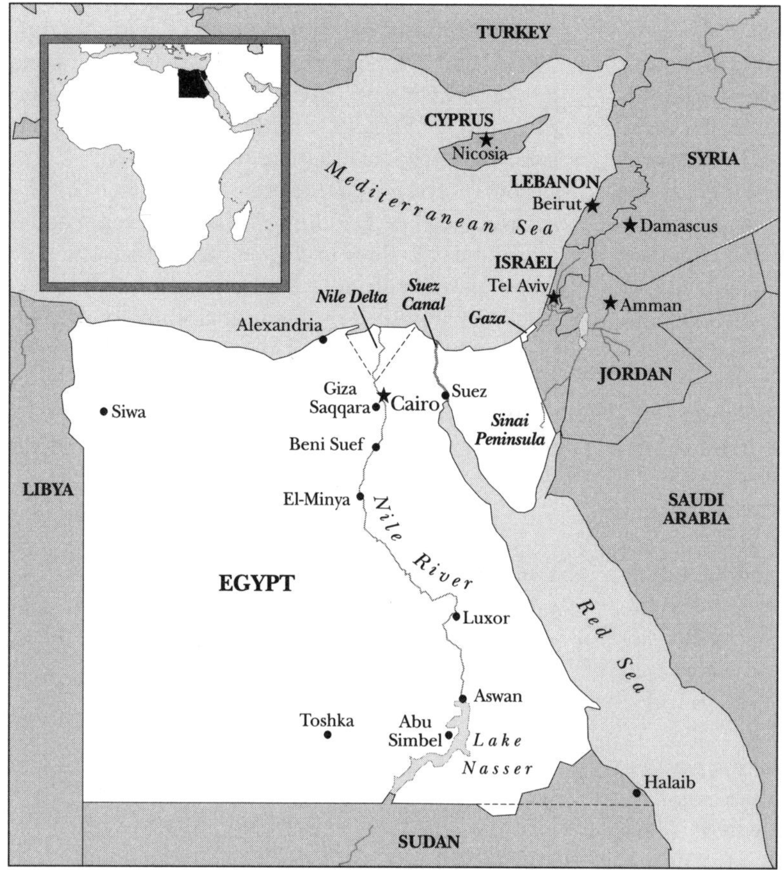

killed and eaten. The government of Egypt sentenced all those who ate the flesh of children to be burned at the stake, but the murders continued. Latif records that he saw the parents of "a small roasted child in a basket" brought to the ruler of Egypt, who condemned them to death. Ironically, the burnt bodies of those executed for cannibalism were released to the starving populace for legal consumption.

The famine spread from the cities to all parts of Egypt. Adults as well as children were in danger of being murdered, even by the wealthy. Workers, brought into homes to perform their duties, and guests, invited to social events, were sometimes killed and eaten by their hosts. The corpses of those who died of starvation filled every town. In Cairo, between 100 and 500 bodies were carried away daily. Latif visited a pile of about 20,000 bodies in order to study human anatomy.

A level of about 28 feet (16 cubits) was considered necessary to produce sufficient crops. According to records kept for six hundred years, the Nile had risen to only 24.5 feet (14 cubits) twenty times and only 22.75 feet (13 cubits) six times. Previous failures of the Nile to reach adequate levels had led to famine. In 1064, a famine that lasted until 1072 resulted in between 25,000 and 40,000 deaths. On September 9, 1200, the Nile reached its highest point for the year, at a level below 22.75 feet (13 cubits).

Knowing that this extremely low flood level would lead to severe food shortages, thousands of Egyptians fled the country to seek refuge in other areas of North Africa and the Middle East. Huge numbers of farmers left their unproductive fields, leading to overcrowding in the cities. By March of 1201, starvation in the cities reached the point where the poor were reduced to eating dogs, carrion, animal excrement, and corpses.

As the famine progressed, children, who were often left unprotected by the deaths of their parents, were

Meanwhile, in April of 1201, the water of the Nile again turned green, a sign that the annual flood would fail to reach the level needed to relieve the famine. In early September of 1201, the Nile's maximum level was about 28 feet (below 16 cubits), then immediately began to drop back. Although not as severe as the extremely low flood level of 1200, the rapid decline of the Nile ensured that starvation would continue.

The second year of the famine resulted in fewer deaths than the first year, mostly because the population of Egypt, particularly among the poor, had been greatly reduced. As an example of the reduced population, Latif records that the number of rush-mat makers in the city of Misr fell from 900 to 15. The population of the cities, so recently increased by refugees, fell so rapidly that rents decreased by as much as 85 percent. Even the price of wheat fell; although there was still a severe shortage of food, the number of buyers had been drastically reduced.

In early 1202, plague broke out in many parts of Egypt. The disease acted so rapidly that farmers fell dead while working their plows. In the city of Alexandria, funeral prayers were said for 700 people in one day. Between July of 1200 and April of 1202, the official number of deaths in Egypt was reported to be nearly 110,000. This number did not include many deaths that government officials failed to record.

In February of 1202, the Nile again turned green, leading to expectations that the annual flood would fail to reach an adequate level. Many Egyptians began to suspect that the source of the Nile had been altered in some way, so that flood levels would never return to normal. On May 20, 1202, a series of violent earthquakes struck Egypt, adding to the number of deaths.

The Nile rose very slowly from the middle of June to the middle of July, discouraging those who hoped for relief from starvation. After the middle of July, however, the Nile rose more rapidly, reaching a level of about 5.25 feet (3 cubits) and remaining steady for two days. The Nile then swiftly increased to a maximum level of about 28 feet (16 cubits) on September 4, 1202. Unlike the flood of 1201, which had declined quickly, the Nile remained at this level for two days, allowing adequate silt to be deposited, then dropped slowly. The return of the Nile to its normal behavior brought two years of devastating famine to an end.

Rose Secrest

For Further Information:

"Famine in Egypt: Failure of Nile Floods Brings Hunger to an Ancient Land." In *Great Disasters: Dramatic True Stories of Nature's Awesome Power.* Pleasantville, N.Y.: Reader's Digest Association, 1989.

Nash, Jay Robert. "Egypt: Famine, 1199-1202." In *Darkest Hours: A Narrative Encyclopedia of Worldwide Disasters from Ancient Times to the Present.* Chicago: Nelson-Hall, 1976.

1601: Russia

Date: 1601-1604
Place: Across Russia
Result: More than 500,000 dead

A combination of drought, traditionally low agricultural productivity, transportation blockages, price inflation caused by greedy grain merchants, and ineffective government military, economic, and welfare policies led to widespread famine throughout Russia from 1601 to 1604. Russian agricultural output was traditionally unreliable due to poor agricultural methods, reliance on peasant and slave labor, and settlement of the Ukraine and trans-Volga steppe lands, where limited rainfall, cold weather, and high winds constantly threatened to turn the region into a dust bowl. A year of drought resulted in famine.

In the years before the famine, war with Russian neighbors caused agricultural labor dislocations and led to restrictions on the movements of peasants and bondsmen. Peasants were prohibited from migrating in search of food when their own nobles could no longer provide. Suspension of these "forbidden years" acts by Czar Boris Fyodorovich Godunov came too late. Godunov also provided Russia's first government famine relief efforts by disbursing food from government storehouses to the starving peasants and slaves. These meager supplies were insufficient to prevent starvation and outbreaks of cannibalism. Desperately hungry peasants and runaway slaves resorted to banditry, bringing transportation of relief supplies to a halt, blocking access to the Baltic ports, and forcing military action to suppress the bandits.

The famine contributed to the transfer of power from the old dynasty to the modern Romanov dynasty. The famine and ineffective famine-relief efforts discredited the Godunov government and paved the way for rule by a series of pretenders to the throne and the chaos of the ensuing "Time of Troubles," eventually leading to the establishment of the Romanov dynasty.

Prior to Godunov, disasters such as famines were seen as acts of God beyond human or the government's ability to prevent or to relieve, although some local relief efforts had been carried out by the Church and generous individuals. Peter the Great, czar from 1696 to 1725, building on the efforts of Boris Godunov, established a series of grain storage houses at strategic points throughout Russia to permit rapid distribution of food to relieve future famines and to prevent future price-gouging in time of need. Peter the Great also experimented with confiscation of private grain stores, control of exports, government regulation of the grain market, and the importation of food from abroad.

Gordon Neal Diem

For Further Information:

Alexander, J. T. *The Time of Troubles.* Translated by S. F. Patonov. Lawrence: University of Kansas Press, 1970.

Dando, W. A. "Man-Made Famines: Some Geographical Insights from an Exploratory Study of a Millennium of Russian Famines." *Ecology of Food and Nutrition* 4, no. 4 (1976): 219-234.

1740: Ireland

DATE: 1740-1741
PLACE: Throughout Ireland
RESULT: 200,000-400,000 dead

Several years of poor potato and oat harvests, a savage winter in 1739-1740, an early and severe frost in 1740 killing the potato crop before it was dug, and grain embargoes and trade disruptions caused by a British war with Spain led to famine and to the deaths of 200,000 to 400,000 peasant farmers and villagers in Ireland in 1740. Famine and fever continued into 1741.

The potato displaced traditional foods in tenant-farming regions of Ireland because it could provide subsistence for a family on a smaller plot of land, thus allowing for the cultivation of more export crops, especially flax for linen. Adults ate up to 10 pounds of potatoes per day. A diet of potatoes plus a cup of milk at each meal yielded 4,000 calories per day, more than the 3,000 calories needed to sustain human health.

The 1740 Irish famine was one of a series of famines in Ireland and throughout Europe during the early 1700's. Food shortages and famines also occurred in 1728-1729, 1744-1745, and 1756-1757. Disruptions in trade due to war hindered minimal British relief efforts. The 1740 famine was the first major Irish potato famine, causing more deaths than the famous Great Irish Famine of 1845-1849, which was the last, best-remembered, and most romanticized of the Irish famines, owing primarily to the massive immigration of Irish to the United States as a consequence.

Gordon Neal Diem

FOR FURTHER INFORMATION:

Connell, K. H. "The Potato in Ireland." *Past and Present* 23 (1962): 57-71.

Crawford, E. Margaret, ed. *Famine: The Irish Experience 900-1900.* Edinburgh: J. Donald, 1989.

Cullen, Louis M. *History of Ireland Since 1660.* London: B. T. Batsford, 1972.

1769: India

DATE: 1769-1770
PLACE: Hindustan, India
RESULT: 3 million dead

An eighteen-month drought caused by a failure of the annual monsoon, together with a breakdown in the complex grain trade and transportation system, led to massive starvation with more than one-third of the province's inhabitants starving to death. Another 3 million died of starvation in neighboring Bengal Province, accounting for one-tenth of the population. In total, authorities estimate that as many as 10 million Indians may have starved in the famine.

Relief efforts were hindered by a complex grain-trading system involving layers of local grain merchants and transporters, regional trade intermediaries, brokers in market towns, wholesale merchants, and local retail shopkeepers. Storage of grain from one harvest season to the next was limited by damage from insects and moisture. The grain transportation system depended on a fleet of small-scale cart drivers and river barges. This system rapidly collapsed with the onset of famine conditions and a drought-reducing river transport.

Gordon Neal Diem

FOR FURTHER INFORMATION:

Banerjee, KumKum. "Grain Traders and the East India Company: Patna and Its Hinterland in the Late Eighteenth and Early Nineteenth Centuries." *Indian Economic and Social History Review* 4, no. 2 (1986): 403-429.

1788: Jamaica

DATE: 1788
PLACE: Plantations in Jamaica
RESULT: 15,000 slaves dead

The American Revolution and British prohibitions on trade with the United States following independence limited the importation of food supplies into Jamaica and other Caribbean islands in 1788. Hurricanes and earthquakes in 1780, 1781, 1784, 1785, and 1786 destroyed the island's food crops of plantains and corn; caused starvation among the slave population; led to outbreaks of dysentery, tetanus, and other infections; and caused wholesale depression within the island's economy.

The economic depression was compounded by 400 percent inflation on the few imported foodstuffs; a price depression in the worldwide sugar market, causing plantations to be unprofitable; inflation in the price of plantation slaves, caused by a monopoly in the slave market; rising shipping and transportation costs resulting from the American Revolution and European wars; physical decay of the plantation infrastructure and equipment because of hurricanes and earthquakes; and uninvolved English and foreign absentee landlords. In spite of their significant value as property, owners failed to provide the subsistence necessary to prevent starvation among the slave population. The disaster led to diversification in Jamaican agriculture, increased black-market importation of food from the United States, and a 1788 law requiring 1 of food crops be maintained for every 4 owned slaves.

Gordon Neal Diem

For Further Information:

Craton, Michael, and James Walvin. *A Jamaican Plantation: The History of Worthy Park, 1670-1970.* Toronto: University of Toronto Press, 1970.

Sheridan, Richard B. "The Crisis of Slave Subsistence in the British West Indies During and After the American Revolution." *William and Mary Quarterly* 33, no. 4 (1976): 615-641.

1790: Skull Famine

Date: 1790-1792
Place: Bombay, India
Result: Thousands dead

The failure of the yearly monsoon led to widespread starvation with an unknown number of dead during the Skull Famine in India in 1790-1792. Cannibalism was rampant. The event is known as the *Piji Bara*, or Skull Famine, because of the cannibalism and because the dead were too numerous to bury. This famine affected a wide area of India, including Hyderabad, Orissa, Madras, and Gujarat Provinces and the city of Bombay. It was one of a series of famines between 1770 and 1800 that are together known as the worst famines in the history of India.

Some British colonial authorities had argued for government migration planning and government price controls on grain as a way to reduce or eliminate famine. Bengal governor-general Warren Hastings argued in the 1780's that a well-regulated state could suffer no famines. British policies remained overwhelmingly in favor of free market and free trade and increased the intensity of the famine.

Gordon Neal Diem

For Further Information:

Ambirajan, Srinivasa. "Political Economy and Indian Famines." *South Asia* 1 (1971): 20-28.

1815: Year Without a Summer

Date: 1815-1816
Place: Areas around Sumbawa, Indonesia; parts of Western Europe, Canada, and the northeastern United States
Result: Total deaths unknown

On April 5, 1815, the 13,000-foot volcano Tambora on the Indonesian island of Sumbawa exploded with a force that modern volcanic indexes classify as supercolossal (7 on the Volcanic Explosivity Index). Eruptions continued for ten days, with that of the greatest magnitude, on April 11, felt for more than 1,000 miles. At least 10,000 people were killed by debris from the explosions, accompanying earthquakes, or tsunamis. For three days, almost total darkness existed as far as 200 miles from Sumbawa, with ash settling in an area of about 800 miles. Crop destruction led to famine and disease, which took approximately 80,000 additional lives on Sumbawa and the nearby island of Lombok. The so-called Year Without a Summer, which occurred less than twelve months later, was ascribed to a drop in global temperatures resulting from Tambora's fine ash, sulphur, and dust particles, which remained in the atmosphere for more than a year.

By late 1815, a few accounts of the Sumbawa disaster had reached Europe, including a detailed report by the acting lieutenant governor of the Dutch East Indies, Sir Thomas Raffles, who had ordered a survey of the affected area. However, no associations were made between this event in a remote part of the world and a series of natural calamities that began to affect parts of Europe, the northern United States, and Canada early in 1816. Among the first to be reported were tremors that were felt in Portugal, Great Britain, and Norway, in February, March, and June, respectively. Ships near the Azores also described an earthquake in that area.

By April, 1816, changes in the weather were becoming evident in North America. From April 12 to 18, daily snowfalls in Quebec totaled 4 feet. Lake Erie was not free of ice until May, and killing frosts were also reported in Pennsylvania and Virginia. Parts of Maine, Vermont, New Hampshire, Rhode Island, and New Jersey experienced a lack of rain. Although fruit trees bloomed in early May in Massachusetts, their potential crops were destroyed by frosts in the middle of the month. New Englanders who found their trees and fields coated in ice eventually learned that similar conditions existed in Virginia and Ohio.

Snow fell in Maine on June 6, beginning one of the worst weeks in that future state's history. Newspaper accounts told a familiar story of destroyed crops, fields covered with frost, and ponds with ice half an inch thick. On the morning of June 8, thousands of songbirds were found frozen to death. Recently sheared sheep died from exposure despite the attempts of farmers to shelter them from the cold. Temperatures rose by June 11, but it was too late to salvage most damaged crops. Newly emerged leaves showed autumn colors and soon began to fall.

Various unusual phenomena were reported from north to south. While Cabbot, Vermont, saw 18 inches of snow on June 8, the year's first hurricane struck the Caribbean islands shortly thereafter, two months ahead of schedule and initiating a season that would last until December. In early July there were heavy frosts in Boston, Albany, and Trenton; snow in Montreal; and coastal ice in the Labrador Sea. A large spot resembling a blemish on the sun led to speculation in American newspapers that it was somehow responsible for the bad weather.

Farmers along the East Coast tried to save the remainder of their crops, with farmers in Maine being forced to work in mittens in the middle of July. Maine, Pennsylvania, and New Hampshire also suffered from drought along with returning cold. New Hampshire experienced four killing frosts in August, while reports from Philadelphia that same month spoke of citizens being able to cross local streams without wetting their feet. Drought had curtailed much of Delaware's growing season, and to add insult to injury, it rained heavily at harvest time. In Amherst, New Hampshire, a long, dry summer was broken by a spectacular August storm, which helped to end the drought and ensured that some late crops survived. With similar weather patterns plaguing Maryland and Virginia, it is not surprising that most vegetables and corn crops were destroyed and the wheat harvest was meager in many areas. These conditions contributed to a growing westward migration, particularly from New England, to Ohio and Indiana. Maine lost as many as 15,000 inhabitants, although this was not a nationwide trend.

	Mean Daily Temperature, 1814-1858	*Daily Temperature, 1816*
May 10	52°	42°
June 10	58°	46°
July 10	63°	55°
August 10	63°	58°
September 10	57°	55°

Mean daily temperatures in London, England, in the nineteenth century compared to the Year Without a Summer.

News from Europe during the same period was bad, if not worse. A cold and excessively wet year led to the loss of much of the grain and vegetable crops in the German states, parts of France, Austria, and Switzerland. France's wine harvests were unusually late because of cold weather. Grain prices soared in Great Britain in anticipation of increased sales of American wheat. There were food-related riots in France. Famine conditions in Ireland would contribute to a typhus epidemic from 1817 to 1819.

Since 1816, scholars in many fields have attempted to link the obvious effects of the eruption of Mount Tambora with a variety of phenomena, ranging from sunspots to the effects of El Niño. Whatever the cause or causes, the Year Without a Summer passed into American and European folk memories and thus became a byword for the extremes of cold weather.

Dorothy Potter

For Further Information:

Dawson, Buck. *When the Earth Explodes: Volcanoes and the Environment.* Commack, N.Y.: Kroshka Books, 1998.

Francis, Peter. *Volcanoes: A Planetary Perspective.* Oxford, England: Clarendon Press, 1993.

Harington, C. R., ed. *The Year Without a Summer? World Climate in 1816.* Ottawa: Canadian Museum of Nature, 1992.

Pierce, Jodie. *Cultural Sensitivity to Environment Change II: 1816, the Year Without a Summer.* Center for Climatic Research, Institute for Environmental Studies Report 15. Madison: University of Wisconsin, 1974.

Stommel, Henry M., and Elizabeth Stommel. *Volcano Weather: The Story of 1816, the Year Without a Summer.* Newport, R.I.: Seven Seas Press, 1983.

1833: India

Date: 1833
Place: Guntur, India
Result: More than 200,000 dead

Poor rainfall caused the crops in Guntur, India, to fail in 1833. The combined failure of the colonial government to plan for migration out of the famine area and the continued free-market, laissez-faire trade policy concerning grain pricing and marketing increased the effects of the famine. About 22 million people were affected by the famine, as well as by the cholera that followed. The combined effects of the two took the lives of more than half of the district's population. It was twenty years before the agriculture and economy recovered.

Gordon Neal Diem

For Further Information:

Datta, Rajat. "Subsistence Crisis, Markets, and Merchants in Late Eighteenth Century Bengal." *Studies in History* 10, no. 1 (1994): 81-104.

Kumar, Dharma. *The Cambridge Economic History of India.* Vol. 2. Cambridge, England: Cambridge University Press, 1983.

1845: The Great Irish Famine

Also known as: The Great Hunger, the Great Starvation
Date: 1845-1849
Place: Ireland
Result: 700,000-1.1 million dead

The Great Irish Famine was the worst famine to occur in Europe in the nineteenth century and the most severe famine in the history of European agriculture. Indeed, some scholars argue that it was one of the greatest human ecological disasters in the history of the world. In addition to mass starvation, the Great Irish Famine changed the social and cultural structure of Ireland through eviction, mass emigration, and a heightened sense of Irish national awareness. It also hastened the end of the centuries-old agricultural practice of dividing family estates into paltry plots capable of sustaining life only through the potato crop.

This natural disaster, caused by a disease known as late blight (*Phytophthora infestans*) resulted in the country's potato-crop failure in successive years between 1845 and 1849. Ireland's population of almost 8.5 million people in 1844 plummeted to 6.5 million by 1850. Although historical sources differ (250,000-2 million dead), during the famine about 1 million people died from starvation, typhus, and other famine-related diseases. In addition, as many as 1.5 million of Ireland's people immigrated to English-speaking countries, such as the United States, Canada, Great Britain, New Zealand, and Australia, because of the famine.

Historical Background. When the New World white potato (Irish potato), native to the Andes Mountains in South America, was introduced into Ireland in the seventeenth century, the new crop flourished in the damp Irish climate, quickly becoming the country's major food supply. Before the introduction of the potato, beef, milk, butter, and buttermilk were the staples of the Irish diet. The potato grew in ever-increasing importance during the 1600's and 1700's, and the population exploded. The lower classes became more and more reliant on the potato they called the "lumper." Before the famine, an average Irish man consumed daily between 7 and 15 pounds of potatoes. Children ate potatoes for their school lunch. Since many did not own knives, one thumbnail was grown long to peel the potato. After the potatoes were boiled, they were strained in a basket. The family would gather and sit around the basket in the middle of the floor. Potatoes, accompanied with buttermilk or skim milk, composed the entire meal, which peasant families ate at every mealtime gathering.

The historical record leading up to the Great Irish Famine, arguably Europe's worst natural disaster of

the nineteenth century, must be examined so the impact of this tragedy can be understood. Since its colonization of Ireland in the twelfth century, Britain's primary economic goal was to extract the greatest amount of resources from its colony for the benefit of British and Anglo-Irish landowners. With the loss of its American colonies in 1775, and with the depression that resulted at the end of the Napoleonic Wars in 1815, Britain's attempts to increase agricultural profits in Ireland escalated. Seeking to force the Irish into greater submission, the British legislated penal laws that denied the Irish the freedom to speak their own language (Gaelic), to practice Catholicism, to attend school, to hold public office, or to own land. A tenant system was introduced into Ireland that gave British and Anglo-Irish landlords control of 95 percent of Ireland's land. Landowners who, for the most part, resided in England became known as absentee landlords and rented land to their Irish tenants, providing each tenant family with a cottage. Each cottage was surrounded by an acre and a half of land.

Some historians blame the ultimate depopulation of Ireland on the Malthusian notion of overpopulation, arguing that because the Irish population was too high, there was not enough food to feed everyone when the potato crops failed. After 1815, the expanding population increased the competition for land and forced peasant holdings to be divided and subdivided into ever-decreasing lots, eventually forcing many people to move to less fertile areas, where only potatoes would grow. The potato crop needed little labor to harvest, and a small acreage furnished a large crop yield. Some families had to survive on a quarter of an acre of land, and the potato was the only crop that would feed many mouths. Even before the famine, during the 1840's, it was common for laborers to hunger in the late summer before harvest. In addition, before the famine, housing and clothing were inadequate, and huts and rags were often the norm for the Irish peasants; a bed or a blanket was a luxury.

By the beginning of the 1840's, almost one-half of the Irish population, especially the poor agricultural communities, relied almost solely on the potato—which supplied vitamin C, amino acids, protein, thiamin, and nicotinic acid—for sustenance. In addition, the other half of the population consumed the starchy vegetable in massive amounts. Researchers explain that because of the nutritive value of the potato, Ireland's population had increased rapidly and reached 8 million by 1841. By then, two-thirds of the population depended on agriculture for sustenance. Simply, the Irish economy became dependent on the potato, and the failure of the potato crop in 1845 had disastrous results.

Causes of the Famine. The causes of famine are numerous and include drought, heavy rain and flooding, unseasonably cold weather, typhoons, and disease. In the late summer of 1845, the *Phytophthora* fungus, an airborne fungal pathogen that destroys both the leaves and roots (the actual potato) of the potato plant, and which originated in North America, established itself in Ireland, where it commenced to destroy the potato crop. The summer of 1845 also saw unusually cool, moist weather. Blight thrives in such climatic conditions and drastically affects even stored crops. In that season, the potato blight destroyed 40 percent of the Irish potatoes. After it struck in 1845, even more potatoes were planted because the pestilence was not expected to strike again. Unfortunately, the potato crop did fail again in 1846, and the results were even worse in 1847, when 100 percent of the crop was ruined. That year, 1847, when suffering reached its climax, is referred to as "Black '47."

In all, the potato harvest failed four years in a row, and the peasants had no food reserves. The famine situation continued unabated because of a deficiency of seed potatoes for new crops and the insufficient quantity planted for fear of continued blight. Unfortunately, the availability of only two genetic varieties of potato in Ireland at that time greatly increased the odds of crop decimation by famine. In hindsight, had other varieties of potato been available in Ireland the entire crop might not have failed.

Potato blight was not unknown in Ireland before 1845. A famine in 1740-1741 killed a quarter of a million people. The island nation struggled through crop failures and subsistence crises throughout the nineteenth century, including 14 partial and complete famines between 1816 and 1842. Because the Industrial Revolution never reached most of Ireland, there was little opportunity for employment other than agriculture.

Effects of the Famine. Although at the beginning of the blight the potato plants appeared green, lush, and healthy, as they did most years, overnight the blight struck them down, leaving acre upon acre of Irish farmland covered with black rot. Leaves curled up and shriveled, black spots appeared on the potatoes, and an unbearable putrefying stench that could be smelled for miles lay over the land. When the fungus had run its course, Irish farmers saw that the crop they relied on for life was destroyed. Ireland was not the only country hit by hardship. Although infected crops were present the United States, southern Canada, and Western Europe in 1845-1846, the results were not nearly as severe or deadly as in Ireland. While other countries turned to alternative food sources, the Irish were dependent on the potato, so the results of the blight were disastrous. As harvests across Europe failed, the price of food soared.

The hardest hit were the landless laborers who rented the small plots of land to feed themselves and their families. When their crops failed, they had to buy food with money they did not have, and prices continued to rise. Although in 1845 only part of the entire Irish potato crop rotted in the fields, as the years went on the blight continued unabated. When much more devastating crop failures followed in 1846 and 1847, millions lost everything: their homes, their few belongings, their families, and eventually their lives. The hardest hit regions were the south and the west of Ireland. During this time, roughly 1 million people, previously well fed on a diet made up primarily of potatoes, died. Peasants forced to eat the rotten potatoes fell ill. People died of starvation in their houses, in the fields, and on the roads.

Disease became rampant and widespread, and most who suffered from long starvation finally surrendered to typhoid, cholera, dysentery, or scurvy. Entire villages fell victim to cholera and typhoid. Indeed, more people died of disease than of starvation. Money became so scarce that the dead were often buried without coffins. Some sources record that during the worst of the famine, peasants died in the night and their bodies would be found in the morning partially devoured by rats. As time went on, unmarked mass graves became the resting place for many Irish. At the worst in 1847, the dead were being buried in trenches. The famine together with the accompanying plagues became known as the Great Famine to the British, the Great Hunger to the Irish middle class, and the Great Starvation to the Irish peasantry.

On this 1880 Harper's Weekly *cover, a woman on the Irish shore beckons for help with her starving family at her feet and the specter of death looming over the country.* (Library of Congress)

Results of the Famine. Before the famine struck, nearly half of all rural families lived in windowless, one-room cottages owned by landlords who were often ruthless. Also before the famine, some peasants were able to grow plots of oats or raise pigs to pay for the rent to their British landlords. After the famine, families who relied on the potato to keep themselves alive were left with nothing and had to choose between either selling their food to pay the rent or eating the food and facing eviction. If tenants failed to pay the landlord, the family was thrown out on the road and their homes were immediately burned to the ground so they could not return. During the Great Hunger, approximately 500,000 people were evicted, many of whom died of starvation or disease, while many others were relocated to poorhouses.

The British government legislated the Coercion Act in support of landlords who evicted those who failed to pay their rent. It also provided British soldiers and a police force to oversee the eviction of tenant farmers. Landlords evicted hundreds of thousands of starving peasants, who then flocked to disease-infested workhouses or perished on the roadside. Many times only grass made up their last meal. The streets swarmed with wretched, unsightly, half-naked beggars or, as they have been called, "the living skeletons" of the Irish. Villages were demolished; Cottages crumbled in ruins, abandoned by their tenants.

Britain provided financial assistance to Ireland in the form of loans amounting to 365,000 pounds sterling. In an effort to encourage an infrastructure to promote industrialization and modernize Ireland and avoid public revolt, the British government set up public works projects. However, these schemes proved useless because they were designed to not interfere with private enterprise. For instance, bridges were built over nonexistent rivers. Today, roads built by impoverished peasants—going from nowhere to nowhere—can still be viewed as part of the Irish landscape. For their efforts, the laborers received such low wages that they could hardly buy enough food to live on. In addition, this work was available to only a small percentage of the population. For example, in one Irish county, Kerry, in 1846, 400,000 people applied for 13,000 public works jobs. In March of 1847, the public works schemes were abandoned.

The responsibility to feed and house the poor fell to various charities. During the famine, 173 workhouses, built adjacent to dangerous fever hospitals, were constructed throughout Ireland. Some were so overcrowded and inadequate that one workhouse in County Limerick, built to accommodate 800 occupants, housed over 3,000 destitute people. Workhouse residents were fed watery oatmeal soup and were forced to wear prisonlike uniforms. Families were split apart into male and female dormitories. Soup kitchens were set up throughout Ireland by religious groups such as the Quakers. However, many times the soup was so weak that it was of little nutritional value. Even this inferior food did not meet the demand as crowds waited for hours outside the distribution centers.

By August, 1847, as many as 3 million people accepted food at soup kitchens. Although soup was given free to the infirm, widows, orphans, and children, the Poor Law Amendment Act of 1847 maintained that no peasant with a holding of one-quarter an acre or more was eligible for relief, which resulted in tens of thousands of farmers parting with their land. In its own efforts to alleviate Ireland's famine, the United States imported cornmeal, or Indian corn, which somewhat eased the food shortage, but the Irish found it unpalatable.

The Emigration of the Irish. Emigration was the only alternative to eviction or the poorhouse. Although the practice predated the famine, emigration rose to over 2 million from 1845 to 1855. When landlords began to issue notices to their tenants to appear in court for nonpayment of rent, the fear of imprisonment caused families to flee their homes for English towns and cities, and if they had the money, to the United States, Canada, New Zealand, and Australia. Most who emigrated did so at their own expense and sent money back to their relatives to follow them. Although during the famine more than 1 million Irish fled their country, many of the Catholic peasantry remained in their native land. The Catholic Church in part discouraged emigration out of fear that the Irish would lose their faith if they lived in Protestant Britain and America.

The famine, however, continued to drive new waves of emigration, thus shaping the histories of the countries where Irish immigrants found new homes. The peak rate of emigration occurred in 1851, when 250,000 left Ireland, continuing through the 1850's and into the 1860's. Centuries after the famine, the far-reaching impact and results are evident in the number of Irish descendants scattered throughout the globe.

Even emigration proved no remedy for the plight of the starving Irish. According to British Poor Laws, landlords were responsible for 12 pounds a year support for peasants sent to the workhouses. Instead, some landlords sent their tenants to Canada at a cost of 6 pounds each. Many of those who survived later made their way across the Canadian border into the United States. Desperate Irish often crowded onto structurally unsafe, overcrowded, understocked, disease-ridden boats called "coffin ships." Thousands of fleeing Irish carried diseases aboard or developed fever on the voyage. Many never saw land again or died shortly after they reached their destination. In several cases, these vessels reached the end of their voyage after losing one-third to one-half of their passengers.

The survivors arrived in North America hardly able to walk, owing to sickness and starvation. The streets of Montreal, Canada, were filled with impoverished emigrants from Ireland, many with typhoid. The Grosse Île, Quebec, fever hospital was overrun with sick and dying infants. In August of 1989, during an address on Grosse Île, Dr. Edward J. Brennan, Ireland's ambassador to Canada, called the Great Famine Ireland's holocaust and the Irish people the first boat people of modern Europe.

Irish Anger Rises. The famine convinced Irish citizens and Irish Americans of the compelling necessity for intensified national awareness and political change. The poor did not readily accept their fate; food riots broke out, and secret political and militant societies increased their activity. Some greatly alarmed Irish believed that the potato would be permanently destroyed. Spiraling crime and disobedience were countered with repression and violence. The unemployed roamed the country, begging and sleeping in ditches. Fifty thousand British soldiers occupied the country, backed up in every town and village by an armed police force. Landlords were shot. During one of the worst famine years, landlord Major Denis Mahon was assassinated by his tenants following his attempt to mass-evict 8,000 of his destitute tenants from his 30,000-acre estate. Ireland was in ruins.

Although the British government spent an estimated 8 million pounds on Irish relief, ineffective measures aimed at alleviating its neighboring island's distress resulted in deep and increased hostilities against British rule. Particularly disturbing was the increased exportation of Irish grain and meat to Britain during this time of famine because the starving Irish people could not afford to purchase these provisions themselves. Landowners continued to make profits through the export of Irish food as well as wool and flax. Historical records show that all through the famine, food—wheat, oats, barley, butter, eggs, beef, and pork—was exported from Ireland in large quantities. In fact, eight ships left Ireland daily carrying food that could have saved thousands of lives. About 4,000 shiploads of food sailed into Liverpool alone in the darkest famine year, 1847.

Despite famine conditions, taxes, rents, and food exports were collected in excess of 6 million pounds and sent to British landlords. During the famine, an average of 2 million tons of wheat was annually shipped out of Ireland, an amount that could have fed the whole population. One scholar claimed that for every ship that came to Ireland with food, there were six ships sailing out. The British government's Coercion Act ensured that British soldiers and a police force were used to protect food for export from the starving.

Responsibility for the Famine. Many historians still place blame on Britain for allowing so many of Ireland's population to die. After all, Ireland was at this time part of the United Kingdom, the wealthiest empire in the world. Although the British government provided relief for Ireland's starving, it was severely criticized for its delayed response; their efforts to relieve the famine were insufficient. For instance, the first step the British took to relieve the catastrophic situation was to send a shipload of scientists to study the cause of the potato failure. The British were further condemned for centuries of political oppression of Ireland as the underlying cause of the famine. Starvation among the peasants was blamed on a colonial system that made Ireland financially and physically dependent on the potato in the first place. The Irish patriot labor leader James Connolly argued that the British administration of Ireland during the famine was an enormous crime against the human race.

No doubt insensitivity toward the Irish contributed to Britain's failure to take swift and comprehensive action in the force of Ireland's disaster. Charles Trevelyn, secretary of the British Treasury during the famine, claimed outright that the government's function was not to supply food, and Lord Clarendon, Viceroy of Ireland during the famine, referred to the evictions and emigrations that resulted from the famine as a blessing for the Irish economy. Additionally, although Prime Minister Sir Robert Peel attempted relief efforts in 1845 and early 1846 by repealing the Corn Laws (protective tariffs that enabled the Irish to import grain from North America), his successor, the liberal Lord John Russell, supported a policy of nonintervention, in keeping with the laissez-faire philosophy that dominated the era's British economic policy. Government officials maintained the belief that it was counterproductive to interfere in economics and placed the burden of relief for the starving peasantry unto the Irish landowners.

Historians today are attempting to shed light on the reasons behind the famine, stressing that although the potato crop failed, a state of famine per se did not exist in Ireland, because other food, such as grain, poultry, beef, lamb, and pork, was available. Basically, there was no shortage of food. Profits, some scholars stress, came before people's needs, and while the blight provided the catalyst for the famine, the disaster was essentially human-made—the Irish people were the victims of economics, politics, and ignorance. Well-known Irish short-story writer Frank O'Connor once observed that "famine" is a useful word used instead of "genocide" or "extermination." The author John Mitchell in 1861 declared that the Irish people died of hunger in the midst of food they themselves had created, and in 1904 Michael Davitt, the founder of the Irish Land League, called the Irish famine a holocaust.

Long-Term Consequences of the Famine. The famine proved to be a watershed in the demographic history of Ireland. Ireland's population continued to decline in the decades following the famine, owing to emigration and lower birth rates, which ultimately allowed for increased landholdings. By 1900, 2.5 million more of Ireland's people had crossed the Atlantic. By the time Ireland achieved independence in 1921, its population was barely half of what it had been in the early 1840's. In their new homes, emigrant men were provided with manual labor jobs on construction sites, roads, and railways, while Irish women were hired as domestics. In time, Irish emigrants found opportunities for success never known in their homeland. For instance, automobile tycoon Henry Ford's grandfather was one such Irish famine emigrant, as was twenty-six-year-old Patrick Kennedy, the great-grandfather of President John F. Kennedy.

The famine was the most tragic and significant event in Irish history. Mary Robinson, the president of Ireland from 1990 to 1997, described the famine as the instrumental event in shaping the Irish as a people, defining their will to survive and their sense of human vulnerability. No one can fully voice the extent or the severity of the suffering endured by the Irish people from 1845 to 1850.

M. Casey Diana

For Further Information:

Foster, R. F. *The Oxford Illustrated History of Ireland.* Oxford, England: Oxford University Press, 1989. Although it only donates two pages to the Great Irish Famine, this book provides the detailed historical background necessary for a deeper understanding of Ireland's disaster. Also considered is the aftermath of the famine and the effects of emigration on English-speaking countries.

Gray, Peter, and Sarah Burns. *The Irish Famine.* New York: Harry N. Abrams, 1995. Richly illustrated volume (150 illustrations) that explains the causes of the catastrophe, the relief efforts from all sides, and the impact of the famine on American history.

Kinealy, Christine. *The Great Calamity: The Irish Famine 1845-52.* New York: Roberts Rinehardt, 1995. Examines in great detail the social, political, and cultural considerations of the famine. The author pays particular attention to the British government's response to the catastrophe.

Laxton, Edward. *The Famine Ships.* New York: Henry Holt, 1997. A journalist of Irish descent, Laxton paints an interesting popular history of the sailing vessels that crossed the Atlantic during and after the famine years. Provides interviews with descendants of emigrants. Color paintings and illustrations and fascinating memorabilia, such as ship artifacts and tickets, support the written text.

O'Cathaoir, Brendan. *Famine Diary.* Dublin: Irish Academic Press, 1998. Absorbing account of the Great Irish Famine from newspaper articles, letters, and official documents that detail evictions, diseases, and the appalling conditions in the poorhouses.

Percival, John. *The Great Famine: Ireland's Potato Famine 1845-51.* New York: TV Books, 1996. Draws on letters, firsthand accounts, and oral tradition passed down through generations. Includes eight pages of color illustrations.

Woodham-Smith, Cecil, and Charles Woodham. *The Great Hunger: Ireland, 1846-1849.* New York: Penguin, 1995. Well-researched and documented text, this is a complete account of the political, social, and cultural environments surrounding the Irish famine. The author pays particular attention to the Canadian emigrant experience, including the horrors of the Grosse Île, Quebec, fever hospital. Although criticized for being scholarly and too dense, the book is rich in historical detail.

1846: The Donner Party

Date: October 27, 1846-April 21, 1847
Place: Truckee Lake (now Donner Lake), California
Result: 42 dead

Starting out on the Oregon Trail, members of the Donner family had every reason to be confident. They had three sturdy wagons stowed with provi-

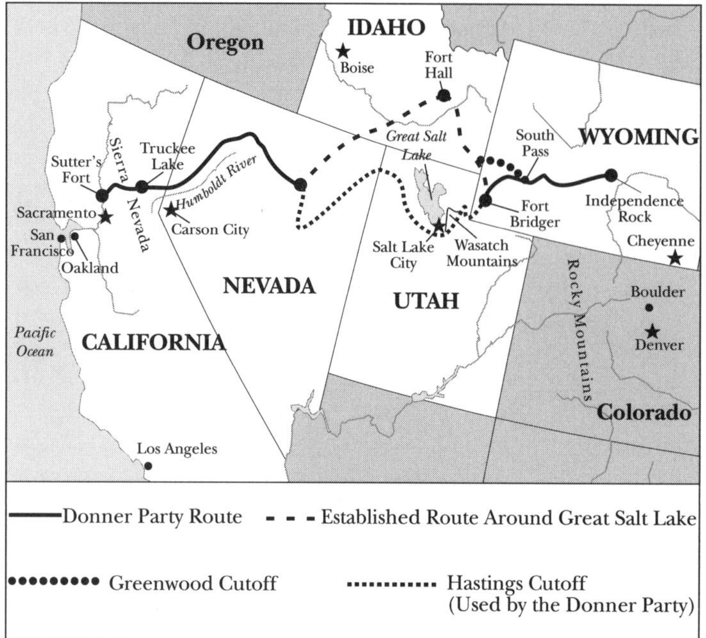

sions, including rations of 175 to 200 pounds of flour and 150 pounds of bacon for each adult. Their friends, the Reed family, also brought similar rations, adding cornmeal, "jerked" (preserved) meat, dried beans, and fruit. No one imagined that a few months later they would be trapped by snow and suffer starvation. They would be reduced to eating ox hide and shoe leather boiled to a gluey consistency, mice, and even their pet dogs before ultimately consuming human flesh.

There were 16 Donners and 7 Reeds, but of these 23 only 7 were adults. Men were hired to drive the oxen, hunt game, and, if necessary, fight Native Americans. The Reeds and Donners joined a larger train for the trip across the Plains. At South Pass in what is now Wyoming, the Donners and Reeds were joined by other emigrants planning to take a new route, the Hastings Cutoff, to Sutter's Fort in the Sacramento Valley. In all, there were 87 people, including seven additional families: the Breens, Eddys, Graveses, Kesebergs, McCutchens, Murphys, and Wolfingers. They selected "Uncle" George Donner to lead. They were mainly well-to-do farm families with no mountain experience, following the directions in *The Emigrant's Guide to Oregon and California* by Lansford Warren Hastings.

Unfortunately, the guidebook failed to reveal that no one, including Hastings himself, had ever taken wagons through the cutoff. Personal ambition motivated Hastings to encourage immigration to California. Mountain man and fort owner Jim Bridger recommended the cutoff, hoping to increase business at his fort. Another mountain man, James Clyman, had warned everyone to follow the established route through Fort Hall, but the Donners and Reeds trusted the guidebook. Reed wrote that he expected to make the 700-mile trip to Sutter's Fort in California in seven weeks. However, the cutoff soon proved to be a disaster. There was no trail, and the steep terrain forced the Donner Party men to build a wagon road. It took sixteen days to travel 36 miles, after which the oxen and people were worn out. Next they faced a long walk over the desert south of the Great Salt Lake. They expected this to take two days and nights, but it took closer to six. They barely survived the caustic alkali dust and thirst; wagons had to be left behind, many cattle and oxen were lost, and, worse, they were almost out of food.

Winter came early in 1846. On October 31, when the travelers reached Truckee Lake in the Sierra Nevada, it was already snowing. They tried to cross the 7,200-foot pass but failed. When the fierce storm finally ended, they were trapped. Family groups established their own territories as they arranged shelter, with the Donners, who had fallen behind, below the lake at Alder Creek. Hunters were unable to find game on the frozen terrain, and most of the remaining oxen, mules, cattle, and horses were killed and frozen for food. As time passed, hoarded food was bartered or sold reluctantly. As the snow increased, the shelters became dark, stinking, vermin-ridden hovels, and the starving people often stayed in bed for days at a time. A group of 15 adults on homemade snowshoes, calling themselves the Forlorn Hope, struggled across the pass to get help. They were the first to resort to cannibalism, and only 7 of them survived. In spite of the four rescue parties who risked starvation themselves, many more people died in camp or during rescue.

One physically healthy man, Louis Keseberg, had been left in the camp until the end because he confessed to eating the sons of two members of the third rescue party. He was also accused of murder. In April, when the last rescue party arrived, Keseberg had filled kettles with human liver, lungs, and blood, while ox meat, uncovered by the snow melt, lay nearby. Because blood can only be obtained from freshly dead bodies, the rescuers concluded that Keseberg had killed Tamsen Donner, who had seemed healthy when she had chosen to remain in camp with her dying husband. Keseberg denied the killing. The woman's body was never found.

Of the dead, single men who were not related to the families died first and so were the first to be eaten. Fourteen males had succumbed by the end of January, but the first female death did not occur until February 2. After that date, children under five years old died at a high rate, in spite of the meat procured by the desperate mothers. Children between the ages of five and nineteen had the highest survival rate.

Spring thaws revealed the mutilated and severed body parts littering the camp. Some of the human remains were later gathered up and buried under a cabin, which was then burned by troops attempting cleanup. Skeletal remains and other artifacts have since been studied by archaeologists to discern the truth behind the conflicting memoirs and historical accounts. The tragedy of the Donner Party remains one of the most fascinating events in the settlement of the American West.

Margaret A. Dodson

For Further Information:

Diamond, J., and M. Paraskevas. "Living Through the Donner Party." *Discover* 13, no. 3 (March, 1992): 100.

Froncek, Thomas. "Winterkill, 1846: The Tragic Journey of the Donner Party." *American Heritage* 28, no. 1 (December, 1996): 28-41.

Hardesty, Donald L. *The Archaeology of the Donner Party.* Reno: University of Nevada Press, 1997.

Houghton, Eliza P. Donner. *The Expedition of the Donner Party and Its Tragic Fate.* Chicago: A. C. McClurg, 1911. Reprint. Lincoln: Bison Books/ University of Nebraska Press, 1997.

Lavender, David. *Snowbound: The Tragic Story of the Donner Party.* New York: Holiday House, 1996.

McGlashan, C. F. *History of the Donner Party: A Tragedy of the Sierra.* 2d ed. Stanford, Calif.: Stanford University Press, 1947.

James and Margret Keyes Reed, surviving members of the Donner Party, in the 1850's. (AP/Wide World Photos)

Stewart, George R. *Ordeal by Hunger: The Story of the Donner Party.* New ed. Boston: Houghton Mifflin, 1960.

1876: India

Date: 1876-1878
Place: Bengal, India
Result: 6 million dead

In one of the most severe famines on record, 3 million people died of starvation and another 3 million died in an outbreak of cholera accompanying the famine in India in 1876-1878. The monsoon failed to occur in southern India in 1876, retarding crop growth. The following year the monsoon in southern India produced so much rain that the crops were flooded, thus preventing a harvest for a second year. That same year, the monsoon failed to occur in northern India, leading to crop failure and famine in both southern and northern India. The two-year famine was worst in the Madras Province, where another 3.5 million people died of starvation. In total, more than 36 million people in India suffered from the 1876-1878 famine.

Indian authorities refused outside aid, especially from Western nations, for fear that borrowing to pay for the aid would bankrupt the national treasury and cause worse problems than the famine itself. India had suffered three additional recent famines, which taxed the authorities' ability to respond with aid relief. From 1866 to 1870, four years of drought over the eastern provinces of Bengal and Orissa spread to the northwest and central Indian provinces, killing 1.5 million people. Famine was followed by an epidemic of fevers in the northwest provinces, killing as much as one-fourth of the population. In 1869-1870, one-third of the population of the Rajputana Province died from famine. Portions of India also experienced famine in 1873-1874. The combined famines from 1866 through 1878 may constitute the longest period of famine on record.

Gordon Neal Diem

For Further Information:

Cronell, James. *The Great International Disaster Book.* New York: Charles Scribner's Sons, 1976.

1876: China

Date: 1876-1879
Place: Northern China
Result: 9.5-13 million dead

During the mid- to late 1870's, a protracted drought in the provinces of northern China precipitated one of the worst famines in recorded history. Five provinces, each with 15 to 25 million inhabitants, were severely struck by famine. In many regions it is estimated that 60 to 90 percent of the population died. All told, somewhere between 9 and 13 million Chinese perished from starvation, disease, and violence. Contemporary witnesses, both local officials and foreign missionaries, agreed that China had never before seen such a devastating famine.

Following three consecutive years of sparse rainfall and months of dry, dusty winds, the famine initially struck large segments of Shantung during the summer of 1876. Massive crop failures led to a desperate search for food. The eating of grass and roots mixed with ground clay resulted in sickness and usually hastened death. Several years into the famine, *The Great Famine* (1879) notes how a Christian missionary graphically described the suffering:

> [T]he people find it difficult indeed to purchase the necessaries of daily life. In all directions they seek these in vain, and try to get the grass covering the ground, in order to allay hunger. So they strip the bark off trees, and pluck up roots and grind the chaff to enable them to live. In ordinary times what the pigs and dogs would not eat, now the people eat, and may they not still be called men, not beasts?

As winter approached conditions worsened. Diseases such as typhoid and dysentery ran rampant. Millions attempted to migrate to neighboring provinces, hoping to escape death. Some residents resorted to pillage and banditry for food. In certain areas hundreds of people huddled together for warmth in huge underground pits. Corpses, too numerous for individual burial, were piled by thousands into mass graves. Countless women and children were sold into slavery and prostitution in an effort to obtain food. Ravenous packs of dogs and wolves roamed the countryside eating the dead and attacking the living. Parents killed their own children and committed suicide to avoid continued suffering. At the height of desperation, many turned to cannibal-

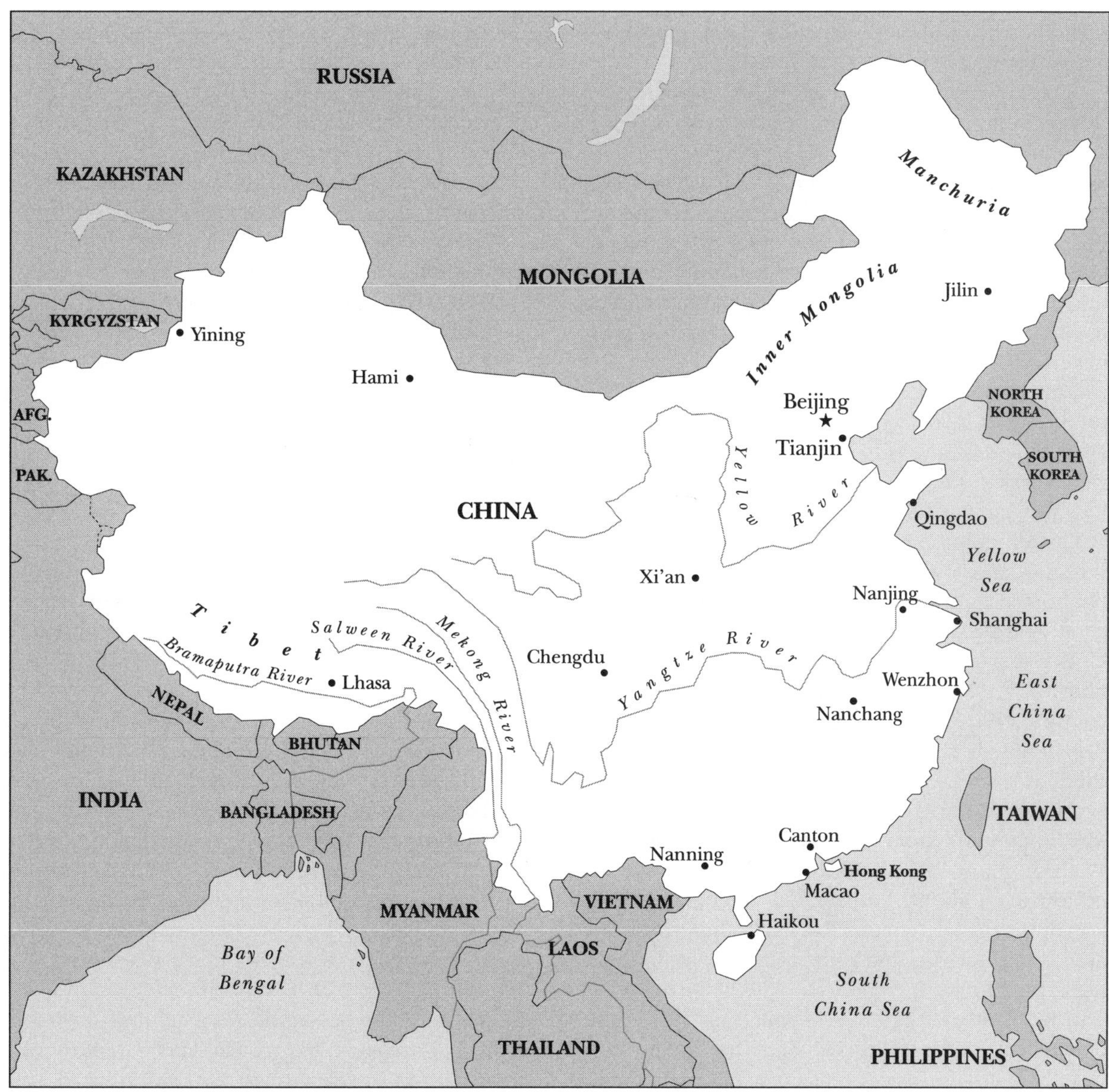

ism. As told in *The Great Famine*, English missionary Timothy Richard remarked in May, 1878:

> The eating of human flesh is a regular thing, and if the people were really dead before, there is little said about it, but if killed then litigations arise. . . . About one fifth only of the children in some places are said to be left, the rest have perished by hunger, disease or—what shall I call it? The butcher's hand! Whole villages are said to have disappeared.

In some areas, local merchants openly sold human flesh at the market; in others, horrific stories circulated of parents killing and eating their own children.

In addition to northwestern parts of Shantung, the famine affected large sections of Shanxi, Shaanxi, Henan, and Chihli. In these provinces, the landlocked and almost entirely mountainous Shanxi experienced the most devastation. Of a population of 15 million, at least 5.5 million perished, and only about 3.4 million received government assistance. Paul Richard Bohr's *Famine in China and the Missionary* (1972) relates how one Westerner described the terrifying scene in Shanxi, with many corpses lying together, remains of wanderers who had huddled together to await death.

Shanxi's dessicated, exhausted soil exacerbated the agricultural impact of prolonged drought. Poor communication combined with government inefficiency and corruption to worsen the famine's effects. Starving residents found it impossible to escape on the narrow, heavily rutted mountain roads. When grain could be transported to starving inhabitants via mules, donkeys, and camels, it was usually too little, too late. Frequently the animals needed for transport were eaten.

Relief efforts of the late Qing imperial government met with many obstacles. Since the late eighteenth century, the rulers in Peking had struggled with a series of massive rebellions and natural disasters. The Taiping Rebellion (1850-1864) destroyed the richest agricultural lands, cut off vast amounts of tax revenues, and cost millions of lives. As famine ravaged the northern provinces in 1876, floods caused major economic dislocation along five coastal provinces. Underlying all these problems, the total population had more than doubled since the mid-eighteenth century; even in good years, China could not produce enough food to sustain its burgeoning hundreds of millions.

Although the government brought in considerable money and grain to famine-stricken provinces, Western missionaries and Chinese commentators critiqued traditional bureaucracy, inefficiency, and corruption. Protestant and Roman Catholic missionaries contributed to the relief of famine victims, as did many Chinese merchants and gentry. In many instances, foreign relief efforts met with resistance from local officials, who believed that Westerners would foment rebellion. Some of the most active missionaries, such as Timothy Richard, pushed for eliminating the underlying causes of famine. Suggestions from Westerners, such as centralizing relief programs and building railways, were often rejected. Although vastly differing in their methods and outlook, Westerners and Chinese came together over humanitarian concerns for the first time during this famine.

Robinson M. Yost

For Further Information:

Bohr, Paul Richard. *Famine in China and the Missionary: Timothy Richard as Relief Administrator and Advocate of National Reform, 1876-1884.* Cambridge, Mass.: Harvard University Press, 1972.

Committee of the China Famine Relief Fund. *The Famine in China.* London: C. Kegan Paul, 1878.

_______. *The Great Famine.* Shanghai: American Presbyterian Mission Press, 1879.

Guinness, M. Geraldine. *The Story of the China Inland Mission.* 2 vols. London: Morgan and Scott, 1894.

Mallory, Walter H. *China: Land of Famine.* New York: American Geographical Society, 1928.

Perkins, Dwight H. *Agricultural Development in China, 1368-1968.* Chicago: Aldine, 1969.

Richard, Timothy. *Forty-five Years in China: Reminiscences.* New York: Frederick A. Stokes, 1916.

1920: The Great Russian Famine

Date: 1920-1922

Place: Russia

Result: Millions dead despite major Western relief efforts, more than 12 million fed by Western aid programs

Russian agriculture has been prone frequently to drought and famine. Indeed, in the years before the Great Famine of 1920-1922, Russia suffered drought and famine in 1891, 1906, and 1911. These were relatively minor events compared to the famine of the early 1920's, however. Several factors contributed to the exacerbation of this latter event. In 1917, already devastated by several years of fighting in World War I, czarist Russia fell to the Bolshevik Revolution. Although Vladimir Ilich Lenin withdrew Russia from the war, soon the Bolsheviks were fighting a civil war of their own against rival groups. Added to the devastation caused by years of war and civil discord, two years of successive drought substantially reduced harvest yields in the Volga River Valley, Crimea, Ukraine, and Armenia. By 1920, conditions in these regions reached critical levels, and, although the new Soviet government was reluctant to tarnish its socialist image, conditions were so desperate Lenin appealed to the world for assistance.

In the aftermath of World War I, many private and charitable organizations bore the brunt of providing the peoples of Europe, the Balkans, and Central Asia with emergency assistance as countries in the war-torn region strove to rebuild themselves. The United States was a major player in provision of relief assistance, and President Woodrow Wilson called upon

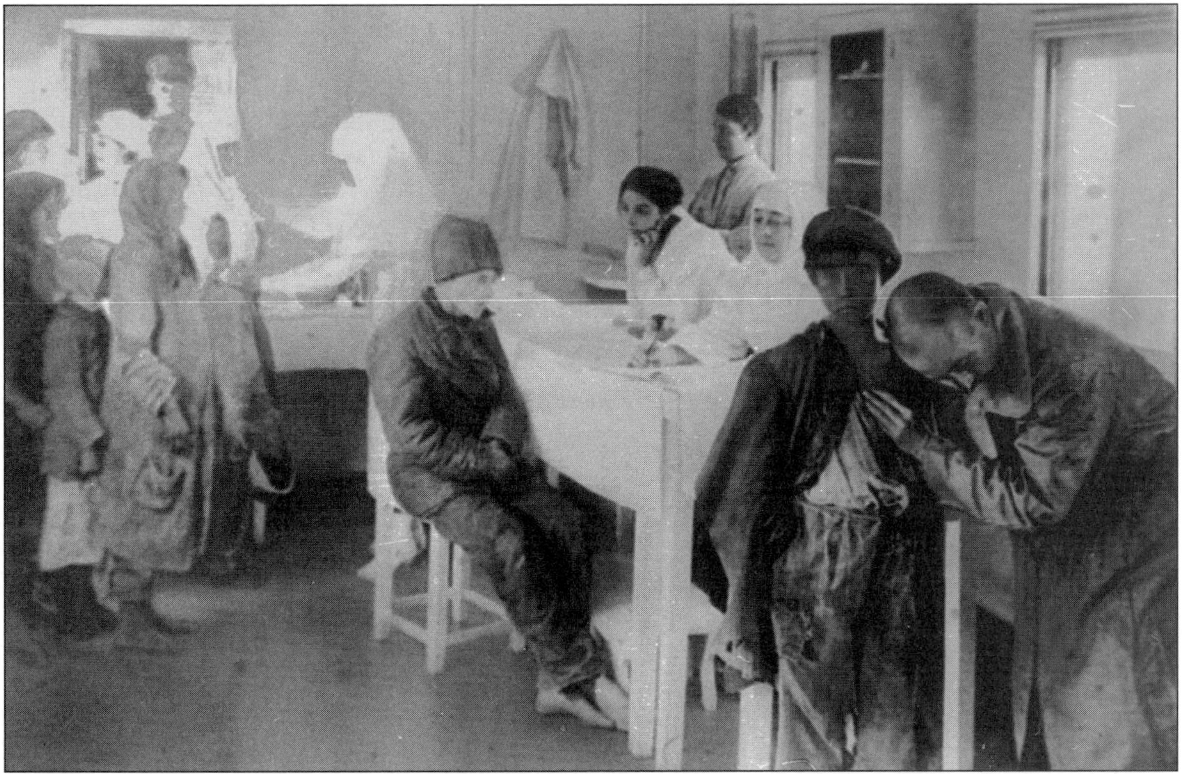

Starving Russians visit a clinic during the Great Russian Famine. (AP/Wide World Photos)

Herbert Hoover near the war's end to head the newly created American Relief Administration (ARA) and its massive relief program to Europe. Although the United States had not yet formally recognized the new Bolshevik regime, Hoover sought to convince the Bolsheviks to sue for peace against rebel forces in return for humanitarian aid, to be funneled through a neutral international relief body headed by the famous Norwegian explorer and philanthropist Fridtjof Nansen. The Russians refused to accept this proposal in 1919, insisting that the civil war must be dealt with first.

A year later, the Bolsheviks emerged victorious from the civil war but found themselves in even worse condition in terms of food supplies. With as many as 20 million people facing starvation, they began serious negotiations with Hoover and with Nansen, who was already leading private philanthropic famine aid programs. Nansen, who was named the High Commissioner for Refugees Coming from Russia by the League of Nations in September of 1921, also headed the International Committee for Russian Relief, which cooperated with Hoover's ARA efforts in assisting nearly 12 million Russians threatened by starvation. The ARA rapidly gained the confidence of Soviet officials, and it provided hundreds of American volunteers and millions of dollars worth of food aid from 1921 to 1923.

The drought broke in 1923, and gradually the ARA phased out relief efforts as grain harvests in the Ukraine recovered. The government of the Soviet Union later honored Hoover and the ARA for the humanitarian efforts exerted on behalf of Soviet citizens held in the grip of famine.

However, the Soviet Union remained prone to drought in subsequent years, and, combined with counterproductive policies requiring the collectivization of agriculture in the early 1930's, the Ukraine suffered from renewed famine. The Russian case illustrates how civil war, agricultural policy, and drought may combine with deadly results. Politics played as much a role as demonstrable need in determining the timing of relief efforts. Because droughts do not happen overnight, there is time to respond to potential famines, but too often governments fail to respond until the starvation and dying is well underway. Nevertheless, in the Great Famine of 1920-1922, intervention was timely enough to save millions.

Robert F. Gorman

For Further Information:

Conquest, Robert. *The Harvest of Sorrow: Soviet Collectivization and the Terror—Famine.* New York: Oxford University Press, 1986.

Marrus, Michael R. *The Unwanted: European Refugees in the Twentieth Century.* New York: Oxford University Press, 1985.

Weissman, B. M. *Herbert Hoover and Famine Relief to Soviet Russia: 1921-23.* Stanford, Calif.: Hoover Institution, 1974.

1959: The Great Leap Forward Famine

Date: 1959-1961
Place: The People's Republic of China
Result: Casualties so vast they can only be estimated at between 15 million and 50 million dead

The greatest famine—and perhaps the greatest natural disaster—in the twentieth century occurred virtually unnoticed in the outside world. So tight was the control of information coming out of the People's Republic of China in the late 1950's that the Great Leap Forward famine was unpublicized. The starving millions in China knew that something was wrong in their area, but the national press was reporting on the spectacular success of the government's programs and acknowledging only food shortages due to bad weather in some localities.

It is hard to say how much knowledge even the Chinese leaders had of this tragedy. Surely the government knew that many of its citizens were hungry, but the lack of a free press meant each leader had to rely on limited personal experience or on government reports from village to county to province to the capital that were inflated every step of the way. In many cases, these reported on bountiful harvests, when the villagers had in fact already eaten the seed needed to plant the next year's crop before the onset of the harsh unproductive winter season. One year the government reported total grain production of 375 million tons when only about 200 million tons had been produced.

In the Great Leap Forward famine, the losses were so great not even the numbers of victims—let alone their names—are known. So far is the world from knowing the exact number of casualties that they can be estimated only by a demographic analysis of the number of "excess deaths." Scholarly estimates of the number of deaths range from a low of 15 million to a high of 50 million, a measure so imprecise as to give a range of deaths that could be off by a factor of three or as much as 300 percent. Thirty-five million people could have died without any record of it.

Geography—both physical and human—contributed to this catastrophe. Since ancient times, China

Food for starving Chinese is unloaded from a ship during the Great Leap Forward. (National Archives)

has been home to the world's largest population and today has well over 1.3 billion people, or about a quarter of the world's total population. China also has the world's third-largest land area—trailing only Russia and Canada. This might seem to be adequate, but well over two-thirds of Chinese land is virtually uninhabitable desert and mountains, so China must feed 25 percent of the world's people with only about 7 percent of the world's arable (farmable) land.

Even in good times, avoiding hunger in China is difficult. With so large a land area, China has too much water (flooding) in some regions and not enough water (drought) in others in any given year. The key to a good national harvest is to have relatively fewer floods and droughts than normal. In 1959-1961, the odds turned against the Chinese in that a higher number than usual of both floods and droughts occurred. The 1960 weather conditions are considered the worst in twentieth century China.

Yet weather is only part of this story, and perhaps not even the most important part. Some scholars attribute only 30 percent of the catastrophe to the weather, reserving the brunt of the blame for failed government policies. To the outside world, the late 1950's anti-Western Chinese Communist system seemed monolithic, and China was thought to have only minor differences with its ally the Soviet Union. In truth, there was a massive split between the two countries, with corresponding differences among the Chinese leaders. They were torn between a highly bureaucratized central planning system recommended by the Russians and a chaotic, voluntaristic path recommended by China's Communist Party leader, Mao Zedong.

While Mao's plan seemed to prevail, conflicts marred its execution in many areas. Mao's Great Leap Forward plan was supposed to stimulate Chinese production so dramatically that China would overtake the British in fifteen years by fostering an ongoing revolutionary fervor among the Chinese. Many Chinese did respond enthusiastically, even accepting Mao's idea that steel production could be stimulated by having villages build backyard iron furnaces. This idea led many to melt down perfectly good iron skillets and dismantle high-quality steel train rails, throw them into backyard furnaces, and turn out third-rate pig iron. While peasants were busy with this unproductive activity, they often failed to plant crops or to harvest ripe yields at the right time, further compounding the catastrophe.

In reality, neither of the paths was suitable for the crisis China faced. While industrial production slipped, grain production plunged disastrously, to about 75 percent of the level before the Great Leap Forward. Worse, much of this grain was siphoned off to pay for "aid" the Chinese were receiving from the Soviets. This meant that the grain available to feed the Chinese people became even less, exposing those most at risk—the sick, elderly, and children—to the horrors of this massive famine. The government's policies clearly aggravated this unprecedented natural disaster.

Richard L. Wilson

For Further Information:

Banister, Judith. *China's Changing Population.* Stanford, Calif.: Stanford University Press, 1987.

Becker, Jasper. *Hungry Ghosts: China's Secret Famine.* London: John Murray, 1996.

Blecher, Marc. *China Against the Tides.* London: Pinter, 1997.

Christiansen, Fleming, and Shirin Rai. *Chinese Politics and Society: An Introduction.* London: Prentice Hall/Harvester Wheatsheaf, 1996.

MacFarquhar, Roderick. *The Coming of the Cataclysm, 1961-1966.* Vol. 3 in *The Origins of the Cultural Revolution.* New York: Columbia University Press, 1997.

_______. *The Great Leap Forward, 1958-1960.* Vol. 2 in *The Origins of the Cultural Revolution.* New York: Columbia University Press, 1983.

Zhao, Kate Xiao. *How the Farmers Changed China: Power of the People.* Boulder, Colo.: Westview Press, 1996.

1972: Africa, Asia

Date: September, 1972-December, 1973, with effects into 1975

Place: The Sahel region of western and eastern Africa, extending from the Atlantic coast through the Horn of Africa, including large areas of Senegal, Gambia, Mauritania, Mali, Niger, Chad, Upper Volta (now Burkina Faso), Sudan, and Ethiopia and smaller portions of nine other independent states; portions of India, Pakistan, and Bangladesh

Result: Estimated 200,000 dead, millions of livestock dead

The early 1970's witnessed a series of exceptionally severe regional famines, none impacting in more devastating fashion or causing as many economic, social, and political upheavals than those of Sahelian Africa. The disaster had been a long time in the making; there were signs of change in West Africa since at least 1968.

The vast Sahel region winds around the southern fringe of the Sahara Desert from the extreme western edge of Africa, around Cape Blanc in Mauritania, to Somalia on the eastern coastal extremity. The region spans anywhere from 125 to 150 miles in width and has long been the transition zone between the Sahara and the lusher equatorial savanna belt. Deriving its name from the Arabic word for "shore," the Sahel is composed of bush, grassland, and sporadic woodlands; the main economic activities are subsistence agriculture and livestock raising, both severely limited at all times by semiarid conditions. Main crops include millet, feed grains, peanuts, and sorghum. The most important pastoralists are the Fulani, estimated to number some 15 million to make them Africa's major cattle-raisers, and the fiercely independent, traditionalist Tuareg.

Certain urban centers are also highly dependent upon rural agricultural production, the most important being Bamako, Mali; Niamey, Niger; Kano, Nigeria; and Ouagadougou, Burkina Faso. The Sahel is an area of extreme weather conditions, with two hot seasons running roughly from February to April and September to November and a short rainy season between May and August. The annual rainfall under "average" conditions could run from 4 to 8 inches per year. From December to January, there is a windy season during which a desert wind called the harmattan brings slightly cooler weather, but at the price of filling the atmosphere with sand and dust.

Drought conditions were first detected in 1968 in northern Senegal, Mauritania, Mali, Niger, Chad, and Upper Volta (now Burkina Faso), and, while this was not unusual in and of itself, it rained much less frequently in the ensuing years. As with any climatic transition zone, the Sahel is vulnerable to even slight alterations, but its fragility was tragically demonstrated in 1972 when there was virtually no rainfall. Deforestation resulting from indiscriminate clearing of trees for firewood, as well as overgrazing of domestic animals in increasingly scarce pasturage, left the soil without a great deal to anchor it in place, and the end product was massive desertification. As the grass withered, the soil became desiccated and was blown away. The Sahara Desert began spreading southward, which resulted in habitat destruction and the eradication of most plant and animal life from the affected areas.

The irreversible damage to the land in turn drove both the nomads and the subsistence farmers to move away. Most of the livestock died along the way, and thousands of humans, weakened by malnutrition and dehydration, also perished. The United Nations Food and Agriculture Organization (FAO) reported in September of 1972 that the unprecedented severe and prolonged drought conditions would produce a humanitarian crisis, but it was not until early 1973, when the coming of the harmattan blew more of the earth away and added to the extent of the devastation, that the global community became aware of the extent of the catastrophe.

Though some $135 million was raised for emergency food and medical supplies, the problems of logistics and distribution kept relief from arriving in time to save many in the more remote areas. The pastoral way of life was placed in serious future jeopardy as many Tuareg and Fulani had to be accommodated in cities and camps. In the camps, especially, more died in epidemics of cholera, measles, and diphtheria.

Throughout 1973 and into 1974, the drought spread eastward into Sudan, Ethiopia, Somalia, and Djibouti, and southward into northern Togo, Dahomey (now Benin), Ghana, Nigeria, Cameroon, Ivory Coast, and Guinea. Human distress caused by the famine and lack of energetic government response to the catastrophe played a significant role in coups that ousted the long-standing regimes in Niger and Ethiopia (1974) and probably in Chad (1975).

On the Indian subcontinent, famine was brought on by a combination of drought and flooding. In India two successive droughts led to food rationing and 25 percent inflation. Pakistan witnessed its worst flooding since the 1890's, resulting in food shortages and steep price increases. The most drastic situation occurred in Bangladesh, where monsoon flooding caused severe loss of life and 100 percent inflation over an eighteen-month period. Europe and Latin America went through double-digit inflation throughout late 1973 and into 1974 as a result of famine-related global food shortages and the Arab oil embargo.

Raymond Pierre Hylton

For Further Information:
Grainger, Alan. *The Threatening Desert: Controlling Desertification.* London: Earthscan/United Nations Environment Program, 1990.
Gritzner, J. *The West African Sahel.* Chicago: Committee on Geographical Studies at the University of Chicago, 1988.

1984: Africa

Date: 1984-1985
Place: Ethiopia, Chad, Mozambique, Mali, Niger, Burkina Faso, and the Sudan
Result: 2 million dead, millions more displaced

A starving child in Ethiopia holds an empty food pot. (AP/Wide World Photos)

When four-year-old Mamush Mekitew reached the American aid camp at Gehowa, Ethiopia, he weighed only 15 pounds. He suffered from acute diarrhea and vomiting and was so weak that he had to be given liquid through a nasal drip. His blind, widowed mother and an elderly uncle crooned to him day and night until he died. "He should not have been alive at all," said a nurse. "It was a miracle he held out for so long."

In many areas, the famine reduced the birthrate, as hungry adult women simply stopped ovulating. A United Nations Children's Fund (UNICEF) relief expedition mounted on camels toured the Sudan's remote Red Sea province and found that childbearing was almost a thing of the past. In a settlement called Bet Utr, not one of the women in thirteen families had given birth during the past year. Three women had died in childbirth, and one had miscarried. In a society where most women give birth every year, Bet Utr should have been teeming with children. In this time of troubles, however, only eight youngsters were left.

At a relief station in the southern town of Doba, Chad, a procession of mothers, their breasts dry and withered, their bodies caked with trail dust, pleaded for food and medicine for the children slung around their shoulders and backs. Doba was in the middle of a war zone, however, and there were few supplies. Two hundred children died from malnutrition in only two weeks. In the harsh semidesert wastes of eastern Chad, hardy desert nomads were reduced to eating the leaves of savonnier trees. Some died because they could not digest the leaves properly.

Like outcasts from the Bible, they trudged out of Tigre, Ethiopia (now a province of Eritria), escaping from a parched, rebel-controlled province that was starved of food supplies by the Ethiopian government. Nearly 200,000 Tigreans fled to camps in neighboring Sudan. There were women too weak to finish the journey on foot, children who listened for water on makeshift hose lines, and children who arrived only to die.

Impact. The famine had two "belts" across sub-Saharan Africa. One belt ran from Mali, Mauritania, and Senegal in the west to Ethiopia in the east. The other belt ran from Somalia on the horn of Africa to Angola, Botswana, and Zambia in southern Africa. As of November, 1984, 50,000 people were dead from famine in Senegal, and 50,000 more were at risk. More than 150,000 cattle had been lost in the previous two years. In Mali, more than 1 million children were suffering from malnutrition, cholera, and measles. A total of 2.5 million people were at risk from famine. In Chad, at least 4,000 people, mostly women and children, had died from famine during the three months preceding December, 1984. Half a million more had been displaced by drought, and relief efforts were hampered by a civil war. In the Sudan, more than 1 million people were threatened by the famine. There had been a great influx of refugees from Chad and Ethiopia, which added to the civil strife already existing in the southern Sudan.

Like much of Africa, Ethiopia has always been subject to ecological disaster. Droughts and famines were reported as early as 253 B.C.E. In the great drought of 1888, a third of the population was said to have died from malnourishment and disease. This calamity in 1984-1985 was part of a thirty-year pattern. The rains have repeatedly failed along the Sahel, the wide swath of land that lies just below the Sahara Desert. As a result, this time there had already been at least 300,000 famine deaths in Ethiopia. A million more people may have been at risk and as many as 6 million people were facing food shortages. In Mozambique, perhaps 200,000 people may have already died from famine. Four million more were in danger largely due to a severe drought and a civil war.

Root Causes. Aside from the lack of rain, these peoples' greatest enemies have been deforestation, booming population, primitive agricultural methods, war, and governmental mismanagement. Black Africa is the world's poorest area, and it is the only region in which the population is growing faster than the food supply. Agriculture never fully recovered from the devastating drought of the early and mid-1970's. In 1982, Ethiopia's per capita food production was only 81 percent of what it was in 1969-1971. In Mozambique, the figure was at 68 percent. Chad's food harvest in 1983 was a disaster. Cereal production plummeted to 315,000 tons, well short of the 654,000 tons needed for minimum living needs. On average, African governments spend four times as much on armaments as they do on agriculture. Primitive farming, in turn, has devastated the environment.

Under increasing pressure for production, traditional fallow periods have been shortened, wearing out the soil. Most farmers have no chemical fertilizers, and the animal dung that they once used to enrich the soil is being burned for fuel, because so many trees have been cut down. In the mid-1960's, 16 percent of Ethiopia's land area was covered by forest. In the mid-1980's, the figure was just 3 percent. "With deforestation, the soil loses much of its capacity to retain moisture and consequently its productivity and resistance to drought," said a U.N. environmentalist. In the twenty years leading up to the mid-1980's, Mauritania lost more than three-quarters of its grazing land to the encroaching sands of the Sahara. Rainfall became another forgotten luxury. The rainfall in 1983 was the lowest in seventy years, and most of the grain crop failed. In some areas, 90 percent of the livestock died.

Ethiopia's leader at the time, Lieutenant Colonel Mengistu Haile Mariam, was warned of impending famine in 1982, in a report from a group of experts headed by Keith Griffin, an Oxford University economist. The Griffin team recommended immediate food rationing and heavy emphasis on rural development. Mengistu ignored the advice. Instead, Mengistu poured 46 percent of Ethiopia's gross national product into military spending, buying at least $2.5 billion worth of arms from the Soviet Union. What investment he did make in agriculture was concentrated on building Soviet-style state farms. Meanwhile, as hundred of thousands starved in 1984 and 1985, Ethiopian officials spent more than $100 million sprucing up their capital, Addis Ababa, and erecting triumphal arches. This expenditure and construction were for the September, 1985, tenth anniversary of the military coup that overthrew Emperor Haile Selassie I.

In Chad before and during the famine, Libya occupied the entire northern half of the country. Meanwhile, a guerrilla conflict in the south rendered that area impervious to relief efforts. At that time, the country had only 60 miles of paved road. The rest of the roads were mostly impassable dirt tracks. The 1984 cotton harvest was the largest in sub-Saharan Africa. Much of the cotton was planted, however, at the expense of food crops. Since no one anticipated the severity of the drought, little of the profit from the abundant cotton crop was saved for emergency food aid. So the cotton money was gone, providing no relief from the killer famine.

The Long-Term Effects. The long-range damage of the famine was the potential effects upon the children who survived. An American child of four to six years old typically consumes 1,600 to 1,800 calories in a daily diet. In the African famine belts, a child the same age took in less than 800 calories per day, a starvation diet. At refugee camps, the basic ration consisted of gruel made from wheat, plus beans, other grains, and vegetable oil. That was not a balanced diet but was far better than anything outside the camps. After months or even years of malnutrition, African children were prey to a host of ailments. Iron-deficiency anemia was prevalent, and in some places a shortage of iodine in the diet caused a mini-epidemic of goiter, an enlargement of the thyroid gland.

For children born and raised at the peak of the famine, blindness was one of the more severe consequences. A lack of vitamin A—which comes from butterfat, eggs, liver, carrots, and leafy vegetables—leads to a condition called xerophthalmia (literally, "dry eye"). Night blindness is an early symptom. Later, sunlight becomes painful. The eyes stop lubricating themselves with tears, and their protective mucous cells dry out. The corneas are scarred and pitted until the victim becomes blind.

Physicians working in famine areas predicted that countless thousands of African children would emerge from the famine with some kind of damage to their mental capacities. Malnutrition can stop the growth of brain tissue, a loss that can not be made up later in life. The belief was expressed that the thousands of orphans created by the famine would pour into towns and cities to scratch out a living as beggars or thieves. Whatever their work would be, many believed that these children would be so handicapped by the famine's effects that they would not be able to compete or make a living for their families.

Relief. Although the rains did eventually arrive in the spring of 1985, the more pressing matter was to get food and medical supplies to relief areas and refugee camps. Getting food into Ethiopia was only half the problem. A moonscape scarred with treacherous canyons and inhospitable mountains, the country is a logistical difficulty. Half its people normally lived a two-day walk from the nearest road. In 1985 there were only about 6,000 trucks in the entire country. At that time only a few hundred of the trucks had been used for relief. Relief supplies did finally begin to show up in quantity. The first food trucks reached the northern town of Korem in a military convoy, for protection against rebels. More than 50,000 people were waiting at the camp for food, and there was not enough to go around. Before the convoy came in, about 100 people were dying every day. Afterward the average dropped to somewhere between 30 and 50 a day. Doctors were forced to perform a gruesome act of triage, selecting only the hardiest refugees to receive food and clothing. The physicians would work their way through crowds. They used pencils to place marks on the foreheads of those who seemed most likely to survive. Aid was not to be wasted on the weak.

A Cooperative for American Relief to Everywhere (CARE) official once described Chad as having nightmarish logistical problems, even worse than Ethiopia's. Chad is a landlocked nation in which the nearest ports are 1,200 miles away, in Cameroon and Nigeria. At that time, food trains took at least three weeks to travel from the seacoast to Chad, and the transport depended on the cooperation of foreign governments. Also, the civil war and the Libyan occupation of Chad continued.

The rains themselves brought a new flood of trouble. Thousands of people in Ethiopia may have died of cold and disease in the rain and hail. Roads and bridges were destroyed, delaying food shipments to many of the country's 8 million famine victims. The rains ruined about 5,500 tons of precious grain at the port of Aseb in Ethiopia. Twenty thousand famine victims in Ethiopia lost their homes to the flooding Shebelle River. Storms also destroyed flimsy shelters in many feeding centers, increasing the threat of epidemics; thousands of people had already died of cholera in Ethiopia. The rains in Mozambique in southeastern Africa destroyed vital food crops, aggravating an already grim situation. By the beginning of May, 1985, more than 200,000 people had died in Mozambique, and 2.5 million people were still in urgent need of food.

Dana P. McDermott

For Further Information:

"An African Nightmare." *Newsweek*, November 26, 1984, 50-55.

"A Cruel Rain for Ethiopia." *Newsweek*, May 20, 1985, 41.

"Famine's New Victim." *Newsweek*, December 3, 1984, 46.

"Hunger Stalks Ethiopia Again—and Aid Groups Fear the Worst." *Time*, December 21, 1987, 34-43.

"The Land of the Dead." *Time*, November 26, 1984, 66-69.

"We Are the Children." *Newsweek*, June 3, 1985, 28-31.

Fires

(AP/Wide World Photos)

Fires occur throughout the world as a result of both human and natural causes. They can inflict devastating damage to natural environments, cities, and buildings, causing billions of dollars in damage. Large fires may be accompanied by many deaths and injuries to people and animals.

Factors involved: Chemical reactions, geography, human activity, weather conditions, wind
Regions affected: All

Science

Fire occurs through the process of combustion. Combustion is an exothermic, self-sustaining, chemical reaction usually involving the oxidation of a fuel by oxygen in the atmosphere. Emission of heat, light, and mechanical energy, such as sound, usually occurs. An exothermic reaction is one in which the new substances produced have less energy than the original substances. This means that there is energy in various forms produced in the reaction. In fires, the energy is released primarily as heat and light.

A fuel is a material that will burn. In most environments, carbon is a constituent element. Many typical fuels must undergo a process called pyrolysis before they will burn. Wood, for example, exists in many buildings in the form of furniture and framing to support the walls and roof. In its normal condition, wood does not burn. It must be broken down through the application of heat into its constituent elements before it can be oxidized. This is the process of pyrolysis.

Oxidation is a chemical reaction in which an oxidizing agent and a reducing agent combine to form a product with less energy than the original materials. The oxygen is usually obtained from the air. The fuel is the reducing agent. For the process to begin, a source of heat must be applied to the fuel. This heat is needed to raise the temperature of the material to its ignition point, or the lowest temperature at which it will burn. Ignition can occur from a variety of natural and human sources. Electric wires or appliances can come in contact with combustible materials, raising their temperature. Natural sources such as lightning can start wildfires. People can deliberately start fires using an accelerant; arson is responsible for many fires throughout the world.

Three factors are necessary for a fire to begin. They are illustrated as the fire triangle of heat, fuel, and oxygen. A fire with these three elements will be a glowing fire. For self-sustaining combustion to occur, a fourth factor, a chain reaction, must be added to the original three factors. This converts the fire triangle to a fire tetrahedral, or four-sided pyramid. A chain reaction occurs when the heat produced by the fire is enough not only to burn the fuel but also to preheat the next segment of fuel so that the fire can grow. As long as the rate of heat production is greater than the rate at which heat is dissipated to the surroundings, more fuel can be ignited and the fire will spread. When the heat produced by the fire is dissipated to the surroundings, the fire will gradually decay.

A fire will continue until the available fuel is consumed, the available oxygen is used, the flames are extinguished by cooling, or the number of excited molecules is reduced. Fire extinguishment and prevention strategies are aimed at breaking or removing one leg of the fire triangle or tetrahedral.

In most fires, either the action of a person or an act of nature, such as a lightning strike or earthquake, are required to bring the factors together for a fire to start. The act of a person may be deliberate, as in the case of arson; accidental, as in the case of someone falling asleep in bed with a lighted cigarette; or an act of omission, such as a building not being constructed in a safe manner.

There are two basic kinds of fires. A fuel-controlled fire is one that has an adequate amount of oxygen but has limited contact with fuel. A ventilation-controlled fire has access to adequate amounts of fuel but has limited contact with oxygen. The National Fire Protection Agency (NFPA) has classified four types of fires. Type A fires involve ordinary combustibles such as wood, paper, cloth, or fiber; they can be extinguished with water or foam. Type B fires involve flammable liquids, such as hot grease, paints, thinners, gasoline, oil, or other liquid fuels; they can be extinguished with a chemical foam or carbon dioxide. Type C fires, electrical fires, can be extinguished with a nonconducting extinguishing agent such as carbon dioxide or a dry chemical. Type D fires involve flammable metals, such as magnesium or sodium alloys, and they can be put out by smothering with a dry powder with a sodium chloride or graphite base.

Four basic mechanisms of heat transfer are involved in fires. Convection is heat transfer within a fluid. In most fires, this occurs within the air. As a fluid is heated, its molecules become less dense and rise. Air at normal density will move into the area of heat, replacing the less dense air that has risen. As this air is heated, it will also rise. This explains the natural movement of fire gases and smoke from lower areas to higher ones. Conduction is heat transfer between two bodies in direct contact with each other. Heat can be transferred through the molecules in a wall by conduction.

A combination of convection and conduction occurs between a solid and a fluid at their boundary. Radiant heat transfer involves heat transfer by electromagnetic waves across distances. A surface, such as a wall, that has been heated by a fire can transfer radiant heat across the room to heat another wall surface or a person's skin even if there is no direct contact. This process occurs in the same way that the heat energy from the sun is transferred to the earth across millions of miles of space. The fourth form of heat transfer involved in fires is latent heat transfer. Latent heat is the heat that is involved in the change of state of a substance. In a fire, water used as an extinguishing agent will be converted to steam, absorbing large quantities of heat energy as it changes from a liquid to a gas.

A conflagration is a fire that spreads from building to building through flame spread over some distance, often a portion of a city or a town. A large group fire spreads from building to building within a complex of buildings. The number of conflagrations and large group fires were substantially reduced in the twentieth century. This decrease is attributed to building codes that require fire-resistant construction of the exterior walls and roofs of buildings in cities, modern fire-department capabilities to extinguish fires, adequate urban water systems that have large quantities of water available for fire extinguishment, and limits on openings between buildings that are located close to one another.

Three main types of conflagrations have occurred since 1950. The first are urban/wild land interface fires. An urban/wild land interface is the area where an urban or suburban area adjoins the natural or undeveloped environment. Fires may start in the wild land and be driven by strong winds and available combustibles into residential or urban areas over a large fire front that cannot be extinguished. The Oakland Hills fire of 1991 is an example of this type of fire. These fires were the most prevalent type of conflagration in the 1990's.

Conflagrations also occur in "congested combustible districts." These fires are typical of urban conflagrations before the 1900's, when the need for streets wide enough for automobiles changed the character of cities around the world. The congested combustible district is one with narrow streets lined with continuous buildings. The Great Boston Fire of 1872 is an example of this type of fire.

Third, conflagrations can be driven by strong winds among houses with wood shingles or other flammable roofing materials. These fires often occur in the southwestern United States. Last, large group fires often occur in old manufacturing districts, where the buildings are abandoned or are poorly maintained. The fire in Chelsea, Massachusetts, in 1908 is an example of this type of fire.

Geography

Fires occur in all geographic regions of the world. Air as a source of oxygen is available in all environments that support human habitation. Fuels are also present in every environment. The trees and grasses in natural environments will become fuels for wildfires; the furnishings in homes, the materials used in the construction of many buildings, and the clothes people wear are all potential fuels in the presence of heat.

Most fires occur outdoors. These are often called wildfires or brushfires. Fires can occur in forests, grasslands, farms (crop fires), and outdoor trash fires. Wildfires can be started either by an act of nature, such as a lightning strike, or by human actions. Many wildfires are started by accident or by carelessness. Examples of this are leaving a campfire unattended or discarding smoking materials through the window of a car into a natural area.

Trash fires, or the burning of debris in land clearings, can also spread beyond the point of origin. Forest management personnel often direct controlled burns in natural areas to burn underbrush, consume fallen limbs and dead plants, and rejuvenate the forest ecosystem. This practice is thought to reduce the hazard of wildfires because a large amount of fuel is consumed in a controlled manner. There are dangers, however, as in the May, 2000, fire in Los Alamos, New Mexico, in which a controlled burn grew into a major conflagation and destroyed hundreds of homes.

Most deaths and injuries from fire occur in homes and garages. Historically, there have also been large numbers of deaths and injuries in public buildings, such as theaters, assembly buildings, schools, hospitals, stores, offices, hotels, boardinghouses, dormitories, and other community facilities. Modern building codes and construction practices have reduced the number and severity of these fires.

The industrial environment poses many serious fire hazards. Industry includes storage, manufacturing, defense, utility, and other large-scale operations. The presence of large amounts of potential fuel or volatile materials such as solvents in an industrial plant in a large open building constitute a potential fire threat.

Fires may also occur in structures that are not buildings, such as bridges, tunnels, vacant buildings, and buildings under construction. While much public fear and awareness of fire is centered on large fires in public buildings, most people who are killed in fires in the United States die in their homes or cars. Approximately 80 percent of fire deaths and 70 percent of fire injuries occur in homes and cars.

The mobile environment is composed of trains, automobiles, airplanes, and other transportation vehicles. Many people die or are injured from fires that occur after vehicles crash or are otherwise involved in accidents. However, it is important to note that only one-sixth the number of people die in vehicle fires as die in home fires each year.

In an urban/wild land interface fire, conflagrations may start in wild lands and be driven by strong winds into urban areas. This phenomenon occurred in the Oakland Hills fire of 1991. (AP/Wide World Photos)

The dangers of fire to people and property are omnipresent. Therefore, strategies for design, fire protection, and fire prevention must reach everywhere. Significant progress appears to have been made in reducing fires involving multiple deaths and large property losses during the twentieth century.

Prevention and Preparations

Fires can be prevented by attacking each leg of the fire triangle or tetrahedral. Sources of heat, particularly open flames, must be isolated from fuels. This can be accomplished in several ways. Rooms that contain sources of heat, such as boiler rooms, mechanical plants, and shops, are usually built with fire-resistant enclosures to contain or compartmentalize the building. Electric wires and electrical appliances must be adequately insulated so the heat produced cannot escape to building materials or furnishings.

Fuels must be limited in wild lands and buildings. Controlled burns, described earlier, provide a method of decreasing fuels in the natural environment. Buildings can be constructed of and furnished with materials that are noncombustible. The amount of fuel in a building is often expressed as the amount of combustible materials by weight compared to an equivalent amount of wood. This is known as a fuel load. Products used in homes and commercial buildings can be redesigned to reduce their fire risk.

Most fires are the result of either careless or deliberate human behavior. Therefore, educating people about fire risks and appropriate fire-prevention strategies is an essential element in fire prevention. Educating the general public could potentially have the greatest impact on reducing the number and severity of fires, but it is perhaps the most difficult strategy to implement. Fire-protection authorities believe that to modify the behavior of the American public with regard to fires requires more than a brief exposure to fire-safety education. The NFPA has produced the "Learn Not to Burn" curriculum material for use in schools across the United States, which consists of a series of exercises with which teachers may teach children of the dangers of fire, fire-prevention strategies, and methods of protecting themselves and their families in the event of a fire. The NFPA reported that in the 1990's only a small percentage of schools actually used this material, however.

The NFPA and many municipal fire departments regularly conduct community meetings and demonstrations of fire protection and prevention techniques, distribute brochures and educational kits, and conduct open houses during Fire Prevention Week activities. These efforts have been aimed at emphasizing actions to prevent fires and appropriate behaviors during fires.

Preparation for fires and protection during a fire can take several forms. Preparing for a fire consists of maintaining buildings to have limited fuels and heat sources. Fuels should be stored in protected areas, and electrical systems and other potential sources of heat must be properly maintained. Access to volatile substances should be limited. A fire-detection system, such as smoke detectors with audible and visible alarms that notify building occupants during the earliest stages of a fire, is an essential preparation component. If the detection system is attached to an automatic suppression configuration, such as a sprinkler system, the fire can be extinguished before it moves beyond the area of origin, reducing its threat to people and property. Providing fire extinguishers, standpipe systems, and other opportunities for manual fire suppression in buildings is also necessary. The fire-detection, alarm, sprinkler, and standpipe systems are called active fire protection systems.

Maintaining a fire department with adequate personnel and equipment is necessary if fires do start and are not suppressed by automatic equipment. A community emergency notification system, such as the 911 telephone line, is required to contact the fire department quickly to ensure that personnel can arrive at the scene with enough time to suppress a fire and rescue people.

Buildings are required to be designed to confine fires to the area of origin by a series of fire and smoke barriers that subdivide a building into a series of compartments. The use of fire- and smoke-resistant walls to confine fire spread is called a passive fire protection method. Other passive fire protection strategies include limiting the use of materials that contribute to fire growth and limiting the size of buildings based on the relative combustibility of their construction systems and contents.

Providing safe ways for people to leave a burning building is an essential method of fire protection. The path from a point inside a building to safety outside the building is called the means of egress. The means of egress consists of three components. The exit access is the unprotected path from any point in a building to an exit. This distance is limited in all buildings so people can move quickly to an exit. An exit is a fire-resistant, smoke-resistant enclosure that leads one from an exit access to the exit discharge, the opening that takes one from an exit to the safety of the "public way." An exit may be a fire stairway in a tall building, a horizontal corridor, or doors that lead directly out of a building in a small, one-story structure. The number and size of exits are determined by how many people will use the building.

It is essential that the exits do not become overly congested during fire evacuations. Fire exits must be illuminated with lights connected to an emergency power source so that when the normal electric service in a building is interrupted during a fire, people can still find the exits in smoke-filled corridors. In very large buildings or in structures such as hospitals, where people cannot be moved out of the building, places of refuge are provided. A place of refuge is an area in a building that is protected from fire and smoke where people can move to await rescue. Conducting fire drills in homes, schools, workplaces, and other buildings is essential so people know how to react in the event of a fire. Many large buildings have voice systems for someone to provide evacuation instructions to occupants through loudspeakers on each floor.

Rescue and Relief Efforts

Injuries and death in fires are primarily caused by the effects of smoke inhalation. Smoke consists of airborne solid and liquid particulates and gases that result from pyrolysis and combustion. The combustion process is never fully complete, so there are also a number of unburned fuel particles and gases in the smoke as well. Many of the particles are about the same size as the wavelength of visible light. Light is scattered by the smoke particles, making vision very difficult in smoke-filled rooms.

Three hazards are posed by smoke: smoke inhalation, burns, and building collapse or explosion. Some of the gases present in a fire, such as carbon monoxide, hydrogen cyanide, and carbon dioxide, are narcotics or materials that cause pain or loss of consciousness. Particles and other gases can cause irritations of the pulmonary system or eyes, ears, and nose. Other gases, such as hydrogen chloride, are toxic in the quantities created during a fire. The combined effects of breathing these gases is called smoke inhalation. It is treated by removing people to a safe environment with clean air and administering oxygen.

Heat is another major product of the combustion process. Typical building fires exceed temperatures of 1,000 to 1,500 degrees Fahrenheit. Human beings cannot sustain temperatures of this magnitude. The skin will receive second-degree burns when exposed to temperatures of 212 degrees Fahrenheit for fifteen seconds. People will go into shock as a result of exposure to heat, irritants, and oxygen deficiency experienced even at the periphery of fires. This condition can lead to elevated heart rates that can bring on heart attacks.

Burns are classified as first, second, and third degree depending upon the damage done to the skin. First-degree burns are characterized by redness, pain, and sometimes a swelling of the outermost layers of the skin. Second-degree burns usually penetrate deeper into the skin than first-degree burns. Fluids accumulate beneath the skin, forming blisters. The skin becomes moist and pink. Third-degree burns result in dry, charred skin that exposes the layers beneath. Third-degree burns are life-threatening and require special treatment.

People can also be injured or die in fires due to collapse of burning buildings and explosions. In some fires in large buildings there have been reports of panicked behavior contributing to fire deaths. The NFPA defines panic as a sudden and excessive feeling of alarm or fear, usually affecting a number of people, which is vaguely apprehended, originates in some real or supposed danger, and leads to competitive, fear-induced flight in which people might trample others in an attempt to flee. Fire investigators state that this type of panic does not occur in many fires.

It is often very difficult for fire rescue workers to remove people trapped in a building. In tall buildings, people must be evacuated by ladders or helicop-

A helicopter douses a forest fire with water, one of many methods of combating the spread of flames. (FEMA)

ters to areas of safety, where initial medical evaluation and treatment can occur. Rescue workers require special fire-resistant clothing and self-contained breathing apparatus to move into a fire scene to remove people without injuring themselves in the process. Fire-department personnel and emergency medical technicians are specially trained to remove people from fires and provide initial first aid. For those suffering from severe smoke inhalation or third-degree burns, special treatment is required. Many hospitals in large metropolitan areas have special burn centers to treat severe injuries. There have been incidents reported in which people have walked away from a fire scene only to die within a few days due to exposure to toxic gases.

Fire department personnel stay at a fire scene until the combustion process has stopped. In a large fire, smoldering can continue under a top layer of ash for some time after the fire has been apparently extinguished, only to restart at a later time when a wind blows some of the ash into contact with a new fuel.

Impact

The short-term effects of fire include damage and destruction of property, including both buildings and natural lands; injury and death to people and animals; and a loss of homes or workplaces, which can have a lasting impact on a community. In the United States there are over 2.4 million reported fires each year. Many estimate that the actual number of fires is much greater than this. There are over 6,000 deaths and 30,000 injuries each year from fires, resulting in over $5.5 billion in fire losses. While there was a decrease in fire deaths in the 1970's and 1980's, attributed to requirements for the installation of smoke detectors in residences, the rates remained relatively constant after that time. The fire death rates in the United States and Canada are almost twice those of other developed countries. Fire remains the second most prevalent cause of accidental death in homes. It is the primary cause of death among children and young adults. Most of the 6,000 fire deaths in the United States each year occur in two segments of the population: the very young and the elderly.

Gary W. Siebein

Bibliography

Branigan, Francis. *Building Construction for the Fire Service.* Quincy, Mass.: National Fire Protection Association, 1992. This book is a primer on fire safety in buildings, written from the perspective of firefighters.

Cote, Arthur, ed. *Fire Protection Handbook.* 18th ed. Quincy, Mass.: National Fire Protection Association, 1997. This handbook by the leading fire-safety association in the world contains detailed chapters on every aspect of fire prevention and control by leaders in the field. It is updated continually and is the definitive work in the area.

Cote, Arthur, and Percy Bugbee. *Principles of Fire Protection.* Quincy, Mass.: National Fire Protection Association, 1995. This book by two noted fire researchers presents a concise summary of fire principles and fire-protection strategies.

Fire Safe Building Design. Emmitsburg, Md.: United States Fire Administration National Fire Academy, 1997. This is an interactive multimedia course and reference on fire-safe building design principles and the basics of fire on a CD-ROM. It presents illustrated, animated material on fire growth, safety principles, and extinguishment and is suitable for students and professionals alike.

Lathrop, James K., ed. *Life Safety Code Handbook.* 5th ed. Quincy, Mass.: National Fire Protection Association, 1991. This is an illustrated annotated guide to the rules and regulations governing life safety in buildings. It includes many illustrations on how to design safety features in buildings.

Lyons, Paul Robert. *Fire in America.* Quincy, Mass.: National Fire Protection Association, 1976. This book presents the history of fires in cities, buildings, and vehicles from ancient times to modern times, in a readable and illustrated format.

Notable Events

Historical Overview

In the history of civilization, humans and fire have been intimately intertwined. Mastery of fire provided a boon to prehistoric humans, and they used it to shape their environment. Primitive peoples used fire to "drive the game," that is, to force wild game into a small area of concentration, where the kill was much easier. As long as humans remained hunter-gatherers, use of fire was central to survival. Indeed, it has been suggested that the growing ability of such people to control the wild game population led to the extinction of many species.

When humankind converted from hunting to agriculture, fire was equally essential, for domestic fire was needed to convert the harvested grains into edible food for humans. The use of fire was at the heart of the growth in technology as well, for the manipulation of raw materials nearly always depended on fire: Pottery needed to be baked to make it usable as con-

Milestones

64 C.E.:	Much of the city of Rome burns.
1666:	About 436 acres of the city of London burn, eliminating the Great Plague.
1679:	Fire affects portions of the city of Boston.
1788:	New Orleans burns.
1812:	Moscow is set on fire by troops of Napoleon I.
1814:	Washington is burned by occupying British troops.
1842:	Most of the city of Hamburg, Germany, burns, leaving 100 dead.
May 4, 1850:	Fire affects large portions of the city of San Francisco.
May 3-4, 1851:	San Francisco again experiences large fires; 30 die.
December 24, 1851:	The Library of Congress is burned.
October 8, 1871:	The Peshtigo fire affects a large area in northern Wisconsin; 1,200 are killed, and 2 billion trees are burned.
October 8-10, 1871:	The Great Chicago Fire leaves 250 dead and causes $200 million in damage.
April 18-19, 1906:	A fire follows the magnitude-8.3 earthquake in San Francisco.
1910:	Wildfires rage throughout the U.S. West in the most destructive fire year in U.S. history to date.
March 25, 1911:	The Triangle Shirtwaist Factory fire occurs in New York City; 145 employees, mostly young girls, die.
November 28, 1942:	The Cocoanut Grove nightclub burns in Boston, killing 491.
July, 1943:	Hamburg, Germany, is destroyed, mostly by fire; 60,000-100,000 are killed.
February 13, 1945:	25,000 die in the destruction of Dresden by fire.
March 9, 1945:	Incendiary bombs destroy 25 percent of Tokyo.
1945:	A large section of Oregon forest ignites in the Tillamook burn.
November 21, 1980:	A fire in the MGM Grand Hotel in Las Vegas kills 84.
Summer, 1988:	Fires affect some 1.2 million acres in Yellowstone National Park and other western forests.
September, 3, 1991:	A chicken-processing plant in North Carolina burns.
October 19-21, 1991:	Wildfires burn much of Oakland Hills, California; 25 die.
April 19, 1993:	A cult compound in Waco, Texas, is destroyed by fire.
July 4-10, 1994:	A Glenwood Springs, Colorado, forest fire kills 14 firefighters.
April 15, 1997:	A fire at a tent city outside Mecca, Saudi Arabia, costs 300 lives.
January-March, 1998:	Large forest fires burn in Indonesia, sickening thousands; 234 die in a Garuda Indonesia plane crash caused by poor visibility from smoke.

tainers, and metals needed to be heated at ever higher temperatures to make the fluid metal that could be transformed into usable items.

Fire is a tricky tool and requires proper management. All too often, fire escapes from the control of the humans wielding it and creates devastation. A vast number of escaped fires were certainly never recorded: Little is known of the fire usages of Mesoamericans prior to the arrival of Europeans at the end of the fifteenth century, although there is archaeological evidence of their use of fire, probably in religious ceremonies. They also used it to manufacture jewelry from the gold they found in the mountains.

One of the earliest recorded instances of uncontrolled fire was the fire that burned much of the city of Rome during the reign of the Emperor Nero, in 64 C.E. Part of Nero's unsavory reputation comes from the story that he amused himself while the city burned and destroyed the homes of hundreds of thousands of its citizens: "Nero fiddled while Rome burned."

Countless unrecorded fires must have taken place during the collapse of the ancient civilization of Rome. At the time, wood was the universal building material, especially for domestic use, and many homes must have burned down when a cooking fire raged out of control. Occasionally such escaped domestic fires had their uses, notably when a large portion of the city of London burned in 1666: The city's population had just been decimated by an epidemic of the bubonic plague, carried by rats. When the houses burned down in the Great Fire of London, the rats burned with them, and the plague was ended.

It is known that the indigenous peoples in America used fire extensively, both to heat their dwellings and, particularly, to modify the environment. They used fire to clear the underbrush in the eastern United States, where otherwise forest cover dominated the landscape. Fire enabled them to rid a small portion of land of trees that they had girdled and of the brush that grew up when the trees died, leaving them a clearing where they could plant the corn, beans, and squash that formed an important part of their diet. They also burned the land to eliminate underbrush within the forest, making travel through it, as well as hunting, easier. These practices were adopted by the European settlers who, in any case, brought with them a tradition of the use of fire for land management.

Fire also shaped the environment without intervention by humans. In the parts of America where rainfall is scarce, lightning often strikes, especially during the summer. The grasslands of the Great Plains are believed to be largely the product of frequent widespread fires that burned over the land often enough to prevent trees from developing. As more American Indians were concentrated on the Great Plains, fire was used by them to manage the great herds of buffalo that grazed there. It was only as the Europeans began to establish settlements on the Great Plains that efforts were made to contain the grass fires.

Meanwhile, fire had become an important tool in warfare. In ancient times, barricades were generally made of wood, and many attempts were made to burn them by tossing burning brands into the area under siege. The development of what came to be known as Greek fire, however, artillery that could toss shells that would burst into flame on contact, made possible a more potent use of fire in sieges. In addition, it became the practice of conquering armies to set fire to urban centers they conquered. Napoleon I's army burned Moscow in 1812, and Washington, D.C., was burned by the British in 1814. In World War II, fire started by aerial bombardment became an important tool. Many fires were begun in London from 1940 through to 1945 as a result of German bombardment. The Allies retaliated by setting fire to both Hamburg, in 1943, and Dresden, in 1945. That same year, incendiary bombs rained down on Tokyo, burning large portions of the city.

As urban concentrations grew, the risk of fire grew with them. Portions of the city of Boston burned as early as 1679. In 1788, the city of New Orleans burned, as did the city of Hamburg in 1842. In 1850 and again in 1851, the city of San Francisco burned. Chicago burned in 1871, allegedly when Mrs. O'Leary's cow kicked over a kerosene lantern. In 1894, a part of the grounds and structures of the World Columbian Exposition in Chicago burned. Much of San Francisco burned again following the devastating earthquake of 1906.

A number of fires in individual buildings became major disasters. Perhaps the most infamous was the Triangle Shirtwaist Factory fire, in 1911, when 145 trapped workers died. On November 28, 1942, the Cocoanut Grove nightclub in Boston burned, causing 491 deaths. The MGM Grand Hotel in Las Vegas burned in 1980, and 84 people died. A chicken-processing plant in North Carolina burned on September 3, 1991, killing 25 workers. Eighty-six people died in 1993, following an extended siege by federal agents at a cult compound in Waco, Texas.

Although the number of victims of building fires in the United States has declined, there were a number of such disasters abroad in the latter half of the twentieth century, in which the death toll exceeded 100. In 1960, a mental hospital in Guatemala City caught on fire, and 225 died. A movie theater in Syria burned the same year, with a loss of 152 persons. The following year, a circus caught fire in Brazil, killing more than 300. In 1971 and 1972, fires in a hotel and nightclub in South Korea and Japan, respectively, each claimed more than 100 victims, as did a department store fire in Japan in 1973.

Large congregations of people are particularly at risk. In 1975 a fire in a tent city in Saudi Arabia resulted in the loss of 138 individuals; 300 pilgrims to Mecca lost their lives in a similar fire in 1997. In 1977, 164 people were killed in Kentucky when a nightclub burned. A fire at a nursing home in Jamaica resulted in the deaths of 157. In 1994, a fire in a toy factory in Thailand killed 213 people, and the same year a theater in China burned, with some 300 losing their lives.

Besides localized fires in buildings, wildfires have been consistent causes of disaster, even though the loss of life has been much less dramatic. The most famous of these was the fire in Peshtigo, Wisconsin, in 1871, when at least 1,200 died. Large forest fires burned the same year in Minnesota and Michigan. In 1881 large portions of the northern half of the lower peninsula of Michigan were engulfed in forest fires. In 1894 fires broke out again in the northern, forested sections of Michigan, Wisconsin, and Minnesota, reappearing in 1908. All these fires were a product of the heavy logging that had taken place in the last thirty years of the nineteenth century and the first decade of the twentieth. By 1910 the north woods of the Great Lakes states were logged out, and the problem was transferred to the heavily timbered regions to the west.

In 1910, wildfires raged throughout the West and the Midwest; more than 6 million acres of national forest land burned, with large acreages of privately owned forest land as well. That year was the worst year in history of losses to forest fires, though it was to be rivaled by the years 1945, 1988, and 1996.

In the dry regions of the United States, as well as elsewhere in the world, forest and brushfires are common in drought years. Nearly every year there are brushfires in California and in the arid Southwest, where the brush accumulations grow rapidly. The spread of settlement into these regions has heightened the risk of disaster, and there is some evidence that arson plays a part. Aerial surveillance has helped to reduce the risk to individuals, and local and national agencies have developed new tools for fighting such conflagrations. Even so, tragedies sometimes occur: In July of 1994, 14 firefighters lost their lives in Glenwood Springs, Colorado, when a sudden wind gust moved a forest fire uphill at a rate of more than 100 feet per second.

The huge forest fires that burned in and around Yellowstone National Park in 1988 attracted the attention of the world through television broadcast. The United States Forest Service, which had for more than fifty years followed a policy of fire suppression, from the massive burns of 1910 until the late 1970's, had then changed its policy. It had become clear that, at least in the West, fire suppression, associated with the popular icon, Smokey Bear, had the effect of allowing large quantities of tinder to build up in the forest. Once a fire got started, the large amounts of fuel made it easy for the fire to expand into a major disaster. Thus the forest service had taken a "let burn" policy, allowing fires that did not threaten people to burn, hoping to keep down the accumulation of brush. However, in 1988 the fires got away from the officials in control, and the public was outraged when more than 1 million acres burned around Yellowstone, America's most-visited national park.

Huge forest fires in Alaska the same year drove the total of burned acreage to more than 3.5 million, and federal officials were forced to revise their fire policy. There was, after 1988, a greater use of what is called controlled burning, deliberately set fires that are confined to a limited area, designed to eliminate the buildup of combustible materials before they create massive conflagrations.

Forest fires will continue to be a problem, especially wherever drought conditions exist. In 1998, drought conditions in Indonesia led to extensive wildfires, some of them escaped fires that had been set by cultivators to open up new areas for farming. The smoke and haze from these fires spread all over Southeast Asia. In 1996, 6 million acres of U.S. forest land burned, the worst fire year since 1952, when the famous Tillamook burn in Oregon took a heavy toll.

One of the worst fire seasons in history occurred in 2000. As many as eighty forest fires were burning at a time in thirteen states in the western United States. Dry summer thunderstorms ignited vegetation that had not seen rain in months. Fires were responsible for more than 6.5 million acres burned, and firefighters were recruited from as far away as Hawaii, New Zealand, and Australia. In California, more than 70 acres of the Sequoia National Forest burned, along with 25,000 acres in Idaho and 20,000 in Nevada. Montana experienced its worst fire season in over fifty years, with 8 deaths from fire by August. The federal government allotted $590 million in emergency funds to combat the conflagrations. Because there had been few fires—and little rain—in these areas in previous years, there was much "fuel" for the fires in the undergrowth and vegetation. As earth's climate warms and drought conditions occur more frequently, more large fires are a probability.

Nancy M. Gordon

64: The Great Fire of Rome

Date: July 19-24, 64 C.E.
Place: Rome, Italy
Result: Thousands dead (accurate records unavailable), thousands of homes destroyed, more than two-thirds of the city destroyed

In the early morning hours of July 19, 64, a fire broke out in a slum district south of the Palatine hill. Due to the high density of poorly built and very flammable insulae (tenement houses), the fire quickly burned out of control. During the next several days acre after acre of the city burned up as the fire spread northward. Panic-stricken residents ran through the streets, where many were suffocated or crushed by crowds of people desperately seeking escape. Adding to the confusion were sudden winds that whipped up the flames in different directions. Supposedly, rescuers and soldiers, instead of trying to stop the conflagration, kindled it even more in greedy hopes of obtaining plunder. To make matters worse, after the original fire subsided, a second fire broke out near the Capitoline hill and lasted for three days. The damage was so extensive that many Romans feared the city would never regain its greatness.

By the time the fire was quenched, 3 of the 14 districts of Rome (as originally laid out by Emperor Augustus) were completely destroyed. Only 4 districts were untouched by the fire. The best ancient sources about the fire, historians Cassius Dio Cocceianus, Suetonius, and Cornelius Tacitus, did not record precise numbers of either lives lost or buildings destroyed. Cassius Dio wrote that "countless" people died in the fire, and it seems likely that hundreds of people perished in the disaster. An ancient letter, purportedly from the philosopher Seneca to the Apostle Paul, mentions that 132 domi (private homes) and approximately 4,000 insulae were destroyed in the flames.

Nero was emperor of Rome at the time, and his role in the disaster and its aftermath has been the subject of many debates on the part of scholars. Nero was at Antium, 35 miles from Rome, when the fire broke out, and he rushed back to his palace in Rome. While watching the fire from his palace, he composed and sang a song, supposedly called "The Taking of Troy," while playing the lyre. He certainly did not "fiddle as Rome burned," as stated in folklore, because violins had not yet been invented. The fact that Nero was not in Rome when the fire started and that when he returned he graciously opened his palace to shelter many who were made homeless by the blaze has led many historians to conclude that he was not responsible for starting the fire.

On the other hand, Cassius Dio, Pliny the Elder, and Suetonius allege arson by Nero. Nero was known to complain about how Rome was aesthetically displeasing. When he purchased 120 acres in the same area where the fire broke out to build an ostentatious palace, it served to confirm the widespread opinion of Roman citizens that Nero had the fire started in order to rebuild the city according to his own liking. The evidence for implicating Nero in starting the fire is, however, primarily circumstantial, and no firm conclusions can be made in this regard.

After the fire, Nero set about making Rome a safer and more beautiful city. New building codes were established, with an emphasis on the use of fireproof materials, and insulae were constructed with greater access to the public water supply. Wider streets were laid out, and Greek-style colonnaded buildings were erected. Nero also began his famous Golden Palace. This prodigious edifice, had it been finished, would have covered nearly a third of Rome. However, Nero's overly ambitious plans for rebuilding Rome resulted in severe financial strain. The growing economic crisis combined with the lingering opinion that Nero was responsible for the fire jeopardized the stability of Nero's rule. With the likelihood of riots and a revolt to his reign becoming ever more threatening, Nero knew that something had to be done. His solution had a profound impact on a new religious group.

Nero's advisers suggested blaming Christians for the fire in order to distract the public. Nero agreed and made a big display of arresting and executing, often by torturous means, many Christians. One of Nero's more hideous methods of killing Christians was to lash them to stakes, tar them, and then turn them into living torches—a supposed example of the punishment fitting the crime. Making Christians the scapegoats for the fire had its desired effect, and the immediate threat of rioting was diffused. The persecution of Christians, however, resulted in the martyrdom of two of Christendom's greatest leaders, the apostles Peter and Paul. The harrowing circumstances facing Christians during this time is revealed in a letter from Peter to fellow believers (written shortly before Peter's execution), in which he writes about their faith being "tried in fire" (I Peter 1:7).

The Great Fire of Rome continued to influence events in the Roman Empire long after the last flames were extinguished. The persecution of Christians did not turn public opinion in Nero's favor, and within the next four years two plots against his life were made. He was able to foil the Pisonian Conspiracy in 65 C.E., but he succumbed to a second plot in 68 C.E., purportedly committing suicide. Nero succeeded in making Rome a more beautiful city, but his Golden Palace was never finished. Furthermore, his fire-prevention plans did not prevent another major fire, in 191 C.E. Nero's blaming of Christians for the disaster resulted in the first official Roman persecution of that religious group. Although Nero's actions were restricted to the city of Rome, this persecution did set a precedent that led to larger and more widespread oppressions of Christians by Roman emperors in the succeeding centuries.

Paul J. Chara, Jr.

For Further Information:

Millar, Fergus. *A Study of Cassius Dio.* New York: Oxford University Press, 1964.

Tacitus, Cornelius. *The Annals and the Histories.* Translated by Alfred John Church and William Jackson Brodribb. Chicago: Encyclopaedia Britannica, 1990.

Tranquillus, Gaius Suetonius. *The Twelve Caesars.* Translated by Robert Graves. Baltimore: Penguin Books, 1957.

1657: The Meireki Fire

Also known as: The Furisode fire
Date: March, 1657
Place: Edo (now Tokyo), Japan
Result: More than 100,000 dead

The city of Edo, located where the eastern part of the central city of Tokyo stands today, became the most important city in Japan at the start of the seventeenth century. In the year 1600, Tokugawa Ieyasu defeated other daimyos (provincial military governors) at the Battle of Sekigahara. Tokugawa established himself as shogun (hereditary military dictator) of Japan, with his headquarters in Edo. Although the emperor of Japan remained in the ancient capital city of Kyoto as the symbolic ruler, the Tokugawa shogunate retained all political power until 1867.

Like all Japanese cities of the time, Edo was built of wood. Fire was always a potential hazard. The first official fire-defense system in Japan was established by the shogunate in 1629. At first, the shogunate employed a small number of resident daimyos to protect important sites within the castle and the family shrines of the shogun. By 1650, this system, known as the *daimyo hikeshi,* was expanded to include firefighters who watched over the residences, shrines, and temples of the daimyos who lived near the castle. This new system was known as the *jobikeshi.*

The Meireki fire took place in March of 1657, the third year of the Meireki era. A year of drought had left the wooden buildings of Edo particularly vulnerable to fire. In addition, a wind blowing from the northwest at hurricane speed ensured that a fire would spread rapidly throughout the city. Because the fire was thought to have been caused by the burning of a *furisode* (young girl's kimono) during an exorcism ceremony, it was also known as the Furisode fire.

The fire began in the Hommyoji Temple in the Hongo District of Edo. It quickly spread to the Kanda District, then south to the Kyobashi District and east

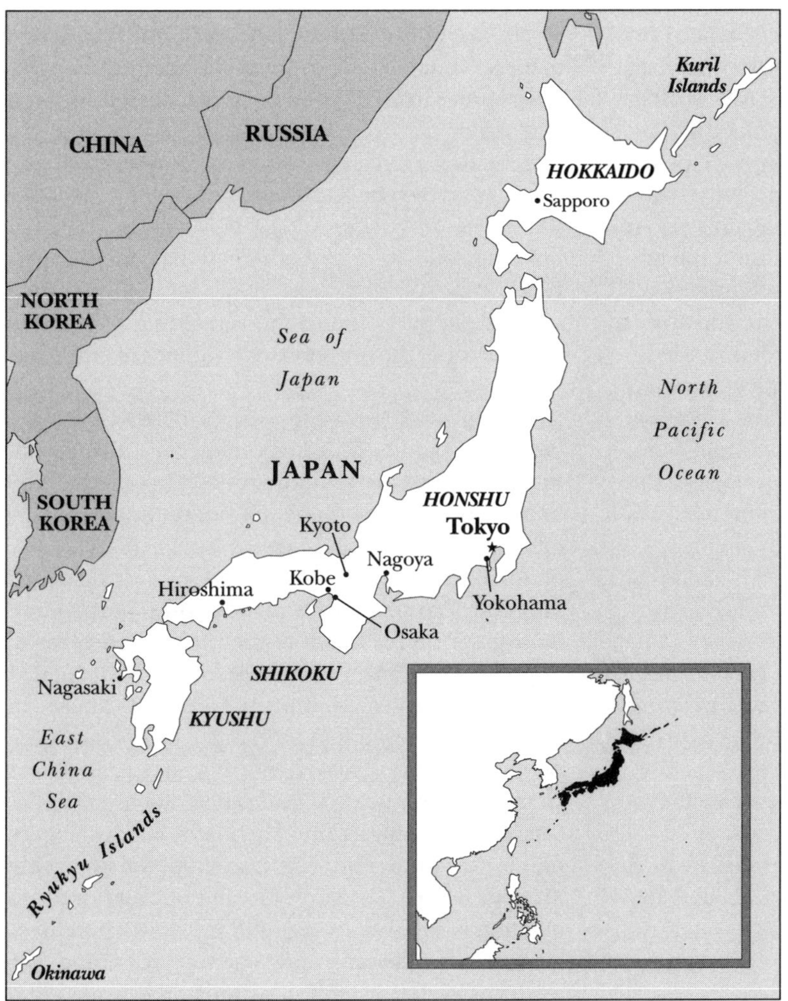

By the end of the third day, the wind and the flames decreased, but the smoke was so thick and the city so full of ruins that it was difficult to move from place to place for several days. Meanwhile, those who had lost their homes in the fire faced severe winter weather. More than 100,000 people lost their lives to the fire, either directly or as a result of exposure to the snowstorm that struck the city the day after the fire. When movement was possible again, the dead were loaded on boats and transported up the Sumida River to the suburb of Honjo. Here they were buried in large pits as funeral prayers were recited by monks of many different sects. A memorial temple, known as the Ekoin, was built on the site and remained until the twentieth century.

The shogunate responded to the disaster by setting up medical facilities and distributing food and money to those left homeless. The rebuilding of the city took two years and depleted the shogunate's treasury. The commercial sections of Edo were the first to be rebuilt, in an effort to restore the economy. The houses of the resident daimyos were not rebuilt; instead, the daimyos were sent back to their home provinces. The restoration of the castle was the last task to be completed. In an elaborate ceremony, the shogun entered the new castle in 1659.

The devastation caused by the fire led to reforms in fire prevention. During the rebuilding of Edo, the width of roads and the spacing of houses were standardized, in order to ease movement during an emergency. Special fire lanes were constructed at various intersections to allow for rapid motion. Laws were passed forbidding the common practice of stacking surplus goods along the banks of rivers, in an attempt to prevent fires from spreading by way of these large piles of flammable objects. The Ryogoku Bridge was built across the Sumida River in 1660, both to allow the city to expand and to ease move-

to the Fukagawa District. Zacharias Waganaer, a Dutch trader who left an eyewitness account of the fire, reported that the heat from the flames could be felt from a quarter of a mile away. He described the approaching wall of fire as a mile wide, with sparks falling from it "like a strong rain." The sun was completely blocked out by the huge amounts of black smoke.

The next day, the wind changed direction. The fire spread north to the Kojimachi District, destroying the houses of the servants of the daimyos. Soon the flames spread to the homes of the daimyos who lived near the castle, burning them to the ground. The castle itself suffered extensive damage. Although the inner section was saved, much of the outer section was destroyed. The castle's central tower, about 200 feet tall, was lost and never rebuilt.

ment across the river. Wide streets were placed on both sides of the bridge, in order to prevent fires from spreading to it. In 1718, volunteer fire-fighting units made up of commoners were organized in Edo. This system was known as the *machi hikeshi.* This system, which eventually included more than 10,000 volunteers, served as the main defense against fire in areas where the common people lived until the late nineteenth century. In 1868, when the emperor regained power from the shogunate, the *daimyo hikeshi* and the *jobikeshi* systems were disbanded, and the *machi hikeshi* system was reorganized into companies of firefighters known as the *shobogumi.* The *shobogumi* were placed under the control of the police in 1881, renamed the *keibodan* in 1939, and renamed the *shobodon* in 1947. In 1948, the first independent, professional fire departments in Japan were created.

Rose Secrest

For Further Information:

Kornicki, Peter. "The Meireki Fire." In *The Cambridge Encyclopedia of Japan,* edited by Richard Bowring and Peter Kornicki. New York: Cambridge University Press, 1993.

"Meireki Fire." In *Encyclopedia of Japan.* New York: Kodansha, 1983.

Sansom, George. "The Great Fire of Meireki." In *A History of Japan, 1615-1867.* Stanford, Calif.: Stanford University Press, 1963.

1666: The Great Fire of London

Date: September 2-6, 1666

Place: London, England

Result: 8 dead; 13,200 homes destroyed; 87 churches destroyed; 44 livery halls, 373 acres within the city walls, and 63 acres outside the city walls burned; more than 100,000 people left homeless; between 6-10 million British pounds in damage

The Great Fire of London, which raged from early Sunday morning, September 2, 1666, until early Thursday morning, September 6, 1666, was regarded by many contemporaries as the worst catastrophe in London's history. Coming shortly after the Great Plague of 1665 and during the Second Anglo-Dutch War (1665-1667), the fire caused substantial changes to be brought to London. Because much of older, medieval London was destroyed—an area 1.5 miles long by 0.5 mile wide—400 streets ceased to exist, and major landmarks such as St. Paul's Cathedral and the Royal Exchange burned, a major rebuilding project overseen by prominent architect Christopher Wren was undertaken. New regulations and strict building codes were implemented that aimed to prevent future conflagrations. Some have argued such massive destruction and the rebuilding of London was a factor in the prevention of additional outbreaks of the plague.

Background. During the 1600's there were a number of substantial fires in London and throughout England. Fires in London in 1630 consumed 50 houses; in 1633 the houses on London Bridge plus 80 more burned; and a gunpowder fire in 1650 killed 27 people, destroyed 15 homes, and severely damaged 26 more. Provincial fires proved to be much more damaging: In 1644, 300 houses burned in Oxford; in 1653, 224 houses in Marlborough; in 1659, 238 houses in Southwold; and in 1665, 156 houses in Newport, Shropshire. The danger of fire was ever-present from household fires; clogged chimneys; and from the businesses of tradesmen, such as bakers, brewers, blacksmiths, and chandlers. No fire departments existed, and fire-fighting equipment was primitive by modern standards. Leather buckets for carrying water, fire hooks for pulling down buildings, ladders, axes, brooms, and "water engines" and "water guns"—devices for drawing water from wells, rivers, ponds, and aqueducts and spraying the fire—were of some use.

London, the largest city in the British Isles and the second largest in Europe, with a population of about 350,000 to 400,000, occupied 458 acres within the city walls and sprawled beyond the walls into the "out parishes" or suburbs. In April, 1665, King Charles II wrote to the lord mayor of London, Sir Thomas Bludworth, and the aldermen of the city, warning them of the danger of fire due to buildings overhanging the streets. He authorized them to imprison people who built overhanging dwellings and to tear the buildings down. Many superstitious people had feared that the year 1666 would bring disaster because of the number 666, which was viewed as a sign of the Antichrist mentioned in the biblical book of Revelation, and there were many predictions issued by self-proclaimed prophets about London's destruction as a result of God's judgment.

View of London in the sixteenth century, before the Great Fire destroyed most of the city. (The Folger Shakespeare Library)

The Fire. The fire started in the house of the king's baker, Thomas Farriner (also spelled Farrinor or Farynor), between 1 and 2 A.M. Sunday morning on September 2, 1666, on Pudding Lane near London Bridge, in what is now EC3 in modern London. The streets in this part of London were congested and narrow, wide enough for only a wheelbarrow. Farriner's family escaped the fire by climbing out an upper-story window to the roof of the next-door building. A female servant's fear of heights prevented her from using this escape route, and she became the first fatality. Wood-frame buildings with pitch on their roofs and combustible materials, such as flax, rosin, oil, tallow, wines, brandy, and other alcoholic beverages, in warehouses on Thames Street fueled the fire, which was blown westward toward the center of the city by a strong wind. Samuel Pepys, the famous diarist, was awakened by Jane Birch, his female servant, at 3 A.M. to see the flames, but he was not concerned by the fire some distance from his residence.

Initially, the fire spread slowly, and most people were able to remove their belongings from their houses. Some ferried them down the Thames River and were charged exorbitant prices; others stored them in churches, only to have to move them again or lose them as the fire spread more extensively than anyone could have imagined. Lord Mayor Bludworth was awakened and surveyed the scene around 3 A.M. and concluded that it was not serious. An inoperative "water engine" near the scene, low water levels, and the failure to pull down nearby buildings allowed the fire to continue to spread. Some contemporaries said that an alderman opposed pulling down the buildings because his home would have been one of the first to be destroyed. The occurrence of the fire on a Sunday caught officials off guard and added to the confusion.

Rumors spread quickly that the fire had been deliberately set by Catholics or foreigners, such as the Dutch or French, and London mobs began assaulting immigrants. A French Huguenot watchmaker, Robert Hubert, later "confessed" to having set the fire. Although his story was full of inconsistencies and changed continuously, he was convicted and hanged in October, 1666.

The fire spread throughout Sunday; the streets were clogged with people fleeing and with household goods. The Thames River became crowded with sightseers on boats and goods floating in the river. The sound of crackling flames, crashing buildings, occasional explosions, and peoples' cries filled the air. King Charles II and his brother, James, duke of York, alerted by Pepys, arrived on the scene and heroically began to supervise and assist the fire-fighting efforts, as did William Lindsay, earl of Craven, who had stayed in London during the Great Plague the previous year.

People from the countryside came to London with carts and wagons to make money by helping to transport peoples' belongings. Some charged 30 pounds for use of a cart, and thievery was commonplace. Some contemporary eyewitnesses were critical of citizens for being more concerned with saving their household belongings than with attempting to extinguish the fire. People rendered homeless by the fire began to congregate in large open spaces and fields in Moorfields, Finsbury and Islington, and Highgate in the north and St. Giles Fields and Soho in the west. Citizens of different social classes, along with whatever possessions they could transport, crowded into these areas. The fire's impact was unlike that of the plague the previous year; the plague killed the poor, while the rich had fled. The fire destroyed the property of both the rich and the poor.

Although the fire had advanced only 150 yards east of Pudding Lane to Billingsgate, damage caused by the northern and westward movement of the fire started to become substantial. Citizens had been reluctant to pull down buildings to create a firebreak because of ordinances requiring people to pay to rebuild any structures pulled down. Eventually, sailors and watermen from the Thames River began pulling down houses with ropes and using gunpowder to blow up buildings. Samuel Pepys was concerned enough by Sunday evening to move his money into his cellar and to have his gold and important papers ready to carry away if flames threatened his home. At about 4 A.M. Monday, September 3, Pepys moved his belonging in carts while riding in his nightgown. By Sunday's end, the fire had burned half a mile westward along the Thames.

The fire's spread on Monday, September 3, continued to cause astonishment, and it seemed as if the air itself had been ignited, with the sky resembling "the top of a burning oven," according to diarist and eyewitness John Evelyn. He also noted that the Thames was still choked with floating goods, boats, and barges loaded with all manner of items. Charles II, concerned about a possible breakdown in law and order and the lack of success in stemming the fire's spread, established eight "fire posts" throughout the city, with the duke of York in charge. These posts, under the command of a nobleman assisted by justices of the peace and constables and supported by soldiers, provided for the protection of property and were a symbol of authority in that chaotic time. Coleman Street in the east; Smithfield, Adlersgate, and Cripplegate to the north; and Temple Bar, Clifford's Inn Gardens, Fetter Lane, and Shoe Lane in the west were the locations of these posts. Militia from the counties surrounding London were called up to be ready to assist.

Hopes that the fire might be stopped along the Thames at Bayard's Castle, a large, tall stone structure, were dashed, as this building burned and the fire continued to move westward along the river. The portions of the city along the river that had been destroyed were the poorer ones, but as the conflagration remained unchecked it began to consume some of the wealthiest portions, including Lombard Street, where many merchants, bankers, and goldsmiths plied their trade. Most of these individuals moved their valuables, mostly money and bonds, to Gresham College much more easily than could the tradesmen who had bulky goods and materials stored in warehouses along the Thames. The most important structure lost to the flames on Monday was the Royal Exchange, the principal location for trading commodities in London, such as pepper and silk. The one bright spot on Monday was the halt of the fire at Leadenhall, a marketplace for grain and poultry products, in what would be EC2 in modern London, which marked the extent of the fire to the north and east. Although the financial center of London had been burned, its relocation along with the city government to Gresham College to the north was a positive development that provided for a semblance of financial and political stability.

The worst day of the fire was Tuesday, September 4. Contemporaries living in the countryside reported that the red glow of the fire could be seen 10 to 40 miles away at night, and residents of Oxford, 60 miles to the west, noted that the smoke obscured the daytime sunlight. A strong east wind blew embers, spreading the fire rapidly. The Guildhall in the north burned, and the fire jumped the city walls and moved into the out parishes. The Fleet River, which ran to the Thames to the west of the city walls, was regarded as a potential firebreak, but the flames leaped across it and continued westward.

St. Paul's Cathedral, the most prominent landmark in London, burned, along with 150,000 British pounds worth of books that booksellers had moved into its basements for safekeeping. Eyewitnesses reported that chunks of stone between 20 and 100 pounds fell from the cathedral, and lead from its roof melted into the streets. The Exchequer (national treasury) was moved to Nonesuch, Surrey, and the Queen Mother, Henrietta Maria, moved to Hampton Court, west of London.

The Tower of London was spared because the nearby buildings had been blown up, preventing the fire from reaching it. Had fire reached the stores of gunpowder in the Tower, a tremendous explosion would have resulted. Samuel Pepys and William Penn, father of the founder of Pennsylvania, dug holes in their gardens to bury their wine and cheese, believing that this would preserve them. Charles II and the duke of York helped to man water buckets and shovels and scattered gold coins among the workers as payment for their effort. Such actions helped elevate popular opinion of the monarchy.

Late Tuesday night the wind began to drop. Because of the abatement of the wind and demolition work, the fire began to be contained on Wednesday, September 5. The Temple, one of the Inns of Court (law school), was the last significant structure to burn. Rumors spread throughout London that the French and Dutch, 50,000 strong, had landed in England and were marching on London. Such notions were fueled by the fact that the postal service from London had been disrupted, and newsletters that were routinely sent to the provinces had stopped, causing puzzlement and suspicion. By Thursday, September 6, when dawn broke, the fire ended after it reached its furthest border at Fetter Lane in the west, where brick buildings halted the flames, Cock Lane in the north and west, and All Hallows Church, Barking, in the east.

Pepys noted that it was "the saddest sight of desolation" that he ever saw. Citizens who walked through the city noted that the ground was hot enough to burn the soles of their shoes; ash was inches deep, and debris was piled up in mounds. Fires smoldered in basements for weeks and even months, and acrid odors permeated the air.

Aftermath. On Wednesday, September 5, 1666, Charles II issued two royal proclamations to begin the process of recovery from the disaster. In order to feed the displaced and homeless, the king ordered local magistrates to bring bread to London. He also had markets set up throughout the city and let people store their goods in public places. The second proclamation urged the inhabitants of surrounding towns to accept refugees and allow them to practice their trades. On Thursday, September 6, the king went to Moorfields to address the thousands of refugees there and explained that the fire was the judgment of God—not a conspiracy of Catholics, the French, or the Dutch. Charles II ordered 500 pounds of navy sea biscuits, or "hardtack," released for the refugees to eat, but the food was too dense for the people who were not used to it. Army tents were used to house the homeless, who also had built makeshift huts or had slept out in the open.

Another significant problem was sorting out the owners of the personal effects, household belongings, business papers, and wares that had been quickly deposited at several locations throughout the city. In the hope of recovering additional misplaced or stolen items, amnesty was declared for people who might have taken property illegally or by mistake. Scavenging among the ruins yielded items that were relatively undamaged or at least usable, especially precious and base metals that had melted. Although some merchants had no hope of such finds, the loss to booksellers was probably the most spectacular, 150,000 pounds, which involved a total ruin for a number of prominent merchants, and many scarce and rare titles were destroyed, leading to a substantial increase in the price of certain desirable volumes. Some contemporaries claimed that the price of paper doubled after the fire.

Another commodity that rapidly increased in price was coal, especially as cold weather would be coming in the following months; accusations of price gouging were common. Because of the massive destruction of housing and the large number of homeless people, competition for housing space was fierce, and rents quickly escalated, as they did for tradesmen seeking to relocate their businesses.

Because of the massive destruction, which left only a few recognizable landmarks standing, people had a completely clear view of the city from west to east, and the Thames River could be seen from Cheapside in the center of the city. The rebuilding of London was a daunting undertaking that started slowly. The London Common Council ordered inhabitants to clear the debris from the streets. Tradesmen and craftsmen were resettled, city offices were relocated, churchwardens were to report those who were in need of assistance, and donations came in from wealthy citizens who were either spared by the fire and from other cities. Because most charitable contributions for other previous disasters had come from London's citizens, the collection of donations was rather modest—16,201 pounds coming from collections in 1666 and 1668. Some provincial cities were concerned that the source of money to aid their plague victims would now be reduced because that money had come from London, which was now in dire straits itself.

Rain on Sunday, September 9, helped dampen the embers, and contemporaries noted that the attendance at church was greatly increased. Ten days of heavy rain in mid-October brought additional misery to the homeless but helped extinguish remaining hot spots. On Monday, September 10, Charles II ordered Wenceslaus Hollar, the prominent landscape designer, and Francis Sandford, a historian and author, to make a survey of the city, and their report formed the basis for most of the statistical information about the extent of the damage caused by the fire. Their work was completed and published later in 1666 and showed a before-and-after perspective to visually indicate the extent of the destruction. The king issued another royal proclamation on Thursday, September 13, 1666, mandating rebuilding with brick and stone, allowing authorities to pull down houses built contrary to regulations, for streets were to be wide and a wharf, which was to be free from houses, was to run along the Thames River. October 10 was established as a day of fasting by royal proclamation. Also on that day, contractors or surveyors were appointed to prepare a list of all the properties destroyed and their owners or renters in preparation for delineating the path and layout of streets.

Within days of the end of the fire, several influential citizens, including John Evelyn and Christopher Wren, had submitted plans for rebuilding the burned area. Town planning was developed as a more serious undertaking in the seventeenth century, and the fire and such widespread physical damage in a major city offered an unprecedented opportunity to put it to the test. Wren was appointed Deputy Surveyor of His Majesty's Works, and he drew up a plan for rebuilding London, which improved access to London Bridge, developed a wharf from the Temple to the Tower along the Thames, set the Royal Exchange as the center of town, and redesigned St. Paul's Cathedral and 51 other churches.

Legislation established a special fire court, which first met on February 27, 1667, to settle disputes over land, rents, and rebuilding. The judges' verdicts were final, and they did not have to abide by ordinary court procedures. They could even order new leases and extend existing ones. The Rebuilding Act (1667) provided for the seizing of any land not built upon after three years and its sale to someone who would rebuild. Four types of houses were permitted: two-story houses built on lanes, three-story houses on streets, four-story houses on larger streets, and four-story "mansion houses" for wealthy citizens. For each style of home the thickness of walls and heights from floor to ceiling were specified. Guild regulations were set aside in order to facilitate rebuilding, and wages and prices of materials were fixed. The revenue for supporting this law was to be financed by a tax on coal of 1 shilling per ton, which was raised in 1670 to 3 shillings per ton. This was London's first major set of building codes.

Despite regulations and legislation, the actual rebuilding went slowly because of the increased cost resulting from the specifications set forth in the codes and the disputes that arose over the widening of streets, which caused a loss of property or a reduction in the size of property. Other factors that caused delay were the difficulties in obtaining building materials such as lead, timber, brick, tile, and stone. This did open up new trade opportunities in the Baltic Sea area, a major producer of timber. By 1667 the streets had been laid out, but only 150 houses had been rebuilt. Almost 7,000 had been completed by 1671, although as late as the 1690's there were fewer houses in London than before the fire. An important development in the rebuilding was Charles II's laying of the first stone for the reconstruction of the Royal Exchange on October 23, 1667, which was completed by September, 1669, when the merchants occupied it. Ironically, the Royal Exchange was destroyed by fire again in 1838.

Another major project was the straightening of the Fleet River and the building of quays on its banks, which became the location for numerous warehouses. The monument to the fire, a 202-foot high Doric column of Portland stone, was erected between 1671 and 1677 and stood 202 feet from where the fire started. An inscription that blamed the fire on Catholics was removed during the reign of Catholic king James II (ruled 1685-1688), the former duke of York. The rebuilding of St. Paul's Cathedral began in 1675 and was completed in 1710.

A number of positive developments resulted from the Great Fire. It destroyed a substantial portion of a very unsanitary city, fire insurance was developed, new fire equipment was purchased, and fires received quicker responses. The London Common Council developed a plan that divided the city into four fire districts, each of which was to provide buckets, ladders, axes, and water engines. In addition, the various merchants' companies were to store fire-fighting equipment. Such plans were copied by other English towns and cities. London's redesign influenced the layout of Philadelphia, Pennsylvania, and Savannah, Georgia.

Mark C. Herman

For Further Information:

Bell, Walter George. *The Great Fire of London in 1666.* London: Bodley Head, 1920. Reprint. Westport,

Conn.: Greenwood Press, 1971. This first scholarly work of the Great Fire of London is lively and quotes extensively from primary sources.

Evelyn, John. *The Diary of John Evelyn.* Edited by E. S. DeBeer. Vol. 3. Oxford, England: Clarendon Press, 1955. This famous diarist and eyewitness of the fire recorded excellent entries about the blaze and the immediate aftermath.

Leasor, James. *The Plague and the Fire: London 1665/1666.* New York: McGraw-Hill, 1961. The author has produced a very vivid account of these two major disasters.

Pepys, Samuel. *The Diary of Samuel Pepys.* Edited by Robert Latham and William Matthews. Vol. 3. Berkeley: University of California Press, 1972. This famous diary contains the observations of an eyewitness who was well connected to the political leaders of the time.

Picard, Liza. *Restoration London.* New York: St. Martin's Press, 1998. In this social history, the fire and the rebuilding of the city are placed in the context of London's history in the late seventeenth century.

Porter, Roy. *London: A Social History.* Cambridge, Mass.: Harvard University Press, 1995. This stimulating work places the fire and its impact within a very broad historical context.

Porter, Stephen. *The Great Fire of London.* Phoenix Mill, Gloucestershire, England: Sutton, 1996. This profusely illustrated work provides a readable scholarly assessment of the background to, events of, and impact of the fire.

1795: Denmark

Date: June 6-7, 1795
Place: Copenhagen, Denmark
Result: 1,300 buildings burned, 18,000 left homeless

Two eighteenth century fires destroyed the central part of Copenhagen, Denmark's capital. A port city on the Baltic Sea, Copenhagen overlooked Sweden to the east and was a Scandinavian trade center during the 1700's. Copenhagen's harbor was home to fishermen, who sold their catches at markets in the city's interior. In 1795 that part of the city reflected approximately eight hundred years of Copenhagen's history through architecture ranging from medieval to Renaissance styles. King Christian IV, who ruled from 1588 to 1648, had ordered the construction of many of the more elaborate structures that were destroyed by fires in 1728 and 1795.

Situated on the islands of Sjælland and Amager, Copenhagen was surrounded by water and connected by bridges and canals. Despite this proximity to water, the nucleus of the city along Stroget, the main thoroughfare, was quickly engulfed in flames in June, 1795. The area that caught on fire was crowded with multistory dwellings and businesses, many of which shared walls or were separated only by narrow alleys or courtyards. Most of the buildings, some dating from the medieval era, were made from timber and had wooden shingled or thatched roofs, which easily were set on fire. Sea breezes spread flames to neighboring houses. The streets resembled mazes because of their tight twists and turns, and structures were compacted closely together.

The fire razed large sections of Copenhagen and burned several churches. Christianborg Slot, the royal family's granite castle, was burned. Fish markets, stocking barrels of herring and eels, burst into flames, as did wharfs, warehouses, and quays by the sea. Approximately 1,300 buildings were leveled by the fire, and 18,000 people became homeless. Copenhagen's population had been 60,000 in 1700, before the bubonic plague had killed a third of the residents, and the city probably had attained that number of citizens again by the turn of the nineteenth century.

Some solidly built structures withstood the flames, and the fire did not damage the earthen fortification walls that encircled Copenhagen. The fire caused building laws to be passed, requiring that houses built on sites where a structure burned in 1795 had to be constructed of stone or brick and that roofs could not be made from wood or straw. Apartment buildings erected where houses burned in the 1795 fire were required to have four separate sides and larger interior courtyards. Streets were redesigned to be wider and straighter with curved corners, so fire engines could maneuver more easily. Surviving buildings from 1795 comprise part of Copenhagen's tourism promotions. Visitors can explore underneath the restored castle compound that houses legislative and judicial bodies to look at artifacts preserved in the burned ruins by the Nationalmuseet.

Elizabeth D. Schafer

For Further Information:

Bendure, Glenda, and Ned Friary. *Denmark.* Oakland, Calif.: Lonely Planet, 1999.

Taylor-Wilkie, Doreen, ed. *Denmark.* Boston: Houghton Mifflin, 1996.

1825: Canada

Date: October, 1825
Place: New Brunswick, Canada
Result: 160 dead, 4 million acres burned

Considered one of the most ecologically damaging forest fires in the nineteenth century, the New Brunswick conflagration was accidently set by lumbermen in the southern part of that Canadian province. It is also known as the Miramichi fire, after the name of the region it razed. Drought conditions during the fall of 1825 exacerbated the fire because dry leaves burned quickly and winds spread the flames to adjacent foliage.

Before the Miramichi fire, New Brunswick experienced several fires in an 8,000-square-mile area between Fredericton, Chaleur Bay, and the southern coast. A hurricane fanned the flames toward the interior, and smoke hovered above the province. A 400-square-mile area near Newcastle was incinerated. At Fredericton, one fire consumed Governor Sir Howard Douglas's house, and a second blaze destroyed most of the town's structures. The fire moved into nearby forests and burned vegetation growing on the banks of the upper Northwest Miramichi River.

The Miramichi fire raged through a coniferous forest, where the resinous needles fueled flames. The waxy covering of other leaves, including holly and eucalyptus, fed the fire. Evergreens and oaks also were quickly consumed. The fire moved into northern Maine and ultimately affected an area of 4 million acres, including several towns and outlying communities. One of the most immediate results was decreased timber production. Total casualties included 160 people killed. In addition to timber being destroyed, the fire affected agriculture, weather, and wildlife in the area. Rivers were polluted with ash. Commercial shipping on the Miramichi River was suspended because communities no longer existed, and most warehouses had been destroyed. Total property damage was estimated to be $40,000. Some businesses, such as the Gilmour Rankin Company, prospered despite the fire's devastation.

Elizabeth D. Schafer

For Further Information:

Webster, J. Clarence. *An Historical Guide to New Brunswick.* Rev. ed. New Brunswick, Canada: Government Bureau of Information and Tourist Travel, 1947.

Wynn, Graeme. *Timber Colony: A Historical Geography of Early Nineteenth Century New Brunswick.* Toronto: University of Toronto Press, 1981.

1842: Germany

Date: May 5-7, 1842
Place: Hamburg, Germany
Result: 100 dead

The Hamburg fire of 1842 began at a store located on Deichstrasse near the harbor. At 1 A.M. on May 5, Hamburg's night watchman ran frantically through the city, shouting warnings about the fire. Cannon fire and church bells signaled the alarm to the city's sleeping residents. A group of 1,000 firefighters futilely utilized 34 fire engines and 11 fireboats against the fire but quickly lost control. The fire gained strength when it reached warehouses on Deichstrasse that contained alcohol, shellac, and rubber. A southern wind spread the flames, which crossed over a canal to Steintwiete.

Firefighter commander Adolph Repsold suggested blowing up several houses in order to establish a gap too wide for the fire to vault. Aware that this technique had successfully prevented damage during a New York fire, Repsold could not convince Hamburg's officials to approve his idea. They worried that property owners might demand financial reimbursement. Without a firebreak, the fire engulfed structures along adjoining streets and soon covered the entire city. Tall, narrow dwellings fueled the fire, which moved swiftly from one building to the next. By noon anxious city officials decided to pursue Repsold's plan, but the fire easily hopped over the exploded rubble.

The fire razed the Nikolai Church and the art and organ it housed. Citizens successfully fought the flames that threatened St. Katherine's Church and

This illustration from The Illustrated London News *from May 14, 1842, shows the destruction of Hamburg, Germany, by fire.* (Library of Congress)

nearby warehouses and homes. On May 6, firefighters used gunpowder to blow up the city hall and other structures, but the fire continued to spread. Volunteers joined the effort, but St. Peter's Church burned on May 7, and the city was filled with scorched linden trees. By May 8, the fire was completely extinguished on the street Brandsende.

Property damages totaled 135 marks, and 50 deaths were reported, with some estimates suggesting at least 100 individuals had been killed. One-fifth of Hamburg's 160,000 residents became homeless because of the fire. Looters reveled in the destruction. Hamburg had recently suffered occupation by French troops, flooding, and outbreaks of cholera and smallpox. The fire delayed the city's economic recovery, although reconstruction included installment of wider canals and stone bridges. Plaques inform modern passersby of the historical significance of the fire's originating and concluding sites.

Elizabeth D. Schafer

For Further Information:

Simon, Edelgard. *Hamburg: A Gateway for the World, 1189-1989.* London: Lloyd's of London Press, 1989.

1848: Turkey

Date: August 6, 1848
Place: Constantinople, Turkey
Result: 200 dead

Fires frequently burned parts of Constantinople during the nineteenth century. Europeans writing travel accounts about their adventures in Turkey often described observing fires and firefighters in various sections of the city. Constantinople was especially vulnerable to destruction by fire because so many of the city's structures were built from wood and closely placed together, often sharing walls. Streets were mazelike, hindering firefighters from reaching blazes quickly and enabling flames to jump between buildings. Many residents were careless with cooking fires, and sparks ignited houses. Observers at the Galata and Bayazid Towers contacted fire companies when a fire was detected and raised a crimson flag to alert residents of the emergency.

In 1848, fire razed the Pera section of Constantinople. Perhaps one of the best accounts of this fire was written by British author Edward Lear, who was known for creating humorous limericks. Writing to his sister Ann, Lear commented that eight fires had occurred since his arrival in Constantinople on August 1. He told her that the fires had consumed several hundred houses and left hundreds of people homeless and impoverished. At about midnight on August 6, a hotel waiter woke Lear, warning him that a fire was burning out of control. Lear went to the hotel roof, protected by moistened carpets, and watched the flames advance, illuminating the city. He heard houses crashing as the fire engulfed them and nervously saw the fire approach the hotel, being extinguished two houses away from his inn. Lear commented that the fire's victims were temporarily living in a cemetery and planned to rebuild wooden homes on the site of their burned domicile.

Elizabeth D. Schafer

For Further Information:

Ekrem, Selma. *Turkey.* New York: Charles Scribner's Sons, 1947.

Freely, John. *Istanbul: The Imperial City.* New York: Viking, 1996.

Mansel, Philip. *Constantinople: City of the World's Desire.* New York: St. Martin's Press, 1996.

1851: San Francisco

Date: May 3-4, 1851
Place: San Francisco, California
Result: 30 dead, $3.5 million in damage

Fire and theft plagued pioneer residents of San Francisco. The 1849 gold rush resulted in mass settlement of the area and quick erection of dwellings, ranging from tents and wooden huts to stone and iron-reinforced houses. The residents included adventurers, convicts, and entrepreneurs who embraced divergent beliefs and ambitions, often sparking conflict. The city's first major fire occurred on Christmas Eve of 1849 and instigated the formation of volunteer fire companies equipped with pumps, ladders, hosecarts, axes, and necessary tools. Many of the firemen had belonged to fire departments in urban communities before they traveled west to hunt for gold.

San Francisco had endured five significant fires before the 1851 conflagration. A May 4, 1850, blaze resulted in ordinances stating that people who refused to fight fires would be fined and that each dwelling must have water-filled buckets prepared. On the day before the 1851 fire, rumors spread that former convicts living near the waterfront planned to set the city on fire on the anniversary of the 1850 fire so they could loot. Just before midnight, flames ignited a paint store located in the city's Portsmouth Square. A sharp wind spread the fire in the business district. The city's raised plank sidewalks funneled the flames to buildings, which were engulfed.

Firefighters exploded structures with gunpowder in futile attempts to stop the fire. Thieves covered their faces with wet cloths to steal while residents were distracted. The fire was so intense that its glow could be seen 100 miles away in Monterey.

After ten hours, the fire was extinguished, having burned 18 blocks of the town's center and razing 1,500 houses. Several brick buildings survived, and employees doused the Dewitt & Harrison warehouse with 80,000 gallons of vinegar it held to save that structure. An area three-quarters of a mile long and a quarter of a mile wide was leveled. The 1851 fire caused greater destruction than the five previous fires totaled, and optimistic businessmen rebuilt their stores with thicker brick walls to fireproof them. Archaeologist Heinrich Schliemann wrote a descriptive account of his experiences during the fire. Authorities arrested Benjamin Lewis, accusing him of arson.

Elizabeth D. Schafer

For Further Information:

Lewis, Oscar. *San Francisco: Mission to Metropolis.* 2d ed. San Diego: Howell-North Books, 1980.

Lotchin, Roger W. *San Francisco 1846-1856: From Hamlet to City.* New York: Oxford University Press, 1974.

Mayer, Robert, ed. *San Francisco: A Chronological and Documentary History 1542-1970.* Dobbs Ferry, N.Y.: Oceana, 1974.

1866: Canada

Date: October 14, 1866
Place: Quebec, Canada
Result: 2,500 homes destroyed, 18,000 left homeless

The city of Quebec suffered several devastating fires in the nineteenth century. Before the 1866 fire, two fires destroyed 3,000 houses in the central part of Quebec. Residents rebuilt their homes, mostly wooden structures, and settlers, many of whom were French immigrants, moved to Quebec to work for local industries. These people were the primary victims of the 1866 fire. Because of the catastrophic fires, officials established the Quebec Fire Brigade on September 16, 1866, and the city financed the purchase of horses, steam engines, hoses, ladders, and a chemical engine.

Despite these efforts, firefighters were unable to contain the fire that ignited Quebec in October. Dry weather contributed to the fire's quick spread through the two districts of St. Roch and St. Sauveur, areas which had caught on fire previously and sustained losses. This section of Quebec was home to artisans and laborers, who lived in primarily wooden dwellings located close together. Industries, convents, and churches were also located in those sections. The districts' narrow, twisting streets delayed firefighters, and ash from the fire set nearby buildings afire.

The neighborhood had exceptionally clean, paved streets free of debris, which may have prevented worse fire damage. Nevertheless, the flames razed 2,500 houses and 17 churches. At least 18,000 people of Quebec's 55,000 residents became homeless. The 1866 fire encouraged Quebec officials to pass regulations regarding the building of wooden structures to reduce fire risks and providing more sources of water to extinguish fires.

Elizabeth D. Schafer

For Further Information:

Doughty, Arthur G., and N. E. Dionne. *Quebec Under Two Flags: A Brief History of the City from Its Foundation Until the Present Time.* Quebec: Quebec News, 1903.

1870: Turkey

Date: June 5, 1870
Place: Constantinople, Turkey
Result: 900 dead

This 1870 fire began at an Armenian home on Feridje Street in the section called Pera. A girl was carrying a tray of heated charcoal downstairs to the family's kitchen when she tripped and dropped the pan. Sparks from the glowing charcoal scattered on the steps and were blown through a window to the roof of an adjacent house. Flames quickly erupted atop the wooden structure and leapt to nearby buildings. Soon, the Armenian and Christian areas of the city were engulfed by fire fanned by brisk winds.

The city's winding streets hampered firefighters, and the fire razed 1 square mile, including 3,000 houses and docks along the Bosporus Strait. Stores, churches, mosques, hospitals, and embassies located near Feridje Street were damaged, although stone walls protected some of the structures. Officials estimated that 900 people died during the fire.

Tourist Edmondo De Amicis published an account of his experiences during the fire, describing how a guard refused to unlock a fountain near the fire until he received authorization to do so. In the meantime, the fire consumed more property while an enraged crowd gathered. He finally relented, but the fire was out of control. Sultan Abdul-Aziz observed the fire from a safe distance with his escorts. The Sisters of Charity tended to victims, and Muslims and Christians cooperated to rescue children. By nightfall the wind subsided, and the fire ended.

Elizabeth D. Schafer

For Further Information:

De Amicis, Edmondo. *Constantinople.* Translated by Caroline Tilton. New York: G. P. Putnam's Sons, 1887.

Mayne, Peter. *Cities of the World: Istanbul.* London: Phoenix House, 1967.

1871: Wisconsin

Date: October 8, 1871
Place: Peshtigo, Wisconsin
Result: At least 1,200 dead, 2 billion trees burned

At 9 p.m. on October 8, 1871, a forest fire that had developed into a rapidly moving firestorm swept over the small lumber town of Peshtigo, Wisconsin. The fire began almost at the same minute as the Great Chicago Fire, which was raging some 240 miles to the south, and a similar forest conflagration burning to the east in Upper Michigan. Within half an hour

Peshtigo was destroyed. The fire that engulfed and destroyed Peshtigo, Wisconsin, ranks as the deadliest fire in United States history to date. More than 1,200 people perished in the fire, and over 2 billion trees covering 1.25 million acres were destroyed. By the morning of October 9, 1871, the Peshtigo and Michigan fires combined to destroy 3.5 million acres of forest lands.

Peshtigo was a company town. The Peshtigo Company sawmill was owned by Chicago entrepreneur William B. Ogden and ran 97 saws, averaging a daily cut of 150,000 board feet of lumber. In addition, Ogden was principal owner of a three-story woodenware factory in Peshtigo. At the time it was the largest woodenware factory in the United States, producing thousands of wooden tubs, pails, shingles, clothespins, and broom handles daily. Lumber company officials, concerned for the safety of the factory and lumber mills located in the area, convened a management council to discuss the possible fire danger, but no decisive plan of action was agreed upon other than to clear a 30-foot-wide firebreak along the north side of the Peshtigo River and to fell trees in the immediate vicinity of the mills.

Conditions Leading to the Fire. During the late 1800's, the practice of clearing scrub brush and slash-and-burning in grassland regions of the eastern Dakotas, compounded by a year of regional drought and atypical meteorological conditions, established an environmental condition that started a chain reaction of unchecked prairie fires that burned through the weeks of August and September, 1871. Driven by the prevailing westerly winds, the fires crossed the Minnesota and Mississippi Rivers into drought-inflicted areas of old-growth timberlands to the east and north. These forest fires spread rapidly by crowning, or traveling between treetops, then dropping to the ground and starting more intensive fires from the additional fuel on the forest floor. Strong thermal updrafts then carry sparks and firebrands to ignite more fires.

Communications in this region of the country were almost nonexistent. It was not uncommon for major fires to take a minimum of several days, and often several weeks, to be reported in metropolitan newspapers. The only warning of swift-moving fires was often issued by stagecoach and railroad passengers, or by those fleeing the fire's rapid advance. As a result, these great fires moved eastward unchecked and relatively unannounced. By September 1, 1871, a series of great interlinked prairie fires stretched from the Canadian border through Iowa and remained unreported to the communities far ahead.

By the end of the first week of September, 1871, the sky from the Straits of Mackinac in Michigan, throughout northern Wisconsin, and as far south as Chicago, Illinois, and South Bend, Indiana, were choking under a cloud of smoke. During the early days of September several small jump fires, caused by burning firebrands carried high into the sky by fire-generated convection currents and then blown downrange by prevailing winds, had occurred west of Peshtigo. The forests surrounding Peshtigo were thick-barked, old-growth timber, which were usually not harmed by ordinary forest fires. Fires were often considered a nuisance rather than a threat.

On September 23, 1871, a jump fire came within several miles of Peshtigo. A firebrand from this fire ignited the main sawdust pile of the Peshtigo Company, but the fire was extinguished by a bucket brigade of 60 men. After this episode the management of the Peshtigo Company, now mindful of the potential danger of the advancing range and forest fires and the unchecked spread of smaller slash fires caused by nearby railroad construction, ordered large barrels of water placed by the side of every business establishment, bunkhouse, and hotel. Flammable goods were packed in crates, moved from company-owned stores to the riverside, and covered with dampened earth. As a lumber town, Peshtigo was constructed almost entirely of timber-frame buildings, wood-shingle roofs, and wooden sidewalks. The roads were covered with sawdust and wood chips to control mud formation and dust. Workers at the local bank dug holes in the soil beside their buildings into which they could dump money and valuables if fire reached Peshtigo. Many families soaked woolen blankets and laid them over their cedar-shingled cabin roofs. However, by September 25, the winds abated, veered to the southeast, and the direct fire threat to Peshtigo was removed.

With the exception of a small fire the next week, ignited by careless railroad workers, mill operations and daily life returned to normal in Peshtigo. Autumn weather in the U.S. upper tier states is dominated by shifting winds as advancing cold fronts plunge southward from the Arctic and meet moist tropical winds moving northward from the Gulf of Mexico. The clash of these air masses typically results in cold rains and churning winds, until winter snows begin. In 1871, however, the autumn rains did not arrive; drought conditions existed throughout the central United States. In the east, as far as New York City and Boston, the air was smoke-laden from the great fires burning unchecked to the west. Great Lakes shipping traffic was being negatively affected by the thick smoke because ships were unable to safely enter harbors due to poor visibility. Yet the fires continued to burn unchecked.

The Fire Reaches Peshtigo. Just prior to 9 P.M. on the evening of October 8, 1871, a fine ash began to drift over Peshtigo. There was no wind, and the ash settled like a fine snow. Residents noted that as the ash fell wild birds and pet animals began to utter noises and act in frantic bursts of behavior. Then the sky to the southwest began to turn a dark red color, silhouetting the surrounding trees against the dark of night. Unknown to the residents of Peshtigo, over 300 families in the nearby Sugar Bush communities were being engulfed in a raging firestorm with flames estimated to have reached a height of over 200 feet. There is no record of what happened in Sugar Bush;

nearly every resident of the communities perished in a matter of minutes as they tried to flee the advancing firestorm along the road to Peshtigo. There was no warning in Peshtigo.

The firestorm raced northeastward, spreading in all directions as it consumed old-growth trees and drought-ridden underlying ground cover. Winds accompanying the advancing fire, and driving it forward, are estimated to have been of hurricane velocity, swirling in gusts of over 100 miles an hour and even higher in the center of the firestorm.

Survivors of the fire reported that the previously still evening air suddenly developed a slight breeze, at which time the air instantly became very hot; survivors equated the rush of heat to that of a blast furnace. This was accompanied by a low moaning sound from the southwest, which grew louder, building to a deep rumbling roar like a train approaching from the distance. It was reported that as the roaring sound escalated, the sky to the west of Peshtigo flashed a brilliant red color almost blinding in its intensity, then faded to a glowing yellow as bright as the sun. Within seconds a violent wind struck the town, and the forest surrounding Peshtigo was engulfed in a wall of rolling and tumbling flames hundreds of feet high, moving at tremendous velocity. The rushing wind was so strong that trees were uprooted, roofs were lifted off of houses, and chimneys blew over.

The Effects of the Fire. Many of the buildings in Peshtigo were reported to have simply exploded into flames; one second they were standing, the next they were blown apart into flaming pieces of debris. The tremendous heat of the oncoming firestorm ignited the wooden bridge and the wooden railroad trestle crossing the Peshtigo River while still nearly a mile away. It has been estimated that the forward edge of the firestorm may have been close to 2,000 degrees Fahrenheit. As Peshtigo erupted into flames the glow could be seen as far away as Menominee and across Green Bay to Door County.

The mill, wooden structures, sawdust-covered streets, and pine-plank sidewalks leapt into flames, cutting off the escape routes of many Peshtigo citizens. Many people tried to seek shelter within buildings. Though the Peshtigo River was being engulfed by walls of flame and jammed with toppled burning logs, it was the only location to offer any hope of safety. Humans, pets, draft and farm animals, and forest denizens all rushed to reach the river's waters. It was impossible to flee from the fire—it was moving too fast. Survivors reported seeing humans and animals running toward the river simply burst into flames. Other eyewitness accounts describe the thermal updrafts and convection currents of the fire as twisting like tornadoes. Others reported that the air seemed to be aflame as balls of fire would appear out of nowhere and suddenly disappear or as hot gases struck a supply of oxygen not yet consumed by the advancing firestorm.

The Peshtigo River was deep, and many of those who reached it drowned quickly. Others were injured by panicked animals, carried away by the current, or struck by logs and debris. Those citizens who reached the river slapped their hands on the water's surface and splashed each other in an attempt to cool their skin and hair. Many stripped off clothing and wrapped it around their heads to keep their hair from bursting into flames from the intense heat. Even with a continuous soaking of water, skin and cloth dried out almost immediately from the terrific heat. Flaming debris falling into the river burst into steam. When the woodenware factory exploded, it showered those in the river with flaming tubs, pails, shingles, and broom handles.

Within the town, anyone who sought shelter in a structure died. In one tavern, over 200 victims were trapped and incinerated. Only those who found refuge in the river and several more who struggled to a nearby marsh survived the inferno. Within twenty minutes, the town of Peshtigo had been obliterated, and at least 1,200 citizens had perished.

After nearly six hours, the few survivors climbed out of the water and waited until dawn for the ashes to cool so the search for possible survivors and noncremated bodies could begin. Three victims were found in a large water tank near the mill, but the water had become so hot that all 3 died. Several people were found dead under similar circumstances at the bottom of a well. Many of the bodies were found huddled at the bases of trees.

Most of the bodies were burned beyond recognition. As a result, 350 victims of the fire were buried in a mass grave. Many victims who were not cremated died of suffocation as oxygen was sucked out of the air and into the firestorm. While the Peshtigo fire was the most deadly fire in American history, its destruction was overshadowed by the Great Chicago Fire that raged out of control the same night. For weeks after the disaster, the nation's press paid little attention to Peshtigo while devoting major coverage to the

Chicago fire. The governor of Wisconsin was eventually forced to issue a special proclamation begging the nation to divert their charity and gifts from Chicago to Peshtigo.

Though much is known about the existing meteorological and environmental conditions at the time of the tragic Peshtigo fire, a new theory was offered in the late 1990's concerning the cause of the super outbreak of firestorms the night of October 8, 1871. Based on eyewitness accounts, regional observations, damage patterns, and the curious circumstance of several large conflagrations all igniting at approximately the same time over a wide, yet confined, geographic area, some investigators suggested the firestorms may have resulted from a Tunguska-like atmospheric meteor explosion.

Randall L. Milstein

For Further Information:

Lyons, Paul R. *Fire in America.* Boston: National Fire Protection Association, 1976.

McClement, Fred. *The Flaming Forests.* Toronto: McClelland and Stewart, 1969.

Pernin, Peter. *The Great Peshtigo Fire: An Eyewitness Account.* Madison: University of Wisconsin, 1999.

Soddens, Betty. *Michigan on Fire.* Thunder Bay, Ontario: Thunder Bay Press, 1998.

1871: The Great Chicago Fire

Date: October 8-10, 1871

Place: Chicago, Illinois

Result: 250 dead, more than 17,420 buildings destroyed, more than 100,000 left homeless, more than $200 million in damage

Undoubtedly one of the most crushing catastrophes ever to strike the city of Chicago, Illinois, was the Great Chicago Fire that raged for three days, from October 8 until October 10, 1871, twice jumping the Chicago River and igniting buildings on the other side. The city, tinder-dry after a virtually rainless summer and early autumn, had grown very rapidly as the United States experienced a great western expansion. Buildings erected quickly to house the heavy influx of new residents and to meet the requirements of the city's burgeoning industrial and commercial enterprises were often flimsy structures that served an immediate and pressing need but could not withstand the ravages of a raging fire propelled by strong winds.

When the final tally was in, 250 people lay dead, thousands were homeless, an estimated 17,420 buildings had been destroyed, and property damage was set at over $200 million, an inconceivably large sum at that time, representing about one-third of the city's total worth. The fire put the mettle of the city to an extreme test. Many thought this catastrophe would mark the death knell of Chicago as a major transportation crossroads and industrial hub. The city, however, soon emerged stronger than ever, fully meeting the challenge posed by its great loss.

The Chicago of 1871. In 1871, Chicago was unquestionably a boomtown. A decade earlier, it had been the site of the 1860 Republican National Convention, at which longtime Illinois resident Abraham Lincoln was nominated to run for the presidency of the United States. By 1870, its population of 334,000 exceeded that of St. Louis, Missouri, the only other contender in the Midwest for the title of metropolis. The city, intersected by the Chicago River, with Lake Michigan on its eastern border, enjoyed a virtual monopoly in transportation, with ships coming from the eastern United States by way of the Great Lakes and railroads from the East converging in Chicago with those serving the West. The city's industries produced meat, lumber, shoes, farm machinery, and scores of other items. Chicago was also among the country's largest distributors of farm products.

In the year of the fire, Chicago sprawled over some 23,000 acres, on which nearly 60,000 buildings had been erected. The overall property value of the city at that time was slightly more than $600 million. Prosperity was evident on every hand, and an ebullient optimism was in the air. People had flocked to Chicago because it offered them a better life than they could find almost anywhere else in the United States, certainly better than they could anticipate anywhere else in the Midwest. Immigrants from Eastern Europe, Scandinavia, Italy, and Greece poured into the city, which could offer them the immediate opportunity of employment.

Beginning and Spread of the Fire. Shortly after 9:00 on the evening of October 8, 1871, a fire broke out in a barn behind the cottage of Patrick and Catherine O'Leary at 137 De Koven Street in the southwestern part of the city, a working-class neighborhood whose humble structures were mostly wooden.

Close to De Koven Street were planing mills, lumberyards, and furniture factories, all of which could add fuel to any flames that might rage near them.

When the alarm was sounded, the fire brigade rushed to the scene, realizing the danger that any such fire might pose when the town was so dangerously dry following a prolonged drought. A mere 2.5 inches of rain had fallen between July 3 and October 8, whereas normal rainfall for that period was between 8 and 9 inches. Only the night before, nervous spectators watched as 5 acres burned violently very close to the O'Leary barn, the site of the new fire.

Persistent legend has it that the fire in the O'Leary barn began when Mrs. O'Leary's cow kicked over a lantern that ignited some nearby hay. This bit of lore has never been substantiated, although it is altogether possible that this was the actual origin of the fire. What is known for sure is that when the fire bells sounded, the firefighters, exhausted from having fought a blaze that destroyed 4 blocks of the city the day before, arrived to find an inferno that was spreading rapidly. It was hoped that when the flames reached the 4 blocks that had been devastated the night before, the fire would be brought under control, but this was not the case, although this 4-block barrier prevented the flames from spreading to the west, which was spared the worst of the damage during the conflagration.

By 10:30 on the evening of October 8, less than two hours after the first alarm was sounded, the fire on De Koven Street was declared out of control. Nearby residents were urged to evacuate their homes, but many, accustomed to hearing the fire warnings several times a week, paid little heed to the admonitions to flee, convinced that the danger was not great. The fire raged so strongly that by 11:30 a wall of flames had jumped the Chicago River and advanced into the business district.

What made the fire of October 8 an extraordinary one was that it was fed by gale-force winds out of the

An 1871 lithograph showing the Great Chicago Fire viewed from the west. (Library of Congress)

southwest that soon caused the great bursts of flames to become walls of fire. The air quickly became superheated; blinding ash and swirling dust were blown into people's faces by the fierce winds, blinding them and making breathing all but impossible; the force of the flames created a roar like that of a runaway locomotive. Soon those who had gone to their beds blandly assuming that this was just another fire found themselves confronted by a situation from which many could find no escape. The wind was so strong that no one could outrun it. Turmoil and confusion gripped all of those downwind from the fire as it proceeded in a northeasterly direction.

Before it was over on October 10, the fire, driven by the strong winds, had twice leaped across the Chicago River, proceeding as far as Fullerton Avenue, the city limits, and stopping only when it reached Lake Michigan to the east. It left a burned area 4 miles long and 0.66 mile wide. An estimated 1,687 acres had been burned by the fire, and nearly everything on those acres had been reduced to ash.

Great Peshtigo and Western Michigan Fires. It is a matter of mere coincidence that as the Great Chicago Fire was raging, another fire brought on by the dry conditions and high winds that plagued the Midwest on October 8, 1871, was raging north of Chicago in Peshtigo, Wisconsin, a small lumbering community north of Green Bay. This fire, once ignited, spread with such rapidity that there was no way to control it. The pine forests that surrounded the town provided ample fuel for the conflagration. As the flames hit the trees, they actually exploded, their sap igniting like gasoline.

As it turned out, the Peshtigo fire, although it is less well known than the Great Chicago Fire, was the most devastating in the history of the United States. It resulted in over 1,200 deaths. Everyone in its path perished. The Chicago fire received more publicity than the Peshtigo fire merely because Chicago was a commercial and transportation center through which many Americans had passed, thereby becoming familiar with it. The Peshtigo fire wiped out an entire small community; the Chicago fire destroyed a major metropolis.

On the evening of October 8, yet another fire erupted in western Michigan. This forest fire in a sparsely populated area claimed few lives, but it left nearly everyone in the area homeless, some 15,000 people losing their residences to the advancing flames. All sorts of rumors circulated about these three coincident fires. Some thought that a comet had struck the earth, but it was soon determined that the cause in each case was a parched landscape that had somehow been ignited. Any parched landscape is vulnerable, sometimes being set ablaze by a lightning strike.

Extent of the Damage. Despite the vast destruction caused by the Great Chicago Fire, a few buildings in the city's central part remained in its wake, among them the Chicago Water Tower, which stands to this day as a city landmark. Ironically, the De Koven Street residence of Patrick and Catherine O'Leary was spared by the fire, although almost nothing was left standing around it. The famed Palmer House was completely destroyed, but the Michigan Avenue Hotel, whose panicked owner sold it for what he could get as the fire advanced, came through unscathed, much to the gratification and profit of its new owner, John B. Drake. It was saved because buildings adjacent to it were demolished before the fire arrived.

Only two of the exclusive residences on the elegant north side of Chicago, home to such notable families as the Ogdens, the Ramseys, the McCormicks, and the Arnolds, remained standing after the fire. The courthouse, which had been built at a cost of $1 million and whose bell had announced such memorable and historic events as the assassination of President Abraham Lincoln in 1865, was destroyed, its bell crashing down from its dome at 2:30 A.M. on October 9. Crosby's Opera House, Hooley's Theater, and the Washington Street Theater also went up in flames. The celebrated Field and Leiter Department Store on State Street was soon consumed by the advancing fire, along with some $2 million worth of merchandise with which it was stocked.

One of the major problems posed by the fire was that the wind propelled it in such unpredictable directions that firefighters often found themselves caught by a raging inferno in front of them and another such inferno behind them. The speed with which the flames spread was phenomenal. The dry, wooden buildings that lay in its path virtually exploded when the fire reached them.

Early Warnings About Flimsy Construction. Chicagoans had been warned well in advance about the dangers inherent in many of the buildings that had been built in great haste to accommodate the city's rapid expansion. *The Chicago Tribune*, whose own headquarters were completely destroyed by the fire, had warned its readers in a blistering editorial a

Frightened residents of Chicago flee the flames of the Great Fire, carrying what possessions they can. (Library of Congress)

month before the disaster that many of Chicago's brick buildings were only one brick thick. Their facades frequently crumbled and fell into the streets below. The cornices on many stone buildings had collapsed as the buildings weakened, sometimes crashing into the street and injuring pedestrians who happened to be in their paths.

Some of Chicago's most imposing buildings were impressive shells whose construction was so substandard that, had the fire not consumed them, they would surely have collapsed in the normal course of everyday use. The city's cast-iron buildings were not well secured on their foundations, so that even they were rapidly deteriorating and in some cases rusting away.

If the buildings in the business district were shoddy, residential construction throughout the city, particularly in the working-class neighborhoods such as De Koven Street, was even worse. Residential construction on the tonier north side of Chicago around Dearborn, Rush, Ontario, Cass, and Huron Streets seemed elegant at first glance, but most of the mansions in these exclusive neighborhoods had been built more for show than for safety.

The houses on the north side of town were filled with valuable furniture, oriental rugs, paintings, statuaries, and tapestries, but these priceless treasures were displayed in buildings that would go up in flames instantly in the sort of dire situation that marked the Great Chicago Fire. It took just flames and a strong wind to turn Chicago's most illustrious neighborhood into a field of smoldering rubble.

Fire-Fighting Methods in 1871. Certainly, given the fire-fighting equipment of that day, there was little chance of controlling a fire that advanced as quickly as the Great Chicago Fire. Much fire fighting at that time was done by bucket brigades, lines of people who passed buckets of water toward a fire. This meant that those fighting the fire, which generated a killing heat and which moved so rapidly as to threaten everything in its path, had to stand close enough to the conflagration to throw water upon it.

By 1871, Chicago was more advanced than many cities in its fire-fighting equipment. It had steam fire engines with steam-powered pumps to direct water onto fires that were burning out of control. However, these pumps were no match for the walls of flame that stretched nearly a mile wide in some places during the Great Chicago Fire.

By 3:00 on the morning of October 9, the pumps of Chicago's waterworks on Pine Street had failed, so the steam fire engines had little or no water to use in fighting the blaze. The only salvation now seemed to be Lake Michigan in the east, where the fire would necessarily stop. This natural barrier was some 4 miles from the fire's origin on De Koven Street.

Looting and Drunkenness in the Face of Disaster. As the Great Chicago Fire advanced, chaos broke out in the city. Distraught citizens poured into the streets. The owners of saloons, fearing that the advancing crowds would ransack their establishments, rolled barrels of whiskey into the streets, where the assembled crowds drank freely from them. Soon the streets were filled with drunkards, many of whom thought that the end of the world was nigh.

Soon wholesale looting began as the less honest of the spectators broke into shops and residences, taking from them anything of value that they could carry away. Some of these miscreants, running away with their loot, misjudged the extent and speed of the fire and were burned in their tracks as they tried to escape.

It was not until October 11 that Lieutenant General Philip Sheridan led five companies of infantry, which had been rushed from Omaha and Fort Leavenworth, into the city where, declaring martial law, they were accorded all of the authority of the police department. The city's most respected citizens welcomed Sheridan and his troops after living for three days in a lawless and chaotic environment. These troops maintained order in the city for the next two weeks.

The imposition of martial law was deemed necessary because, although there was little left in the city to loot, many citizens feared that professional criminals and confidence men might flood into town trying to rifle buried safes and vaults and trying to exploit the homeless. Some thoughtful citizens, however, feared that it was dangerous to place a city under martial law in peacetime because soldiers had not been trained to deal with urban populations. They had been schooled to deal with enemies, and it was feared that they might now, under martial law, act as though innocent citizens were the enemies.

End of the Fire. On the morning of October 10, the fire was beginning to burn itself out. At its northeastern extreme, it had been stopped by Lake Michigan. On the morning of the 10th, a steady rain fell upon the city, quenching most of the lingering flames.

As survivors straggled along the shores of Lake Michigan trying to find friends and family, they found that people, blackened by the smoke, were virtually unrecognizable. Many who had fled toward the lake as the flames moved in an easterly direction sought refuge on the beaches, but these beaches became so overheated that the only way for people to survive was to immerse themselves in the freezing waters of the lake, sometimes staying immersed for hours.

The morning was brisk and damp. Survivors of the fire huddled in shock in a cemetery near Lake Michigan that had recently been emptied of its corpses so that a park, eventually to become Lincoln Park, could be built. As they began to take stock, they realized not only that some 250 lives had been lost and many of the city's business establishments and residences destroyed but also that art museums, archives, public records, libraries, and other valuable and irreplaceable assets had been lost to the flames.

Personal property entrusted to bank vaults for safekeeping had been mostly destroyed. The Federal Building at the northwest corner of Dearborn and Monroe Streets, which housed a major post office and a customs house, was no more. Inside it, over $1 million in currency had been incinerated. It is not surprising that some people thought Chicago could not rise from its ashes, but those who thought the matter through realized that its ideal location as an inland port would assure its endurance as a city of considerable note.

Aftermath. Remarkably, despite the massive havoc that the Great Chicago Fire wreaked, the city's infrastructure remained virtually intact. The water and sewer systems continued to operate, despite the temporary disabling of the Chicago Waterworks during the fire. Transportation facilities, both ships and trains, still connected Chicago with the rest of the country.

Had the sewer system been destroyed by the fire, epidemics might have broken out. Had the water system been severely compromised, the city would have been brought to its knees. As it turned out, however, Chicago was in an excellent position to rebuild. Before rebuilding, however, legislature would pass ordinances that imposed stringent building codes upon those who were to reconstruct the city.

One of the outcomes of the fire was the election the next month of Joseph Medill as mayor of Chicago. Medill ran on a platform of stricter building codes and fire prevention and won handily, although one might question the validity of the vote—voting records had been lost in the fire so that allowing people to vote was a matter of faith. People who showed up at the polls and claimed to be registered voters were permitted to vote as long as they met two requirements: They had to be male and they had to be or appear to be of age.

The central business district of Chicago was laid waste by the fire. This main part of the city was built south and west of the Chicago River and extended as far as the railroad that ran along Lake Michigan to the east. Besides being the city's main shopping district, with its array of department stores and specialty shops, it was the home of a number of national corporations and of the renowned Chicago Board of Trade. This part of the city was now a shambles. A total of 3,650 buildings were destroyed in the central part of the city alone. Some 1,600 stores went up in flames, and 60 factories that employed thousands of people were totally destroyed. Temporary headquarters had to be set up for many businesses as plans were made to rebuild, this time with structures that passed the strict new fire codes that had been put into place as a result of the recent disaster. Six thousand temporary structures were quickly erected to house the thousands of homeless and to provide at least minimal shelter for the businesses whose buildings had been destroyed.

The elegant north side of Chicago accommodated almost 14,000 dwellings before the fire, ranging from the lakeside mansions of the rich to the humble cottages of those who served them. This section of town incurred the most substantial damage from the fire. When the flames had subsided, only 500 structures were left standing.

Rebuilding Chicago. Before long, a postfire building boom was under way. Such architects as Dankmar Adler, Daniel H. Burnham, and Louis H. Sullivan worked tirelessly to create a new Chicago that would be the architectural envy of the rest of the nation. It is in this refurbished section of town that the first steel-frame skyscraper was erected. The Home Insurance Company Building, opened in 1885, was the first of such skyscrapers to be built. Within the next decade, 21 new steel-frame buildings ranging from twelve to sixteen stories in height graced the downtown area, which now has some of the highest buildings in the world, including the famed Sears Tower that rises more than a hundred stories above the street.

As an aftermath of the fire, Chicago's public transportation system also underwent a great revitalization. Trams—horse-drawn, cable-drawn, and electric—began to appear on city streets. The elevated train, which serves thousands of commuters every day, was erected to provide rapid transportation to the Loop.

Within three years of the fire, Chicago had rebuilt sufficiently to regain its stature as the preeminent city in the midwestern United States. Workers poured into the devastated city to help rebuild it. It was not unusual to see hundreds of new houses being built simultaneously in a given area. About 100,000 construction workers raced to build some 10,000 houses as quickly as they could.

R. Baird Shuman

For Further Information:

Goodspeed, E. J. *Chicago's Holocaust.* Chicago: Author, 1871. Despite its age, this book, which is still readily accessible in many libraries, is one of the best on the subject of the Great Chicago Fire because it has the virtue of immediacy. Goodspeed tells the story of the fire with great verve and authority.

Holli, Mervin G., and Paul R. Green, eds. *The Mayors: The Chicago Political Tradition.* Carbondale: Southern Illinois University Press, 1986. The essay by David Protess entitled "Joseph Medill: Chicago's First Modern Mayor" reveals how the Great Chicago Fire catapulted mayoral candidate Medill, who ran a campaign based on fire prevention and strict building codes, into office. He was elected in November, 1871, a month after the fire.

Hutton, Paul Andrew. *Phil Sheridan and His Army.* Lincoln: University of Nebraska Press, 1985. The section about General Sheridan's marshaling five companies to go into Chicago within days of the fire and establish martial law is particularly relevant and cogent. Hutton's presentation is clear and concise.

Lewis, Lloyd, and Henry Justin Smith. *Chicago: The History of Its Reputation.* New York: Harcourt Brace Jovanovich, 1992. This overall history of Chicago reveals a great deal about the effects of the Great Fire on the city's eventual development. It treats the fire as one of the crucial events in the growth and ascendancy of the city.

Lowe, David. *The Great Chicago Fire: In Eyewitness Accounts and Seventy Contemporary Photographs and Illustrations.* New York: Dover, 1979. This well-illustrated, oversized volume contains excellent pictures from the period of the fire as well as the firsthand accounts of ten Chicagoans who lived through the catastrophe and had vivid memories of it.

Pauly, John J. "The Great Chicago Fire as a National Event." *American Quarterly* 36 (Fall, 1985): 668-683.

Pauly treats the Great Chicago Fire in a broad context, demonstrating its national implications. He shows how the city arose from its rubble to become one of the world's greatest metropolises.

Sawislak, Karen. *Smoldering City: Chicagoans and the Great Fire, 1871-1874.* Chicago: University of Chicago Press, 1995. This is perhaps the best extant contemporary book on the subject of the Great Chicago Fire. It is extraordinarily thorough and readable.

Waskin, Mel. *Mrs. O'Leary's Comet! Cosmic Explanations for the Great Chicago Fire.* Chicago: Academy Chicago, 1984. One of the more amusing explanations of three fires that took place on October 8, 1871, was that a comet had struck the Midwest, causing these coincidental blazes, one of which, in Wisconsin, took 1,200 lives, nearly ten times the toll of the Great Chicago Fire.

1872: The Great Boston Fire

Date: November 9-10, 1872
Place: Boston, Massachusetts
Result: 13 dead, 776 buildings destroyed, $75 million in damage

The Great Boston Fire originated in the basement of a warehouse on the corner of Kingston and Summer Streets near the bottom of an elevator shaft that extended to the attic. The warehouse was about 72 feet high, including a wooden mansard roof, and covered an area of 50 by 100 feet. As soon as the flames entered the shaft, they were carried upwards with tremendous convective force and burst through the roof shortly afterward.

The fire spread from the original building throughout the downtown area of the city by five major mechanisms. The primary mechanism of fire spread was from roof to roof by firebrands. A firebrand is a piece of burning material from a building that is carried by convective forces, such as wind, to a nearby building. The firebrands would land on the flammable wooden mansard roofs of adjacent buildings and spread the fire. The second method of fire spread was large tongues of flame that burst through window openings and spread the fire across narrow streets. Third, gas mains exploded in buildings and started new fires in adjacent buildings. It was not until hours into the fire that the gas mains were finally turned off. Fourth, heat was transferred by radiation from buildings on fire across the narrow streets. The fifth means of fire spread was explosions used by untrained personnel in an attempt to make firebreaks.

From Summer Street the fire raged north, consuming large areas of Franklin, Milk, Water, and State Streets before being stopped at the doors of historic Faneuil Hall. To the east it spread rapidly along High and Purchase Streets, destroying the waterfront area. The help of fire departments from 30 cities from as far away as New Haven, Connecticut, and Biddeford, Maine, was needed to bring the fire under control. This finally happened at 4 P.M. on Sunday, when it reached Washington, Broad, and State Streets because the engines could draw their water supply directly from the large water mains located there. A large number of water streams could finally be directed at the tops of the burning buildings with adequate pressure to reach the mansard roofs and penetrate through the windows into the interior of the buildings to extinguish the fire.

The factors that contributed to the conflagration are discussed in four major categories: urban planning and infrastructure, building and construction, natural factors, and fire service.

The streets were very narrow, with relatively tall buildings on all sides. Fire can spread across the narrow openings by convection and radiation once one building is fully involved in a fire. The tallness of the buildings limited the angle at which hose streams could be projected at them.

There was an insufficient water supply in the district where the fire occurred. The area had originally been a residential neighborhood, and the water mains and hydrants were drastically undersized for the amount of combustibles present in the warehouses. Water reservoirs were located under some of the streets, but their capacity was not adequate either. The hoses and hydrants had couplings of different sizes, which prevented the many fire departments assisting in the fire from coupling directly to the hydrants without using adapters. The pipes, which were only 6 inches in diameter to begin with, were restricted to 5 inches in diameter due to corrosion in the aging pipes. The hose streams projected at the buildings could not reach the upper stories or the roofs because of the limited pressure and the older-style hydrants. This was a major factor in the spread of the fire. Once an adequate quantity and pressure of water were available, the fire could be extinguished.

The mansard roofs were constructed of wood rather than the stone of the French buildings from which they were copied. The wood frame on the roof presented a large combustible surface to the fire, allowing it to spread rapidly above the heads of the firefighters. Wood trim around windows and doors, as well as timber floors, contributed combustible material to the fire. The granite veneers used on many buildings heated up and broke off or split apart, and the facades collapsed as the veneers separated from the main structure. The warehouse buildings were large, open-plan structures that were filled with great amounts of flammable contents. Compartmentation of the warehouses would have reduced the spread of the fire within the buildings.

Another problem was the warehouses' continuous vertical openings from the basement of the buildings to the roof. Once a fire begins in an open shaft, convective forces will naturally push the fire upwards. The fire will then spread onto intervening floors, moving horizontally as well as vertically, finally penetrating the roof.

Natural factors also existed. There was a 5- to 9-mile-per-hour wind the evening of the fire. Currents of air created by the fire gave the appearance of a firestorm or fierce wind. Large amounts of oxygen were drawn into the fire, creating local convective currents.

There was a critical delay in sounding the alarm for the fire because the policemen were between shifts. This allowed enough time for the fire to become fully developed in the building of origin before fire department personnel arrived on the scene. Many of the horses used to pull the fire engines were sick, and the engines and pumpers had to be pulled by firefighters from the stations to the fire. The firefighters became fatigued after fighting the fire for over twenty-five hours. The chief engineer could not command the entire fire front on foot.

As a result of the hearings held after the fire, the department was reorganized and placed under the Board of Fire Commissioners. All companies in high-value areas were staffed with full-time personnel. A number of new companies, including a fireboat company, were placed in service. Modern equipment was purchased, and additional hydrants were installed on larger pipes to improve water pressure. The fire-alarm system was transferred to the fire department, and district chiefs were made permanent. The board instituted a training program and a separate maintenance department.

In 1871 a bureau for the survey and inspection of buildings was established as the first agency to regulate building in Boston. Its authority was greatly expanded after the fire. Strict regulations were put into effect with regard to the thickness of walls and the materials to be used on the exposed portions of buildings. The fire service was reorganized. Boston thus entered the modern age of fire protection for its citizens after learning a valuable lesson in fire prevention from the disaster of 1872.

Gary W. Siebein

For Further Information:

Bugbee, James M. "Fires and Fire Departments." *The American Review*, July, 1873, 112-141.

Lyons, Paul R. *Fire in America*. Boston: National Fire Protection Association, 1976.

Sammarco, Anthony Mitchell. *The Great Boston Fire of 1872*. Dover, N.H.: Arcadia, 1997.

1894: Minnesota

Date: September 1, 1894

Place: Hinckley, Minnesota, and surrounding communities and countryside

Result: More than 440 dead, more than 300,000 acres burned in Pine County and swaths in 4 neighboring counties, at least $25 million in damage

On September 1, 1894, a disastrous forest fire struck the east-central Minnesota lumber and railroad town of Hinckley, on the Grindstone River in Pine County. In minutes, it devastated Hinckley and surrounding settlements, and it eventually rolled across 20 miles of countryside.

The disaster was similar in pattern to many other fires that struck the Great Lakes states between 1870 and 1920. Human activities had set the stage: Dry fuel was plentiful owing to slash (wood debris) left behind by loggers and to storage of wood in lumberyards and at railroad sidings. Ignition sources were also plentiful because farmers commonly used fire to clear land, and fires were frequently started by sparks from trains. Further, fires often persisted in peat bogs. Thus, fire was a common and familiar occurrence.

Another typical element of Great Lakes states fires was drought, and 1894 was no exception. At St. Paul, less than 80 miles away, only 2.2 inches of rain fell from May through August—16 percent of normal rainfall. Temperatures had been high, and relative humidity had been low all summer.

Pine stumps were smoldering that summer in the swamps and cutover land around Hinckley and nearby towns. In addition, fires burned along the two railroad lines that passed through Hinckley—the Eastern Railway of Minnesota/Great Northern line, and the St. Paul and Duluth Railroad (later to become the Northern Pacific). These railroad fires were thought to be a major cause of the disaster. Yet, ironically, trains were also the means by which many people were saved.

Early on the afternoon of September 1, a stiff southwest wind fanned smoldering flames. Efforts by the Hinckley fire department to fight blazes on the edge of town proved futile. Shortly after 3 P.M., Hinckley received word that Brook Park, 9 miles southwest on the Great Northern line, was burning and that some of its inhabitants had died. At about the same time, another fire was burning its way toward Mission Creek, 3 miles south of Hinckley, on the St. Paul and Duluth line. The two fires converged at Hinckley.

A great black cloud arriving from the south impelled Hinckley's inhabitants to flee, many to the Eastern Minnesota Railroad depot. There, a passenger train and a freight train were hastily coupled together. More than 350 boarded as the depot itself began to burn and the paint on the sides of the cars blistered. By 4 P.M., the train was steaming northward, through burning brush and trees, as flames engulfed the town. The Grindstone River Bridge, just outside Hinckley, was already burning when the train crossed. The train then took aboard another 40 refugees. At Sandstone, 9 miles north of Hinckley, the train stopped briefly to warn the inhabitants, but they paid little heed. Leaving Sandstone, the train crossed another burning bridge, this time across the Kettle River. Minutes later, the bridge began to collapse. The train proceeded to safety in West Superior, Wisconsin.

Many of those who remained in Hinckley died, including 127 who took refuge in a swampy clearing near the Grindstone River. This spot was the deadliest in the fire area. Of those who ran to the river itself, a few survived, but others drowned. The fate of about 100 who fled to a gravel pit holding shallow water was better: All but one survived. Some people sought refuge in wells or root cellars, only to suffocate there.

Some 200 other Hinckley residents fled north along the tracks of the St. Paul and Duluth Railroad. Thirty-three of them succumbed to flames. Then a southbound train stopped and took the survivors aboard. Rather than continuing south, into the advancing fire front, the train's engineer reversed gears and headed back toward Skunk Lake, a swamp 6 miles north of Hinckley. As it reached the lake, the train broke into flames, but nearly all of the 300 passengers and refugees reached safety in the lake.

Hinckley was badly burned. At least 248 people were killed—the highest death toll in the fire's area—and the town's main lumber mill was destroyed. Sandstone was also destroyed, and the death toll there and in the surrounding countryside, at more than 60, was the second highest in the fire. Many of those who survived in Sandstone had taken refuge in the Kettle River. In Brook Park, 28 people, or more than one-fifth of the population, died. Twenty-three Ojibwa Indians died near Mille Lacs Lake. Mission Creek was destroyed, but the townspeople survived in a large potato patch. The town of Partridge (now Askov) was destroyed, but the death toll was low. Not only towns but also logging camps, homesteads, and farms burned. Large tracts of virgin white pine were destroyed.

By midnight on September 1, relief parties and provisions were on the way. The following day, corpses were found all across the charred landscape. In a field 1 mile east of Hinckley, 248 bodies, many of them unidentified, were buried in trenches. Several years later, a monument was erected there to commemorate the disaster.

Telegraphed accounts of the fire brought newspaper reporters from all quarters to the burned area. Their reports generated sympathy, and money and supplies poured in from around the country. The Minnesota governor appointed a State Fire Relief Commission to supervise distribution of aid to victims. Despite the fact that they had previously experienced many forest fires that had devastated towns and settlements, it was the Hinckley disaster that started Minnesotans talking about prevention. A little was done, but it was many years before effective measures were put in place.

Jane F. Hill

For Further Information:

Anderson, Antone A. *The Hinckley Fire.* New York: Comet Press, 1954.

Garrison, Webb. *Disasters That Made History.* Nashville: Abingdon Press, 1973.

Holbrook, Stewart H. *Burning an Empire: The Story of American Forest Fires.* New York: Macmillan, 1943.

Larsen, Lawrence Harold. *Wall of Flames: The Minnesota Forest Fire of 1894.* Fargo: North Dakota Institute for Regional Studies, 1984.

Swenson, Grace Stageberg. *From the Ashes: The Story of the Hinckley Fire of 1894.* Stillwater, Minn.: Croixside Press, 1979.

1900: New Jersey

Date: June 30, 1900
Place: Hoboken, New Jersey
Result: 326 dead, 250 injured, $2.2 million in damage

The piers of Hoboken played a key role in the American economy in 1900. With no tunnel underneath the Hudson River to connect Manhattan Island with the mainland to the west, all goods bound to New York had to be taken off railcars at Hoboken and transported to cargo boats. It was, in all likelihood, from one of these cargo boats that a crew member threw a burning bale of cotton overboard, mistakenly thinking it would hit the water and that the flames would be put out. Instead, it hit a wooden pier, quickly lighting it.

The fire spread to three German liners, the *Main*, the *Bremen*, and the *Saale*, which were quickly burnt in a fire endangering the other ships in the harbor as well. Another German ship, the *Kaiser Wilhelm der Grosse*, was damaged. A coda to the tragedy was added when the Hawkhurst Land Company sued the North German Lloyd line for trespassing on its land, which it had used to try to separate the burning ships from the other vessels in the harbor.

Nicholas Birns

For Further Information:

The New York Times, July 1-6, October 19, 1900.

Newberry, Lida, *New Jersey: A Guide to Its Present and Past.* New York: Hastings House, 1977.

1904: Maryland

Date: February 7, 1904
Place: Baltimore, Maryland
Result: 140 acres destroyed, estimated $125-$150 million in damage

The most memorable fire in the history of Baltimore began on a frigid Sunday morning in February of 1904. Eerily, it occurred almost exactly one hundred years after what had previously been Baltimore's most destructive conflagration, in 1804. The 1904 fire started in the basement of the warehouse of John E. Hurst and Company, a major local commercial concern which sold dry goods to other businesses.

Almost instantly, noxious gas began to overwhelm the firemen who had responded to the initial crisis. Sensing that a major catastrophe was at hand, fire departments from neighboring cities were contacted but made little headway against the blaze. A fierce wind from the northeast exacerbated the fire, rendering useless the water hoses that were mustered against it. The historic wooden houses of Baltimore's central city were obliterated, and most of the city's

A view of downtown Baltimore after the devastating fire of 1904. (AP/Wide World Photos)

traditional downtown was completely destroyed. The fire was finally stopped when it could not cross Jones Falls, which feed into Baltimore's harbor.

Nearly 1,600 buildings, containing up to 2,500 businesses, were wiped out by the fire. The Maryland Institute, a well-known college of art which had been in operation for seventy-five years, was completely burned. Both people's homes and Baltimore's economic base were devastated, though there was only one confirmed death: Mayor Robert M. McLane committed suicide in the wake of the fire. In the opinion of many, the fire inflicted a level of psychological as well as physical damage on Baltimore's inner city, which led to the deterioration and poverty characterizing that area for much of the twentieth century.

Some heartening developments emerged from the fire as well. In the past, Baltimore volunteer firefighters had been famed for placing more stress on fighting among themselves in political factions than in quelling fires. In the 1904 fire, though, the firefighters showed great bravery, often trying to save a threatened building until it became clearly impossible, and even then barely escaping with their own lives, leaving their equipment behind. They employed such strategies as dynamiting buildings so that they collapsed before spreading the fire onto neighboring sites; though this approach did not work, it was important in the evolution of fire-fighting techniques.

Almost immediately, plans for rebuilding were implemented; over 400 homes and office buildings were built within the next few years. Local insurance companies paid most of the outstanding policies, which expedited the reconstruction. The industrialist and philanthropist Andrew Carnegie supplied most of the money for the rebuilding of the Maryland Institute.

Nicholas Birns

For Further Information:

The New York Times, February 8-9, 1904.

Owens, Hamilton. *Baltimore on the Chesapeake.* Garden City, N.Y.: Doubleday, 1941.

1908: Massachusetts

Date: April 12, 1908, Palm Sunday
Place: Chelsea, Massachusetts
Result: More than 12 dead, 85 missing, 17,450 homeless, $6 million in damage

At 11 A.M. on Sunday, April 12, 1908, a fire was reported in the facilities of the Boston Blacking Company in this suburb of Boston. Although the fire department of the city of Chelsea attempted to contain the fire, gale winds of 40 miles per hour caused sparks to jump from the Boston Blacking Company building to some of the frame houses nearby, and the flames rapidly spread out of control to the entire center of the city of Chelsea.

Chelsea was located on a peninsula surrounded on three sides by water: Boston harbor on the west, Chelsea Creek on the south, and Mystic River on the north. The lowlands bordering these bodies of water were occupied by industrial facilities near the water and by small, closely packed wooden houses immediately adjacent to the factories. The houses were occupied by workers in the factories; they were mostly immigrants who had recently come to the United States, particularly Jews from the Russian Empire.

The fire spread rapidly through the wooden houses, while the occupants tried to rescue some of their belongings. Throughout the day people dragged household possessions from the houses in the path of the fire and carted them off to a relief area. The fire spread rapidly from the small wooden dwellings occupied by factory workers to the central business district, which it almost totally demolished. Even buildings made of granite crumbled from the intensity of the fire. In all, one-fourth of the city of Chelsea burned, some 350 acres. The fire was contained when it reached the Mystic River and the Boston and Maine Railroad tracks.

The fire destroyed 13 churches of almost every denomination. Nine schools and several public libraries were also destroyed. The flames could be seen as far away as Portland, Maine. The fire threatened to move across the water to Boston itself. The shoreline contained several oil facilities on both sides of the water. Those on the Chelsea side eventually caught fire and burned. Tugs attempted, in vain, to tow some barges loaded with oil containers away from the shore, but the intensity of the fire was so great that all the tow lines burned through before the barges could be towed out of harm's way. On the Boston side, the Boston fire department struggled all day to prevent the Standard Oil facility from being engulfed as well. Although several oil tanks at the water's edge caught

The great fire that engulfed Chelsea, Massachusetts, in 1908. (AP/Wide World Photos)

fire, the Boston fire department succeeded in saving the main installation.

The fire evoked a nationwide response. Within two weeks, some $300,000 had been contributed for relief for the homeless, largely immigrant families. Many organizations joined in the relief effort, particularly the Knights of Columbus, the Knights of Pythias, the Odd Fellows, the Elks, and the Eagles. The Central Relief Committee, located in the new high school, was formed to coordinate the relief effort. Many owners of autos volunteered to transport donations to the relief center.

Reconstruction began immediately and was largely completed by 1910. After the fire, some of the older ethnic elements in Chelsea moved out to other Boston suburbs. Their place was taken by new immigrants, so that by 1915, 84 percent of Chelsea's population consisted of immigrants and their families.

Nancy M. Gordon

For Further Information:

Boston Globe, April 13, 1908, p. 1.

Souvenir Book of the Great Chelsea Fire, April 12, 1908. Boston: New England Paper and Stationery, 1908.

1909: Illinois

Date: November 13, 1909
Place: Cherry, Illinois
Result: 259 dead

The Cherry Mine is about 100 miles southwest of Chicago at Cherry, Illinois. Opened in 1904 by the St. Paul Mining Company, a subsidiary of the Chicago, Milwaukee and St. Paul Railroad, the mine existed solely to supply fuel for the railroad. Cherry, named for James Cherry, the railroad engineer in charge, was built to house miners. Almost all of the town's approximately 2,500 inhabitants consisted of miners or their families. On the morning of the disaster, 484 men went underground in the mine.

Up-to-date, well-managed, and prosperous, the Cherry Mine was a sought-after place to work. It was dry, gas-free, and, with the railroad as its owner, largely immune from seasonal layoffs. Also, the Cherry Mine was one of the first lit by electricity. Unfortunately, however, the electrical system shorted out three weeks prior to the disastrous fire, and oil torches were put temporarily into use. Such torches were, at the time, widespread in coal mines.

The Layout of the Mine. The Cherry Mine was entered through two shafts. The "second vein" (Illinois Springfield Number 5 Coal), a 5 foot, 2 inch seam mined at 316 feet, was the principal coal source when the mine burned. Beneath this, the lowermost of the three horizontal coal seams in the mine, the 3.5-foot "third vein" (Illinois Colchester Number 2 Coal) was mined at a depth of 486 feet. The "first vein" (Illinois Number 7, Streator Coal) at 271 feet was not mined in the Cherry Mine.

On both levels, miners were isolated far from the shafts. The main shaft hoist connected the second level to the tipple, or head frame, but did not run down the shaft to the third seam. A second hoist in the ventilation and escape shaft connected the second and third seams but did not reach the surface. Thus, men and cars from the lower level were lifted to the second level, proceeded 200 feet past the mule stables to the main hoist and, at this point, were lifted to the tipple. There was no hoist in the air shaft above the second level, but an enclosed wooden stairway and ladders allowed miners to climb from the bottom to the top of the shaft. Two tunnels, mined through coal, passed around the stables to connect the shafts. These passages were propped with pine timbers and were partially lined with pine planks. About 75 mules were used to haul wooden mine cars between the working faces and the hoist landings. A "pillar" of unmined coal surrounded and supported the two shafts, stables, and entries.

The second level of the Cherry Mine was worked by the room-and-pillar method. Nearly a mile of "main entries," or tunnels, extended in an east-west direction from the shaft. Additional entries crossed the main entries at right angles to outline rectangular panels for mining. As coal was mined, "pillars," left in a rectangular arrangement, supported the "back," or roof.

The third seam was mined by the long-wall method because the seam was so thin that rock had to be excavated from the roof to permit men and mules to pass. Haulage entries radiated outwards from the shaft, and working tunnels branched out at acute angles. Here men had to crouch under a 3.5-foot "back." As the coal mining proceeded, the roof was allowed to collapse behind the miners, with only the tunnels remaining open. Miners on both levels were dependent on messengers for communication.

The Fire. At about 1:30 P.M. on November 13, 1909, a carload of hay was apparently ignited by kerosene dripping from the open torch at the second vein air-shaft landing. This small fire was ignored by miner Emil Gertz as he hurried to catch the 1:30 hoist. "Cagers," or hoist operators, Alex Rosenjack and Robert Dean continued hoisting coal for several minutes after they knew about the fire. Minutes later, Rosenjack and two others tried unsuccessfully to dump the burning car down the air shaft. Eventually, aided by a group of miners from the third vein, they pushed the car into the air shaft, where the fire died in the water-filled "sump" at the shaft bottom.

Meanwhile, however, timbers in the second level entries had ignited, and dense smoke already prevented miners from reaching the only water supply in the mine—a hose in the stables that supplied water for the mules. The fire raged out of control. At least forty-five minutes—too late for many to escape—passed before all men at the remote mining faces heard the warning. One cageload of men came up from the lower level before the cager fled, and a few additional men climbed the escape shaft stairs. Some second-vein men reached the hoist shaft from the side opposite the fire and escaped before smoke and flame blocked the shaft. Pit boss Alex Norberg then ordered the fan reversed to draw air down the main shaft, and mine manager John Bundy organized twelve volunteers to go down on the hoist to rescue trapped miners. After six successful trips, the seventh ended when the rescuers burned to death in the cage. Tragically, the hoist engineer, John Crowley, delayed lifting the men because signals from below were confused. At 8 P.M. the mine was sealed to smother the fire.

Recovery Efforts. Soon mine inspectors, firefighters, and rescue experts arrived to supervise further rescue and recovery. On November 14, R. Y. Williams and his assistant, from the University of Illinois, were lowered to the second level in the ventilation shaft

Smoke billows from the Cherry Mine after a fire there killed 259. (AP/Wide World Photos)

wearing oxygen helmets and suits, but smoke and steam forced them out, and the shafts were again covered. The next day temperatures were fairly comfortable, but there was still too much smoke and steam underground. In an attempt to use the main shaft hoist, the fan was repaired to pull air down the main shaft. Ventilation, however, revived the fire, so both shafts were once again covered. On the fourth day, although the main shaft still retained excessive temperatures, a decision was made to enter the air shaft, and a temporary cage was constructed.

The next day, November 18, the "helmet men" retrieved a body from the air shaft. Also, a hose was lowered down to the second level late in the day, and fire fighting began. Chicago firefighters led the effort west of the main shaft all that night, and on the 19th they recovered 4 more bodies. Also, explorers got around cave-ins to reach the south entry and penetrated east almost to the air shaft. Repairs to timbering and removal of roof falls were done on these passages during the night. By the end of the first week, the fire was apparently under control in areas accessible from the main shaft landing.

Finally, on November 20, when the workings (tunnels and shafts) were stabilized and it appeared that no live men remained underground, the remaining mining inspectors left at 10:30 A.M. However, shortly after noon, 21 survivors, led by George Eddy and Walter Waite, were found on the second level. These men had sheltered behind barriers they erected to preserve breathable air, and all but 1 eventually recovered. After survivors were found, the mine inspectors hastily returned. Rooms east of the main south entry were explored that night and through Monday the 22nd, without finding additional living miners: About 100 bodies were removed. On November 23 and 24, the northwest entries were searched without recovering men or bodies. Northern workings east of the shaft, where many men had been employed, remained inaccessible. At this point, smoke began issuing from the main passageway connecting the west shaft with the air shaft. This passage was temporarily blocked by a roof fall and a temporary barrier. Exploration of the northwest section immediately ceased, the barrier was removed, and a hose was turned into the passage, dousing the fire.

Also on November 24, four men reentered the third vein for the first time since the fire began and found 3 to 4 feet of water in the workings. Groups of bodies were discovered in dry places. However, pumping preparations halted when fire began encroaching behind the shaft lining south and east of the main shaft. These fires could not be suppressed, so smoke spread west, practically driving out the rescuers. In addition, dense coal smoke from burning pillars aroused fear of noxious gases. Thus, after a unanimous decision that no survivors remained in the mine, both shafts were sealed with steel rails and concrete in order to smother the fire on November 25, 1909, two weeks after the fire began.

During the crisis, the Red Cross sent supplies and workers. The Catholic Church sent nuns to help the bereaved, and other churches organized relief committees. The *Chicago Tribune* gathered money and contributed food.

The Aftermath. Restoration began February 1, 1910, after temperatures dropped to normal and the mine was ventilated. Finally, the fire was extinguished, and the lower level was drained. By March 5, 82 bodies had been recovered from the second level, and on April 12, 51 bodies were removed from the third level. Four to 6 men remained unaccounted for. Next, the second level was walled off, everything of value removed, and it was abandoned. By September 3, some third-level entries were cleared to the coal face, and the mine was expected to reopen October 10, 1910—one year and thirty-one days after the fire.

Results of the Cherry Mine disaster were many and varied. Public indignation made it necessary to bring in the militia to guard mine officials. Also, cagers Rosenjack and Dean fled the town, and hoist engineer Crowley was placed under protection. In all, 187 bodies were found on the second vein: 51 on the third vein and 12 victims burned to death during rescue efforts. Three of 256 dead listed in the state mining inspector's report were "American," 233 of diverse nationalities, and 20 of unreported nationality. The youngest miners were only fifteen and working in violation of the Factory Act, which prohibited those under sixteen from mining.

The Cherry Relief Commission collected a total of $256,215.72 from the state legislature and death benefits from the United Mine Workers, as well as money from the railroad, from churches, and from many individual donors. Also, an additional $400,000 settlement was negotiated with the mining company. These funds provided widows with lump-sum payments and, until they remarried, modest pensions, as well as child support for children too young to work. In 1910 and 1911 the Illinois state legislature passed several bills in response to the Cherry disaster. These required improved fire-fighting and prevention measures, telephones connecting the faces and cages with the surface, improved workers' compensation laws, and establishment of regional fire and rescue stations. The Cherry Disaster also was crucial in establishment of the Federal Bureau of Mines.

As of 1999, Cherry's annual memorial services and museum continued to draw large attendance. After the disaster, the St. Paul Mining Company continued with many of the original miners until 1927. By then unmechanized long-wall mines were obsolete, and the mine closed. In 1928, Mark Bartolo reopened the mine until its final closure during the Depression. Bartolo salvaged buildings and equipment and began to farm the site. As of 1999, the family still farmed the land.

M. Casey Diana

For Further Information:

Buck, F. P. *The Cherry Mine Disaster.* Chicago: M. H. Donohue, 1910.

Burns, Robert Taylor. "The Cherry Mine Disaster." *Outdoor Illinois* 8, no. 4 (1967): 36-40.

Curran, Daniel J. *Dead Laws for Dead Men.* Pittsburgh: University of Pittsburgh Press, 1993.

Hudson, Thomas. "The Cherry Mine Disaster." In *Twenty Ninth Annual Coal Report of the Illinois Bureau of Labor Statistics.* Springfield: Illinois State Journal, 1911.

Wyatt, Edith. "Heroes of the Cherry Mine." *McClure's Magazine* 34, no. 5 (March, 1910): 473-492.

1918: Minnesota

Date: October 12, 1918

Place: Cloquet-Moose Lake-Duluth region, Minnesota

Result: 453 dead, 85 badly burned, 52,371 injured or otherwise affected, at least 32 towns or villages wholly or partially destroyed, at least 4,089 houses and 6,366 barns destroyed, 250,000 acres burned, more than $30 million in property damage

On October 12, 1918, a number of fires struck an agricultural and timber region of northeastern Minnesota. The fires were similar to many other disastrous fires that struck the Great Lakes states between 1870 and 1920. Dry fuel was plentiful, owing to slash (wood debris) left behind by loggers and to storage of wood in lumberyards and at railroad sidings. Sparks from trains frequently set fires, and fires often occurred in peat bogs.

The area affected by the 1918 disaster extended from north of Duluth southwestward a total of more than 60 miles, through Cloquet to the Moose Lake-Kettle River and Sturgeon Lake areas, and westward more than 45 miles, from north of Duluth to west of Floodwood. A series of dry years, culminating in a drought the summer and fall of 1918, made conditions ripe for disaster. The immediate trigger was a passing cold front, bringing dry northwest winds and low humidity. The disaster was later attributed mainly to the railroads. Ironically, trains were also the means of saving many people. Those people beyond reach of the railroads, mainly farm families, sought refuge in open fields, streams, lakes, swamps, culverts, and ditches. More disastrously, they went into root cellars and wells, where many suffocated. Winds reached 60 to 80 miles per hour.

There were five or six major fire areas and several smaller ones. The largest, which was called the Cloquet fire, and the Duluth-area fire damaged the most property and affected the most people. The second-largest fire, in the Moose Lake and Kettle River area, caused at least half the deaths in all the fires that day.

Fires had smoldered north and west of Cloquet, along the Great Northern Railroad line, for weeks before the disaster. Although all contributed to the Cloquet fire, one stood out in public opinion as the primary source of that blaze: a fire at Milepost 62, 4 miles west of Brookston. Railroad crewmen could not extinguish this fire. By 11 A.M., October 12, rising winds were fanning the flames, which ignited huge piles of wood stored at the siding there. By 1:40 P.M., the fire had spread south and east, across the Fond du Lac Indian Reservation. Farms and homes of both Ojibwa and settlers there were destroyed, but no Ojibwa were killed. The fire also spread eastward along the railroad tracks to Brookston. Just after 4 P.M., a Great Northern relief train carried about 200 of Brookston's 500 inhabitants out of town. A stop in Cloquet, 20 miles down the St. Louis River, allowed the passengers to alert the local people of the fire. The train eventually reached safety in Superior, Wisconsin.

By 6 P.M., a light ash was raining on Cloquet. Then the fire roared into town. By 9 P.M., strong winds were

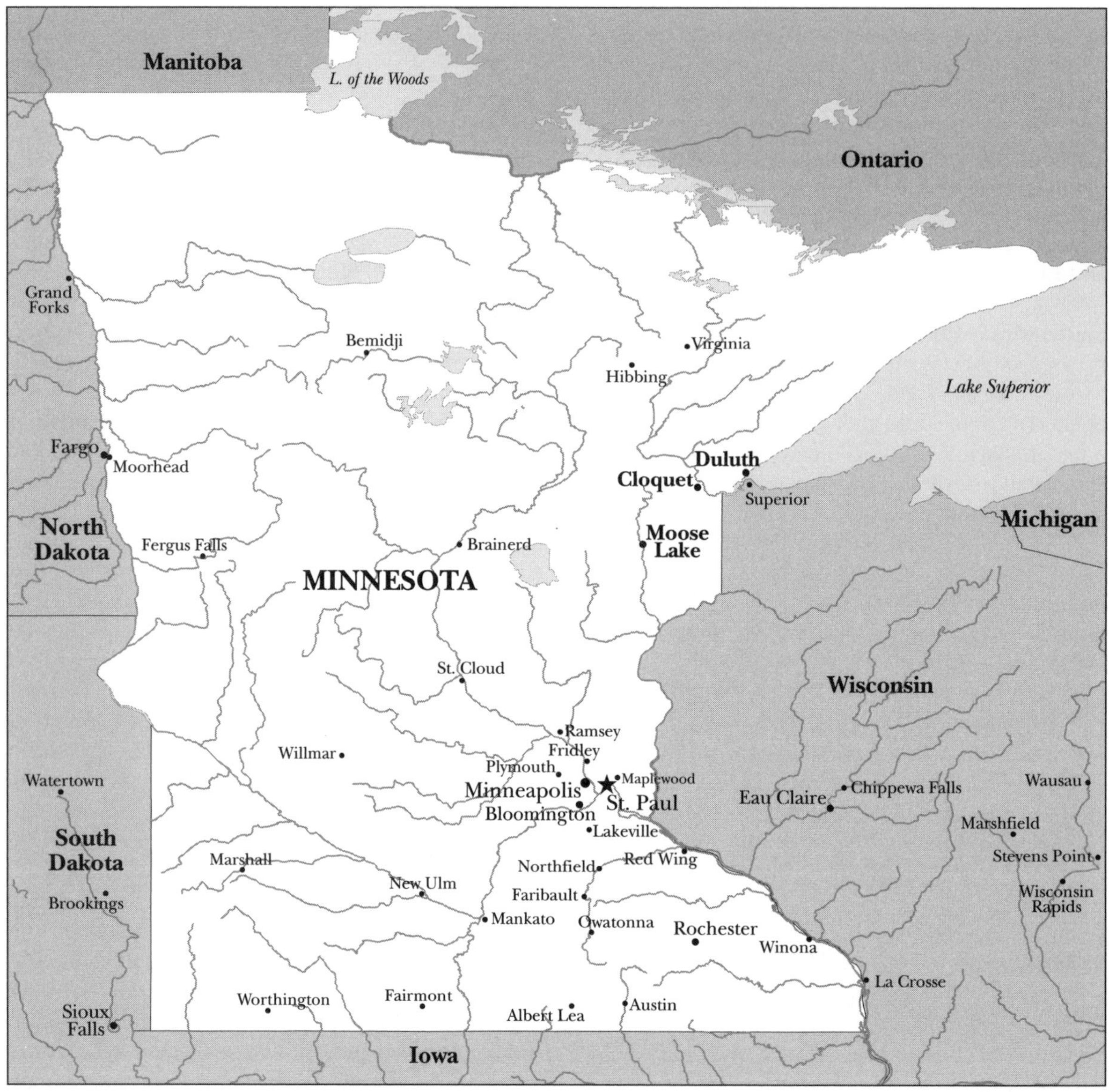

lifting flaming boards from the lumberyards and dropping them across the city. From the hills came great masses of flaming wild hay, which landed on rooftops. Four trains were assembled to evacuate the Cloquet townspeople, who made their way calmly to the tracks. A total of 7,800 people—the vast majority of the city's population—were taken to safety by rail.

Fifty men stayed in Cloquet to fight the fires. Their efforts, aided by a wind shift, helped save 3 of the city's 5 sawmills and a pulp and paper plant. Fewer than 6 people probably died in the city, even though Cloquet itself was burned severely. In contrast to the "miracle of Cloquet," deaths in the surrounding countryside from the Cloquet fire were estimated at more than 100.

In the western fire area, which included Kettle River and Moose Lake, about 25 miles southwest of Cloquet, numerous fires were identified along local railroad tracks. The most severe were along the Northern Pacific and the Minneapolis, St. Paul, and Sault Ste. Marie lines. The day of the disaster, railroad—and peat-bog—fires flared up. Some of them merged, forming larger fire fronts.

One of the worst disasters in all the fires that night occurred in the Kettle River area of the western fire region. Panicked townspeople drove toward the town of Moose Lake on a narrow, dirt road. In the thick smoke, many crashed at a spot later named "Dead Man's Curve." Flames killed up to 100 of those stranded there. Many people also died in nearby areas. A mass grave was later dug at Moose Lake.

Three relief trains took more than 300 people from Moose Lake and Sturgeon Lake before those towns burned. Some residents of Moose Lake survived by taking refuge in nearby Moose Head Lake.

Fires that night also damaged communities and farms closer to Duluth. A major source of these blazes was the Milepost 62 fire on the Great Northern line, which probably joined with fires along other rail lines, forming an irregular, eastward-burning fire front 10 miles wide. Although many farms, dairies, and houses were destroyed, Duluth largely escaped the fire.

The disaster's long-term effects, like its more immediate impact, varied by region. Cloquet rebounded, but in the hard-hit areas around Kettle River and Moose Lake, some communities simply withered. Kettle River and Moose Lake eventually thrived, however.

The U.S. Railroad Administration, which ran the railroads during World War I, was held legally responsible for the fires. The courts eventually awarded victims a total of nearly $30 million. The fires prompted the adoption of some fire-prevention measures. A network of firebreaks was established in the region, fire lookout towers were erected, and fire-fighting equipment was brought in.

Jane F. Hill

For Further Information:

Carroll, Francis M., and Franklin R. Raiter. *Fires of Autumn: The Cloquet-Moose Lake Disaster of 1918*. St. Paul: Minnesota Historical Society Press, 1990.

Holbrook, Stewart H. *Burning an Empire: The Story of American Forest Fires*. New York: Macmillan, 1943.

1923: Northern California

Date: September 17, 1923
Place: Berkeley, California
Result: 2 dead, $10 million in damage

Considered at the time to be the worst conflagration to strike a California city since the 1906 San Francisco earthquake and fire, the 1923 Berkeley blaze devastated that college community. Unusually hot temperatures exacerbated conditions as strong winds blew flames from Centra Costa Ridge, a residential area north of Berkeley, toward the University of California campus. Residents of homes in northeastern Berkeley neighborhoods used garden hoses and buckets to douse the fire but abandoned their houses when their attempts proved futile. Merchants in downtown businesses evacuated their stores as cinders landed on buildings, spreading the fire.

The northeastern part of Berkeley was engulfed by flames, which moved southeast through the town, often leaping erratically between buildings and leaving some houses standing while everything around them was razed. A United States Postal Service pilot reported that he had seen brushfires around San Francisco as he flew there from Reno, Nevada, and that the fire's heat was so intense that he increased his altitude. The pilot observed that the fire was nearing both the university and waterfront and said that the Berkeley blaze appeared to be the most horrible of all the fires he had detected. University officials prepared to extinguish the fire as it approached the north and west sides of the campus.

Fallen palm trees and downed wires blocked roads, impeding firefighters. Firefighters from Oakland and San Francisco joined the battle against the fire, and university students also volunteered. Firefighters detonated dynamite to create firebreaks to block the fire's forward movement toward the campus. When the blaze reached the university's gates, a sudden wind shift redirected the fire away from the school. National Guard and Army troops arrived to ward off looters, and students and citizens were deputized to monitor stricken areas and remove debris. They also quickly stopped two minor fires that occurred after the main blaze was deterred.

City officials blamed an insufficient water system for obstructing firefighters' efforts. The fire leveled 1,000 houses in a 50-block area, leaving half of the university faculty homeless as well as hundreds of students who had lived in fraternity and sorority houses that were also destroyed. Although most reports said that no one died during the fire, an initial article stated that 2 people had been killed falling through a roof on campus. Almost 100 of the city's 60,000 residents (including 5,000 university students) were missing or injured, including national tennis champion Helen Wills. Total property damage was estimated at $10 million.

Elizabeth D. Schafer

For Further Information:

"Berkeley Is Swept by a Great Fire; University Saved." *The New York Times*, September 18, 1923, p. 1.

"Berkeley Prepares for Reconstruction." *The New York Times*, September 20, 1923, p. 1.

"1,000 Homes Burned, Loss of $8,000,000 in Berkeley Fire." *The New York Times*, September 19, 1923, p. 1.

1934: Japan

Date: March 21, 1934
Place: Hakodate, Japan
Result: 1,500 dead

In 1934, a Wednesday evening windstorm knocked down a chimney on a house, setting it on fire. Gale-force winds quickly spread the flames to nearby structures, and the blaze grew out of control as wooden houses dry from drought caught fire. The fire leapt across streets and gaps between dwellings. Residents of Hakodate, a densely populated city of 200,000 located north of Tokyo on Hokkaido Island, hurried from their homes toward the harbor. Eyewitnesses said the stampede was reminiscent of scenes from the 1923 Great Kwanto Earthquake in Tokyo because people rushing to the waterfront discarded bundles containing possessions to move more quickly. Refugees crowded onto ships and steamers, seeking safety from the conflagration.

As citizens evacuated Hakodate, military troops arrived to fight the fire and protect property from looters. The fire intensified during the night as it consumed most of the city's public and business buildings and extended into residential suburbs. At 1:30 A.M., the city's mayor contacted the prefectural governor by radio, telling him that 17,000 to 20,000 houses had burned.

On Thursday morning, the fire finally waned as winds subsided. The central part of the city was almost completely razed, with only walls of larger structures standing among ashes. Destruction included stores on the main shopping street of Ginza, which had been believed to be fireproof. The blaze destroyed telegraph offices, and fire reports were sent to Tokyo via the wireless station at Ochiishi. Total fire casualties included 1,500 dead and 200,000 homeless. Many of the dead suffocated or died from exposure while waiting for rescue along the waterfront. Survivors were miserable as cold weather and snow intensified their ordeal while they waited for delayed relief supplies to arrive.

Elizabeth D. Schafer

For Further Information:

Byas, Hugh. "1,500 Japanese Die in Hakodate Fire; 200,000 Homeless." *The New York Times*, March 22, 1934, p. 1.

"Tokyo Speeds Aid to Fire-Swept City." *The New York Times*, March 23, 1934, p. 15.

1949: China

Date: September 2-3, 1949
Place: Chungking, China
Result: More than 1,700 dead, 100,000 left homeless

Set by a pro-Communist arsonist, this fire symbolized the political chaos of post-World War II China. Nationalists led by Chiang Kai-Shek countered the Communists, represented by Mao Zedong, who wanted to control major cities, including Chungking in Sichuan Province, which was the Nationalist capital.

The fire began in one of the city's slums during the late afternoon. The flames appeared in several different areas, indicating that it probably was intentionally set.

The fire roared through residential areas toward Chungking's business district. Strong winds fed the flames. Residents rushed toward the Jialing and Yangtze Rivers, hoping to escape in boats. The fire outraced people, killing many before they reached the docks. Others drowned trying to elude the flames. The fire burned for eighteen hours before it was stopped. Casualties included 1,700 dead, 100,000 homeless, and at least 10,000 structures leveled. Thousands of people were injured.

The exact cause of the fire remained a mystery. Some people thought that the Nationalists had started the blaze to create a backlash against the Communists. Others assumed Communists had begun the conflagration to scare the Nationalists. Several suspects known to be active in the underground Communist movement were arrested and interrogated, and one man was executed. Tensions were heightened, and, one month later, the Nationalists were forced to evacuate to the island of Taiwan while the Communists secured Chungking. The 1949 fire represents the extreme carnage inflicted during China's twentieth century civil war.

Elizabeth D. Schafer

For Further Information:

"Chungking Fire Kills 1,700." *The New York Times*, September 9, 1949, p. 12.

"Five Held in Chungking Blaze." *The New York Times*, September 13, 1949, p. 17.

"1,000 in Chungking Die in 18-Hour Fire." *The New York Times*, September 5, 1949, p. 1.

1956: Cleveland National Forest

Date: November 24-25, 1956
Place: Cleveland National Forest, California
Result: 11 dead, 40,000 acres burned

Extremely dry timber and brush caught on fire at the Cleveland National Forest in San Diego County in November of 1956. Gusty northeastern winds fanned the flames into an unmanageable wall of fire that consumed as many as 2,000 acres per hour at its most intense period. Approximately 100 people living in rural places near the town of Ramona were evacuated, while 1,600 volunteers began to combat the rapidly spreading blaze, which consumed 12 houses. Firefighters included 500 sailors from the San Diego Naval Training Center and a group of prisoners.

The fire burned 40,000 acres located near the Mexican border and 2 state parks. Eleven firefighters were killed when the wind erratically shifted and a wave of flames separated them from other volunteers who watched as the fire pushed and trapped the men against a steep cliff they could not scale. The dead included United States Forest Service workers, a prison employee, and prisoners from California and several other states.

Experienced firefighters admitted that this fire was unusual because it was so quiet and unpredictable. The lack of moisture in the brush meant that the fire did not produce crackling noises. Despite their efforts, firefighters realized that the fire could not be stopped unless the wind subsided and a significant amount of rain fell. Firefighters managed to gain some control of the conflagration on the southwest edge of the forest, which was adjacent to Lakeside, a San Diego suburb. The fire continued to rage along a 40-mile section to the south until it burned out.

Elizabeth D. Schafer

For Further Information:

"11 Killed by Forest Fire on Coast; 1,400 Fighting Three-Day Blaze." *The New York Times*, November 27, 1956, p. 39.

"Fire out of Control: Blaze in California Forest Destroys 12 Houses." *The New York Times*, November 26, 1956, p. 1.

1983: Australia

Date: February 17, 1983
Place: The states of Victoria and South Australia
Result: 75 dead, 800 injured, 350,000 farm animals killed

Australia's dry terrain and its relatively rare areas of dense vegetation have often rendered the continent vulnerable to fire. The fires of February, 1983, were remarkable in that they wrought major damage upon sizably populated areas. Ironically, the fires took place on Ash Wednesday, the beginning of Lent; they were thus dubbed the "Ash Wednesday fires."

Although there were up to a dozen major fires on that day, the two most important were the Otway fire and the Gambier (or Clay Wells) fire, which affected the states of Victoria and South Australia, respectively. The Clay Wells fire was larger, though the Otway fire affected more people. Both began with a sudden shift in the direction of wind after a cold front had replaced dry summer breezes (February is in the Australian summer). The spread of the fire was hastened

The Cockatoo school, 30 miles east of Melbourne, Australia, burns in one of a dozen fires in the area. (AP/Wide World Photos)

by a drought that had afflicted these regions in the preceding months and had left a large amount of dry fuel on the floors of forested gullies close to major farming and population centers. Sporadic brush fires had been occurring from November, 1982, onward.

The Ash Wednesday fires seemed to be on this level at first, but wind speed (averaging 55 miles per hour, with some gusts reaching 80 miles per hour) caused the fires to quickly combine. When electric power lines began to catch fire, it became clear that a major disaster was underway. Over 16,000 firefighters participated in the struggle against the combined brush fires, using not only fire engines and water but also helicopters and airplanes as well as computerized fire location and scanning technology. Fortunately, the winds shifted direction around twelve hours after the onset of the fires, and the various fires quickly became isolated from each other and died down.

Damage was immense, especially near the densely populated Victorian city of Geelong. Houses burned down, and forests and livestock essential to the regional economy were decimated. It took years of government assistance and insurance claims before these areas were fully returned to normal.

Nicholas Birns

For Further Information:

Pyne, Stephen. *Burning Bush: A Fire History of Australia.* New York: Henry Holt, 1991.

1987: China

Date: May 6-27, 1987
Place: Northern China
Result: 193 dead

Beginning on a Wednesday afternoon in 1987, this forest fire raced through Mohe County in Heilongjiang Province in northeastern China because inept Forestry Bureau workers were ineffective at stopping the first sparks. Initial reports released by Chinese officials indicated that 100 people had already perished in the blaze. By Friday night, the fire had leveled an estimated 2,000 square miles of forest. Satellite images revealed that the conflagration had burned along a path 62 miles long and 25 miles wide and that the city of Xilinji had been razed.

Within a week, thousands of firefighters managed to cease the fire's eastward movement and slowed its advance toward the west. The Weather Forecasting Center in Beijing estimated that 2,350 square miles had been destroyed in the Great Khingan Mountains region, close to the Soviet Union border. The fire moved south toward forests near the city of Mangui in Inner Mongolia, where a wilderness reserve and the sole reindeer farm in China were located. Firefighters dug a firebreak to protect the city. At Uma, 75 miles away, a separate forest fire in the Soviet Union threatened to cross the Argun River into China. Firefighters from Inner Mongolia monitored that blaze to prevent it from joining the Chinese forest fire.

By late May, the Xinhua News Agency announced that the fire had been extinguished in Daxinganling Forest. This forest fire was designated the worst known forest fire to strike China. While aircraft were used to seed clouds to produce precipitation to dampen the flames, thousands of people fought the blaze on the ground. Casualties totaled 193 dead; 221 injured; 2.47 million acres razed, including agricultural and forest land; and numerous communities leveled. More than 51,000 people became homeless because of the fire. Chinese leaders dismissed Yang Zhong, China's Forestry Minister, for ineffective management during the fire.

Elizabeth D. Schafer

For Further Information:

"China Finally Halts Its Worst Forest Fire." *The New York Times*, May 27, 1987, p. A3.

"China's Forestry Chief Is Dismissed over Fire." *The New York Times*, June 7, 1987, p. 20.

"100 Lost in Forest Fire." *The New York Times*, May 10, 1987, p. 13.

1988: Yellowstone National Park

Date: Summer, 1988

Place: Mainly Yellowstone National Park, located predominantly in northwestern Wyoming and partly in southern Montana and eastern Idaho; also, surrounding national forests in the northern Rocky Mountains

Result: 2 dead; approximately 1.2 million acres burned, 793,000 in Yellowstone National Park itself; more than $3 million estimated in damage

The summer of 1988 saw the largest forest fire complex ever recorded for the Greater Yellowstone area, the largest in the northern Rocky Mountains for decades, and one of the most severe in U.S. history. The fires, which burned 36 percent of the more than 2.2-million-acre Yellowstone National Park and a total of 11 percent of the Greater Yellowstone area, triggered the nation's most expensive fire-suppression effort and a heated debate about national park fire management policy.

Over the millennia, many conflagrations as large as the 1988 fires have swept across the vast volcanic plateaus of Yellowstone National Park. The fires have affected mostly the large stands of lodgepole pine, which dominate the high-elevation areas. These stands constitute 80 percent of the park's forests and cover nearly 60 percent of the park. The recurring, major fires are responsible for the mosaic landscape of different-aged pines. Tree-ring research shows that fires of this magnitude last struck in the early 1700's.

Crescendo of Fires. The 1988 fire season in the Greater Yellowstone Area began on May 24, when lightning ignited a blaze that rain quickly extinguished. Over the next six months, lightning and careless people triggered 247 more fires in the area. Early in the season, officials in Yellowstone National Park stuck to their policy, begun in 1972, of allowing lightning-ignited fires to burn in the backcountry, under certain guidelines. From 1972 through 1987, such fires had burned only 33,759 acres, and all these blazes had died naturally. Park staff did not foresee the extreme weather conditions that would develop in the summer of 1988.

The previous six summers had all been wetter than average, and rainfall in April and May of 1988 had been above average. However, the winters since 1982 had been consistently dry, and it is mainly the snowpacks in the mountains that moisten the park's plateaus. Weather experts were saying that the period leading up to 1988 was becoming the driest since the 1930's Dust Bowl. The summer of 1988 proved to be the driest in the park's history. Precipitation in June, July, and August was 20 percent, 79 percent, and 10 percent, respectively, of normal.

The failure of the usual June and July rains amplified the early fires. By July 15, 8,600 acres had burned; by July 21, more than 17,000 acres were ruined. The fires drew the attention of park visitors and the national media. On July 21, in a departure from policy, park officials decided to suppress all fires, whether caused by lightning or by humans. Nevertheless, within a week, fires in the park covered nearly 99,000 acres. By the end of July, dry fuels and high winds made the larger fires nearly uncontrollable.

In August, with almost no rain, temperatures remaining high, and a series of dry, cold fronts bringing strong, persistent winds, there was a marked decrease in moisture in forest debris. This dry fuel engendered near-firestorm conditions. By August 15, a total of 260,000 acres had burned. On August 20, the single worst day—dubbed "Black Saturday"— winds as high as 70 miles per hour pushed fire across more than 150,000 acres in and around the park. Walls of flame reached 100 to 300 feet high. More acreage burned in a single twenty-four-hour period than had burned during any previous decade in the park's history.

Firefighters and soldiers poured into Yellowstone National Park. Aircraft, both for transporting firefighters and supplies and for dropping water and fire retardant on the flames, arrived from around the nation, and dozens of trucks were brought in. Firefighters cleared firebreaks and set backfires. National news reporters also arrived in force. Local businesses became alarmed at the prospect of lost tourist income. The park's fire-management policy came under heated debate, from park border towns to the U.S. Congress, as the conflagrations raged on despite the fire-fighting effort.

Fires in Yellowstone National Park in 1988 destroyed 36 percent of the trees. (AP/ Wide World Photos)

Spot fires, caused by burning embers carried up in the smoke, were breaking out up to a mile and a half ahead of the fires, mocking firebreaks. Even marshes and swamps burned, as well as young, green forests, which park ecologists had not expected to ignite. Some days, the seven major fire complexes, which in the end were responsible for more than 95 percent of the burned acreage, advanced as much as 10 or 12 miles. Of these seven, three had been started by human beings, and park staff had attempted to suppress them from the outset. These three were ultimately responsible for more than half the area burned.

By August 31, 550,000 acres had burned. At that point, park officials abandoned traditional, direct attacks on the fires and withdrew firefighters to developed areas, to try to protect only life and property. On September 7, 100,000 acres burned. On September 10, park authorities evacuated several towns, including Mammoth Hot Springs, the park's headquarters. That night the wind turned north, and by morning it was snowing. The fires lost their strength, although they did not die out completely until the onset of winter, in November. After September 11, firefighters were gradually sent home.

A total of more than 25,000 firefighters, as many as 9,000 at one time, fought the fires in the Greater Yellowstone area, at a total cost of about $120 million. They hand-cut a total of 665 miles of fireline and cut 137 miles of bulldozer lines, including 32 miles in Yellowstone National Park itself. Two of the firefighters were killed outside the park, one by a falling tree and the other while piloting a plane transporting other personnel.

Effects and the Recovery Process. After the fires, Congress funded the restoration of fire-damaged facilities, which included 67 destroyed structures, and studies of the long-term impact of the fires. Although the 1988 tourist season was cut short by the blazes, visitors returned in 1989.

Scientists, eager to study the ecological effects of severe fire in a natural laboratory, set to work examining the impact on wildlife and plants. From the start it was clear that the 1988 Yellowstone fires burned in a heterogeneous pattern, owing to variations in fuels, winds, and terrain. Substantial areas were untouched by fire or only lightly burned by fast-moving ground fires that left most of the trees alive. Other areas were completely blackened by fierce fires that reached into the canopy and burned the treetops.

Most of the severely burned land, however, defied theories that fires of this magnitude would "sterilize" the soil by killing root systems and seeds, opening the way for invading weeds. Although flames consumed the aboveground parts of grasses and other herbaceous plants, even the hottest fires rarely burned more than the top inch of soil, leaving viable seeds, bulbs, roots, and rhizomes below that depth. By the spring of 1989, grasses and flowers were growing abundantly.

The heaviest fires were in the huge stands of aging, diseased, highly combustible lodgepole pine. These fires promoted new growth by releasing nutrients long locked up in the old trees, by opening the forest canopy and permitting sunlight to reach the young plants, and by clearing deadfall. Unlike many of the park's herbaceous plants, most trees do not regenerate by sprouting from their roots. Rather, they depend on seeds, and lodgepole pine is a master at this method in fire-affected landscapes. The cones of many, though not all, lodgepole pines are sealed by resin until the intense heat of fire melts the resin and releases seeds that have been stored in the cones for many years. This produces a large crop of young pines to take advantage of the abundant water, nutrients, and space that become available after a fire. This cone adaptation, called "serotiny," resulted in the development of the even-aged pine stands covering much of the Rocky Mountains, where fires are frequent. By the spring of 1989, lodgepole pine seedlings were establishing themselves abundantly. Ten years after the fires, many of them were knee- to shoulder-high.

Fire also affected the park's lower elevation areas, characterized by sagebrush grasslands interspersed with forests of Douglas fir and aspen. The Douglas firs, which dominate only a small percentage of the landscape, came back more slowly than the lodgepole pines but, a decade after the fires, were emerging above the shrubs. The park's scattered groves of aspen, the only deciduous tree common in the park and declining there for decades, sprouted profusely from the roots, but the new shoots were grazed by elk. Regeneration of willows, which typically line the streambanks, and sagebrush also may have been fire-stimulated. Ten years after the fires, grasslands had recovered to prefire conditions.

As new plants of many kinds became established, the populations and kinds of insects and larger animals feeding on the abundant new food supplies increased. The rapid rebound of plants and animals throughout the park surprised many ecologists.

The fires' toll on large animals was relatively small. Many animals survived by moving away from the flames. Postfire searchers found, both within and outside the park, carcasses of 335 elk (of a herd estimated at more than 30,000), 36 deer, 12 moose, 6 black bears, and 9 bison, mainly in areas where fast-moving flames prevented escape.

Fires in the sagebrush grasslands on the park's northern range, which supplies critical winter forage for the park's largest herds of elk and buffalo, diminished these animals' food supply for the winter of 1988-1989. Many of the animals starved, but their deaths were attributed more to the severe winter and to the 1988 summer drought's effects on forage than to fire.

Some birds and many small mammals were killed by the fires. A few small fish kills occurred as a result of heated water or fire retardant dropped on the streams. The fires caused physical and food-web changes in the streams, but these did not seem to affect fish adversely.

Causes and Fire Policy. After much debate, many scientists concluded that the most significant factor causing the 1988 Yellowstone fires was the combination of drought and sustained, strong winds. Their position was bolstered by the dating of charcoal in park lakebeds, which indicated that, over the past fourteen thousand years, the recurrence interval of major fires is fifty to five hundred years and is related mainly to drought. According to this view, abundant fuel, in the form of accumulated deadwood and old, diseased pines, would exacerbate, but not cause, the fires.

In contrast, a more traditional hypothesis holds that fuel buildup is a major factor leading to severe fires. Some scientists argued that Yellowstone National Park's fire-suppression policy, in force from 1872 until 1972, augmented the forest fuel buildup and thus made a severe conflagration more likely. However, most think that suppression, which was effectively carried out for only some thirty years, had little effect, especially at the higher elevations.

Many scientists concluded that the origin of the fires—natural or human-made—was less important than weather and fuel in determining overall fire severity. Fire experts also concluded that the massive fire-fighting effort probably did not significantly reduce the acreage burned, although it saved many buildings.

As a result of the controversy over federal fire policy touched off by the 1988 Yellowstone fires, national parks and forests suspended and updated their fire-management plans. In 1992, Yellowstone National Park again had a wildland fire-management plan, but with stricter guidelines for allowing naturally occurring fires to burn.

Jane F. Hill

For Further Information:

Baskin, Yvonne. "Yellowstone Fires: A Decade Later—Ecological Lessons Learned in the Wake of the Conflagration." *BioScience*, February, 1999, 93-97.

Carrier, Jim. *Summer of Fire: The Great Yellowstone Fires of 1988.* Salt Lake City: Gibbs-Smith, 1989.

Despain, Don G. F. "The Yellowstone Fires: Ecological History of the Region Helps Explain the Damage Caused by the Fires of the Summer of 1988." *Scientific American*, November, 1989, 36-45.

Sholly, Dan R., with Steven M. Newman. *Guardians of Yellowstone: An Intimate Look at the Challenges of Protecting America's Foremost Wilderness Park.* New York: William Morrow, 1991.

Vogt, Gregory. *Forests on Fire: The Fight to Save Our Trees.* New York: Franklin Watts, 1990.

1991: The Oakland Hills Fire

Date: October 19-21, 1991
Place: Oakland Hills, California, and vicinity
Result: 25 dead, 150 injured, 2,843 single-family homes destroyed, 433 apartment units destroyed, $1.5 billion in damage, 1,520 acres burned

The area of Oakland Hills is extremely susceptible to fires for many reasons. Oakland Hills is a small community near San Francisco located between Berkeley and Oakland and the hills that surround them. The houses located there are sheltered by trees, with narrow roads leading up steep hillsides to different subdivisions. Most of the houses in the Oakland Hills area in the 1990's were million-dollar dwellings that people had worked a lifetime to afford.

The Oakland Hills area is known as a wildland-urban interface. This is where human-made developments and wildland fuels meet at a boundary that is susceptible to wildfires because of the accumulation of dense fuels. In the late twentieth century, the number of people moving to the wildlands increased dramatically. Wildfires are actually beneficial to the natural cycles of many types of ecosystems, when they are not close to human settlements. They remove the weak and dead vegetation that are potential fuels for larger fires if they are allowed to accumulate and allow for a chance for renewal in the forest. The cleansing effects of the fires present dangers when homes are built in these wild areas, however.

In wildland-urban interface areas, city services such as fire protection and water supply are not always fully provided. Procedures for controlling wildfires often include sacrificing some areas in order to set up a perimeter firebreak. This procedure requires sacrificing some homes and property to save others.

The remains of dozens of homes burned in the Oakland Hills fire. (AP/Wide World Photos)

The Oakland Hills area was well known for fires in the past. In September of 1923 a wildfire started northeast of Berkeley and spread quickly. It burned 130 acres, consuming 584 buildings and causing $10 million worth of damage. After the fire, the city council passed legislation requiring fire-resistant wood coverings for roofs but rescinded the legislation before it could take effect. Another fire started in September of 1970 southeast of the University of California Berkeley campus. It destroyed 38 homes and damaged 7 others. The total cost of damage was $3.5 million. Yet another fire began just north of where the Oakland Hills fire started in December of 1980. This fire destroyed 6 homes and injured 3 people in only twenty minutes.

In 1982, Berkeley designated a section of the city as the Hazardous Hill Fire Area after an extensive inspection program. Four months before the fire, in June of 1991, Berkeley passed an ordinance that required all houses in this area to have Class-A roofs. This ordinance did not include the area of the Oakland Hills fire.

It is essential for communities to prohibit dangerous building practices; mandate regular inspections to ensure adequate clearing of plants, shrubs, and trees away from homes; and seek support to implement these policies to protect people living in the wildland-urban interface. California has a law that designates hazardous fire areas as places covered by grass, grain, brush, or forest, whether publicly or privately owned, and regions that are so inaccessible that a fire would be difficult to suppress. The area of Oakland Hills was not considered hazardous because all the residences were accessible by paved roads, even though they were narrow and winding.

The Oakland Hills Fire. The story of the Oakland Hills fire actually begins the day before the fire started. On October 19, 1991, a fire of suspicious origin started near 7151 Buckingham Boulevard. The wind was not strong enough that day to push the fire very far. Firefighters were able to keep the blaze under control and thought they had extinguished it. The heat from the fire on October 19 that had been extinguished caused pine needles to drop from the trees, laying down a fresh layer of kindling. A type of debris called duff fell around and inside the area of the first burn. Duff is the pine needles, often up to a foot thick, that have accumulated under the trees; it is highly flammable. The water used by the firefighters extinguished the flames that burned on top of the duff, but the duff combined with ash and dust to form a crust. The fire continued to smolder under the crust. Firefighters followed prudent procedures by leaving their hoses in place overnight and returning periodically to the fire scene to check for signs of renewed fire.

At approximately 10:45 the next morning, as 25 firefighters were finishing up after the fire of the previous day, sparks burst out of the duff. They were carried by winds ranging from 16 to 25 miles per hour, with some observers estimating winds up to 65 miles per hour. The wind brought them to a tree that instantly burst into flames. Convective currents and strong winds allowed the fire to move out of the northeast region and spread to nearby vegetation. By 11:15 in the morning, the fire was raging out of control. The fire went uphill from the place of origin. The winds changed suddenly and blew the fire in many directions at once. A warm, dry wind blowing in the valleys of a mountain, called a foehn, pushed the fire back downhill just as fast as the fire was spreading uphill.

Minutes later, the winds changed again. This time the fire started spreading eastward, toward the Parkwood Apartments and the Caldecott Tunnel. Another change in the wind direction sent the fire to the southwest. Many pine trees and other shrubs burst into flames. Homes were becoming threatened, and firefighters struggled to contain the fire. The fire spread across Highway 24 and headed toward Lake Temescal. At the same time, another flame front started moving northwest, toward the Claremont Hotel and the city of Berkeley. The fire turned into numerous large fires because of spotting. Firebrands were carried by the fire to areas remote from the original fire. The winds caused the fire to descend along the ridge between Marlborough Terrace and Hiller Highlands. The winds accelerated the motion of the fire down the ridge, causing it to consume everything in its path.

Within one hour the fire had consumed 790 structures. The area south of Highway 24 and the area near the Caldecott Tunnel caught fire. An area called Upper Rockridge caught fire because of winds and spotting. By noon, 40 percent of the total affected area was burned. As the fire began spreading south and west, it reached flatter, more open ground and started slowing. The fire reached temperatures as high as 2,000 degrees Fahrenheit. Although this temperature can boil asphalt, this fire was not as fierce or hot as most wildfires.

Attempts at Extinguishing the Fire. Weather conditions and the rapid spread of the fire in many directions at once made it extremely difficult to extinguish the blaze. The fire hoses were mostly ineffective because the wind was so strong that it bent the water streams 90 degrees on 500-gallon-per-minute hoses. For the first three hours, air attacks were also ineffective because of strong winds, heavy smoke that obscured vision, and the continuous fuel chain available to the fire.

Fire units ran out of water during the fire owing to five primary factors. Large quantities of water were used by firefighters suppressing the fire; homeowners were wetting their roofs and vegetation with large quantities of water as well. Water pipes had burst, and water was freely flowing in destroyed homes. Tanks and reservoirs could not be refilled due to electrical power failures caused by the fire. There was also a problem with matching hoses to the fire hydrants. Some of the hoses from out-of-town fire brigades did not fit on the hydrants. Some had adapters that could be put on the hydrants, but many of the adapters were left on the hydrants as the fire overtook the perimeters.

Many of the homes had roofs covered with wooden shingles or shakes. Flaming embers were blown by the wind from houses that were already on fire onto the roofs of nearby homes, which then caught on fire. According to observers, homes burned to their foundations in ten minutes or less. The steep hillsides presented difficulties to the firefighters. Hoses and other equipment had to be dragged up the hills. The streets were very narrow. As firefighters were moving large trucks up the streets toward the fire, homeowners were moving away from the fire to evacuate the area, causing bottlenecks.

The first tactics the firefighters used were to retreat to the perimeter, attack the fire, and summon help. The fire was spreading so fast that the firefighters could not establish an effective perimeter. The units coming to assist the initial crew found other areas burning, so they stopped to fight those fires. However, they were overrun eventually by the fire. The fire departments had a difficult time communicating with other fire departments around the state because there were too many units trying to use the same radio channel and too few channels were available. The hilly terrain also caused interference with the radio signals, making it difficult to coordinate the attack.

The coordination of the firefighters improved as time passed. It was possible to establish good perimeter areas as the weather conditions became better and the fire reached areas where water was available. The firefighters were able to suppress the ignition of homes by breaking the chain of combustibles that was responsible for the earlier destruction of houses, allowing the firefighters to save many homes.

The Oakland Hills fire developed firestorm conditions within fifteen minutes. Firestorms are produced when the gases, heat, and motion of a fire build up to a point that they begin to create their own convection currents independent of external conditions. Oxygen is pulled into the base of the fire in great quantities, producing large convection columns when the air is heated at the fire. When the intensity of a fire reaches firestorm levels, a fire front can develop that is able to move away from the direction the wind is blowing.

The Oakland Hills and Berkeley fire departments were not the only ones to assist in extinguishing the fire. They were joined by 88 engine strike teams, 6 air tankers, 16 heliac units, 8 communications units, 2 management teams, 2 mechanics, and more than 700 search-and-rescue personnel from other municipalities. In addition, 767 law enforcement officers assisted.

Effects of the Fire. As a result of the fire, Assemblyman Tom Bates introduced a bill, later known as the Bates Bill, requiring the California Department of Forestry and Fire Protection, along with local fire authorities, to identify places in the Local Responsibility Areas that were considered to be "very high fire hazard severity zones." Terrain, foliage, building construction, and lack of adequate access were among the factors considered in establishing these zones. Once the hazardous areas were identified, the local authorities either adopted the state fire marshal's model ordinance, adding or subtracting areas from the identified zones; indicated that they already met or exceeded the Bates minimum; or a combination of these responses.

Most of the ordinances that were adopted required that all the dwellings in endangered areas must have at least a Class-B roof. A defensible perimeter around the home was also required. This included a 100-foot-wide area around the building where grass and ground cover could not exceed 3 inches in height. Specimen trees were allowed as long as they were at least 15 feet apart and no closer than 15 feet from the house. Access roads must be at least 10 feet wide and have 13 feet, 6 inches vertical clearance to allow passage for fire-fighting apparatus. In 1994, more legislation was passed, which raised the roofing requirement to a Class-A roof. Other directives included planting "fire-resistant" vegetation, requiring sprinklers in new homes where access is limited, requiring one-hour construction on the exterior of homes in high-risk areas, providing standard hydrant connections, and improving communication systems for emergency workers.

Gary W. Siebein

For Further Information:

Darlington, David. "After the Firestorm." *Audubon* 95, no. 2 (March/April, 1993): 2-12.

Report of the Operation Urban Wildfire Task Force. Washington, D.C.: Federal Emergency Management Agency, United States Fire Administration, FA-115, 1992.

1993: Southern California

Date: October 28-November 3,1993
Place: The metropolitan Los Angeles area, especially Malibu
Result: 3 dead, 111 injured, 1,084 homes destroyed, $500 million in damage

Fire meant double trouble for the inhabitants of the metropolitan Los Angeles area in the fall of 1993. No sooner had a belt of fires on the fringe of urban Los Angeles, from Santa Barbara in the north to Oceanside in the south, raged and been extinguished than a new set broke out in the coastal area of Malibu.

Most of the areas afflicted by the first set of fires were on land that is heavily forested but often dry and subject to fierce, torrid Santa Ana winds. Yet it was strongly suspected that many of the fires did not arise from natural causes. Investigators believed that many of the fires resulted from arson, the result of vagrants and homeless people building fires for warmth, which then blew out of control. In Altadena, for instance, the transient Andres Huang was arrested for arson on October 27. Huang had set a fire in the early morning and then, unable to see, had fallen over a cliff, though not fatally. There soon was a ring of fire ranging across five counties and requiring the attention of

5,000 firefighters. Many houses a century old were destroyed, and families lost most of their belongings.

Most of these fires were put out as of November 1. The next day, though, a series of wind gusts drove fires of unknown origin toward the affluent beachside enclave of Malibu. Again, houses and land of considerable value were destroyed. Given the density of this area's population and the relative shortage of premium land, these fires were proportionally more devastating in their impact than they would have been in most other regions. The most prominent fatality was Duncan Gibbins, who had directed the 1991 science-fiction thriller *Eve of Destruction.* Gibbins was overcome when he tried to return home to save his cat; the cat was later found slightly singed but alive. Several others also died, and many thousands more were forced out of their homes, most of which either faced months of extensive rebuilding or were completely ruined. On November 4, Donald Manning, the head of the Los Angeles Fire Department, pronounced the fire emergency finally over.

Nicholas Birns

For Further Information:

Edwards, Megan. *Roads from the Ashes.* Los Angeles: Trilogy Books, 1999.

Facts on File, November 4, 1993, 824.

1997: Indonesia

Date: September 24-26, 1997

Place: Indonesia, with resulting smoke affecting neighboring Malaysia

Result: 263 dead from related accidents

It was not fire in the conventional sense that caused the twin tragedies—a plane crash and a shipwreck—that afflicted Indonesia in September, 1997. Rather, it was the haze generated by numerous small forest fires across the archipelago that comprises Indonesia as well as the Asian mainland. The fires themselves were not the problem—indeed, many of them had been deliberately set by Indonesian crop growers and

Fires in Laguna Beach, California, in 1993 destroyed many homes but left this one untouched. (AP/Wide World Photos)

A rainforest in Borneo, Indonesia, is reduced to ashes after a fire. (AP/Wide World Photos)

timbermen to clear the land. Normally, these fires would have been extinguished by the prodigious monsoons that swept across the region in September. However, severe and persistent drought, along with a delay in the arrival of the monsoons that most meteorologists attributed to the weather phenomenon El Niño, meant that the fires continued to roar and to produce the throttling haze.

The haze first was viewed as having reached disastrous proportions on September 24. On this day, the United States and Canada evacuated most of the personnel in their embassies in the Malaysian capital of Kuala Lumpur, and Indonesia began to commit military troops as well as firefighters to combat the myriad blazes. In many parts of the region, people could not see for more than 2 feet in front of them. People were dying not only from smoke inhalation but also from the thirst and starvation caused by the drought as the haze impeded most relief efforts. On September 25, both Canada and Japan offered the use of advanced fire-fighting techniques, including water cannons.

Before this aid was implemented, however, a tragic collision occurred in the straits separating Indonesia and Malaysia on September 26. An oil tanker collided with a cargo vessel, killing 29 of the latter's crew; only 5 survived. Provisional assessment of the cause blamed the smoke, which had shrunk the navigable horizon to less than a mile; a formal government investigation later tended to ratify this view.

An even bigger disaster occurred the same day, as Garuda Indonesia Airline flight 152, an Airbus 300-B4 flying from Jakarta to Medan in Sumatra, crashed near Buah Nabar, most likely because of low visibility. A radio transcript of the conversation between the cockpit and the Sumatra control tower revealed confusion on the part of the pilot as to which way he should turn the plane. Visibility was less than 300 feet, which almost certainly affected the pilot's mistaken landing on rough ground deep in a ravine rather than upon the airport runway. All 234 passengers were killed on impact. Aside from the haze and pilot error, blame was also placed on the Sundstrand Corporation, an American firm which made the Garuda plane's ground warning system, which should have prevented the plane from landing anywhere but the runway. The Garuda crash is considered one of the twenty worst air disasters, in terms of the loss of human life, to date.

Nicholas Birns

For Further Information:

Facts on File. October 2, 1997, 704-705.

2000: New Mexico

Date: May 4, 2000
Place: Los Alamos, New Mexico
Result: 200 homes destroyed

On May 4, 2000, the National Park Service attempted a controlled burn in the Bandelier National Monument in Los Alamos, New Mexico. Disaster struck the next day when 45-mile-per-hour winds blew the flames out of control. By May 8, 2,000 acres had burned, and 500 houses in the vicinity had been evacuated. In addition, the fire was approaching the Los Alamos National Laboratory, the site of nuclear weapons research.

One week after the fire's start, 14,000 people were evacuated, and 18,000 acres with 150 homes in Los Alamos were destroyed by flames. The nearby towns of Espanola, White Rock, and Abiqui, the onetime home of artist Georgia O'Keefe, were evacuated as well. The more than 1,100 firefighters were helpless against the heat, and the winds only became stronger the following day, preventing attempts at containment. President Bill Clinton declared the town a disaster area and promised relief to the residents. The National Guard was called in to prevent looting and maintain order.

Also on May 11, park superintendent Roy Weaver was suspended from his job for ordering the controlled burn. Intended to clear brush from the park and thereby prevent fires, the controlled burn was begun in spite of a drought and forecasts of strong winds. Inquiries were being made amid accusations that negligence on the part of Weaver and the Park Service resulted in 400 families being made homeless in the area. Interior Secretary Bruce Babbitt released a report criticizing the actions of the Park Service and banned all prescribed burns for a month.

The Los Alamos National Laboratory escaped serious harm, with no threat to bunkers containing explosives or nuclear materials. However, 40 trailers and small buildings on the laboratory site were destroyed, including one with chalkboard notes about the construction of the first atomic bomb. Although there was no release of radiation because of the fire, on May 27 scientists examining the results of the fire identified about six former dumps that would possibly release low-level nuclear and chemical waste into rivers after July rains. The brush that held the soil in check was burned off in the fire, allowing for runoff.

Lauren Mitchell

For Further Information:

Drogin, Bob. "Toxic Runoff Feared After Blaze at Los Alamos." *Los Angeles Times,* May 27, 2000, p. A1.
Sterngold, James. "As Fire Rages, Park Service Action Is Questioned." *The New York Times,* May 12, 2000, p. A1.
"Wildfire out of Control in Los Alamos." www.cnn.com/2000/US/05/11/nmex.fires.06/. May 11, 2000.

Floods

(AP/Wide World Photos)

Floods occur when streams or rivers overflow their banks and inundate the adjacent floodplain. They have caused enormous destruction of property and loss of life ever since human societies settled in large numbers along river valleys.

Factors involved: Geography, human activity, plants, rain, snow, temperature, weather conditions
Regions affected: Cities, forests, islands, mountains, plains, rivers, towns, valleys

Science

Floods are difficult to define. This is partly because there are no natural breaks in nature and partly because flood thresholds are selected based on human criteria, which can vary. The common definition of a flood is the result of a river overflowing its banks and spreading out over the bordering floodplain. The scientific definition would be in terms of discharge, which is the volume of water moving past a given point in the stream channel per unit of time (cubic feet per second).

Two aspects that are instrumental in flood occurrence are the amount of surface runoff and the uniformity of runoff from different parts of the watershed (a region that drains to a body of water). If the response and travel times are uniform, then the flow is less likely to result in a flood. Conversely, watersheds that have soils and bedrock with higher infiltration rates are prone to flooding. Flood magnitude depends on the intensity, duration, and areal extent of precipitation in conjunction with the condition of the land. If the soils in the watershed have been saturated due to antecedent precipitation, the flooding potential is much greater. For example, the unusual occurrence of Hurricanes Connie and Diane in 1955 striking so close together in time resulted in substantial flooding along the Delaware River in New Jersey and Pennsylvania because the ground was already saturated from the first storm.

Floods are caused by climatological conditions and part-climatological factors. Climatological conditions include heavy rain from tropical storms and hurricanes, severe thunderstorms, midlatitude cyclones and frontal passages, and rapid snow and ice melt. Part-climatological factors consist of tides and storm surges in coastal areas. Other factors that may cause floods are ice- and logjam breakups, earthquakes, landslides, and dam failures.

Flood-intensifying conditions include fixed basin characteristics, such as area, shape, slope, aspect (north- or south-facing), and elevation; and variable basin characteristics, including water-storage capacity and transmissibility in the soil and bedrock, soil infiltration rates, and extent of wetlands and lakes. Channel characteristics, such as length, slope, roughness, and shape, also may intensify floods, as may the human effects of river regulation: conjunctive use of groundwater, interbasin transfers, wastewater release, water diversion and irrigation, urbanization and increases in impervious cover, deforestation and reforestation, levees, and land drainage.

Because floods are capable of such extensive damage, knowledge of the magnitude and frequency of these events would be very useful. Accordingly, hydrologists use statistical methodology to obtain estimates of the probability that a flood of a certain size will occur in a given year. The estimates are based on historical stream-flow records, and special graph paper is used. The peak discharge for each year of record is plotted on the vertical Y-axis, which is scaled arithmetically. The horizontal X-axis on the bottom is scaled in probability terms, which provides the percent probability that a given discharge will be equaled or exceeded.

The plotting position for each annual peak flow is calculated using a special equation. A straight line is drawn through the array of data points on the graph, which then becomes a flood-frequency graph for a location (gauging station) on a particular river. The horizontal X-axis at the top of the graph provides the return period in years (or recurrence interval), which is the inverse value of the probability percentage on the bottom X-axis. Thus, a discharge associated with a value of 5 percent means that this discharge is expected to be equaled or exceeded in five out of one hundred years. In this example of a 5 percent probability value, the return period is twenty years, implying that on the average, this particular discharge is estimated to be equaled or exceeded once every twenty years. This frequency estimate can also be called the twenty-year-flood.

Note that the flood estimate is stated in probability terms. This has confused some people, who believe that if a twenty-year-flood event occurred, then the next flood of that magnitude will not occur again for another twenty years. This is incorrect, as two twenty-year-floods can occur in the same year, even though the probability is low. A fifty-year-flood and hundred-year-flood have a probability of being equaled or exceeded of only 2 and 1 percent, respectively.

The longer the historical record of floods, the more confidence may be taken in the estimated flood frequencies. However, the historical period of record for many bodies of water of fifty or even seventy-five years is considerably shorter than the total time the water has been flowing. In addition, many watersheds have been extensively changed by urbanization, farming activities, logging, and mining to such an extent that previous discharges may not be in accord with current conditions. Also, climatic change, particularly near large metropolitan areas, may have been great enough to make quantifiable changes in discharge. Thus, forecasts that are based on past flows may not be suitable for estimating future flows.

Flash floods differ from long-duration floods of large streams in that they begin very quickly and last only a short time. They often occur with torrential thunderstorm rains of 8 to 12 inches in a twenty-four-hour period over hilly watersheds that have steep ground and channel slopes. Three climatological situations are associated with flash floods. One is a hurricane that occurs over a landmass, which happens often in the eastern United States. The second situation occurs when moist tropical air is brought into a slow-moving or stationary weather front, which is common in the central and eastern United States.

The third occurs in the mountainous western states, as typified by the flash floods caused by winter storms in California.

The hydrologic effects of urbanization on flooding potential are substantial. Roofs, driveways, sidewalks, roads, and parking lots greatly increase the amount of impervious cover in the watershed. For example, it is estimated that residential subdivisions with lot sizes of 6,000 square feet (0.14 acres) and 15,000 square feet (0.34 acres) have impervious areas of 80 and 25 percent, respectively. Commercial and industrial zones have impervious areas of 60 to 95 percent. A typical suburban shopping center with its large expanse of parking area has about 90 percent impervious cover.

As the impervious cover increases, infiltration is reduced and overland flow is increased. Consequently, the frequency and flood peak heights are increased during large storms. Another change related to urbanization is the installation of storm sewers, which route storm runoff from paved areas directly to streams. This short-circuiting of the hydrologic cycle reduces the travel time to the stream channel, reduces the lag time between the precipitation event and the ensuing runoff, and increases the height of the flood peak. In essence, an increasing volume of water is sent to the stream channel in a shorter period of time.

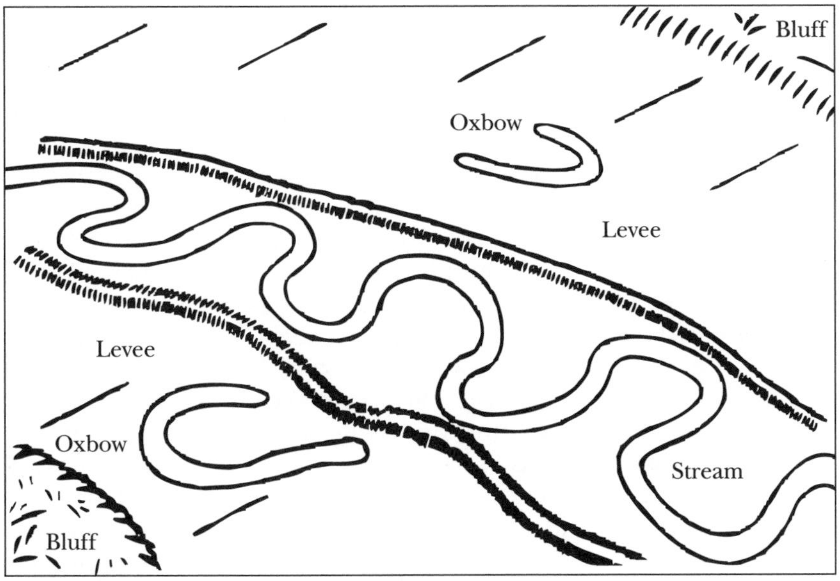

Geography

Floods are one of the most common and damaging of natural hazards. They can occur anywhere in the world but are most prevalent in valleys in humid regions when bodies of water overflow their banks. The water that cannot be accommodated within the stream channel flows out over the floodplain—a low, flat area on one or both sides of the channel. Floodplains have attracted human settlement for thousands of years, as witnessed by the ancient civilizations that developed along the Nile River in Egypt, the Yangtze and Yellow Rivers of China, and the Tigris and Euphrates Rivers in Mesopotamia (now Iraq). More people are living in river valleys than ever before, and the number is increasing. About 7 percent of the United States consists of floodplains that are subject to inundation by a hundred-year-flood. Most of the largest cities of the nation are part of this 7 percent. Even as flood damages increase, development in the floodplain has been growing by about 2 percent a year.

Large areas of the floodplain not only are inundated but also are subjected to rapidly moving water, which has enormous capacity to move objects such as cars, buildings, and bridges. If the flood is large enough, the water will inundate even stream terraces, which are older floodplains that are higher than the stream. For example, Hurricane Agnes in 1972 caused the Susquehanna River to rise nearly 16 feet above flood stage, inundating the downtown portion of Harrisburg, Pennsylvania, which was built on a terrace.

Floods can also be devastating in semiarid areas where sparsely vegetated slopes offer little resistance to large volumes of overland flow generated by a storm event. For example, the winter storms in January, 1969, in Southern California and the consequent flooding resulted in 100 deaths. Floods also occur in coastal and estuarine environments. A winter storm in 1953 resulted in severe

Levees are structures designed to contain stream flow, oxbows are bodies of water that were detached from the stream, and bluffs are the boundaries of a floodplain.

coastal flooding in eastern England and northwestern Europe (particularly the Netherlands), causing the deaths of over 2,000 people, the destruction of 40,000 homes, and the loss of thousands of cattle. Bangladesh is particularly vulnerable to coastal flooding. Most of the population of over 115 million in an area about the size of New York State live in the downstream floodplain of the Brahmaputra and Ganges Rivers. In addition, its location at the head of the Bay of Bengal only accentuates the storm surges that frequently occur in this area from tropical storms. For example, coastal storm surges killed 225,000 people in 1970 in Bangladesh.

Prevention and Preparations

Societies have made many attempts over the years to prevent floods, most of which involve some form of structural control. For example, the Flood Control Acts of 1928 and 1936 assigned the U.S. Army Corps of Engineers the responsibility of building reservoirs, levees, channels, and stream diversions along the Mississippi and its major tributaries. As a result of this legislation, 76 reservoirs and 2,200 miles of levees in the Upper Mississippi River basin alone were built by the Army after the late 1930's. State and local governments constructed an additional 5,800 miles of levees in the same watershed. The U.S. Natural Resources Conservation Service (formerly the Soil Conservation Service) built over 3,000 reservoirs on the smaller tributaries in the basin. All these very expensive efforts on the Mississippi and similar efforts on other watersheds still did not prevent the disastrous floods in 1993 on the Mississippi and in 1997 on the Red River in North Dakota and Minnesota.

Flood-abatement measures can be divided into structural and nonstructural approaches. The structural approach involves the application of engineering techniques that attempt either to hold back runoff in the watershed or to change the lower reaches of the river, where inundation of the floodplain is most probable. The nonstructural approach is best illustrated by zoning regulations.

One form of a structural measure is to treat watershed slopes by planting trees or other types of vegetative cover so as to increase infiltration, which thereby decreases the amount of overland flow. This measure, when combined with the building of storage dams in the valley bottoms, can substantially reduce the flood peaks and increase the lag time between the storm event and the runoff downstream. Another very common type of structural measure is to build artificial levees (or dikes) along the channel. They are usually built of earth, may be broad enough to contain an automobile trail, and should be high enough to contain the design flood. During high water on the Mississippi at New Orleans, it is possible to see ships sailing above when standing at the foot of the levee.

Starting in 1879 with the Mississippi River Commission, a large system of levees was constructed in the hope of containing all floods. This levee system has been expanded and improved so that it totals over 2,500 miles in length and is as high as 30 feet in some places. One problem with the levees is that the river channel aggrades or builds up over time so that it is higher than the bordering floodplain. If the levees fail, the water in the channel will rush into the floodplain, which is at a lower elevation, and create a disastrous flood. For example, the Yellow River in China in 1887 flooded an area of 50,000 square miles (nearly the size of England), which resulted in the direct deaths of nearly 1 million people and the indirect deaths of millions more by the famine that followed.

Another structural measure that has been tried by the Army Corps of Engineers on the Mississippi is to cut channels (also known as cutoffs) across the wide meander loops, which shortens the river length. This reduction in length increases the river slope, which correspondingly increases the average velocity of the water. As velocity increases, more water can move through the channel, and the flood peak can be reduced. Although the technique was initially successful, the river responded by developing new meanders, which only increased the length.

Where feasible, selected portions of the floodplain may be established as temporary basins that will be deliberately flooded in order to reduce the flood peak in the main channel. A related structural measure, which is used in the delta region of the Lower Mississippi, is to use floodways that divert water from the channel directly to the ocean. For example, the Bonne Carre floodway upstream of New Orleans is designed to divert excess water to Lake Pontchartrain, which is adjoined to the Gulf of Mexico.

As an alternative to structural flood abatement measures that involve engineering solutions, the nonstructural approach is to view floods and the damages they cause as natural events that will continue in the future even after expensive and elaborate engineering structures have been built. Levees

Dikes are built across rivers to contain floodwaters. When they rupture, as this one in China did in 1998, lands are inundated. (AP/Wide World Photos)

that were designed for a hundred-year-flood will fail if a flood of greater magnitude, say a two-hundred-year-flood, occurs. The real problem is the ongoing urban, commercial, and industrial development in the floodplain. Consequently, the nonstructural measure that has received increasing attention is floodplain zoning, which restricts development in flood-prone areas. This type of planning allows some agricultural activity and recreation in the floodplain as these types of land use call for occasional flooding. Under this form of zoning, permanent structures such as houses, schools, businesses, and industries would not be permitted in the flood-prone portions of the floodplain.

One of the major nonstructural techniques that has developed over the years in the United States to reduce flood losses is flood insurance. The notion of an insurance program that provides money for flood losses appeared to be reasonable because the pooling of risks, collection of annual premiums, and payments of claims to those property owners who suffer losses was similar to other types of insurance programs, such as fire insurance.

The first attempts to begin a federal flood insurance program began after flooding of the Kansas and Missouri Rivers in 1951. Legislation was introduced over the years and resulted in the National Flood Insurance Act of 1968. This act created the National Flood Insurance Program, which is administered through the Federal Emergency Management Agency (FEMA). The objectives of the program are to have nationwide flood insurance available to all communities that have potential for flooding, try to keep future development away from flood-prone areas, assist local and state governments in proper floodplain use, and make additional studies of flood hazards. One of the useful outcomes of the program has been the preparation of maps showing the approximate delineation of the area that would be covered by the hundred-year-flood. These maps are made available to all floodplain communities and provide essential information to realtors and mortgage-lending institutions. The flood insurance program is meant to be self-supporting.

However, there is some controversy about flood insurance. For example, although one of the intents of the program is to assist people who cannot buy insurance at private market rates, the effect has been to encourage building on the floodplain because people feel that the government will help them no matter what happens. Some people would even like to move their homes and commercial facilities to higher land in another location, but property owners can only collect for damages if they rebuild in the same flood-prone location. If these criticisms are correct, this policy of rebuilding on the floodplain will only perpetuate the problem.

As distinct from an earthquake, which occurs without warning, major storms and the associated possibility of flooding can be learned of in advance. Satellites and specially equipped reconnaissance airplanes can track storms over the ocean that may be heading for land and provide early warning of potentially heavy rainfall and storm surges. The River and Flood Forecasting Service of the U.S. National Weather Service maintains eighty-five offices at various locations along the major rivers of the nation. These offices issue flood forecasts to the communities within their region. The flood warnings are disseminated to local governmental agencies, who may then close roads and bridges and recommend evacuation of flood-prone areas. Parts of coastal Florida have evacuation routing directions on highway signs.

Rescue and Relief Efforts

The U.S. Army Corps of Engineers has been actively involved in flood control efforts since 1824, and much more so after 1890. This involvement in flood fighting was broadened in 1955, when Congress authorized them under Public Law 84-99 to engage in preparation and emergency response to floods. The Corps became responsible for implementing precautionary measures when there was an imminent threat of potentially serious flooding, providing any necessary emergency assistance during floods so as to prevent loss of life and property damage, providing immediate postflood assistance, and rehabilitating any flood-control structures that were damaged.

In order to respond quickly and provide assistance under emergency conditions, the Corps established emergency-response plans in conjunction with training of personnel for emergency response and recovery activities. These plans are tested by conducting exercises with state and local governments and other federal agencies, such as FEMA. When flooding is imminent or has already occurred, the Corps has the authority to provide state and local governments with technical assistance, supplies and materials, and equipment. Emergency construction—which includes stream obstruction removal; temporary levee construction; and the strengthening, repairing, and increasing of the height of existing levees—may also be included. Sandbagging levees to protect buildings during a flood constitutes 90 percent of the emergency assistance. For example, about 500,000 sandbags were used during the 1986 flood near Tulsa, Oklahoma.

As soon as the flood subsides, the Corps is authorized to remove debris that blocks critical water supply intakes, sewer outfalls, and key rail and road arteries. Restoration of public services and facilities is also provided for.

The nonengineering relief efforts are handled by other agencies. Foremost among them is the American Red Cross, which started in 1905 to establish shelters for the homeless and arrange for meals for flood victims and rescue workers. Other civic and religious organizations join in the rescue effort with food, clothing, miscellaneous household goods, and money. These organizations can also assist in cleanup and rebuilding operations.

Impact

Among the natural hazards in the world, floods rank first in the number of fatalities. An estimated 40 percent of all the fatalities that occur from natural hazards are attributed to flooding. People are attracted to river valleys for water supply; navigation; arable, level land; and waste disposal—yet these are the same lands that are the most susceptible to floods. Flood damages tend to be more in terms of property loss and less in fatalities in industrialized societies because the latter have the technology for better monitoring, storm and flood warnings, and evacuation procedures. In contrast, developing countries, particularly those with high population densities, suffer greater loss of life, because prevention and relief efforts are less well organized. The estimated distribution of fatalities and property losses from flooding is 5 and 75 percent in developed countries, respectively, as compared to 95 and 25 percent in developing countries, respectively.

These differences can be illustrated by the Great Mississippi River Flood of 1993 and several historical floods in China. Unusually heavy rain in the Upper Mississippi River basin in the late spring and early summer of 1993 was the immediate cause of the flood. For many locations, monthly rainfall totals were the highest ever measured in over a century. Levees failed and allowed enormous volumes of water to spread out over the floodplain, inundating an area of over 15,000 square miles (nearly the size of Switzerland). An estimated 70,000 people were driven from their homes, 50 lives were lost, and the property damage topped $12 billion. Historical records for floods in the densely populated floodplain of the Yellow River in China estimate an astonishing 900,000 and 3.7 million deaths in 1887 and 1931, respectively—a sad world record.

Obviously, water is the key element in flood damage. The water overflowing the stream channels inundates land that has buildings, equipment, crops, roads and rails, and communications that were not intended to operate underwater. In addition, the high velocity of floodwaters has extra capacity to carry sediment and debris, such as parts of buildings, which damage other structures in its path and are later dumped at some inconvenient location.

The most dramatic damage from floods is loss of human life. Other forms of damage include loss of livestock in rural areas; destruction of crops, buildings, transport facilities, and stored materials, such as seed, fertilizer, and foodstuffs; and soil erosion by the rapidly moving water. Even the coffins in cemeteries may be scoured out and destroyed, as was the case in the Great Mississippi River Flood of 1993.

Robert M. Hordon

Bibliography

Beyer, Jacqueline L. "Human Response to Floods." In *Perspectives on Water*, edited by David H. Spiedel, Lon C. Ruedisili, and Allen F. Agnew. New York: Oxford University Press, 1988. This is a well-written chapter that focuses on flooding and how societies respond to its danger.

Dunne, Thomas, and Luna B. Leopold. *Water in Environmental Planning*. New York: W. H. Freeman, 1978. This is a classic book that contains several very useful chapters on runoff processes, flood hazard calculations, and human adjustments to floods.

Dzurik, Andrew A. *Water Resources Planning*. 2d ed. New York: Rowman & Littlefield, 1996. In addition to other material on planning issues in water resources, this book contains a good chapter on floodplain management.

Hornberger, George M., Jeffrey P. Raffensberger, Patricia L. Wilberg, and Keith N. Eshleman. *Elements of Physical Hydrology*. Baltimore: The Johns Hopkins University Press, 1998. Contains a chapter that provides a technical discussion on streams and floods from an engineering perspective.

Jones, J. A. A. *Global Hydrology*. Essex, England: Longman, 1997. A well-documented book on hydrology and environmental management, including a chapter on floods and magnitude-frequency relationships.

Myers, Mary Fran, and Gilbert F. White. "The Challenge of the Mississippi Floods." In *Environmental Management*, edited by Lewis Owen and Tim Unwin. Malden, Mass.: Blackwell, 1997. This chapter provides a readable account of the issues involved in the destructive 1993 Mississippi floods.

Paulson, Richard W., Edith B. Chase, Robert S. Roberts, and David W. Moody, comps. *National Water Summary 1988-89*. U.S. Geological Survey Water-Supply Paper 2375. Denver, Colo.: Books and Open-File Reports Section, 1991. Although this lengthy report (591 pages) deals with floods and droughts for each state for 1988-1989, there are several highly informative introductory chapters on flooding issues.

Strahler, Alan H., and Arthur N. Strahler. *Modern Physical Geography*. 4th ed. New York: John Wiley & Sons, 1992. One of the better standard college books that has useful text and illustrations on runoff processes and floods.

White, Gilbert F. *Choice of Adjustment to Floods*. Department of Geography Research Paper 93. Chicago: University of Chicago, 1964. This is a classic paper that deals with the social-science aspects of settlement on floodplains, including the increasing damages from floods in the face of ever-larger expenditures for flood control.

Notable Events

Historical Overview

Flooding of rivers and coastal areas has been a natural phenomenon ever since the earth cooled sufficiently for water to accumulate on its surface. Floods are important in numerous geological processes, such as erosion of the continents, transport of sediments, and the formation of many fluvial and coastal landforms. There are a number of causes of flooding in historic times. The most common cause is an excess of precipitation in a drainage basin, which then leads to rivers overflowing their banks and inundating the surrounding areas. In general, rivers flood about every one to two years. This type of flooding may be very local, in the case of flash flooding, or it may be more widespread, as when large-scale storms dump great quantities of rain over extended areas for long periods of time. A second common reason for flooding is the movement of typhoons or hurricanes into coastal areas, which often causes severe coastal flooding. Flooding may also be caused by the collapse of human-made structures, such as dams or levees. Finally, there are a few examples of flooding caused directly by humans as an act of war or terrorism.

Perhaps the most spectacular example of large-scale flooding occurred during the Pleistocene epoch (the Ice Age) in eastern Washington and Idaho, when an ice dam in western Montana broke and released a torrent of floodwaters. The floodwaters raced across eastern Washington at velocities of 98 feet (30 meters) per second and scoured much of the area down to bedrock. The discharge of the floodwaters was estimated at about 179 million cubic yards (13.7 million cubic meters) per second, and the total water released in this catastrophic flood is estimated to be approximately 81.7 million cubic yards (25,000 cubic meters), an amount about equal to five times the water held in Lake Erie. The flood may have lasted as long as eleven days. Many other ice-dam collapses probably resulted in similar, if less catastrophic, floods during the ice ages, but the record of the eastern Washington flood is the best preserved.

When humans began to live in towns and cities, they commonly chose sites along rivers. The rivers provided water, transportation, and food, and the floodplains had fertile soils. Civilizations arose along the Tigris (western Asia), Euphrates (western Asia), Nile (eastern Africa), and Yellow (northern China) Rivers. Each of these civilizations depended directly or indirectly on the flooding of these rivers. The yearly floods brought nutrients to the floodplains, which became the early agricultural bases for these civilizations. As populations grew after the agricultural revolution began, more and more people moved into areas that were inundated periodically by floods. Floods are the most widespread of the natural hazards, and, because of the extensive development in the floodplains, floods are the most commonly experienced natural disaster. For centuries, floods were seen as necessary but completely uncontrollable acts of nature.

However, this view changed when people realized that some floods might be controlled by constructing levees and dams. Chinese engineers have tried to control the flooding of the Yellow River for over 2,500 years. Levees have been built along this river to control the river during high water flow, but the program requires constant expansion and maintenance. The Yellow River is the muddiest river in the world, and it continually deposits sediment in its channel, thus raising the level of the river water. This aggradation of the channel bed requires that even higher levees be constructed. The levees do control moderate-size flooding events but have frequently broken during higher flow levels.

The Yellow River has broken through its levees 1,593 times since the year 1800. Each levee breach causes a flood, many of which have been catastrophic. In 1887 more than 900,000 people lost their lives as the Yellow River flooded, and an additional 2 to 4 million people died later as the result of the flooding. The Yellow River flooded again in 1921, 1931, 1938, and 1939. Millions of Chinese have died during the flooding of this river known as "China's Sorrow." The 1938 flood was created by the Chinese army as it dynamited the levees in order to cause a flood southward to stop the advancing Japanese troops. The strategy worked, but at a great cost. Over 1 million Chinese people died in this human-made flood, and many more suffered for years afterward due to hunger and disease caused by the inundation of the agricultural areas.

The Yellow River has not been the only danger in China. Flooding of the Yangtze River in China has also caused extensive damage and great loss of life. In India, the Ganges and Brahmaputra Rivers annually flood because of the enormous amount of rain and snowfall in the Himalayas, which are the source area for these rivers. Monsoon conditions add to the flooding during most years, and rivers commonly in-

Milestones

1228:	Flooding in Holland results in at least 100,000 deaths.
1333:	The Arno River floods Venice, with a level of up to 14 feet (4.2 meters).
1642:	More than 300,000 people die in China from flooding.
1887:	The Yellow River floods, covering over 10,000 square miles of the North China Plain. Over 900,000 people die from the floodwaters and an additional 2 to 4 million die afterward due to flood-related causes.
1889:	A dam bursts upstream from Johnstown, Pennsylvania, and the floodwaters kill over 2,200 people.
1911:	The Yangtze River in China floods, killing more 100,000 people.
1927:	Extensive flooding of the Mississippi River results in 313 deaths.
March 12, 1928:	The St. Francis Dam collapses in Southern California, leading to about 450 deaths.
1938:	Chinese soldiers are ordered to destroy the levees of the Yellow River in order to create a flood to stop the advance of Japanese troops. It works, but at a terrible cost to the Chinese people; more than 1 million die.
1939:	Flooding of the Yellow River kills over 200,000 people.
1947:	Honshū Island, Japan, is hit by floods that kill over 1,900 people.
November 1, 1959:	Over 2,000 people die in floods in western Mexico.
October 10, 1960:	Bangladesh floods kill a total of 6,000 people.
October 31, 1960:	Floods kill 4,000 in Bangladesh.
November 3-4, 1966:	Flooding in Florence, Italy, destroys many works of art.
January 24-March 21, 1967:	Flooding in eastern Brazil takes 1,250 lives.
July 21-August 15, 1968:	Flooding in Gujarat State in India results in 1,000 deaths.
October 7, 1968:	Floods in northeastern India claim 780 lives.
June 9, 1972:	Heavy rainfall over Rapid City, South Dakota, causes an upstream dam to fail and release floodwaters, and 238 people lose their lives.
July 31, 1976:	A flash flood rushes down Big Thompson Canyon, Colorado, sweeping 139 people to their deaths.
July, 1981:	Over 1,300 people die in the flooding of Sichuan, Hubei Province, China.
June-August, 1993:	Largest recorded floods of the Mississippi River occur; 52 people die, over $18 million in damage is inflicted, and more than 20 million acres are flooded.

undate large regions along the lower stretches of these rivers. Yearly flooding of the lowlands in Bangladesh is often compounded by coastal flooding caused by oceanic storms moving inland. In October of 1960, two separate floods killed 6,000 people and 4,000 people, respectively. In August of 1968 more than 1,000 people perished in a flood in the Gujarat State, India, and this was followed by another deadly flood three months later in northeastern India, which resulted in the death of 780 people.

Owing to the enormous population growth in Asia and the relatively low level of flood control in many parts of the region, damage and death from flooding in this area have historically been great. It is estimated that in the twenty-year period between 1947 and 1967 more than 154,000 people were killed by floods in Asia.

Flooding in Europe has also caused damage, suffering, and loss of life. Records indicate that a flood in Holland in 1228 killed an estimated 100,000 residents. On November 4, 1333, Florence experienced one of its greatest floods when the Arno River overflowed its banks and inundated the city to a depth of 14 feet (4.2 meters). In 1966, Florence was once again flooded by the Arno River, but to the even greater depth of 13 feet. In total, 24 people perished in the flood. This flood also damaged priceless paintings, sculptures, tapestries, books, and maps.

On October 9, 1963, Italy suffered a devastating flood caused by the overtopping of a high arch dam in Vaiont. The flood was caused by an enormous rockslide that rushed into the reservoir behind the dam. The rock debris filled the reservoir and displaced the water toward the dam in waves as high as 230 feet (70 meters). The water flowed over the dam (which was not destroyed) and down the river valley at great speeds. A total of 1,800 people died. In the period from 1947 to 1967, floods took 10,540 lives in Europe (excluding the Soviet Union).

Flooding has also been extensive in the United States. One of the great tragedies in the late nineteenth century was caused by the collapse of the dam above Johnstown, Pennsylvania. In the western part of the state another dam collapse occurred in 1928, when the St. Francis Dam in Southern California ruptured, sending a flood downstream. More than 450 people in the Santa Paula area died from this flood.

Regional flooding of the Missouri-Mississippi drainage basin has long caused problems for the midwestern part of the country. Flooding of the lower stretches of the Mississippi River in the late 1800's caused engineers to design extensive levee systems to hold back the floodwaters. In 1927 the river rose to its then-historic high water level, causing extensive damage in the southern states. The river breached its levees in 225 locations, and 313 people lost their lives. The Mississippi again flooded in 1943 and 1944.

In 1972, Hurricane Agnes moved onshore and northward through the eastern part of the country, dumping enormous quantities of rain in the region and causing extensive flooding east of the Appalachian Mountains from North Carolina to New York State. A total of 113 people lost their lives in these floods. Estimated damages were in excess of $3 billion, the largest flood disaster in United States history at that time. Also in 1972, the devastating Rapid City, South Dakota, flood occurred. A tremendous thunderstorm broke over the area, dumping up to 15 inches (38 centimeters) of rain in less than six hours. The upstream dam was overtopped, and the river inundated the floodplain and much of Rapid City. The death total was 238, and damages exceeded $160 million.

The following year, the Mississippi River flooded extensively again, resulting in over $1.155 billion in damage. However, the extensive flood-control measures and early evacuation kept the death toll to a low level. In 1976, a thunderstorm dropped over 7.5 inches (19 centimeters) of rain in four hours over Big Thompson Canyon in Colorado. The flash flood that resulted killed 139 people. Only a few days earlier the Teton Dam in Idaho had collapsed, killing 11 people.

The largest flood of the Mississippi River in the 133 years of record keeping occurred in 1993. High-water marks were recorded at St. Louis, and the river broke through or overtopped 1,083 levees in the upper part of the basin. More than 20 million acres were flooded, and damages exceeded $18 billion. At least 52 people died in the floods.

Jay R. Yett

2400 B.C.E.: The Great Flood

Also known as: The Great Deluge
Date: Approximately 2400 B.C.E.
Place: Worldwide
Result: According to the Bible, all human and land-based animal life drowned, except for those on Noah's ark

The Great Flood is described in the Bible, Genesis 6-8. The story relates how God destroyed the existing world but saved Noah and his family and representatives of each animal species in an ark. Noah had built the ark under God's orders, and the occupants of the vessel were the only survivors after forty days and forty nights of torrential rain. Noah sent out a raven and a dove. The dove returned with an olive branch. After the waters subsided, the ark came to rest on Mount Ararat, in modern-day Turkey. Noah took his family from the ark, released the animals, and offered sacrifices to God. Noah symbolically began the world over again by signing a contract (covenant) with God promising to obey his word. In return God promised not to send another flood, a promise signaled by the appearance of a rainbow.

The tradition of the Flood, which is very old, was retold by many peoples in Mesopotamia to show a concern with sins and the destruction they can bring when the gods become angry with human behavior. Despite many attempts by scientists and historians to find evidence of a worldwide flood, none has been discovered. Some experts have speculated, however, that a large regional disaster contributed to the story of the Great Flood. In 2000, explorer Bob Ballard uncovered a 7,000-year-old settlement under the Black Sea that was inundated by rising Mediterranean waters, perhaps as a result of melting glaciers.

Leslie V. Tischauser

For Further Information:

Lambert, W. G., and A. Millard. *Atrahasis: The Babylonian Story of the Great Flood.* New York: Oxford University Press, 1969.

1228: Netherlands

Date: 1228
Place: Friesland, the Netherlands
Result: More than 100,000 drowned

By the 1200's the area around Friesland had a large population of farmers, growing crops and cutting peat or turf for sale as fuel. Peat cutters frequently cut the soil all the way to the system of dikes, the earthen walls built to keep the sea waters away, that protected the territory from the water and storms of the North Sea. The 1220's exhausted much of the peat supply, and the constant digging had undermined the earthen dike system, so much so that pounding waves and water could easily break apart the dikes. Many attempts were made to limit peat cutting, but by this time it was almost too late. Long stretches of the dike had been badly weakened.

A fierce storm early in 1228 sent huge waves into the dike system, which crumbled under the water's heavy impact, flooding the surrounding lowlands with massive amounts of water. Whole towns were swept away by the water's might, and thousands of people were drowned in their homes and fields. Community life was shattered, and where peaceful villages once stood the tides now had free rein to advance daily into the inland. Re-diking began shortly after most of the floodwaters subsided, but further storms and tides devastated the area throughout the thirteenth and fourteenth centuries. The huge numbers of deaths resulting from the 1228 flood did not deter settlers from reentering the region and trying again to make a living in the rich, but very dangerous, lowlands adjacent to the stormy North Sea.

Leslie V. Tischauser

For Further Information:

Lambert, Audrey M. *The Making of the Dutch Landscape: An Historical Geography of the Netherlands.* London: Academic Press, 1985.

1421: Netherlands

Date: April 17, 1421
Place: Dort, the Netherlands
Result: More than 100,000 dead, 20 villages never found again

The flood that swept through 72 villages in the Dutch lowlands adjacent to the North Sea was the second worst in the history of the Netherlands. The area, which the Dutch called the Grote Waard, had experienced serious flooding resulting in thousands of deaths in 1287, 1338, 1374, 1394, and 1396. On all these occasions, however, the flooded areas had dried out, and the dikes, the earthen walls built to keep the sea waters away, were sealed. On April 17,

1421, a fierce storm, backed by a powerful wind, sent huge waves into the dikes, and finally the waters broke through. Despite the long history of flooding, the area was heavily populated with an average of 500 people per square mile in 1421.

As water burst through the massive dikes, floodwaters raced through the city of Dort, killing about 100,000 of its residents. Seventy-two farming villages were flooded, and 20 of them disappeared forever beneath the raging ocean. The town of Dordrecht found itself permanently separated from the mainland when the waters subsided. The whole economy of the mainly agricultural region was devastated for many years. Many wealthy landlords and noble families were reduced to total poverty. Not until 1500 were the dikes fully rebuilt.

Leslie V. Tischauser

For Further Information:

Lambert, Audrey M. *The Making of the Dutch Landscape: An Historical Geography of the Netherlands.* London: Academic Press, 1985.

1570: Netherlands

Date: November 1, 1570
Place: Friesland, the Netherlands
Result: More than 50,000 dead

A huge storm in the North Sea, fueled by gusting winds from the north, sent tremendous waves over the extensive series of dikes the Dutch had built to protect them from the ocean. Salt water tore through the earthen dikes, smashing through more than 30 farming communities in the region and the wealthy city of Friesland. About 20,000 deaths were counted in that city alone, and the total reached more than 50,000 before the waters subsided. This devastation took place in the same region where just forty years earlier more than 400,000 people drowned in floodwaters raging over and through the dike system.

The 1570 storm came during a Dutch war with Spain, and many Christians in Spain said the flood was God's punishment of the Dutch for starting the conflict. That the devastation took place on All Saints Day, a major religious holiday at this time, added to the conviction that God's vengeance was behind the disaster. The powerful storm created such ruin and devastation that many destroyed villages were never rebuilt and the bodies of the dead were never found, most of them swept away violently into the depths of the sea.

Leslie V. Tischauser

For Further Information:

Lambert, Audrey M. *The Making of the Dutch Landscape: An Historical Geography of the Netherlands.* London: Academic Press, 1985.

1574: The Flood of Leiden

Date: August 3, 1574
Place: Leiden, the Netherlands
Result: More than 10,000 Spanish troops dead, siege of Leiden lifted

Disasters can come from many sources. Nature can create massive devastation and suffering. Accidents can destroy life on a massive scale. Wars stand out as examples of human-made disasters inflicted upon others. Yet very rare is the disaster that is purposely inflicted upon oneself yet is still declared successful and welcome. The flooding of Leiden in 1574 fits the latter description.

The origins of the Leiden flood lay in the recent outbreak of war between the Dutch and the Spanish, with the Dutch hoping to attain national independence from the Habsburg Empire. Several disagreements triggered the war. First, the Dutch, manifesting a growing nationalism, increasingly demanded a measure of internal self-rule. Dutch ports were vital to the economic health of the Habsburgs, and the Dutch believed their economic contribution deserved a measure of political influence. The Habsburgs, centered in Vienna, were not willing to share political decision making. Second, the Dutch had widely embraced the expanding Protestant religious movement sweeping through northern Europe and began to demand religious tolerance. The Habsburg Dynasty, the champion of Roman Catholicism in southern Europe, vehemently rejected this. Catholic authorities in the Netherlands did not persecute Dutch Protestants, but the intransigence of the Habsburg leadership angered the Dutch.

Last, a change in royal leadership alienated Dutch allegiance to the Habsburgs. For years a member of the Habsburg Dynasty had ruled central Europe as the Holy Roman Emperor, whose domain included direct political leadership of the Netherlands. In 1555, however, Holy Roman Emperor Charles V transferred political control of the region to his son, Philip II of Spain. Philip established his court in the Netherlands until 1559, when a series of grievances caused him to return to Spain. First, Philip was an ardent Catholic who viewed Protestants as heretics to be eradicated (Philip II sent the Spanish Armada to destroy England and also financed many of the religious wars in Europe). Second, Philip was accustomed to ruling by decree in Spain and could not deal with the Dutch representative legislature, the Estates General. Philip's attempt to rule by decree alienated even his Catholic Dutch subjects. Third, Philip imposed heavy taxes and military conscription upon the Dutch to participate in wars against Protestants elsewhere in Europe. Last, after Philip II moved his court back to Spain in 1559, the Dutch would not tolerate an absent monarch ruling their lives from a distance. The Dutch, Catholic and Protestant alike, banded together to fight for their independence in a war that would last eighty years (1568-1648).

Initial Spanish attempts to quell the uprising had only mixed results. Spanish troops commanded by the duke of Alva captured Brussels, but only by starving thousands of the city's inhabitants to death, an act which brought even more Dutch into the rebellion. In 1573, Philip II appointed a new military commander to the Dutch campaign, Don Luis de Requesens. Requesens instituted a strategy of isolating the predominantly Protestant northern Dutch cities from the mainly Catholic southern provinces (modern-day Belgium) in the hope he could compel the Catholic rebels to put down their arms and declare loyalty to their Catholic king. In pursuit of this goal, Requesens sent a Spanish army under the command of General Luis Valdez up the Oude River Valley to seize the city of Leiden. On May 26, 1574, Valdez surrounded the city, began the construction of sixty-two fortifications, and prepared for a lengthy siege of Leiden. Soon the attack had taken its toll, and the starving defenders were on the verge of surrender.

After failing to expel the Spanish by fighting as separate provinces, in 1572 the Dutch rebel armies elected William the Silent (Prince William I of Orange) as overall commander of their military effort. Eager to cut off Spanish intrusions into the southern provinces, Prince William made the relief of Leiden his primary objective. A hastily assembled land army failed to lift the siege, however, and William was forced to use more drastic means. Perhaps the most famous feature of the Netherlands was its system of dikes and dams used to reclaim land from the sea. Crowded into a corner of northwestern Europe, the growing Dutch population could obtain arable land only by constructing dikes in shallow coastal areas, pumping out the water, and reclaiming the land from the sea. While an effective means of increasing land area, the system of dikes left much of the country below sea level. William proposed to sever the dikes at the mouth of the Oude River, drown Valdez's army, and resupply Leiden with a Dutch fleet riding at sea beyond the dikes.

With no other alternative available to relieve Leiden, William ordered the breaching of the dams. On August 3, 1574, a wall of seawater, estimated by some to be 20 feet high, rolled up the Oude River Valley. Stunned by the Dutch act of desperation, General Valdez pulled his army back from Leiden's walls, weakening his attack. Although many of his troops drowned, Valdez still had a sizable force, and not until October 3 did the Dutch fleet under the command of Louis de Boisot finally lift the siege, forcing Valdez to retreat back to the North Sea coast. The siege operation and flooding had cost Valdez more than 10,000 troops and had halted the Spanish advance into the southern provinces.

Although the war would drag on for several decades, the Flood of Leiden demonstrated to the Spanish the resolve of the Dutch. The willingness purposely to inflict a disaster upon one's own country demonstrated the Dutch determination to fight, a determination that ultimately led to Dutch independence in the 1648 Treaty of Westphalia.

Steven J. Ramold

For Further Information:

Exercise of Arms: Warfare in the Netherlands, 1568-1648. Leiden, Netherlands: E. J. Brill, 1998.

Israel, Jonathan I. *The Dutch Republic: Its Rise, Greatness, and Fall, 1477-1806.* Oxford, England: Clarendon Press, 1998.

Motley, John L. *The Rise of the Dutch Republic: A History.* New York: Harper, 1874.

Parker, Geoffrey. *The Dutch Revolt.* New York: Penguin Books, 1985.

Schiller, Frederick. *History of the Revolt of the Netherlands.* London: Bohn, 1871.

1642: China

Yangtze River
Date: 1642
Place: Hunan Province, China
Result: More than 300,000 dead

There are three sources of potential flooding in Hunan Province. The two major streams of the province proper, the Yuan River and the Xiang River, rise in the highlands of southern Hunan or beyond and empty into Dongting Hu Lake, on the northern, or downstream, border of the province. The second source is the Yangtze River, which has its headwaters in the Tibetan highlands and derives a significant amount of its flow from snowmelt from Tibet and adjoining mountainous areas. The Yangtze flows through extensive highlands, which include the famous Three Gorges, where the giant dam and water project was under construction at the end of the twentieth century. The Yangtze exits the highlands and flows across the broad, flat plains of eastern China near Shashi, in Hubei Province, Hunan's neighbor to the north.

Upon reaching the flat plain, the Yangtze is inclined to overflow into a whole series of lakes before entering the ocean. The first of the large lakes is Dongting Hu, which is where the Yuan and Xiang Rivers join the Yangtze. Dongting Hu Lake is natural, but it has been "enhanced" by embankments in order to hold more water and to prevent overflows during smaller floods. Nothing can prevent the Yangtze River and Dongting Hu Lake from overflowing in a giant flood, however, such as occurred in 1931. Then, the entire plain near the course of the Yangtze becomes a lake, and the loss of life and vital crops is immense.

It is possible for Hunan Province to be in a drought, with dry uplands in the Yuan and Xiang River basins, and still experience flooding from the Yangtze River and the overflow of Dongting Hu Lake, which would cause backwater flooding along the lower courses of the Yuan and Xiang Rivers. This would also be disastrous to the fertile plains of northern Hunan, which in the seventeenth century were just beginning to assume importance as part of the rice bowl of China, during the final days of the Ming Dynasty.

The period from 1640 to 1645 was believed to have the most severe weather of the Ming Dynasty. Repeated floods occurred from 1637 to 1641. Hunan was a frontier region at this time. Most of the southern, and upland, portions of the province were more sparsely populated, and people supported themselves by hunting and fishing or by dry-land farming on the uplands, where mountain crops were easier to grow with small investments of capital and labor. Paddy-rice production, providing surpluses for export to other parts of China, could only have been carried out near the Yangtze River and Dongting Hu Lake, accompanied by a relatively high density of population.

It is unlikely that the flooding in 1642, with a high loss of life—more than 300,000—could have been the consequence of high waters on Hunan's smaller rivers. Moreover, one reconstruction of climate for the period indicates drought for most of the uplands. This era, at the end of the Ming Dynasty, was also a period of great unrest, with peasant revolts, marauding armies, and a general breakdown of control by a strong central government, which typically results in a lack of attention to the maintenance of dike and flood-control systems. The similarity to circumstances surrounding the great Yangtze River flood of 1931 is striking and suggests that the flood of 1642 was caused by high waters from the headwaters and highlands of the Yangtze River basin. Such a disaster could explain the huge loss of life to famine downstream along the Yangtze.

Neil E. Salisbury

For Further Information:

Heijdra, Martin. "The Socio-economic Development of Rural China During the Ming." In *The Ming Dynasty, 1368-1644, Part 2.* Vol. 8 in *The Cambridge History of China,* edited by Denis Twichett and Frederick W. Mote. Cambridge, England: Press Syndicate of the University of Cambridge, 1998.

Perdue, Peter C. *Exhausting the Earth: State and Peasant in Hunan, 1500-1850.* Cambridge, Mass.: Harvard University Press, 1987.

1824: Russia

Neva River
Date: November 19, 1824
Place: St. Petersburg, Russia
Result: More than 10,000 dead, millions of dollars in property damage

In the bitterly cold winter of 1824 a huge ice jam on the Neva River blocked the flow of water behind it for several weeks. Then, on November 19, the water raged over the dam and into the streets of the great Russian city of St. Petersburg, killing more than 10,000 citizens. This was the worst flood in the city's history, as water rose to the first-story windows of homes and other buildings. Even the Winter Palace of Czar Alexander I was damaged. Hundreds of carriages and horses were swept away by the icy waters, and about 400 soldiers drowned as they waited to be rescued on the roofs of their barracks.

In the nearby port of Kronshtadt, home of the Russian navy, hundreds of sailors were killed as the city was inundated by the Neva waters. The floodwaters picked up a hundred-gun ship and left it several hundred feet away in the middle of the marketplace. St. Petersburg, constructed by Czar Peter the Great in the early 1700's as Russia's new capital city, faced millions of dollars in property damage. Many works of art in the city's extensive museums were badly damaged, thousands of books in its great libraries were waterlogged, and thousands of homes were completely swept away.

Leslie V. Tischauser

For Further Information:

Sutton, Ann, and Myron Sutton. *Nature on the Rampage.* Philadelphia: J. B. Lippincott, 1962.

1887: Switzerland

Date: July 10, 1887
Place: Zug, Switzerland
Result: 70 dead, more than 600 left homeless

On the morning of July 10, 1887, a new $80,000 dam constructed on a small river above the village of Zug began to break apart. Eventually a wall of concrete more than 80 feet high crumbled, and thousands of tons of water rushed through the valley, sweeping aside trees, houses, and hundreds of animals.

About a dozen people in a café heard the noise of the wall of water, rushed out to see what was happening, and were crushed to death by the floodwaters. Two rescue boats were battered about in the raging stream, and the occupants all drowned. Dozens of huts disappeared, and their occupants were found in the flood's aftermath dead or badly bruised and injured. Seventy citizens died, and most of Zug's remaining 600 villagers were made homeless. The morning after the catastrophe, however, rescuers came upon a cradle floating in the subsiding waters. In the cradle they found a baby, still alive, having survived a long night alone on the floodwaters.

Leslie V. Tischauser

For Further Information:

The New York Times, July 11-12, 1887.

1887: China

Yellow River
Date: September 28, 1887
Place: Cheng-chou, China (now Zhengzhou, People's Republic of China)
Result: Approximately 900,000-7 million dead, approximately 1,500-2,000 villages and towns destroyed, estimated 10,000 square miles of land flooded

During the past three thousand years, the Yellow River—known as "China's Sorrow"—has flooded its banks more than fifteen hundred times, most disastrously during September and October of 1887. Heavy spring rains in the North China Plain had dangerously swollen the Yellow River, which villagers had tried to hold back with an ancient system of dikes reinforced by kaoliang bales. Unfortunately, this system had eroded, and villagers' pleas for its repair were ignored by the local government.

On September 28, 1887, at a sharp bend near Cheng-chou in Henan Province, the Yellow River surged through a weak dike wall—a breach that proved fatal for a tragically high number of villagers in the surrounding area. Within minutes, the gap widened from a few feet to 100 yards and then to 0.5 mile as an entire section of the dike fell away. Floodwaters 20 feet deep immediately engulfed Cheng-chou, making it impossible to turn the river back. Rolling eastward, it spread in a 40-foot swath across Henan and Shandong Provinces, reaching into Anhui Province as it destroyed crops, cattle, and entire towns.

Inundated by floodwaters up to 50 feet deep, villagers were left homeless and starving, clinging to rooftops and treetops as they waited for help. However, communication systems in China at that time were so poor that the first eyewitness accounts of the disaster did not reach the outside world until early November. By then, the Yellow River had roiled across the countryside for more than a month, leaving survivors not only physically emaciated but also psychologically devastated, overwhelmed by the sudden destruction of their communities.

By all accounts, the toll of death and loss was horrendously high: approximately 900,000 to 7 million lives lost, approximately 1,500 to 2,000 towns and villages destroyed, and an estimated 10,000 square miles of land flooded. Even when the flood finally subsided (after splitting into channels at the Huai River and the Lower Yangtze), the villagers' suffering was not over. In its wake, the Yellow River left a desert of yellow sand up to 10 feet deep. The fall harvest had been ruined, new crops could not be grown, and famine spread across the land. As the Chinese government and foreign missionaries tried to feed and house refugees from the North Plain, Chinese engineers directed the monumental task of mending the Cheng-chou breach that had started the flood.

From 1888 to 1889, hundreds of workers moved thousands of tons of earth, sand, silt, and stones to repair the dike. Their efforts were largely successful (the Yellow River would not break through again until 1911), but during the same period, an estimated 500,000 lives were lost to the cholera that followed flood and famine. Even as villagers rebuilt their homes and replanted the land, they knew that the Yellow River's power over their lives had not been conquered.

Mary Louise Buley-Meissner

For Further Information:

Allaby, Michael. *Floods.* New York: Facts on File, 1998.

Clark, Champ. *Flood.* Alexandria, Va.: Time-Life Books, 1982.

Davis, Lee. *Natural Disasters: From the Black Plague to the Eruption of Mt. Pinatubo.* New York: Facts on File, 1992.

Ward, Kaari, ed. *Great Disasters: Dramatic True Stories of Nature's Awesome Power.* Pleasantville, N.Y.: Reader's Digest Association, 1989.

1889: The Johnstown Flood

Date: May 31, 1889
Place: Johnstown, Pennsylvania
Result: About 2,209 dead, 1,600 homes lost, 280 businesses destroyed, $17 million in property damage

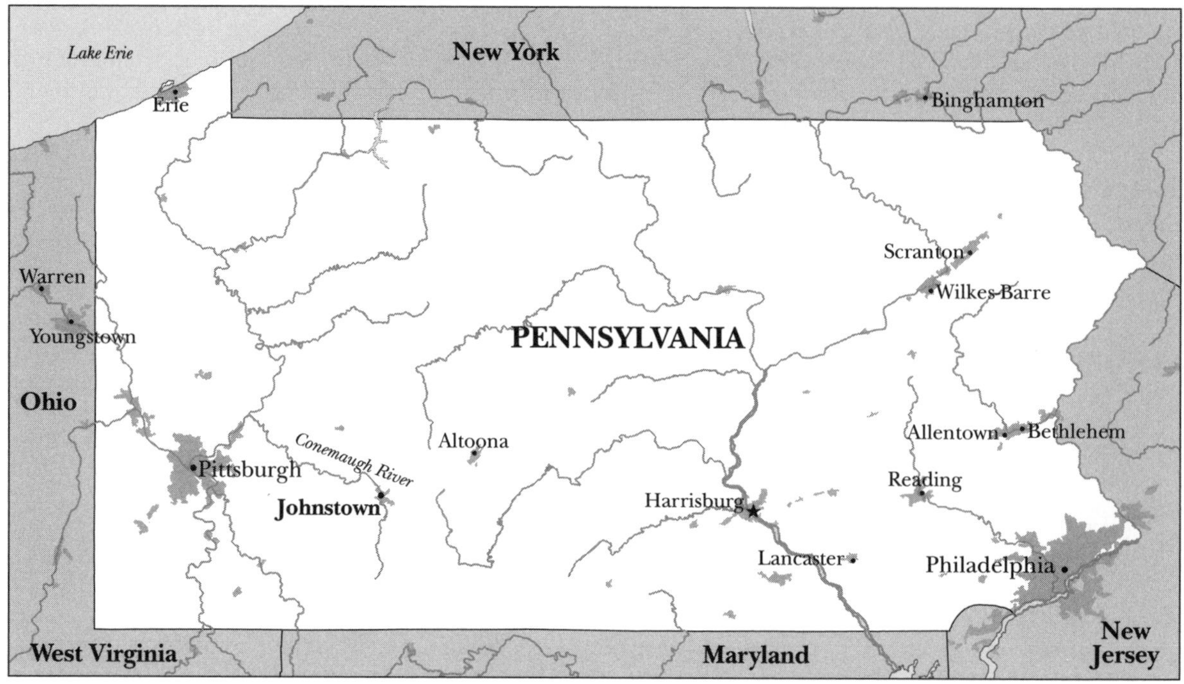

Strictly speaking, the Johnstown Flood of 1889 was not a natural disaster. Nature was only partly responsible; neglect and human error also contributed. Without the latter two, the disaster would not have occurred.

Flooding in the narrow valley of western Pennsylvania was a common occurrence, and while creating a certain amount of water damage in buildings, it also led to a casual attitude about these natural events. The great loss of life, however, was the result of a tremendous wave caused by the breaking of a dam 14 miles upstream from Johnstown.

Johnstown, Pennsylvania. The first white settlers came to the valley around 1771, but the area was abandoned several times before it became a backwoods trading center. Population started growing when the canal system from Philadelphia to Pittsburgh was finished, and by 1889, ten thousand people lived in Johnstown, with a total of thirty thousand crowded in the narrow valley. Johnstown was built on a nearly level floodplain at the confluence of the Little Conemaugh and Stony Creek Rivers in Cambria County. In the early 1800's, Pennsylvania's canal system, when completed, had too little water in the summer to be usable; in 1836 the state legislature appropriated $30,000 for a reservoir dam on the South Fork River. The final cost was $240,000, and it was completed in 1852, six months before the Pennsylvania Railroad was built from Philadelphia to Pittsburgh, making the canal obsolete. The canal system was put up for sale in 1854 and in 1857 was bought by the Pennsylvania Railroad for $7.5 million.

In June, 1862, the dam broke after heavy rains. Little damage resulted downstream as the reservoir was only half-full, and a watchman had opened the valves and released much of the pressure before the break. The reservoir, then only about 10 feet deep, was abandoned until Congressman John Reilly bought it in 1875 for $2,500. Four years later he sold it to Benjamin F. Ruff, a onetime railroad tunnel contractor, coke salesman, and real-estate broker, for $2,000. Before selling it, Reilly removed the cast-iron discharge pipes and sold them for scrap.

The dam had been constructed according to the best engineering knowledge of the day. It was composed of layers of clay covered with an inner and outer coating of stones. A spillway, 72 feet wide, was cut at the eastern end of the rock of the mountain. The dam breast was more than 900 feet long and 20 feet wide, and the dam itself was 850 feet high with a 270-foot base, at the center of which were five cast-iron sluice pipes, each 2 feet in diameter and set into a stone culvert. These pipes were controlled from a nearby wooden tower. It was these sluice pipes which had been removed by Reilly, and the control tower burned in 1862.

In 1879, Ruff persuaded fifteen Pittsburgh men to buy shares in the venture, and on November 15 the South Fork Fishing and Hunting Club was chartered in Pittsburgh. Members, eventually numbering 61, included Andrew Carnegie; Henry Clay Frick, the coke king associated with him; several other Carnegie associates and officials; banker Andrew Mellon; Robert Pitcairn, the powerful head of the Pittsburgh division of the Pennsylvania Railroad; and other industrial, commercial, and political leaders from Pittsburgh. Named president, Ruff boarded up one side of the stone culvert and dumped rock, mud, brush, hay, and anything else he found, including horse manure, into the hole left by the pipes; lowered the height of the dam several feet to provide a roadway wide enough for two carriages to be driven abreast on its top; installed a bridge over the spillway and under it a screen of iron rods to keep in the fish with which the lake was to be stocked; and built a clubhouse, boathouses, and stables. Sixteen members added private summer homes. Renamed Lake Conemaugh, 450 acres, 1 mile across and 2 miles long, it drained 60 square miles of mountainside, including many creeks, was 70 feet deep in the spring, and contained water weighing 20 million tons.

Watching this activity with some concern was Daniel J. Morrell, head of the Cambria Iron Works downstream, which had about $50 million invested in the valley. In November, 1880, Morrell sent John Fulton, an engineer and his designated successor, to look over the dam. Fulton's report, a copy of which Morrell sent to Ruff, noted that "repairs were not done in a careful and substantial manner, or with the care demanded in a large structure of this kind." He reported that the lake had no discharge pipe nor any other method to reduce or take the water out of the lake, and that it had been repaired badly, leaving a large leak at its center. In a brusque answer, Ruff maintained that there were no leaks, the weight of the water had been overestimated by Fulton, and the Iron Works was in no danger from the dam. He was later to declare that the "leaks" were springs at the base of the dam.

Still unsatisfied, Morrell in a second letter offered to cooperate in the work, helping financially to make the dam safe. The offer was declined, with renewed assurances of safety. Morrell died in 1885 and Ruff in 1887; two years later, Colonel Elias J. Unger, a retired Pittsburgh hotel owner, was named club president and manager and took up full-time residence at the lake.

In February, 1881, heavy rains caused serious damage, and in June of the same year during a flash flood rumors flew that the dam was about to break. These rumors were renewed each year but for the next eight years proved groundless, leading to an attitude of complacency on the part of everyone in the area.

The first record of a flood in Johnstown is from 1808, when a small dam across Stony Creek, put in as a millrace for one of the first forges, was breached. As the years went by, floods became more serious because timber was being stripped off the mountainsides to provide lumber for building, and the river channels were narrowed to make room for buildings and bridges. Thus, there was less river to handle more runoff. From 1881 to 1888, seven floods were recorded, three of them serious.

The Year of the Johnstown Flood. In April of 1889, 14 inches of heavy snow fell, then melted rapidly in the warm weather. In May rain fell for eleven days. On May 28 a storm that had originated out of Kansas and Nebraska caused hard rains over a wide area. On May 29 the U.S. Signal Corps warned the mid-Atlantic states that they were in for severe local storms, and parts of Pennsylvania had the worst downpour ever recorded; at the South Fork Club 7 inches fell.

On Thursday, May 30, a fine rain fell for most of the day, but by 4 P.M. the sky was lighter and the wind was up. People who lived in areas that had been flooded assumed the storm was over and the waters would recede. However, by 11 P.M. heavy rain and high winds had returned. During the night, families in the valley heard "rumbling and roaring" sounds as the heavy storm water tore big holes in the saturated ground. Crops washed away, roads became creeks, and little streams rampaged torrents.

By Friday morning the rain had eased off, but the sky was very dark and a thick mist hung in the valley. Rivers were rising faster than 1 foot an hour, and by 7 A.M., when men arrived for their shift at the Cambria mills, they were told to go home and take care of their families. By 8 A.M., much debris was observed in the lake, and it was rising rapidly. At 10 A.M. schools were let out. The Chicago and Pittsburgh trains arrived on time at Johnstown, but some areas of track were already in precarious condition, and at 11 A.M. a log boom burst up the Stony Creek, sending logs to jam against the massive Johnstown stone railroad bridge. By noon the water level in Johnstown was at a record high, and after the Stony Creek ripped out the Poplar Street and Cambria City bridges, George T. Swank, editor and proprietor of the *Johnstown Tribune,* started a running log of events.

Meanwhile, at the dam, young John G. Parke, Jr., new resident engineer for the South Fork Club, was busy that morning supervising twenty Italian laborers who were installing a new indoor plumbing system. Parke noted about 7 A.M. that the water level of the lake was only about 2 feet from the top of the dam, while the previous day it had been 4 to 6 feet below. He heard a sound from the head of the lake like "the terrible roaring as of a cataract." He went inside to have breakfast and then with a young workman took out a rowboat and surveyed the incoming creeks, finding the upper quarter of the lake filled with debris.

When Parke returned to shore, he was told he was needed at the dam immediately, and he saddled his horse to ride there. He found nearly fifty people observing the sewer diggers trying without much success to throw up a ridge of earth to heighten the dam. At the west end a dozen men were trying to cut a new spillway through the tough shale of the hillside but succeeded in providing a trench only knee-deep and about 2 feet wide. Local onlookers advised Colonel Unger, who was directing the work, to tear out the bridge and the iron-mesh spillway, but he did not want to lose the fish. At 11 A.M., the lake water was at the level of the dam, eating at the new ridge, and there were several large new leaks at the base.

Around 12:15, when Unger ordered the spillway cleared, it was too late: Debris had piled up to the extent that the bridge and mesh were jammed in, and the spillway was virtually blocked. At 12:30, Parke considered cutting a new spillway through one end of the dam, but he did not want to take the responsibility for ruining the dam. He reasoned that there would be no way later to prove the dam had been about to break. He went into the clubhouse for dinner. By 2 P.M. the water was running over the center of the dam, at its lowest point.

A man sits on a tree trunk that pierced a house during the Johnstown Flood. (AP/Wide World Photos)

The Flood Itself. The dam gave at 3:10 P.M. John Parke insisted it did not break, it "just moved away." It took about forty minutes for the entire lake to empty. Civil engineers later calculated the velocity was akin to "turning Niagara Falls into the valley." They blamed the lack of outlet pipes, the lowered height of the dam in relation to the spillway (which was itself crammed with debris), and the fact that due to earlier damage the dam was weakest and lowest at its center.

The men stood and watched as huge trees were snapped off the ground and disappeared and the water scraped the hill down to bedrock to a height of 50 feet; the farmhouse and buildings belonging to George Fisher vanished in an instant; and Lamb's Bridge and the buildings of George Lamb climbed the 60-foot crest, then rolled and smashed against the hill. Then the valley turned sharply to the right and blocked their view. The Fisher and Lamb families had escaped minutes before, but at South Fork, Michael Mann, who lived in a shanty on the creek bank, was the first casualty. His body was found a week later, 1.5 miles downstream, stripped of all clothing and half buried in mud. South Fork Village, stacked on the hillside in a bend in the valley, suffered little damage: About 20 buildings, a planing mill, and the bridge were swept away and then deposited about 200 feet upstream by the water's backwash as it slammed into the mountain on the north side of the Little Conemaugh River. However, the 40-foot "mountain" of water, moving about 10 to 15 miles per hour, claimed another 3 lives.

For the first mile of its 14-mile journey to Johnstown, the river had only railroad tracks and equipment to swallow up. As the valley narrowed and twisted, the water height grew to over 60 feet. As it hit the tremendous stone viaduct built fifty years earlier and still used for the main line of the Pennsylvania Railroad, there was a booming crunch as debris piled up and momentarily formed another lake. Then the bridge collapsed all at once, and the water exploded with concentrated power down the valley, taking with it the entire small village of Mineral Point. Fortunately, most of the inhabitants had left earlier in the day as the water rose due to normal flooding, but the death toll reached 16 as those left went racing off downstream on their own rooftops or were caught in the maelstrom.

As the water advanced down the valley (average decline in elevation, 33 feet per mile), the debris caught in various places, damming up the water and then releasing it to flow more violently. The debris and the friction with the hillside also caused the top water to travel more rapidly, so that a "surf" effect developed, pounding debris and bodies deep into the mud and making later retrieval difficult. Now several hundred freight cars, a dozen or more locomotives, passenger cars, nearly a hundred more houses, and quite a few human corpses were part of the wave that surged on down the valley. Past East Conemaugh, the flood was on a straightaway, and it began to gather speed. Woodvale with its woolen mill was wiped out, along with 314, or 1 of every 3, people in town. Miles of barbed wire from Gautier Works were added to the wreckage, which swept into Johnstown at 4:07 P.M.

In Johnstown, the floodwaters had actually begun to recede. Most people, perched in upper stories, never saw the water coming, but they heard it. It began as a deep, steady rumble and accelerated into a roar. Those who actually saw the wall of water, now an estimated 40 feet high, remembered "trees snapped off like pipestems" and "houses crushed like eggshells." Most impressive was the cloud of dark spray that hung over the front of the wave. Preceding the spray was a high wind.

The water hit Johnstown harder than anything it had encountered in its 14-mile course from the dam. It bounced off the mountain in its path and washed back up it 2 miles, carrying debris and people with it. The devastation took just ten minutes. However, the suffering and loss of life were more protracted.

The massive stone-arched Pennsylvania Railroad bridge on the downriver side of Johnstown had been protected by a curve in the river and held. Debris piled up 40 feet high against it, to an area of 40 acres, and as night came on it caught fire. Editor Swank, who had been watching everything from his *Johnstown Tribune* office window, wrote that the fire burned "with all the fury of the hell you read about—cremation alive in your own home, perhaps a mile from its foundation; dear ones slowly consumed before your eyes, and the same fate yours a moment later."

The finest and newest hotel in town, the Hulbert House, had been used as a place of refuge by many people seeking safety. It collapsed almost the instant it was hit by the flood. Of the 60 people inside the building, only 9 got out alive.

It was later wondered if so many lives were lost because no warning was given. Most of the blame for loss of life can be placed on the fact that flooding was

Johnstown residents gather on rooftops amid the wreckage caused by the flood of 1889. (AP/Wide World Photos)

common in the valley, and each year brought rumors that the dam was going to fail, but in the nine years since the lake had been filled no major upsets had occurred. Unger sent Parke to South Fork at 11:30 A.M. with a warning of danger, but two local men who had just gone to the dam said there was nothing to worry about. Sometime before 1 P.M., the East Conemaugh dispatcher's office received a message to warn the people of Johnstown that the dam was liable to break. He set it aside without reading it; his assistant read it and laughed. An hour later another message was sent to East Conemaugh, Johnstown, and Pittsburgh, and in thirty minutes another. Still, no one was unduly alarmed.

The only meaningful warning was received in East Conemaugh, when a railroad engineer whose crew was repairing tracks just upriver heard the water coming. He jumped into his engine, tied down the whistle and steamed down the tracks. Nearly everyone in East Conemaugh heard the whistle and understood almost instantly what it meant. Otherwise, as one telegraph operator noted of the messages, people paid no attention to the few warnings. As a matter of fact, the common attitude was that anyone taking any precautions was at best gullible and at worst a coward.

Aftermath and Cleanup. Dawn on Saturday, June 1, was dark and misty, and the river was still rising. A few random buildings stood amid the wreckage that was piled as high as the roofs of houses. Every bridge was gone except the stone bridge, and against it lay a good part of what had been Johnstown, in a blazing heap. Below the bridge the Iron Works, though damaged, still stood, but at least two-thirds of the houses in Cambria City had been wiped out, and a tremendous pile of mud and rock had been dumped the entire length of the main street.

Amid the wreckage were strewn corpses and portions of corpses of horses and humans. Rescue parties had worked through the night to free people trapped alive in the burning pile, but an estimated 80 died. Now others helped bring the marooned down from rooftops and searched among the ruins for signs of life. Roads were impassable. The railroad had been destroyed. Every telegraph and telephone line to the outside was down. There was no drinkable water, little food, and no stores from which to obtain either.

Five Pittsburgh newspapers had sent journalists, and the first newspapermen arrived on foot at about 7 A.M. on June 1. The presence of reporters at the scene the following day and for several weeks to come, as well as later remembrances by people who lived through the event, provided records of individual experiences. Many of the contemporary newspaper accounts, however, were sensationalized and based on rumor as much as fact.

By noon rafts were built; people on the hillsides whose homes had escaped harm and farmers from miles out in the country began coming into town, bringing food, water, and clothing; unclaimed children were looked after. At 3 P.M., a meeting was called at the Adams Street schoolhouse. Arthur J. Moxham, a young, self-made, wealthy, and popular industrialist was put in charge of business. He immediately organized committees to establish morgues, remove dead bodies from the wreckage, establish temporary hospitals, organize a police force, and find supplies and funds. A fear of typhoid as well as concern for the survivors made retrieval, identification, and burial of the bodies imperative. Those who were not identified were numbered, their descriptions recorded, and they were buried. One out of every 3 bodies would never be identified. Hundreds of people who were lost would never be found; it is supposed that some simply walked away and never came back. Not for months would there be any realistic count of the dead, and there would never be an exact, final count. Two bodies were found as late as 1906. Ninety-nine whole families had been wiped out, 98 children had lost both parents, and hardly a family had not suffered a death. The flood had killed about 1 out of every 9 people.

On Sunday the weather eased off. Bodies were taken across the Little Conemaugh in skiffs and buried in shallow graves. A post office was set up, and all survivors were instructed to register. The first patients were cared for in a temporary hospital, and the first train came through. Supplies and volunteers, more newspapermen and police, doctors and work crews, a shipment of tents, an eleven-car train containing nothing but coffins with more to come, and a Pittsburgh fire department arrived, extinguishing the fire at the bridge by midnight. At the end of the day more than 1,000 people had arrived to help the 27,000 who needed aid. Thousands more were on their way.

On Tuesday, Moxham resigned, and James B. Scott, head of the Pittsburgh Committee, took over as civilian head of the area. From Washington, D.C., came nurse Clara Barton and her newly organized American Red Cross to set up tent hospitals and six hotels with hot and cold running water, kitchens, and laundries. In five months she distributed nearly half a million dollars worth of blankets, clothing, food, and cash. Upon her departure she was presented with a diamond locket by the people of Johnstown, and she was later feted in Washington at a dinner attended by President Benjamin Harrison.

By the end of the month a book on the disaster had been published, and within six months, a dozen would appear. Newspapers carried sensational stories for weeks and published extra editions, all of which sold out. Songs were written about the flood, several of which became best-sellers. Sightseers with picnic baskets arrived and bought souvenirs. In all, cash contributions from around the world would total more than $3.7 million.

In spite of assiduous cleanup, including the sprinkling of four thousand barrels of lime over the area, typhoid broke out, affecting 461 people and killing 40. Everyone took it for granted that Johnstown would be rebuilt, and on its original site, and so it was. John Fulton made public the faults of the dam. In Pittsburgh, members of the South Fork Club met and officially decided that it would be best to say nothing about their role in the disaster. Suits were brought against them, but the club had nothing except the now-worthless site and widespread negative publicity; no one was awarded anything. Cyrus Elder, who had lost his wife and daughter and his home, and who was the only local member of the club, concluded, "If anybody be to blame I suppose we ourselves are among them, for we have indeed been very careless in this most important matter and most of us have paid the penalty of our neglect."

Erika E. Pilver

For Further Information:

Degen, Paula, and Carl Degen. *The Johnstown Flood of 1889: The Tragedy of the Conemaugh.* Philadelphia: Eastern Acorn Press, 1984. Primarily a photographic history, this illustrated text tells the story of the flood through period photography.

Gambee, Budd Leslie. *Frank Leslie's Illustrated Newspaper, 1855-1860: Artistic and Technical Operations of a Pioneer Pictorial News Weekly in America.* Ann Arbor, Mich.: Author, 1963. A forerunner of today's tabloids, it contains sensational text and engravings.

McCullough, David. *The Johnstown Flood.* New York: Simon & Schuster, 1968. The author is a well-known historian, and this work remains the definitive history of the flood. An extensive bibliography is included.

______. "Run for Your Lives!" *American Heritage Magazine* 16, no. 4 (1966): 5-11, 66-75.

Walker, James Herbert. *The Johnstown Horror!!! Or, Valley of Death.* Philadelphia: H. J. Smith, 1889. Although difficult to find, this book provides much information on the Johnstown Flood.

1890: Mississippi River

Date: February-April, 1890

Place: The Upper Mississippi River (particularly Tennessee, Ohio, and Kentucky) and the Lower Mississippi River from Illinois to New Orleans

Result: Almost 100 dead, 50,000 homeless, development of consolidated flood plan for the Mississippi River

The story of the Mississippi River flood of 1890 begins in February of that year on the Upper Mississippi River. The weather grew surprisingly warm, and thunderstorm after thunderstorm followed in Tennessee, Ohio, Kentucky, and the neighboring states. The rivers began to rise and enclose people with a wall of water that took some to their deaths. Train and steamboat travel were stopped, and businesses were damaged or totally destroyed. By March water-gauge readings along the Lower Mississippi from Illinois to New Orleans were at dangerously high levels.

Thousands of dollars had been spent on levees along the Lower Mississippi, with engineers bragging about the strength of the levees and how safe it was to live along the river. Yet in early 1890 the country for miles around was underwater, with hundreds of farms and homes completely submerged. One entire family and their home in Indiana was taken away by the river. The list of dead was growing, and by April levees were beginning to crumble and break. The levees' capability to protect the people and the country from being overwhelmed was of great concern. By the end of the 1890 flood season there would be almost 100 people dead and 50,000 homeless. With these figures, some river engineers understood that science, education, and past mistakes would play a major role in future Mississippi River flood-control planning.

In 1891, William Starling, one of the Mississippi River Commission's (MRC) best engineers, reflected on the effects of the flood of 1890. It must have seemed to him that the outcome of almost two hundred years of flood control was almost insignificant. The river's power was still enormous, and it had proved its might by devastating the lower valley with an intense flood. Starling perceived that the Mississippi was unique from other rivers only in size, and that modern science, skill, and money would be useless if there was not cooperation between federal, state, and local governments.

Although the 1890 flood must have been discouraging to the engineers of the MRC, in truth, they still had accomplished much by the beginning of the twentieth century. The political horizon had become much brighter because of the MRC's efforts to persuade federal, state, and local governments to work together for the same goals. The administrative structure of river control was much more coherent than it had ever been, understanding of methods of flood control had become more scientific and less empirical, and men with superior educations had been groomed to fill top positions of leadership within the MRC. Methods of levee construction had been refined and almost perfected, given the limitations of nineteenth century earth-moving technology.

Altogether, these advancements allowed the MRC to confront the Mississippi River, and, while they had not been able to stop flooding, the engineers' ability to manage damage was better than it had ever been. During the 1890 flood, for example, only 5 levee breaks occurred in the Lower Yazoo district, where the MRC had concentrated much of its energy, and none of those was due to water overflowing the levees.

Nevertheless, even though the 1890 flood did not equal the massive flood of 1882, which would not be equaled until the twentieth century, it was still very serious. The MRC had been arguing in favor of higher levee grades since 1888, and the flood of 1890 made clear the importance of stouter levees. The 1890 flood ultimately created 53 new crevasses. As it had done after previous floods, the MRC used the levels of the 1890 flood to establish new reference lines for new grades. This meant that complete levee lines had to be raised, and work began immediately. This time, the MRC chose to establish levee grades that were in relationship to the real flood height, not to the calculated confined height of the flood. The two flood levels were different because the true height was influenced by the crevasses that inevitably formed. The MRC adjusted levees to this grade by raising the levees in the vicinity of crevasses to grades thought to be adequate for the full discharge of the river.

The 1890 flood brought into focus the progress that supporters of comprehensive river management had made. Its devastation caused Congress to pass a new River and Harbor Act, which marked a major change in national policy concerning the Lower Mississippi. As had happened previously, changes in national policy usually came about because of the effects of a particularly damaging flood. The new policy ended the practice of defining levee building solely in terms of improvement of navigation, instead allowing flood-control structures to be built solely for the purpose of the protection of property. The MRC no longer had to justify all levee construction by somehow tying it to navigation improvement. This change was reinforced in 1891 by a joint resolution of Congress that further emphasized the government's interest in flood-control work designed to protect property.

Loralee Davenport

For Further Information:

Starling, William. "The Improvement of the Mississippi River." *Transactions of the American Society of Civil Engineers* 20 (March, 1889): 108.

_______. "Keeping the Mississippi Within Her Banks." *Engineering Magazine* 1 (April, 1891): 3-4.

_______. "The Levees of the Mississippi River." *Engineering News* 35 (January 30, 1896): 77.

1903: Kansas and Missouri Rivers

Date: May 26-June, 1903

Place: Kansas, especially Lawrence; Missouri, especially Kansas City

Result: 200 dead, 8,000 left homeless

Two weeks of heavy spring rains brought huge amounts of water to the Kansas River and Lower Missouri River Valleys. The Kansas River began to overflow its banks on May 26, sending floodwaters into the business district of Lawrence, Kansas. By May 30 traffic across the bridges lining the northern and southern parts of the city came to a halt. Torrents of water continued to pour into businesses and homes along the river, carrying many buildings downstream. The two parts of the city were cut off from each other for several days, and communication was interrupted. Perhaps 100 people lost their lives in the worst flood in Lawrence's history.

As the floodwaters moved downriver they continued to leave behind death and destruction. The Missouri River rose 35 feet above flood stage and knocked out every bridge in Kansas City. Every animal in the city's vast stockyards was drowned. The raging waters drowned another 100 people as they moved through central Missouri. After six weeks the waters had subsided, and recovery became possible. The United States Army Corps of Engineers surveyed the damage and estimated more than $20 million in property had been destroyed. The flood made 8,000 people homeless, many of them losing their houses permanently. It was many years before the region's economy recovered from the flood of 1903.

Leslie V. Tischauser

For Further Information:

Knight, F. M., photographer. *Views of the Great Kansas River Flood.* Lawrence, Kans.: Author, 1903.

1903: Oregon

Willow Creek

Date: June 14, 1903

Place: Heppner, Oregon

Result: 325 dead, $250 million in damage

Rain and hailstorms in the foothills of the Blue Mountains north of the small town of Heppner, Oregon, led to a violent cloudburst over Willow Creek. The storm lasted for only an hour but turned the normally calm creek into a raging river. A wall of water more than 20 feet high headed for Heppner, knocking down everything in its path. When the water reached the village it surged through, destroying more than 200 homes and businesses, one-third of the total number in the town, in less than an hour. Property damages were estimated at more than $250 million. About 200 people were swept away by the torrent in Heppner alone. Another 125 victims disappeared from farms, which were also inundated by the floodwaters. The force of the wall of water disrupted and destroyed many lives in just one hour.

Leslie V. Tischauser

For Further Information:
The New York Times, June 15-16, 1903.

1904: Colorado

Arkansas River
Date: August 7, 1904
Place: Eden, Colorado
Result: 96 dead

A flash flood on the Arkansas River, caused by several days of very heavy rain, washed out an old wagon bridge a short distance from the railroad trestle in Eden, Colorado, crossed daily by the *Denver-St. Louis Express,* operated by the Denver and Rio Grande Railroad Company. The train was moving faster than usual because it was six minutes behind schedule. Debris from the wagon bridge smashed into the front of the train, and it gave way under a torrent of water. The locomotive pulling the seven-car express pulled the baggage car and several passenger and sleeping cars into raging water below, but a porter in the rear three cars pulled the emergency air brakes, and they stopped just inches from the collapsed bridge.

Ninety-six passengers, including the engineer, were swept to their deaths, making this the worst train disaster caused by a flood to date. Several passengers in the chair car managed to save themselves because the raging water had torn a hole in the car's roof and they were able to swim to safety. Bodies of the victims floated downstream for several miles, where they lay under several feet of mud until rescuers found them the next day. The arms of one of the passengers stuck through the muddy grave, and as the rescuers dug for his body they uncovered many more. They found the body of one young woman 23 miles downriver. The railroad cars in the river were badly mangled and were beyond repair. The force of the water had been so great that it even tore open the door of a large safe in the baggage car.

Leslie V. Tischauser

For Further Information:
The New York Times, August 8-9, 1904.

1911: China

Yangtze River
Date: September, 1911
Place: Chinese provinces of Hubei and Hunan; most of the cities of Shanghai and Yichang
Result: More than 100,000 dead

Early in September, 1911, the mighty Yangtze River in China burst over its human-made earthen embankments, causing one of the most destructive floods in modern history. The river valley became an inland sea covering 700 square miles in the Chinese provinces of Hubei and Hunan and most of the city of Shanghai. More than 2 million people lived in the area, most of them very poor peasants and farmers. More than 100,000 people died in the first hours of the flood as raging waters swept over much of the countryside.

The aftereffects of the flood, mainly starvation and famine, caused by complete destruction of the region's rice crop, were just as devastating. Perhaps another 100,000 Chinese died of hunger over the next several weeks. The entire economy was destroyed. Bandits and starving people raided the countryside, stealing food and supplies from wherever they found them, and murdering hundreds more. Missions, hospitals, and businesses were attacked and burned to the ground. Floodwaters surged through the largest cemetery in the region, unearthing thousands of wooden caskets and sending them down the river, adding further horrors to the scenes of devastation and destruction. Hundreds of thousands of Chinese remained homeless for weeks and even months after the waters finally began to subside; many refugees fled the region, never to return, seeking higher ground in Mongolia and Manchuria.

Leslie V. Tischauser

For Further Information:
The New York Times, September 11-20, 1911.

1912: Mississippi River

Date: April, 1912
Place: Along the Mississippi River from Cairo, Illinois, to Bolivar County, Mississippi
Result: 250 dead, 30,000 homeless, $45 million in damage

Very late and extremely heavy snowfalls in the spring of 1912 led to a huge runoff as warm weather caused the snow cover to melt suddenly in early April. Major tributaries to the Mississippi River, including the Missouri, Kansas, Wisconsin, Illinois, and Des Moines Rivers, rose rapidly due to the melting and swelled into the Mississippi. The river broke through its banks near Cairo, Illinois, just above the place where the Ohio River joins the Mississippi, on April 10. Army troops called out to build dikes arrived too late to save many towns downriver. Many people had been warned of the troubles upriver and had abandoned their homes by time the water struck. The Mobile and Ohio Railroad tracks adjacent to the river were totally covered with water, and Cairo, a city of about 8,000 people, was filled with water swirling through its streets.

Several dozen people drowned in Cairo. In northwestern Kentucky, the Real Foot Lake levee collapsed after three days of attack by the flood, and the town of Hickman was destroyed. By April 20, floodwaters had reached Benoit, Mississippi, drowning citizens. The entire county of Bolivar was covered with water, 200 of its residents died, and $10 million worth of property in this single county alone was destroyed. All together, at least 250 people died as a result of this flood, 30,000 people were made homeless, and $45 million worth of property was damaged. An area of about 2,000 square miles was flooded in total, from Cairo to Bolivar County.

Leslie V. Tischauser

For Further Information:
The New York Times, April 16-22, 1912.

1913: Ohio, Indiana, Illinois

Date: March 25-27, 1913
Place: Ohio, Indiana, and Illinois, especially Dayton, Ohio, and the Miami River Valley
Result: More than 500 dead, hundreds missing, more than $100 million in damage ($100 million in the Miami River Basin alone)

At the end of winter and into spring, the atmosphere over Middle America is in turmoil. Warm, moisture-laden, tropical air masses move northward up the Mississippi River Valley as the cold Arctic air of winter recedes poleward, following the path of the westerly jet streams. Numerous cyclonic storms follow this track, bringing what are usually the heaviest snowfalls of winter and the first of the excessively heavy rains of summer. If conditions are right, in the clash of the air masses both "winter" and "summer" conditions may occur within the same storm system.

Such was the case in late March of 1913. A "Colorado low," said to have originated in southwestern Utah, began to track eastward, in the usual fashion of the westerlies. By Sunday morning, March 23, the storm had reached Denver, Colorado, and moved across the Great Plains of Colorado and Kansas, bringing blizzard conditions behind the front and severe dust storms before it. The contrast between this air and that moving northward in the Mississippi Valley created ideal conditions for the development of tornadoes, one of which pressed northward from Oklahoma and reached Omaha, Nebraska, by Sunday evening, accompanied by rain, hail, and lightning. Omaha was especially hard hit, with perhaps 115 dead and hundreds injured. The city was cut off from communication with the rest of the world for four hours.

Many smaller towns were nearly wiped out, and tornadoes generated by the front moving eastward killed many more in Iowa, Illinois, and as far east as Terre Haute, Indiana. The cold wave following brought snow, adding to the misery of the homeless. The storm's center moved northeastward into Canada, but the tail of the system developed new storms that moved eastward, up the Ohio River Valley. This resulted in the third heavy rainfall in ten days, with disastrous impact in Indiana, Ohio, and eastward.

Hardest hit was Dayton, Ohio, and the Miami River Valley, with a loss of more than 360 lives and damage to property in excess of $100 million. Approximately 15 square miles of the city were inundated before the flood crested at midnight on March 26 and the waters began to recede. During the two days of highest water levels, 65,000 people were marooned, cut off from food, water, and escape. At least 8 buildings in the central business district were destroyed by fire, high waters keeping firefighters 2 miles away from the scene. Although several dams in the region did collapse and levees generally were unable to restrain floodwaters, false reports of a dam failure upstream of Dayton added panic to the problems. As the hours without rescue mounted, some people despaired and committed suicide.

In a disaster of this scale, particularly before the advent of effective and reliable wireless communications, counting the victims and identifying the location of the most serious problems are nearly impossible. Immediate estimates of casualties are usually exaggerated, and the final numbers are downscaled. Thus, at the height of the flood and before communications could be restored across flooding rivers, it was thought that many thousands may have died. In addition to Dayton, Columbus and most of the medium-size cities of Ohio, as well as Indianapolis and Peru, Indiana, were especially hard hit. Numerous smaller communities unfortunate enough to be located in the rivers' floodplains were also engulfed by the raging waters, adding to the death toll and property losses.

While casualty figures generally decline as better information becomes available with the recession of the storm waters, economic damages include more than simply destroyed or damaged buildings, and the toll often mounts as the reality of the situation sinks in. In addition to heavily industrialized Ohio and Indiana, the storms moved east and caused severe flooding in Pennsylvania and New York. Closed factories impacted workers as well as corporations. Travel in 1913 was essentially by rail; all-weather roads did not exist. The railroads suffered more than $25 million in losses as tracks and bridges were destroyed or damaged, which also delayed relief supplies.

Communication over long distances in this era was by telegraph in Middle America. Telegraph systems suffered the same losses as railroads, and the experience of the March, 1913, flood hastened the expansion of wireless communication systems throughout the United States. Another result was the establishment of the Miami Conservancy District in 1915, leading to the construction of flood-control dams, which proved quite successful in preventing further flood damage in that basin. The Ohio River system as a whole was not as fortunate, experiencing disastrous floods for more than a quarter century after 1913.

Neil E. Salisbury

For Further Information:

Leopold, Luna B., and Thomas Maddock, Jr. *The Flood Control Controversy: Big Dams, Little Dams, and Flood Management.* New York: Ronald Press, 1954.

The New York Times, March 23-28, 1913.

1915: China

Zhu River
Date: July, 1915
Place: Canton, China
Result: More than 100,000 dead

The city of Canton, China, was devastated by floodwaters from the Zhu River in the summer of 1915. The large number of deaths that resulted occurred because more than 1 million of the city's 3 million residents lived on riverboats and had little protection from the river's surging waters. The poorly maintained dikes along the Zhu were at the root of the great flood. Hunger and poverty had driven a large number of poor peasants to the river's edge, where they sought to grow maize (corn) in small plots. The riverbanks had been largely deforested in the nineteenth century, however, and this caused the erosion of the soil upstream. Thus, as the floodwaters caused by extremely heavy monsoon rains advanced toward the city, there was little to hold them back. The dikes were not strong enough to hold the mass of water from Canton's streets and neighborhoods.

The terrible flood of 1915 killed 100,000 people by drowning and gave rise to diseases that killed thousands more as raw sewage littered the streets long after the waters receded. China remained far too poor, however, to take any effective action against the conditions that caused the flood. Land-hungry peasants continued to cut down trees and grow crops in the floodplains of China's major rivers. Thousands of Chinese continued to live in cheaply made houseboats in Canton even after many of their friends, neighbors, and relatives had been swept away by the murderous floodwaters of 1915.

Leslie V. Tischauser

For Further Information:

Gernet, Jacques. *A History of Chinese Civilization.* Cambridge, England: Cambridge University Press, 1982.

1916: Netherlands

Date: January, 1916
Place: North Sea coast of the Netherlands
Result: 10,000 dead

In the winter of 1916 a severe, blustery winter storm turned the North Sea coast of the Netherlands into a raging fury. Huge waves slammed into the dikes protecting small villages, towns, and farms from the fury of the sea. Once the dikes were broken through, however, a torrent of water spilled into the lowlands, sweeping away thousands of homes, animals, and people. The death toll from the January flood reached over 10,000, adding to the atmosphere of death that surrounded a Europe engaged in the bloody disaster of World War I. The area of the Netherlands that lay below sea level was devastated and covered by water several feet deep, as it had been during many previous floods. The freezing waters of the North Sea did not recede for several weeks, and when they did they left behind mud, death, and misery. Many of the ruined towns would not be rebuilt until the 1920's, two years after the Great War finally came to an end. The dikes would eventually be rebuilt, awaiting yet another assault by the powerful waters and winds of the North Sea.

Leslie V. Tischauser

For Further Information:

Lambert, Audrey M. *The Making of the Dutch Landscape: An Historical Geography of the Netherlands.* London: Academic Press, 1985.

1916: Southern California

Date: January, 1916
Place: Otay Valley, California
Result: 22 dead, $10 million in damage

Heavy winter rains battered rivers and creeks in the Otay Valley of California, to the east of San Diego, causing several, including the Otay, San Diego, Cottonwood, Sweetwater, and others, to rise out of their banks. Massive pressure from the floodwaters caused several breaks in the newly constructed Otay Dam. Raging water broke through in several places, and soon the entire dam burst, sending a giant wall of water down the valley. The swirling mountain of water caught many residents of the valley in their homes and moved on so quickly that few people had time to escape. Twenty-two people living in the lowest areas of the valley were swept instantly to their deaths. The Otay Valley, which produced large quantities of fruits and vegetables, suffered more than $10 million in damages to farmland, crops, and houses. The avalanche of water did most of the damage in a span of less than an hour after crashing through the dam.

Leslie V. Tischauser

For Further Information:

The New York Times, January 16, 1916.

1921: Colorado

Arkansas River
Date: June 2-3, 1921
Place: Pueblo, Colorado
Result: 120 dead, $25 million in damage

The year 1921 was one of the worst for floods in the history of the United States. The deadliest flood that year hit Pueblo, Colorado, on June 2. Excessive rain turned the Arkansas River into a raging torrent. Recently constructed earthen levees were no match for the floodwaters as they spilled wildly into the streets of downtown Pueblo. The citizens were not prepared for the wall of water that raced into their homes and businesses. Despite days of steady rain, few had sought refuge on higher ground. The water reached second-story windows in some areas, and debris and raw sewage released by the water added to the city's woes.

About 120 people drowned in the first hours of flooding, and the water took more than a week to recede. The governor called out the National Guard to protect against looting, although none was reported, and to assist in the rescue efforts. Hundreds of frightened victims were taken by boat from the heaviest hit areas, and many lost everything they had, either to the water or to the mud. After the floodwaters receded, property damage was assessed at more than $25 million. A new system of levees was constructed shortly after the devastation was revealed. The 1921 flood is remembered as the worst in the history of the state of Colorado.

Leslie V. Tischauser

For Further Information:
The New York Times, June 3-6, 1921.

1921: Texas

San Antonio River
Date: September 7-11, 1921
Place: San Antonio, Texas
Result: 51 dead, $5 million in damage

The flood on the San Antonio River in 1921 came a day after the heaviest single rainfall recorded in American history, 23.11 inches at Taylor, Texas, a small town about 30 miles to the northeast of the city of San Antonio. The heavy rain resulted from a hurricane smashing through the Gulf of Mexico toward the Mexican coast. The slashing rain sent the San Antonio River entirely over its banks, adding to the floodwaters created by the immense amount of rainwater already filling the streets. The river flooded so rapidly, however, that many residents were caught totally unprepared. One moment they were standing on what seemed to be dry ground, and the next they were swimming in water up to their necks.

Buses, trucks, and cars were abandoned by their drivers, who were forced to climb buildings to save themselves. Many streets were covered with 5 to 9 feet of water. Most downtown buildings were flooded and badly damaged, and more than $5 million in property damage was reported. The 51 people killed were washed away in the early moments of the disaster. San Antonio remained underwater for almost a week before the floodwaters began to recede. In the aftermath, city officials decided to improve the levee system along the river, although that project took more than ten years to complete. The 1921 flood was the worst in the city's history.

Leslie V. Tischauser

For Further Information:
The New York Times, September 8-13, 1921.

1927: Mississippi River

Date: April, 1927
Place: Seven states along the Mississippi River, especially Mississippi, Arkansas, and Louisiana
Result: 313 dead, 700,000 homeless, $300 million in damage

It began raining in late March in the Mississippi River Valley, and it seemed to never stop. Along with the rain came tornadoes and earthquakes that caused a tremendous amount of additional damage. The United States Weather Bureau reported that the flood of 1927 was the worst in the area in more than two hundred years. Heavy rains, however, were not the only reason for the flood. Human activities, such as logging and farming, contributed to the damage. The forests along the Mississippi's main channel and major tributaries had been cut repeatedly by loggers over many years, and farmers cleared the land of all trees to expand their acreage. When the rains came in 1927, the water had no place to pause, rushing directly into the streams. As the tributaries filled, the mass of water poured into the main channel, breaking over and through the levees that extended all along the river to the Gulf of Mexico. Two major breaks in the levees occurred on April 21, at Mound Landing, Mississippi, and Pendleton, Arkansas. People in these towns reported that when the water broke through it roared like a wild animal; others said it sounded like a tornado or a runaway freight train.

The flood damaged farmland in seven states, although Mississippi, Arkansas, and Louisiana suffered the most destruction. For a distance of 1,000 miles, from Cairo, Illinois, to the Gulf, floodwaters spread out to a distance of more than 100 miles from the Mississippi's main channel. More than 16.5 million acres were flooded in 170 counties in 7 states. About 162,017 homes were flooded, 41,487 buildings were totally destroyed, and the 33,000 Red Cross volunteers who aided the relief effort fed 311,922 people. Deaths were officially established at 313, though some experts believed that as many as 500 people may have drowned in one of the worst floods in the twentieth century in the United States.

Leslie V. Tischauser

For Further Information:

Daniel, Pete. *Deepin' as It Come: The Great Mississippi Flood.* New York: Oxford University Press, 1977.

1927: Kentucky River

Date: May 29-30, 1927
Place: Northeastern Kentucky, especially Morgan and Harlan Counties
Result: 89 dead, 12,000 homeless, $7 million in damage

Heavy rains sent the Kentucky River over its banks in dozens of places in May, 1927, as floodwaters raced over sandbags and dikes. The swollen river flooded for most of its 259 miles. When its waters reached the Ohio River in Carroll County the raging stream added to the woes of people still suffering effects from the Mississippi River flood of 1927. In that April flood, the entire Mississippi River system, including the Ohio, had backed up into a lake hundreds of miles across and several feet deep, causing millions of dollars in damages.

The area heaviest hit in the May flood was Morgan County, in the northeastern part of Kentucky, and its county seat of West Liberty. Most of the 89 victims lived in small communities along the river. The area was among the poorest counties in the state. Lack of adequate roads and shortages of rescue equipment hampered relief efforts. Another hard-hit county was Harlan County, in the center of Kentucky's coal-mining region. Damages to homes and crops, mainly tobacco, reached more than $7 million before the waters began to recede. The flood of 1927 was one of the worst in the state's history. The areas hit hardest were among the poorest counties and towns in the United States; recovery would be very difficult, and many victims saw most of their possessions washed away, never to be regained.

Leslie V. Tischauser

For Further Information:

The New York Times, May 30-June 2, 1927.

1927: New England

Date: November 3-4, 1927
Place: Vermont, particularly the Green Mountains; also New York, Massachusetts, and Connecticut
Result: 200 dead, $28 million in damage

A late-season tropical storm heading north from the Caribbean swept through western New England early in November, 1927. The warm humid air of the storm was trapped between two cold fronts moving east out of Canada. These weather conditions brought very heavy rains, lasting several days, to the Hudson River Valley and the Green Mountains of Vermont. Towns in the Green Mountains suffered the most deaths—84—and the worst damages as water from the Winooski River swept over its banks and flooded the entire valley.

All together, 200 people were drowned by floodwaters in the states of Vermont, New York, Massachusetts, and Connecticut. Property damage was heaviest in Vermont as thousands of people were made homeless by the swirling waters of rivers and streams that jumped their banks and spread over thousands of acres of farmland. Many small towns had water in their streets and buildings for two or three weeks after the rain finally stopped. The New England flood came at the end of one of the worst flood years in American history, beginning with the Mississippi River flood in the spring. In New England, property damage was assessed at more than $28 million.

Leslie V. Tischauser

For Further Information:

The New York Times, November 4-6, 1927.

1928: St. Francis Dam Collapse

Date: March 12, 1928
Place: Near Saugus, California
Result: About 450 dead; 1,200 homes and other buildings severely damaged or destroyed; almost 8,000 acres of farmland stripped of livestock,

orchards, crops, and topsoil; $15 million in damage

The St. Francis Dam, named after the San Francisquito (little Saint Francis) Canyon and Creek where it was located, was designed and built by William Mulholland, chief engineer for the Los Angeles Department of Water and Power (DWP) from 1886 to 1928. Its purpose was to create a 600-acre reservoir as a reserve water supply for the city of Los Angeles. Mulholland had devoted much of his life to making sure his beloved city had enough water to grow and prosper. Los Angeles had never had a reliable water supply until 1913, when Mulholland achieved world renown with the completion of the Owens Valley Aqueduct, at that time the longest aqueduct in existence. Its series of tunnels and concrete-lined channels transported 258 million gallons of water every day from the green Owens Valley south to the thirsty city of Los Angeles.

A boon to the growth of Los Angeles, the aqueduct brought death to the Owens Valley as the drought-plagued city sucked the Owens River dry. Owens Valley residents fought to prevent Los Angeles from taking all of their water. When peaceful means failed, a few desperate ranchers resorted to violence. The first dynamiting of the aqueduct occurred in May, 1924, and it continued sporadically throughout the remainder of the decade. Understandably, Mulholland began to worry about the fate of Los Angeles if the water supply were cut off for long periods of time. Because the aqueduct crossed the San Andreas fault, it was not just vulnerable to sabotage—potential earthquakes were another hazard. Mulholland's solution was the St. Francis Dam, with a reservoir big enough to hold an emergency supply of water capable of meeting the city's needs for at least one year. In fact, to ensure an adequate supply in drought years, the original 175-foot height of the dam was increased by 11 feet to allow for additional water storage eleven months after construction had begun. The base of the dam was not widened, however, a risky oversight in a gravity dam like St. Francis, which resists the enormous pressure of its pent-up waters through sheer weight alone.

The dam was completed in May, 1926. The St. Francis Dam was a massive curved concrete wedge about 200 feet high and 700 feet long. It was 156 feet

The broken water barrier of the St. Francis Dam after the flood of 1928. (AP/Wide World Photos)

thick at its base and 18 feet thick at its crest, and it contained over 134,000 cubic yards of concrete. Despite its imposing size, leaking cracks appeared in the dam during its initial filling in 1926-1927. Mulholland claimed they were caused by the curing of the concrete and had them sealed. In February, 1928, as the water level rose again with winter rains, fresh leaks appeared, which increased in intensity with the spring runoff.

The Dam Breaks. On March 7, 1928, the dam reached its maximum holding capacity of 38,168 acre feet (over 12 billion gallons), with water lapping within 3 feet of the parapet and wind-driven waves breaking over the spillways near the top. The previous year's leaks reopened, keeping Mulholland's work crews busy. By Monday, March 12, the dam had been holding up its towering wall of water for five days. That morning, Tony Harnischfeger, the damkeeper, phoned Mulholland to report a new leak. Mulholland arrived at 10:30 A.M. with his assistant, inspected the dam for the next two hours, and left after assuring the damkeeper that the dam was safe. The damkeeper and his small son would be the first victims of the dam's collapse twelve hours later. Their bodies were never recovered.

The St. Francis Dam burst at 11:57 P.M., unleashing a 185-foot wave of destruction into the canyon below. About 50 miles to the south in Los Angeles, night owls who noticed their lights flicker momentarily had no idea they were witnessing the first signs of the deadliest disaster in Southern California history. Closer to the dam, at the Saugus substation of the Southern California Edison Company, the local electric power utility, one of the transmission lines shorted out, blowing up a switch and triggering an emergency alert. Edison personnel had no idea what had happened either.

At the electrical powerhouse directly below the dam, workman Ray Rising, a native of the Midwest's "Tornado Alley," awoke to the sound of what he thought was a tornado. Running to the door, he saw a 140-foot-high wave loom out of the darkness. He managed to resist being engulfed by climbing onto a rooftop that he rode like a raft through the twisting canyon, calling for his wife and children, until it dashed against the canyon wall, where he jumped to safety. Only 3 people survived out of 28 workmen and their families at the powerhouse. The powerhouse itself, a 65-foot concrete structure, was crushed like an eggshell by the wave 10 stories high.

Rolling over the Harry Carey Ranch near Saugus, the deadly tide, now 80 feet high, swept up miles of barbed wire ripped from the ranch's pastures. By 12:40 A.M. Tuesday, Edison employees at the Saugus substation knew the dam had failed and tried to phone a warning to an Edison work camp of 150 men 8 miles downstream from the dam on the banks of the Santa Clara River. The phone rang, but there was no answer, and then the line went dead. They knew what had happened this time. The flood arrived in Castaic Junction, a little town 40 miles from Los Angeles, at 12:50 A.M. and wiped it off the face of the earth. The lone survivor, George McIntyre, lived by grabbing the branches of a cottonwood tree. The bodies of his father and brothers were found near Santa Paula, 30 miles downstream.

At 1:30, highway patrol officer Thornton Edwards got an emergency call that would make him the Paul Revere of Santa Paula as he set out on his motorcycle with screaming sirens to warn the townspeople to evacuate. To his horrified amazement, he reached the Willard Bridge spanning the Santa Clara River only to see it crammed end to end with excited people waiting for the show to begin. He ordered the bridge cleared, posted a guard at either end, and drove on.

The flood reached the bridge by 3 A.M. As the flood surged over the top of the bridge, the latter snapped in half and disappeared. Meanwhile, Deputy Sheriff Eddie Hearne responded to his call by racing his squad car up the Santa Clara Valley toward the oncoming flood with both sirens wailing and lights flashing, first to Santa Paula and then to Fillmore. He got as far as crossing the Pole Creek bridge on the edge of Fillmore when he saw the road ahead inundated by a wide expanse of water, mud, trees, wreckage from buildings and vehicles, and other debris. He immediately raced back to Fillmore to phone a warning to evacuate the city of Oxnard and the adjacent plain.

The entire Santa Clara Valley was awake by now and evacuating to higher ground. At Saticoy, a rancher woke 19 transients sleeping under a bridge to warn them. One refused to head for higher ground, saying there was not enough water in Southern California in which to take a bath, much less fill up the dry bed of the Santa Clara River. His body was found soon after daylight. By now, the speed of the water had decreased from 18 to around 5 miles per hour, but the flow had spread out to about 2 miles wide, consisting of about half water and half mud and trash. The flood narrowly missed Oxnard as it flowed to the sea. As dawn broke, hundreds gathered on the hills above Ventura to watch the final leg of the flood's journey. It left a dirty gray streak all the way out to the Channel Islands, over 20 miles from shore.

After the Flood. Within an hour of the St. Francis Dam's collapse, the entire reservoir had emptied, with a peak discharge rate of over 1 million cubic feet per second. The flood swept a path of devastation 55 miles through the Santa Clara Valley from the dam in San Francisquito Canyon to the Pacific Ocean between the towns of Ventura and Oxnard. The death toll from the flood—comparable to California's greatest natural disaster until that time, the 1906 San Francisco earthquake and fire—would have been much higher in a more populated area. However, the damage was still awesome.

The land lay in ruins. Bodies, both human and animal, were strewn everywhere. Forests had vanished, buried in silt. Orange, lemon, and walnut orchards were flattened. Towns were in shambles. Many valley residents staring at the wreckage the flood had left behind that Tuesday morning had never even heard of the dam that had wreaked such unbelievable carnage. Many wandered around aimlessly in shock. Fortunately, the Red Cross and other relief agencies had begun to arrive by 3:45 A.M. Doctors, nurses, and emergency equipment poured in from Los Angeles and San Francisco, but the doctors and nurses had little to do because there were very few people injured, aside from some suffering from exposure after being outside all night with little or no clothing. Fortunately or unfortunately, this unusual situation was due to the violent nature of the flood. Once caught in the floodwaters, most victims perished. The majority of survivors were either lucky or alert enough to escape before the deadly tide reached them and thus avoided injury. Many victims were never found, forever buried under tons of mud; the mounting number of mud-encrusted corpses was overwhelming to the survivors.

Bodies were transported from the lowlands in farm trucks, unloaded and stacked in piles near mortuaries, and washed down with garden hoses to make identification possible. One valley resident was so angry and disgusted that she stopped trying to shovel the mud from her home long enough to paint a sign she stuck in her front yard for all to see. The sign said, Kill Mulholland!

Did the state's greatest human-made disaster have to happen? Although William Mulholland accepted full responsibility for the tragedy that ruined his career, many DWP officials and others, including Mulholland himself, suspected that the dam might have been dynamited by Owens Valley terrorists. However, the overwhelming consensus is that the collapse was due to human error in the construction of the dam.

To avert further criticism, city officials decided to settle all claims for damages and loss of life as soon as possible without going through the courts. The city council passed an ordinance providing $1 million—an enormous amount of money in 1928—to start rebuilding and settling claims. About 2,000 workers with hundreds of tractors and other heavy equipment tackled the huge mess. It took ninety days working around the clock to finish the cleanup. All that remained were the broken pieces of the dam itself. Fourteen months after the disaster, an eighteen-year-old boy fell to his death while climbing on the ruins, and the city decided to demolish them. Mulholland's most infamous engineering project thus became an unremarkable pile of concrete rubble lying just upstream of where the dam once stood.

Despite the tragic proportions of the flood, the disaster had some positive outcomes. Among them were the formation of the world's first dam-safety agency, the adoption of uniform engineering specifications for testing of dam materials still in use around the world, a reassessment of all DWP dams and reservoirs, and an extensive retrofitting of the St. Francis Dam's twin, Mulholland Dam (renamed Hollywood Dam after the 1928 flood destroyed Mulholland's reputation). Perhaps most beneficial was the development of an efficient process for settling wrongful-death and damage suits that influenced disaster-relief legislation used extensively by victims of later floods, earthquakes, hurricanes, and other natural calamities.

Sue Tarjan

FOR FURTHER INFORMATION:

Davis, Margaret Leslie. *Rivers in the Desert: William Mulholland and the Inventing of Los Angeles.* New York: HarperCollins, 1993.

Nunis, Doyce B., Jr., ed. *The Saint Francis Dam Disaster Revisited.* Pasadena: Historical Society of Southern California and the Ventura County Museum of History and Art, 1995.

Outland, Charles F. *Human-made Disaster: The Story of the St. Francis Dam.* Rev. ed. Glendale, Calif.: Arthur H. Clark, 1977.

Reisner, Marc. *Cadillac Desert: The American West and Its Disappearing Water.* New York: Penguin, 1993.

1931: China

Yangtze River
Date: Late July to mid-September, 1931
Place: Southern China
Result: 3.7 million dead

Following a stormy period in April, 1931, during which southern China experienced its most disastrous floods in years, July brought continuous heavy summer rains to most of eastern China. Flooding was common from Manchuria south to Canton as the summer monsoon pressed inland. By July 24, the Yangtze River was flooded for 500 miles downstream from the river port of Shashi, where the Yangtze leaves the western hill and mountain country and flows across a broad, flat plain. This is rich farming land, the heart of rice production in China, essential for feeding tens of millions of people, and by the end of July thousands of acres of cropland had been ruined by one of the worst floods in sixty years. Moreover, this region is densely populated, not only by small villages but also by great cities, especially Wuhan (formerly Hankow, Wuchang, and Hanyang) and Nanjing (Nanking), the capital city for Chiang Kai-Shek's Chinese Nationalist government.

Early August saw a short-lived subsiding of flood levels near Hankow, but the saturated dike system had been weakened and collapsed in many places. Over 500,000 people were reported homeless, with refugees pouring into the large cities, especially Hankow. By August 6, the flood level was still below the sixty-year-old record, demonstrating that the flooding was largely the consequence of years of neglect of the embankments and dikes. Funds (taxes) that normally were earmarked for the maintenance of the dike system had been diverted to the military; South China had seen warfare since 1924. In 1926, Chang Kai-shek led his army from Canton to the Yangtze to unify China. Conflict and dissension were more common than unity, however; the province of Hunan became communist, and Chiang's forces also battled those of various warlords. In a hydraulic society such as China's, strong centralized government seems to be necessary for the maintenance of the river and canal system, including the dikes and embankments.

As the rivers annually carry more sediment from their headwaters, only a portion of this makes it to the ocean. A natural stream deposits most of its sediment on the floodplain. Dikes confining the water to an unnatural channel result in the sediment load being deposited within the channel itself, raising the likelihood that the river will flood. The Yellow River of North China carries carries the largest sediment load of any major river on earth; the Yangtze is not far behind. As the dikes are raised to higher and higher levels to prevent flooding, sediment builds up in the channel. Maintenance of the system requires removal of this sediment as well as repair and strengthening of the dikes. Both the Yellow River and the Yangtze actually flow on a bed level that is, in places, higher than the adjoining plains, a recipe for disaster.

Monsoon showers are intense, but they are frequently scattered, leaving much of the land without significant rainfall. Thus, two-thirds of Hunan Province, less than 100 miles upstream from Hankow, was said to be suffering from flooding, with ten million people affected. Yet many counties of the province were actually suffering from drought and were barren of vegetation. Crops in the more fertile areas next to the exotic rivers (which derived their flow from their headwaters) were destroyed by flooding.

In Hankow, August 7 saw the beginning of five days of torrential thunderstorms. Water levels began to rise once more, damaging or destroying food stores. More refugees poured in from small villages that were flooded out. There was no food in Hankow to share, and the death toll reached 1,000 per day. The decaying corpses of farm animals festered in the water, to be joined by those of the newly dead humans, floating downstream to the ocean for lack of anyplace else to put the bodies. Worst of all, this was the only water available for drinking for the million inhabitants of Hankow and the hundreds of thousands of refugees. Not surprisingly, typhoid fever and dysentery were rampant, with fears of a cholera epidemic.

By August 14, the Yangtze was at a record high level, and dikes were collapsing with great loss of life, as well as those buildings taller than flood levels which had served as temporary refuges for people. The river continued its rise until at least the 19th; by August 23 the waters began to recede, but it was projected that it would take weeks for Hankow and Nanking to dry out. Under such circumstances, it was impossible to make an accurate count of casualties. The projection was that 2 million would die before new autumn crops could help feed them. Another 2 million were doomed to die along the Grand Canal. Most of these deaths would be attributed to starvation or disease, indirect effects of the flooding, rather than to drowning. The impact upon the economy was staggering. Recovery was hindered by the resumption of military operations after the main flood wave had passed and by the fact that severe flooding occurred throughout eastern China.

Neil E. Salisbury

For Further Information:

The New York Times, July 24-September 7, 1931.

The Times (London), August 5-September 15, 1931.

1937: U.S. Midwest

Ohio River

Date: January, 1937

Place: The Ohio River basin, south from West Virginia and west to Cairo, Illinois; also south along the Mississippi River to Helena, Arkansas

Result: 300 dead, more than 900,000 evacuated in Ohio Valley, $418 million in damage, including Lower Mississippi River Valley

The Ohio River basin meanders through the hills and mountains of Appalachia, a region of heavy winter precipitation. Somewhere in the basin, every year, some river floods. Most of these floods are of little consequence; they are expected, and few lives are lost, with minimal damage. January, 1937, proved to be an exception. Flooding was at record levels, entire cities were evacuated, and costs, as well as misery and disruption of the lives of the valley's inhabitants, were extremely high.

The rains began on December 26, 1936, and continued at relatively low intensities until January 19, 1937. These rains saturated the ground and were followed by six days of excessive precipitation of relatively high intensity over the area near the main stem of the Ohio River and the lower portions of its larger tributaries: the Kentucky, Green, Cumberland, Tennessee, and Wabash Rivers. The upstream tributaries had generally smaller and shorter periods of flooding but emptied their waters downstream to raise the level of the Ohio River's main stem. Record-breaking floods occurred in a belt generally less than 100 miles wide along and south of the Ohio River from West Virginia west to the mouth of the Ohio at Cairo, Illinois, and then south along the Mississippi River as far as Helena, Arkansas. The Ohio was above flood stage January 22 to 27 from Pittsburgh, Pennsylvania, 1,000 miles downstream to Cairo.

Kentucky was the hardest hit in terms of death and damage, but it is difficult to separate loss of life due directly to flooding from indirect casualties as a result of disease and exposure. Cincinnati, Ohio, recorded a river stage 4 feet higher than the previous record and was about 10 percent flooded. Louisville, Kentucky, had the highest stage above the previous record, 10.4 feet; two-thirds of the residential areas and nearly all of the business district were flooded. Evansville, Indiana, was more than 50 percent flooded, with the river 5.4 feet above the previous record. Paducah, Kentucky, was 95 percent flooded, and nearly all of its population of 35,000 was evacuated by a flood stage 6.3 feet above the record. Many smaller cities fared about as badly as Paducah. The only saving grace of the flood is that it was short-lived. By the first week of February the water levels began dropping, and life began to return to normal, with an immense task of cleaning up facing the valley's inhabitants.

Neil E. Salisbury

For Further Information:

The New York Times, January 15-February 16, 1937.

United States Geological Survey. *Floods of Ohio and Mississippi Rivers: January-February 1937.* Water-Supply Paper 838. Washington, D.C.: U.S. Government Printing Office, 1938.

1938: Montana

Custer Creek

Date: June 19, 1938

Place: Near Terry, Montana

Result: 46 dead, about 60 injured

The passenger train Olympian Special *crashed into Custer Creek following a flash flood in Montana.* (AP/Wide World Photos)

Flash floods, characterized by "walls" of water rushing down on the victims with extremely short warning times, occur most commonly in small stream basins. Larger stream basins, with areas of hundreds or thousands of square miles, absorb more easily the discharge of numerous small tributaries. Flash floods are generally the result of either high-intensity (frequently thunderstorm) rainfalls focused on a small area or of dam breaks.

The *Olympian Special*, a train of the Chicago, Milwaukee, St. Paul, and Pacific Railroad, had the misfortune to encounter a flash flood on Custer Creek, a tributary of the Yellowstone River, on the night of June 19, 1938. Custer Creek is about 25 miles long and flows from upland badlands of the Great Plains into the Yellowstone River. The accident occurred near the creek's mouth. Custer Creek had been reported practically dry by a railroad track walker shortly before the accident. Then, an intense rainstorm in the creek basin created a wall of water that washed out a steel and concrete bridge, causing the engine car and several passenger cars to hurtle into the raging floodwaters below. Two sleeper cars were largely covered by the muddy floodwaters of the creek, making rescue efforts difficult. Two passengers and train porters managed to lead survivors to safety in the pitch-black night. The rear cars of the train broke free of the wreck and remained above the flood, saving their occupants.

This tragedy points up the difficulty of issuing warnings for floods resulting from infrequent intense rainstorms. There are literally many thousands, perhaps millions, of small stream basins worldwide that are subject to flash flooding, far too many to monitor the flooding of specific basins with stream gauges. Consequently, attention in the late twentieth century was directed toward forecasting possible flash flood-creating storms with advanced radar systems.

Neil E. Salisbury

For Further Information:

The New York Times, June 20-28, 1938.

1939: China

Yellow River

Date: August-November, 1939

Place: Chinese provinces of Hebei and Shandong

Result: 200,000 estimated dead, 25 million homeless

The world's most dangerous place, in terms of lives lost to natural disasters, is the North China Plain, stretching south from Beijing to Shanghai and the Yangtze River. Most of this lowland is actually the alluvial fan or floodplain of the Yellow River, so-called for the color of the heavy silt it carries from the hills and plateaus to the west. The earliest date of flooding recorded for the Yellow is 2297 B.C.E. The Chinese attempted to control the floods by building levees, which forced the stream to deposit much of its silt load on the river's bed. The result is that the Yellow now flows to the ocean on a streambed 25 feet above the level of the plain, in a 12-mile-wide belt between the levees. Any summer of exceptionally heavy monsoon rains threatens to overtop the levees, exposing millions of Chinese on the plains below the riverbed to raging torrents. In 1938, Chinese troops, in an effort to slow the advance of Japanese invaders, deliberately breached the levees, causing an estimated 500,000 civilian deaths.

A year later, heavy monsoon rains flooded much of the northern portion of the plain. The Yellow has changed course several times in recorded history. From 2356 to 602 B.C.E. the great river flowed northeast across the plain through the city of Tianjin to the Bo Hai, a large embayment of the Yellow Sea. The lower portion of this course is now occupied by the Hai River, and this flooding caught the attention of Western journalists because of the presence of concessions occupied by European and U.S. nationals. Japanese troops controlled Tianjin and restricted the actions of the Westerners in the last weeks of August, 1939, just before World War II erupted in Europe. As the Hai River rose, thousands of Chinese swarmed into the concessions, adding to the chaos.

Most Westerners were evacuated as the floodwaters reached depths of 10 to 15 feet and more, wiping out not only settlements but also the summer crops of the northern plains. It is always difficult to make an accurate count of casualties in a great disaster, because disease spreads quickly when sanitation is destroyed, and famine frequently follows, as in this case. The best estimate is that 200,000 Chinese died, and perhaps 25 million were affected by the floods. The levee system was not restored, and the Yellow returned to its present course after World War II, in 1947.

Neil E. Salisbury

For Further Information:

The New York Times, August 4-27, September 15, 1939.

Waltham, Tony. *Catastrophe: The Violent Earth.* New York: Crown, 1978.

1948: U.S. Northwest

Columbia River

Date: May-June, 1948

Place: Oregon, Washington State, Idaho, and Montana; British Columbia, Canada

Result: 51 dead, $100 million in damage

The Columbia River rises in the Rocky Mountains of British Columbia, Montana, and Idaho. Most of its discharge comes from the melting of winter snowfall, after the period of maximum precipitation for the region. Its average discharge is second only in the United States to that of the Mississippi River. Disastrous floods occur when the winter months are especially cold, snowy, and long; there is an abrupt shift in temperatures from cold to warm in the spring; and heavy rains coincide with the warm temperatures, speeding the melting of the snowpack. This sequence is not unique to the Columbia River but is characteristic of all the snowbelt rivers of North America.

The sequence occurred in a larger flood in 1894, when the floodplain was largely unsettled, and again in May and June, 1948, after extensive development of the floodplain had taken place. The Columbia and its tributaries rose quickly above flood stage in western Montana, northern Idaho, eastern Washington, and British Columbia by May 30. Thousands of refugees and 15 deaths were reported by that date. On May 31, the flood wave passed through Portland, Oregon, near the mouth of the river, and broke through a railroad embankment that was serving as a dike or levee, although it had not been designed for this task. Vanport City, a suburb of Portland with a population of 18,500, was wiped out. Incredibly, there was relatively little loss of life considering that the break of the dike created flash flood-like waves of water that struck with little warning.

The river was above flood stage for forty-three days at Portland before the danger was past and rebuilding could begin. As it happened, 1948 was a presidential election year, and President Harry S Truman and the Republican-dominated Congress clashed over

Residents of Vanport, Oregon, struggle through floodwaters on May 30, 1948. (AP/Wide World Photos)

the extent to which federal expenditures could prevent the recurrence of such disasters. Although two large dams, Bonneville and Grand Coulee, were constructed before the 1948 flood, both were multipurpose with an emphasis upon hydroelectric-power generation. Flood-control dams must be essentially empty of stored water to be effective in a flood of this size. By the late 1990's several dams had been constructed on the Columbia and its tributaries.

Neil E. Salisbury

For Further Information:

Hoyt, William G., and Walter B. Langbein. *Floods.* Princeton, N.J.: Princeton University Press, 1955.

The New York Times, May 30-June 14, 1948.

United States Geological Survey. *Floods of May-June 1948 in Columbia River Basin.* Water-Supply Paper 1080. Washington, D.C.: U.S. Government Printing Office, 1949.

1950: China

Huai and Yangtze Rivers

Date: March-August, 1950

Place: Anhui Province, China

Result: 489 dead, 10 million homeless, 5.2 million acres of cropland inundated

The flood season began in March in northern Anhui Province, despite the efforts of 1 million peasants who had been at work since at least January strengthening and repairing the dike systems of the Yangtze and Huai Rivers. China was in the grip of its most serious famine in seventy-two years, largely as a consequence of 1949's extraordinary flooding—the worst in many years on the Yangtze—and the most severe drought in the northeast since 1921. Not since 1878 had both occurred together. As many as 30 million Chinese were on the brink of starvation.

The early March flooding was followed by a two-month drought, then a three-week period from June 27 to July 16 with 20 inches of rain. As a consequence, the Huai River flooded again, exceeding the record levels of the 1931 floods. Compounding the problem was the fact that rivers were flooding elsewhere in China, and resources were stretched thin. Flooded land does not produce food. By mid-August, Chinese Communist newspapers announced that 5.2 million acres had been inundated in the Huai River area, on 3.7 million acres of which the crops had been completely destroyed; on the rest, production was only 10 to 30 percent of normal. There was silence, however, on the question of how many Chinese had succumbed in the famine. In October, plans were announced for flood-control measures to tame the annual destructive flooding of the Huai River.

Neil E. Salisbury

For Further Information:

The New York Times, March 16, 20; July 17, 25; August 9, 15; October 15, 25, 1950.

1950: Nebraska

Date: May-July, 1950

Place: Eastern Nebraska, especially Lincoln and Beatrice

Result: 23 dead, 60,000 acres inundated, $60 million in damage

Southeastern and east-central Nebraska was struck by a series of flash flood-producing thunderstorms in May and July, 1950, causing the worst floods in fifty years. This part of Nebraska is covered with rolling loess-mantled hills, originally prairie grassland, which by 1950 had been converted mostly to corn fields.

Thunderstorms produce most of the precipitation that supports the rural farming economy, but they are a hazard as well as a resource. These storms are usually described as "scattered," meaning there is a lot of space between the downpours, and a single storm generally delivers 3 to 5 inches of rain at the most. Occasionally, conditions in the upper atmosphere block the usual movement of the storm cell eastward, and as the storm stalls or sits in place, exceptionally high amounts of rainfall result. One cell in the May 8 storm dropped 14 inches of rain, and another in the July 10 storm totaled over 13 inches.

This is too much water for the small stream basins to handle, and flash floods rip across highways and through towns, generally without warning in the early stages of the flooding. Many of the 23 people who lost their lives in these storms were trapped in automobiles or buses. Three medium-size basins were hit hardest: Salt Creek, near Lincoln; the Big Blue River, which flows south to the Kansas River and was hit by both the May and July storms; and the Little Nemaha River, flowing east to the Missouri River. Beatrice, on the Big Blue River downstream of the major rainfall, had time to prepare for the July flood wave, which had less serious impact as a result.

Neil E. Salisbury

For Further Information:

Hoyt, W. G., and W. B. Langbein. *Floods.* Princeton, N.J.: Princeton University Press, 1955.

The New York Times, May 10, 12; July 10, 12, 1950.

United States Geological Survey. *Floods of May-July 1950 in Southeastern Nebraska.* Water-Supply Paper 1137-D. Washington, D.C.: U.S. Government Printing Office, 1953.

1951: Kansas and Missouri Rivers

Date: July, 1951

Place: Manhattan, Topeka, Lawrence, and Kansas City, Kansas; Kansas City, Missouri

Result: 19 dead, 500,000 homeless, $870 million in damage

The plains of Kansas and adjacent states had a wet spring in 1951, with broad areas receiving more than 10 inches of rain in June alone, and smaller, scattered storms dropping up to 16 inches. The ground was saturated, setting the stage for disaster when a storm system lingered over the Kansas River basin from July 13 to 19. In this system, three bursts of heavy rain delivered as much as 14 inches of rain, with unofficial records of as much as 17.5 inches. This resulted in record-breaking floods along all the streams draining the areas of heavy rainfall.

The Kansas River began flooding on July 11, soon filling the bottomlands from bluff to bluff. The flood wave worked its way downstream, flooding first

Manhattan, Kansas, then Topeka, next Lawrence, and finally Kansas City, Kansas, and Kansas City, Missouri, where the river empties into the Missouri River. The bottomlands in the two Kansas Cities are the site of a major industrial and railroad concentration, and here the damage was greatest in monetary terms—over $200 million in Kansas City, Kansas, alone. Compounding the problem were fires caused by exploding oil storage tanks in the refineries. The flood wave moved downstream on the Missouri River, inundating mostly agricultural land. In the entire flood, nearly 2 million acres of farmland were under water. The flood wave continued downstream past St. Louis and into the Mississippi River Valley, with some minor flooding.

The impact of floods upon the infrastructure is often overlooked, as well as the costs entailed by people and businesses outside the flood area. Transportation was essentially halted for weeks. Passenger trains were stalled, with their clients trapped for four days. Many firms, especially meat-packing plants, closed their doors, never to reopen. This was the most costly flood to date in the United States. Arguments as to how to prevent future disasters raged between political camps, those devoted to ending "pork-barrel" expenditures such as flood control, and the engineers who were charged with the responsibility of curtailing the impact of events such as this. In the latter half of the twentieth century, more dams and levees were constructed in the region, reducing the impact of all but the largest of floods, such as the Great Mississippi River Flood of 1993.

Neil E. Salisbury

For Further Information:

The New York Times, July 1-31, 1951.

United States Geological Survey. *Kansas-Missouri Floods of July 1951.* Water-Supply Paper 1139. Washington, D.C.: U.S. Government Printing Office, 1952.

The Central Industrial District of Kansas City, Missouri, was under water in 1951. (AP/Wide World Photos)

1951: Italy

Po River
Date: November 7-29, 1951
Place: Po River Valley, Italy
Result: At least 150 and perhaps 1,000 dead, 270,000 acres of cropland flooded, $200 million in damage

Winter is the rainy season in the Mediterranean, and the Po River Valley, the agricultural heartland of Italy, suffered its most disastrous flooding of modern times in November of 1951. The headwaters of the Po, in the hills of Piedmont and the Italian Alps, experienced heavy rains on November 7. By the 9th, there was widespread loss of life and damage as far east as Milan. By the 12th, the flooding had reached the Adriatic coast at the mouth of the valley, where high tides added coastal flooding to the overflow of the rivers.

Landslides caused by rain-weakened hillsides also killed many, making it difficult to ascertain the exact number of flood victims. Estimates ranged from 150 dead to more than 1,000. As is usually the case with flooding, many of the deaths occurred in automobiles or rail cars. The collapse of buildings in the high water also killed many, including some who had taken refuge in hospitals and churches.

Dike and levee breaks caused flash flood-like waves of death and destruction. By November 17, entire cities near the mouth of the Po and other rivers had been isolated, and evacuation of as many as 200,000 inhabitants was aided by the military, including British and American North Atlantic Treaty Organization (NATO) forces. Every type of watercraft available was pressed into service, as well as helicopters. Some dikes had to be blown up deliberately to divert floodwaters to the Adriatic. Small villages were sacrificed to save larger cities, such as Rovigo.

Compounding the authorities' problems were roving gangs of looters and the interference and demonstrations of the Communist Party and its sympathizers, who demanded that expenditures for armaments be directed to flood relief. The government had already determined that funds scheduled for social programs and land reform would have to be used instead for relief and rebuilding. By November 28, the floodwaters began receding.

Neil E. Salisbury

For Further Information:
The New York Times, November 13-30, 1951.

1953: North Sea

Date: February 1, 1953
Place: The Netherlands, Great Britain, and Belgium
Result: 1,853 dead

Although the greater portion of the devastation wrought by the North Sea storms and flooding of late January to early February of 1953 occurred in the southwestern provinces of the Netherlands, considerable damage and loss of life also took place in the low-lying coastal regions of eastern Great Britain and coastal Belgium.

The people of the Netherlands, though seasoned through a centuries-old history of progress and setback in their struggle with the North Sea and prepared for ordinary emergency situations, were confronted in February, 1953, with an unprecedented set of circumstances that unleashed overwhelming natural forces on their coastal defenses.

The Flood in Great Britain. By the early hours of January 30, 1953, an exceptionally severe atmospheric depression had developed in the North Atlantic Ocean roughly 250 miles northwest of the Isle of Lewis in Scotland's Outer Hebrides. It gave rise to formidable gale winds, which had moved into the North Sea by the morning of January 31 and had assumed a south-southeasterly course.

After having caused gale-force winds and high tides in Scotland and along the Irish coast, the storm shifted to the northern sector of the North Sea, pushing large masses of water southward. Such depressions, with severe storms, are not an unusual occurrence in the North Sea region. The difference in this instance was that, whereas most depressions pass across the North Sea itself quite rapidly, the 1953 depression moved very slowly. This allowed the buildup of an exceptionally massive amount of water that, driven southward by the gale winds and coinciding with the high, seasonal spring tides, led to an unforeseen calamity.

Along the coast of east England, gales were recorded at the highest velocity up to that date for Great Britain—113 miles per hour. The evening of

January 31 and the morning of February 1, 1953, is when most of the destruction and resultant deaths occurred.

In Great Britain the areas most devastated were the coastal regions and the lowlands of the main river estuaries, stretching roughly from the Humber in Yorkshire to the Thames, a distance of approximately 180 to 200 miles. Particularly vulnerable low-lying areas were totally submerged, including the tourist resort towns of Mablethorpe and Sutton-on-Sea, and nearly the entire Lincolnshire coast. Sea walls were breached at Heacham, Snettisham, and Hunstanton, while those at Salthouse, Cley, Great Yarmouth, and Sea Palling were heavily damaged.

Massive evacuation was undertaken, with at least 32,000 individuals being removed, including virtually the entire population (13,000) of Canvey Island in the Thames estuary and all the inhabitants of Mablethorpe and Sutton-on-Sea along the coast. In Norfolk, east England, the Ouse River overflowed its banks, covering the historic town of King's Lynn with over 7 feet of water. Further south, where the Orwell River overflowed, Felixstowe was also inundated. In Suffolk, property damage was most extensive at the ferry port of Harwich, as well as at Tilbury, Great Wackering, and Jaywick Sands. Foulness Island in Essex was completely submerged.

In the Thames region, severe pollution problems occurred when the three major oil refineries at Coryton, Isle of Grain, and Shellhaven suffered substantial damage. Spreading south down the Kentish coast, the gales and tides submerged parts of Gravesend, Herne Bay, Dartford, Margate (where the harbor lighthouse was destroyed), and Birchington. Sheerness's naval dockyard and facilities were also rendered useless.

Aftereffects. On February 2, 1953, Prime Minister Winston Churchill declared the storm to have created a state of "national responsibility." Attempts at collecting relief funds and supplies for the afflicted coastal and river areas were spearheaded by the London Lord Mayor's appeal fund, which raised some 5 million pounds sterling.

The death toll in Britain reached 307, 156,000 acres were flooded (one-third of the total acreage went under salt water), and the total for lost livestock—mainly cattle and sheep—was estimated in the hundreds of thousands. About 500 domiciles were completely demolished and another 25,000 damaged. Monetary loss through damage was estimated at between 40 and 50 million pounds sterling.

On March 5, 1953, a special committee under the chairmanship of Lord Waverly was appointed by Queen Elizabeth II and Churchill to investigate the causes for the catastrophe and issue recommendations. The Waverly Committee released its findings and recommendations in August of 1953. It was decided to implement an early gale warning system along the east coast to be in effect from September 15 to April 30 each year.

The tragedy led to the passage of the Coastal Flooding (Emergency Provisions) Act on May 20, 1953. Special river boards throughout the east coast were appointed and then granted extraordinary powers in case of emergency. The minister of agriculture was further granted the authority to compensate and otherwise provide relief to farmers and farm families whose property had sustained damage as the result of flooding.

The Flood in Belgium. In Belgium between January 30 and 31, 1953, the same tidal storm caused 22 deaths and wreaked devastation in the low coastal plain between the ferry port of Ostend and the Dutch border. The Schelde River overflowed its banks, breaking the dike at Antwerp and flooding a part of the metropolitan area. Massive damage was inflicted upon the town and harbor of Ostend as well as Zeebrugge, where the lock of the sea canal was battered. Although the dikes at Malines were breached, damage to the town itself was not as extensive as elsewhere. The greater proportion of the domiciles in the towns of Knokke, Blankenberge, and La Zoute were heavily damaged.

The disaster in Belgium had serious political repercussions as King Baudouin had made a trip to the French Riviera in order to recuperate from a bout with influenza. His absence during a time of national emergency was much resented and vehemently criticized in the Belgian press. The royal family, and the monarchy itself, were in considerable jeopardy in the wake of the 1951 abdication crisis centering around former king Leopold III. The political atmosphere was so charged that King Baudouin felt compelled to return for a three-day tour of the devastated area before going back to the Riviera on February 12.

The Netherlands. By far the most massive blows dealt by this catastrophe fell on the Netherlands, which had been waging a continual, centuries-old battle to reclaim its low-lying agricultural land (polders) from the North Sea and was particularly vulnerable to the inroads of storm tides because of the sheer amount of land lying below sea level. Of these, the spring tides had usually been the highest and the most dangerous. Storm tide depredation had been a recurring peril along the lower islands of Zeeland Province and the estuaries of the Meuse, Rhine, Schelde, and Ijssel Rivers. The most destructive of these storm tides had occurred in 1421-1424, 1570, 1682, 1715-1717, 1808, 1825, 1863, and 1916. The 1953 storm tide would surpass all others since 1570 in the sheer scope and dimensions of its devastation.

The potential for future danger had been acknowledged in the 1930's, when plans were formulated for the construction of a more modernized series of protective dikes, dams, and bridges along the estuaries of both the Schelde and the Meuse. These plans had been interrupted by the Nazi invasion of the Netherlands in June, 1940, and the subsequent German occupation from 1940 to 1945. By 1953, the construction schemes were virtually forgotten.

The combination of the delayed, northeasterly gale winds causing the North Sea to rise to unprecedented levels and the spring tides led to most of the inundation. Estimates of the dead and missing vary slightly, but the figure of 1,524 is conventionally accepted (for a total of 1,853 when tallied with the tolls for Britain and Belgium). An estimated 988,400 acres of land were saturated, some 50,000 buildings were destroyed or damaged, 89,000 to 100,000 individuals were evacuated, and 300,000 were left homeless. In monetary terms the damage was estimated to have totaled 1.5 billion guilders. Nearly 6 percent of the farmland in the Netherlands, mainly in the provinces of Zeeland, Brabant, and South Holland, was left under water. The loss of enormous numbers of cattle, chickens, and sheep brought forth major concerns over the danger of epidemics caused by rotting carcasses and wastes.

Almost entirely inundated were the islands Schouwen and Duiveland, Overflakkee, Walcheren, Tholen, North Beveland, and South Beveland. Flushing Town suffered flooding of up to 9 feet in its center, after the sea wall had fractured in five separate places. The largest urban centers effected were Rotterdam and Dordrecht, which had extensive flooding in the outlying districts, though not in the center. At Rotterdam, the Hook of Holland Canal was destroyed, as was the Moerdijk Bridge.

North Holland Province sustained far less damage and loss of life but nevertheless experienced substantial coastal flooding in resort areas The Netherlands' largest and most popular seashore resort, Scheveningen, was flooded, and much of its beach was temporarily washed away.

As a general rule most of the fatalities occurred in situations where either there was no warning or the reports of danger were taken too lightly. Many remembered wartime flooding in 1944-1945, which was not as severe as had been feared, and therefore downplayed the magnitude of the 1953 storm and underestimated the perilous nature of their situation. The village of Goedereede (population 2,000) proved to be a model of vigilance and cooperation. The majority of the villagers fled to the upper rooms of their houses, reacted calmly, and assisted one another in the survival and evacuation processes. Goedereede sustained no casualties as a result of the tragedy.

Relief Efforts in the Netherlands. Relief efforts were directed from the Zeeland center of Middelburg, which had escaped the flooding, by the Dutch Red Cross through communications with the local burgomasters (mayors) and other available authorities. The speed and effectiveness of the assistance varied according to the degree of damage and isolation of a given village or community. Helicopter units of the British royal air force, the U.S. Air Force, and the Swiss air force were sent in to assist the Dutch military in its rescue efforts. Some 2,000 stranded individuals, many trapped on the roofs of their houses, were rescued.

Ironically, the Dutch government, only days prior to the flooding disaster—on January 27, 1953—had informed the United States government that the Netherlands had sufficiently recovered from the ravages of World War II and had no further need for U.S. financial assistance, thus terminating the Marshall Plan in that country. On February 6, 1953, the Dutch requested a temporary resumption of U.S. aid under the Marshall Plan to recoup from the storm-tide catastrophe. February 8 was proclaimed by Queen Juliana a day of official mourning, and on February 16 the state of emergency was lifted.

In the wake of the disaster the schemes of the 1930's were revived in the form of the Delta Plan. The Delta Commission, appointed to recommend and accelerate improvements, rendered its report on July 10, 1953. By the end of the year, setbacks in April and November due to high tides notwithstanding, there had been remarkable progress made in the region's recovery. The last of the breaches in the dikes were closed in September, the Schouwensee Dike had been raised 16 feet, and a mobile storm defense was set up at the mouth of the Ijssel estuary, just east of Rotterdam. Reclamation of polderland, augmented by the efforts of a motley collection of international student volunteers and the use of concrete caissons of World War II vintage, was completed by early December.

Raymond Pierre Hylton

For Further Information:

Studies in Holland Flood Disaster 1953: Prepared and Edited by the Institute for Social Research in the Netherlands Under the Sponsorship of the Committee on Disaster Studies of the National Academy of Sciences. 4 vols. Washington, D.C.: National Research Council, 1955.

1954: Rio Grande

Date: June 27-July 3, 1954
Place: Southwestern Texas and northern Mexico
Result: 16 dead and 728 homes destroyed in Texas, more than 200 dead and 15,000 homeless in Mexico

Throughout the early 1950's Texas experienced a major drought. The drought was at its worst in 1953. That year, the U.S. Army Corps of Engineers completed Falcon Dam near Brownsville. Locals wondered at the logic of building such an expensive dam during the years of drought. Project officials estimated that it would take several years for the reservoir behind the dam to be filled.

Then, on June 26, 1954, Hurricane Alice moved into Mexico just south of Brownsville. The storm hit the coast less than twenty-four hours after its formation. At the height of the storm, Hurricane Alice had winds of only 80 miles an hour, just 5 miles above hurricane strength. While not a particularly severe storm, the small hurricane precipitated one of the worst floods in Texas history. One positive outcome of the hurricane was that Falcon Dam filled up in a matter of days.

The heavy rains of Hurricane Alice not only filled the dam but also resulted in a major flood disaster. The Rio Grande along the border of Texas and Mexico began to swell. As the water rose, bridges were washed out. The flooding began with heavy rains on Sunday, June 27. A train was stalled on the tracks between Langtry and Comstock, Texas, due to the flooding of the Pecos and Devils Rivers. Some 300 passengers were stranded and had to be airlifted out by helicopter due to road closings in all directions. Newspapers reported that there were several automobiles stranded across southern Texas due to the washout and closings of highways and county roads.

The small Texas town of Ozona was the first community to experience problems, when a flash flood hit the town at 3:00 A.M. on June 28. Almost half of the buildings in the community were destroyed. The wall of water washed families out of their beds. Over 100 homes were demolished, and more than 200 more were damaged. There were reports of families riding out the flood on the river while attached to logs and tree limbs. Sixteen people lost their lives in Ozona that night.

The river rose over 40 feet at Del Rio, Texas. One indication of the enormity of flooding is to measure the change in daily discharge of water at specific spots along rivers. At Del Rio, where the river reached an all-time record in July, the comparison of water in the Rio Grande before and during the flood is astounding. The mean daily discharge of the Rio Grande in June of 1954 was 1,571 cubic feet (44.5 cubic meters) per second. In July the Rio Grande discharged at a mean rate of 18,787 cubic feet (532 cubic meters) per second. At Comstock, Texas, the discharge of the Rio Grande averaged over 900,000 cubic feet per second in one day.

The river reached over 62 feet at Laredo on June 30. The city of Laredo received the brunt of the flooding where the river's crest covered 390 city blocks. An American Red Cross survey indicated that 605 homes were destroyed in Laredo and more than 1,700 were damaged. There was no loss of life in the city, in part because citizens received advanced warning and evacuated. City water was lost for several days, and over 1,500 people became homeless. One newspaper report indicated that more than 5,000 people were evacuated from their homes, sheltered in schools throughout Laredo. The local health department began a mass prevention program against typhoid, and over 50,000 people were immunized.

At the same time the Rio Grande was flooding, the Pecos River, which runs into the Rio Grande from New Mexico, rose rapidly. An 86-foot wall of water rushed out of the Pecos, washing out bridges in its path, including the International Bridge between Laredo, Texas, and Nuevo Laredo, Mexico.

The worst damage caused by the flooding was in Mexico. In Ciudad Acuña, across the river from Del Rio, Texas, 10,000 of the 14,000 residents were left homeless. Martial law was declared at Nuevo Laredo when approximately one-third of the town was flooded. The United States government entered into a cooperative agreement with Mexican officials to help the flood victims in the three major Mexican towns along the Rio Grande, the communities of Ciudad Acuña, Nuevo Laredo, and Piedras Negras. Units of the American Red Cross and the United States Army were flown into Mexico and assisted with food, medical, clothing, and water-purification supplies. Within a few days, a pontoon bridge had been built between Laredo and Nuevo Laredo, which helped speed up the disaster relief efforts in Mexico.

The flood of 1954 was one of the worst floods in Southwest history. Severe damage to towns, bridges, and roads in Texas and the country of Mexico led to hundreds of thousands of dollars in repair costs. Hundreds of homes in Texas were destroyed, and thousands were badly damaged. Mexico was hardest hit, with more than 200 lives lost and thousands left homeless.

Judith Boyce DeMark

For Further Information:

American Red Cross. *Southwest Texas Flood of June, 1954.* n.p.: Author, 1954.

Carr, John T., Jr. *Hurricanes Affecting the Texas Gulf Coast.* Report 49. Austin: Texas Water Development Board, 1967.

Dunn, Gordon E., and Banner I. Miller. *Atlantic Hurricanes.* Baton Rouge: Louisiana State University Press, 1960.

Garcia, Rolando. "Residents Recall Worst Drought on Record." *Brownsville (Tex.) Herald,* July 26, 1998.

International Boundary and Water Commission. *Flow of the Rio Grande and Related Data.* IBWC Water Bulletin 24. El Paso, Tex.: Author, 1954.

"Season's First Hurricane Hits Texas Border City." *The New York Times,* June 26, 1954, p. 6.

"200 to 500 Believed Dead in Piedras Negras Flood." *Laredo Times,* June 30, 1954, p. 1.

1954: Tibet

Date: July-August, 1954
Place: Southern Tibet, especially Xigazê and Gyangtse
Result: 500 to 1,000 dead

The highest mountains on earth are the Himalayas, where southern Tibet and India share a border with Nepal and Bhutan. This is also the region with the world's greatest precipitation, most of which falls during a few months in the summer monsoons. Heavy snowfall in the winter of 1953-1954 melted quickly with the advent of the warm season rains, and flooding was widespread throughout the region.

The trading center of Gyangtse, on the Namchung River, population 10,000, was washed away on July 23. More than 300 troops and government officials in a fort clinging to the steep valley walls above the Namchung were buried when the structure collapsed. On August 10, the same fate was suffered by 500 Chinese troops in a barracks in Xigazê, the second most populous city of Tibet. The old palace of the Panchen Lama (the chief spiritual adviser of the Dalai Lama) also collapsed. The Panchen Lama was safe, however, having been invited, along with the Dalai Lama, on an extended visit in Beijing, China.

Neil E. Salisbury

For Further Information:

The New York Times, July 27; August 13; December 2, 1954.

The Times (London), July 24, 27; August 5; September 4, 1954.

1954: Iran

Date: August, 1954
Place: Farazhad, Iran
Result: 2,000 dead

The earth's dry lands are particularly vulnerable to flash flooding because most of these regions receive the bulk of their precipitation from thunderstorms or high-intensity rainfall. Add to this the facts that dry lands have sparse vegetation to hold back runoff and their surfaces are frequently bare rock or clay-filled badlands, neither of which are capable of absorbing much rainfall, and the potential for disaster is clear. Topography often contributes to the risk, for dry lands are well known for their deep and narrow canyons.

All these factors were present at the Muslim shrine of the Imam Zadeh David, located at the bottom of a steep, rocky gorge some 30 miles northwest of Tehran. Flash floods had already killed more than 150 people three weeks earlier in Iran. This was not sufficient warning for the pilgrims visiting the shrine. A heavy thunderstorm filled the gorge with a wall of water 90 feet high, engulfing the shrine and the 2,000 pilgrims who had sought refuge there. Few who were in the gorge managed to climb to safety. The rest were swept away and buried in the mud.

Neil E. Salisbury

For Further Information:

The Times (London), August 23, 1954.

1955: Northern California

Date: December, 1955-January, 1956
Place: Yuba City, California
Result: 74 dead (61 in California, 13 in Oregon), 50,000 homeless, $150 million estimated in damage

Worldwide, most places receive their heaviest precipitation during the warm season, or summer; thus, flooding is generally a warm-season event. In the so-called Mediterranean climates, which include California, the reverse is true; most rain—and snow, at higher elevations—arrives in winter, as do the floods.

December, 1955, was an exceptionally bad time for Northern California, because the high-altitude jet stream swung farther south than usual, collecting warm, tropical, moisture-laden air off Hawaii and delivering it to the state's river basins. Heavy rains persisted for days, and the warm rains melted the 6-foot-deep snowpack in the Sierra Nevada, increasing the flood levels of streams that headed in the mountains. This included the American, Feather, and Yuba Rivers, the last two joining at the twin cities of Marysville and Yuba City.

By December 22, all the rivers of northwestern California and the northern Sierras were overflowing, as were rivers in southern Oregon and western Nevada (Reno). The Eel and Klamath Rivers were especially hard hit by these early storms; thousands of people were evacuated, and 2 small towns were destroyed. By the 24th, the Sierra Nevada snowmelt floods had forced the evacuation of Marysville (population 12,500) and its neighbor Yuba City (population 8,000) for fear that the dikes would break. About 1,000 men remained in Marysville to strengthen the dikes, which held and saved the city from serious flooding.

Yuba City was not so fortunate, however; the dikes broke and flooded the city to a depth of 6 to 8 feet or more. Ironically, the dike break at Yuba City lowered the flood level, helping to save Marysville. Sacrificing small towns or farmland by breaking the dikes to lower flood levels is a common strategy in fighting floods, but here the effect was accidental. By the following day, Christmas, the floods were receding after California's worst natural disaster since the 1906 San Francisco earthquake. New flood levels returned to Yuba City on the 26th and 27th, contributing to the contamination of water supplies and the closing of the sewage plant. On January 14, 1956, Yuba City was evacuated again in the face of a new flood threat, but this time the dikes held.

As is often the case, not only in the United States but also worldwide, natural disasters encourage political parties and groups to assail each other with alternative views concerning responsibility for the tragedy or for the government's involvement in rescue and rehabilitation efforts. Some held that had the proposed Oroville Dam been built as part of the Feather River Project, designed to send excess water south to water-needy Southern California, it could have controlled the Yuba City flooding. Much damage had been prevented by dams, such as Shasta, Folsom, Friant, and others, it was suggested. Democrats blamed Republicans for failing to fund flood-control projects, a cry that had been raised at the time of the Columbia River flood of 1948. Of note is the fact that President Dwight D. Eisenhower, a Republican, proposed an experimental flood insurance program as a consequence of the California floods. This type of program was in place by the early 1970's. The Oroville Dam on the Feather River and several smaller dams on the Yuba River helped protect Yuba City and Marysville from a repeat of the 1955-1956 event.

Neil E. Salisbury

For Further Information:

The New York Times, December 21, 1955-February 26, 1956.

1959: Malpasset Dam Collapse

Date: December 2-3, 1959
Place: Above Fréjus, France
Result: Estimated 412-421 dead

When dams collapse, they create flash floods. Stream valleys that ordinarily encounter only nuisance high-water levels during rainy spells are transformed into killers, trapping people who cannot escape the rushing waves or even walls of water that are suddenly released from confinement behind the dam. Six days of heavy rain on the French Riviera filled a relatively new dam for the first time on the night of December 2, 1959, and the rock beneath the structure was unable to accommodate the added pressure. The dam burst with such force that windows and doors were blown out of the damkeeper's cottage a mile downstream. A wall of water roared down the narrow gorge of the Reyran River, sweeping the remains of farms and orchards with it, and then spread out on the plain below on a path as much as 6 miles wide, engulfing the town of Fréjus and its inhabitants.

After the flood, 3 feet of silt covered the plain, destroying the roads and rail lines and burying the victims. Fréjus was originally constructed by Julius Caesar in 49 B.C.E. and was the most important seaport on the French coast. Today its harbor has been silted up by rivers to such an extent that the town is 2.5 miles from the ocean.

Two factors, the isolation of the disaster area and the difficulty in locating the dead, are characteristic of flash floods of all types: those due to high-intensity rainstorms in small stream basins, those resulting from dam breaks, and those associated with rapid mass wasting of earth materials, such as rock avalanches. Isolation makes rescue efforts difficult; helicopters may snatch people from the floodwaters, but heavy equipment is required to move debris. The difficulty of locating bodies buried in mud prolongs the agony of those who maintain hope that their families might have survived and leads to ever-increasing and imprecise death tolls as time progresses. There is usually a "missing persons" category associated with flood disasters—bodies never recovered, or in this instance, actually swept out to sea.

The Malpasset Dam collapse was a tragedy of such proportions that the attention and assistance of not only the usual agencies but also the French and U.S. fleets were involved in supporting the rescue efforts. Artist Pablo Picasso donated two paintings to be auctioned for the relief of victims of the flood.

Neil E. Salisbury

For Further Information:

The New York Times, December 3-22, 1959.

Waltham, Tony. *Catastrophe: The Violent Earth.* New York: Crown, 1978.

1962: Germany

Date: February 16-25, 1962
Place: The German coast, particularly Hamburg and Bremerhaven
Result: 309 dead, tens of thousands homeless, $250 million in damage

It is difficult to distinguish the impact of storm-surge floods, in which the ocean is whipped up along a coastline, from river floods, which result from rain or snowmelt inland. This is particularly true where coastal lowlands are easily flooded by both simultaneously as rivers are prevented from discharging into the ocean by the high storm waves. Such is the case in Hamburg, Germany, at the head of the estuary of the Elbe River; in Bremerhaven, on the Weser River estuary; and in Bremen, 20 miles upstream.

Winter is the stormy season along this North Sea coastline, which extends westward to the especially low-lying areas of the Netherlands. Although the Netherlands is particularly well known for reclaiming land from the sea, holding back the waters by an elaborate system of dikes, similar procedures have been used along most of the river estuaries of northwestern Europe. A fierce storm on February 16-17, 1962, with winds of hurricane force (in excess of 75 miles per hour) combined with high tides to break the dikes in many places along the German and Dutch coastlines and rivers. Storm effects were said to be felt as far as 60 miles from the coastline. Houses were smashed by the waves, farmlands were inundated, and entire communities were isolated. Compounding the problem of evacuation of tens of thousands of people was the darkness created by the failure of the power systems.

For the inhabitants of the region, the scene recalled the air raids of World War II. A great difference, however, was in the rescue efforts, which involved British, Dutch, West German, and U.S. military. Helicopters proved especially useful in rescuing isolated and marooned victims and in delivering food and supplies.

Neil E. Salisbury

For Further Information:

The New York Times, February 17-25, 1962.

1962: Spain

Date: September 26, 1962
Place: Barcelona and environs, Spain
Result: 700 estimated dead, $50 million or more in damage

The Mediterranean region is characterized by dry summers, with rain and snowfall mainly occurring in the winter. In 1962, the summer's drought was broken on the night of September 26 by a fierce nine-hour storm that flooded the Barcelona area. This is the major industrial center of Spain, and much of the damage was to textile mills and other factories, destroying a good portion of the economic base that sustains the population. Some 15,000 workers were left without jobs, many of whom also lost their homes.

Hardest hit were the hill towns of Tarrasa, Sabadell, and Rubi, each about 10 miles from Barcelona, which escaped major damage. The area is hilly and, in some areas, mountainous, which allows rainfall runoff to collect quickly and roar down the valley with disastrous results for the population below. In Tarrasa, 78 were killed in one textile mill alone as it was engulfed by floodwaters before the workers could escape. Many others were drowned as they slept. Mass burials were common as the death toll rose in succeeding days. Many bodies are never recovered from the flood deposits or are washed out to sea; thus the ultimate death toll of 700 is only an estimate. Offers of aid came from other European nations and the American military stationed in Spain. Spanish-born artist Pablo Picasso donated one of his best paintings to be auctioned for flood relief.

The rainy season was not over on September 26; on October 12 the ancient city of Gerona, Spain, some 50 miles up the coast from Barcelona, was hit by a flood that displaced 600 people. On November 8, as the area was rebuilding from the worst natural disaster to hit Spain in modern times, another flood hit Barcelona and Sabadell, destroying another 800 homes and slowing the region's recovery.

Neil E. Salisbury

For Further Information:

The New York Times, September 27; November 7-8, 1962.

1965: Great Plains

Arkansas and South Platte Rivers
Date: June 17-28, 1965

Place: Colorado and Kansas
Result: 23 dead, at least $100 million in damage

The southern Rocky Mountains (Sangre de Cristo Mountains of New Mexico and southern Colorado, and the Front Range in Colorado) experience the second highest number of thunderstorms annually in the United States; only Florida has more. These mountains, rising as high as 14,000 feet, comprise the headwaters of the Arkansas River, which then flows east across the plains of Colorado and Kansas. From June 16 to 18, 1965, thunderstorm activity along the Rockies from New Mexico to Montana caused flash floods to roar out of the mountains onto the floodplains of the Great Plains. While most of the monetary damage was along the South Platte River near Denver, the Arkansas River experienced the longest-lived flood and the greatest number of people displaced from their homes.

By June 17, the flood wave had reached La Junta, Colorado, driving dozens of families from their homes. By the 18th, the flood crest had reached Syracuse, Kansas, and evacuations had been ordered from Pueblo, Colorado, at the foot of the mountains, to the Kansas border. The flood wave moved slowly, about 2 miles per hour, but once the high water arrived, despite the warning, people were shocked by the rapidity of the water's rise—14 feet in one hour in Dodge City on the 20th—and risked being trapped in buildings. By the time the flood wave reached Great Bend, Kansas, on June 23, floodwaters threatened the levee system, but it had been reinforced with sandbags and held. Downstream, the flood wave reached Hutchinson on the 26th and Wichita, Kansas, shortly after; in both cities flood-control levees held.

Federal flood aid of millions of dollars was dispatched to the Arkansas and South Platte River Valleys to assist in rebuilding public works and highways destroyed by the flooding, as well as to alleviate private losses. President Lyndon Johnson signed the first flood-aid bill of June 30, obviously impressed by his view of the flooding as he flew over the river on his way to San Francisco. Upland fields of wheat in Kansas benefited from the rains, which resulted in higher yields, but individual farmers in the path of the flood saw their crops wiped out.

Neil E. Salisbury

For Further Information:
The New York Times, June 16-July 4, 1965.

1966: Brazil

Date: January 11-13, 1966
Place: Rio de Janeiro and environs, Brazil
Result: 239-400 estimated dead, 45,000 evacuated

The heaviest rainfall in eighty years, 9 inches in less than twelve hours, saturated hillsides in Rio de Janeiro and surrounding areas in January of 1966, causing landslides and mudflows. The steep hillsides are crowded with poorly built shanties, which accounted for most of the deaths as these were swept downhill with their inhabitants inside. Especially hard hit were the Copacabana and Ipanema Districts, where the contrast between the poverty-stricken shanty towns on the hillsides and the rich neighborhoods below is particularly dramatic.

By January 13, some low-level buildings were destroyed by mudflows. The Maracano River flooded some areas to a depth of 7 feet. The urban services of the city were interrupted; 40 percent of the population was without water. Typhoid, always a risk during floods, was feared, and shots were given to both refugees and others with poor water supplies.

It is virtually impossible in this kind of disaster to distinguish between victims of river floods and mudflows. In severe floods, there is no pure water; a continuum exists between river floodwaters and mudflows. Similarly, it is difficult to determine the total number of deaths. Many bodies are buried by the mud and never recovered.

Neil E. Salisbury

For Further Information:
The New York Times, January 12-22, February 13.

1966: Italy

Date: November 3-4, 1966
Place: Florence, Italy
Result: 24 dead; 50,000 homeless; 1,300 artworks and 700,000 books, manuscripts, and drawings destroyed or damaged; 4,000 buildings weakened or destroyed; more than $4 billion estimated in damage (exclusive of art)

October, 1966, had been an unusually wet month in all of northern Italy. November promised to be much

the same. Little did the residents of Florence realize that the light drizzle of November 3 would turn into the worst flood in the city's fifteen-hundred-year history. The main characteristics of the great Florence flood of 1966 were its short duration—only about twelve hours—the extensive destruction of property, and the small loss of human life.

On the evening of November 3, 1966, a cyclonic storm driven by 90 mile-per-hour winds hit Italy south of Florence and moved northeast across the country, dumping thousands of tons of water over a 38,000-square-mile area mainly in the region drained by the Arno and Po Rivers. Because of the intervening Apennine Mountain chain, the storm dropped most of its water to the west, in the Arno drainage area. The drizzle in Florence turned into a rain that fell in sheets. By 10 A.M. on November 4, the usually placid river had risen more than 30 feet, broken through its dikes and embankments, and surged into the city, reaching a depth of 18 feet in places.

The flood can be compared to an enormous sheet of water bearing down on the city, carrying with it vast amounts of debris and dead animals from outlying farms and villages. Florence itself is located in a natural basin surrounded by hills. The city became a churning lake, the water capped by the oily scum of the contents of thousands of uprooted fuel-oil tanks. Before the water swept on to the sea, it left behind most of the debris: 40,000 dead animals, 10,000 ruined automobiles, and 100,000 tons of silt and mud. There was no great loss of life because November 4 was a holiday; many of the shops and artisan ateliers were therefore closed.

The financial and physical results of the flood, however, were appalling. In the historic Church of the Holy Cross, water rose to the height of 13 feet, destroying the *Crucifixion* of Giovanni Cimabue, one of its greatest treasures. In the plaza of the cathedral in the center of the old city, the water swirled with such force that it loosened five of the ten panels of the bronze doors to the baptistry executed by Lorenzo Ghiberti and considered by many the city's greatest single art treasure. The fence surrounding the building prevented the panels from being washed away but not from being damaged.

More than 1,300 works of art were lost or damaged. The greatest lasting damage was done to the archives of the National Library. More than half a million historic books; 9,000 prints and drawings; many thousands of portraits, maps, and letters; 200,000 manuscripts; and over 3,500 very old works were either destroyed or so water-soaked it would take years to restore them. Fortunately, most of the collections of the Uffizi and the Pitti, Florence's major museums, were in galleries on the second floor of their buildings and were comparatively safe. Those stored in the basements and restoration ateliers were not so lucky. The watch collection in the Science Museum was lost, as was most of the Etruscan collection in the Archaeological Museum.

The floodwaters receded as rapidly as they rose. They crested by 11 the evening of November 4. By the afternoon of November 6, the level of the Arno had dropped 18 feet. Florence was prostrate, without water, telephones, heat, gas, or electricity. Damage had been done to the foundations of the famed cathedral and its adjoining bell tower. Some of the older buildings, their foundations undermined, began to tilt ominously. Streets were choked with mud, debris, carcasses of animals, and destroyed automobiles. Dark, sticky, smelly petroleum clung to everything, augmented by the pervasive smell of sewage because of the blocked sewers.

A great loss in property was suffered by the artisans and shopkeepers of Florence. Their shops were, for the most part, small, usually dealing in a single luxury item. The inundated basements were not only their workspaces but also their storage areas. Virtually no one had flood insurance. The water rose so swiftly there was no time to save property. About 6,000 of the 10,000 shops of Florence were wiped out. The floodwaters swept through the jewelers' shops on the Vecchio Bridge, carrying away their valuable stock.

Help was quick to arrive. The government in Rome appropriated large sums in flood relief and instituted measures to help distressed merchants and artisans. It sent soldiers, earthmovers, bulldozers, and trucks to help clear the mud and debris. Flamethrowers were used to dispose of the dead animals. Surrounding cities such as Milan and Turin also gathered millions of lira in assistance. In the United States, the International Committee to Rescue Italian Art was quickly formed and raised more than half a million dollars in aid. Britain's Italian Art and Archives Rescue Fund followed the American example—as did nearly every other European country. Students and volunteers converged on Florence, helping to rescue the art. Florentines set about patiently restoring their beloved city. By the end of the month the superintendent of the Florentine galleries gave assurance that historic Florence had withstood the fury of the elements and would be saved for posterity.

Nis Petersen

For Further Information

"Disaster in Italy: Damage Done by Flood." *Newsweek*, November 21, 1966, 110-111.

Kent, N. "Florence: A Disaster Area." *American Artist*, January, 1967, 1-2.

Sobel, Lester A., ed. *Facts on File Yearbook, 1966.* Vol. 26. New York: Facts on File, 1967.

Taylor, Katherine Kressman. *Diary of Florence in Flood.* New York: Simon & Schuster, 1967.

1967: Brazil

Date: January 24-March 21, 1967
Place: Rio de Janeiro and São Paulo, Brazil
Result: 1,250 dead

Heavy tropical rainstorms flooded Rio de Janeiro and its environs on three separate occasions roughly a month apart, with results that were reminiscent of the 1966 storms that killed as many as 600. On January 23-24, rains flooded the Maracana River and caused hillside mudflows that destroyed homes. The President Dutra Highway, linking Rio de Janeiro with São Paulo, was flooded, with several buses and numerous automobiles reportedly swept into the Paraíba River. Power and water were in short supply. Death toll estimates ranged from 150 to more than 600. On February 20, two apartment houses, one of them eight stories tall, collapsed after an 11-inch rainfall. The death toll was estimated at 119. In addition, 30,000 were without shelter. On March 21, heavy rains caused a landslide in the seaside town of Caraguatatuba, leaving another 100 dead. The total death toll from heavy rains and associated flooding and mudflows was estimated at 1,250.

Neil E. Salisbury

For Further Information:

The New York Times, January 23-24; February 20-21; March 19, 1967.

1967: Portugal

Date: November 25-26, 1967
Place: Lisbon area, Portugal
Result: 457 or more dead, thousands homeless

A 350-square-mile area with Lisbon at its center was hit by an all-day rain, followed by 3.5 inches between 6 P.M. and midnight. About 6 feet of water ran down the street, swamping automobiles. Flood levels reached 13 feet on some buidings. Moviegoers in a theater were surprised by floodwaters suddenly filling the lower floor. Approximately 150 patrons were rescued from the balcony. In some districts, only those who lived in two-story houses survived. Hardest hit were the poorer parts of the city and some of the small towns in the region.

When the sunshine returned the next day, not all the survivors were happy. An independent newspaper complained that the authorities had failed to control recurrent flooding, despite the knowledge of which areas would be hardest hit. Students complained that the government obstructed the students' relief efforts and engaged in censorship of information related to the flood. They maintained that the extent of the disaster was not related to natural conditions, but rather to social, economic, and administrative conditions. Specifically, the students were concerned that the government allowed shacks in the area, which could not withstand the flooding, rather than building housing for the poor.

Neil E. Salisbury

For Further Information:

The New York Times, November 27-28, 30; December 4, 1967.

The Times (London), November 27-28, 1967.

1968: India

Date: July 21-August 15, 1968
Place: Gujarat, India
Result: 1,000 people and 80,000 cattle dead

A seven-day monsoon flood struck the state of Gujarat, about 100 miles north of Bombay, in the summer of 1968, leaving death and destruction. More than 1,000 people were thought to have died, along with 80,000 cattle. The situation was worsened by the rotting of the cattle carcasses and impure water. Road and rail transport to the area was cut off as more than 700 square miles were submerged; food grains had to be air-dropped to prevent starvation. Hundreds of thousands were left homeless.

This was a summer of troubles for India. On July 14 monsoon floods killed more than 200, and millions were homeless in East Pakistan and four In-

A railroad track that was twisted and uprooted by the 1968 flood in Gujarat, India. (AP/Wide World Photos)

dian states following six days of rain. Six weeks earlier people were dying in this same region from heat and lack of water before the monsoon rains arrived. On October 7 it was reported that floods and landslides caused by four days of torrential rains in sub-Himalayan northeastern India had killed between 780 and 1,000 people, mostly in Darjeeling.

Neil E. Salisbury

For Further Information:

The New York Times, August 9, 15; October 8, 1968.

The Times (London), July 15, August 13, 1968.

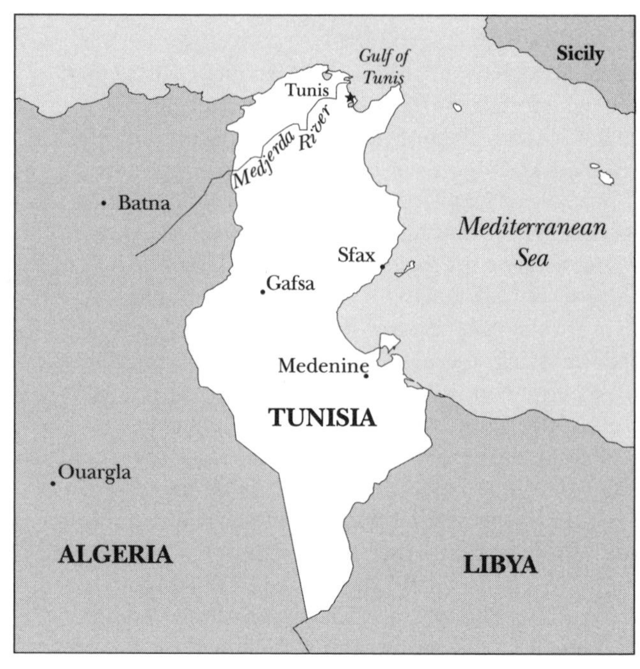

1969: Tunisia

Date: September 29-October 28, 1969
Place: Across Tunisia
Result: 542 people and 1 million livestock dead, 100,000 homeless

Although Tunisia has a lengthy coastline on the Mediterranean Sea, it is not a country with a lot of water. There are few major rivers in Tunisia, and the largest one, the Medjerda, has a small drainage area. The average amount of annual rainfall ranges from 20 inches in the northern and eastern areas closest to the Mediterranean to 7 inches in the desert areas of the south. The terrain tends to be more dry than wet, and typically drought is a more plausible threat to Tunisian agriculture than flooding.

Thus the ferocity of the floods that struck the country in 1969 was almost totally unexpected. The country received over 16 feet of rainfall in slightly over a week; the amount of precipitation that could have reasonably been expected to accumulate in a decade was instead compressed into a far smaller period. The lack of drainage combined with the incredible amount of sudden, pronounced rainfall to create both river flooding and flash flooding. Tunisia had very few human-made reservoirs, and there was a shortage of flood pools; similarly, a scarcity of levees meant that the spread of the water faced little opposition.

The floods themselves were tremendous, with both the Medjerda and the large, normally shallow lakes in the southwest of the country cresting to unprecedented heights, but it was the lack of preparation for them that was the greater catastrophe. The flat landscape and low river drainage of much of Tunisia meant that there were few natural obstacles to the progress of the flood's ravages. Ten of Tunisia's 13 provinces (containing most of the country's population) were inundated, destroying roughly 50,000 homes and farms and rendering between 300,000 and 550,000 people homeless. Again, preparation was a factor, as very little of the Medjerda Valley was dammed and few farmers had taken precautions to guard either their homes or their crops from potential flooding. The flooding lasted over a week, finally subsiding on October 8.

Olive farmers composed the largest group in Tunisian agriculture; their crops were particularly hard hit as rainfall, normally a boon in the variable Tunisian climate, wiped out an entire season's harvest. More localized products such as tomatoes, chickpeas, and sugar beets also suffered, as well as crops, such as barley, grown in the near-desert south that depended on low rainfall to flourish. Besides the collateral damage incurred, the destruction of the soil made the cultivation of the primary crop much harder in the years immediately following.

It was not only Tunisia's agriculture that was buried, but also aspects of the country's natural resources production communications infrastructure. The production of oil and phosphates, which had been increasingly important factors in an economy that had been improving in recent years, was disrupted severely. Roads, railways, bridges, and viaducts were all swept away; by one count, 33 bridges and 29 roads were put out of commission by the flooding.

Exacerbating the problems caused by the flood was uncertainty in Tunisia's political situation. Tunisia had been independent from France for only slightly more than ten years and was still not entirely on its own feet organizationally or economically. Habib Bourguiba, Tunisia's founding president, had taken ill earlier in the year. Although Bourguiba lived for a good many years more, the doubts about his health in 1969 led to fears of a power vacuum. More immediately impacting the industries affected by the flood was the forced resignation of Ahmed ben Salah, the minister for economic planning, who had been in charge of the collectivization of certain areas of Tunisian agriculture. Ben Salah's planning, though, certainly could not be blamed for floods that were acts of nature.

The international community responded rapidly to the chaos caused by the flooding. The United States, Germany, France, Belgium, Spain, many Arab countries, the International Development Bank, the Red Cross, and the Red Crescent promised aid. This was not only in the form of loans and credits but also in the form of more immediately needed tangible resources, such as trucks, aircraft, helicopters, and temporary harbors and bridges. Much of the repair activity was centered in southern Tunisia, as well as large cities such as Tunis, the country's capital, and Sfax, as well as the Gafsa, Kairouan, and Gabès regions.

Food and provisions were also donated: Blankets, tents, canned goods, flour, oil, milk, and sugar were provided to people who had to assure their own and their families' survival as well as, in many cases, regenerate devastated farms that were the backbone of their country's economy. All of Tunisia's development plans had to be recalibrated, and the damage done by the floods would restrain Tunisian economic productivity for years to come.

Tunisia had been caught by surprise once, but it would not happen again. Immediately, President Bourguiba ordered his planners to formulate strategies to prevent future disasters. It was, however, not until the 1980's that a series of dams was constructed in the Medjerda watershed, which promised to forestall damage from future floods equal to the devastation of the autumn of 1969.

Nicholas Birns

For Further Information:

Ashford, Douglas. "End of an Era for Tunisia?" *Africa Report*, January, 1970, 28-29.

Moudoud, Ezzeddine. *Modernization, the State, and Regional Disparity in Developing Countries: Tunisia in Historical Perspective, 1881-1982.* Boulder, Colo.: Westview Press, 1989.

Simmons, John. *Village and Family: Essays on Rural Tunisia.* New Haven, Conn.: Human Relations Area Files, 1974.

"Tunisia: Disastrous Floods." *Africa Research Bulletin*, September 15-October 14, 1969, 1477.

1972: West Virginia

Buffalo Creek
Date: February 26, 1972
Place: Logan County, West Virginia
Result: 125 dead, 4,000 homeless, $10 million in damage

The hills of West Virginia are wet every winter, like the rest of the Ohio River basin. West Virginia, along with its Appalachian neighbors, has coal in those hills. Coal mining produces millions of tons of refuse, tailings (residue from the coal), and overburden (material overlying the coal), which have to be dumped somewhere, and the narrow valley bottoms do not leave many options. Nearly all the refuse ends up in the stream bottoms or perches precariously on the hillslopes above. The United States has thousands of dams, the vast majority of which are earth-filled with whatever soil and rock is available locally. In West Virginia many dams are composed of the refuse of coal mining, which is not the most stable material to hold water.

At 8:01 A.M. on February 26, 1972, after three days of heavy rain in the valley of Buffalo Creek, one such dam failed, sending a wall of water 10 to 20 feet high roaring down the valley, through 17 towns and a dense rural population. Of the 4,000 people in the valley, 125 died, and many of the survivors suffered from what would later be called post-traumatic stress disorder. The rain was not unusual for that region, but the flood occurred because the refuse piles were not properly engineered, experts claimed. The refuse became saturated and simply gave way. Two smaller breaks had occurred several years earlier, without serious damage, and consequently many of the valley inhabitants ignored warnings that they were in danger.

Blame for the disaster was difficult to fix; the coal company stated it was an act of God but settled claims for nearly $30 million. Official hearings brought out conflicting opinions, which echoed those of the survivors. Some of the valley's inhabitants felt they themselves were partly to blame, because they had mined the coal whose refuse composed the dams.

Neil E. Salisbury

For Further Information:

Davies, William E., James F. Bailey, and Donovan B. Kelly. *West Virginia's Buffalo Creek Flood: A Study of the Hydrology and Engineering Geology.* Geological Survey Circular 667. Washington, D.C.: U.S. Geological Survey, 1972.

The New York Times, February 27-March 19, 1972.

Nugent, Tom. *Death at Buffalo Creek: The 1972 West Virginia Flood Disaster.* New York: W. W. Norton, 1973.

1972: South Dakota

Rapid Creek
Date: June 9, 1972
Place: Rapid City, South Dakota
Result: 238 dead, $160 million in damage

Rapid City, South Dakota, was settled along Rapid Creek by white settlers in 1876. The town was situated by the relatively small and quiet creek that drains from the Black Hills. When gold was discovered in the Black Hills, a rush ensued that led to the formation of the town. The area had been home to the Sioux Indians, and they had given the name "Minnelusa" to the creek. The Sioux name means "running water," because the creek sometimes ran wild. Rapid Creek flows from the higher elevations in the Black Hills down through a series of tilted resistant rocks (a hogback) and cuts a narrow water gap through the Dakota sandstone. After passing this point, the creek flows through a floodplain that progressively widens from only 656 feet (200 meters) below the water gap to almost 3,280 feet (1,000 meters) downstream.

The early settlers were also wary of settling in the floodplain of the river. They rarely camped in the floodplain for fear of being caught in a flash flood. The fear of flooding led the early residents to construct most of the town south of the floodplain. The wisdom of this choice was shown when Rapid Creek flooded extensively in 1902. The memory of this flood and subsequent smaller floods led the residents to seek some form of flood control.

A number of flood-control methods were suggested in the 1940's, but they were deemed too expensive. In 1952 Pactola Dam was constructed about 9.9 miles (16 kilometers) upstream of the city. Many people considered the river floodplain in Rapid City to be flood-proof, and Pactola Dam did provide significant protection from small flood events. This flood control led to extensive urbanization of the floodplain after 1952. By 1972 the city had grown to a population of approximately 50,000, and almost the entire floodplain was covered with shopping centers, mobile-home parks, houses, and car lots. The folly of such development was tragically demonstrated on June 9, 1972.

The meteorological conditions that developed on the evening of June 9 set the stage for a tremendous flash flood. Warm, moist air was being brought from the Gulf Coast region, and, simultaneously, cold air was coming down from the northwest. The two air masses collided on the eastern edge of the Black Hills. The orographic effect of the Black Hills helped to form tremendous thunderheads that towered up to 9.9 miles (16 kilometers) into the atmosphere. There was no jet stream at higher altitudes to disperse the clouds, and when it began to rain the system was stationary for a number of hours.

For hours the rain pelted the eastern Black Hills, and in some areas as much as 15 inches (38 centimeters) of rain fell in only six hours. The streams of the eastern Black Hills quickly flooded, and much of the water was channeled into Rapid Creek. The waters filled the reservoir behind Pactola Dam to the spillway level, but it was choked with debris. The reservoir continued to rise behind the dam to as much as 10.5 feet (3.2 meters) above spillway level; as the flood crest arrived, the dam finally failed. The peak discharge of the river at Rapid City was measured at about 50,500 cubic feet (1,430 cubic meters) per second. Statistical analysis of historic flooding on Rapid Creek indicates that this discharge should be approximately equal to that of a hundred-year-flood. The floodwaters released soon inundated the floodplain at Rapid City with force.

In total, 238 people died in the flood. Damage on the floodplain was very extensive. Most of the buildings within the floodplain were destroyed or damaged. The total damage was estimated by the U.S. Army Corps of Engineers to be about $128 million. Since the residents of area thought that the river was flood-proof, none of them had flood insurance.

Following this devastating flood, the residents of Rapid City began to look seriously at new flood-control measures to ensure that this type of disaster would not occur again. The Army Corps of Engineers investigated the possible construction of a large flood-control dam at Dark Canyon, just above Rapid City. Since much of the rainfall that caused the flood occurred downstream from Pactola Dam, a large dam further downstream might provide more flood protection. The economic analysis of the project, however, showed that it was not feasible.

Because there would be no structure to protect the floodplain, the city council took the Army Corps of Engineers' suggestion to develop a floodplain management program. The program required that there be no new residential or commercial development in the floodplain. The few buildings in the floodplain that survived the flood were later moved to higher ground or destroyed. In place of urban development, the city council decided to create a green belt consisting of parklands, a golf course, ice rinks, and several settling ponds used to recharge the groundwater system. This floodplain management program is designed to prevent deaths during flooding and at the same time provide recreational opportunities for the residents of the area. It is unlikely that the death and damage tolls of future floods will approach those of the 1972 flood.

Jay R. Yett

For Further Information:

Abbot, Patrick L. *Natural Disasters.* Dubuque, Iowa: Wm. C. Brown, 1996.

Lundgren, Lawrence. *Environmental Geology.* Englewood Cliffs, N.J: Prentice-Hall, 1986.

Rahn, Perry H. "Flood-Plain Management Program in Rapid City, South Dakota." *Geological Society of America Bulletin* 95 (1984): 838-843.

1972: Philippines

Date: July 18-August 12, 1972
Place: Manila, Philippines
Result: 536 dead, 1.2 million refugees, 6 million affected, $225 million in damage

Summer monsoon rains had already caused 32 deaths and widespread flooding when dikes failed in the main agricultural district of Luzon, north of Manila, Philippines, on July 13, 1972. A typhoon moved across the island five days later, bring thirty hours of intensive rainfall and the worst flooding in decades. By July 20, dikes had given way across 5 provinces, 142 were already known dead, and flooding had impacted 1.8 million victims. The death toll rose day by day, with little knowledge of conditions in outlying villages. Both Philippine and United States military personnel aided in rescue efforts, but the dimensions of the disaster were overwhelming. Government efforts to prevent starvation among the victims met with resistance and hoarding of food supplies. By August 1, with monsoon rains following the typhoon, all major highways and ground transportation links were flooded. July rainfall in Manila totaled 68.6 inches; farther north in hilly and mountainous terrain around Baguio, 15.6 feet of rain was recorded in July, causing landslides that buried even more victims.

Such conditions are ideal for the spread of disease, and in early August both cholera and typhoid were identified in the population. Inoculations could not reach the entire area, and at least 33 died from cholera. By August 4 the floodwaters began to recede, but most of the rice crop had been lost, and food riots were breaking out. Gangs of looters added to the death toll and to civilian unrest. Communist guerrillas were reported to be moving into the flood area and supporting the resistance of the more than 100,000 squatters who were being evicted from their housing on the waterways of Manila. Their presence on these drainage pathways had hampered flood-control efforts. Massive foreign aid was sought by Philippine authorities to aid in rebuilding and the recovery of the economy.

Neil E. Salisbury

For Further Information:

The New York Times, July 19-August 16, 1972.

1973: Mississippi River

Date: March-May, 1973

Place: Mississippi River, especially from southern Louisiana north to the junction of the Missouri River

Result: 33 dead, $1.155 billion in damage, more than 12 million acres flooded, record 77 consecutive days (St. Louis) to 88 days (Vicksburg, Mississippi) above flood stage

In giant river basins like the Mississippi's, floods do not arise from one day of rain or even the offspring of one week of storms. Most often, they are the consequence of a significant period of steady or exceptional rainfall or snowmelt. These floods depend upon antecedent moisture, the hydrologist's term for the conditions that cause the soil to be near saturation so that when a particulary heavy rainy period stalls over the basin, flooding is inevitable.

Such was the case with the Mississippi River basin in the spring of 1973. The entire basin recorded above-normal precipitation from October, 1972, to February, 1973. Much of the upper and western parts of the basin had more than 150 percent of normal precipitation. Although the Ohio River basin precipitation for this same period was below normal, that basin received 8 to 12 inches of moisture in the winter of 1972-1973. Had the Ohio River experienced the exceptional moisture of the Mississippi River basin, the flood would have been much more disastrous.

Thus, by March, 1973, the stage was set for unusually high and long-lasting floods. March was extremely wet in the Mississippi River basin. The lower Missouri River basin experienced four times its normal rainfall, and the upper Mississippi River basin (upstream of St. Louis) received twice its normal precipitation. April conditions continued to be very wet in the Tennessee Valley, in the Iowa-Wisconsin-northeastern Illinois region, and in the lower Mississippi River basin. This extraordinarily high monthly precipitation was the result of many days of rainfall caused by a succession of frontal storms, which would have resulted in a major flood even without the antecedent moisture of winter. Winter had left the flood-control reservoirs of the basin filled and the fields and soil saturated.

The major tributaries of Iowa, Missouri, Wisconsin, and Illinois were already full with stream flow when the prolonged rainy spell of March and April began. The reserved water emptied into the main stem of the Mississippi River. Finally, the week ending April 22 saw heavy rainfall in the basin as far north as Wisconsin, which exacerbated the flooding already in progress and contributed to the record peak river stage (flood level) recorded at St. Louis. The river stages were the highest ever recorded from Cape Girardeau, Missouri, upstream for 370 miles. Downstream of Cape Girardeau, the water levels were the highest since the disastrous 1937 flood, which had encouraged Congress to authorize a system of flood-control reservoirs and other engineering works in the Mississippi River basin.

Large basins like the Mississippi River basin are characterized by slow, steady increases in main stem flood levels, which are highly predictable and should afford plenty of time for evacuation. Damages will still occur to buildings and croplands, but flash flooding is not possible except on some tributary streams. The larger the basin, the less its tributaries flood. This differs from the flash flooding of smaller basins caused by heavy rainstorms or dam breaks, which overwhelm the population with their short warning times. They also lead to violent destruction of property and people being trapped by the flood, as opposed to the relatively slow and gradual soaking of buildings by rising water levels in the slower-paced large-basin floods.

Large floods are more benign; there is time to evacuate people, unless the levees break. In this case the waters rise faster, frequently with flash flood-like waves; people may be trapped; and loss of life is greater than in slow-rising flooding. It is a gamble that engineers, planners, and political decision makers take: Building levee systems will protect people and their possessions from smaller and more frequent floods but will leave them exposed to more hazardous flooding if the levees fail during infrequent large floods. Hydrologists believe that there is always a bigger flood coming in the future. No levee system has ever been built that will save a river floodplain from the largest floods.

The first serious consequences of the 1973 flood occurred in mid-March, in the Lower Mississippi River basin. By April 2, 6 million acres had been flooded south of St. Louis, with the Mississippi Delta-Yazoo River basin of northwestern Mississippi the hardest hit. Entire towns were isolated, and widespread evacuations were ordered. By April 4, levees were crumbling from southern Louisiana north to the junction of the Missouri River. The Army Corps of Engineers estimated that levees and flood walls had prevented $150 million in damages, but flooding was still widespread. St. Louis had not taken the necessary steps to make its citizens eligible for the new federal flood insurance under the National Flood Insurance Act of 1968, and in all of Missouri only 303 families were insured.

The Bonnet Carre floodway was opened north of New Orleans to divert floodwaters to nearby Lake Pontchartrain and the Gulf of Mexico. Even this could not halt the rising waters, and on April 17 the Morganza Dam was opened to increase water flow down the Atchafalaya River floodway. To create the floodways, easements were purchased, farmers moved out, and hunting clubs moved in to search for game. As estimated 2,000 deer were drowned as waters in the floodway rose, but 200 were saved. Inevitably, people living near the floodways or in flooded rural lands objected to the plan that saved New Orleans at the risk and expense of the less densely settled areas.

By April 29, the flood crest passed St. Louis at a record high level. The river did not drop below flood stage, however, until May 25, making this a record seventy-seven-day-long flood. Downstream, the river was above flood stage for as long as ninety-three days.

Neil E. Salisbury

For Further Information:

Belt, C. B., Jr. "The 1973 Flood and Man's Constriction of the Mississippi River." *Science*, August 29, 1975, 681-684.

Chin, Edwin H., John Skelton, and Harold P. Guy. *The 1973 Mississippi River Basin Flood: Compilation and Analyses of Meteorologic, Streamflow, and Sediment Data.* U.S. Geological Survey Professional Paper 937. Washington, D.C.: U.S. Government Printing Office, 1975.

The New York Times, March 16-May 29, 1973.

1974: Australia

Date: January 26-30, 1974
Place: Queensland, Australia
Result: 12 dead, 8,000 homeless, $160-$320 million in damage

To empty its floodwaters, a river has to flow either downhill, into the main stream if it is a tributary, or into the ocean if it is the main stream. If the body of water already has a high water level, the new floodwaters have no place to drain to, and backwater flooding results. This results in both higher flood stages and more extensive and long-lasting flooding. This was the case in January of 1974, when high tides and storm surges of tropical Cyclone Wanda (a hurricane in Western Hemisphere terminology) combined to prevent the rivers of eastern Australia from emptying their floodwaters into the ocean.

In the two weeks preceding the Queensland floods, New South Wales, adjoining to the south, had experienced extensive flooding that resulted in 1,000 homeless, 6 or more dead, and about $100 million in damage. Brisbane, the capital of Queensland, was hit by 24 inches of rain in forty-eight hours on January 25-26, with rains continuing. About 8,000 inhabitants were forced out of their homes, with more than one-third of the city under water. By the 29th, the weather had cleared and the floods began receding, but 90 percent of public transportation had been immobilized, food stocks had been destroyed in warehouses, and looting had become rampant. The coastal cities had been hard hit by the cyclone's rainfall. Moreover, vast areas (250,000 square miles) of the flatter interior were also under water in the worst flood in Australia since 1893.

Neil E. Salisbury

For Further Information:

The Times (London), January 28-31, 1974.

1974: Brazil

Tubarão River
Date: March 24, 1974
Place: Tubarão, Brazil
Result: 500-1,000 dead, city of Tubarão 70 percent destroyed, $250 million in damage

Torrential tropical rains over a two-week period in March, 1974, caused the worst recorded floods in Brazil's history. Hardest hit was Tubarão, a farm center squeezed between the mountains and the coast, and villages in its environs. Estimates of the dead were difficult to verify, as most of the city was buried in mud and bodies were carried out to sea. Water raced through the streets after strong ocean waves built up by an east wind prevented the Tubarão River from discharging its floodwater, whereupon it flowed through the city.

An estimated 70 percent of the city was destroyed, and another 20 percent was damaged. At least 10 percent of the population, particularly those who were wealthy, fled the city, many vowing never to return. Starvation was imminent for many, particularly in rural areas, which were cut off and could not be reached by rescue forces. Ironically, a ten-year development plan for the area had been completed just a week before the disaster. Afterward, survival was the major concern.

Neil E. Salisbury

For Further Information:
The New York Times, March 28-April 1, 1974.

1974: Bangladesh

Date: July to mid-August, 1974
Place: Bangladesh
Result: 2,000 or more dead, two-thirds of the nation flooded, 80 percent of summer crop lost

The country of Bangladesh was established in 1971 after unrest following the cyclone of 1970, which was responsible for the deaths of about 1 million persons. After that event, East Pakistan became Bangladesh, largely because of local dissatisfaction with the response of West Pakistan to the impact of the cyclone.

Bangladesh was subject to heavy flooding given its location near two major rivers. The Brahmaputra and Ganges Rivers flow south from the Himalayas and join in a giant delta at the head of the Bay of Bengal. Both rivers reach their peak flow in August, although they sometimes flood in July, as was the case in 1974. By early August, 1974, fifty days of flooding and related

Women in Tubarão, Brazil, await the distribution of medicine, flour, and other foodstuffs following severe nationwide flooding. (AP/Wide World Photos)

Victims of the 1974 Bangladesh flood leave their homes in search of dry land. (AP/Wide World Photos)

cholera had resulted in the deaths of over 500 people. Eventually, more than 2,000 may have died, but more serious is the fact that 80 percent of the summer crop—40 percent of the food supply—was lost. Starvation then took its toll, with foreign aid slow in coming and the distribution of food hampered by the lack of transport. People believed the delay in arrival of foreign aid was due to corruption and mismanagement of the government, which misdirected supplies once they had been delivered to the new nation.

Neil E. Salisbury

For Further Information:
The New York Times, July 31-August 18, 1974.

1976: Teton Dam Collapse

Date: June 5, 1976
Place: Near Rexburg, Idaho
Result: 11 dead, 1,000 injured, 30,000 homeless, 4,000 homes and businesses destroyed, $1 billion in damage

When dams fail, deadly flash floods are often created. The recently completed Teton Dam failed around noon on June 5, 1976. People were able to respond to the three-hour warning of trouble, but warning systems are rarely completely efficient, and 11 people lost their lives. The potential loss of life, however, was 35,000, making the fatality rate less than 0.1 percent. As the floodwaters receded, the anger of the survivors and other interested parties who had tried to block construction of the dam was as great as if many more had perished. A 35-mile-long strip of irrigated farmland and 6 communitites had been inundated, with an estimated loss of 4,000 homes, farmsteads, and businesses. Idaho Falls, a larger community downstream on the Snake River plain, had also suffered from flooding.

Most of the organized opposition to the dam's

construction had come from people who lived some distance from the dam site, largely from environmental groups who were concerned about both safety and ecological impact and who challenged the economic assumptions that supported the Bureau of Reclamation's decision to proceed with the project. They had failed in court, which ruled that the requirements of the Environmental Impact Assessment had been met.

In addition, questions had been raised by geologists concerning the nature of the bedrock underlying the 300-foot-high, 3,000-foot-long earth-filled structure. More than one investigative group examined the flood; an independent panel concluded that the dam failure was the result of poor engineering work by the Bureau of Reclamation. Specifically, according to the panel, "water from the reservoir traveled through fissures in the canyon wall, penetrated protective barriers that were supposed to block those fissures, and then traveled to the core of the dam where it eroded tunnels that weakened the sturcture and caused it to fail." The federal government paid hundreds of millions of dollars in claims and reimbursements.

Neil E. Salisbury

For Further Information:

Boffey, Philip M. "Teton Dam Verdict: A Foul-up by the Engineers." *Science* 195 (January 21, 1977): 270-272.

The New York Times, June 6-15, 29; July 8, 15; September 7, 19, 25, 1976.

1976: Colorado

Big Thompson River
Date: July 31-August 1, 1976
Place: Big Thompson Canyon, Loveland, Colorado
Result: 139 dead, $35 million damage

The Colorado Front Range and its southern extension, the Sangre de Cristo Mountains of southern Colorado and northern New Mexico, present ideal conditions for the development of late-day and evening thunderstorms. Generally, these storms form over the mountains and then move to the east, over the lower elevations of the Great Plains.

On the evening of July 31, 1976, huge convective thunderstorms exploded to heights of 62,000 feet above sea level, fed by unusually moist air at the ground surface. However, aspects of the storms were different from the usual scenario: Winds were light, and the storms failed to move east. The storms were stationary, and, instead of spreading 1 or 2 inches of rain along a long track, they dumped 6 to 12 inches in an hour or two on the foothills between Estes Park and Loveland, Colorado. The canyon of the Big Thompson River in the foothills is narrow, and the valley walls are steep. Moreover, the vegetation is transitional to the dry lands of the plains, and neither the soil nor the underbrush beneath the pines has great capacity for absorbing heavy rainfalls. The conditions were prime for a disastrous flash flood.

July 31 was a weekend night, and the canyon was crowded with as many as 4,500 people—tourists, campers, weekenders, and locals; the Big Thompson is a major route up to Rocky Mountain National Park. At 6:00 P.M., almost no rain was falling on the foothills. Within two to three hours, walls of water had rushed down the valley bottoms, sweeping automobiles, houses, and their inhabitants toward the plains in a mix of water, rocks, and mud. A total of 139 persons died and 5 remained missing, a hearteningly low toll considering the circumstances and the lack of warning. Many people, with difficulty, scrambled up the steep slopes to avoid the onrushing torrents.

All narrow mountain valleys are at risk for flash floods; survivors followed the warning signs erected along Colorado's highways that state, Climb to Safety. It took several days for helicopters to rescue people from the mountainsides. The highway was gone, destroyed in the flood. It took days to recover the victims' bodies from the debris. The known dead numbered 65 immediately after the flood, 98 on August 11, climbing to 130 on August 31, with the last victim recovered after September 27. Removal of the storm debris cost $1.6 million. There were serious questions raised as to whether the canyon should be reopened for transport and habitation, but flooding is a normal occurrence in all canyons. Rather than depopulate the mountains, the highway and the buildings were replaced.

Neil E. Salisbury

For Further Information:

McCain, Jerald F., et al. *Storm and Flood of July 31-August 1, 1976, in the Big Thompson River and Cache la Poudre River Basins, Larimer and Weld Counties,*

Colorado. Geological Survey Professional Paper 1115. Washington, D.C.: U.S. Government Printing Office, 1979.
The New York Times, August 2-October 3, 1976.

1978: India

Yamuna and Ganges Rivers
Date: September 4-29, 1978
Place: Northern India
Result: 1,291 dead, 1.5 million dwellings destroyed or damaged, 43 million displaced

In what became known as the worst monsoon in decades, flooding was scattered in northern India in July and August, 1978, with several casualties. September marked the beginning of the more serious events, at both ends of the Ganges River Valley. At the southern end, close to the Bay of Bengal, flash flooding on local streams west of Calcutta led to reports of 10,000 to 15,000 people being swept away. These figures were never confirmed, despite eyewitness accounts of "hundreds of bodies" being carried by the rivers. Such reports point up the difficulty of establishing accurate records of death and destruction, especially in developing nations, where dense rural populations become scattered by evacuation and communication is slow and imperfect under the best of conditions.

The major, large-river flooding occurred on the Yamuna and Ganges Rivers far to the west, where they exit the Himalayas and begin their journey to the sea. The Yamuna breached dikes in the Delhi area, disrupting transportation and causing the evacuation of 200,000 people. By September 9, the flooding had moved downriver, easing the situation in Delhi and New Delhi but threatening Agra, the location of the Taj Mahal and Varanasi. Temples and shrines were under water, although the Taj Mahal escaped destruction, and another 250,000 people were evacuated. By the 11th, the flood wave moved downstream, with waters receding from Delhi, Mathura, Agra, and Allahabad, where the Yamuna joins the Ganges.

The military was active in rescue efforts, but government actions were not without controversy, as Prime Minister Indira Gandhi and her party were campaigning against the Janata Party. Among other complaints, Gandhi pointed out that boats, which were in short supply, were not available for the rescue and evacuation of the poor. By the 15th, both the Yamuna and the Ganges Rivers had burst through their banks, engulfing hundreds of villages and isolating 15,000 more. As the flood wave moved downstream toward Calcutta, tens of millions of people were said to be displaced. The flood threat eased slightly on the 19th, but renewed rains flooded the Calcutta region on the 26th through the 29th, cutting off the city. The heavy monsoon rains were continental in scope: Laos, Vietnam, Burma, Nepal, and Afghanistan were flooded.

Neil E. Salisbury

For Further Information:

The New York Times, September 4-29, 1978.
The Times (London), September 4-29, 1978.

1981: China

Yellow River
Date: August 14-September 7, 1981
Place: Shanxi Province, China
Result: 764 dead, 5,000 injured, 200,000 homeless

Shanxi Province is immediately west of the North China Plain, where the Yellow River has historically taken a number of paths to the sea. The Yellow River flows along the southern and western borders of the hilly and mountainous province, but it was not the major culprit in the flooding of 1981. Although Shanxi Province is largely grassland used for grazing, the valleys are intensively cultivated, with high population densities. Like southern China and India, this dry land is dependent upon the summer monsoon for most of its moisture. The amount of rain, and its arrival time, is highly variable on the dry-land borders.

Heavy rains commenced on August 14, yielding up to 24 inches in a short time, more than the average annual amount. This resulted in flash flooding on the smaller streams of the mountainous terrain, with 250 villages swept away and more than 250,000 acres flooded. About 1.25 million people were affected by the flooding, with more than 200,000 of them left homeless. On this dry-land border, few forests exist under natural conditions, so deforestation can hardly be blamed for the floods, as is the case elsewhere in China. However, extensive expansion of terracing of the hillsides to permit crop growing probably increased sediment yields from the flood—silt that will end up in the Yellow River.

Neil E. Salisbury

For Further Information:
The New York Times, September 7, 1981.

1982: Nicaragua, Honduras

Date: May 26-28, 1982
Place: Nicaragua and Honduras
Result: 225 dead, 70,000 homeless

Five days of torrential tropical rainfall in the mountains of Nicaragua and Honduras left 15,000 people homeless and at least 10 dead by May 26, 1982. The next few days found the toll mounting. Troops took food to thousands who had been isolated for four days. On May 27, the governments of Honduras and Nicaragua appealed for international aid. By this time, 177 were known dead and 55,000 were homeless. The final toll after eight days of rain was 225 dead and an estimated 70,000 homeless.

The United States had cut off aid to Nicaragua in January, 1981, charging that the Sandinista government was supplying leftist rebels in El Salvador; however, it considered the request from the Nicaraguan government. The United States embassy in Managua, Nicaragua, had responded earlier with a $25,000 donation and 44 tons of food and supplies. Aid was forthcoming in response to the disaster, and much later relations between the two governments were smoothed over, not without political consequences in both nations.

Neil E. Salisbury

For Further Information:
The New York Times, May 26-29, 1982.

1982: India

Ganges River
Date: August 29-September 13, 1982
Place: India
Result: 700 dead, thousands of villages damaged or destroyed, millions evacuated

India expects hundreds of deaths each year as monsoon rains exceed the drainage capacities of the rivers. Evacuation of dwellings and farms is an annual event in the richest farming regions. On this basis, conditions in 1982 were about "normal," although that term must take into account the fact that different places are impacted to varying degrees. In 1982, the state of Orissa, southeast of Calcutta, suffered from both flash flooding and slower river-rising floods, the worst in memory. Flash floods derive from the hilly nature of the terrain, the Eastern Ghats, where small basins can flood quickly from torrential rains. Orissa is outside the major lowland of the Ganges Plain but has medium-size streams that flood in similar fashion, that is, more slowly and predictably.

Uttar Pradesh and Bihar were flooded by the annual rise of the Ganges River, with scores of villages inundated by the end of August. The flow of the Ganges usually peaks in August to September, and by the time the runoff receded in mid-September more than 30 million villagers had been affected by the flooding and at least 700 were dead.

Neil E. Salisbury

For Further Information:
The New York Times, August 29-September 9, 1982.
The Times (London), September 2-13, 1982.

1983: Bangladesh

Ganges and Brahmaputra Rivers
Date: May 1-4, 1983
Place: Bangladesh
Result: 75 dead, 50,000 homeless

Floods in Bangladesh, especially those with high death tolls and damage, generally stem from either runoff from the Himalayas via the Ganges and Brahmaputra Rivers or storm surges funneled from tropical cyclones moving up the Bay of Bengal. Often such disastrous floods are a combination of both these causes. The lowlands of eastern Bangladesh lay beneath another funnel, one created by the east-west trending Khasi Hills and the north-south trending mountains bordering Myanmar. This region of eastern India and Bangladesh may well have the world's heaviest precipitation year after year. Some parts receive over 400 inches of precipitation annually, with a record of more than 1,000 inches in a twelve-month period. This is a consequence of moisture-laden monsoonal air being uplifted over the highlands as it moves onshore.

The result in early May, 1983, was several days of particularly heavy storms, which killed 75 people and left 50,000 homeless. A period of flooding, evacuation, and homelessness is an almost annual event for many in this region, but to the outside world these miseries are overshadowed by the giant floods of the Ganges-Brahmaputra Delta. Such was the case in 1983, when elsewhere in Bangladesh, September storms killed 877 and drove nearly 1 million from their homes.

Neil E. Salisbury

For Further Information:

The Times (London), May 4, September 30, 1983.

1985: Italy

Date: July 19, 1985
Place: Stava, Italy
Result: 224 dead

A dam used to purify minerals from a fluorite mine collapsed shortly after noon in a narrow valley in the Dolomite Alps of northern Italy. A 150-foot-wide swath cut through the tourist village of Stava, destroying 3 hotels and part of a fourth, as well as 24 houses.

Although all life in the river was said to have been killed by pollution from the mine dam, the picturesque valley drew many tourists. Angry reactions from the Communist Party and citizens' groups blamed both offícals and the mine-dam owners for the tragedy. Questions arose concerning inspection of the earthen structure and enforcement of environmental rules. The dam's owners and some officials were arrested, reflecting feelings of frustration with the political process and the adherence to regulations.

Neil E. Salisbury

For Further Information:

The New York Times, July 20-29, 1985.

1988: Bangladesh

Date: July-September, 1988
Place: Bangladesh, especially the capital city of Dhaka
Result: About 2,400 dead, 30 million homeless, $1 billion in damage

Unusually heavy monsoon rains, rather than tropical cyclones, were to blame for the widespread and long-lasting flooding of the Ganges, Brahmaputra (which becomes the Jamuna), and Meghna Rivers that devastated Bangladesh in 1988, with floodwaters covering three-fourths of the nation at one point. By July 10, 121 people had been killed, 5 million were displaced or injured, and all roads were flooded in some districts. The worst flooding began in late August, with 32 inches of rain falling in three days. By September 1, 680 people were dead, 25 million had been displaced, and the capital city of Dhaka had been virtually cut off from the rest of the nation. By September 3, half of Dhaka was under water, mostly in the poor and middle-class districts. A renewed appeal was made for international relief aid, but it was difficult for supplies to be delivered because the Dhaka airport was under water.

By September 6, it was clear that Bangladesh had received the worst flooding in seventy years, with a cost of rebuilding that would exceed that of the 1987 flood, $4.5 billion. Although water levels began receding on the 7th, many people died from gastrointestinal problems or from snakebites. Water was contaminated, people were living on rooftops, and food was in short supply. The problem was regional; India had also experienced a death toll in the hundreds.

The Brahmaputra had a hundred-year-flood, that is, a discharge that could be expected only once in one hundred years. The Ganges and Meghna Rivers had fifty-year-floods. Rains on September 10 worsened the flooding. On the flat, low-lying landscape of Bangladesh, there was simply no place for the water to go after it reached its peak level—most of the nation is a floodplain or delta.

Although some experts believe that the flood was caused by human agency, research suggests it was largely natural in origin, resulting from the three rivers reaching their peak flows at the same time. Because most of the water in the rivers came from India, Bangladeshi authorities blamed deforestation in India's hills and mountains for the floods. They sought a multinational plan to control the annual flooding, involving also India, Nepal, Bhutan, and China, the headwaters (sources) of the streams that reach the ocean by passing through Bangladesh. India proved to be resistant to the plan, so Bangladesh made its case to the United Nations General Assembly in October, pointing out that the 1988 flood had destroyed 1.25 million homes and 8 million people were still homeless.

Neil E. Salisbury

For Further Information:

Brammer, H. "Floods in Bangladesh I: Geographical Background to the 1987 and 1988 Floods." *Geographical Journal* 156 (March, 1990): 12-22.

_______. "Floods in Bangladesh II: Flood Mitigation and Environmental Aspects." *Geographical Journal* 156 (July, 1990): 158-165.

The New York Times, August 28-September 22; October 11, 1988.

Smith, Keith, and Roy Ward. *Floods: Physical Processes and Human Impacts.* Chichester, England: John Wiley & Sons, 1998.

1991: China

Yangtze River
Date: July, 1991
Place: Southeastern China
Result: 1,781 dead, estimated $7.5 billion in economic losses

The summer rains came twenty days early in 1991, and they were torrential, flooding rivers, including the Yangtze and the Huai, in several southern and eastern provinces. Jiangsu Province, near the coast, and Anhui Province were the hardest hit. Nanjing on the Yangtze, and Shanghai, at the mouth of the Yangtze, suffered, as well as many smaller cities. In Yangzhou city, 610,000 people were evacuated. Overall, about a million acres of farmland were under water, putting the fall grain harvest at risk. For the first time in Communist government history, an appeal was made for international aid. Responses were quick from Hong Kong, which supplied 80 percent of the aid, and from Taiwan, where Chiang Soong Mei-ling, widow of former Chinese president Chiang Kai-Shek, pledged $782,000.

The death toll was lower than the average annual flood toll of 3,000, but economic costs were extremely high. The army regained some respect for its rescue efforts, but the highest government officials were criticized for doing "too little, too late." By July 24, typhoons were moving into the southern coastal areas, bringing heavy rains and more death.

Neil E. Salisbury

For Further Information:

The Times (London), July 10-24, 1991.

1993: The Great Mississippi River Flood of 1993

Date: June-August, 1993
Place: Primarily Minnesota, Wisconsin, Iowa, Illinois, and Missouri
Result: 52 dead, 74,000 homeless, $18 billion in damage

Unlike other natural disasters, it is extremely difficult to pinpoint the actual starting point of the Great Mississippi River Flood of 1993. The river's upper basin experienced above-normal rainfall levels in the spring that resulted in some earlier flooding, and fall weather produced subsequent flooding as well. Yet since the greatest carnage occurred during the heavy rains from June through August, 1993, most experts use these parameters as the official beginning and end of the great flood of 1993.

Causes. The flood of 1993 can be attributed to the record rainfall that dominated the Midwest's weather during the summer of 1993. Other surface meteorological conditions, however, also played a pivotal role. Prior to the flood, the ground was already saturated, as soil moisture levels remained exceptionally high. Heavy winter snowmelt and spring rains further increased the dangers of flooding as the Mississippi River's vast tributary system began emptying its excess into the river. This water, moreover, substantially increased the chances of daily precipitation, since evaporation tends to be recirculated in the form of rainfall. From June through August, the Upper Mississippi River basin rainfall was 200 percent above normal, and the 20 inches of rain was the highest recorded total dating back to 1895. Along the Iowa shores alone it exceeded 36 inches. This problem was further exacerbated by the unusual number of cloudy days that not only inhibited the sun's ability to dry the land but also increased the likelihood of daily showers.

Human and Property Costs. The flood primarily affected the Upper Mississippi River basin in the area located north of Cairo, Illinois. While the damage affected commerce, industry, and housing in over one-third of the United States, the heaviest flooding occurred in various river towns in Minnesota, Wisconsin, Iowa, Illinois, and Missouri.

This event represented the most costly flood on record in American history. Although the flood of 1927 resulted in the loss of 313 lives, compared to 52 in 1993, the property damage was much more extensive. Floodwaters significantly ruined various portions of the physical landscape, wreaked havoc on river ecosystems, and destroyed crops. Its impact on the transportation system and agricultural income ravaged the region. Barges were unable to travel on the river for eight weeks. Major roads and highways were closed, often forcing people to miss work. Millions of acres of prime farmland remained under water for weeks, significantly weakening the country's food production, and soil erosion destroyed some of the best farmland in the country. Homes, farms, industries, and entire towns were obliterated by the river's rising waters. Communities fought to stave off the flood by organizing sandbagging activities to reinforce and raise the capacity of levees, and while some succeeded, over 1,000 levees eventually ruptured. All this carnage compelled President Bill Clinton to declare the region a disaster area, but local, state, and national agencies struggled to meet the demands of unprecedented relief efforts. While some individuals eagerly accepted assistance and attempted to rebuild their lives, many simply relocated to higher ground, believing that an idyllic life along the river's banks was no longer possible.

Infrastructure Costs. This flood also produced dire consequences for the entire ecosystem along the Mississippi River. Herbicides from flooded farms were washed into the river and eventually threatened fisheries in the Gulf of Mexico. Deforestation occurred, and trees that survived remained highly vulnerable to disease, insect attack, and stress. Flooding provided various pest species, such as mosquitoes, with ample breeding grounds. When a fish farm

Two bridges over the Mississippi River were washed out during the 1993 flood. (FEMA)

flooded on one of the river's tributaries, the Asian black carp escaped and endangered mussels and clams. Finally, ducks, which traditionally migrated to the region just in time for hunting season, bypassed the region because all the natural habitats and food sources were destroyed in the flood.

Agricultural and livestock production significantly declined as well and generated almost $9 billion in losses. Minnesota farmers burned wheat fields because they were too saturated to harvest. Corn and soybean yields dropped by 30 percent. These losses aided farmers in Indiana, Ohio, and other states that remained dry, but overall the loss of agricultural income decimated many state economies and forced the federal government to assume responsibility for disaster relief.

Other record losses shattered the transportation network. Damages to the infrastructure and revenue losses totaled $2 billion and forced many people out of work. Barges carry approximately 15 percent of all freight in America, with most of this traffic taking place along the Mississippi River. With the flood, however, over 2,900 barges and 50 towboats were stranded. Once the river reached the flood stage in June, the U.S. Army Corps of Engineers halted all barge traffic, and by the end of July this industry was losing $3 million per day. This also caused widespread unemployment in St. Louis as over 3,200 dockworkers were laid off.

The railroad industry experienced similar problems; its losses amounted to $241 million. Tracks, bridges, and signals were decimated and forced companies to close or to seek alternate routes. Industry leaders such as Union Pacific and Canadian Pacific were forced to halt operations from Wisconsin to St. Louis. Amtrak's Memphis-to-Chicago run had to be diverted 900 miles off course in order to complete its journey.

States were also forced to close roads and highways. More than 100 flooded roads and 56 bridges were shut down in Wisconsin, and in Missouri, many workers faced hours of delay in their daily commute to work. Finally, and most threatening, bridge traffic came almost to a halt. In early July, bridges were closed in Hannibal, Missouri, and Keokuk, Iowa. When the Quincy, Illinois, levee broke on July 15, there was no way to cross the river for a 250-mile area north of St. Louis. Coupled with the inability of ferries to operate in this weather, trucks and buses were forced to add over 200 miles to traditional delivery and transportation routes. Damage in this sector alone spawned over $1 billion in repair costs.

Personal Losses. Nothing, however, outweighed the personal tragedies. More than 74,000 people lost their homes, heirlooms, and belongings. As water levels swelled and levees ruptured, entire communities were eliminated, and for many the carnage was so immense that they decided to never return to the river's edge. While the flood claimed many victims, the river towns did not go down without a fight. Communities built temporary levees with sandbags, plywood, and concrete. As the river continued to rise, people risked their safety to remain on the levees checking for seepage, leaks, and sand boils. These attempts, however, were highly unsuccessful. Over 80 percent of all state and local levees failed, causing many towns to evacuate.

Other towns were decimated beyond repair. Residents of Grafton, Illinois, along one of the most scenic stretches of highway in America, the Great River Road, were forced to flee as water covered the rooftops of many two-story homes. Roads in Alton, Illinois, were impassable, and water virtually obliterated many of the town's historic landmarks. In Valmeyer, Illinois, the community labored to save the town, only to see it completely demolished by the flood. In fact, when the waters receded, Valmeyer residents decided to relocate their entire town to a bluff overlooking the river instead of rebuilding on the banks. The entire island of Kaskaskia, Illinois, was covered with over 20 feet of water after its 52-foot-high levee broke. Most residents felt confident that they could withstand this disaster, but their plight clearly reveals the power of the Mississippi. At 9:48 A.M. on July 22, the levee ruptured, and since the island's bridge had previously been flooded out, everyone was forced to flee on two Army Corps of Engineers barges. Many livestock could not get out and drowned. By 2 P.M. Kaskaskia Island was entirely covered by water.

Effects on Towns. Both the devastation and personal courage that the flood generated can be observed in the story of one community. As the water traveled south down the river, the historic town of St. Genevieve, Missouri, was directly threatened. The home of several historical landmarks, including a number of two-hundred-year-old French colonial buildings, this town was the first European settlement west of the Mississippi River. It had experienced tragic floods in the past and had responded by building an elaborate set of levees and flood walls. It had survived the flood of 1973 when the river crested at 43 feet, and it had already begun to recover from a brief period of flooding in April. Yet nothing in its history could prepare St. Genevieve for its upcoming battle with the river.

Largely a town filled with quaint bed-and-breakfast inns, restaurants, and antique shops, St. Genevieve depended upon tourism for its survival. While the flood eliminated this industry and virtually destroyed the town's economy, it did not diminish the community's energetic struggle to avoid disaster. By the middle of July, Governor Mel Carnahan ordered in the National Guard in an effort to save one of America's most valuable historic treasures. The media quickly flocked to Missouri to cover this event, and St. Genevieve was featured on every major news network. The governor also allowed local prison inmates to work on the levee, and volunteers flocked to Missouri to fill sandbags and offer relief help. For the rest of July, the nation watched as St. Genevieve fought for its survival.

The river, however, continued to rise. By the end of July, as the water level reached 48 feet, one levee ruptured, sending more than 8 feet of water over sections of the town, damaging a number of homes and businesses and knocking some buildings right off their foundation; the people continued to fight. Volunteers worked at a feverish pace to raise the main levee to 51 feet and staved off disaster when the river crested at a record level 49 feet on August 6. Employees at a local plastic plant saved their factory by volunteering their time to build a levee around their plant. Yet the flood claimed several casualties. Forty-one historic buildings were damaged, tourism became nonexistent, and all the levee work had significantly undermined the town's service infrastructure.

The city of St. Louis, however, was spared. Once the river exceeded the 30-foot flood level, water started to steadily creep up the steps of the Gateway Arch. Several barges, including one containing a Burger King restaurant, broke away and crashed into the Popular Street Bridge. Oil refineries and petroleum processing plants threatened to dump poisonous chemicals into the river. Yet despite springing several leaks, the 50-foot flood wall held. Cities such as Des Moines, Iowa, and Kansas City and St. Joseph, Missouri, suffered record losses, but St. Louis's riverfront property remained dry.

The Great Mississippi River Flood of 1993 was the most costly flood in recorded history to date. Some experts claim it represents a five-hundred-year-flood of unprecedented proportions due to its length, volume, and carnage. It permanently eliminated numerous small towns, obliterated historical treasures, and destroyed priceless memories such as wedding pictures, souvenirs, high school yearbooks, and family correspondence. While the Midwest's struggle with the raging river held the nation's attention for only a few months, the devastation it wrought will be forever remembered as one of the most costly natural disasters in history.

Robert D. Ubriaco, Jr.

For Further Information:

Burnett, Betty. *The Flood of 1993: Stories from a Midwestern Disaster.* Tuscon, Ariz.: Patrice Press, 1994. This text is a collection of articles from various journalists covering the flood. It is an informative source on the social history of the disaster and provides many worthwhile personal recollections.

Changnon, Stanley, ed. *The Great Flood of 1993: Causes, Impacts, and Responses.* Boulder, Colo.: Westview Press, 1994. A series of academic articles, this source analyzes the causes and the impact of the flood and is especially helpful for those interested in weather conditions and infrastructure costs. Also furnishes an extremely valuable chronology of the flood.

"In Their Own Words." *St. Louis Post-Dispatch,* September 5, 1993, p. C1. This article contains several stories from the experiences of volunteers, residents, and officials during the flood, which offer special insight into the personal side of this tragedy.

National Weather Service. *The Great Flood of 1993.* National Disaster Survey Report. Washington, D.C.: National Oceanic and Atmospheric Administration, 1994. This text serves as the official scientific source on the flood.

1995: California

Date: January, 1995
Place: Primarily Northern California but also as far south as San Diego
Result: 11 dead, $300 million in damage

El Niño was blamed for heavy rains affecting much of California, particularly the coastal counties, in early January, 1995. Flooding began to affect the Russian

River town of Guerneville on the 8th, with the Petaluma and Napa Rivers near flood stage. By the 9th, the Eel, Smith, Van Duzen, and Sacramento Rivers were also near or above flood stage. The next day, the storm had swept south; Santa Barbara received 8 inches of rain in twenty-four hours and 14 inches in eight days. This one storm would deliver nearly the average annual rainfall to that area.

Twenty-four counties were declared disaster areas, and ten more would be added two days later, meaning that more than half of California was eligible for federal assistance in rebuilding after the floodwaters receded. Before the sun came out, however, the storms had spread from the Oregon border south to near San Diego. Mudslides were common; large trees, including redwoods, were uprooted from the saturated soil, causing death and damaging property. Roads and schools were closed, and several thousand people were living in shelters.

The Interstate 5 bridge near Coalinga, California, was washed out on March 10, 1995. (AP/Wide World Photos)

A new storm renewed flood pressures in Northern California on January 13 and 14. The Sacramento area was particularly hard hit, with flooding occurring in the Rio Linda area north of the city. Despite billions of dollars being spent on flood-control measures (the Sacramento River ranks second to the Mississippi River on flood-control expenditures), floods recur as people move onto floodplains after dams are built, giving them a false sense of security. High levees and flood walls protect settlements from smaller, more frequent flooding but cause more serious risks when the levees break, as they often do. The policy of allowing floodplain development, even encouraging it with federal flood insurance, was questioned after this flood event.

Although the 1995 storm was not as severe as that of 1986, 1995's storm season was not over. In March, severe storms, worse than January's in some places, again affected more than half of California.

Neil E. Salisbury

For Further Information:
The New York Times, January 9-15, 1995.

1995: Northern Europe

Date: January-February, 1995
Place: Belgium, France, Germany, and the Netherlands
Result: 30 dead, $2 billion in damage

Rivers rose to record levels in northwestern Europe as a result of days of rain and warm weather melting the snowpack. The rivers generally rise late each winter, but 1995 was a particularly wet year. On January 31, the Rhine River at Cologne crested at its highest level since the eighteenth century, flooding the riverside restaurants. The only traffic in the city was on boats. Embassies, including that of the United States, were closed in Bonn.

Downstream in the Netherlands, conditions were even more severe. Weakened dikes forced authorities to order the evacuation of 200,000 people. Farm animals were moved out of harm's way. Shipping along the waterways, both rivers and canals, was halted for fear of crumbling the dikes. The dikes are composed of sand and clay and fail when the water levels drop rapidly, as was the case on February 2 and 3. The Rhine River is the world's busiest waterway, and the nearby rivers and canals are important; consequently, the impact on the economies of these European nations was severe. Total damages may have approached $2 billion, with indirect costs difficult to calculate.

For such a large flood, the death toll was relatively low, about 30. This is because the rivers rose slowly and predictably and authorities had time to warn the inhabitants of threatened areas. In contrast, when the sea dikes failed in the Netherlands in 1953, waters rushed in quickly, as in a flash flood, and more than 1,800 people died.

Neil E. Salisbury

For Further Information:
The New York Times, January 30-February 4, 1995.

1996: Spain

Date: August 7-8, 1996
Place: Northern Spain
Result: 70 campers dead in the Pyrenees

A flash flood killed at least 70 campers and injured 200 more in a crowded campground near Biescas in the Spanish Pyrenees. About 650 people, mostly Spaniards, were in the campground when torrential rains caused an avalanche. Mud and rocks tore through the campsite, tossing cars and campers about. Eight bodies were recovered from a reservoir 9 miles down the Gallego River, attesting to the strength of the floodwaters.

Deaths from flash floods are not uncommon in Spain in summer; the previous year 11 were killed in a storm. The Green Group political party accused the government of criminal negligence for licensing the campground. The government's response was that it is impossible to predict flash floods. This is true in the timing of the floods; rainstorms are random in their occurrence, although rains have a seasonal preference in different regions. Improved radar may aid in "real-time" predictions, allowing for warnings to be issued.

Neil E. Salisbury

For Further Information:
The New York Times, August 8-9, 1996.

1996: U.S. West Coast

Date: December 26, 1996-January 7, 1997
Place: Washington State, Oregon, California, and Nevada
Result: 36 dead, $2-3 billion in damage

The U.S. West Coast receives most of its precipitation in the winter; snow high in the mountains, rain at lower elevations. Of critical importance in determining whether or not flooding will occur is not only the total amount of precipitation and the intensity with which it falls but also the temperature of the air mass that delivers the moisture. Cold air, with an origin near Alaska, usually brings snow to the chillier high elevations of the mountain ranges, with rain at the warmer lower elevations below the freeze line. A storm of this type is less likely to produce flooding than a "warm" storm, because most of the snow will be stored on the mountain slopes until spring.

The storms of late December, 1996, and early January, 1997, were the offspring of a "Pineapple Express," or warm, tropical air following the path of the jet stream straight from Hawaii. Warm air holds more moisture and yields heavier snowfall, which does not wait until spring to melt, but rushes down the mountain slopes to increase the likelihood of flooding.

In western Washington, around Seattle, by December 27 snow and freezing rain had paralyzed the city and the region. The three motor routes across the Cascade Mountains were closed by heavy snowfall, airplane flights were canceled with hundreds stranded in the airport terminal, 300,000 homes were without power, and downtown Seattle resembled a ghost town on this Friday after Christmas. Only the coffee shops remained open. Two days later a second storm struck, with 2 feet of snow, sufficient to collapse some roofs and close additional roads in the region extending down to Portland, Oregon. The last days of 1996 brought a calm between storms; airports and roads were reopened, but 65,000 homes were still without power.

Seattle is a hilly city and one that is unaccustomed to heavy snows (some residents boast that Dallas has higher average winter snowfall). Buses and automobiles were stalled everywhere, especially at intersections and the bottoms of hills. By this time the two storms had killed 11 people and caused an estimated $125 million in damage, and a state of emergency had been declared in western Washington. More storms and more rain would bring flooding and mudslides. It was the region's most serious natural disaster in years.

The first days of 1997 brought more rain and snow, which in the higher elevations melted rapidly in the warm air. Flood warnings were issued for every western slope river north of San Francisco. The effects of the storms extended south to Yosemite National Park, where 2,500 people were trapped by snow and the flooding Merced River. About 50,000 people were evacuated from Yuba City and Maryville, California, the site of large-scale flooding in 1955-1956, when it was feared the levees would not hold back high waters flowing from the Oroville Reservoir. Although that project, constructed after the 1955-1956 disaster, was supposed to provide flood protection, the dimensions of the 1996-1997 floods were overwhelming reservoirs elsewhere.

Giant sinkholes opened up on some of Seattle's roads, and mudslides were feared in some of the more hilly and affluent neighborhoods. The storm's impact extended eastward to Reno, Nevada, where the twenty-four-hour casinos were closed for the first time in recent memory as the Truckee River flooded downtown. Flooding and mudslides isolated communities in Idaho. January 3 brought some respite, floods began receding, and the Yosemite tourists were freed, but many highways and rail lines were still blocked. The governors of the five states had declared a state of emergency in ninety counties. Rivers began receding from their highest levels, and businesses struggled to reopen.

On January 4 the sun began shining as the storms moved eastward. An estimated 1,500 to 2,000 homes had been destroyed, and even in the calm, the weakened levees were giving way to the still-high water levels, bringing additional flooding to the Central Valley of California communities and those of western Nevada. Outside the storm area, Southern California was affected because it receives much of its water from Northern California. These northern flooded waters were now polluted by dead farm animals; agricultural pesticides and other chemicals; the inundation of sewage plants; and saltwater intrusion from San Francisco Bay into the source canals of the delta.

Neil E. Salisbury

For Further Information:

The New York Times, December 28, 1996-January 7, 1997.

1997: Red River

Date: April, 1997
Place: North Dakota and Minnesota
Result: Most of Grand Forks under water, nearly 1 million acres of farmland flooded

The Red River Valley of the North Dakota-Minnesota border is not a typical river valley. No high bluffs define the alluvial bottoms; indeed, there are scarcely any alluvial bottoms. The rivers are incised only a few feet below what is arguably the largest, flattest surface in North America: the lake plain known as the leavings of glacial Lake Agassiz. Compounding any potential flooding of the Red River is the fact that it flows northward to Canada; it is part of the Arctic Ocean drainage. This area is cold in winter, and most floods arise because of melting snow. The waters flow north to still-frozen Canada, backing up in floods because there is no place for the water to drain.

The winter of 1996-1997 was especially snowy, at least twice the normal for the valley as a whole, with three times the normal snowfall in places. Meltwater flooding had already begun in the northern plains when a blizzard struck on April 5, 1997, building drifts up to 20 feet high and leaving levee workers piling sandbags. The dikes failed at Breckenridge, Minnesota, near the headwaters of the Red River on April 6, causing the evacuation of hundreds of people. By the 11th, the flood had crested at Fargo-Moorhead, the twin cities of North Dakota and Minnesota, without serious flooding, although the river was at its highest stage in over one hundred years. The Army Corps of Engineers, responsible for most flood efforts in the United States, had predicted high flood levels because of the heavy snowpack and had been at work for several weeks, raising and strengthening the dikes.

A man stumbles through high waters in East Grand Forks, Minnesota, after the 1997 flooding of the Red River. (AP/Wide World Photos)

On the 18th and 19th, the dikes at Grand Forks-East Grand Forks, North Dakota, some of which were 50 feet high—the biggest hills in the Red River Valley—were overtopped, and most of the 50,000 residents of Grand Forks and 8,500 from the Minnesota side were evacuated. Fires in downtown Grand Forks complicated the process. President Bill Clinton was on the scene on April 22, promising a Marshall Plan approach to recovery and rebuilding, including a request to Congress for more relief funding. About 70 percent of Grand Forks was flooded. Because nearly 90 percent of the homes were above the hundred-year-floodplain level, no federally supported flood insurance was available to them.

The floods moved north to the Canadian border, where the normal 300-foot-wide river had swollen to 20 miles in width. About 24,000 people were evacuated on the Canadian side of the border, and Winnipeg's flood defenses held. Grand Forks residents were finally allowed back to their mud-encased homes at the end of April to begin the task of rebuilding, aided by a $2,000 donation per flooded family from an anonymous donor. Federal funds were slower in coming; floods are often seen as an opportunity for political wrangling. A disaster-relief bill in Congress was held up for weeks as Republicans attached unrelated amendments in an attempt to bypass President Clinton's veto. He vetoed the bill anyway, the Republicans capitulated, and the disaster-relief bill was finally passed on June 15.

Neil E. Salisbury

For Further Information:

The New York Times, April 5-27; May 1, 6-8, 22, 24; June 10, 13, 1997.

1997: Central Europe

Rhine and Oder Rivers
Date: July-August, 1997

Place: Central Europe, especially Poland and the Czech Republic
Result: 104 dead, $6 billion in damage

The region of Europe between the Rhine and Oder Rivers was ravaged by forty floods between 1945 and 1999. As late as 1996, the Rhine reached a flood stage of 33 feet (10 meters) in Cologne, Germany. Yet observers called the flood of July, 1997, which affected all of Central Europe, the "flood of the century." Beginning on July 5 and lasting for five days, rain poured from the skies over Central Europe. This was followed ten days later by another rainstorm, which swelled the rivers beyond their banks, particularly the Oder, which originates in the mountains of Moravia in the Czech Republic and flows north until it empties into the Baltic Sea near Szczecin.

Weather experts note that the disaster was caused by what the specialists describe as an exaggerated "5b" phenomenon. This is the typical weather front that brings to the eastern Alps region rain in the summer and snow in the winter. However, in 1997 the cold front was unusually cold, and the warm front in the Mediterranean was uncommonly hot. A cold front over Great Britain sent cold polar air to the Adriatic region on July 4. In Italy the cold front mixed with warm air and moved to the eastern regions of the Alps in Austria and the Czech Republic, where it met hot, moist air coming from Greece in the Balkans. In Greece it had been unusually warm, with temperatures reaching 104 degrees Fahrenheit (40 degrees Celsius), ensuring the evaporation of massive amounts of sea water.

The mixture of cold and moist, warm air resulted in torrential rain over the Carpathian Mountains and the Giant Mountains of the Czech Republic between July 6 and 10. The Czech weather station in the northwestern Carpathian Mountains recorded the rainfall during this five-day period and discovered that it was equal to the total amount of annual precipitation in the German state of Brandenburg. Some experts argue that the intensity of the rain may reflect a greenhouse effect. They note that after 1930 the number of low-pressure systems over the North Atlantic and Europe doubled, and the amount of rain increased because of warmer temperatures in the Mediterranean regions.

All of Central Europe was affected by these massive rainstorms, which caused billions of dollars of destruction and resulted in the death of over 100 people. Austria suspended barge traffic on the Danube for 60 miles between Linz and Krems because of high water. In some areas in lower Austria, near Vienna, water reached the rooftops. One motorcyclist was killed after skidding on a flooded road. In Romania, rivers across the state broke their banks in late July, causing 1 death by drowning. Even in Italy the foul weather spawned a tornado in the beach resort of Bibione near Venice, injuring 40 people.

Poland and the Czech Republic suffered the most fatalities. In the Czech Republic the flood was responsible for the death of 46 people. Two-fifths of the Czech Republic was affected by the flood, resulting in damage to thousands of homes and communities at a time when the country already faced major economic problems. Poland registered the largest loss of lives, and the state declared a day of national mourning for the 56 dead. The rain from the Czech mountain area, where many trees died because of pollution, gorged the Oder, which flows through southwestern Poland. By July 22, 1.3 million acres of land were flooded and 140,000 people had been evacuated. Southwestern Poland, where one-quarter of the population lives, suffered the most. It is an area that produces 26 percent of the national income.

The German state of Brandenburg, which shares the Oder River as a border with Poland, also suffered massive material losses, although no direct deaths were caused by the flood. The dikes on the German side were endangered in three different places, but the most critical area was the Oderbruch, an area of former marshland 15 miles wide and 55 miles along the Oder, which was turned into agricultural land in the eighteenth century. Thousands of German soldiers worked frantically to plug the dikes.

Much help came from the German and Polish armies and the Red Cross. German television and radio stations collected funds, and the German post office issued a special stamp to raise funds for the victims. There was, however, also much recrimination. Poles blamed Czechs for emptying reservoirs, which added water to the Oder, and Germans blamed Poles for not providing enough information about the situation in the upper Oder regions. The Polish prime minister, Wlodzimierz Cimoszewicz, even scolded Polish citizens who had not purchased flood insurance.

In addition to the loss of billions of dollars of property, massive pollution resulted from dead animals, sewage, and flooded gas stations. Swedish experts warned of danger to the Baltic Sea, and Polish scientists cautioned against the excessive use of chlorine. Aside from the material reconstruction, there was also the need for long-term solutions, particularly since as early as 1994 a Polish official had warned of a lack of flood protection. One plan was to establish an international flood warning system similar to that of the Rhine. Dike repairs were also essential, but many scientists urged the reconstruction of natural marshes along the Oder and massive reforestation in the Czech Repulic. As in other regions of the world facing similar problems, the perplexing issue was how to protect the population living in the floodplain.

Johnpeter Horst Grill

For Further Information:

Boyes, Roger. "Kohl Tries to Keep Head Above Flood." *The Times* (London), July 29, 1997, p. 11.

Collcutt, Deborah. "Collapse of Dike Forces Germans to Flee." *The Times* (London), July 24, 1997, p. 16.

_______. "Germans Put on Alert for Flood Exodus." *The Times* (London), July 19, 1997, p. 14.

Cowell, Alan. "River Rises: So Does German Mettle." *The New York Times*, July 19, 1997, p. A4.

_______. "With Nearly 100 Dead, Floods Keep Raging in Central Europe." *The New York Times*, July 21, 1997, p. A6.

Walker, Ruth. "Bursting Levees Strain Europe's New Democracies." *The Christian Science Monitor*, July 28, 1997, p. 1.

1997: Arizona

Colorado River
Date: August 12, 1997
Place: Antelope Canyon, Arizona
Result: 11 dead

A thunderstorm 15 miles away sent an 11-foot wall of water down Antelope Canyon, a tributary of the Colorado River near Page, Arizona, killing 11 hikers. The only survivor was the guide to a group of hikers, who clutched a ledge as he was washed downstream, his clothing torn off by the ferocity of the floodwaters. The canyon is one of several near the upper portion of the Grand Canyon that are particularly photogenic, with near-vertical, narrow, twisting, brightly colored walls that draw tourists and photographers from around the world. Nine of the victims were Europeans who may have been unaware of the dangers posed by thunderstorms; severe storm warnings had been issued for the area, and several people warned the hikers of danger. Two days earlier, 650 residents and tourists had to be airlifted out of the Havasupai Indian Reservation, located on the south rim of the Grand Canyon, because of flash flooding.

More sophisticated technology for warnings in remote regions has been developed but is often thwarted by vandalism or by the difficulties posed by deep canyons and valleys in receiving radio transmissions. On the Colorado plateaus, including the Grand Canyon area, summer is the time of dangerous monsoon rainstorms, and narrow canyons should be avoided.

Neil E. Salisbury

For Further Information:

The New York Times, August 10-18, 1997.

1998: China

Yangtze River
Date: July 27-August 31, 1998
Place: China
Result: 3,000 dead, millions homeless, $20 billion economic loss

Flooding from the summer rains affected many areas in China in 1998, most seriously along the Yangtze River and in Heilongjiang Province in the north. Large lakes along the lower course of the Yangtze have been used for some time as overflow outlets during floods, thus relieving pressure on the larger cities. Dongting Hu Lake in Hunan Province, where the Yangtze begins its exit from the hilly and mountainous terrain of the interior, is an example.

The year 1998 brought the worst flooding in forty years, overwhelming the capacity of the lake, which had been reduced by a third because of siltation from upstream erosion. Thus, the lake itself became flooded by July 27, and 300,000 refugees spent weeks living precariously on its dike system. On August 5, the army, which was deeply involved in both rescue operations and flood-control measures, began opening dikes and deliberately flooding farmland in order to save the large cities downstream, particularly Wuhan, an industrial center with a population of 7 million. Needless to say, the farmers objected; 60,000 people evacuated on short notice from the area were now homeless.

By August 21, the Yangtze had experienced its sixth flood crest, and Wuhan was still at risk. Meanwhile, in Heilongjiang Province in the north, flooding endangered not only the farm and urban population but also the nation's largest oil field. The Yangtze River problem was especially acute, because one potential but controversial solution, the construction of the Three Gorges Dam, would absorb most of the money that could be used for alternative flood-control measures. The Chinese government conceded three major mistakes in policy and announced sweeping changes. Deforestation in the upper reaches of the Yangtze undoubtedly contributed to flooding; logging would cease and reforestation would begin. Human invasion of the wetlands along the river had been allowed, indeed encouraged, by drainage projects; the lakes and wetlands would be restored. The upkeep of the dikes had been badly neglected, the necessary resources having been diverted into the Three Gorges Dam project.

President Jiang Zemin made protection of the river's main dikes the first priority. Logging was halted immediately, and reforestation, which employs only a third as many workers as logging, commenced. The province was to receive funding to aid in the transition to a nonlogging economy. At the same time, local officials in former wetland zones anticipated that farmers would move back in and rebuild once the floodwaters drained, regardless of the government's pronouncements.

Neil E. Salisbury

For Further Information:

The New York Times, July 27-August 31; September 3, 27, 1998.

1998: Texas

Date: October 17-21, 1998
Place: Southern Texas

A soldier carries a child through floodwaters in Wuzhou, China, in 1998. (AP/Wide World Photos)

Result: 31 dead, at least 1,500 evacuated in 60 counties

In 1998 South Texas was suffering from extreme heat and drought, resulting in some water restrictions and rationing. Then, on August 23, Tropical Storm Charley from the Gulf of Mexico dumped 18 inches of rain on Del Rio, which had averaged only 17 inches in a full year. The result was a flood, which destroyed 625 homes and severely damaged another 937. Additional damage was sustained on the Mexican side of the border, and all together at least 15 deaths were attributed to the floods. In Laredo 3 bridges between the two countries had to be closed.

The worst was yet to come. On October 17 a Pacific cold front stalled over south-central Texas and began drawing tropical moisture from two hurricanes off the west coast of Mexico. The resulting storms spawned tornadoes near Caldwell and Corsicana that killed 2 people. Over the weekend as much as 2 feet of rain caused the waters of the Colorado, Guadalupe, San Marcos, and other rivers to rise as much as 30 feet above flood stage in a matter of hours. In some places the Colorado River grew to 6 miles wide, as did the Guadalupe River. Flooding affected one-fourth of the Lone Star State and resulted in twenty counties being declared disaster areas by President Bill Clinton at the request of Governor George W. Bush, and later five more counties were added. Early reports said at least 22 had died and property damage was estimated at over $400 million. Later the Texas Department of Health placed the official death toll at 31.

San Antonio, the largest city affected, received nearly 17 inches of rain during the first twenty-four hours. This was more rain than had previously fallen all year long and was the heaviest twenty-four-hour rainfall ever recorded in the city since such records were first kept, in 1885. The National Weather Service reported that October became the wettest month on record. Previously, the worst flooding in the city's history took place in 1921. Resulting floodwaters rose without warning and swept away vehicles, homes, and businesses. Streets and highways were closed, and power was cut off for thousands of residents.

A 4-mile stretch of highway was closed near Olmos Dam, located in the heart of the city, which was at its capacity of 48 feet. The dam, which was usually dry, had been built for flood control. National Guard units were called upon to aid police and emergency-response officials. People had to be evacuated, some from rooftops, as did their pets. Because of the special circumstances, several Red Cross shelters, contrary to their usual policy, allowed the animals to remain with their owners. A state and federal disaster field office was opened, and a mobilization center was established at Fort Sam Houston, which was supported by the Defense Coordinating Element.

Approximately halfway between San Antonio and Austin, the college town of San Marcos received more than 22 inches of rain. However, damage was not as extensive there as it was a little farther south in the city of New Braunfels, which is 35 miles north of San Antonio on the Guadalupe River. Floodwaters forced at least 1,400 people to seek shelter after the river crested at a record 30 feet. The Red Cross opened forty-seven shelters to accommodate the people who fled their homes. When it was over, 115 homes were reported destroyed and another 665 were damaged.

Seguin, a city of about 19,000 inhabitants east of San Antonio, also suffered extensive damage. The Red Cross reported that 253 homes were destroyed and an additional 1,000 were damaged. All city water had to be shut off because of contamination.

Perhaps the hardest hit town was Cuero, a town of about 6,700 people southeast of San Antonio. The October flood was the worst in its history, surpassing the great flood of 1936. Three-fourths of Cuero was swamped when the Guadalupe River crested nearly 30 feet above its 20-foot flood stage. At least 2,000 people were left homeless when 643 homes were destroyed. This represented 26 percent of the city's housing units, and more than 43 percent of the remaining houses suffered some damage. About 1 mile northeast of town at the Stevenson Unit, a correctional facility, inmates had to be moved to cells on the upper floor.

Downstream, 100 miles south of San Antonio, the city of Victoria had time to prepare for the flood, and people were evacuated in a timely manner. The water crested at 36 feet Wednesday morning, breaking the 1936 record by 4 feet. At least 600 homes were completely or partially submerged. Crests of from 3 to 15 feet above previous flood levels were reported in Cuero, Gonzales, New Braunfels, Seguin, and Victoria.

Population centers were not the only places to suffer from the floodwaters. Ranchers along the San Marcos River reported hundreds of miles of fences flattened, resulting in at least 5,000 to 10,000 cattle roaming the country looking for high ground.

Ground transportation was severely affected by the flooding. Cars, buses, and trucks were detained or rerouted because of the closing of roads and bridges, and trains were similarly affected by water on the tracks. Amtrak was forced to halt trains in south Texas, and Union Pacific's key Sunset Route between El Paso and San Antonio/Houston was shut down while 40 trains were detoured over other lines, including Union Pacific's Golden State Route between El Paso and Herington, Kansas. Amtrak's Texas Eagle from Chicago had to turn back at Fort Worth, and the eastbound Sunset Limited out of Los Angeles was trapped 15 miles west of San Antonio by a 45-foot washout.

Philip E. Lampe

For Further Information:

Herrick, Thaddeus. "Texas Floods Attain Mammoth Proportions." *Houston Chronicle*, October 21, 1998, pp. 1A, 12A.

MacCormack, John. "Water Roaring Towards Gulf." *San Antonio Express*, October 20, 1998, pp. 1A, 6A.

1999: Mexico

Date: August 27-October 26, 1999
Place: Eastern and southern Mexico
Result: 404 dead, approximately 350,000 homeless

Beginning in late August, 1999, Mexico and much of Central America was beset by torrential rains. Some of these rains were the result of early tropical storms, such as Hurricane Bert, while others were just excessive seasonal rainstorms. The rain quickly brought river levels to flood stage, and 5 people were killed in areas southeast of Mexico City when local rivers overflowed their banks.

As people struggled to recover from this first deluge, another series of storms struck Mexico, culminating with an unnamed tropical depression, the eleventh of the season, which hovered in the Gulf of Mexico off the coast of Veracruz on October 5. This depression brought 10 to 15 inches of rain to the already saturated region, causing the Grijalva and Usumacinta Rivers in the state of Tabasco to overflow their banks. In all, nearly 53,000 people in 150 communities had to flee to higher ground. By October 6, flooding had spread to the states of Hidalgo, Puebla, Veracruz, and Chiapas.

A flood survivor floats his belongings through water-filled streets in Villahermosa, Mexico. (AP/Wide World Photos)

Rain continued into October 7. By the end of that day the flooding extended to cover nine central and southern states. The Mexican government called out the military to help with the relief efforts. In the more mountainous regions of central Mexico, the floodwaters triggered massive mudslides, destroying several villages and killing approximately 100 people. In the village of Teziutlán at least 40 bodies were pulled from the mud, while 31 more were recovered in Tetela de Ocampo. Many of the mudslides were a result of the combination of torrential rains and heavy deforestation of the mountainsides.

Rains continued through October 11, causing reservoirs throughout the region to exceed their normal capacity. In order to protect dams at several locations, the government was forced to release additional water into the already swollen rivers. The additional flooding hampered relief efforts, especially in the southern state of Oaxaca, which had also suffered a major earthquake on September 30. The city of Tenango, in Puebla, was evacuated when a foot-wide crack was discovered in the dam above the city. In the city of Villahermosa, the flooding resulted in the presence of crocodiles in the streets.

The rains temporarily let up on October 12, giving the region a brief respite. However, it was only a short break, as the rains returned a week later; 5 more inches of rain fell on October 21, forcing hundreds of thousands to flee their homes again. The new rains forced additional water releases from the already swollen reservoirs, further adding to the record river levels. The new flooding led to a riot at the Center for Social Readaptation, a prison in Villahermosa, further hindering relief efforts.

When the storms finally subsided after October 26, the official death toll was 404. It was impossible to tally a final total as the floodwaters and mudslides swallowed many villages entirely, leaving no trace of the occupants.

Jacob P. Kovel

For Further Information:

Dillon, Sam. "From Ravaged Villages, Forlorn Mexicans Trek for Help." *The New York Times*, October 15, 1999.

Lopez, Luis. "In Flooded Area of Mexico, Waters Rise, Prisoners Riot." *The Detroit News*, October 23, 1999.

Riley, Michael. "When the Earth Moves." *Newsweek International*, November 1, 1999.

1999: Venezuela

Date: December 15-18, 1999

Place: The coast of the Vargas region, Venezuela, especially the cities of Caracas and La Guaira

Result: 5,000-30,000 dead, 340,000 homeless, 200,000 jobs lost, millions of dollars in damage

In the Venezuelan capital city of Caracas and its environs, shantytowns called *ranchos* cling to the sides of 6,000-foot-high mountains. The shacks are constructed of whatever materials are available, they do not conform to building codes, and they are illegal. They may collapse during heavy rains, drinkable water is not common, and the rates of violent crime in these neighborhoods are among the worst in Latin America. However, they are the only housing available to the thousands of migrants who flock to the city from the countryside, seeking work or improvement in economic conditions.

This has become the norm in most of the large cities of Latin America and East Asia, where rural economies will no longer support the migrants. In a typical rainy reason, 200 or more of Caracas's shanties will be swept away, and hundreds may lose their lives. About 70 percent of Caracas's population is said to live in the *ranchos*. An estimated 80 percent of Venezuela's population lives in poverty; in the *ranchos* that figure approaches 100 percent.

On December 15, three days of heavy rainfall struck the city, an out-of-season storm that was not totally unexpected. The first debris avalanche occurred in the early morning of the 16th, as a wall of mud and rocks 20 feet high swept down the mountainside, carrying shanties with it. Debris avalanches rushing down the mountainsides mixed with floodwaters, producing a barren landscape of rocks and mud not unlike that left by the torrents flowing down the flanks of Mount St. Helens, Washington, during its eruption in May, 1980. Observers of the Washington site described it as a "moonscape." The Caracas scene differed only in that the fans of debris covered hundreds of dwellings, with towers of high-rise buildings surrounded by the muck.

The hardest hit area was a 60-mile stretch of the coast in Vargas state. Affluent neighborhoods also suffered, both in Caracas proper and in the port city of La Guaira, where a golf course, country club, and marina were destroyed. Thousands remained stranded on rooftops, trying to avoid the raging rivers. Chaotic conditions prevailed, exacerbated by poor communication and transportation systems, as well as the lack of a well-prepared civil defense organization.

Relief efforts began immediately, with dozens of nations sending aid. The evacuation of the Vargas area became an air-and-sea rescue operation involving 13,000 troops, 5,000 volunteers, 40 helicopters, and 16 warships. About 70,000 people were evacuated in this operation, and thousands more walked along the beach to La Guaira, where they were bused or flown to temporary shelters. Most of Vargas, which is half the size of Rhode Island, would have to be razed and turned into parks. The survivors were to be moved to new settlements away from the coast, based around agricultural communities and business parks inland. To many, this sounded like the kind of life they had abandoned to move to Caracas for want of work.

In all, 23,000 homes were lost, and 140,000 people remained homeless for a week following the storms. It appeared that reconstruction and relocation would take several years and cost perhaps $15 billion. Fortunately, unlike most tropical nations that suffer major natural disasters, Venezuela has resources that aid in its survival. It is America's leading foreign source of oil and has the largest reserves in the Western Hemisphere.

Neil E. Salisbury

For Further Information:

The New York Times, December 19, 1999-January 15, 2000.

Time, December 31, 1999.

U.S. News and World Report, January 3, January 10, 2000.

2000: Mozambique

Date: Mid-February to mid-March, 2000

Place: Along the Limpopo River in Mozambique

Result: Hundreds dead, more than 12,000 evacuated, 300,000 homeless

Mozambique occupies the southeastern coast of Africa, between Tanzania to the north and South Africa in the south. This location is relevant to the flood disaster for both physical and historical-political reasons. Physically, Mozambique possesses the broadest coastal plain of Africa, south of the Congo. Two major rivers, the Limpopo and the Zambezi, plus the significant Save River, cross this plain. North of the Zambezi, the coastal plain narrows, and the higher plateaus of Africa creep closer to the ocean.

The flood disaster was concentrated on the broad floodplains of the Limpopo and Save Rivers, where some of the richest farmland is situated and, consequently, the farm population is dense. The uplands between the rivers are dry and subject to drought. The historical-political significance of Mozambique's location stems from the fact that it adjoins South Africa. After Mozambique gained its independence from Portugal in 1975, civil war broke out and lasted for sixteen years. South Africa supported the rebels. A United Nations-sponsored peace accord took effect in 1993, and after that the nation's economy grew at a rapid pace.

Flooding had resulted from especially heavy rainfalls in February, not only in Mozambique but also in neighboring South Africa, Zimbabwe, and Botswana. On February 22, a tropical cyclone struck the coast, causing additional flooding on the Limpopo River. A lull occurred, bringing a false sense of security to the region. Then, on the 26th, Cyclone Eline hit, creating a wall of water that moved downstream on the Limpopo from the highlands in Zimbabwe, carrying away hundreds of villages and thousands of people. Many ended up in treetops—there was no high ground to which to flee—and awaited rescue, some for five days, before helicopters from South Africa reached them. In all, South African helicopters rescued over 12,000 from the floodwaters by March 3, often from treetops. One woman gave birth in a tree after being trapped there for several days. On the Save River 164 were known dead. Throughout Mozambique it was estimated that 300,000 were homeless or had lost their livelihood.

The United Nations estimated that one-third of the corn crop—a staple—had been destroyed. The government stated that crops on 250,000 acres had been washed away, and 40,000 cattle drowned. Nearly 1 million of the 17 million people in Mozambique had either lost housing, farms, or food supplies. At least 500,000 people would be unable to feed themselves for the next six months.

By March 5, the floodwaters were subsiding and 250,000 people were safe from the waters in 72 refugee camps, but food and medicines were slow in coming. The transportation infrastructure, roads and bridges, had been badly damaged and slowed the movement of supplies. American relief forces arrived in early March to augment the South African efforts and were joined by Germans, British, and Spanish forces by March 7. Many locals complained that relief was too slow in coming from the Western powers, which may have caused additional loss of life. On March 13, it was announced that the United States, Great Britain, Italy, Spain, and Portugal would forgive the remaining debt owed by Mozambique in the hope of aiding the recovery process and seeing a return to the excellent progress the nation had been making before the disaster.

Neil E. Salisbury

For Further Information:

The New York Times, February 23-March 14, 2000.

Fog

(AP/Wide World Photos)

Fog can be a transportation danger because it reduces visibility. It is particularly hazardous in situations where heavy use of a transportation artery occurs.

Factors involved: Geography, temperature, weather conditions
Regions affected: Coasts, especially those where a cool ocean current is present; mountains; cities; towns

Science

Fog occurs when the temperature of any surface falls below the dew point of the air directly above it. There are a number of different kinds of fog, depending on the circumstances that lead to its generation. Radiational fog occurs in the early morning hours, when the cooling of the ground has created a temperature differential between the ground and the moist air directly over it. The lower ground temperature (at lower temperatures the air is less able to hold moisture) causes the moisture in the air immediately above it to condense into tiny droplets. Massed, the droplets make visibility impossible. By definition, fog exists when visibility is less than 0.6 mile (1 kilometer).

Advectional fog occurs when moist air moves over colder water. This is the kind of fog common along coasts, especially those where a colder ocean current tends to parallel the coast. If wind speeds increase, the density of this kind of fog also tends to increase, unless the wind speed is such as to blow away the moist air mass constituting the fog. For that to occur, wind speeds greater than 15 knots are needed.

Upslope fog occurs in areas in which the prevailing winds blow over a large surface area from a moist region toward a region of increasing altitudes. As the wind blows upslope, it creates the temperature gradient between the ground and the moister air that can induce fog.

Occasionally, precipitation in the form of drizzle can turn into fog. This can occur if the drizzle is falling through cool air that becomes saturated as a result of the drizzle. Such fogs can become very dense and are most apt to occur in places where relatively high rainfall is the norm.

In high latitudes, what are known as ice fogs are rather common. In these cases, below-freezing temperatures cause moisture in the air to become suspended ice crystals that dominate the atmosphere, creating the effect of fog. For such fogs to form, very low temperatures are needed—at least minus 25 degrees Fahrenheit.

The fog that comes off the surface of a body of water in early winter is often warmer than the air above. Even though the vapor pressure of the water is higher (the reverse of the normal condition creating fog) droplets will sometimes move upward from the water creating the effect of fog. Such fog is called steam fog.

Geography

Radiational fog may occur anywhere if the proper temperature differential exists, but it is most common in areas where there are different elevations. This type of fog tends to concentrate in depressions or river valleys. It tends to burn away during the early morning hours if the day is sunny—the heat of the sun dries up the condensed water vapor.

Advectional fog is most common along coasts and most frequent along coasts where a cold ocean current flows and creates the necessary temperature dif-

Although pilots can land planes by radar, airports often shut down during heavy fog. (AP/Wide World Photos)

ferential. The cold ocean current is the defining factor, and for this reason fog is very common on seacoasts where such currents exist. The west coast of the United States, from San Francisco northward, is subject to such conditions, with the prevailing wind blowing the moisture off the ocean onto the land. The Pacific coast of North America has at least sixty days of dense fog each year.

The east coast of Canada, especially Newfoundland and Labrador, is notorious for its dense fogs. These fogs result from the cold Labrador current that runs up that coast. Even further south, on Cape Cod, Massachusetts, fogs are fairly common, although they lack the intensity of those along the east coast of Canada.

Iceland and the British Isles are notorious for their fogs, again resulting from the temperature differential between the land and the surrounding ocean. On the other hand, fogs are rare in the lower latitudes farther south in Europe, although radiational fog may exist in, for example, the Alpine valleys of Switzerland.

Although fog is rare in tropical areas, there are two regions that do experience it. One is the Peruvian coastline, where, although there is little actual precipitation, vegetation can survive in an essentially desert climate from the condensation of the moisture contained in the fogs. Another tropical area that experiences fog is the coast of Somalia, in eastern Africa, where some unusual coastal currents create the necessary temperature differential.

Arctic fogs have created problems for weather-gathering stations in Greenland for a number of years. They are particularly intense on the east coast of Greenland.

Although the reduction in the use of coal-fired steam engines has reduced the amount of steam vented into the atmosphere around cities, auto exhausts and emissions from power plants can, if added to natural fog, produce what is often called smog. This mixture of natural fog and emissions can be a hazard. Some cities, located where prevailing winds cannot disperse such atmospheric collections because of adjacent mountains, have severe problems with smog—Denver and Los Angeles are examples.

Prevention and Preparations

Because of the hazard to transportation, especially air transport, at various times efforts have been made to try to disperse fog, especially at transportation hubs. Seeding a fog with salt has been found effective but has some obvious environmental drawbacks. Another method, creating a blast of hot air along the runways of airports, has been used in some critical situations but demands an extremely large fuel input. However, when temperatures are below freezing (below 25 degrees Fahrenheit), success has followed seeding of fog with solid carbon dioxide crystals. Another method occasionally used has been spraying with propane gas. However, when temperatures are above freezing (and most fogs form under such conditions), no satisfactory method has been found to disperse fogs at airports.

Foghorns have been the traditional method of warning vessels both at sea and on large bodies of inland waters, such as the Great Lakes. The most effective antidote to fog has been the development of radar, which sees through fog. This methodology has become increasingly successful in handling air traffic, although the radar devices have had to become more exact as the volume of traffic has grown. Even so, and even though all commercial pilots now must be able to land a plane solely with the use of instrument indicators, fog can shut down air operations. Most pilots prefer being able to see a runway before they land. Even localized fogs can disrupt the schedules of virtually all airlines because they interrupt interconnecting flights.

Although airplane crashes in the United States resulting from fogs are now relatively rare because the flights are regularly shut down when fog closes in an airport, there is always an intensive investigation by the Federal Aviation Administration (FAA) if there is a crash. Because the federal government controls all the airline flights through its air traffic control system, flights are routinely canceled when a serious fog situation exists.

Fog continues to be a problem in automobile travel, although the development of the interstate highway system, with its dual road structure, has helped reduce the dangers. However, the majority of roads remain two-lane roads, and it is up to the individual motorist to drive with exceptional care in foggy conditions.

As shipping has become more a system for moving freight than for moving people, the risk of marine accidents is no longer what it once was. Still, in certain areas fog continues to be a problem for oceangoing traffic despite the assistance of radar.

Impact

As the amount of air travel has grown, so has the danger posed by fog conditions. The layout and siting of airports can be helpful in mitigating the effects of fog, but the standard response is still to shut down flights until the air clears. The airlines are proud of their safety record—it is far safer to travel in a commercial airplane than in a car—and they do not want to risk their reputation. Few people survive an airplane crash; far more survive an automobile accident.

Nancy M. Gordon

Bibliography

Barry, Roger G., and Richard J. Chorley. *Atmosphere, Weather, and Climate.* London: Routledge, 1992. A strongly scientific presentation that treats fog as condensation. Provides numerous maps showing water vapor content at various locations.

Gedzelman, Stanley David. *The Science and Wonders of the Atmosphere.* New York: John Wiley & Sons, 1980. Contains numerous diagrams and maps. Provides descriptions of the climate in various geographical areas, with the resulting vegetation. Numerous photographs.

Hidore, John J., and John E. Oliver. *Climatology: An Atmospheric Science.* New York: Macmillan, 1993. Contains four excellent diagrams of the process of fog formation. A solid, scientific-based presentation for the general reader.

Lockhart, Gary. *The Weather Companion.* New York: John Wiley & Sons, 1988. Contains some information on foghorns. Otherwise, a compendium of popular weather lore.

Lydolph, Paul E. *The Climate of the Earth.* Totowa, N.J.: Rowman & Littlefield, 1985. Although a generalized text on climatology, this text contains good material on the different kinds of fogs.

Notable Events

Historical Overview

Although fogs can occur anywhere in the world under the appropriate conditions, they are more common in the northerly latitudes, especially along seacoasts. Consequently, they began to pose a major problem as the inhabited world spread northward from the Mediterranean. They constitute a hazard for travelers, and as the development of new vessels made people more venturesome on the sea, fog became more of a risk factor. At the same time, vessels tended to hug the shoreline, where the lack of visibility in a fog (fog is defined as a condition in which visibility is less than 3,281 feet, or 1,000 meters) posed the risk of running aground on a difficult-to-see coast.

As European fishermen braved the Atlantic to fish in the rich waters of the Grand Banks off Newfoundland, the fogs that often enshroud that peninsula became deadly. Breton fishermen risked their lives in search of cod as early as the fifteenth century, and thousands of fishermen have lost their lives in shipwrecks brought about by the inability of the crewmen to see. In the lobby of one of the principal hotels on the French island of Miquelon, one of the few remaining possessions of France in the Western Hemisphere, there is a chart listing more than 300 wrecks that have occurred along the Newfoundland coastline, most as a result of fog. The locals maintain that the list significantly undercounts the number of wrecks that have cost fishermen their lives.

Throughout the nineteenth century, as residents of coastal areas of New England went to sea to make a living, the risk of shipwreck along the rocky New England coast remained great. In the middle of the nineteenth century the whaling vessels of New England numbered more than 700. Because the ships possessed only relatively rudimentary navigational instruments and navigated by sight, fogs posed a real danger. Even the adoption of foghorns at many risky coastal points did not relieve the danger for sailing vessels.

New technology, especially the invention of wireless radio in the late nineteenth century enabling ship-to-shore communication, reduced some of the risks posed by fog. Radio communication from shore stations to vessels during fog was only introduced gradually, however; the first such signal on the Great Lakes was sent in 1925. The invention of radar in World War II vastly reduced the risks of fog at sea, as it enabled vessels to "see" even under conditions of heavy fog.

Marine disasters under foggy conditions did not disappear with the introduction of wireless radio, however. On May 29, 1914, the *Empress of Ireland* was struck by a Norwegian steam freighter on the St. Law-

Milestones

January 19, 1883:	357 die in fog-related collision of steamers *Cimbria* and *Sultan*.
1901:	Transatlantic wireless radio sends first signal to receiver in St. John's, Newfoundland.
1925:	First radio signal to warn of fog is sent to ships on the Great Lakes.
December 23, 1933:	Two trains collide in fog near Paris, killing 230.
1945:	Radar is used for tracking civilian traffic in ships and planes.
December 5-9, 1952:	Heavy smog in London kills 4,000 people.
July 25-26, 1956:	The Italian liner *Andrea Doria* sinks after being struck by Swedish vessel in fog.
July 31, 1973:	A Delta Airlines jet crashes while attempting to land at Boston's Logan International Airport in fog; 89 die.
March 27, 1977:	Two airliners collide in fog in Tenerife, Canary Islands; 583 die.
April 10, 1991:	138 die in crash of ferry *Moby Prince* and oil tanker *Agip Abruzzo* in Italy.

rence River; when the Norwegian vessel backed off, the *Empress of Ireland* quickly filled with water and went down within fifteen minutes. Although 444 people were saved, more than 1,000 died. All passengers were rescued when the *George M. Cox* struck Isle Royale in Lake Superior in 1933, despite foghorn warnings. Even the presence of radar did not prevent a collision between two vessels on Lake Michigan in October, 1973, although no one was injured.

The most spectacular shipping disaster attributed to fog was, however, the sinking of the Italian liner *Andrea Doria* in July of 1956. The Swedish liner *Stockholm* struck the *Andrea Doria* just after 11 P.M. in heavy fog. The Swedish ship had a reinforced prow, and, despite being equipped with numerous watertight bulkheads, the *Andrea Doria* could not be saved; it sank in the Atlantic eleven hours later. All passengers who survived the impact were saved, however, by other ships that came to the rescue.

Fog, when mixed with suspended particles in the air, can be a killer on its own. The famous London fogs, mixed with suspended particulate matter and called "smogs," proved to be particularly intense between December 5 and 9, 1952. They are thought to be responsible for the deaths of more than 4,000 individuals.

Fog also poses a danger to surface transportation. The greatest problems have arisen in situations where numerous trains use the same track and are dependent on signals that may not be readily visible in heavy fog. London has a history of train disasters due to fog and smog. In 1947, in South Croydon, an overcrowded suburban train was rammed from behind by a faster-moving train. The signaling equipment, only partly automated, failed to alert the faster train to the presence of the suburban train on the same track. In 1957, on a day when fog reduced the visibility to as little as 66 feet (20 meters), an express train struck an electrified suburban train at St. John's, outside of London, killing 92 people. The introduction of fully automated signaling equipment has helped prevent such disasters, although as late as 1966 a passenger train crashed into the rear of a freight train in Villafranca, Italy, causing the death of 27 people.

Fog is a major hazard to airplane traffic. Although most airplane accidents in the United States are not attributable to fog, in part because the stringent rules of the Federal Aviation Administration require that airports with severely reduced visibility be shut down, the danger is great. The crash of a Delta jet attempting to land at Logan International Airport in Boston on July 31, 1973, brought home the dangers posed by fog. Eighty-nine people lost their lives. Since then, airports have been shut down entirely when they are enveloped in fog, and incoming flights are diverted to other airports. The flight control system maintained by the federal government is entirely based on radar, which is unaffected by fog.

Nancy M. Gordon

1883: North Sea

Ship collision
Date: January 19, 1883
Place: Off the island of Borkum, the Netherlands
Result: 357 dead in collision between steamers *Cimbria* and *Sultan*

The liner *Cimbria* was a small 3,037-ton, 329-foot-long steamship of the Hamburg-Amerika Line built in 1867 for the immigrant trade. It departed Hamburg on January 18, 1883, with 302 passengers and 120 crew members. Most of the passengers were Russian, Prussian, Austrian, and Hungarian immigrants intent on a new life in the United States, but also on board were a group of French sailors bound for the naval base at Harvé and a group of Chippewa Indians returning home after performing in a touring "Wild West" exhibition.

Early on January 19, a dense fog arose off the Dutch coast. Despite the deteriorating visibility, the ship's captain did not alter the *Cimbria*'s course or speed. Off the Island of Borkum, lookouts heard a foghorn but could not discern the bearing of the oncoming ship until it loomed out of the fog. It was the passenger liner *Sultan*, of the Hull and Hamburg Line, under the command of Captain Cuttill. The *Sultan*'s bow smashed into the *Cimbria*'s left side just ahead of the foremast, opening a hole deep under water and causing heavy flooding. Backing away from its victim, *Sultan* found its own situation to be very serious, with a 7-foot hole in the bow and rapid flooding. Faced with the very real possibility that the *Sultan* would sink, Cuttill did not lower his boats or do anything else to succor the *Cimbria*, and the two stricken ships drifted apart.

Aboard the *Cimbria*, the situation was serious. Sleeping passengers were pitched from their bunks by the impact. They soon found the ship listing to the right and settling low in the water. The passengers were quickly herded on deck, and, there being no question that the ship was going to sink, the crew began lowering the lifeboats. Seven were successfully launched before the list became too great to lower the last few, although apparently none of the lifeboats was full. One of the boats capsized as it reached the sea, throwing the passengers into the water. The crew of the *Cimbria* remained in very good discipline, making every effort to save the passengers, even to the point of cutting loose spars to serve as flotation devices for those unlucky enough to find themselves in the water. Unfortunately, the ship sank before all the preparations could be made. Many of the passengers went into the sea, and in the chilly waters they quickly succumbed to hypothermia. In the heavy fog, the lifeboats drifted apart, and three simply disappeared.

Two boats containing 39 survivors were picked up by the sailing ship *Theta* on January 21, 1883. Another boat with 17 survivors was picked up by the British ship *Diamant*, and a final boat made landfall on Borkum with 9 aboard. In the end, these 65 persons were all that were saved of the 422 passengers and crew. The majority of the 72 women and 87 children aboard the *Cimbria* were lost.

An official inquiry was held at Hamburg to determine the cause of the loss of the *Cimbria*, and Captain Cuttill was questioned at length concerning his failure to render aid to the stricken liner. He explained that he felt at the time that the *Sultan* had suffered the worse damage and that the *Cimbria* was therefore obliged to render him aid. Further, with the heavy fog, he could not see the *Cimbria*, and he feared he would lose his lifeboats if he put them in the water and sent them to its aid. As the two ships drifted apart, he was unaware of the tragedy that overtook the *Cimbria* and was completely absorbed by the problems of saving his own ship. Subsequently, calculations proved that had the ship taken on another foot of water in its hold, the *Sultan* would also have been lost.

Thomas R. Stephens

For Further Information:

Hocking, Charles. *Dictionary of Disasters at Sea During the Age of Steam, Including Sailing Ships and Ships of War Lost in Action, 1824-1962.* London: Lloyd's Register of Shipping, 1969.

1883: North Atlantic

SHIP COLLISION
DATE: September 27, 1883
PLACE: Off the coast of Newfoundland
RESULT: 322 dead in collision between sidewheeler *Arctic* and steamer *Vesta*

The Collins liner *Arctic* was one of four sister ships built in 1850 to challenge the British monopoly on the trans-Atlantic passenger service. Although built with an obsolescent wooden hull and devoid of watertight internal compartments, these ships' 15-mile-per-hour (13-knot) speed made them among the fastest vessels afloat, usually making the Atlantic crossing in ten days. With its luxurious cabins, the Collins line was popular with high society.

The *Arctic* left Liverpool, England, on September 20, 1883. When the ship entered a heavy fog on the morning of the 27th, Captain James Luce failed to slow his speed, order a foghorn blown to warn approaching ships, or post extra watchmen. At 12:15 P.M., the *Arctic* crossed the path of the iron-hulled French liner *Vesta*, with Captain Alphonse Puchesne commanding. The *Vesta* lost nearly 10 feet of its bow in the ensuing collision, while the *Arctic* received at least three holes below the waterline.

Captain Luce took immediate steps to aid the *Vesta*, which he believed to be the more badly damaged ship. Captain Puchesne lowered two lifeboats, one of which capsized, drowning several passengers. As this disaster was taking place, Luce learned that his own ship was flooding. He tried to patch the holes by lowering a sail over the side, but the protruding debris from the *Vesta*'s bow prevented any sort of seal from forming. In an attempt to raise the damaged area above the waterline, Luce tried releasing the anchors and their heavy chains. The flooding continued unabated.

In a desperate effort to save the *Arctic*, Luce decided to abandon the *Vesta* and make a run for the coast and beach his ship. As the *Arctic* got underway, it inadvertently ran down the second of Vesta's lifeboats, killing all aboard save one, Jassonet François, who was saved by a rope thrown to him from the deck of the *Arctic*.

Unfortunately, the run for shore actually increased the flooding of the *Arctic*. Rising water extinguished the boiler-room fires while the ship was still 35 miles offshore. Captain Luce ordered women and children into the boats, but part of his crew mutinied and took the boats for themselves. One crew member who tried to stop them was killed. Luce led those remaining aboard in a last-minute attempt to build a raft, to which 72 people clung when the ship finally sank at 4:45 P.M. Only 1 person aboard the raft survived. Among the 59 survivors were the ship's captain, the first mate, and François, the survivor of the *Vesta*'s lifeboat.

Thomas R. Stephens

FOR FURTHER INFORMATION:

Hocking, Charles. *Dictionary of Disasters at Sea During the Age of Steam, Including Sailing Ships and Ships of War Lost in Action, 1824-1962.* London: Lloyd's Register of Shipping, 1969.

Ritchie, David. *Shipwrecks: An Encyclopedia of the World's Worst Disasters at Sea.* New York: Facts on File, 1996.

1887: English Channel

SHIP COLLISION
DATE: November 19, 1887
PLACE: Off the coast of Dover, England
RESULT: 132 dead in collision between liner *W. A. Scholten* and SS *Rosa Mary*

The thirteen-year-old Dutch liner *W. A. Scholten* was traveling from Rotterdam to New York with 156 passengers and 54 crew members. On the night of November 19, 1887, the *W. A. Scholten* was steaming about 4 miles off the coast of Dover, England, when it struck the bow of the anchored collier *Rosa Mary*, which was waiting for the fog to clear. The collier was badly damaged but remained afloat until dawn, when it entered the harbor on its own power and docked.

The *W. A. Scholten* was in much worse condition. The collision tore an 8-foot hole in its bow, and it immediately began to sink and list sharply to port, disappearing below the waves within twenty minutes. Only two lifeboats were launched, but many of the passengers were provided with life belts and were able to remain afloat until picked up by the passing British steamer *Ebro* and a private boat that also came to the rescue. Eventually, 78 survivors were picked up, leaving 132 dead, including the ship's captain and first mate.

Thomas R. Stephens

For Further Information:

Hocking, Charles. *Dictionary of Disasters at Sea During the Age of Steam, Including Sailing Ships and Ships of War Lost in Action, 1824-1962.* London: Lloyd's Register of Shipping, 1969.

1890: English Channel

Shipwreck
Date: March 30, 1890
Place: Off the coast of England
Result: 100 dead in wreck of the ferry *Stella*

The nine-year-old, 1,059-ton ferry *Stella* made its first run of the Easter holiday season on March 30, 1890, with 174 passengers and 43 crew members. Soon after leaving the English Channel, the ship encountered heavy fog. Captain W. Reeks, wishing to reach Guernsey before dark, maintained the ship's top speed of 22.4 miles per hour (19.5 knots).

About 4 P.M., the lookout spotted rocks ahead and heard the warning horn of the Casquets lighthouse. The captain ordered the ship hard-a-port, without changing speed. The *Stella* continued its new course for a short time and then struck Black Rock, one of the Casquets islands. The damage done to the hull was severe, and the ship began to sink at once. The evacuation of the ship was characterized by the calm order in which it was carried out, with the men aboard the ferry allowing the women and children to enter the lifeboats first. The ship sank within twenty minutes, taking 100 passengers and crew to their deaths.

Thomas R. Stephens

For Further Information:

Hocking, Charles. *Dictionary of Disasters at Sea During the Age of Steam, Including Sailing Ships and Ships of War Lost in Action, 1824-1962.* London: Lloyd's Register of Shipping, 1969.

Ritchie, David. *Shipwrecks: An Encyclopedia of the World's Worst Disasters at Sea.* New York: Facts on File, 1996.

1914: Canada

Ship collision
Date: May 29, 1914
Place: St. Lawrence River, Canada
Result: More than 1,000 dead in sinking of *Empress of Ireland* following collision with *Storstad*

The fame and historical significance of some disasters certainly overshadow other tragedies and accidents. Such is the case regarding the loss of the *Empress of Ireland.* The nationality, location, and date of the disaster all contributed to a general lack of knowledge about the ship's loss, despite the unpleasant fact that more passengers lost their lives in the accident than in more famous incidents.

Empress of Ireland (completed in 1907) and its sister ship *Empress of Britain* were constructed by the Fairfield Shipbuilding and Engineering Company of Glasgow as flagships of the Canadian Pacific Line. At 14,200 tons, *Empress of Ireland* carried more than 1,000 passengers—310 first class, 350 second class, and 800 third class—on the Quebec-to-Liverpool route. For eight years the ship enjoyed a distinguished reputation for service and reliability and never once was involved in any sort of accident.

Empress of Ireland, with 1,057 passengers and 420 crewmen aboard, left Quebec on May 28, 1914. Many of its passengers were prominent leaders of the Canadian Salvation Army, on their way to Europe to attend the organization's worldwide convention. At approximately 1 A.M., Captain Henry Kendall, commanding the *Empress of Ireland* for the first time, paused to drop off pilot Adelhard Bernier at Rimouski, Quebec, at the point where the St. Lawrence River widens before the approach to the open sea. At about the same time, the Norwegian collier *Storstad* was approaching Rimouski to take on its pilot before entering the narrow portion of the river. The *Storstad*'s 7,000-ton displacement was further burdened by 11,000 tons of coal scheduled to be unloaded in Quebec the next day. On the *Storstad*'s bridge First Mate Alfred Toftenes stood watch, peering into the darkness as intermittent fog began to develop over the river.

Not long after passing Rimouski, the two ships sighted each other. In the darkness without any visual references, both ships misjudged the bearing and speed of the other, with disastrous results. Before signals could be launched and positions verified, a blanket of fog obscured both vessels' view of the other,

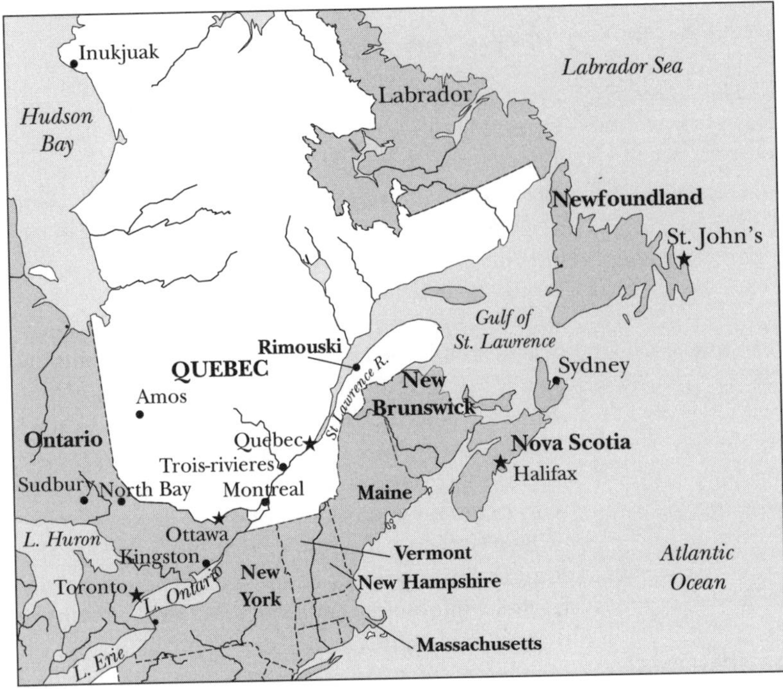

leaving the ships groping toward each other in the darkness. Both officers then took actions intended to prevent a collision, but which in retrospect proved the opposite. First Mate Toftenes, obeying the established maritime rules, proceeded on his original course and speed, presuming the other ship would do the same and pass cleanly to port.

Captain Kendell, however, did almost the opposite. He initially ordered all his engines to stop in order to allow the other vessel to pass ahead of him. The immense mass of the ship, however, carried the vessel forward anyway. To compensate, Kendall ordered the engines to full reverse to halt the *Empress of Ireland's* forward momentum, announcing his intent to the unseen ship by three long blasts from his steam whistle. When First Mate Toftenes heard the whistle, he realized the danger of his situation. He immediately reduced forward speed and called the *Storstad's* commanding officer, Captain Thomas Anderson, to the bridge. Anderson had just arrived on the bridge when the massive starboard side of the *Empress of Ireland* suddenly appeared out of the fog less than 100 yards dead ahead. Captain Anderson immediately reversed engines, while Captain Kendall went to full speed to avoid a collision, but their efforts were in vain. *Storstad* rammed the *Empress of Ireland* amidships, nearly cutting it in two.

Captain Kendall, realizing his ship was doomed, immediately ordered the helmsman to turn the ship toward shore and prepare the passengers for evacuation. Despite direct action, the *Empress of Ireland* and many of its passengers had no chance. The deep wound caused by the *Storstad* had flooded the boilers, and the *Empress of Ireland* came to a dead stop in the channel. Electrical power also failed, plunging the ship into darkness and disabling the public address system needed to alert sleeping passengers and crew. The gash in its side also admitted tons of water into the ship. Only ten minutes after the collision, the *Empress of Ireland* capsized, floated bottom up for several minutes, then sank in 150 feet of water.

Because of the loss of power and the quick demise of the ship, the death toll was staggering. Of 1,057 passengers, only 217 survived. More crewmen survived the tragedy because they were awake and working, but 172 of the 420 crewmen lost their lives. An additional 20 crewmen aboard the *Storstad* also died. Eager to place blame, a Canadian court of inquiry cleared Captain Kendall of all responsibility for the disaster. A Norwegian inquiry subsequently cleared the *Storstad* of any fault. In actuality both were to blame. Captain Kendall had acted indecisively and had not followed established maritime rules by failing to maintain his course. First Mate Toftenes also deserved blame for not summoning his commanding officer until the situation had deteriorated.

The loss of the *Empress of Ireland* has slipped into obscurity for several reasons. First, its loss was overshadowed by the sinking of the *Titanic* two years earlier. *Empress of Ireland* also sank in the St. Lawrence River instead of on the higher-profile passenger routes in the North Atlantic. Finally, the growing war scare in Europe that would result in World War I only three months after the loss of *Empress of Ireland* dominated the news more than the loss of a passenger liner on a Canadian river.

Steven J. Ramold

For Further Information:
Bonsall, Thomas E. *Great Shipwrecks of the Twentieth Century.* Baltimore: Bookman, 1988.
Croall, James. *Fourteen Minutes: The Last Voyage of the "Empress of Ireland."* London: Sphere Books, 1980.
Marshall, Logan. *The Tragic Story of the "Empress of Ireland."* Harrisburg, Pa.: Minter, 1914.
Wood, Herbert P. *Til We Meet Again: The Sinking of the "Empress of Ireland."* Toronto: Image, 1982.
Zeni, David, *Forgotten Empress: The "Empress of Ireland" Story.* Tiverton, N.Y.: Halsgrove, 1998.

1917: English Channel

Ship collision
Date: February 21, 1917
Place: Near the Isle of Wight
Result: 636 dead in collision between transport *Mendi* and steamer *Darro*

The fourteen-year-old, 4,230-ton steamship *Mendi*, under command of Captain Henry A. Yardley, was pressed into service as a transport during World War I. In January, 1917, it was part of a convoy of six ships, escorted by the armored cruiser *Cornwall*, carrying South African and Australian troops to France. The first part of the journey was accomplished without serious incident, although the German raider *Wolf* shadowed the convoy briefly before deciding not to risk an encounter with the *Cornwall*. The convoy reached Plymouth, England, in mid-February.

On February 21, 1917, the *Mendi* left Plymouth for Harvé with 806 officers and men of a South African labor battalion and 88 crew members. The ship encountered a heavy fog, and Captain Yardley took the precautions of reducing speed and sounding the ship's foghorn. However, the *Mendi* proceeded without navigational lights in order to avoid German submarines. Around 5 A.M., she was struck by the 11,000-ton liner *Darro*. The much more massive *Darro*'s bow sliced into the forward right side troop deck, killing many of the sleeping men. The ship took on a heavy list, which prevented the launching of its lifeboats, and sank within twenty minutes. Fatalities included 607 officers and men of the labor battalion and 29 crew members. The *Darro*, fearing an enemy submarine attack, immediately proceeded on its way without rendering assistance.

Thomas R. Stephens

For Further Information:
Hocking, Charles. *Dictionary of Disasters at Sea During the Age of Steam, Including Sailing Ships and Ships of War Lost in Action, 1824-1962.* London: Lloyd's Register of Shipping, 1969.

1933: France

Train collision
Date: December 23, 1933
Place: Near Paris, France
Result: 230 dead, approximately 70 injured in collision involving *Nancy Express* and a commuter train

A combination of ice and heavy fog conspired to create extremely hazardous conditions near Lagny, some 15 miles east of Paris, on December 23, 1933. A commuter train carrying some 300 passengers, mainly families traveling to Paris for the holidays and soldiers and sailors going home on Christmas leave, had reduced speed because of the limited visibility. It was struck from behind by the *Nancy Express*, moving at full speed. The caboose and last four coaches of the commuter train were almost completely destroyed, killing 230 passengers and leaving the rest with varying degrees of injuries.

The express train, made of heavy steel coaches pulled by a powerful "Mountain" class steam engine, survived the crash with very modest damage. No one aboard the *Nancy Express* was badly injured. In contrast, the lightly built wooden coaches of the commuter train were utterly destroyed.

The French railroad had safeguards in place that should have prevented the disaster. First, a system of block signals, tripped automatically by the passage of a train, should have warned the crew of the *Nancy Express* that they were approaching another train. Further, in foggy weather a detonator was automatically placed on the track, which was set off by the passage of a train's wheels and gave an audible warning of an obstruction ahead. The crew of the commuter train testified that the safeguards were operating properly as they traveled down the track, but the crew of the express train claimed that the safeguards had failed to operate. The entire engine crew of the *Nancy Express* was taken into custody and charged with negligence following the wreck.

Thomas R. Stephens

For Further Information:
The Times (London), December 27, 1933, p. 10.

1945: New York City

Plane crash
Date: July 28, 1945
Place: Empire State Building, New York City
Result: 14 dead, 26 injured, $500,000 in damage when an airplane crashed into the building

On the morning of Saturday, July 28, 1945, New York City was covered with a blanket of low-lying clouds. Visibility from the ground extended up to about 600 feet. The top of the Empire State Building, 1,250 feet high, was immersed in fog. A U.S. Army B-25 twin-engine bomber was on a routine flight from Bedford, Massachusetts, to Newark, New Jersey. The pilot had radioed LaGuardia Airport to ask for weather information and was warned about the low cloud ceiling. While over Manhattan, the plane descended briefly below the clouds, presumably for the pilot to see the ground and to get his bearings. According to observers on the street, the plane had just ascended back into the clouds when they heard the sound of a violent explosion. The B-25 had struck the side of the Empire State Building at the seventy-ninth floor.

The fuselage of the airplane made a 20-foot-diameter hole in the north face of the building and became embedded there. One of the engines broke

The holes made in the Empire State Building after a bomber crashed into it in heavy fog in 1945. (AP/Wide World Photos)

off, smashed all the way through seven interior walls and out through the south side, falling onto the roof of a neighboring twelve-story building, where it caused considerable damage. The other engine crashed through the door of an elevator shaft and dropped eighty floors to the basement.

The worst damage was from a searing fire caused by gasoline released from the ruptured fuel tanks. Several office workers on the seventy-ninth floor were trapped in the fire with no chance to escape. Their bodies were incinerated beyond recognition. Firefighters responding to the alarm found that the water supply system up to the sixtieth floor of the building was undamaged. Carrying their hoses up the next eighteen flights of stairs, they were able to bring the blaze under control in less than an hour. Thousands of onlookers on the street below were held back by uniformed police to avoid injuries from falling fragments of metal, masonry, and glass.

In the 1940's, elevators were not automatic but had to be started and stopped manually by an elevator operator who rode up and down with the passengers. A female operator had just opened the elevator door one floor below that of the airplane's impact. Her clothing caught on fire, but it was extinguished by nearby office workers who also provided first aid. They took her to another elevator that was still functioning in order to transport her down to ground level so she could get medical help. As the car started downward, the supporting cable snapped with a sound like a rifle shot. The elevator with its operator and the injured woman aboard fell from the seventy-fifth floor to the sub-basement. Firemen cut a hole into the fallen car and miraculously found the two women alive, although seriously injured. Apparently, automatic safety equipment had functioned to retard the downward motion of the elevator and to cushion its impact at the bottom.

The accident took place on a Saturday morning, when many offices were unoccupied. A spokesman for the Empire State Building estimated that there were less than 1,500 people in the building at the time of the crash. On a typical weekday, there would have been about 5,000 office workers plus another 10,000 visitors. The number of casualties likely would have been much larger on a business day. Fourteen people died, including the 3 military personnel on the airplane, several staff members of the Catholic War Relief Services on the seventy-ninth floor, and one employee on the seventy-eighth floor. Injuries due to burns and smoke inhalation occurred mostly to people above the eightieth floor. They could not be evacuated until the fire had been extinguished.

Temporary scaffolding was erected to close the hole made by the airplane's impact. The rest of the building was declared safe for occupancy. By Monday morning, all the offices in the Empire State Building, except on two floors, were able to open for business again. An Army investigation established that the accident was due to pilot error, not equipment failure. Monetary compensation for medical expenses and for damage repair at that time required a separate congressional act for each individual claim.

Any building over twenty stories tall is called a skyscraper. Because Manhattan is an island with limited land area, the way to increase the office space available for business was to build higher. Between 1902 and 1929, almost two hundred skyscrapers were built in New York City, making it the skyscraper capital of the world. At the height of the stock market boom in 1929, a group of investors decided to build the tallest skyscraper ever attempted. Using steel beam construction, the builders were able to erect the framework for several floors at one time, then add the elevators, walls, and windows later. The whole structure was completed in only eighteen months, reaching a height of 102 stories. Unfortunately for the owners, the stock market crash and the depression that followed it left much of the building unoccupied. Operating revenue during these lean years was generated from visitors who paid an entrance fee to ride the elevators up to the top. The Empire State Building was a major tourist attraction as the highest building in the world until it was surpassed by the World Trade Center in 1972 and the Sears Tower in 1973. The Petronas Twin Tower in the city of Kuala Lumpur, Malaysia, became the highest structure in the world when it was completed in 1997.

Hans G. Graetzer

For Further Information:

"Bolt from the Fog." *Newsweek* 26 (August 6, 1945): 35-36.

James, Theodore, Jr. *The Empire State Building.* New York: Harper & Row, 1975.

The New York Times, July 29, 1945.

"Skyscraper Crash." *Life* 19 (August 6, 1945): 31-32.

Tauranac, John. *The Empire State Building.* New York: St. Martin's Press, 1997.

1956: North Atlantic

Ship collision
Date: July 25-26, 1956
Place: Off Nantucket
Result: 52 dead in collision between liners *Andrea Doria* and *Stockholm*

The Italian luxury liner *Andrea Doria* was considered among the most graceful and opulent ships afloat. It was also considered extremely safe. Its hull was divided into eleven watertight compartments, and it was believed that it could remain afloat even if two compartments were flooded.

On the evening of July 25, 1956, the *Andrea Doria*, commanded by Captain Piero Calamai, was on the last leg of its nine-day crossing from Genoa, Italy, to New York, carrying 1,134 passengers and 572 crew members. It entered a heavy fog off the coast of Nantucket, Massachusetts, and, near midnight, collided with the Swedish liner *Stockholm*, steaming on a reciprocal course. Both ships had radar, and each was aware of the presence of the other. However, the radar in use at the time was able to provide only the relative position of other ships, not their speed and heading. As a result of misinterpretations aboard both ships, it was not realized until the last moment that the ships were on a collision course.

The *Andrea Doria* cut across the bow of the *Stockholm*, which struck it squarely on the right side just behind the bridge. The reinforced ice-breaker bow of the *Stockholm* tore a hole 30 to 40 feet wide and nearly as deep in the side of the *Andrea Doria*. A young girl asleep in her cabin aboard the *Andrea Doria* survived being flipped from her bed onto the deck of the *Stockholm*. However, 47 other passengers and crew aboard the Italian liner were killed as a result of the impact. Despite its safety features, the *Andrea Doria* at once took on a severe list, which made it impossible to launch its left-side lifeboats. In order to avoid a panic among the passengers, Captain Calamai did not sound an alarm. He did send out an SOS requesting the assistance of all available ships.

The collision left the *Stockholm* badly damaged, with 69 feet of its bow crushed, 3 of its crewmen dead and 2 more dying. Furthermore, the damage to the bow ripped open the chain locker, allowing the reserve chain for the anchor line to fall to the bottom. Because the chains were still attached to the anchors aboard the ship and the loose ends were entangled on the seafloor, the *Stockholm* was held firmly in place. Fortunately, however, the crew was able to restrict the flooding to a single compartment, and the ship was never in danger of sinking. Captain H. Gunner Nordenson of the *Stockholm* responded to the *Andrea Doria*'s distress call by offering to take on survivors.

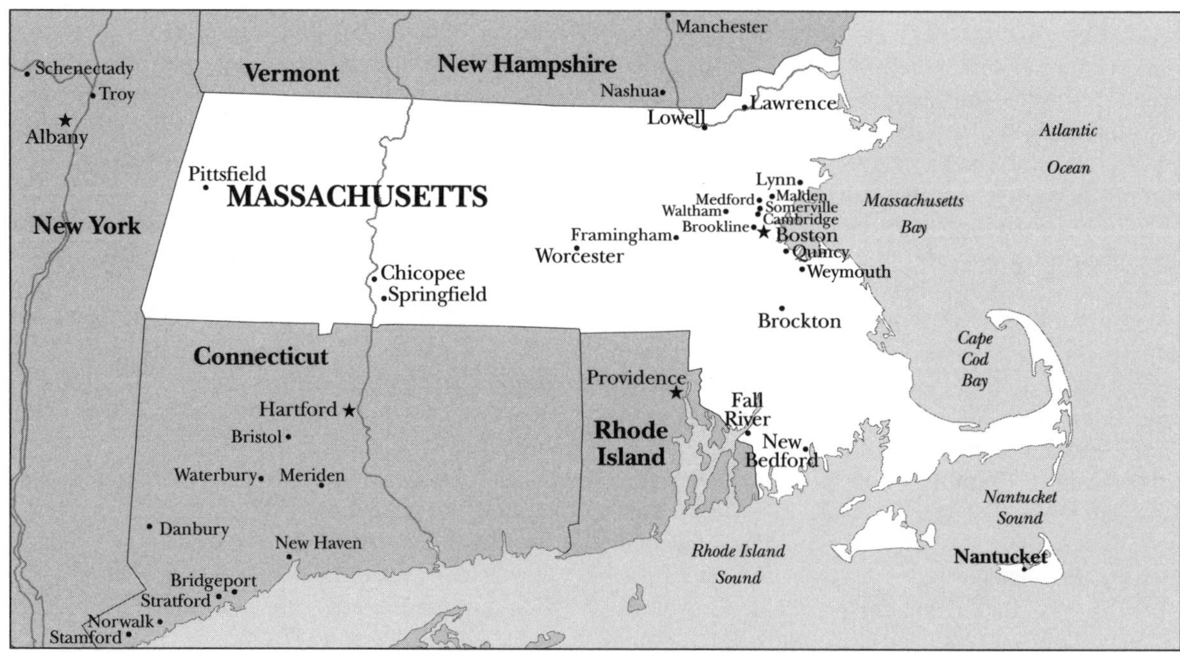

The Italian cruise liner Andrea Doria *sinks off the coast of Nantucket after colliding with the Swedish liner* Stockholm. (AP/Wide World Photos)

The *Stockholm* launched half its lifeboats and took aboard the first of the survivors just after midnight. The crew of the *Stockholm* was amazed to find that of the 545 survivors they received from the *Andrea Doria,* 234 were members of the crew, nearly all of whom came in the first wave of lifeboats.

Other ships that responded to the call for help included the oil tanker *Robert E. Hopkins,* the United States transports *Cape Ann* and *Private William H. Thomas,* the destroyer escort USS *Edward H. Allen,* the Coast Guard tug *Hornbeam,* and the French luxury liner *Ile de France.* Although not the first to arrive, the *Ile de France* played a key role in the rescue. To reassure the passengers of the *Andrea Doria* that help had arrived, the captain of the *Ile de France,* Baron Raoul de Beaudéan, pulled his vessel to within 400 yards of the listing wreck and turned on all the ship's lights. Beaudéan then had the ship's lifeboats assist in the evacuation of the stricken *Andrea Doria.* The first boats left the *Ile de France* around 2 A.M., and an hour later the last of the passengers and crew, except a salvage crew of 40 volunteers, were safely off the ship.

The captain remained aboard his ship awaiting the arrival of the Coast Guard tug until 5:30 A.M., when the list became so great that it was feared the ship might capsize at any moment. At that point, he and the last of his crew boarded the lifeboats. The *Andrea Doria* continued to float for several hours, but there was no hope that it could be saved. At 10 A.M. the ship rolled over on its side and then slipped beneath the waves.

The subsequent investigation into the loss of the Andrea Doria indicated that the *Stockholm's* bow struck the right side of the main fuel tanks of the Italian ship. The tanks on the left side of the ship remained intact and full of air. If these tanks could have been flooded somehow, the ship would have settled on an even keel and then would have been able to use all of its lifeboats or possibly even have survived the collision. Unfortunately, the only way to vent the air and flood these tanks was by way of controls located at the end of a tunnel running through the centerline of the ship. The tunnel flooded instantly, and there was no way to access the controls. With no way to correct its list, *Andrea Doria* continued to roll further as it settled in the water, until it finally capsized.

Thomas R. Stephens

FOR FURTHER INFORMATION:

Hocking, Charles. *Dictionary of Disasters at Sea During the Age of Steam, Including Sailing Ships and Ships of War Lost in Action, 1824-1962.* London: Lloyd's Register of Shipping, 1969.

Moscow, Alvin. *Collision Course: The Classic Story of the Most Extraordinary Sea Disaster of Our Times—The Collision at Sea of the S.S. "Andrea Doria" and the M.S. "Stockholm."* New York: Grosset & Dunlap, 1981.

Ritchie, David. *Shipwrecks: An Encyclopedia of the World's Worst Disasters at Sea.* New York: Facts on File, 1996.

1957: England

TRAIN COLLISION
DATE: December 4, 1957
PLACE: St. John's, England
RESULT: 92 dead, 187 injured in collision between electric train *Charing Cross* and steam train *Cannon Street*

Fog played a major role in one of the worst train accidents in the history of Great Britain's Southern Region Railroad. The 5:18 *Charing Cross*, an electric train with ten cars loaded with a mix of commuters and Christmas shoppers, was stopped at a signal in a thick fog. It was struck from behind by the 4:56 *Cannon Street*, a steam train. The steam train plowed into the rear of the electric train, then jackknifed, swinging out to strike a steel beam supporting a viaduct carrying other rail traffic. The stone viaduct collapsed on two coaches of the steam train, crushing them to about half their normal height.

Local citizens and firefighters rushed to the site of the accident, the civilians providing tea and blankets to the injured while the firemen worked to pull survivors from the wreckage. Rescue efforts were hampered by the instability of the damaged viaduct, and late in the morning all work was suspended until daylight to ensure that the viaduct was not accidentally knocked down. The large number of injured overwhelmed the three hospitals closest to the accident, forcing many to be transported further into London.

Thomas R. Stephens

FOR FURTHER INFORMATION:

The Times (London), December 5, 1957, p. 10.

1960: New York City

PLANE COLLISION
DATE: December 16, 1960
PLACE: Staten Island and Brooklyn, New York City
RESULT: 133 dead in collison of United and TWA airplanes

There was snow on the ground and a heavy fog in the air in New York City on the morning of December 16, 1960. Above Idlewild Airport (now John F. Kennedy Airport), two planes were in holding patterns waiting to land. The first was United Airlines flight 826, a DC-8 carrying 77 passengers and 7 crew members from Chicago's O'Hare Airport to Idlewild. The second was Transworld Airlines (TWA) flight 266, a Lockheed Super Constellation with 44 people aboard, traveling from the Cleveland Airport to New York's LaGuardia Airport.

Both planes were at 5,000 feet. The TWA plane was cleared by air traffic controllers at LaGuardia, who directed the pilot toward the narrow course leading to the landing strip. Due to the heavy fog, clouds, and drizzle, visibility was difficult. Meanwhile, the United plane had overshot its holding pattern by 12 miles and was traveling at a speed much higher than that necessary to maintain the usual holding pattern. The controller advised the TWA pilot of the existence of a plane 1 mile away, which the controller presumably believed to be traveling at a different altitude. At 10:23 A.M. the two blips representing the planes on the controller's radar screen merged, as the two planes collided.

The LaGuardia controller communicated with Idlewild Airport, which told him that one of its planes, a United DC-8, was missing. The United plane had indeed crossed the flight path of the TWA plane, its right wing tearing open the TWA's fuselage and sending one TWA passenger directly into one of the DC-8's engines. The TWA Constellation was reportedly knocked up on its tail with its propellers upward, then spiraled down toward Staten Island with one of the DC-8's engines in tow. The broken Constellation spread debris over 4 miles of Staten Island, much of which hit Miller Army Airfield. The airfield's controller recalled watching three large sections of plane flying through the overcast sky; two of the engines on these pieces exploded before they hit the ground, which caused the wings and tail to break off. The field was filled with smoke, flames, huge pieces of shrapnel, and parts of dismembered bodies falling from the sky. After impact, those passengers still strapped to their seats were ejected, turning the snow on the ground red.

Emergency workers removed the 3 live passengers to a hospital. Only 1 reached the hospital alive but died several hours later. At the crash scene, workers fought fires and attempted to identify and remove the bodies and debris strewn on the ground and in the trees. There were no survivors. Remarkably, all debris fell in unoccupied spaces such as the Miller Airfield and an empty playground, and there were no casualties besides the passengers and crew members.

The United plane, now missing an engine, continued on for 8 miles, trying desperately to reach LaGuardia Airport. It lost altitude quickly as it flew northeast over Brooklyn. At 10:30 A.M., the plane careened directly into Sterling Place, between Sixth and Seventh Avenue in the Park Slope neighborhood of Brooklyn. The plane sheared off the top of a sixteen-family apartment building, and the nose collided into the Pillar of Fire Church. The plane's tail ended up in a nearby intersection. The plane narrowly missed crashing into St. Augustine School, one block away from the crash site, where hundreds of children sat in their classes.

All passengers and crew were dead except an eleven-year-old boy, Steven Baltz, who had been flying from his home in Illinois to join his family in New York. Baltz crawled out of the flaming debris, burned and with broken bones, and was rushed to Methodist Hospital, where he died twenty-seven hours later. There were 5 casualties among Park Slope residents, killed when the debris hit: a Christmas tree seller, a dentist, the caretaker of the Pillar of Fire Church, a butcher, and a snow shoveler.

As with the TWA plane, the area was littered with metal wreckage, rubble from buildings, passengers' clothing, and bodies. The trees and fire escapes were littered with clothing and light debris. An emergency disaster signal notified the entire city of the tragedy. Workers controlled the fires, then began identifying and removing bodies.

The National Transportation Safety Board—assisted by the Federal Aviation Administration (FAA), airline manufacturers, and the pilot's union—and the airlines were responsible for investigating the crash. Investigation of the United/TWA crash, aided by the DC-8's flight data recorder found in the Pillar of Fire Church, was consistent with radar and radio data that showed that the United plane had gone past its holding pattern and was traveling at too high a speed. Additionally, one of the pilot's navigational radios was not functioning. These factors were assigned as the official primary cause of the accident. The fog prevented TWA from seeing the United plane, but this was not viewed as a source of blame. Primary blame was assigned to United Airlines, but skepticism over New York City's air traffic control system led to a final liability assignment of 61 percent responsibility to United, 24 percent to the United States government (responsible for the FAA air controllers), and 15 percent to TWA.

The crash did not result in many new aviation rules, although it did instigate the rule of reporting nonfunctioning navigational equipment to the air traffic controller. Inside information from FAA investigators claimed that the cause of the crash was inappropriate training of United pilots and that repeated written complaints by FAA investigators about poor training and other unsafe factors were not heeded. Documents supporting these claims exist in an FAA hearing, the investigator's private documents, and government records. These claims have not changed the official reason behind the crash, but they could if criminal charges were to be brought against United Airlines.

Michelle C. K. McKowen

For Further Information:

Jamieson, Wendell. "The Forgotten Disaster." *Newsday*, December 15, 1991, 1.

Stanley, Stewart. *Air Disasters*. London: Ian Allen, 1986.

Zautyk, Karen. "Red Snow: The Brooklyn Air Crash, 1960." *Daily News*, September 29, 1998, p. 47.

1977: Tenerife

Plane collision
Date: March 27, 1977
Place: Tenerife, the Canary Islands
Result: 583 dead in collision of two jumbo jets, including 335 of 396 onboard Pan American Boeing 747-121 and 248 onboard KLM Boeing 747-206B

Around 1:29 A.M. Greenwich mean time (GMT)—all times here correspond to this reference—on

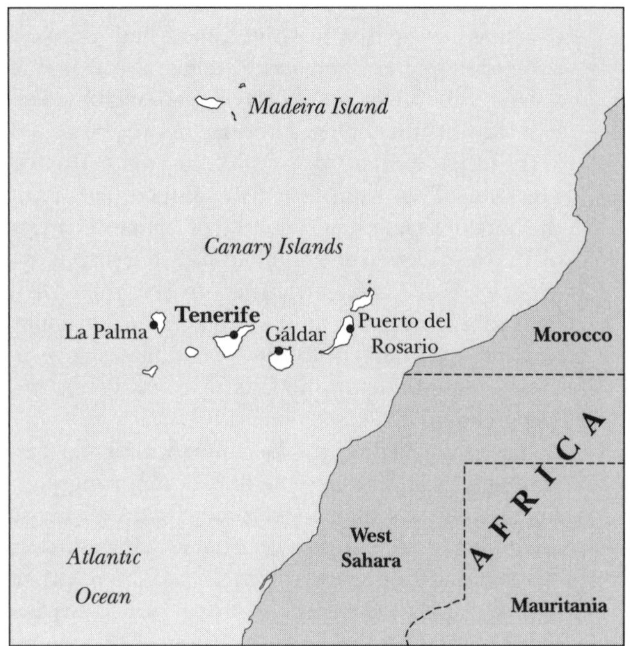

March 27, 1977, Pan American (Pan Am) flight 1736 took off from Los Angeles for a flight to Las Palmas, Spain, via New York. The Pan Am flight arrived at New York's John F. Kennedy (JFK) International Airport at 6:17 A.M., where it landed briefly for a change of crew and refueling prior to its transatlantic flight. Flight 1736, captained by veteran pilot Victor Grubbs, took off from JFK airport at 7:42 A.M. en route to Las Palmas. Around 9:31 A.M. on March 27, 1977, Royal Dutch Airlines (KLM) flight 4805, captained by KLM's chief 747 training pilot Jacob van Zanten, took off from Amsterdam for a flight to Las Palmas.

At approximately 12:30, a bomb exploded in the Las Palmas Airport's passenger terminal, and the airport was closed for security purposes. Consequently, KLM was diverted to Tenerife, an island owned by Spain that is the largest of the Canary Islands. It landed at Los Rodeos Airport at 1:38 P.M. Around 2:15, Pan Am was also diverted to Tenerife because of the bomb scare at Las Palmas Airport, and it arrived at Tenerife shortly before 3 P.M.

Around 3, Las Palmas Airport was once again opened to air traffic. Because the Pan Am flight had just arrived at Tenerife, and all of its 396 passengers and crew were still on board, the flight made preparations to leave at once. However, the taxiways were congested by twenty to thirty airplanes that had been diverted from Las Palmas. According to Dorothy Kelly, senior flight attendant of Pan Am and crash survivor, almost 400 passengers on the Pan Am flight had been up all night and did not know what was occurring. The Pan Am cockpit crew could hear KLM Captain Van Zanten complain on the radio about the delays and his anxiousness to take off.

At 4:15, the KLM airplane began refueling and passenger reboarding. This was completed, all but one passenger having reboarded, around 4:45. Now both Pan Am and KLM were parked parallel at the entrance to runway 12, away from the takeoff end. While the KLM flight was refueling, the Pan Am copilot and flight engineer stepped outside and found the wingtip clearance between the two aircrafts to be 12 feet short of the minimum required; hence the Pan Am flight had to wait.

Meanwhile, the air traffic control tower radioed instructions that KLM was to first taxi up runway 12 to the takeoff end and turn around 180 degrees. Pan Am was to follow KLM up runway 12 but clear the runway at the third taxiway and report back to the control tower. At 4:59, KLM received clearance to taxi up runway 12. Three minutes later Pan Am was cleared to follow KLM. As the plane moved, a thick fog descended upon the runway, rendering visibility extremely poor. Around 5:05, KLM reported ready for takeoff.

Cockpit voice recorder tapes indicate that at this time, an overanxious KLM Captain Van Zanten pushed his engines to full throttle, in preparation for takeoff, even though he did not have control tower clearance. The recorder tapes reveal a distressed first officer cautioning the captain that he does not have clearance. After the first officer requested clearance, air traffic control granted it. However, around the same time, a message from Pan Am informing the tower that it was still taxiing the runway was lost in noise recorded in the KLM cockpit. Around 5:06, the control tower instructed Pan Am to report when the runway was clear, to which Pan Am agreed.

Despite these audible interchanges and the fact that at 5:06 the control tower specifically instructed KLM to stand by for takeoff, Captain Van Zanten pushed the throttle back up, and the plane started to roll toward Pan Am, which was not visible in the fog. According to the cockpit voice recorder, the KLM flight engineer asked Captain Van Zanten in desperation whether Pan Am was still not clear off the runway, to which the response was *jawel* (an emphatic yes).

Within the next few seconds, the Pan Am captain and copilot noticed the KLM lights shaking—indicating movement—in the distance and made a desperate effort to get their plane off the runway. Moments before the impact, they saw the KLM landing lights, indicating that KLM had started to take off when it collided at full throttle with the hapless Pan Am.

Both aircrafts burst into flames on impact, with the top of Pan Am virtually sliced off. Many passengers on Pan Am were trapped in the flaming inferno with no escape route. Miraculously, however, 61 of 396 passengers and crew onboard Pan Am survived. KLM had no survivors among its 234 passengers and 14 crew members.

A joint investigation by Spanish investigators, the National Transportation Safety Board (NTSB), Pan Am, Boeing, KLM, and the Dutch government concluded that the main cause, though exacerbated by bad weather, of the worst aviation disaster in history was the irresponsible overanxiousness of the Dutch pilot, who chose to go ahead with takeoff despite serious uncertainties about air traffic control tower clearance to do so, even among his own cockpit crew.

Monish R. Chatterjee

For Further Information:

Carroll, R. "Collision Course: Runway Crash of KLM and Pan Am Jets at Tenerife Airport, Canary Islands." *Newsweek* 89 (April 11, 1977): 49-51.

Drake, S. "After the Holocaust: Crash of Pan Am and KLM Jets on Tenerife Runway." *Newsweek* 90 (September 26, 1977): 10.

"New Questions About Air Safety: With Views on Canary Islands Collision." *U.S. News and World Report* 82 (April 11, 1977): 35.

1991: Italy

Ship collision
Date: April 10, 1991
Place: Livorno, Italy

The damaged Italian tanker Agip Abruzzo *after being struck by the Italian ferry* Moby Prince. (AP/Wide World Photos)

Result: 141 dead in collision between ferry *Moby Prince* and oil tanker *Agip Abruzzo*

The ferry *Moby Prince* left the port of Livorno, Italy, at 10:30 p.m. on April 10, 1991, carrying 74 passengers and 68 crew members. A heavy fog severely restricted visibility. Most of the passengers and crew remained in their cabins watching a soccer match on television. Only 3 miles out of port, the ferry struck the anchored oil tanker *Agip Abruzzo.* Immediately following the collision, the *Moby Prince* reversed course and sent out an SOS over the radio.

Fire broke out aboard both ships, and the *Moby Prince* was engulfed by the quickly spreading flames. Oil from the blazing tanker spilled into the sea, surrounding the ferry with a ring of burning oil that prevented passengers and crew from jumping overboard. Only a single steward's mate, Alessio Bertrand, survived the conflagration, stumbling to the back of the ship and clinging to a rail. Temperatures within the ferry were believed to have reached over 1,000 degrees, frustrating rescue attempts.

Thomas R. Stephens

For Further Information:

The Times (London), April 11, 1991, p. 1.

Heat Waves

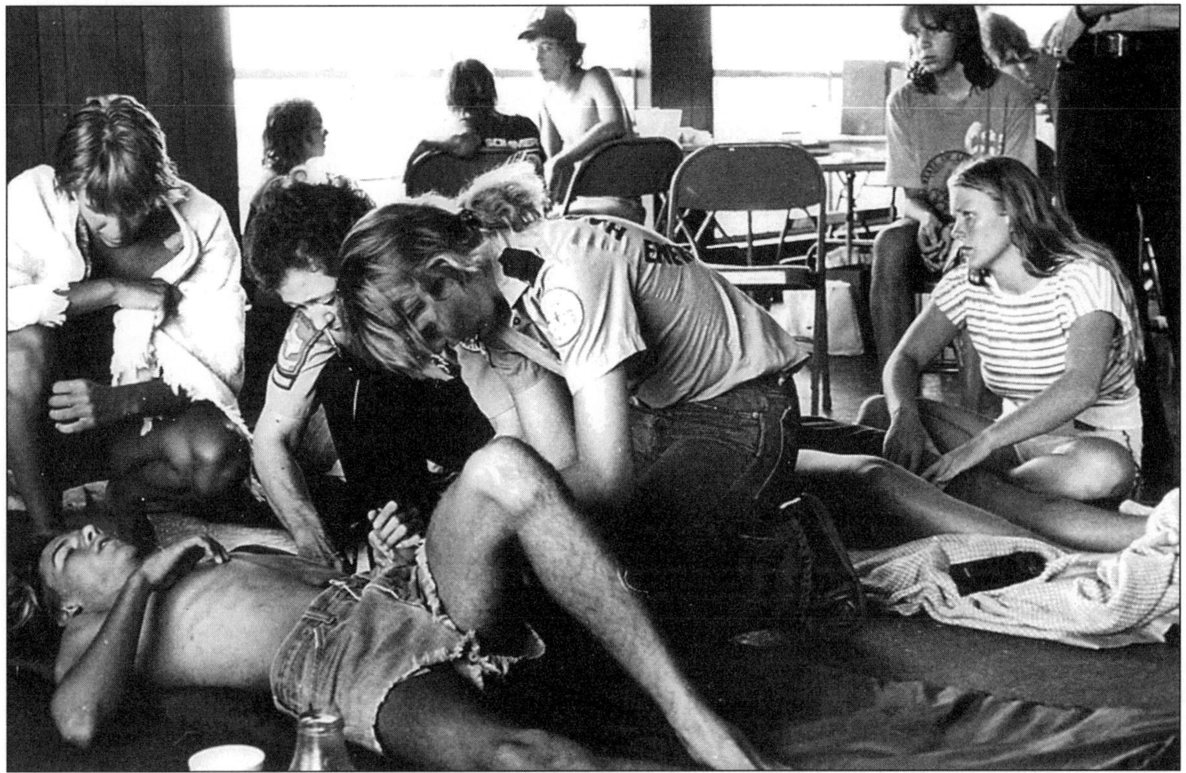

(AP/Wide World Photos)

Heat waves occur when the air temperature remains abnormally high for an extended period of time over a region. Heat waves destroy crops; damage infrastructure, such as roads, buildings, and railroad tracks; and cause both animal and human deaths.

Factors involved: Chemical reactions, geography, human activity, temperature, weather conditions, wind
Regions affected: Cities, coasts, deserts, plains, towns, valleys

Science

Heat waves are the result of a combination of natural factors and human activity. Natural factors include the normal heating of the earth's atmosphere by short-wave radiation from the sun and long-wave radiation from the earth, the flows of heat that make up the net radiation balance, the tilt of the earth, and the chemical makeup of the atmosphere above the surface of the earth. Human activity, mainly the burning of fossil fuels, is capable of changing the chemical makeup of the atmosphere and thus affects the heating of the earth's atmosphere.

Normal heating of the earth's atmosphere occurs when radiant heat, or short-wave radiation, from the sun begins to heat the earth shortly after dawn. Radiation is defined as the transmission of energy in the form of electromagnetic waves. The short-wave radiation is absorbed by the earth. The earth then emits long-wave radiation, which is absorbed by the atmosphere as heat. (Wavelength refers to the distance between the wave crests of successive waves.) In summary, the sun's rays heat the earth, the earth passes some of this heat to the air, or atmosphere, that surrounds it, and the atmosphere becomes warm. As the air near the earth warms, it rises, and cooler air descends. This rising and lowering sets air currents in motion in the atmosphere. These air currents carry the heat that under certain circumstances can become a heat wave.

A wide variety of factors can affect the amount of short-wave radiation that is absorbed by the earth. About 30 percent of the short-wave radiation coming to Earth is reflected by clouds or dust particles and never reaches the earth's surface. Another 17 percent of the radiation is absorbed by clouds and other particles in the atmosphere. Thus, a change in the amount of clouds or particles in the atmosphere will affect the amount of radiation that reaches Earth. The condition of the earth's surface also influences how much radiation is absorbed. The color, composition, and slope of the surface determine how much radiation is absorbed or reflected. Rays that strike the earth perpendicularly are less likely to be reflected. Rays that strike dark soil or dark surfaces are more likely to be absorbed than if they strike light-colored areas.

Carbon dioxide, water vapor, and ozone are the three major components of the atmosphere that absorb the long-wave radiation emitted by the earth, with carbon dioxide absorbing the most. The higher the concentration of these substances becomes in the atmosphere, the more heat is absorbed and the hotter the air becomes. High concentrations of these chemicals also provide a blanket effect over the earth, preventing radiation and heat from escaping. This blanket effect results in a phenomenon called the "greenhouse effect." In a greenhouse, the sun's rays pass through the glass and warm the air within the greenhouse. The glass, however, then prevents the heat from escaping. Similarly, the sun's radiation passes through the atmosphere, warming the earth and the air, and then the atmosphere stops the heat from escaping.

Although the greenhouse effect occurs naturally, it can be influenced by human activity. When fossil fuels are burned, enormous quantities of carbon dioxide are produced and released into the atmosphere. Over the last one hundred years, human beings have increased their use of fossil fuels drastically. Generating electricity, heating buildings, and using automobiles are all human activities that currently depend on burning fossil fuels. Debate continues among scientists as to what role the higher levels of carbon dioxide in the atmosphere and the greenhouse effect play in global warming trends.

When the radiation that leaves the earth is subtracted from the radiation that reaches earth, the amount of radiation left over is called the net radiation. Net radiation affects the earth's climates and is a source of heat for earth. Thus, all factors that affect radiation to and from the earth will influence the possible development of heat waves.

Geography

Heat waves can occur anywhere on Earth. A wide range of countries have reported heat waves, including the United States, Canada, Russia, India, Japan, many European countries, many African countries, Australia, and Cyprus. Heat waves generally occur over land masses rather than over the oceans. More energy is required to raise temperatures over water than over land, so temperature fluctuations are more prevalent over land. Thus, islands that are surrounded by large bodies of water do not experience heat waves. Since air cools as the altitude increases, mountainous areas are less susceptible to heat waves than are lower areas.

Urban areas tend to have higher rates of heat-related deaths than do rural areas. The heat retention of urban structures contributes to the natural heat of the heat wave. Also, the tall buildings and the pollution of urban areas stagnate the movement of air, thus intensifying the effects of a heat wave.

Many areas of the United States have been affected by heat waves. In 1901, 9,508 heat-related deaths occurred in the midwestern states. During the brutally hot summer of 1936, 15,000 to 20,000 people perished from the heat. As late as July, 1995, heat in the Midwest killed almost 500 Chicago residents. Heat waves have devastated the southern states and have wreaked havoc in both New England and California. As of 1999, neither Hawaii nor Alaska had recorded a heat wave. Although Hawaii is located near the equator, the Pacific Ocean surrounding Hawaii moderates its temperatures. Alaskan summer days can be hot, but they only go above 90 degrees Fahrenheit occasionally.

Prevention and Preparations

Human beings are powerless to control the natural forces, such as radiation, that affect heat waves. However, human beings can control the amount of fossil fuels they burn, and thus somewhat control the carbon dioxide in the atmosphere. Numerous international conferences have been held to discuss this issue.

Although heat waves are not preventable, both individuals and communities can prepare for heat waves and reduce their harmful effects. Individuals should discuss with family members what they would do during a heat wave and should identify the coolest places to be while at home, at work, or at school. They should learn about places in the community where people can go for help, plan daily activities for the coolest time of day, and refrain from working during the midday hours. Wearing lightweight, light-colored clothing and staying out of the sun can reduce the effects of a heat wave. People should talk to their doctors about any medications or medical conditions that would affect their ability to tolerate heat, as well as learn the signs and symptoms of heat stroke and heat exhaustion and first-aid treatments for these conditions.

On the community level, appropriate support programs can greatly reduce loss of life. Those most at risk are the elderly, the poor, and those with health conditions that reduce the ability to tolerate heat. Obtaining air conditioners and fans for those who need them has been effective in saving lives. Establishing "cool centers," areas that are air-conditioned, where people without air-conditioning can go to cool down, can also help reduce fatalities. Media announcements, especially television and radio, inform and alert people to the dangers of heat waves. During the Chicago heat wave of 1995, police officers even went door to door to check on elderly citizens.

Rescue and Relief Efforts

To save lives, rescue and relief efforts must be started as soon as the heat wave hits. The two dangerous medical conditions that result when heat waves occur are heat exhaustion and heat stroke, the latter being the more serious. When someone is exposed to hot weather for an extended time and does not take in adequate water and salt, heat exhaustion occurs. The human body cools itself by sweating; the evaporation of water from the skin reduces body heat. Excessive sweating causes the body to lose large amounts of water and salt. Extended exposure to heat requires the

The effects of a heat wave may be lessened by staying out of the sun, wearing lightweight clothing, and being in air-conditioned environments when possible. (AP/Wide World Photos)

body to sweat profusely in an effort to get rid of heat. If the water and salt lost in this process are not replaced, the body's attempts to cool itself eventually become ineffective, and heat exhaustion occurs.

The symptoms of heat exhaustion include pale, clammy skin, rapid pulse and breathing, headache, muscle cramps, dizziness, and a sick and faint feeling. If heat exhaustion occurs, the victim should lie down in as cool a place as possible with his or her feet raised slightly, loosen tight clothing, and replace lost fluids by drinking water. One level teaspoon of salt added to each quart (or liter) of water will help to replace the salt lost during excessive sweating. Heat exhaustion must be treated immediately or it will progress to heat stroke.

Heat stroke, also called sunstroke, occurs when the body's temperature regulation mechanism fails. This mechanism, which is located in the brain, normally helps the body maintain a constant temperature by telling the body to shiver if it needs to become warmer or to sweat if it needs to cool. If a person suffers a heat stroke, this mechanism stops functioning and the body temperature starts to rise to 104 degrees Fahrenheit (40 degrees Celsius) or higher. This is a medical emergency, and medical help should be sought immediately.

The symptoms of heat stroke include flushed, hot, dry skin; strong, rapid pulse; confusion; and ultimately unconsciousness. To treat heat stroke until medical help arrives, victims should be moved to the coolest place possible. Their clothing should be removed, they should be sponged with cool or tepid water, and they should be fanned by hand or with an electric fan. A blow-dryer set on cool may also be used. When the body temperature is reduced to about 101 degrees Fahrenheit (38 degrees Celsius), victims should be turned over onto their stomachs with one leg bent slightly, arms raised to the level of the head, and the head tilted back, keeping the chin lower than the body. The entire process must be repeated if the body temperature begins to climb again.

Impact

In the United States alone, heat waves have been responsible for the loss of billions of dollars and thousands of human lives. Heat waves damage property, both privately and publicly owned. They kill cattle and destroy crops. Excessive heat causes roads to buckle and crumble, and it warps metal, causing, for example, railroad tracks to bend, resulting in train derailments. Heat waves have been connected to increased cases of riots, violence, and homicides. Sustained heat waves are very difficult for the human body to tolerate. When heat waves occur, normal daily activity must be adjusted in order for humans to survive.

Louise Magoon

Bibliography

Abrahamson, Dean Edwin. *The Challenge of Global Warming.* Washington, D.C.: Island Press, 1989. Provides a through discussion of the greenhouse effect.

American Red Cross. *Heat Wave.* Stock Number NOAA/PA 94052. Rev. ed. Washington, D.C.: U.S. Dept. of Commerce, 1998. This pamphlet gives very practical advice on how to survive a heat wave.

Clayman, Charles B., M.D. *The American Medical Association Family Medical Guide.* 3d ed. New York: Random House, 1994. Offers a thorough description of heat exhaustion and heat stroke and the first-aid treatments for these conditions.

DeBlij, H. J., and Peter O. Muller. *Physical Geography of the Global Environment.* New York: John Wiley & Sons, 1993. This geography textbook describes the heating of the earth's atmosphere, global distribution of heat flows, the greenhouse effect, and climate changes.

Graedel, T. E., and Paul J. Crutzen. *Atmosphere, Climate, and Change.* New York: W. H. Freeman, 1995. This book gives a very easy-to-read description of weather, temperature, and climatic changes.

_______. *Atmospheric Change: An Earth System Perspective.* New York: W. H. Freeman, 1993. Details the chemistry of the atmosphere and climate and describes ancient climate histories.

Lyons, Walter A. *The Handy Weather Answer Book.* Detroit: Visible Ink Press, 1997. Using a question-and-answer format, the author gives short, simple answers to questions that are posed.

Oliver, John E. *The Encyclopedia of Climatology.* New York: Van Nostrand Reinhold, 1987. Provides a good discussion of the effects of temperature extremes.

Notable Events

Historical Overview

Throughout history, extremes in temperature have greatly affected human existence. From 543 to 547 A.D., the entire Roman world suffered from plague. Great heat in the area contributed to the spread of the disease. Hot weather caused the flea that transmitted the bubonic plague to speed up its life cycle. The European countries were also affected by wave after wave of disease from 1348 until 1665. Again, the hot summers furthered the spread of the disease.

Detailed weather records from early times do not exist. Information about weather is inferred from the reports of travelers and food availability. Weather reports from the sixteenth century have survived. However, reports based on instrument readings did not appear until the seventeenth century. These records show that periods of high temperature have been recorded for many areas on earth, including Europe, Africa, China, India, Australia, and North America. As time progressed, the records became much more detailed. Thus, much of the information available on heat waves relates to events occurring after the middle of the nineteenth century.

Heat waves have been a contributing factor in human migration patterns. In Ireland, in 1845, hot summer temperatures favored the growth of the or-

Milestones

1348-1350:	Hot summers contribute to the spread of bubonic plague in Europe.
1665-1666:	Very hot summers in London exacerbate the last plague epidemic.
1690:	Siberia experiences extreme heat, probably due to southerly winds; at this time, Europe is abnormally cold.
1718-1719:	Great heat and drought affect most of Europe during the summers of these years.
1845:	Moist, southerly winds and a hot summer provide the perfect growing conditions for the potato blight fungus, resulting in the Irish Potato Famine.
1902:	Willis H. Carrier designs the first system to control the temperature of air.
1906:	The term "air-conditioning" is used for the first time by an engineer named Stuart W. Cramer.
1936:	Dust Bowl conditions arise in the central United States; 15,000 to 20,000 die.
1968-1973:	Drought occurs in the Sahel region of Africa.
1972:	A heat wave affects Russia and Finland.
1975-1976:	Heat waves are recorded in Denmark and the Netherlands.
1980:	A heat wave in Texas produces forty-two consecutive days above 100 degrees Fahrenheit.
1990:	The United Nations' Intergovernmental Panel on Climate Change (IPCC) predicts that greenhouse gases and carbon dioxide emissions produced by human activity could raise world temperatures by 32.5 degrees Fahrenheit (0.25 degree Celsius) per decade.
August, 1994:	A severe heat wave and drought parches Japan; blocks of ice are put in subway stations for travelers to rub their heads against.
July, 1995:	A heat wave in the midwestern United States kills almost 500 people in Chicago alone, as well as 4,000 cattle.
1995:	The IPCC predicts carbon dioxide and greenhouse emissions to raise earth's temperatures between 33.4 and 38 degrees Fahrenheit (0.8 and 3.5 degrees Celsius) within one hundred years.
July, 1998:	A heat wave hits the southwestern and northeastern United States; daytime temperatures in Texas hit 110 degrees Fahrenheit, with forty-one days of above-100-degree weather, causing huge crop losses and 144 deaths.
July, 1998:	Worldwide, July is determined to be the hottest month in history to date.
August, 1998:	India reaches 124 degrees Fahrenheit; 3,000 people die in the worst heat wave to hit India in fifty years.
August, 1998:	50 people die in Cyprus, and 30 die in Greece and Italy; grapes die on vines.
August, 1998:	In Germany, record heat produces severe smog, and cars lacking antipollution devices are banned.

ganism that caused the potato blight fungus. Failure of the potato crop resulted in widespread famine. Over the next six years around 1 million people died in Ireland. Although an epidemic of typhus contributed to the death toll, hunger played a significant role. Believing that there were more opportunities elsewhere, thousands of Irish immigrated to the United States.

In the United States, heat waves have been responsible for thousands of deaths and the loss of billions of dollars in the twentieth century alone. The century began with a very hot summer in 1901. It is reported that 9,500 people died that summer. The summer of 1936 was brutally hot; an estimated 15,000 to 20,000 people lost their lives. Those who survived often lost their farms and everything for which they had worked. Again, heat waves influenced migration; families left the "Dust Bowl" area of the middle United States and moved toward the coasts, where more fertile land was to be found.

The air-conditioning of homes began in the 1930's, but it was not in prevalent use. In 1980, only 30 percent of the homes in the United States had air-conditioning, which greatly reduces death tolls during heat waves.

The heat wave of 1980 in the midwestern United States killed 1,265. The heat wave of 1988 resulted in 10,000 casualties. In 1995, almost 500 people in Chicago died within one week. The same heat wave killed 4,000 cattle. The increasing frequency and severity of heat waves worldwide in the last half of the twentieth century generated tremendous concern in the scientific community. Much effort went into studying weather patterns in an attempt to determine whether these heat waves are just part of a natural fluctuation of weather or if human activity is contributing to the warming of the earth.

The damage done by heat waves does not affect all socioeconomic classes to the same degree. The economically disadvantaged suffer more dire consequences when heat waves hit than do those with resources. During the heat wave that struck Chicago in 1995, most of the fatalities were people who were poor and elderly. Most lived in the top floors of old apartment buildings that were not air-conditioned. People with resources obtained air-conditioning or left the city. Farmers are another group of people who are hard hit by heat waves. When heat waves destroy crops or kill cattle, the farmer's livelihood is destroyed as well. Meanwhile, an accountant who lives in an air-conditioned home in the city pays a bit more for hamburger but hardly notices. Thus, heat waves affect some social classes more than others.

Louise Magoon

1911: New York, Pennsylvania

Date: July 3-11, 1911
Place: New York City and central Pennsylvania, especially Pittsburgh
Temperature: 104 degrees Fahrenheit
Result: 380 dead

The summer of 1911 was hot throughout the North Temperate Zone (the region between the Arctic Circle and the tropic of Cancer), as both Europe and North America experienced record highs. The American Northeast even surpassed many record highs, often enduring sweltering, 100-degree heat. The temperature soared to 104 degrees at Vernon, Vermont, and North Bridgton, Maine, and to 105 degrees at Nashua, New Hampshire, to establish all-time highs for those three states. Afternoon highs of 101 at Boston, 101 at Albany, New York, and 100 at Portland, Maine, were precedent-setters for those cities. North of the border, Rocklesse, Ontario, saw a temperature of 108.

The impact of the heat was most severe in New York City and its surroundings. A warm front traveled eastward from New Jersey at the pace of 3 miles an hour. Citizens looked for thickening clouds, hoping they would bring the relief of rain, but felt only a few scattered drops here and there.

The New York City Department of Health attempted to advise the populace on the cause, prevention, and treatment of sunstroke and heat prostration. New York mayor William J. Gaynor expressed concern that ice dealers, who provided the ice responsible for cooling perishable food in prerefrigeration times, would not be able to get ice to their customers. However, no serious drought or food spoilage occurred. Finally, a warm front from Canada dispersed the heat as a major thunderstorm predicted by the United States Weather Service never materialized.

On July 13, the death total from the heat wave was reported at 211. The heat afflicted all ages; most of those who died from the heat succumbed in their homes. Most of the victims were males, a phenomenon that newspaper reports and editorials struggled to analyze. An actor named Robert Crook, disoriented by the heat, overdosed himself with strychnine. This heat wave also claimed victims in Pittsburgh and Philadelphia (the latter city reporting a total of 159 fatalities on July 16) and indirectly across a wide swath of central Pennsylvania, when a thunderstorm bringing respite from the heat hit that area, killing 5 and providing yet another reminder of the unpredictability of nature.

Nicholas Birns

For Further Information:

"Heat Mounts to 95 and Kills 22 Persons." *New York Tribune*, July 11, 1911.

1916: Chicago

Date: July 20-29, 1916
Place: Chicago and environs, including Wisconsin
Temperature: 100 degrees Fahrenheit
Result: 380 dead

The heat wave that burdened Chicago and environs in the summer of 1916 was caused by a large warm front camped over Lake Michigan for the balance of a week, which barely moved an inch in that time. The life and energy of the city, as well as in outlying towns and nearby cities in Wisconsin, such as Kenosha, also ground to a halt. The temperature reached 100, and the humidity was at nearly 80 percent; the usual jokes about hell being no hotter than Chicago in summer gained a new relevance.

Railroad cars had considerable trouble operating, given that the heat had warmed the tracks to near-unacceptable levels of danger, and being inside the railroad cars was so uncomfortable that travel dwindled to a minimum. The immigrant community was particularly affected, and the city's then-meager network of social services was strained to the maximum. The Catholic diocese, to which many of the immigrants belonged, took a leading role in helping organize relief for these communities.

No one can know how many deaths were advanced by the torrid weather, how many diseased or aging hearts surrendered that under better conditions would have continued functioning. This is especially true in conditions such as prevailed in Chicago in 1916, when so many citizens were potentially vulnerable to the heat. The high casualty level of 380, though, cannot wholly be blamed on the absence of modern amenities and government planning, as a similar heat wave in 1995 claimed an even larger number of victims.

Nicholas Birns

For Further Information:

Chicago Tribune, 1916.

United States Weather Bureau. *Climatic Guide for Chicago, Illinois Area.* Washington, D.C.: Author, 1962.

1917: New York City

Date: July 27 to August 3, 1917
Place: New York City, as well as rural areas of New York State, New Jersey, and Connecticut
Temperature: 103 degrees Fahrenheit
Result: 190 dead

As American troops prepared to ship off to Europe to fight in World War I, New York City was suffering through a torrid stretch of weather during the height of summer. As opposed to earlier and later heat waves, in which the majorities of the damage and deaths were in the city itself, during July and August of 1917 it was the rural areas of New York State, New Jersey, and Connecticut that bore the brunt of the heat.

In Long Island, for instance, a region that was then heavily agricultural, the potato crop failed in the heat. The heat wave unfortunately transpired in the crucial weeks leading up to the beginning of the harvest, far too late in the crop cycle to repair or undo the damage. At least one proprietor of a Suffolk County potato farm declared that he was economically ruined and intended to sell out as soon as possible. However, not all was sorrowful in New York-area agriculture. Winemakers in Long Island and the upstate Finger Lakes regions reported that the high temperatures and dry weather would increase the quality of their vintages for the year, making them one of the few groups to enjoy the oppressive weather of the summer of 1917.

The sweltering heat in the rural areas did not mean that the city was spared. Stifling heat caused New York Yankees fans watching the baseball team at Hilltop Park to faint in the stands, and several of the city's major department stores reported cases of heat prostration among their customers. It was nearly impossible to travel in the city's subway system because of the stifling underground heat. An outside observer would have found it hard to believe that the world's busiest and most sophisticated city could be stopped in its tracks by the natural forces of heat, but the heat was all too real for the New Yorkers trapped in its midst. A cold front from Canada brought relief, but not before the summer weather had taken an unusually high toll on the city, leaving 190 dead.

Nicholas Birns

For Further Information:

New York Sun, August 1-3, 1917.
The New York Times, August 1-3, 1917.
New York Tribune, August 1-3, 1917.

1931: United States

Date: June 27-July 2, 1931
Place: Throughout the United States, especially midwestern and southern states
Temperature: Average of 106 degrees Fahrenheit
Result: 1,016 dead in 12 states

During the summer of 1931 there was a tremendous hot spell followed by a drought, which resulted in such severely dry conditions that winds began blowing the soil around in what became known as the Dust Bowl. June 27, 1931, began an intense period of temperatures repeatedly reaching 90 degrees or more. Between June 30 and July 2 in Vermont, temperatures reached 90, 96, and 93 degrees Fahrenheit consecutively.

In various states throughout the country, record-setting temperatures were reached. In Monticello, Florida, a record temperature of 109 degrees was reached on June 29, 1931. The temperatures eventually averaged out at 106 degrees. The Midwest was es-

pecially hard hit since a heat wave had also occurred during the summer of 1930. Rainfall in early 1930 had been about average, however, while it was markedly reduced during 1931. As the hot temperatures continued with little rainfall, people succumbed to the heat, and eventually 1,016 died due to the intense heat.

Heat kills by taxing the human body beyond its limits. Approximately 175 Americans die due to the demands of summer heat during an average year, according to the National Weather Service (NWS). The NWS defines a heat wave as a period of three or more days with temperatures over 90 degrees. During modern times, with the luxuries of central air and public swimming pools to beat the heat, average casualties rarely reach 250.

During 1931, record temperatures were reached. Throughout the entire year, Lincoln, Nebraska, recorded sixty-two days with temperatures over 90 degrees. These were not consecutive days, but such temperatures greatly contributed to the climate conditions during 1931. Lincoln also recorded fifteen days with temperatures of 100 degrees or more. Las Vegas, Nevada, reached an all-time record temperature of 118 degrees in mid-July, 1931.

To add to the problems, warm winds from the west, blowing across the Pacific, picked up moisture from the ocean. However, as these winds crossed the Rocky Mountains, they lost their moisture, becoming very dry. During 1931, rainfall averaged about 7 inches less than normal for the area. Crops failed, and the usually hardy prairie grasses began dying. As vegetation died, the roots that held the soil in place also disappeared.

With the hotter temperatures and the warm westerly winds the heat wave intensified. During the summer of 1931, the Midwest was literally baking. With no rainfall, which cools both the earth and the air temperature, the actual temperature was probably higher than the thermometer readings. Although the winds crossing the Rocky Mountains were dry, meaning the humidity was lower, the heat from those dry winds intensified the actual air temperatures. Both the heat and blowing dust caused health problems for many people, especially children and the elderly.

Also, the midwestern farmers were especially hard hit by the economic depression gripping the nation. These farmers had gone from bumper wheat crops to an abundant supply, which drove prices down. At the beginning of the Depression, farmers fought to keep their farms. As the heat destroyed crops, the physical condition and health of farm families declined, which also led to a greater number of deaths during the heat wave of 1931.

The 1931 heat wave led to the drought on the Great Plains, which lasted until 1938. The drought became so bad farmers left in swarms for California. With the soil parched and overworked from bumper crops during post-World War I farming, the clods of soil broke down into fine dust. As winds picked up, dust storms began. The first occurred in 1932. They became more severe as the weeks and months of dry, hot days continued, summer after summer. Soon, the blowing sand became so bad the storms looked like black blizzards and soil had to be shoveled out of houses and away from doors. The Midwest became known as the Dust Bowl.

Though the heat wave of 1931 ultimately led to the drought and Dust Bowl conditions in the American Midwest, this event had a profoundly positive effect on American society. With the "dust blizzards" reaching extremes in the mid-1930's, revolutionary agricultural policy was developed. The Soil Conservation and Domestic Allotment Act was voted into existence in 1936, once legislators experienced the "black blizzards" as dust blew from the Great Plains all the way to the Capitol. The Soil Conservation Service enacted measures to refurbish the Great Plains.

Lisa A. Wroble

For Further Information:

Allaby, Michael. *Dangerous Weather: Droughts.* New York: Facts on File, 1998.

Henson, Robert, with Steve Horstmeyer et al. "The Twentieth Century's Top Ten U.S. Weather and Climate Events." *Weatherwise,* November/December, 1999. Also at wwww.weatherwise.org/99.nd.20thcent.html.

National Weather Service. "Heat Index Program." www.nws.noaa.gov/er/mhx/heatwvg.htm.

"Record Breaking Heat of July." *Science News* 80 (August 10, 1934): 135.

Thornley, B. "Riding the Heat Waves." *Collier's,* July 26, 1930, 19.

Ward, Kaari, ed. "Drought and Despair in Mid-America." *Great Disasters.* Pleasantville, N.Y.: Reader's Digest Association, 1989.

Watkins, T. H. "Dust, Drought, and Displacement." In *The Great Depression.* Boston: Little, Brown, 1993.

1948: New York City

Date: August 24-30, 1948
Place: New York City
Temperature: 100 degrees Fahrenheit
Result: 33 dead

As their newspapers blared headlines concerning the crisis between the United States and the Soviet Union over the fate of West Berlin in 1948, New Yorkers were worrying about problems closer to home. A dense fog heralded a rush of warm gulf air, which infiltrated the New York area in late August, causing fire hydrants to be opened and municipal swimming pools to be overwhelmed with bathers seeking relief. Thousands even slept on the beaches to escape the ovenlike heat of their homes. The heat set off burglar alarms in many apartments, creating additional havoc and confusion. The suburbs also felt the impact of the drought as aquifers and underground water tables subsided. Because New York City relies for its water supply on reservoirs in upstate New York rather than on wells or any other form of groundwater, the risk of drought did not cause any particular water shortages or rationing, but the persistence of the heat still generated concern.

August 26 saw the temperature reach 108 degrees, the hottest day since 1936 and the third hottest day on record in the history of New York City. There were over 30 fatalities throughout the region, most of them occurring in multifamily dwellings in the inner city. Although not all deaths at the time were traceable to the heat, the city's health department noted a substantial rise when compared to the previous year. Press editorials debated whether heat quickened or aroused mental instability. With the new respectability of psychology in American society, discussion of the mental effects of heat waves became part of public discussion of these weather phenomena for the first time, opening an important new angle in studying the impact of weather on human society.

Just as public concern about the heat peaked, additional anxiety was created by news that a large hurricane was on its way up the eastern seaboard with the potential to strike New York City. Fortunately, the hurricane stayed away, and the influence of a low-pressure front on its periphery brought cooling rain sorely yearned for by New Yorkers.

Nicholas Birns

For Further Information:

"Mercury Tops 91 in Month's Hottest." *New York Sun*, August 26, 1948.
New York Herald Tribune, August 20-30, 1948.
The New York Times, August 20-30, 1948.

1951: Texas

Date: August 1-18, 1951
Place: Eastern and central Texas
Temperature: 102-104 degrees Fahrenheit
Result: 42 dead

The summer of 1950 had yielded uncomfortable hot stretches, but the entire summer of 1951 was one long sustained heat wave for Texas, as it stayed hot almost continuously for three long months. The beginning and middle of August were particularly severe. Drought and extreme heat affected an expanding area of the south that summer, being particularly severe in Texas and Oklahoma. Texas estimated over $105 million in agricultural losses. Overall economic costs were predicted to be two to three times the agricultural losses. Also, at least 42 heat-related deaths occurred statewide.

This was one of the driest and warmest April-July periods on record for Texas, with mean temperature of 76 degrees Fahrenheit (almost tying the 1925 record) and a remarkably low mean precipitation of 4.51 inches. In San Antonio, it was over 100 degrees Fahrenheit for five straight days; in Del Rio, temperatures were over 100 for a week. Austin and the normally fertile hill country of central Texas received less than a third of its usual rainfall. Dallas was the community most seared by the heat, as the temperature surpassed 100 for nine consecutive days. A cooling weather pattern surged in from the Great Plains by mid-August. Average temperatures, though, remained in the nineties, strong enough to seriously harm that fall's agricultural harvest.

Nicholas Birns

For Further Information:

Bomar, George. *Texas Weather.* Austin: University of Texas Press, 1985.

1955: California

Date: August 31-September 8, 1955
Place: Central and Southern California
Temperature: 100-110 degrees Fahrenheit
Result: 107 dead

Californians, used to long periods of temperate, warm weather, were reacquainted with the trials of temperature extremes by the heat wave that hit the southern and central regions of the state at the end of the summer of 1955. In Los Angeles, the heat was exacerbated by the city's rampant smog, which made the air almost unbreathable at times. Morning fog, visible in Los Angeles and surrounding areas, promised relief from the heat but did not deliver.

Los Angeles experienced a record stretch of consecutive 100-degree days, reaching at one point a two-year high of 101. The densely populated coastal areas averaged between 96 and 101 degrees Fahrenheit; remote inland areas such as Barstow and Brawley saw the mercury reach at least 110 degrees. In the agricultural Central Valley, the heat harmed crops and endangered the irrigation system pivotal to the health of California's agriculture. Governor Goodwin Knight inspected several drought-devastated areas in early September. By September 10, a cool sea breeze from the Pacific had crested inland, alleviating the heat but not eliminating the impression it had made upon the land and people of California.

Nicholas Birns

For Further Information:

DeMarrais, Gerard A., George C. Holzworth, and Charles R. Hosler. *Meteorological Summaries Pertinent to Atmospheric Transport and Dispersion over Southern California.* Washington, D.C.: U.S. Government Printing Office, 1965.

Pitt, Leonard, and Dale Pitt. *Los Angeles A to Z.* Berkeley: University of California Press, 1997.

1957: Western Europe

Date: July 2-8, 1957
Place: Western Europe, particularly Italy, West Germany, Austria, and the Netherlands
Temperature: 96 degrees Fahrenheit
Result: 340 dead

In early July of 1957, a high-pressure front of warm Mediterranean air filled the skies over Western Europe and remained for almost a week. By Tuesday, July 9, deaths from the heat wave had reached a count of 340. At least 147 people were killed in Italy from Sunday to Tuesday. Particularly affected were residents of senior citizens' homes; 95 such victims died in the northern Italian cities of Venice, Padua, and Milan. Sixty-eight casualties occurred in West Germany, 35 in Austria, and 29 in the Netherlands. These deaths resulted from dehydration, heat stroke, heat-induced heart attacks, and traffic jams caused by citizens trying to escape to cooler beach or mountain climates.

Traffic was also a big problem in England, where temperatures were cooler in absolute terms but seemed relatively high to the English, who considered the high eighties scorching. Major highways in England were clogged with motorists trying to escape the heat. Temperatures went as high as 96 in Paris, the highest temperature in nine years, and July 4 witnessed the hottest temperature ever recorded in France on that date.

Nicholas Birns

For Further Information:

Facts on File 1957, July 4, 1957-July 10, 1957.

"96 Degrees in Paris." *The Times* (London), July 5, 1957, p. 10.

1958: Saudi Arabia

Date: June 28, 1958
Place: Mecca, Saudi Arabia
Temperature: 111 degrees Fahrenheit
Result: 35 dead

The hajj (pilgrimage) to the Islamic holy sites in Mecca, Saudi Arabia, is a peak experience in the life of any devout Muslim. It also creates one of the most densely populated temporary concentrations of humanity on the planet. Pilgrims come from all over the Muslim world, of varying ethnicity, language, and sect. Every Muslim is under a theoretical obligation to make the hajj, and some save money their entire lives to journey to Mecca. This mass of nonindigenous peoples from foreign lands already in a heightened emotional state was apt to be unusually upset by the severe heat that parched Saudi Arabia in late June, 1958.

A very low relative humidity of less than 10 percent caused severe shortages of drinking water, exacerbating the situation. On Friday, the official Muslim day of prayer, the heat, the thirst, and the confusion all came to a head, and 35 fatalities occurred. Limitations of the availability of drinking water and the absence of large-scale shelters compounded the problem. The pilgrims who had sought to honor their religion and its shrines were instead forced to confront nature's haphazard ways.

Nicholas Birns

For Further Information:

Peters, F. E. *The Hajj: The Muslim Pilgrimage to Mecca and the Holy Places.* Princeton, N.J.: Princeton University Press, 1994.

1960: India

Date: June 1-21, 1960
Place: Northern India
Temperature: 109 degrees Fahrenheit
Result: 395 dead

The usually fertile and temperate Indo-Gangetic plain of northern India was saddled with nearly three weeks of stifling heat in June, 1960. Cities such as Varanasi (106 degrees Fahrenheit), Agra (109 degrees Fahrenheit), and Lucknow (108 degrees Fahrenheit) experienced precedent-setting highs in temperature. June is not normally very rainy in northern India, but it was even worse than usual in 1960, with rain levels perched near an all-time low, averaging under 2 inches (50 millimeters) in the major communities of the region. Despite substantial efforts by government authorities and individuals to save as many lives as possible, the sustained heat eventually broke down resistance and killed hundreds. Drought and thirst were judged to be as responsible for the deaths that occurred, as was the heat itself.

Nicholas Birns

For Further Information:

India Meteorological Office. *Hundred Years of Weather Service, 1875-1975.* Poona, India: India Meteorological Department, 1976.

1965: India

Date: June 16, 1965
Place: Assam and Meghalaya provinces, India
Temperature: 91-104 degrees Fahrenheit
Result: 144 dead

The mountainous areas of Assam and neighboring provinces normally have cool temperatures in June, averaging about 68 degrees Fahrenheit. A warm front swept in from the Bay of Bengal and hovered over the area cities. Gauhati and Jorhat, as well as Shillong in neighboring Meghalaya, reported record-breaking highs, with Shillong reaching 104 degrees Fahrenheit. What is the notoriously rainiest region of India, one with some of the highest precipitation levels worldwide, suffered from an unaccustomed assailant—heat. Those who were killed by the heat were mainly traders who had to travel long distances for their work; they died largely of exposure. A cholera epidemic given ballast by the heat killed far more, bringing the total death toll to over 1,000.

Nicholas Birns

For Further Information:

Telegraph (Calcutta), June 17-18, 1965.

1965: Brazil

Date: December 27, 1965
Place: São Paulo, Brazil
Temperature: 95 degrees Fahrenheit
Result: 135 children dead, many injured

December is the height of summer in equatorial São Paulo, Brazil. Summers are hot there but not severe, because São Paulo's slightly inland location removes it from the immediate zone of the Brazilian coast and its often boiling heat. The heat that came in from the northeast was fierce and came in a package of fetid, torpid air, a blanket of warmth that was unmoving. A high relative humidity, consistently over 90 percent, did not help conditions.

The stagnant atmosphere of the heat wave trapped the already polluted air, severely affecting crowded alleys and shanties of the inner city. Holiday festivities had brought many people to the city, with many families visiting friends and relatives over the

Christmas break. While this meant that fewer people were isolated in their homes, an often dangerous condition during a heat wave, the population was outside, bearing the brunt of the sun's force. Very few residents had air-conditioning in 1965; among these were 135 children who died of heat exhaustion.

Nicholas Birns

For Further Information:

The New York Times, December 28, 1965.

São Paulo, Brazil. Translated by Wordware Agencia de Traducoes. São Paulo, Brazil: Callis Editora, 1995.

1966: India

Date: June 4-11, 1966
Place: Bihar, northern India
Temperature: 102 degrees Fahrenheit
Result: 300 dead

The winds that blow through the province of Bihar, India, in the spring or "hot season" are ususally rather slow, but in June of 1966 they were virtually nonexistent, as a static, stagnant heat lingered over the area for an entire week. Patna, the capital of Bihar, reported record highs of 102 degrees Fahrenheit, as well as a rainfall of 2.2 inches (56 millimeters), which was only about 35 percent of the normal amount received by the city. By the time cool winds from the southeast dissipated the heat on Saturday, June 11, hundreds of people had died of sunstroke and dehydration. In the northwest region of India, it was announced on June 14 on All-India Radio that 69 people had succumbed to the heat. It is likely that when the rainy season finally arrived in 1960, citizens of India appreciated it more than usual.

Nicholas Birns

For Further Information:

Telegraph (Calcutta), June 9-14, 1966.

1966: New York City

Date: July 1-13, 1966
Place: New York City, especially Brooklyn
Temperature: 102 degrees Fahrenheit
Result: More than 200 dead

At first the citizens of New York City did not even particularly notice the slow, steady heat in July of 1966. By July 11, though, it was impossible to ignore, as the city simmered in triple-digit temperatures, straining the resources of local electric and water utilities. The African American community of New York was particularly affected, especially in the Bedford-Stuyvesant and East New York neighborhoods of Brooklyn.

Because of the recent racial tensions occurring in the wake of the Civil Rights movement, the heat became a potential political issue as well as a public health concern, as riots like those contemporaneously occurring in other major cities were feared. Mayor John Lindsay noted that many citizens did not use or seek air-conditioning, because of either poverty or the cultural conditioning of growing up in times when air-conditioning was unavailable. The heat wave occasioned a 24 percent increase in the death rate when compared to the same period during the previous year.

Nicholas Birns

For Further Information:

The New York Times, July 13, 1966.

1967: Mexico

Date: May 10, 1967
Place: Guadalajara, Jalisco, Mexico
Temperature: 95 degrees Fahrenheit
Result: 70 dead

It was a double dose of severe weather in 1968 for several states of Mexico that earlier that year had experienced heavy snowfall. The state of Jalisco was particularly afflicted. Guadalajara, the capital of Jalisco, is in what is termed the *tierra templada*, which is between 328 yards (600 meters) and 1,969 yards (1,800 meters) in altitude. This terrain usually does not suffer severe heat, but the absence of the usual flow of cooling air from the Pacific meant that summer came unusually early on May 10, 1967, killing approximately 70 people (30 in Guadalajara itself, the rest in surrounding areas where the temperature rose as high as 102 degrees Fahrenheit) and seriously straining local and federal relief services.

Nicholas Birns

For Further Information:

The New York Times, May 11, 1967.

Roure, José Maria Muria. *A Thumbnail History of Guadalajara.* Translated by Michael Mathes. Guadalajara, Jalisco, Mexico: Editorial Colomos, 1983.

1968: Mexico

Date: May 29, 1968
Place: Durango, Mexico
Temperature: 95 degrees Fahrenheit
Result: Approximately 70 children dead

There was no escaping the heat wave stemming from the warm front that swept in from the Gulf of Mexico on a sultry Wednesday in May, 1968. The only cool places in Durango were the deep-hewn *quebradas* (canyons) beneath the surrounding mountains, where no one lived. The already low riverbeds were reduced to a trickle as Durango's inhabited sections endured a short but punishing barrage of heat. This heat wave was made calamitous only partially by the temperatures themselves; much of the impact was due to the logistical unpreparedness of the local authorities, as the government found it difficult to help many people in need. Approximately 70 children died in an overcrowded schoolroom.

Nicholas Birns

For Further Information:

The New York Times, May 30, 1968.

The South American Handbook. Chicago: Rand McNally, 1969.

1968: Japan

Date: July 22, 1968
Place: Honshū, Japan
Temperature: Unknown
Result: 72 dead

In the last ten days of July, 1968, the subtropical high was stronger than normal near Japan, and the nation experienced hot and sunny days. Monthly mean temperatures were normal in northern and eastern Japan and above normal in western Japan (including most of the nation's densely populated areas) and the Ryukyu Islands. Monthly precipitation amounts were far less than normal, creating near-drought conditions unusual for a nation as northerly located as Japan.

Although the heat was strongest in terms of temperature in the southern island of Kyūshū, it was not here that tragedy struck. A group of Japanese seeking respite from the heat by bathing in the ocean off western Honshū island suffered death by drowning. They drowned within a hundred feet of the shore while helpless onlookers watched, unable to halt the current that carried out 72 people to their watery grave. Seven people were also reported missing. A cold front from Siberia known by Japanese meteorologists as an "Okhotsk high" eventually drove out the heat by the end of the month.

Nicholas Birns

For Further Information:

Chiriin, Kokuro. *The National Atlas of Japan.* Tokyo: Japan Map Centre, 1997.

The New York Times, July 23, 1968, p. 20.

1969: Rio de Janeiro

Date: November 10, 1969
Place: Rio de Janeiro and the coastal plain, Brazil
Temperature: 106 degrees Fahrenheit
Result: 35 dead, 440 injured

Given the tropical climate of Rio de Janeiro, located virtually on the equator, it could easily be assumed that its inhabitants were unfazed by the heat wave that struck their city. This was far from what happened, however. The Cariocas (natives) of Rio reeled from a heat wave that swooped in from the Atlantic, unaccompanied by the normal heavy winds of this time of year, which despite their ferocity had the advantage of keeping the heat from rising to unendurable levels.

The most seriously impacted community was the *favelas,* or shanty-dwellings, in Rio, whose flimsy homes offered no resistance to the fierce heat. Thirty-five of the city's poorer inhabitants died, about half from infectious diseases spurred on by the heat, and over 400 were injured due to collapsing structures weakened by the unceasing heat.

Nicholas Birns

For Further Information:

Mitchell, James W. *Crucibles of Hazard: Mega-cities and Disasters in Transition.* New York: United Nations University Press, 1999.

1972: Argentina

Date: January 3-13, 1972
Place: Buenos Aires and environs, Argentina
Temperature: 100 degrees Fahrenheit
Result: Approximately 100 dead

Buenos Aires is located in what Spanish-speaking meteorologists term the *tierra caliente,* low-lying coastal areas adjacent to the sea. January is summer in Southern Hemisphere countries such as Argentina, but, even so, Buenos Aires was unprepared for the severity of the heat wave of 1972. This was especially true of the way the heat persisted through the nighttime; usually it is hot in Buenos Aires only during the day. On January 4, the temperature reached 100 degrees Fahrenheit. Some attributed the higher temperatures not just to weather patterns but also to anthropogenic (human-induced) atmosphere changes, linked largely to industrial pollution and visible in the clotted haze besetting Buenos Aires at this time.

Approximately 100 people died, mainly from exposure and heat-generated heart failure, although 3 children died of dehydration. The impact of the heat wave was felt by Porteños (Buenos Aires residents) long after it had ended because of water shortages and government-mandated water conservation measures. The seriously diminished levels of rivers, wells, and reservoirs also affected the availability of water resources for energy production, among other impacts. As 50 percent of Argentinean electricity is produced through hydraulic generation, the heat wave at the beginning of 1972 impinged upon Argentine economic productivity for months thereafter.

Nicholas Birns

For Further Information:

Buenos Aires Herald, January 2-7, 1972.
Ross, Stanley R., and Thomas F. McGann. *Buenos Aires, Four Hundred Years.* Austin: University of Texas Press, 1982.
Villrock, Andres. *Report of the Argentine Delegation to the International CLIVAR Conference, Paris, 2-4 December 1998.* Paris: CLIVAR, 1999.

1972: India

Date: May, 1972
Place: India
Temperature: 99 degrees Fahrenheit
Result: More than 800 dead

April and May are usually the hottest months in India, and the region's world-famous heavy rains—monsoons—clear and cool off the hot air in the latter part of the summer. Southern cities such as Bangalore, Mysore, and Madurai are well used to average highs of over 86 degrees Fahrenheit during this time. In 1972 the accustomed weather patterns were jolted by a combination of very high temperatures with excessive humidity, which simply never sufficiently concentrated to erupt as a thunderstorm. Temperature ranges moved into the high nineties on the Fahrenheit scale, and life came to a virtual standstill in what is typically the region's most pleasant season. Hundreds of people were killed, most of them either itinerant merchants or poor people who lacked shelter.

A series of cool breezes from the Himalayas eventually dispelled the torpid residue of the heat. The north central region was not spared, as people baked under the heat in New Delhi; local groups tried to dispense water, but to little avail. In the eastern part of the country, the West Bengal region suffered 247 deaths within the space of two weeks. Relief Minister S. Roy stated the region had suffered the equivalent of $105 million in damage.

Nicholas Birns

For Further Information:

Bhattacherje, Satya Bikash. *Encyclopaedia of Indian Events and Dates.* New York: Apt Books, 1986.

Lengerke, Hans J. von. *The Nilgiris: Weather and Climate of a Mountain Area in South India.* Wiesbaden, West Germany: Steiner, 1977.

1980: United States

Date: June-August, 1980
Place: Mainly the southwestern and midwestern United States
Temperature: 107 degrees Fahrenheit
Result: 1,265 dead, $20 billion in damage

The American Southwest suffered its worst heat in a quarter-century in 1980, when Texas alone had forty-two consecutive days of 100-degree temperatures. A high-pressure area stalled over the region from late June to mid-July, remaining virtually immobile as it parked above farms, houses, and cities, holding them all in unremitting, static torpor. Dallas set what was at that time its heat-wave record with forty-two consecutive days above 100 degrees, from June 23 to August 3. In other areas of Texas, the temperature went below 100 for a few days in early July, spurring hopes that the worst was over, but this lull was succeeded by a volley of further triple-digit-temperature days.

Similar conditions prevailed in many other cities stretching across a wide swath of the south central United States. Not only the relentlessness but also the wide distribution of the heat wave among a number of different climate zones and diverse terrains gave this heat wave a particular impact.

Weather afflicts all people in a given area equally, but people react in different ways. In 1980 air-conditioning was still not available to all. This was especially true of the elderly, who sometimes felt that they did not really need air-conditioning even if they could afford it, and the poor. It was also reported that many elderly people preferred to keep their doors locked out of fear of robbery or attack, and thus often became dehydrated or suffocated. Although the urban poor received most of the attention in the media's coverage of the heat wave, rural poor, such as sharecroppers and migrant workers, were equally devastated by the heat. Given the centralization of the population in cities, however, relief efforts were easier to mount there.

National Guardsmen searched for elderly residents in St. Louis, Missouri, and attempted to deliver

A man attempts to stay cool in a fountain in Boston Common in the summer of 1980. (AP/Wide World Photos)

fans to the poor in the state's other major urban center, Kansas City. Some innovative solutions to this problem were suggested, among them a proposal that a tax break be given to people with air-conditioning willing to take elderly or handicapped people into their homes. This did not prevent a significant amount of deaths in these cities; in St. Louis alone, one count tabulated 113 fatalities, and Kansas City nearly kept pace with 111 deaths as of July 21. In early August, the U.S. Congress passed measures moderately increasing energy aid to the inner-city poor. On a more long-term level, the U.S. government sought to find ways to implement drought planning for arid and semiarid regions.

The National Oceanic and Atmospheric Administration (NOAA) advised citizens to contact state and local relief agencies. The victims of the heat were not merely the old and infirm. A soldier stationed at Fort Sill, near Lawton, Oklahoma, fainted from heat exhaustion during a review parade, and several high school and college athletes were also among the victims, though most of the latter group survived.

Though the heat wave was concentrated in the Southwest, the Midwest and Middle Atlantic areas also suffered. At first it looked as if the heat wave would be as severe in the Midwest as in the Southwest, but by early July it was clear that the Midwest was only experiencing an "average" heat wave, which gave no immediate comfort to the regions' inhabitants but prevented the summer from passing into legend. The situation was more severe in the Washington, D.C., area, where on July 18 the temperature reached 102 degrees, followed up by two more 100-degree days within the next week. A three-year-old child died in a parked car, while 2 runners collapsed from heat stroke during the middle of a race and died shortly thereafter. In neighboring agricultural areas, over 500,000 chickens were said to have died on the eastern shore of Maryland, devastating that area's staple poultry crop, while Fairfax County, Virginia, farmers were threatened by severe drought.

The heat wave occasioned extensive crop and livestock damage nationwide, and cattle ranchers, especially, feared that entire herds would be lost. Though there was a significant amount of livestock fatalities, fears that this would cause meat shortages and negatively affect the economy were unfounded. Though food and beef prices did rise, these increases were of fleeting duration. Part of the reason for the moderate impact of the heat and drought was the speed with which southwestern farmers harvested their grain crop, even though this meant getting the crop in one or two weeks early. Some parts of the economy were actually helped by the heat, as soft-drink sales surged, especially those from carts and vending machines in St. Louis, Dallas, and Kansas City.

Meteorologists debated various explanations for the severity of the heat wave, attention centering on small alterations on the pull exerted on the earth by either the sun or the moon. Although the popular imagination leapt on the nearly contemporaneous eruption at Mount St. Helens, Washington, no scientific evidence was found to support a correlation.

President Jimmy Carter sent millions in disaster aid to the affected states, the urgency being heightened by his campaign for reelection as well as fears that crop and beef shortfalls would seriously impact the economy. Although the uncomfortable weather was not a major factor in the results of the 1980 elections, it surely contributed to an existent mood of national discontent.

Nicholas Birns

For Further Information:

Burnes, Brian. "Summer 1980 Echoes in Heat Wave Memory." *Kansas City Star,* July 31, 1999, p. A1.

"Death Toll from Severe Heat Wave in U.S. Exceeds 760." *Washington Post,* July 17, 1980, p. A2.

"National Weather Service Says July Was the Hottest Ever in D.C. Area." *Washington Post,* August 1, 1980, p. B1.

The New York Times, June 20-July 15, 1980.

"U.S. Heat Wave to Raise Meat Prices." *Christian Science Monitor,* July 24, 1980, p. 6.

1995: India

Date: June 15-19, 1995
Place: Assam, India
Temperature: 104 degrees Fahrenheit
Result: 1,200 dead

On June 20, 1995, the official All India radio station related that 560 people had died from heat stroke in temperatures as high as 122 degrees Fahrenheit. These temperatures were the highest recorded in India in the twentieth century. The heat wave was finally broken by monsoons in midsummer, whose devastating effect almost equaled that of the heat wave. Assam's provincial chief minister, Parafulla Kunmar Mahunta, was active in trying to provide shelter and protection for people suffering from exposure to the heat. The death toll was later estimated to have risen to 1,200, counting deaths from exposure and collateral deaths.

Nicholas Birns

For Further Information:

Keesing's Record of World Events. London: Longman, 1995.

Telegraph (Calcutta), June 20-21, 1995.

1995: U.S. Midwest, Northeast

Date: July 12-17, 1995
Place: Midwest and Northeast, especially Chicago and Milwaukee
Temperature: Up to 106 degrees Fahrenheit
Result: More than 1,000 dead (465 in Chicago, 129 in Milwaukee)

In July of 1995 an unusually strong upper level ridge of high pressure slowly moved across the Great Plains and came into contact with exceptionally humid conditions at ground level. The slow progression of the air mass created good opportunities for daily heating and the accumulation of humidity. Working together, these two factors produced extraordinarily hot and humid weather in the Midwest and on the East Coast. When this air mass came into contact with the urban sprawl of Chicago, Milwaukee, and other cities, the results became particularly deadly. The concrete and steel buildings trapped the heat, while the lack of a breeze made for stifling conditions. Further, even the daily low temperatures remained unusually high, preventing nighttime cooling from helping to dissipate the daytime heat buildup.

The Temperatures Climb. Temperatures across the Midwest and East Coast soared during the record-breaking event. The National Weather Service (NWS) issued the first heat advisory for Chicago on July 12, 1995. By July 13 Chicago experienced temperatures of 104 degrees Fahrenheit at O'Hare airport and 106 degrees Fahrenheit at Midway. Both represented the highest daily temperatures ever recorded at those locations up to that point, and the city witnessed the second-highest summer temperatures in its history to that date, falling just one tenth of a percentage point short of the overall record. Taking into account the Heat Index, which reached 119 degrees Fahrenheit on July 12 and continued to climb, it became the worst summer on record for Chicago. The intense heat caused a section of Interstate 57 in downtown Chicago to buckle, closing an intersection for repairs.

Milwaukee also witnessed extreme temperatures, experiencing a high of 101 degrees Fahrenheit on July 14. As the air mass moved eastward, other cities reported record-breaking heat. Philadelphia hit 103 degrees Fahrenheit on July 15, while New York City hit 102 degrees the same day. Baltimore had a city record of 102 degrees, and Danbury, Connecticut, also set a city record with 106 degrees. Washington, D.C., had to close the Washington Monument for several days to prevent heat exhaustion in tourists.

The Death Toll. As the temperatures soared, people suffered physically from the heat, and the first injuries and deaths were soon reported. Because the heat came early in the summer, before people's bodies became acclimated to hotter temperatures, residents, especially of northern locations, suffered more from the heat, with some succumbing to death. Heat caused the heart to pump blood more forcefully, because of the expansion of blood vessels to cool the body. Hearts needed time to become fully acclimated to the extra exertion. When the heat wave happened suddenly, as in 1995, heart attacks and other physical distress resulted.

Dr. Edmund Donoghue, the Cook County medical examiner during the summer of 1995, established three specific criteria for determining if a fatality resulted at least in part from the heat. Donoghue maintained a death was attributable to the heat if one of the factors was indicated at the time of death. If the body temperature had risen to at least 105 degrees at or shortly after the time of death, if there was evidence of elevated temperatures at the location where the victim was discovered, or if the victim was seen alive for the last time at the height of the heat wave and subsequently found in a decomposed state, then Donoghue called the death heat-inspired. His findings were later adopted by the NWS to establish the death toll for the heat wave of 1995.

Although people died in other locations, such as the 11 who died in New York City and the 21 in Philadelphia, the worst fatalities occurred in Chicago and Milwaukee. In Chicago, 435 people officially died during the heat wave, with 162 being recorded on July 15 alone. Others were rushed to local hospitals. At one point, 18 hospitals in Chicago placed their emergency rooms on bypass status, as they were unable to handle any more patients because of the overwhelming numbers from the heat wave. The Cook County coroner's office filled the 222-bay morgue and needed to use 7 refrigerated tractor trailers to store additional corpses awaiting autopsies. Everyone at the morgue worked overtime to clear the backlog of heat-related cases. In Milwaukee, 129 people officially died during the event. Bodies were directed to local funeral homes when the medical examiner's office became full. Many of the dead had body temperatures in the range of 107-108 degrees. Emergency rooms in Milwaukee also experienced an upsurge in patients, with some closing for short periods of time because of the caseload.

Two of the dead were three-year-old boys left inside a locked van for an hour when their caregiver forgot about them when she took several other children into a mall on a field trip. Most of the people who died from the heat were senior citizens, especially those living alone or who had apartments on the second floor and higher. They often died with their windows closed and doors locked. A. D. and Willie May Gross of Chicago, both in their sixties, died together in their home, which did not have air-conditioning. Rescuers found the doors and windows bolted and shut, with the temperature inside the house at 125 degrees Fahrenheit. The Chicago Housing Authority never placed enough air-conditioning units into the public housing projects, even though managers asked for units in recreation rooms and common areas to provide a cool area for residents. Many residents, especially of public housing, feared the crime outside their apartments more than the heat and refused to open doors and windows to allow air circulation. The homes of many of the dead were in the range of 100 to 120 degrees Fahrenheit.

Other victims declined assistance even when it was offered to them. One eighty-seven-year-old casualty, Mabel Swanson, could have gone to stay at a neighbor's air-conditioned apartment in Chicago, but she preferred to stay in her own home. She died during the night from the heat and was discovered by a neighbor the next morning. Chicago established designated cooling stations where residents could enjoy air-conditioning and get relief from the oppressive conditions, but these centers went largely underused during the crisis. One center had room for 200 people but was empty during the heat of the day.

Most of the dead lacked air-conditioning in their homes and apartments and used fans instead. In Kansas City, Missouri, which also saw its share of deaths, Arthur Castlebery died at home with three fans blowing on him. When the mercury rose above 90 degrees and the humidity was above 35 percent, fans acted like a convection oven, heating the room further by circulating the hot air, rather than cooling it off. The temperature in the room was 110 degrees when Castlebery's body was discovered.

Other Effects. Commonwealth Edison Company, the local electric company for Chicago, demonstrated an inability to handle the increased demand for electricity during the heat wave. Several substations caught fire or otherwise failed, and the company resorted to rolling blackouts to ration the power throughout the city without notifying consumers in advance. During these rolling blackouts, residents experienced two- to four-hour power outages over the course of the day. In other instances, substations failed entirely, leaving tens of thousands of residents without electricity for up to forty-eight hours. This critical situation contributed to some fatalities. Although eighty-nine-year-old Florentine Aquino had air-conditioning in his home, a rolling blackout halted his electric service. His wife awoke to discover him lying dead next to her in their bed the next morning. After the event, lawyers filed a class-action lawsuit against Commonwealth Edison because of the outages.

Most of the victims of the heat wave suffered from diseases exacerbated by the high temperatures. Diabetes, pulmonary heart disease, upper respiratory problems, and high blood pressure contributed to their deaths. Others had more unique problems. Eight-year-old Kyle Garcia from Kenosha, Wisconsin, died from dehydration. Garcia was in a full body cast, covering his chest to his feet, and his body could not process liquids, making it unable to prevent death. Mental illness also contributed to a number of deaths. An antipsychotic medication given to schizophrenics prevented perspiration and impaired their ability to dissipate heat, causing heat exhaustion and death for some. Twelve of the dead in Milwaukee took these psychotropic or mind-altering medications, with fatal consequences.

The heat wave of 1995 initiated a spate of research into deaths caused by heat exhaustion and related causes. The NWS conducted a study for later emergency disaster procedures in the event of future heat waves. It found that, although heat waves annually killed more Americans than hurricanes, tornadoes, or blizzards, the general public lacked awareness of the deadly potential. In particular, the NWS implemented a series of policies, such as better warning systems and the establishment of cooling stations, to handle heat waves and to prevent the high casualty rate of the summer of 1995.

James B. Seymour, Jr.

For Further Information:

Chicago Sun Times, July 12-31, 1995.
Chicago Tribune, July 12-31, 1995.
Kansas City Star, July 23, 1995.
Madison Capital Times, July 17, 1995.
Milwaukee Journal Sentinel, July 12-31, 1995.
U.S. Department of Commerce. *Natural Disaster Survey Report, July 1995 Heat Wave.* Silver Springs, Md.: National Weather Service, 1995.

1996: Pakistan

Date: June 16-19, 1996
Place: Karachi and other parts of Sind Province, Pakistan
Temperature: 108 degrees Fahrenheit
Result: 37 dead

The effect of the 1996 heat wave in Pakistan was exacerbated by the environmental problems besetting the country at the time, especially in terms of contaminated water and pollution. Pollution had stripped mangrove trees of the layers of leaves that had cushioned the impact of previous heat waves on the Indus River delta and Karachi; the decrease of mangrove-covered areas meant that heat had more chance to sink into the environment. The same sort of problem proceeded from the heavy felling and stripping of the few forest areas along Pakistan's generally arid coast.

The contaminated water being supplied by the Karachi Water and Sewerage Board also posed a serious threat to the health of Karachiites. Usually the upper classes are spared the brunt of the misfortune during heat waves, but everyone in Karachi was affected by the water problem. Water pipelines were submerged in the sewerage water in several places in the city, where there was leakage and mixing of potable water with sewage. After much panic, it was determined that the polluted water was being supplied from the Manchar Lake, which contained a dangerous level of minerals and chemicals. This contributed severely to the death toll during the heat wave.

What was notable about the response to the Karachi heat wave of 1996 was that it was coordinated not only by the Pakistani and local governments but also by nongovernmental organizations, such as Health Oriented Preventive Education (HOPE) and the Community Health Sciences department of Aga Khan University. These agencies were crucial in sparing lives and providing relief, making this heat wave far less catastrophic than it could have been, though these positive portents were for the moment muted by awareness of the high death toll from the heat wave.

Nicholas Birns

For Further Information:

Daily Dawn (Karachi), June 16-19, 1996.

1996: Oklahoma, Texas

Date: July 1-10, 1996
Place: Southern Oklahoma and northeastern Texas
Temperature: 105 degrees Fahrenheit
Result: 22 dead

Whereas for most of the United States the summer of 1996 was rainy and temperate, for the southwest and south central portions of the country this generalization hardly held. These regions suffered excruciatingly hot temperatures periodically throughout the summer. The worst manifestation of this heat occurred between July 1 and 19. It was more the cumulative impact of the heat waves than extremes of temperature on any one day that had such a searing effect, although there were a number of days over 100 degrees, which verged on setting records. On

July 1, the mercury went over 100 degrees for the first time that summer in Oklahoma City.

Once the heat wave arrived, it settled in for a long stay. As is typically the case, the poor and elderly were the most vulnerable to the heat. Eighty-year-old Sylvia Gough Harris had refused the entreaties of her children to buy herself an air conditioner; she suffered for this refusal, becoming one of the heat wave's first victims in Oklahoma. Carol Yeahquo, an elderly man with Alzheimer's disease who had wandered from his nursing home before the heat wave's arrival, was found dead after the seventh consecutive day of triple-digit temperatures. Those elderly who had air-conditioning and survived were faced with massive electricity bills, which many of them could not pay.

By July 10, Oklahoma officials announced at least 7 people had died of hyperthermia (excessive heat). Many lives were saved because most Oklahomans had air-conditioning in 1996; air-conditioning was publicly credited by local officials, including Governor Frank Keating, for making a difference in numerous cases. Air-conditioning was proven to be not just a modern convenience but also a vital public health resource.

The heat wave also affected Texas, where even more lives were lost. By July 5, temperatures at the Dallas-Fort Worth airport had matched a record high of 105 degrees, and the heat had claimed its first fatality, seventy-seven-year-old Verne Bownds of the central Oak Cliff area. Over a dozen more deaths followed, all of them linked by the Dallas County Medical Examiner's Office to the heat, as the sun continued to broil Dallas and Tarrant Counties. Some managed to escape the warmth, however; employees at the Reddy Ice Company, a large firm in Dallas, found they appreciated their chilly work surroundings more than usual.

The heat wave finally broke in both Texas and Oklahoma because of a massive thunderstorm, which, while cooling the air considerably, caused power outages for thousands. This region survived its share of uncalm weather in the summer of 1996.

Nicholas Birns

For Further Information:

Christian Science Monitor, August 2, 1996.

Daily Oklahoman, July 1-10, 1996.

McKenzie, Aline. "Temperatures Fall, but They're Still Dangerous." *Dallas Morning News,* July 11, 1996.

1998: U.S. South

Date: May-September, 1998
Place: U.S. South, especially Texas and Oklahoma
Temperature: Daily highs of at least 100 degrees Fahrenheit in many cities
Result: 200 or more dead, $6-9 billion in damage

In the south central United States, after April, 1998, had brought cooler-than-normal weather to a number of cities, May brought not only smoke from forest fires in Mexico and Central America but also a high-pressure system with hot air. On May 2, Del Rio, Texas, had a high temperature of 103 degrees Fahrenheit, and Laredo had a high of 107. The May heat continued and occurred far beyond Texas. Monroe, Louisiana, had a May record high of 104 on May 31, and Little Rock and New Orleans each set May records for high average temperatures. Along with the heat came drought: While much of the West Coast had more than 200 percent of normal precipitation in May, less than 50 percent of the normal fell in an area from north Florida and Alabama through Mississippi, Louisiana, southern Arkansas, Texas, most of Oklahoma, New Mexico, and much of Arizona.

As June began, high temperatures and dry weather continued in Oklahoma and Texas, until a cold front brought relief from the heat, without, however, bringing much moisture. The Dallas-Fort Worth metroplex, which had experienced a high of 101 degrees on June 1, had a high of only 73 on June 6, the same day on which Amarillo, Texas, recorded a low of 41. Unfortunately, the cool weather failed to last, and, after a gradual warming, a weather phenomenon called the Bermuda High stagnated over much of the southern part of the United States. With that event, the main period of the heat wave of 1998 began.

Although none of the cities in the south central or southeastern United States came especially close to Death Valley's high of 129 degrees on July 17, many of them set or came close to setting their own records. College Station, Texas, for instance, had a high of 100 on May 31, which tied a May record. Furthermore, the high of 107 on June 14 set a College Station record for any day in June, and the high of 106 for July 17 missed the pre-1998 record summer high by only 4 degrees. For the 153 days from May 1 through September 30, 1998, College Station had 51 days on which the high was at least 100 degrees, 42 other days on which the high was at least 95, and (not counting 2 days with missing data) only 23 days on which the low was less than 70. For 30 consecutive days, from July 6 through August 4, the high in College Station was never less than 100, nor was the low ever less than 73. Meanwhile, May and June set College Station records for low rainfall in those months, and July was also abnormally dry.

The story of the heat and drought in the long summer of 1998, however, is one of human suffering—200 or more deaths—not just of meteorological statistics. On July 12, when the high in Dallas County, Texas, reached 110, 6 people died there from the extreme heat. The heat took a sad toll elsewhere, as well, often on the elderly, the sick, the poor, and those who mistakenly thought they could endure prolonged high temperatures indoors or outdoors. Sometimes people died after they refused to turn on their fans or their air conditioners. In a strange tragedy, a nine-year-old boy from Randlett, Oklahoma, died from primary amoebic meningoencephalitis, which he contracted while swimming in the warm, stagnant water of Lake Arrowhead in Wichita Falls, Texas.

With the suffering came efforts at relief, federal and local. Among the latter efforts were those in Dallas County, where health-department officials established a telephone line for people who wanted advice about avoiding heat exhaustion and heat stroke. Community centers in the county welcomed people who wanted to escape from hot homes into cool buildings, and charities gave electric fans and window air conditioners to the poor. Moreover, through the Low Income Home Energy Assistance Program, President Bill Clinton promised $100 million in aid for 11 states. The federal funds were to help the poor pay their electric bills and buy fans and air conditioners.

Beyond the immediate threat to life and health posed by the heat was the damage done by the drought that accompanied it. When most people living in cities and towns thought of the effects of the hot, dry weather, they thought of their parched lawns and gardens, the inconvenience of water rationing, occasional disruptions in water service because of broken mains, and widespread bans on outdoor burning, including the use of charcoal in grills. For residents of a large area in Florida, however, the drought led to massive forest and brush fires.

For ranchers and farmers in Texas, Oklahoma, and elsewhere, the drought was also a disaster, as ponds shrank and even dried up entirely, the yield per acre of crops such as soybeans and corn declined significantly, and grasshoppers threatened to eat whatever greenery was left in the fields. Hay became such a treasure that Governor Frank Keating of Oklahoma wrote to the governors of Arkansas, Missouri, Kansas, and Colorado, asking for gifts or sales of hay from farmers there and promising that the Oklahoma National Guard would transport it. In addition to planning Operation Haymaker, Governor Keating also asked Oklahomans to pray for rain.

Eventually, in early August, rain fell in parts of Texas and Oklahoma, providing some relief from the heat as well as the drought. Later in August, Tropical Storm Charley arrived in Texas, but the rain of 17.03 inches on August 23 caused a deadly flood in Del Rio, which had earlier in the year experienced sixty-nine days with highs of at least 100. The end of August and the beginning of September brought reheating to the south central region, with temperatures in some cities climbing again past 100 degrees. In Oklahoma, McAlester had a high of 110 on September 4 and Walters had the same high the next afternoon. In mid-September, Tropical Storm Frances brought rain that dropped temperatures, but only with the coming of autumn did the heat wave of 1998 actually end.

Victor Lindsey

For Further Information:

Daily Oklahoman, May 15-September 30, 1998.

1999: U.S. Midwest, East Coast

Date: July 19-31, 1999

Place: U.S. Midwest and East Coast, from Missouri and Illinois through New England

Temperature: Over 100 degrees Fahrenheit

Result: 257 dead

Following a period of drought for the eastern seaboard, an extreme heat wave hit the Midwest and East Coast of the United States in July, 1999. Temperatures in excess of 100 degrees Fahrenheit were regularly reported. States from Missouri and Illinois through New England were affected. The heat wave brought New York City its hottest July on record. The extreme weather phenomenon was blamed on a stalled high-pressure system in the Atlantic Ocean, which usually is found far to the southeast, over Bermuda.

A hint of what was to come was seen over the 100-degree Fourth of July weekend. Temperatures then dipped to only slightly above normal until mid-July, when they started to climb toward 100 again. Record-setting temperatures and multiple-day records were reached across the regions. On July 31 Philadelphia hit 99 degrees for a ninth day of above-90-degree readings. The heat also prompted scattered thunderstorms that dropped hail. Rain did occur, but it often fell too fast to be absorbed by the ground, thereby doing little to diminish the drought conditions. Even Wisconsin saw over 100-degree weather, which helped spawn deadly thunderstorms.

Prior to the official start date of July 19, extreme heat had claimed victims in the Northeast earlier in July, and New York City had suffered a power outage for approximately eighteen hours. The heat wave and accompanying drought forced water rationing in New Jersey. The drought and heat wave hit farmers especially hard, prompting emergency farm relief aid from the federal government. The extreme temperatures prompted heat advisories and warnings to be issued. Officials across the stricken region called for people to check on neighbors and relatives to make sure they were well.

The heat wave caused deaths from Alabama to Michigan. One victim in North Carolina, a migrant farm worker, had a body temperature of 108 degrees. By the end of July, 50 people in Chicago had perished because of the heat and 39 had died in Missouri. Hardest hit were the elderly and people who did not have fans or air-conditioning. In many instances elderly victims had air-conditioning but believed it would be too expensive to run. New York City and other areas established "cooling centers," air-condi-

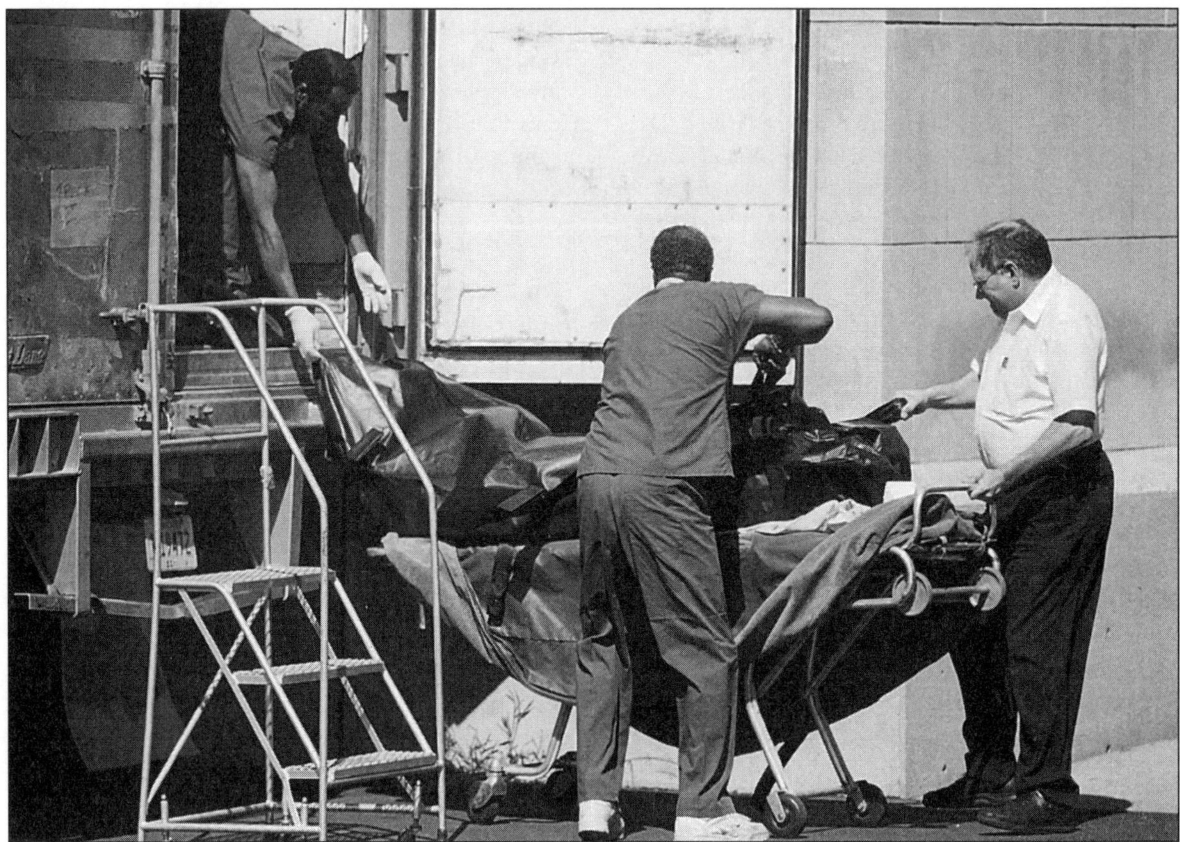

A victim of the 1999 heat wave in Chicago is removed by medical personnel. About 50 people died in Chicago as a result of high temperatures. (AP/Wide World Photos)

tioned buildings where people could take refuge. Roads to beaches were clogged with people trying to escape the heat.

The heat wave finally ended with a cool front that pushed through the region, bringing temperatures back down into the eighties. The front brought temperatures in Chicago down from 104 to 81 degrees. In the 1990's, the Midwest had been hit more than once with such extreme weather. In 1995 Chicago lost more than 400 citizens to a heat wave. Although not as deadly as the earlier heat wave, the July, 1999, heat wave claimed more than its share of victims.

Jennifer S. Lawrence

For Further Information:

The New York Times, July 24, 29; August 1-3, 1999.

Hurricanes, Typhoons, and Cyclones

(National Oceanic and Atmospheric Administration)

Hurricanes, typhoons, and cyclones are cyclonic storms formed over tropical oceans. A single storm can cover hundreds of thousands of square miles and has interior winds of 74 to over 155 miles per hour. Hurricanes are known as the "greatest storms on earth," and destruction goes beyond wind damage, as storm surges and subsequent flooding have caused many of the greatest natural disasters in the world. Hurricane damage in the United States continues to rise as more people move to coastal areas; however, the loss of life has decreased due to better forecasting and evacuation methods.

Factors involved: Geography, gravitational forces, rain, weather conditions, wind
Regions affected: Cities, coasts, forests, islands, oceans, rivers, towns

Science

A hurricane (from the Caribbean word *huraka'n*), also called a typhoon (a combination of *t'ai feng*, Chinese for "great wind," and *typhon*, Greek for "whirlwind") requires warm surface water, high humidity, and winds from the same direction at a constant speed in order to form. All hurricanes begin as cyclonic tropical low-pressure regions, having a circular motion that is counterclockwise in the Northern Hemisphere and clockwise in the Southern Hemisphere. These depressions can only develop in areas where the ocean temperatures are over 75 degrees Fahrenheit (24 degrees Celsius). The eye structure of a hurricane, which must be present in order for a storm to be classified as a hurricane, demands temperatures of 79 to 80.6 degrees Fahrenheit (26 to 27 degrees Celsius) to form.

In hurricane formation, heat is extracted from the ocean, and warm, moist air begins to rise. As it rises, it forms clouds and instability in the upper atmosphere. The ascending air then begins to spiral inward toward the center of the system. This spiraling movement causes the seas to become turbulent; large amounts of sea spray are then captured and suspended in the air. This spray increases the rate of evaporation and helps fuel the storm.

As the vortex of wind, water vapor, and clouds spins at an increasing rate, the eye of the hurricane forms. The eye, which is at the center of the hurricane, is a relatively calm area that experiences only light winds and fair weather. The most violent activity in the hurricane takes place in the area right around the eye, called the eyewall. In the eyewall, the spiraling air rises and cools and moisture condenses into droplets that form rainbands and clouds. The process of condensation releases latent heat that causes the air to rise and form more condensation. The air rises rapidly, resulting in an area of extremely low pressure close to the storm's center. The severity of a hurricane is often indicated by how low the pressure readings are in the central area of the hurricane.

As the air moves higher, up to 50,000 feet, it is propelled outward in an anticyclonic flow. At the same time some of the air moves inward and into the eye. The compression of air in the eye causes the temperature to rise. This warmer air can hold more moisture, and the water droplets in the central clouds then evaporate. As a result, the eye of the hurricane becomes nearly cloud-free. In the middle and upper levels of the storm, the temperature in the eye becomes much warmer than the outside. Therefore, a large pressure differential develops across the eyewall, which helps to establish the violence of the storm.

Waves of 50 to 60 feet are common in the open ocean from the hurricane winds. Winds in a hurricane are not symmetrical around the eye. Facing the direction the hurricane is moving, the strongest winds are usually to the right of the eye and can move at speeds up to 200 miles per hour. The radius of hurricane winds can vary from 10 miles in small hurricanes to 100 miles in large hurricanes. The strength of the wind decreases in relation to its distance from the eye.

Depending on the size of the eye, which can range from 3 to 40 miles in diameter, a calm period of blue skies and mild winds can last from a few minutes to hours as the eye moves across a given area. The calm is deceiving because it is not the end of the storm but a momentary lapse in intensity until the winds from the opposite direction hit.

Storms resembling hurricanes but that are less intense are classified by their central pressure and wind speed. Winds up to 39 miles per hour (34 knots) are classified as tropical depressions, and winds of 40 to 73 miles per hour (35 to 64 knots) are called tropical storms. To be classified as a hurricane, storms must have sustained winds of 74 miles per hour or higher.

All hurricanes in the Northern Hemisphere have a general track, beginning as a westward movement in response to the trade winds, veering northward because of anticyclonic wind flow around subtropical high-pressure regions, and finally trending northeastward toward polar regions in response to the flow of the prevailing westerly winds. The specific path of travel of each storm is very sporadic. Some will travel in a general curved path, while others will change course quite rapidly. They can reverse direction, zigzag, veer from the coast back to the ocean, intensify over water, stall, return to the same area, make loops, and move in any direction at any given instant of time.

The path of a hurricane is affected by pressure systems of the surrounding atmosphere and the influence of prevailing winds and the earth's rotation. Hurricanes can also be influenced by the presence of high- and low-pressure systems on the land they invade. The high-pressure areas act as barriers to the hurricanes, and if a high is well developed its outward spiraling flow will guide the hurricane around its

A satellite view of Hurricane Hugo as it approaches the United States. The cyclonic motion of the "arms" and the eye of the hurricane are visible. (AP/Wide World Photos)

edges. Low-pressure systems tend to attract hurricane systems.

The greatest cause of death and destruction in a hurricane comes from the rise of the sea from a storm surge. As the hurricane crosses the continental shelf and moves to the coast, the water level may increase 15 to 20 feet. The drop in atmospheric pressure at sea level within the hurricane causes the storm surge. The force of the reduced pressure allows the hurricane to suck up the seas and allow the winds in front of it to pile the water up against the coastline. This results in a wall of water that can be up to 20 feet tall and 50 to 100 miles wide. This wall of water can sweep across the coastline where the hurricane makes landfall. The combination of shallow shore water and strong hurricane winds makes for the highest surge of water.

If the storm surge arrives at the same time as the high tide the water heights of the surge can increase an additional 3 to 4 feet. The height of the storm surge also depends upon the angle at which the storm strikes the coast. Hurricanes that make landfall at right angles to the coast will cause a higher storm surge than hurricanes that enter the coast at an oblique angle. Often the slope or shape of the coast and ocean bottom can cause a bottleneck effect and a higher storm surge.

Water weighs approximately 1,700 pounds per cubic yard, and when lifted to any great height its weight can be a very destructive force. The storm surge is responsible for 90 percent of the deaths in a hurricane. The pounding of the waves caused by the hurricane can easily demolish buildings. Storm surges can cause severe erosion of beaches and coastal highways. Often, buildings that have survived hurricane winds have had their foundations eroded by the sea surge or have been demolished by the force of the waves. Storm surges and waves in harbors can destroy ships.

The salt water that inundates land can kill existing vegetation, and the residual salt left in the soil makes it difficult to grow new herbage.

Precipitation from hurricanes can be more intense than from any other source. The amount of rainfall received during a hurricane depends on the diameter of the rain band within the hurricane and the hurricane's speed. A typhoon in the Philippines in 1944 caused 73.62 inches of rain to fall in a twenty-four-hour period, a world record. Heavy rainfall can cause flash floods or river-system floods. Flash floods last from thirty minutes to four hours and are caused by heavy rainfall over a small area that has insufficient drainage. This causes excess water to flow over land and overflow streambeds, resulting in damage to bridges, underpasses, and low-lying areas. The strong currents in flash floods can move cars off roads, wash out bridges, and erode roadbeds.

River-system floods develop more slowly. Two or three days after a hurricane, large rivers may overflow their beds because of excessive runoff from the saturated land surface. River floods cover extensive areas, last a week or more, and destroy both property and crops. When the floodwaters retreat, buildings and residences can be full of mud. Often, all furnishings, appliances, wallboard, and even interior insulation within the structure must be completely replaced because of the infiltration of the mud.

Rain driven by the wind in hurricanes can cause extensive damage to buildings because of leakage around windows, through cracks, and under shingles.

Hurricanes often spawn tornadoes. The tornadoes associated with hurricanes are usually about half the size of tornadoes in the Midwest and are of a shorter duration. The area these tornadoes affect is small, usually 200 to 300 yards wide and not quite 1 mile long. Yet even though they are smaller tornadoes they can be very destructive, ruining everything in their path. Tornadoes normally occur to the right of the direction of the hurricane's movement. Ninety-four percent of tornadoes occur within 10 to 120 degrees from the hurricane eye and beyond the area of hurricane-force winds. Tornadoes associated with hurricanes are most often observed in Florida, Cuba, the Bahamas, and the coasts of the Gulf of Mexico and the south Atlantic Ocean.

Geography

Because hurricanes need temperatures of 79 to 80.6 degrees Fahrenheit (26 to 27 degrees Celsius) to form they will rarely develop above 20 degrees latitude because the ocean temperatures are never warm enough to provide the heat energy needed for formation. In the Northern Hemisphere the convergence of air that is ideal for hurricane development occurs above tropical waters when easterly moving waves develop in the trade winds. The region around the equator is called the "doldrums" because there is no wind flow. Hurricanes, needing wind to form, can be found as little as 4 to 5 degrees away from the equator. At these latitudes the Coriolis effect, a deflecting force associated with the earth's rotation, gives the winds the spin necessary to form hurricanes.

Hurricanes evolve in specific areas of the west Atlantic, east Pacific, south Pacific, western north Pacific, and north and south Indian Oceans. They rarely move closer to the equator than 4 or 5 degrees latitude north or south, and no hurricane has ever crossed the equator. In the Northern Hemisphere hurricanes are common from June through November, and in the Southern Hemisphere the hurricane season occurs from December to May.

In the Western Hemisphere these storms are called hurricanes. They are referred to as typhoons in the western Pacific, cyclones in the Indian Ocean, Willy Willys near Australia, and *baguious* in the Philippines. The swirling motion of these storms is cyclonic or counterclockwise in the Northern Hemisphere and clockwise in the Southern Hemisphere.

Prevention and Preparations

Hurricanes cannot be prevented; therefore, steps need to be taken to try to avoid loss of life and destruction of property. Persons in hurricane areas need to be aware of and respond to hurricane watches and warnings that are forecast by the National Hurricane Center, National Weather Service, and local media. The National Hurricane Center is responsible for forecasting hurricane watches and warnings for the Atlantic and eastern Pacific north of the equator. Although both warning capacity timing and accuracy have greatly improved, predictions can still be inaccurate by as much as 100 miles in a twenty-four-hour period.

Before a watch or warning is forecast, residents need to prepare a home evacuation plan. This involves determining where the family will go if a hurricane threatens. The options could be with friends or relatives who live outside of the area or public shelters. Evacuation supplies such as extra cash, hygiene products, drinking water, batteries, bedding, clothing for wet and cold conditions, prescriptions, canned foods, and road maps should be kept on hand and should provide a three-week supply for each person and pet. Restoration supplies should also be organized and stored together for use after residents are able to return home. Restoration supplies include rope and chains, brooms and shovels, rolls of heavy plastic, duct tape, tools, nails, pruning shears and saws, large-capacity garbage bags, nonperishable foods, folding lawn chairs, mosquito spray and netting, and chlorine bleach to be used for purifying water.

In order to protect homes in hurricane areas, shutters should be installed to protect windows. In some cases thin plywood can be used to cover large windows. Masking tape or duct tape applied to windows can help control some of the shattering in window breakage. Gas grills and propane gas tanks should be stored in a safe place so they are not damaged or do not explode during the storm. It is recommended that dead vegetation around the house be cleared and any coconuts removed from the trees so that they will not become destructive debris in the middle of the hurricane. All objects kept outside should be tied down, and all electricity, water, and gas should be turned off at the main panel if a hurricane warning is issued. Insurance policies, inventory records, and important documents should be kept in safe-deposit facilities. Trees and shrubbery should be cut in such a manner as to allow air to flow through them so that they will survive in hurricane winds.

If a hurricane watch is issued, windows should be covered and backup systems such as portable pumps to remove floodwater, alternate power sources, and battery-powered lighting should be made available. Because a hurricane watch means that a hurricane is possible in twenty-four to thirty-six hours, residents should be prepared for evacuation if one is called.

A hurricane warning indicates that a hurricane will reach land within twenty-four hours. All utilities should be turned off and loose items secured. Small items inside the house should be placed on countertops in order to avoid damage in case of flooding. Cash, social security cards, drivers' licenses, wills, medical records, bank account information, small valuables, and photo albums should be put in waterproof bags to ensure their safety. Garbage cans, lawn furniture, and bicycles should be brought inside so as not to be blown around and cause damage in the hurricane winds. Cars should be filled with gas and contain evacuation maps; if evacuation is called for, then emergency plans should be put into action.

One way to survive a hurricane is to build a "safe room" or shelter in the house. The shelter must be built where it cannot be flooded during a hurricane. It must be anchored to the foundation of the house in such a way as to resist uplift or overturning in the storm. All the connections in the shelter must be strong enough to resist structural failure and penetration by wind-blown debris.

Rescue and Relief Efforts

Devastation after a hurricane can range from light to catastrophic, depending on the storm's intensity. After a hurricane millions of cubic yards of debris can be left in its wake. Before residents are allowed to return to a hurricane area, emergency management personnel make search and rescue and preliminary damage assessments. Residents are not allowed back until it is determined safe. Dangling wires, fallen trees, debris, and washed-out roads can make travel back into the area difficult or impossible until cleanup has been accomplished.

Debris can consist of trees, shrubs, building materials, and hazardous waste, such as paints, solvents, batteries, and insecticides. As this debris is cleaned up Emergency Management and Environmental Resource Management personnel, with the help of the U.S. Army Corps of Engineers, will need to authorize and manage the disposal of the debris. Task forces work with regulatory agencies to determine the impact of incineration and other disposal methods.

The Red Cross and other volunteer agencies help provide needed relief. Often there is deterioration or contamination of water supplies, and the Red Cross brings in bottled water as well as nonperishable foods. Shelters may be set up for those left without homes.

Residents are advised to not enter their homes or businesses before officials have checked for structural damage. They are told to beware of such outdoor hazards as downed power lines, weakened limbs on trees, or damaged overhanging structures. People need to be aware that poisonous snakes are often driven from their dens by high water and seek refuge in trees and structures. Residents are encouraged to take as many photographs of the damage to their property as possible for insurance purposes. If their homes are livable, the long process of cleanup takes place.

Impact

The Saffir-Simpson Hurricane Scale categorizes the storm intensity of hurricanes into five levels. Level 1 hurricanes are considered weak and have sustained winds of 75 to 95 miles per hour. They cause minimal damage to buildings but do damage unanchored mobile homes, shrubbery, and trees. Normally they cause coastal road flooding and minor damage to piers. Storm surges seen in Level 1 hurricanes are usually 5 to 7 feet above normal.

Level 2 hurricanes, with wind speeds of 96 to 110 miles per hour, damage roofing materials, doors, and windows on buildings. They also cause substantial damage to trees, shrubs, mobile homes, and piers. Utility lines can be blown down, and vehicles may be blown off bridges. Flooding of roads and low-lying areas normally occurs two to four hours before the center of the hurricane arrives. Storm surges are estimated to be 8 to 12 feet high under these conditions.

Level 3 hurricanes are considered strong and boast winds of 111 to 130 miles per hour; large trees can be blown down. These storms destroy mobile homes and can cause structural damage to residences and utility buildings. Small structures can be destroyed, and structures near the coastline can sustain damage from battering waves and floating debris. Flooding from this level of hurricane can destroy small structures near the coast, while larger structures normally sustain damage by floating debris. There can be flooding 8 miles or more inland. Coastal areas can see storm surges that average 11 to 16 feet.

Level 4 hurricanes are categorized as very strong, with winds of 131 to 155 miles per hour. These storms can blow down trees, shrubs, power lines, and antenna towers. They cause extensive damage to single-family structures and cause major beach erosion. They can damage lower floors of structures, and the flooding can undermine foundations. Residences often sustain roof structure failure and subsequent rain damage. Land lower than 10 feet above sea level can be flooded, which would cause massive evacuation of residential areas up to 6 miles inland. Storm surges reach levels of 14 to 20 feet at this level.

Level 5 hurricanes are classified as devastating, sustaining winds greater than 155 miles per hour.

Hurricane Andrew caused billions of dollars in damage to homes, property, and boats. (AP/Wide World Photos)

Evacuations of residents living within 5 to 10 miles of the shoreline may be required. This strong a hurricane can cause complete roof failure on residential and industrial buildings, as well as some complete building failures. Major utilities are usually destroyed in this level of hurricane. Structures less than 15 feet above sea level can sustain major damage to lower floors, and massive evacuations of residential areas usually occur. Storm surges associated with these severe hurricanes can be 18 feet or higher.

The devastation of hurricane winds is exemplified by the fact that the wind force applied to an object increases with the square of the wind speed. A building 100 feet long and 10 feet high that has 100-mile-per-hour winds blowing against it would experience 40,000 pounds of force being exerted against its walls. This is because a 100-mile-per-hour wind exerts a force of approximately 40 pounds per square foot. If the wind speed was 160 miles per hour, the force against the house would be 100,000 pounds. Additionally, winds in a hurricane do not blow at a constant speed. The wind speeds can increase and decrease rapidly. The wind pressure on the house and fluctuating wind speed can create enough stress to cause connections between building components to fail. Often the roof or siding can be ripped off the house, or windows may be pushed in. Structures that fail because of the effects of extreme winds often look as if they have exploded. Rain blown by the wind also contributes to an increase of pressure on buildings and can help cause structure failure.

Flying debris, often referred to as "windborne missiles," can be thrown at a building with enough force to penetrate the walls, windows, or roof. A 2-by-4-inch piece of wood that weighs 15 pounds can have a speed of 100 miles per hour when carried by a 250-mile-per-hour wind. This will enable it to penetrate most reinforced masonry.

The impact of hurricanes goes beyond the destruction of homes and property. Agricultural loss, oil platform and drilling rig damage, and destruction of boats can range into millions and even billions of dollars. Property loss alone in 1992's Hurricane Andrew was approximately $25 billion. Agriculture, petroleum industry, and boat losses in Florida and Louisiana amounted to another $1 billion.

The marine environment is also impacted by hurricanes. There can be changes in near-shore water quality, as well as bottom scouring and beach overwash. Fuel from damaged boats can discharge into the water for days. Often, sponges, corals, and other marine life will be severely impacted.

Dion C. Stewart and Toby R. Stewart

Bibliography

Bryant, Edward A. *Natural Hazards*. Cambridge, England: Cambridge University Press, 1991. Provides a solid scientific treatment for the educated student. Readers should have a basic understanding of mathematical principles to fully appreciate this book. Contains a glossary of terms.

Pielke, R. A., Jr., and R. A. Pielke, Sr. *Hurricanes: Their Nature and Impacts on Society*. New York: John Wiley & Sons, 1997. A very informative and well-written book by father and son meteorologists. Focuses on the United States, integrating science and social policies in response to these storms.

Robinson, Andrew. *Earth Shock: Hurricanes, Volcanoes, Tornadoes, and Other Forces of Nature*. London: Thames and Hudson, 1993. An informative book written for high school students or general adult readers. Provides an interesting mix of science, individual event summaries, and noteworthy facts and figures.

Tufty, Barbara. *1001 Questions Answered About Hurricanes, Tornadoes, and Other Natural Air Disasters*. New York: Dover, 1987. This text has a logical flow to it. Excellent illustrations to accompany the text.

U.S. Department of Commerce. *Hurricane Andrew: South Florida and Louisiana, August 23-26, 1992*. Silver Springs, Md.: National Weather Service, 1993. An interesting overall view of Hurricane Andrew, its development, and its impact. Contains excellent color pictures and graphs.

_______. *Hurricane Opal*. Silver Springs, Md.: National Weather Service, 1996. Particularly interesting in its treatment of the "reporting" of hurricanes by the news media, and how it can change the impact. In the case of Opal, the hurricane forecast was almost overlooked in the wake of other breaking news.

U.S. Park Service. *Hurricane Andrew, 1992*. Denver: U.S. Department of the Interior, 1994. An excellent account of the response and impact of Hurricane Andrew in south Florida.

Notable Events

Historical Overview

Hurricanes are major tropical storms that originate in the Atlantic Ocean off the west coast of Africa between June and November. Similar storms can develop in the Pacific Ocean, where they are called typhoons, and in the Indian Ocean, where they are called cyclones. Hurricanes have clearly existed since the end of the last ice age, but their impact on humans has been markedly enhanced by the growth of population in the coastal areas impacted by these storms.

The Atlantic Coast and the coastline of the Gulf of Mexico are the two areas most affected by Atlantic hurricanes. The tail end of such a storm may have destroyed the remains of the Spanish Armada in 1588, when it sought to escape the victorious English fleet by sailing around the British Isles.

Hurricanes have had a profound impact on the vegetation of the Atlantic coastline. These "disturbances," as ecologists classify them, have the effect of destroying so much of the vegetation that the process of ecological succession must start over in the areas affected by hurricanes. There is, on average, one hurricane per century at any particular point on the Atlantic coast; in the twentieth century, a Category 4 hurricane struck the Atlantic coast once every six years, on average. Hurricanes are classified according to wind speed from 1 to 5; Category 4 hurricanes have windspeeds of 131-155 miles per hour.

What is known about hurricanes before the twentieth century comes mainly from descriptive records. It is known, for example, that what has been described as a "hurricane" struck the coastline of Rhode Island and Massachusetts in 1635, and another hit about a century later, in 1727. In 1752, the Carolinas were hit, and in 1769 and again in 1783 hurricanes struck the Atlantic coastline from South Carolina to New England. How much destruction was done by these hurricanes, or how many may have lost their lives, is unknown because records of that sort were not kept at that time.

Scientists are sure that a hurricane that missed New Orleans on August 10, 1856, wiped out the settlement on Last Island, off the Louisiana coast. The Federal Weather Bureau was created in 1890, and in 1898 an early warning network was set up in the West Indies—the first steps in the system that, by the end of the twentieth century, succeeded in reducing the loss of life from hurricanes. Notwithstanding, these early warning efforts did not prevent what is still, from the standpoint of loss of life, the most devastating hurricane in U.S. history, the one that struck Galveston, Texas, on September 8, 1900; estimates of the death toll (arising as much from the following storm surge) reach 12,000.

Deaths by drowning are a common feature of some of the earlier known hurricanes, a hazard that has been mitigated by the evacuation of communities in the path of a hurricane. A storm that hit the Miami, Florida, area in 1926 left some 200 people dead. More than 4,000 died in 1928 when, as a consequence of the storm named for it, Lake Okeechobee overflowed. This disaster led to the construction of a levee around the lake.

Only 47 were killed in 1933 when a hurricane struck the mid-Atlantic coast. This hurricane led to further actions on the part of government to prevent the loss of life from hurricanes. Notwithstanding preventive measures, the 1930's saw one of the most destructive hurricanes of the twentieth century, when the Great New England Hurricane of 1938 struck New England and pushed inland, killing more than 600 people and causing extensive damage, particularly to the forests of New England. Even though this hurricane only qualified as a Category 2 storm, the extent of the damage etched it in the minds of the inhabitants of New England.

Major changes in the government's handling of hurricane alerts resulted from technological advances in the 1930's and particularly during World War II. The radio made advance warning of large populations much easier as it became popular in the 1930's. World War II, however, with its extensive use of airplanes, revolutionized the handling of hurricane information. With airplanes, it became possible to fly over the disturbances as they progressed from the Atlantic Ocean off the coast of Africa toward the Atlantic coastline of the Western Hemisphere. It thus became customary to follow the path of a hurricane and to forewarn threatened populations by radio. Because the radio message was easier to understand when it had a name attached to it, the practice of naming hurricanes began in 1953.

In 1965 U.S. president Lyndon Johnson reorganized the government's weather monitoring system. Prior to that, in 1955, two new facilities had been created: the National Hurricane Center in Miami and the Experimental Meteorology Laboratory, also in Miami. The latter performs meteorological research, and the former tracks the paths of hurricanes as they develop. They subsequently became part of the National Oceanographic and Atmospheric Administration (NOAA). In 1978 the Federal Emergency Management Agency (FEMA) was added by President Jimmy Carter to the governmental organizations designed to deal with hurricanes and other natural disasters.

The devastation wrought by Hurricane Camille, which struck the Gulf coast on August 17, 1969, made clear the importance of united societal action. Although Camille only caused 258 deaths—as compared with predecessors Audrey in 1957, in which more than 500 people lost their lives, and Hilda, which killed 304 people in 1964—but the value of the property destroyed by Camille soared into the billions and focused people's minds on the problem of hurricanes.

Hurricanes have been quite erratic in where they strike land (they generally quickly lose force once they move over land), but the Gulf coast has been a favorite target. In August of 1970 Hurricane Celia struck Texas and Florida; in September of 1979, Hurricane Frederic landed on the Gulf coast (in 1979 men's names as well as women's began to be used), in 1985 Hurricane Juan struck the Gulf coast, and in September of 1988 Hurricane Gilbert hit the Caribbean and Mexico. In 1992 Hurricane Andrew hit chiefly South Florida but also went on to Louisiana, and in 1998 Hurricane Georges struck first in the Caribbean and then traveled to the Gulf coast.

Analysis of the history of hurricanes indicates that, during the second half of the twentieth century, intense hurricanes in the Atlantic Ocean decreased. There is no scientific justification for linking hurricanes to global warming, although many people draw such a connection. There is some connection between the formation of hurricanes and the heat over the Sahel in Africa, but it provides no indication as to where any hurricanes that might form will strike land in North America.

It has been found that the number of deaths caused by hurricanes can be dramatically reduced by evacuating the residents of an area in the path of a hurricane. If a hurricane strikes the coast of North America in a relatively uninhabited area, destruction will probably be extensive but few lives will be lost. However, the rapid growth of coastal populations makes it less and less likely that hurricanes will come ashore where few people are. Even though Hurricane Hugo in 1989 struck a portion of the South Carolina coast that was lightly inhabited, it caused the deaths of 75 people; the more intense Hurricane Andrew resulted in the deaths of only 50. Massive evacuation efforts were made once it became clear where Hurricane Andrew would strike the Florida coast,

Milestones

1588:	A major storm destroys Spanish Armada seeking to escape English navy under Sir Francis Drake.
August 15, 1635:	A colonial hurricane strikes Massachusetts and Rhode Island coastal settlements.
September 27, 1727:	A hurricane strikes the New England coast.
September 15, October 1, 1752:	Two hurricanes strike South and North Carolina.
September 8-9, 1769:	The Atlantic coast, from the Carolinas to New England, is hit by a hurricane.
October 22-23, 1783:	A hurricane strikes the Atlantic coast, from Carolinas to New England.
August 13, 1856:	A hurricane striking Last Island, Louisiana, results in a death toll of 137.
1890:	The Federal Weather Bureau created.
1898:	A hurricane warning network is established in the West Indies.
September 8, 1900:	A hurricane in Galveston, Texas, leads to the highest death toll from a hurricane to date, from the following storm surge.
September 15-22, 1926:	The Great Miami Hurricane strikes Florida and the Gulf states, resulting in 243 dead.
December 17-18, 1944:	A typhoon in the Philippine Sea kills 790.
September 4-21, 1947:	A hurricane impacts the Gulf states, leaving over 50 dead.
1953:	The system of naming hurricanes is adopted.
October 12-18, 1954:	Hurricane Hazel strikes Atlantic coast, causing 411 deaths and $1 billion in damage.
June 27-30, 1957:	More than 500 die when Hurricane Audrey hits the Louisiana and Texas coastlines.
September 6-12, 1960:	The Atlantic coast's Hurricane Donna results in 168 dead and almost $2 billion in damage.
August 15-18, 1969:	Hurricane Camille rages across the southern United States; 258 die.
June 21-23, 1972:	122 die during Hurricane Agnes.
September 7-14, 1979:	Hurricane Frederic strikes the Gulf coast states, causing $1.7 billion in damage.
September 12-17, 1988:	Hurricane Gilbert kills 260 in the Caribbean and Mexico.
September 10-22, 1989:	75 die as Hurricane Hugo strikes the Caribbean, then South Carolina.
April 30, 1991:	A cyclone hits Bangladesh and kills more than 131,000.

August 22-26, 1992:	Hurricane Andrew strikes southern Florida, leaving 50 dead and $26 billion in damage.
July 5-15, 1996:	Hurricane Bertha hits the Caribbean and the Atlantic coast; winds exceed 100 miles per hour.
November 3, 1997:	Typhoon Linda kills more than 1,100 in Vietnam.
June 9, 1998:	A cyclone hits the Indian state of Gujarat; more than 1,300 are killed.
September 16-29, 1998:	400 die when Hurricane Georges strikes in the Caribbean, then the Gulf coast; winds exceed 130 miles per hour.
October 27, 1998:	Hurricane Mitch hits Central America; the death toll exceeds 11,000.
February 11, 1999:	Cyclone Rona strikes Queensland, Australia; 1,800 are left homeless.

and there is no doubt that many lives were saved because of this.

In countries where the governmental infrastructure is less well developed than in the United States, the kinds of policies followed in the United States will not particularly help. A cyclone that hit Bangladesh in 1991 killed 131,000 people. A typhoon that landed in Vietnam in November of 1997 killed 1,100. A cyclone in the Indian state of Andhra Pradesh in November, 1996, caused the deaths of more than 1,000 people, and when a cyclone hit the Indian state of Gujarat in June of 1998 more than 1,300 people lost their lives. Hurricane Mitch, which hit Central America in late October of 1998, killed more than 11,000 and totally devastated the economies of Honduras and Guatemala. Experts have estimated that in Asia alone, the number of people at risk for death from cyclones is somewhere between 12,000 and 23,000.

Although actions taken by society have succeeded, at least in the United States, in reducing the effects of hurricanes on humans in the latter portion of the twentieth century, the costs of hurricanes have risen dramatically. Hurricane Camille, which struck the Gulf coast in 1969, and Hurricane Betsy, which landed in the Bahamas, South Florida, and Louisiana in 1965, produced damages estimated to run in the neighborhood of $1 to $2 billion.

In contrast, the damage caused by Hurricane Andrew, in 1992, totaled more than $25 billion. The largest part of this consisted of damage to private property, but many public structures and roads were also affected. The damage caused by Andrew bankrupted a number of insurance companies, and many more restricted the amount of coverage they would provide in hurricane-prone regions. As the value and number of properties in coastal areas grow, the risk of major economic dislocation from future hurricanes grows. Although some governments have attempted to restrict development along hurricane-prone shores, this has proven unpopular and has not been highly successful. Most experts agree that future disasters caused by hurricanes are inevitable.

Nancy M. Gordon

1281: Japan

Typhoon
Date: August 14-15, 1281
Place: Hakata Bay, Kyūshū, Japan
Result: More than 100,000 dead, 2,000 ships destroyed in a Mongol armada

On the night of August 14-15, 1281, an extraordinarily severe typhoon struck Kyūshū, the southernmost of the four islands that constitute Japan. For the Japanese people, this storm occupies a special place in their history, for it virtually annihilated a Mongol invasion force and thereby played a critical role in preventing at least a portion of their beloved homeland from falling under foreign domination.

The instigator of the ill-fated Mongol campaign against Japan was Kublai Khan (1215-1294). Best

This entire operation was to take place during Japan's typhoon season. Kublai and his commanders were well aware of this and clearly understood that ships caught on the open seas by a typhoon had no chance of survival. It was therefore critical that the Mongol flotilla complete its sea journey as quickly as possible, and it was to this end that Kyūshū, rather than Honshū, the seat of the Kamakura government, was selected as the target of the attack.

Although the unexpected death of the commander of the Chiang-nan Division delayed the scheduled rendezvous of the two Mongol armies, Kublai's forces ran into no weather difficulties and reached the coast of Kyūshū unscathed. Once ashore, however, the invaders confronted fierce resistance from Japanese warriors, who were expecting the invasion. For six weeks, the fighting dragged on, until August 14, when, as the Mongols were preparing what they hoped would be a decisive assault, a typhoon suddenly sprang up.

known as the first Mongol emperor of China, and thus the founder of the Yüan Dynasty, Kublai aspired to have Japan's rulers, the Kamakura shogunate, recognize his sovereignty and pay tribute. When efforts to achieve his objectives by diplomatic means failed—the Japanese brutally executed his envoys in both 1275 and 1279—the emperor decided to use military force to compel the rebellious Japanese to submit.

In June, 1281, a Mongol invasion force consisting of two armies set out for Japan. The Eastern Route Division, 40,000 soldiers strong, sailed on 900 ships from Korea, while the larger Chiang-nan Division, made up of 100,000 soldiers and transported on 3,500 ships, embarked from recently conquered southeastern China. Kublai's plan was for these two forces to rendezvous at sea and then carry out a concentrated assault against Kyūshū.

Had this been an ordinary typhoon, there is a good chance that the Mongol fleet, which was securely moored, would have survived with minimal damage. The evidence, the extent of the destruction in particular, indicates that this was no ordinary typhoon. One historian, writing in 1921, concluded that this storm was the equivalent of the 1906 typhoon that devastated Hong Kong.

Contemporary records show that the wind blew from the north and west and that the storm's vortex traveled northeastwardly through the Tsushima Strait. As the storm moved parallel to Kyūshū's coast, it blew ashore and wreaked havoc. The powerful wind drove many of the Mongol vessels into the narrows, where they were jammed and destroyed. When the storm finally subsided, the sea was littered with wreckage. Bodies of men and horses floated in a tangle of masts and lumber so densely intertwined that survivors could walk out on the surface of the sea. The numbers speak for themselves. In a single night, more than 100,000 Mongol soldiers were killed and more than 2,000 ships were destroyed. What remained of Kublai's armada returned to Korea. Never again would the Mongols undertake an invasion of Japan.

In the immediate wake of the August, 1281, typhoon, Japan's Shinto priests explained that the homeland had been saved by divine intervention. Specifically, they claimed that the *Kami* (gods) of Ise Shrine, the major shrine of the Shinto faith, had sent the great storm. Henceforth, the Japanese people referred to the typhoon of 1281 as the *Kamikaze* (divine wind).

It should be noted that the storm of August, 1281, marked the second occasion within a decade that the *Kamikaze* had thwarted a Mongol invasion of Japan. Nearly seven years before, in November, 1274, Kublai Khan had dispatched a smaller military force (nine hundred ships and forty thousand soldiers) to attack Kyūshū. This assault, like the attempted invasion of 1281, ended in disaster for the invaders when a ferocious storm struck Hakata Bay. While there is some debate about the precise nature of that storm—it is unclear whether it was an out-of-season typhoon—and about the location of the Mongol fleet at the time it struck, there is no doubt that on two separate occasions in the late thirteenth century adverse weather disrupted attempted Mongol invasions of Japan.

Bruce J. DeHart

For Further Information:

Ballard, G. A. *The Influence of the Sea on the Political History of Japan.* Westport, Conn.: Greenwood Press, 1972. Originally published in 1921, this work contains an entire chapter on the two attempted Mongol invasions of Japan, which includes interesting information about the 1281 typhoon.

Benson, Douglas S. *The Mongol Campaigns in Asia: A Summary History of Mongolian Warfare with the Governments of Eastern and Western Asia in the Thirteenth Century.* Chicago: Bookmasters, 1991. The section "The War with Japan, 1281" offers a concise description of the events of August, 1281.

Hall, John W., Marius B. Jensen, Madoka Kanai, and Denis Twitchett, eds. *The Cambridge History of Japan.* Vol. 3. Cambridge, England: Cambridge University Press, 1990. Based exclusively on Japanese sources, chapter 3, "The Decline of the Kamakura Bakufu," by Ishii Susumu, offers an excellent account of the destruction of the Mongol armada and the role weather played.

Rossabi, Morris. *Kublai Khan: His Life and Times.* Berkeley: University of California Press, 1988. This biography of Kublai offers a readable account of the origins, course, and aftermath of the Mongol invasions of Japan. Rossabi points out that weather was only one of several factors that doomed Mongol aspirations to bring Japan within their sphere of influence.

Saar, John. "Japanese Divers Discover Wreckage of Mongol Fleet." *Smithsonian Magazine,* December, 1981, 118-129. Saar both recounts how Japanese divers discovered the remains of Kublai's fleet in the summer of 1981 and tells the story of the invasion and typhoon.

Sansom, G. B. *Japan: A Short Cultural History.* Rev. ed. London: The Cresset Press, 1952. Although older, this still-useful work is based on primary sources and offers a narrative and analysis of the 1281 typhoon.

1502: Dominican Republic

Hurricane
Date: June 29-July 1, 1502
Place: The Dominican Republic and Haiti
Result: More than 500 dead

Explorer Christopher Columbus arrived on his fourth and last voyage to the New World shortly before an approaching storm hit his base on the island of Santo Domingo, now Hispaniola, or the Dominican Republic and Haiti. Columbus had probably experienced a hurricane on his second voyage in 1495. As he was departing for Spain after completing that expedition, a terrible storm devastated the same island; three of his ships were sunk.

By his fourth voyage, Columbus apparently could tell the signs of a hurricane because he requested permission from the island's governor to shelter his small fleet in a river along the coast. His request was refused, so he sent a second message warning of the coming storm and pleading that the governor at least delay the sailing of a large fleet of naval vessels scheduled to return home. That request was also refused, and the fleet sailed under the command of Admiral Bobadilla. The weather, as is generally the case just before the arrival of a hurricane, was quite calm. Columbus's warnings proved right, however, and the winds and waves destroyed the fleet, with losses totaling more than 500 sailors. Only 1 ship survived. Columbus's ships, on the other hand, were finally brought to refuge and suffered only minor damage.

Leslie V. Tischauser

For Further Information:

Barnes, Jay. *Florida's Hurricane History.* Chapel Hill: University of North Carolina Press, 1998.

1559: Florida

Hurricane
Date: August 21-22, 1559
Place: Tampa Bay, Florida
Result: More than 600 dead

In 1559 King Philip II of Spain sent a fleet headed by Admiral Tristan de Luna to establish a port on the western coast of Florida. The admiral first sailed to Veracruz, Mexico, to pick up sailors and supplies. He left the coast of Mexico on June 11 with 13 ships, more than 1,000 sailors, and 200 horses. Early in August the fleet sailed along the west coast of Florida, along the Gulf of Mexico, and found a suitable site to build a fort, close to the present-day city of Tampa Bay.

Just a week after his crew landed on the coast and began building a fort, a powerful hurricane devastated the coast, knocking down trees and most of the half-completed buildings. More than 600 of the admiral's men were killed by the gigantic waves and storm surge that hit the beaches. The savage force of the storm crushed plans for creation of a new Spanish outpost. King Philip II issued orders to abandon the project and gave up all ideas of future settlement on the Gulf coast because too many of his men were killed by the hurricanes that struck that region. The king ordered the admiral to build along Florida's Atlantic coast instead; as de Luna's small fleet edged up the Atlantic another powerful storm struck, killing the admiral and all of his men.

Leslie V. Tischauser

For Further Information:

Pielke, Roger A. *Hurricanes: Their Nature and Impact on Society.* New York: John Wiley, 1997.

1622: Cuba

Hurricane
Date: September 6, 1622
Place: Havana, Cuba
Result: More than 2,000 dead

Late in July, 1622, an expedition of more than 50 ships left Madrid, Spain, bound for Cuba. The ships ran into a hurricane off the east coast of Florida and took more than thirty-nine days to reach Havana. When they reached port, the ships were overrun with rats, the drinking water was foul, and many sailors lay dead on the decks. This was not the only loss for Spain caused by this massive storm. Another 50 ships that had left Cuba on their way to Spain were also devastated by the hurricane.

The storm swept through Havana, flooding its streets and drowning hundreds of residents. Eighteen ships from the fleet that were headed to Spain made it back to harbor with their masts broken. Hundreds of sailors had been swept off the ships, drowning at sea. Fifty survivors made it to the Dry Tortugas, and 60 more floated on rafts to the Florida Keys, where they were rescued. One survivor was found hanging onto a hatch cover a few miles off the Keys. He told his rescuers that he had survived by eating a sea gull that had landed on his crude raft. The Spanish navy lost 9 ships and 550 sailors, many of them eaten by sharks, on this expedition, as well as hundreds of bars of gold and silver. The total number of victims of this storm was never precisely determined, though Spanish authorities made estimates of more than 2,000 deaths.

Leslie V. Tischauser

For Further Information:

Dunn, Gordon L. *Atlantic Hurricanes.* Baton Rouge: Louisiana State University Press, 1960.

1666: West Indies

Hurricane
Date: August 4, 1666
Place: Guadeloupe, Martinique, and St. Kitts
Result: More than 2,000 dead

A violent hurricane in 1656, and another one eight years later in 1664, devastated the island of Guadeloupe. However, the most destructive storm to hit the island came on August 4, 1666. Every ship in its harbors and each boat along its coast were smashed to bits by the intensity of the wind and waves. The nearby islands of Martinique and St. Kitts were also struck by the storm. The sea rose to such heights that the 6-feet-thick walls of a fort were totally washed away, as were the 14-pound guns that stood behind them. A Spanish fleet carrying more than 2,000 sailors was totally lost except for 2 survivors. The cotton and tobacco crops on the islands were also totally destroyed. The tremendous force of the wind, waves, and waters knocked down almost every house and building on the three islands; survivors said it was the most intense storm they had ever experienced.

Leslie V. Tischauser

For Further Information:

Pielke, Roger A. *Hurricanes: Their Nature and Impact on Society.* New York: John Wiley, 1997.

1703: England

Hurricane
Date: November 27, 1703
Place: England
Result: More than 30,000 dead

A gigantic Atlantic hurricane swept through the south of England in November of 1703 with high winds and gales that lasted for two weeks. The famous English writer Daniel Defoe talked to many survivors and left behind in vivid detail a record of the enormous destruction caused by the storm. Rainstorms first hit the coast on November 14 and did not stop for fourteen days. The wind blew debris from houses and buildings with such great force that bricks were imbedded 8 inches into the earth. Wooden beams flying through the air killed hundreds of people in the port towns of Plymouth, Hull, Yarmouth, Cowes, Portsmouth, Bristol, and Grimsby.

Giant waves flooded the Thames River, and an estimated 300 naval vessels were destroyed. The fury of the storm caught ships from the French and Russian fleets seeking refuge in English harbors. Government officials estimated that at least 30,000 sailors from the English, French, and Russian navies were drowned. The tide produced by the storm was so huge that water rose 6 to 8 feet higher than anyone in England had ever seen. The storm surge flooded the streets of many riverside towns and totally destroyed more than 5,000 houses. Many people in those houses had no chance to escape and were carried away to their watery graves.

Leslie V. Tischauser

For Further Information:

Tannehill, Ivan. *Hurricanes: Their Nature and History.* Princeton, New Jersey: Princeton University Press, 1956.

1713: North Carolina

Hurricane
Date: September 16-17, 1713
Place: North Carolina
Result: At least 70 dead

One of the earliest recorded hurricanes in the colony of North Carolina's history struck far into the interior on September 16-17, 1713. Heavy winds caused massive damage to the coastal towns, especially around the Cape Fear River. The city of Port Royal suffered massive flooding, and houses in Charleston, along the Atlantic coast in South Carolina, were swept into the sea with their occupants still inside. Several ships were carried far inland by the storm surge and ended up 3 miles from the shore in the middle of a marsh. Another large boat was found 10 feet up in a tree. Thousands of trees were blown down like matchsticks. The winds were so great that an 80-foot-tall lighthouse on an offshore island was broken into two pieces as the building snapped apart at the middle.

Most of the 70 deaths occurred along the coast as people were drowned by the tremendous waves and storm surge. Heavy rains and winds lasted for two days, adding more misery to the unlucky inhabitants of North Carolina. It was only a matter of luck that the strongest winds and highest floodwaters hit rather sparsely settled regions of the colony, or the death toll would have been much higher.

Leslie V. Tischauser

For Further Information:

Barnes, Jay. *North Carolina's Hurricane History.* Chapel Hill: University of North Carolina Press, 1996.

1715: Florida

Hurricane
Date: July 31, 1715
Place: Near the east coast of Florida, from Cape Canaveral to Fort Pierce
Speed: 75 miles per hour
Result: 700-1,000 dead, 11 ships and 14 million pesos lost initially

Spanish treasure fleets carried the wealth of the New World to Spain from the fifteenth to the eighteenth century. In the eighteenth century, Spanish silver and gold from the Americas served as the most important source of Spanish wealth and provided the backing for most of the currency of Europe. Consequently, the treasure fleets were crucial to the Spanish economy as well as to the entire European economic structure. The fleets were organized so that

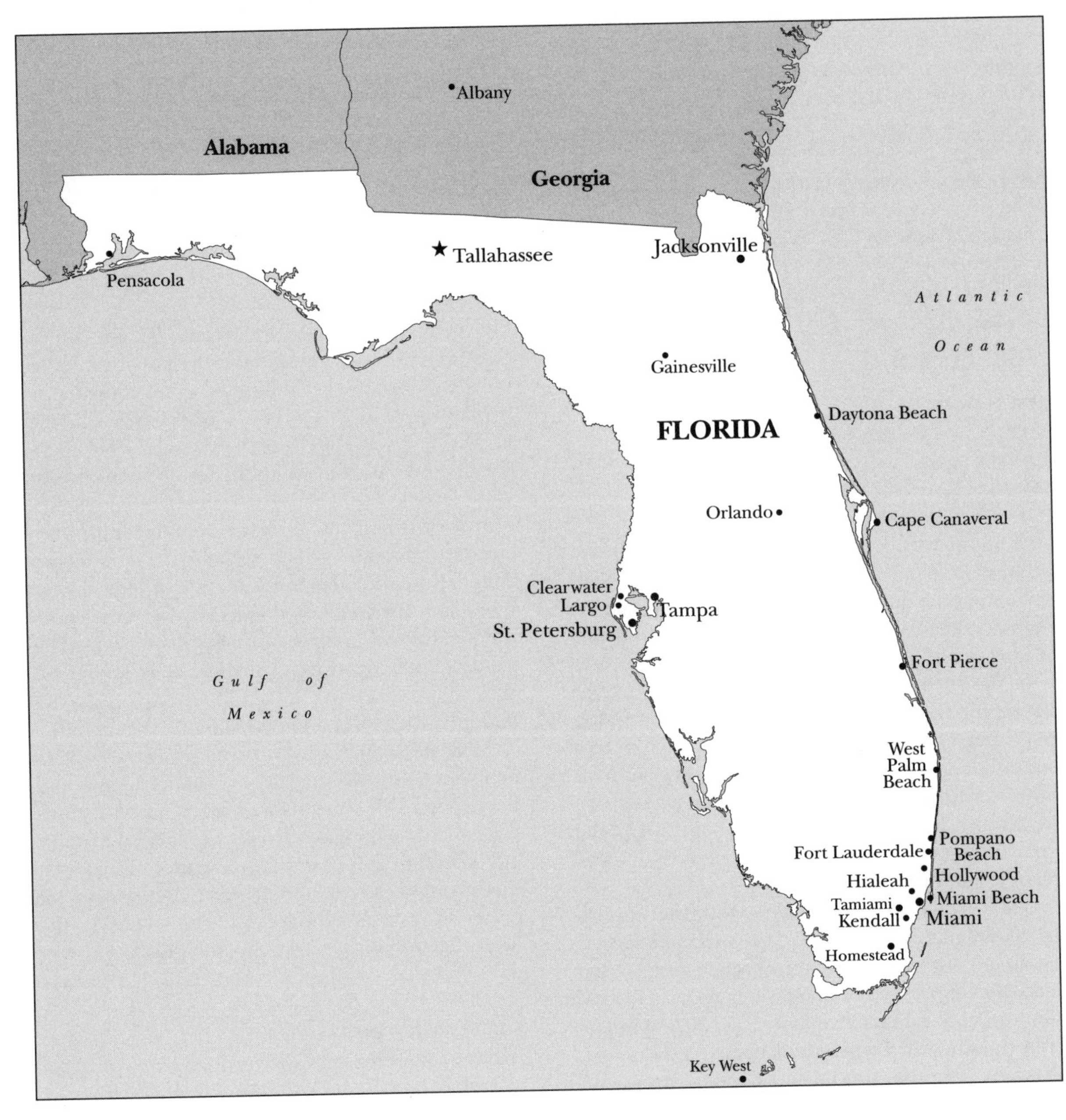

two fleets left Spain at different times of the year: The New Spain or *Flota* fleet sailed to gather the gold and silver of present-day Mexico in the spring, and the *Tierra Firme* fleet sailed in late summer to collect the riches of South America at Cartagena, in present-day Colombia. The combined fleet would meet in Havana for the return voyage. The two greatest enemies of the fleets were pirates and weather. In order to combat piracy, treasure fleets were well-defended by protective convoys. To avoid the threat of hurricanes, the combined fleet was to leave in the spring before summer brought the hurricane season.

Though the Spanish usually sent treasure fleets every year, from 1701 to 1714, during the War of the Spanish Succession, Dutch and English enemies hampered the successful delivery of riches. In 1712, as the war was ending, King Philip V of Spain ordered that the New Spain fleet be sent out as soon as possible to fill his depleted treasuries. The New Spain fleet left Spain on September 16, 1712, reaching Veracruz on December 3. The fleet was not to leave that port for nearly two and a half years. Meanwhile, the *Tierra Firme* fleet left Spain on July 19, 1713, and reached Cartagena on August 29. After picking up cargo from Cartagena and Portobelo, the squadron reached Havana on October 2, 1714. The New Spain fleet, which had been delayed in Veracruz, did not arrive in Havana until June of 1715.

A month later, the combined fleets, numbering 12 ships—11 Spanish and 1 French, the *Grifón*—left Havana for a dangerously late return voyage to Spain on July 24, 1715. The Spanish fleets took the standard route along the coast of Florida, following the Gulf Stream before heading east. The journey was uneventful until July 30, when the air became uncomfortably humid and the winds blew erratically. The weather grew increasingly violent, with strong winds, huge waves, dark skies, and horrendous downpours. The rain soon ceased, but terrific gales punctuated the evening. By midnight five gales had pounded the ships.

The worst was yet to come. Wind, rain, and high waves broke off masts and rendered the ships uncontrollable. At 2 A.M. the winds reached over 75 miles per hour. The *Nuestra Señora de la Regla* hit bottom, the superstructure tearing away from the hull. Passengers and cargo, including 120 tons of silver coins, sank to the bottom of the sea. More than 200 persons from that ship alone were drowned. The *Santo Cristo de San Román* suffered similar damage, with 120 lost. The *Nuestra Señora del Rosario* was smashed to pieces by the storm, resulting in 124 fatalities. Another large ship, the *Nuestra Señora del Carmen* sank, but most of the passengers and crew made it to shore. In all, 11 ships were lost and 700 to 1,000 passengers and crew drowned in one of the greatest shipwrecks in history.

Only 1 ship—the French ship *Grifón*—survived. It had sailed northeast of the fleet and escaped the hurricane completely. About 1,500 passengers and crew swam or floated on wreckage and made it safely to shore. Survivors and wreckage were washed up along the shore for 30 miles of the Florida coast. After the storm had ended, commanders surveyed the damage, collected the groups of survivors, and brought them to a single camp at Barra de Ays. They then salvaged the ships with the least damage in order to sail for help. The first ship embarked for St. Augustine, Florida, the nearest settlement. Those people with the worst injuries were evacuated with the small crew who went to seek help. Two more salvaged ships were sent: one to St. Augustine with injured people and one to Havana carrying men of high rank.

Help from St. Augustine in the form of food, tools, and small boats arrived at the survivors' camp. In addition, a number of American Indians were brought to help the 1,400 survivors. The Indians built shelters, hunted small animals, foraged for food, and taught the settlers how to smoke and dry meat. Once the news of the tragedy reached Havana, 7 ships were fitted to sail to the Florida coast. The vessels held supplies for the shipwrecked and diving gear to try to salvage the treasure lost to the sea. Thirty Indian divers were hired to assist in the retrieval of the riches. When the cargo was unloaded, the remaining survivors boarded the ships and sailed to Havana. It was now September 10, 1715, nearly a month and a half since the hurricane.

The salvaging operation began once the hurricane victims were evacuated. About 80 percent of the registered treasure was recovered between September, 1715, and April, 1716. Salvage continued until 1718, with little further success. The remaining treasure was buried under the sand and encrusted with coral until its discovery by Florida treasure hunters nearly 250 years later.

Bonnie L. Ford

FOR FURTHER INFORMATION:

Burgess, Robert F., and Carl J. Clausen. *Gold, Galleons, and Archaeology: A History of the 1715 Spanish Plate Fleet and the True Story of the Great Florida*

Treasure Find. New York: Bobbs-Merrill, 1976.

Marx, Robert F. *Sea Fever.* Garden City, N.Y.: Doubleday, 1972.

Marx, Robert, and Jennifer Marx. *New World Shipwrecks, 1492-1825.* Dallas: Ram, 1994.

Walton, Timothy R. *The Spanish Treasure Fleets.* Sarasota: Pineapple Press, 1994.

1722: Jamaica

Hurricane
Date: August 28, 1722
Place: Port Royal, Jamaica
Result: At least 400 dead

The British colony of Jamaica suffered huge losses in life and property from a powerful hurricane that hit the island and its major city, Port Royal, on August 28, 1722. Just thirty years earlier a violent earthquake had largely destroyed the same area. Residents of the wealthy English sugar colony had rebuilt many homes and businesses after the quake, but nature struck again with great severity. Twenty-six ships were lost after being battered and bashed by the powerful winds of the storm. More than 400 people were killed in the city of Port Royal from raging floodwaters and waves. Trees were blown down like matchsticks, and at least one ship was found the next day with its anchor suspended high in a tree. The great violence of the hurricane destroyed much of Jamaica's sugar crop and brought economic ruin to many planters. Other sugar growers responded to the difficulties created by the storm by cutting back on the food and supplies offered to slaves.

Leslie V. Tischauser

For Further Information:

Tannehill, Ivan Ray. *Hurricanes: Their Nature and History, Particularly Those of the West Indies and the Southern Coasts of the United States.* New York: Greenwood Press, 1986.

1737: Bay of Bengal

Cyclone
Date: October 7, 1737
Place: Countries along this part of the Indian Ocean
Result: 300,000 dead

On October 7, 1737, an enormous cyclone struck with all its strength at the mouth of the Hooghly River, which empties into the Bay of Bengal. Striking at high tide, the cyclone created a storm wave that reached a height of 40 feet as it moved nothward toward the densely populated low-lying shore and seaports. This surge destroyed at least 20,000 ships and caused 300,000 fatalities.

David M. Soule

For Further Information:

Cornell, James. *The Great International Disaster Book.* New York: Charles Scribner's Sons, 1976.

Nash, Jay Robert. *Darkest Hours.* Chicago: Nelson-Hall, 1976.

1775: The Hurricane of Independence

Date: September 2-9, 1775
Place: U.S. East Coast, from North Carolina to Nova Scotia
Result: More than 4,170 dead

During the week of its existence, the so-called Hurricane of Independence destroyed many lives and huge amounts of property all along the Atlantic coast, from North Carolina to Nova Scotia. The violent winds and huge waves created by the storm killed hundreds of people on the North Carolina shores, including more than 150 residents of the coastal town named Bar. The hurricane headed north through Virginia, Maryland, and Pennsylvania, causing tornadoes and heavy flooding along the way.

American militiamen heading out to fight the British Redcoats in these early days of the American Revolution instead had to fight raging rivers and streams. Floodwaters, hail, and wind destroyed much of the corn crop in the affected states and caused hardship long after it the storm had run its course. When the hurricane reached Canadian waters, hundreds of fishing boats were caught off the coast of Newfoundland and capsized, drowning hundreds of fisherman in the icy waters. Death tolls reached 4,000 in Newfoundland alone. Losses of ships, merchandise, and buildings reached the worst levels for a single hurricane in Canadian history. Many towns reported that residents lost everything they had; total losses were in the millions of dollars.

Leslie V. Tischauser

For Further Information:

Dunn, Gordon. *Atlantic Hurricanes.* Baton Rouge: Louisiana State University Press, 1960.

1780: The Great Hurricane of 1780

Date: October 10-16, 1780
Place: The Caribbean, particularly Barbados and the West Indies
Result: 20,000-22,000 dead

The Great Hurricane of 1780 is the deadliest Western Hemisphere storm and the deadliest hurricane on record to date, according to the National Hurricane Center. During the same month, two other killer hurricanes struck, one in Jamaica and one in the eastern part of the Gulf of Mexico. Over 1,000 lives were lost in the first, and over 2,000 in the second.

The Great Hurricane of 1780 struck a number of islands in the Caribbean Sea, devastating Barbados, Martinique, and St. Lucia. It is estimated that around 22,000 people died from the storm, most from drowning. About 9,000 lives were lost in Martinique, 4,000 to 5,000 died in St. Eustatius, and over 4,000 died in Barbados. In addition, thousands died on ships at sea. The number of fatalities from the 1780 hurricane exceeds the cumulative loss of any other year and in all other decades. The storm was responsible for more deaths than any other recorded storm.

At the time the storm hit, the American Revolution was underway, and British and French fleets were sailing the Caribbean area in an attempt to gain control of sea access to the new country. Both fleets suffered heavy losses of ships and men. The fleet of British admiral George Rodney, sailing to the West Indies from New York, was badly damaged and scattered. When he arrived in Barbados, he found that he had lost 8 of 12 warships that he had left moored there, and most of the crews had drowned.

It has been estimated that up to the year 1825, because of the extent of navigation to the New World and the vulnerability of ships at sea and in port, 5 percent of the ships sailing in the West Indies were lost, mainly due to storms. Those lost at sea were generally counted as fatalities in statistics on the storm.

Colleen M. Driscoll

For Further Information:

Burns, A. C. *History of the British West Indies.* Barnes & Noble: New York, 1954.
Clark, G. *Hurricanes of the Caribbean Sea.* Miami: National Hurricane Center, 1988.
Millas, J. C. *Hurricanes of the Caribbean and Adjacent Regions, 1492-1800.* Miami: Academy of the Arts and Sciences of the Americas, 1968.
Schomburgk, Robert H. *The History of Barbados.* Longman, Brown, Green, and Longmans: London, 1848.

1806: Guadeloupe

Hurricane
Date: September 9, 1806
Place: Guadeloupe
Result: 131 dead, hundreds missing

On September 9, 1806, a tremendously powerful hurricane swept over the French West Indian colony of Guadeloupe, leaving behind a mass of debris, destruction, and death. The storm surge and massive waves left 5 to 6 feet of mud and sand covering parts of the two islands of Guadeloupe. The Roseau River overflowed its banks, flooding the streets of the island's largest town, Basse-Terre. The torrent of floodwaters knocked down houses and buildings and drowned more than 50 citizens. The bodies of the victims were washed into the sea and never recovered.

The total number of deaths was never recorded, although newspapers reported that 131 bodies had been found. The number of people missing, many of them African slaves, was said to be in the hundreds. The whole countryside was devastated, and the tobacco and cotton crops were ruined. The 1806 storm was regarded as the most violent to hit Guadeloupe and the nearby island of Dominica, which reported more than 100 lives lost, in the nineteenth century.

Leslie V. Tischauser

For Further Information:

Tannehill, Ivan Ray. *Hurricanes: Their Nature and History—Particularly Those of the West Indies and the Southern Coasts of the United States.* New York: Greenwood Press, 1932.

1819: Gulf Coast

Hurricane
Date: July 27-28, 1819
Place: Mobile, Alabama; Florida; Mississippi; and Louisiana
Result: More than 200 dead

One of the most intense storms to hit the United States in the nineteenth century lashed into Mobile, Alabama, at 8 P.M. on July 27, 1819. The winds, storm surge, and intense rain destroyed much of the city. The eye of the hurricane swept over the area at about midnight, and the wind increased to levels no one in the city had witnessed before. The storm reached all the way to New Orleans, but that city received only minor damage compared to other cities along the Gulf coast. Floodwaters 6 feet deep raced through Bay St. Louis and Pass Christian, Mississippi. Only three buildings were left standing in Pass Christian—all the others were demolished.

Dozens of bodies were swept away, never to be recovered. The storm waters left behind giant snapping turtles and alligators in the streets of Mobile. Many ships in the city's harbor were found blocks away from the coast, having been tossed around like toys by the angry sea. The crews of these vessels were never found. The storm also did great damage to Pensacola, Florida. The city was still in Spanish hands, as Florida would not become part of the United States until a few months later, and no official casualty figures were made public by authorities in the city. It is estimated that the total number of deaths from this extremely intense storm was well above 200.

Leslie V. Tischauser

For Further Information:

Barnes, Jay. *Florida's Hurricane History.* Chapel Hill: University of North Carolina Press, 1998.

1825: Puerto Rico

Hurricane
Date: July 26, 1825
Place: Puerto Rico
Result: 374 dead, 1,210 injured

It is customary in Puerto Rico to name a hurricane after the particular saint's day on which it occurs. July 26, 1825, was Santa Ana's Day, and on it one of the most severe hurricanes in the history of Puerto Rico blew across the island. The wind, flooding, and huge waves did great damage to the island and to the neighboring island of Guadeloupe, where the barometer fell a staggering 1.86 inches in one minute. Hurricane-force winds knocked down more than 7,000 buildings on Puerto Rico alone and crashed their way across the length of the island. More than 374 people were drowned in the storm, and 1,200 were left homeless. It took both islands years to rebuild from the damages.

Leslie V. Tischauser

For Further Information:

Tannehill, Ivan. *Hurricanes: Their Nature and History.* Princeton, N.J.: Princeton University Press, 1956.

1831: Caribbean, Gulf Coast

Hurricane
Date: August 10-11, 1831
Place: West Indies, Barbados, the Gulf of Mexico, and Louisiana
Result: More than 1,500 dead, $7.5 million in damage

One of the most devastating hurricanes of the nineteenth century began near Barbados on August 10, 1831. Its powerful winds and giant waves swept through the West Indies, Haiti, Cuba, and the mainland of Louisiana, close to New Orleans. More than 1,500 people were killed by the storm, a total that pales in comparison to the 20,000 victims of a 1780 hurricane that devastated Barbados. However, property damage caused by the 1831 storm proved much worse, making it one of the worst hurricanes on record.

A newspaper reporter on Barbados described the damage as the worst he had ever witnessed. The terrible wind leveled every tree; the floodwaters turned every patch of green into an ugly, muddy brown. The island looked as if a tremendous fire had scorched it: Buildings were totally destroyed, and houses were filled with mud as water levels reached the tops of their roofs. Several islands along the Louisiana coast were completely covered by water when a gigantic wave smashed across them. The islands, once the homes of pirates, including the famous Jean Lafitte, remained under water for weeks after the storm had worn itself out. One interesting aftermath of this storm was the writing of one of the first scientific and historical studies of hurricanes, *An Attempt to Develop the Law of Storms* (1838) by Lieutenant Colonel William Reid of the Royal British Navy, a survivor.

Leslie V. Tischauser

For Further Information:

Pielke, Roger A. *Hurricanes: Their Nature and Impact on Society.* New York: John Wiley & Sons, 1997.

1835: Florida

Hurricane
Date: September 12-18, 1835
Place: Florida Keys
Result: More than 100 dead

The powerful hurricane that drenched the Florida Keys in September, 1835, originated near Jamaica and blew across that island and Cuba before hitting the Keys. Massive winds, waves, and rain pummeled the islands for two days before moving off to Georgia and South Carolina, where it inflicted more damage. On Key Biscayne, which averages only about 9 feet above sea level, 4 feet of water filled the streets. The heavy winds blew dozens of ships onto the beaches of Key West and other members of the island chain off the south coast of Florida. Homes and buildings throughout the Keys were knocked over by the force of the tremendous wind associated with this hurricane.

Accurate records of the deaths and damages were not kept by any agency or bureau at this time, but about 100 people lost their lives during the storm. One reason casualty figures were not higher was that the eye of the storm swept through a lightly populated area. Many people in the area blamed the storm and the rash of tornadoes and severe thunderstorms in the region on the expected visit of Halley's comet in 1835. There is no scientific evidence to support this view.

Leslie V. Tischauser

For Further Information:

Barnes, Jay. *Florida's Hurricane History.* Chapel Hill: University of North Carolina Press, 1998.

1837: West Indies

Also known as: The Racer's Storm
Hurricane
Date: August 2, 1837
Place: St. Thomas, U.S. Virgin Islands
Result: 500 dead, 20,000 injured

St. Thomas, the second largest of the U.S. Virgin Islands, is a 32-square-mile island in the Caribbean Sea. It has a natural deep-water harbor that makes it an important Caribbean port.

On August 2, 1837, a hurricane struck the island of St. Thomas, causing extensive damage to the city and ships in the harbor. A visitor to the island who was delivering mail subsequent to the hurricane described the devastation he saw. He said that the hurricane seemed to have sent all of its fury against the harbor and the port city, the damage, in his words, defying description. He reported that 36 ships and vessels had been destroyed in the harbor, 12 having sunk. At least 100 seamen drowned as a result of the storm, probably from storm surges. Storm surges of 20 to 30 feet have been the cause of some of the largest losses of life in tropical coastal cyclones. The surges occur because the force of a hurricane creates wind and pressure, which cause the water to rise. Called the "Racer's Storm," the 1837 hurricane also slammed into the coast of North Carolina, wrecking ships moored in the harbors and those sailing at sea.

Colleen M. Driscoll

For Further Information:

Marx, Robert. F. *Shipwrecks in the Americas.* New York: Dover, 1987.
Reid, W. *Law of Storms.* London: John Weale, 1841.

1841: The October Gale

Hurricane
Date: October 3, 1841
Place: Truro, Massachusetts
Result: 57 dead

A very powerful hurricane moved up through the mid-Atlantic, making landfall when it reached the coast of Massachusetts. The storm caught 7 fishing boats as they tried to race back to their harbor in Truro, Massachusetts. The storm smashed into the ships with its full force as they were attempting to turn toward Cape Cod. Gigantic waves and winds hit the small boats. Several overturned, drowning their entire crews, while the other boats were smashed to pieces as they were driven into rocks along the shore. Fifty-seven fishermen died on October 3, all from the small village of Truro. The storm was called the October Gale by survivors.

Leslie V. Tischauser

For Further Information:

Elsner, James B., and A. Birol Kara. *Hurricanes of the North Atlantic: Climate and Society.* New York: Oxford University Press, 1999.

1844: Mexico

Hurricane
Date: August 4, 1844
Place: Matamoros, Mexico
Result: More than 70 dead

An extremely violent hurricane took an unusual path across the Gulf of Mexico and struck many villages and towns along the Rio Grande River Valley in August, 1844. Matamoros, a large city on the Mexican side of the river about 25 miles from its mouth, received the heaviest blow. Brownsville, Texas, which lies across the river from Matamoros, was also heavily damaged by the wind, torrential rain, and flooding. The eye of the storm hit the Mexican city at about 10 P.M. on August 4, 1844. Gigantic waves and powerful winds knocked down almost every building in the city except for a recently built church. Although no official count was made, officials guessed that at least 70 people were drowned by the terrible storm. It was the deadliest hurricane to hit Mexico in the nineteenth century.

Leslie V. Tischauser

For Further Information:

Pielke, Roger. *Hurricanes: Their Nature and Impact on Society.* New York: John Wiley & Sons, 1997.

1846: Florida

Hurricane
Date: October 11-12, 1846
Place: Key West, Florida
Result: More than 40 dead

A massive hurricane that originated in the Caribbean blew across Cuba on October 10, 1846, sinking 92 vessels in Havana harbor before heading back to sea. The next day it struck the Florida Keys, knocking down more than 600 buildings and causing at least $200,000 in damage. Key West was hit the hardest, and most of the 40 deaths reported from the storm occurred on that island. Fourteen deaths resulted from the collapse of a lighthouse on the southern end of the Key. Six people standing on a wharf were swept away by a huge wave and never seen again.

Most buildings in the harbor were washed away. An ancient stone fort, built by the Spanish in the 1600's, was turned to rubble by the force of the waves and wind. Houses, lumber, and ships were dashed to pieces and carried away by the angry waters. A U.S. Navy vessel was almost broken into two pieces by huge waves but managed to stay afloat because of the heroic efforts of its crew. No accurate measure of wind speed was made, but the barometric pressure fell to 27.06 inches, more than 2 inches below normal. The lower the pressure, the more violent the storm.

Leslie V. Tischauser

For Further Information:

Barnes, Jay. *Florida's Hurricane History.* Chapel Hill: University of North Carolina Press, 1998.

1856: Louisiana

Hurricane
Date: August 13, 1856
Place: Last Island, Louisiana
Result: 137 dead

In the week preceding the hurricane of August 13, 1856, more than 13 inches of rain fell on Last Island, off the coast of Louisiana. When the storm hit with heavy winds and huge waves, the entire island was submerged, and every building on it was destroyed. The storm killed 137 people. The only survivors managed to reach a steamship anchored in the harbor.

The violent wind and the slashing rain, which hit people like hailstones, killed men, women, and children. The wind blew sand into people's faces so hard that many were blinded temporarily and could not get to higher ground, where they might have been able to survive. The submerged island remained under several feet of water for many days, and no sign of life was seen except for the few survivors who managed to cling to the steamship as it struggled to remain afloat in the storm-tossed sea.

Leslie V. Tischauser

For Further Information:
Tannehill, Ivan. *Hurricanes: Their Nature and History.* Princeton, N.J.: Princeton University Press, 1956.

1862: Massachusetts

Also known as: The February Blow of '62
Hurricane
Date: February 24, 1862
Place: Gloucester, Massachusetts
Result: 122 dead

Gloucester was one of the oldest fishing villages in the United States, having first been settled in 1623. On February 24, 1862, a powerful storm swept through the city while most of the fishing fleet was out at sea. The unusual, late-season hurricane hit 70 fishing boats along Georges Bank, a sandbank east of Massachusetts and south of the Canadian province of Newfoundland. The storm struck the ships so quickly that they were unable to lift their anchors and sail away.

The ships were struck by huge waves that capsized the boats, one by one, sending all of their crews into the angry sea. Fifteen ships were never found again, and several others were broken apart and abandoned. At least 122 fishermen died in the disaster, and many others were badly injured. The number of deaths from drowning included several fishing-boat captains. Survivors of the gale limped back home to Gloucester with few fish and many horrifying tales to tell of the death and destruction resulting from this terrible storm, which sailors referred to as the "February Blow of '62."

Leslie V. Tischauser

For Further Information:
Elsner, James B., and A. Birol Kara. *Hurricanes of the North Atlantic: Climate and Society.* New York: Oxford University Press, 1999.

1862: China

Typhoon
Date: July 27, 1862
Place: Canton and Huangpu, China
Speed: Winds of 107 miles per hour
Result: 37,000 dead

The 1862 Chinese typhoon's staggering death toll resulted from not only the storm's intensity but also the lack of preparation caused and lack of even limited warning of impending disaster. A measure of the storm's intensity is that it struck so far inland, for Canton and its principal port, Huangpu, are miles from the sea. Canton is on the north bank of the Pearl River and is bounded on the west by the Zengbu River. Originally founded as a village over two thousand years ago during the Qin Dynasty (220-207 B.C.E.), Canton was located upstream from the Portugese island enclave of Macao and the British-held island of Hong Kong. While Macao had existed for three hundred years by this time, Hong Kong had only been in British hands for a quarter of a century by the time of this catastrophe. Population and casualties were light in those areas.

By 1862, Canton had been China's principal southern seaport for hundreds of years. The inner city walls, started in the eleventh century and com-

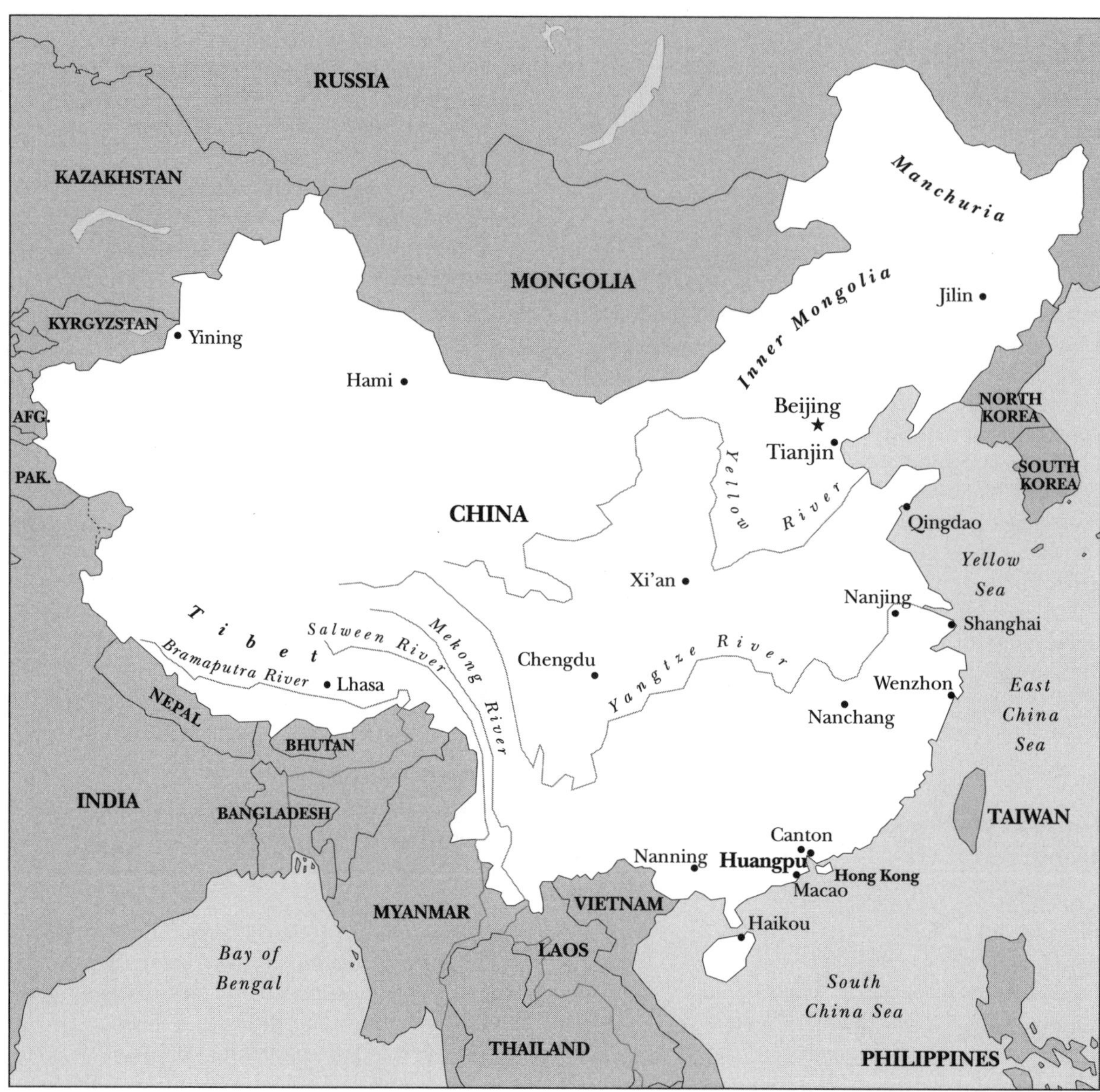

pleted in the sixteenth, were about 10 miles long, 25 feet high, and 15 to 25 feet thick. To the west (farther upstream) and unprotected by the city walls were the wealthy Chinese merchant homes and the residences of all foreigners, who were restricted to living on a small island, Shamian, southwest of the old walled city. While the city walls did give some protection from the high breaking waves along the shore, the 7 inches of rain and 107-mile-per-hour winds were devastating even inside the walls; this typhoon would have been rated severe by modern classification systems.

Outside the walls, where the vast majority of the more than 37,000 casualites occurred, there was virtually no protection, and the results were catastrophic. Hundreds, if not thousands, of fishermen were at sea when this typhoon first arose and were overwhelmed and drowned. This storm was devastating later that afternoon even for those in port. Canton had acquired strong wooden piers, brick warehouses, and even stone quays in the hundreds of years that it served as a Chinese port. All were heavily damaged by the storms and often reduced to rubble. Dozens of fragile wooden Chinese sampans and

Western clipper ships had their masts ripped off and sunk, and this storm also threw upon the shore 6 coal-burning steamships. Two were declared a total loss.

Richard L. Wilson

For Further Information:

Longshore, David. *Encyclopedia of Hurricanes, Typhoons, and Cyclones.* New York: Facts on File, 1998.

Samagalski, Alan, Robert Strauss, and Michael Buckley. *China.* South Yarra, Victoria, Australia: Lonely Planet, 1988.

1866: Georgia

Hurricane
Date: October 2-3, 1866
Place: Near Tybee Island, Atlantic Ocean
Result: 261 dead

Tybee Island lies off the southeast coast of Georgia at the mouth of the Savannah River. On the night of October 2, 1866, the side-wheeler and sailing vessel *Evening Star* was about 180 miles east of the island on its regular run from New York City to New Orleans. The *Evening Star* carried 270 passengers and crew and was considered one of the most luxurious ships of its time. On the evening of October 2 it ran straight into the full fury of a hurricane as it was passing Tybee. For seventeen hours the ship fought the high winds and heavy seas, but finally the vessel began to break apart. To quiet the frightened passengers and crew, a troop of singers and acrobats performed in the ship's saloon.

At about 6 A.M. on October 3 the ship began to sink. Most of the lifeboats had been blown into the ocean, so a mad scramble for the remaining boats took place. As the *Evening Star* went down it carried most of the passengers and crew with it. Only 9 people, including 2 women, made it to the single lifeboat that remained afloat. The 9 survivors floated without food or water for two days. They were finally spotted and rescued by the British steamship *Fleetwing.* The final death count stood at 261 passengers and crew.

Leslie V. Tischauser

For Further Information:

Dunn, Gordon. *Atlantic Hurricanes.* Baton Rouge: Louisiana State University Press, 1960.

1867: San Narciso Hurricane

Date: October 29, 1867
Place: Puerto Rico and the U.S. Virgin Islands
Result: More than 1,100 dead

One of the most powerful hurricanes of the nineteenth century hit the Virgin Islands and Puerto Rico on October 29, 1867. The barometer on St. Thomas fell to 27.95 inches just prior to the storm hitting. More than 600 people drowned in the Virgin Islands before the hurricane blew across Puerto Rico. In Puerto Rico, falling houses and trees killed hundreds of people in what was considered the most violent storm ever to hit the island. The center of the storm passed over the town of Caguas, where there was a frightful calm that lasted ten to twelve minutes before the violent winds and waves struck, killing at least 500 residents. Eyewitness accounts of the storm indicate that it was of rather small diameter, but that it moved rapidly with great destructive power.

Leslie V. Tischauser

For Further Information:

Tannehill, Ivan. *Hurricanes: Their Nature and History.* Princeton, N.J.: Princeton University Press, 1960.

1869: Sexby's Gale

Hurricane
Date: October 5, 1869
Place: Massachusetts
Result: At least 50 dead

One of the most powerful hurricanes ever to hit the northeastern United States was called Sexby's Gale, after one of the ship captains drowned in the storm. The storm hit every New England state with its tremendous winds and heavy rain, but Massachusetts suffered the greatest number of deaths and largest amount of property loss. Fifty ships were smashed to pieces by the furious wind, including several very large cargo ships that had sought refuge in the numerous bays along the coast. Twenty-seven ships were broken apart and sunk in Rumney Bay alone. The hurricane killed more than 50 people, mostly fishermen who had been caught in the violent sea. Damage to houses, buildings, and ships was estimated to be more than $1 million, a huge amount of money at the time.

Leslie V. Tischauser

For Further Information:

Elsner, James B., and A. Birol Kara. *Hurricanes of the North Atlantic: Climate and Society.* New York: Oxford University Press, 1999.

1872: Zanzibar

Hurricane
Date: April 14-15, 1872
Place: Zanzibar
Result: 200 dead

This Zanzibar hurricane lasted from 11 P.M. on April 14 to about 1:30 P.M. the next day, when it rested for about thirty minutes. It then began anew, with more intensity, and lasted for another three hours. All ships in the harbor, with the exception of a steamship from London that had been sent to Zanzibar on a search mission for explorer Dr. David Livingstone, were demolished. Zanzibar Town was destroyed, and about two-thirds of the coconut trees on the island were ruined. Nearly all the island's clove trees, a large source of the country's economy, were uprooted. These trees were replanted the following year, the same year that slavery was officially abolished there.

Michelle C. K. McKowen

For Further Information:

Lyne, Robert Nunez. *Zanzibar in Contemporary Times: A Short History of the Southern East in the Nineteenth Century.* London: Hurst and Blackett, 1905.

Sheriff, Abdul. *Slaves, Spices, and Ivory in Zanzibar: Integration of an East African Commercial Empire into the World Economy, 1770-1873.* London: J. Currey, 1987.

1873: The Great Nova Scotia Hurricane

Date: August 24-25, 1873
Place: Nova Scotia, Canada
Result: 600 dead, $5 million in damage

The Great Nova Scotia Hurricane originated in a tropical region, between Bermuda and Hatteras, but in an unusual fashion it rose northeastward past Georgia up to Maine, then to Nova Scotia, entering at Newfoundland's Avalon Peninsula. It raged throughout Newfoundland, Labrador, Prince Edward Island, and New Brunswick, destroying more than 1,200 ships and fishing boats. Most victims were seafarers who were caught by surprise by the hurricane. The 1873 hurricane was one of the worst in Canadian history.

Michelle C. K. McKowen

For Further Information:

Tannehill, Ivan Ray. *Hurricanes: Their Nature and History.* Princeton, N.J.: Princeton University Press, 1938.

1886: Texas

Hurricane
Date: August 19, 1886
Place: Indianola, Texas
Result: 176 dead

A powerful hurricane hit Indianola, Texas, on the evening of August 19, 1886. Winds reached speeds of 72 miles per hour by the morning, and townspeople sought protection in the signal station. Unfortunately, this building weakened, and people were forced to leave. Some time after, the building collapsed, trapping the weather observer and a doctor inside.

A fire began from fuel lamps knocked over in the station, and it spread through the town in spite of the heavy storm. People fled the buildings to escape the fire, and many were carried away by deluges of water and fierce winds. All records were burned or otherwise mutilated in the signal station, and all town buildings were destroyed. As a result, few details remain about the event.

Indianola had been severely attacked by another hurricane in 1874, which demolished about three-quarters of the town. It was rebuilt and became economically healthy, only to be completely destroyed in 1886; it was not rebuilt after the 1886 hurricane.

Michelle C. K. McKowen

For Further Information:

Tannehill, Ivan Ray. *Hurricanes: Their Nature and History.* Princeton, N.J.: Princeton University Press, 1938.

1893: The Sea Islands Hurricane

Also known as: The Savannah-Charleston Hurricane
Date: August 28, 1893
Place: Georgia, North Carolina, and South Carolina
Result: More than 1,000 dead, 30,000 homeless

The Sea Islands Hurricane was perhaps the most severe of all hurricanes in Georgia, where it killed about 500 people and flooded rice crops. The hurricane then entered South Carolina at Hilton Head Island near Charleston, where it took residents of the coastal communities by surprise, drowning somewhere between 1,000 and 2,000 people. The storm altered the shape of the islands off the coast of the Carolinas—hence the hurricane's name. It caused great financial distress to residents; about 30,000 people were left without homes, and food supplies ran short.

The hurricane moved inland through Charlotte and Wilmington, North Carolina, bringing destruction to property and people. Along the coast and in Georgia, high tides wrecked ships and deposited many inches of rainfall.

Michelle C. K. McKowen

For Further Information:

Barnes, Jay. *North Carolina's Hurricane History.* Chapel Hill: University of North Carolina Press, 1995.

1893: U.S. South

Hurricane
Date: September 27-October 6, 1893
Place: Louisiana, Mississippi, and Alabama
Speed: Estimated winds of 120 miles per hour
Result: Estimated 2,000 dead

The second of two severe hurricanes to strike the southern United States in 1893, the storm that ravaged Louisiana, Mississippi, and Alabama made landfall on October 1, 1893. With winds over 120 miles per hour, the hurricane left a vast amount of devastation in its wake. The storm went ashore between New Orleans and Port Eads, Louisiana, and observers said a large storm surge washed countless people out to sea. Houses collapsed, boats sank, and over 1,500 trees fell along one 15-mile stretch of road. Moving inland, the hurricane dumped vast quantities of rainfall; residents of Mobile, Alabama, had to wade through water reaching their shoulders to reach safety. Approximately 2,000 people perished in the disaster, and millions of dollars in damages were reported in its wake.

James B. Seymour, Jr.

For Further Information:

Flexner, Stuart, with Doris Flexner. *The Pessimist's Guide to History.* New York: Avon Books, 1992.

Tannehill, Ivan Ray. *Hurricanes: Their Nature and History.* 1938. Reprint. Princeton, N.J.: Princeton University Press, 1956.

1899: San Ciriaco Hurricane

Date: August 3, 1899
Place: Puerto Rico
Classification: Category 4
Result: 3,000 dead, $20 million in damage

The San Ciriaco Hurricane was born on August 3, 1899, near the Cape Verde Islands. It swept through a large part of Puerto Rico, bisecting the island from the southeast at 7:30 A.M. in the town of Arroyo, where a barometric reading measured 27.75 inches. It reached the northwest at about 12 P.M., leveling much in its path. In the port at Humacao, a giant wave destroyed almost all houses. Between 1 and 2 P.M. the hurricane's center reached the western coastal town of Aguadilla and then left the island. Winds reached speeds of 135 miles per hour, and the twenty-eight solid days of rain and 13-foot storm surge surrounding the event left 3,000 dead, mostly due to drowning, and thousands more without food, shelter, or employment. Damages were estimated at $20 million.

The San Ciriaco Hurricane was particularly catastrophic in the nation's farmlands, most notably the coffee-growing regions in the mountains. As the region was already suffering from poverty and social tensions, the hurricane added to the island's woes and affected the social and political climate of the next few years.

Michelle C. K. McKowen

For Further Information:

Tannehill, Ivan Ray. *Hurricanes: Their Nature and History.* Princeton, N.J.: Princeton University Press, 1938.

1900: Galveston Hurricane

Date: September 8, 1900
Place: Galveston, Texas
Classification: Force 12 on the Beaufort Scale; Category 4
Speed: At least 84 miles per hour, estimated 110-120 miles per hour
Result: 3,000-12,000 dead

The hurricane that swept in from the Gulf of Mexico and devastated Galveston, Texas, on Saturday, September 8, 1900, killed more people than any other natural disaster in the history of the United States at the time. It was a turning point in the lives of the people of the Upper Texas Gulf coast.

Galveston Island was a low sand-barrier island, almost 28 miles long and from 1.5 to 3.5 miles wide. Its surface at that time rose to an average height of 4 to 5 feet above mean tide level. The average rise and fall of the tide at Galveston was 1.1 feet. The harbor at Galveston, on the bay side, served Texas and the Trans-Mississippi West Railroad. Rail connections, including those of the Southern Pacific and the Santa Fe along with smaller rail lines, focused upon Galveston.

The Formation of the Hurricane. In the first week of September, 1900, an air mass from the north cooled the island after a stifling period of heat. The weather front was known as a "norther." It was accompanied by a line of dark clouds from the northwest. At the same time a hurricane was reported first in the Caribbean Sea and then across Cuba in the Gulf of Mexico. It moved across Key West and then turned in a westerly direction, headed almost straight for Galveston. The cool front kept the slow-moving hurricane out over the Gulf of Mexico, where it gathered strength.

Until September 4, the storm had not developed a very destructive force. It did cause rough seas and heavy rains, however, dropping 12.5 inches of rain in twenty-four hours as it passed over Santiago, Cuba. On September 6, the center of the storm was reported a short distance northwest of Key West. In 1900, the Weather Bureau relied solely on information from its stations ashore. There were no reports radioed from ships at sea. Not until December 3, 1905, did a ship radio a weather observation to be received by the U.S. Weather Bureau. Not until August 26, 1908, was a hurricane report radioed from a ship, the SS *Cartago* off the coast of Yucatán.

The central office of the Weather Bureau ordered storm and hurricane warnings from Port Eads, Louisiana, on the Gulf to Cape Hatteras on the Atlantic. On Friday morning, September 7, the center of the hurricane was estimated to be southeast of the Louisiana coast. The hurricane flags were hoisted in Galveston that morning. Increasing swells were observed to the southeast, and cirrus clouds marked the blue sky.

The Effects of the Storm. By noon of Saturday, September 8, it was evident that the hurricane was bearing down on Galveston. The hurricane flags flew over the Levi Building, which held the Weather Bureau offices, and across the island. Families along the beachfront boarded up their residences and moved to higher ground in the city. The winds were rising constantly, and it rained in torrents. By 3 P.M. the waters of the Gulf and the bay met, covering the low areas across the island. By evening the entire city was submerged. Gigantic waves destroyed the houses nearest the beach first. Debris from these structures was then hurled into the next rows of houses. The wreckage from each street was then thrown by the pounding surf into the next. These buildings also fell and offered more wreckage for the storm to cast against the next block of buildings. The east and west portions of Galveston for three blocks inland were swept clean of residential and commercial structures.

Slate from the roofs flew through the air to endanger anyone out in the torrent. A disastrous fire in 1885 had destroyed a large section of the city, so slate roofs became a requirement in building construction. In the storm these were lethal weapons, but so were falling bricks and wood carried by 100-mile-per-hour winds. From 5 P.M. until midnight, the people were caught where they were, in homes and in buildings, until these collapsed around them under the pressure of the hurricane-force winds. The public

The Galveston hurricane severely damaged Sacred Heart Church on Thirteenth Street. (Courtesy Galveston County Historical Museum)

buildings, courthouse, customs house, and hotels offered apparent safe refuge. They rapidly became overcrowded, however. Telephone, telegraph, and electric-light poles snapped, and the wires were strewn across the streets, which were becoming impassable. Corpses of people, horses, mules, and pets began to float through the streets. The collapse of buildings and the cries for help could not be heard above the roar of the wind.

Nearly 1,000 people gathered in the large Ursuline Convent, two blocks from the beach. A 10-foot wall around the convent crumbled. People, animals, and debris were being washed against the walls of the building. Four expectant mothers gave birth during the storm in the nuns' cells. The babies were baptized immediately, for no one knew if they would make it through the night.

Shortly after 8:30 P.M., the wind blowing from the southeast shattered the east windows on the top floor of the city hall. The crowd that had gathered there nearly stampeded. The front part of the building collapsed shortly thereafter. Police Chief Edwin Ketchum was able to quiet the crowd at first, then lost control. Only music could quiet those who remained in the building. A few blocks away in the Telephone Building, the telephone operators were frantic until they began to sing. Strangely enough, one song was heard repeatedly—"My Bonnie Lies over the Ocean." The operators moved from room to room as the windows were smashed and the plaster began to give way.

Between 8 and 9 P.M., the water reached its maximum depth over Galveston Island. It was 15.6 feet deep above mean tide on the east side of the city at St.

Mary's Infirmary. Downtown, the depth was 12.1 feet at the YMCA Building and 10.5 feet at the Union Passenger Station. Of the sick in St. Mary's Infirmary, together with the attendants, only 8 survived. St. Mary's Roman Catholic Orphans' Home on Fifty-seventh Street fell in portions—the east wing collapsed and then the roof and remaining part of the structure fell—during the height of the storm. All the children and the nuns, along with 2 workmen, perished. Many of the bodies were tied together with ropes, one nun to several children, in an apparent attempt to survive the storm. The numbers of dead children and refugees were never accurately ascertained.

Fort Crockett on the west side of the city near the beach was flooded. It held a heavy battery of 10-inch guns, a battery of eight 10-inch mortars, and a rapid-fire battery. Manning these guns were Battery 0 soldiers of the First Artillery. The men there rode out the first part of the storm in the barracks, but most soon left for higher ground and the safety of the Denver Resurvey School; three drowned on the way. The barracks building was destroyed, and the other men were lost. The shoreline at Fort Crockett had moved back about 600 feet. All fortifications except the rapid-fire battery at Battery 0's Fort San Jacinto on Fort Point, on the eastern bay side of the island, were practically destroyed. At the fort every building except the quarantine station was swept away. Twenty-eight men of the Battery 0 were lost in the storm.

Damage to Ships. The 2-mile channel between Bolivar Peninsula and Galveston Island was the only passage for ocean-going ships into Galveston harbor. The channel was protected by two jetties extending from the peninsula and the island. Moored in the Bolivar Roads across from Fort San Jacinto and the quarantine station were three English steamships—the *Taunton*, the *Hilarious*, and the *Mexican*—in quarantine. The American *City of Everett* was also anchored in the Bolivar Roads. The federal government dredge boat *General C. B. Comstock* was tied up at the U.S. Army Corps of Engineers coal wharf, which was built out into the water from the south jetty near the quarantine station on Galveston Island.

Twelve other steamers were in port at Galveston, moored along the wharf on the bay side of the city. Among them was the English steamship *Kendal Castle* at Pier 31, on the west of the port facility. The American ship *Alamo* was docked at Pier 24, the Norwegian *Guyller* at Pier 21, the English ships *Benedict* and *Roma*, as well as the *Norna*, at Pier 15. The *Comino* was moored at Pier 14, and the *Red Cross* rested at Pier 12 on the east side of the wharf front. By midday, most of the ships were ordered to put out extra mooring lines. Later, the water on the rising tide began to submerge the wharves. The bay was rough, and a drenching rain soaked everything. Smaller craft—shrimpers, tugs, barges, and schooners—were dashed against the wharves.

Every ship in port battled for survival. The *Taunton* was driven by the wind 30 miles to Cedar Point on the mainland. The *Roma* broke its last moorings when the anchors parted from the chains. The ship was carried up the channel broadside to the current. The *Roma* careened into the *Kendal Castle*, then went broadside into the three railway bridges. It finally came to a stop between the last railroad bridge and the 2-mile-long wagon bridge that ran from Virginia Point to the island.

Galveston's rail traffic was cut off from the mainland for several days. The *Guyller* also plowed into the *Kendal Castle*, which began to drift when its lines broke. The ship was blown across Pelican Island, which was completely submerged, into the shallow water at the port of Texas City on the mainland. After the storm the *Kendal Castle* rested in 3 feet of water in the wreckage of the Inman Pier. The *Guyller* became stranded between Pelican Island and Virginia Point. The *Alamo* and the *Red Cross* broke loose and were driven across the channel to run aground on the eastern edge of Pelican Island. The *Comino* and the *Norna* stayed in their berths but were extensively damaged. For 10 miles inland from the shore on the mainland it was common to see small craft such as steam launches, schooners, and oyster sloops.

At the Bolivar Point Lighthouse, near the entrance to the harbor, people began to gather, because it was the best-built structure across the channel on the Bolivar Peninsula. About 125 people sought refuge from the storm there Saturday evening. The supply of fresh water was exhausted in a short time. An effort was made to collect rainwater in buckets tied to the top of the lighthouse. The lighthouse was 115 feet high, but the saltwater spray was blown over 100 feet in the air, mixing with the rainwater that fell into the buckets.

At 5:15 P.M., the U.S. Weather Bureau's anemometer blew away. The last recorded velocity was 84 miles per hour for the five-minute period the Weather Bureau accepted as official. The weathermen estimated winds later at a velocity of 110 or 120 miles per hour during the period from 6 P.M. to 10:45 P.M., after which they began to subside. Gusts were much higher.

At 7:30 P.M. the barometer fell to 28.05 inches. It then began to rise slowly. Galveston was awash in flood tide and debris; the water reached a depth of 8 feet on Strand Street, the heart of the financial district, by 10 P.M. The wind was in a southerly direction and diminishing. Then the water began to ebb and ran off very rapidly. By 5 A.M. of the next day, the center of the street was free of water. Slime an inch thick covered everything. People emerged, trying to find their loved ones. Others just wandered aimlessly through the streets.

Recovery Efforts. Death estimates ranged from 3,000 to 12,000 people. A partial list of the dead compiled by the Galveston *Daily News* after the storm comprised more than 4,200 names. Hundreds more were never identified. The best estimate is that more than 6,000 people lost their lives in Galveston and approximately 2,000 died on the coastal mainland. Morrison and Fourmey, publishers of the *Galveston City Directory,* also gave a figure of approximately 6,000 people dead.

Great piles of corpses, uprooted vegetation, household furniture, and fragments of buildings themselves were piled in confused heaps in the main streets of Galveston. Along the Strand close to the bayfront, where the big wholesale warehouses and stores were situated, great piles of debris lay in massive heaps where the tide had left them. The warehouses became tombs, holding human bodies and animal carcasses. The masses of debris were not confined to any one particular section of the city. There was hardly a family on the island whose household did not suffer loss or injury. In some instances entire families were washed away or killed. Hundreds who escaped from the waves did so only to be crushed by falling structures.

The days following the storm were ones of privation and sadness. There were enough provisions on hand to feed the remaining population in Galveston for a week, but the problem was in properly distributing the supplies. There was an immediate rush to obtain food and water, but this slacked off in time. After finding food and water, attention turned to the wounded and the dead. All pretense at holding in-

Debris left by the Galveston hurricane. (Courtesy Galveston County Historical Museum)

quests was abandoned. More than 2,000 bodies were carried by barge, weighted, and thrown into the Gulf. Hundreds were taken to the mainland and buried at Virginia Point. Ninety-six bodies were buried at Texas City, all but 8 of which had floated to the mainland from Galveston during the storm. Cases were known where people buried their dead in their yards. As soon as possible, the work of cremating bodies began. Vast funeral pyres were erected, and the fire department personnel supervised the incineration.

An estimated 4,000 houses were destroyed, as were many commercial, religious, and public buildings. The first three blocks closest to the water, running the entire length of the city, were completely destroyed on the Gulf side of the island. The water works' powerhouse was ruined, as was the electric plant, so that the city recovered from the storm without fresh water and in the dark. Every structure in the city suffered some storm damage, as the seawater completely covered the island to a depth as much as 15.2 feet above the mean tide. The highest elevation on the island at that time was about 8 to 10 feet above sea level.

After the railway bridges were repaired in a few days, Houston served as the center of relief distribution. It also served as the way out of Galveston for people seeking inland shelter over the next few weeks. Hundreds of refugees passed through every day. Free transportation was furnished to any point in Texas, provided people had relatives who would care for them. Clara Barton, head of the American Red Cross, came to Galveston to personally direct the Red Cross relief effort in cooperation with other agencies, such as the Salvation Army. She wrote during that first week:

> It would be difficult to exaggerate the awful scene that meets the visitors everywhere. . . . In those parts of the city where destruction was the greatest there still must be hundreds of bodies under the debris. At the end of the island first struck by the storm, and which was swept clean of every vestige of the splendid residences that covered it, the ruin is inclosed by a towering wall of debris, under which many bodies are buried. The removal of this has scarcely even begun.

This description written by a lady who had witnessed many disasters provided a singular image of a city in desperate straits.

The 1900 hurricane that devastated the Gulf coast caused a reduction in the volume of business in the South. Prices of staple commodities were higher during the weeks following the storm. There was a sharp rise in the price of cotton, which reached a ten-year high. There was little change in the price of manufactured products, however.

Mayor W. C. Jones took decisive measures in the days immediately following the storm. He organized the General Committee of Public Safety, which took charge of the early restoration of services in Galveston. The water-supply system was put back into order and was cleared of contamination. The mayor imposed price controls. Laborers were brought into the city to replace skilled mechanics in deposal of the bodies; they were then free to return to their regular jobs and repair of the industrial and residential structures and the infrastructure. The work of opening the streets and disinfecting them was pursued vigorously—the debris and garbage were removed by 250 vehicles of every description. They carried the waste out of the city, and it was burned. Eleven hundred tents were received by the Board of Health. All except 300, which were retained for hospital purposes, were distributed through the various ward subcommittees to shelter the homeless. As the rail bridges were repaired, Thomas Scurry, Adjutant General of the State of Texas, arrived with 200 volunteer guardsmen. The governor placed Galveston under martial law.

Galveston civic leaders had organized the Deepwater Committee in the late nineteenth century to promote the port facilities. In the first days after the storm, the Deepwater Committee was able to gain the attention of the Texas state legislature. Leaders such as I. H. Kempner proposed that Galveston be ruled by a commission system of government. The old mayor and ward system did not seem able to marshal the confidence and strength to start the reconstruction of Galveston. With the new system, each of four commissioners had control over one city department: finance and revenue, water and sewers, streets and public property, and fire and police departments. The Galveston model became one for the progressive movement in combating the "political machines" that ran many city governments at the time.

Looking to the Future. The new city government hired General Henry M. Robert and two other engineers, Alfred Noble and H. C. Ripley, to devise some means of protecting Galveston from future storms. Robert had recently retired from the Army Corps of Engineers and had gained fame as the author of *Robert's Rules of Order* (1876). Their recommendation included a seawall and a grade raising of the city's elevation. Galvestonians approved a bond issue to raise the money to begin the work on the seawall. The state also agreed to rebate taxes for thirty-five years to help them finance the grade raising. The seawall was to extend from the east end of the island to Fort Crockett. The work began on October 27, 1902, and was finished on July 30, 1904. The seawall, 16 feet wide at the base and 17 feet high, was constructed of cement and stone around a network of steel pilings and reinforcement bars. Large blocks of granite from central Texas comprised a stone breakwater on the beach side of the wall.

The United States Army also planned to construct a protective seawall at Fort Crockett. Galveston County gave land to the federal government that expanded the fort by 25 acres. This allowed the Army seawall to connect with that on the Gulf side of the city. The Army agreed to fill in the gap and extend the seawall to Fifty-third Street. When completed, the seawall connected with the south jetty at the channel entrance to Galveston harbor at Eighth Street and Avenue A, angled to Sixth and Market, followed Sixth to Broadway, angled again from Broadway to the beach, then ran along the beachfront to Fifty-third Street.

The Goedhart and Bates engineering firm started work on raising grade level on the island around the time the first section of the seawall was completed. The contractors dredged a canal into the heart of the city, then built dikes around sections of the city. They filled the sections with silt their dredges had acquired from the bottom of the bay and the Gulf. Each existing structure was jacked up into place. The filled areas took weeks to dry. Residents had to walk to and from their houses on frame catwalks. The fill simply spread under the houses that had been raised above ground level.

Houses, churches, and commercial buildings all went through this process at the owners' expense. Some sizable masonry buildings were jacked up to new elevations. The grade raising took six years and was finished in July, 1910; all the streets had to be rebuilt. Utilities had to be relocated, and all the planting of trees and shrubs had to be done after the grade raising. The Galveston City Railway Company reestablished public transportation, completing the conversion to electricity from mule-drawn trolleys in 1905.

There was talk of restoring the wagon bridge after its destruction in 1900. Instead, the Texas Railroad Commission condemned the wooden railway trestle and ordered the construction of a causeway to carry rail traffic and automobiles, which were coming into widespread use. The causeway was modeled on a viaduct along the Florida Keys, utilizing twenty-eight concrete arches with 70-foot spans. In the center, a rolling lift gave a stretch of 100 feet for boat traffic to pass through. The bridge accommodated two railroad tracks, interurban rails, a highway for cars, and a 30-inch water main for Galveston from mainland wells. The causeway opened in 1912.

The population of Galveston increased again in the first decade of the twentieth century. The census of 1910 placed the total at 36,981, making Galveston the sixth largest city in the state. Its port facilities continued to be of importance to the U.S. Southwest. Galveston also grew as a popular tourist resort. All the rail lines serving Galveston ran excursions from Houston on Sunday mornings; there continued to be three sets of rail tracks. The railroads cut back on their excursion schedules when the Galveston-Houston Interurban service started in 1911. The Galvez Hostel opened in 1911 to provide visitors with beachfront accommodations on a grander scale than previously known in Galveston. Twenty-six passenger trains were going in and out of Galveston every day by 1912. Thus, in the twelve years after the great Galveston Hurricane, the people of the city had completed a massive seawall, raised the level of the city, continued to compete as a deep-water port, and strengthened transportation links with the mainland.

A hurricane in 1915 proved to be of comparable strength to that of the 1900 storm. Tides were slightly higher, and the wind velocity was about the same. The storm came ashore on August 16, 1915, and the winds and tides continued to buffet the city through the next day. The hurricane washed away the earthen approaches to the causeway and broke the water main; every ship in the harbor suffered damage. At Galveston 8 people died, while elsewhere on the mainland the death toll was 267—compared to the 1900 storm, the loss of life was minimal. The protective devices built after the 1900 hurricane were successful in protecting the city in the 1915 storm. Flooding did take a toll, but this was almost entirely from the bay side. The seawall and the grade raising kept the storm losses at a bearable level. Other major hurricanes in 1943, 1961, and 1983 caused considerable damage but little loss of life. Technology had ensured that Galveston would continue to thrive as a city.

Howard Meredith

For Further Information:

Alperin, Lynn H. "When Disaster Strikes." In *Custodians of the Coast: History of the United States Army Engineers at Galveston.* Galveston, Tex.: United States Army Corps of Engineers, 1977.

Coulter, John, ed. *The Complete Story of the Galveston Horror.* New York: United Publishers of America, 1900.

Garriott, E. B. "The West Indian Hurricane of September 1-12, 1900." *National Geographic* 2 (October, 1900): 384-388.

Halstead, Murat. *Galveston: The Horrors of a Stricken City.* New York: American Publishers' Association, 1900.

McComb, David. "The Great Storm and the Technological Response." In *Galveston: A History.* Austin: University of Texas Press, 1986.

Ousley, Clarence, ed. *Galveston in 1900.* Atlanta: William C. Chase, 1900.

Weems, John Edward. *A Weekend in September.* College Station: Texas A&M University Press, 1980.

1906: Florida

Hurricane
Date: October 18, 1906
Place: Florida Keys
Classification: Category 2
Result: 129 dead

A small but intense hurricane's center passed through Cuba on October 17. The next morning at 3 A.M., the hurricane arrived at Key West, Florida. Here it changed direction, as high pressure on the North Atlantic coast prevented its further northeasterly course. The town of Sand Key was hard hit; winds there reached 75 miles per hour. In Jupiter, winds sped to 60 miles per hour. Measuring stations in Florida recorded high precipitation levels of 2.74 inches in Key West and 3.13 inches in Jupiter. Deaths were almost exclusively of workers who were building the Florida East Coast Railroad and had been living in houseboats. After the hurricane passed Jupiter, it died out.

This hurricane was one of four to hit Florida in 1906. Because of the greater-than-normal number of storms, citizens around the nation began calling any tropical storm a "Florida hurricane," which temporarily sullied Florida's reputation as a land of sunshine.

Michelle C. K. McKowen

For Further Information:

Tannehill, Ivan Ray. *Hurricanes: Their Nature and History.* Princeton, N.J.: Princeton University Press, 1938.

1909: Caribbean, Mexico

Hurricane
Date: August 20-27, 1909
Place: The Caribbean, especially Haiti, and northeastern Mexico
Result: More than 1,500 dead

A hurricane originated in the Atlantic, east of the Windward Islands, on August 20, 1909. It headed westward, destroying houses at Môle Saint-Nicolas, Haiti, with its high waves. It gained intensity and reached the Yucatán Channel on August 25, where winds were estimated by a ship captain at 100 miles per hour. This same captain wired a message to New Orleans on August 26, the first real-time wireless news report of a hurricane. On August 27 the hurricane moved inland to northeastern Mexico, causing mass floods and loss of life and property.

Michelle C. K. McKowen

For Further Information:

Tannehill, Ivan Ray. *Hurricanes: Their Nature and History.* Princeton, N.J.: Princeton University Press, 1938.

1909: U.S. South

Hurricane
Date: September 10-20, 1909
Place: Louisiana, Mississippi, and Alabama
Classification: Category 4
Result: 350 dead

On September 10, 1909, a hurricane developed as pressure fell quickly over the Leeward Islands. The storm moved westward, crossing Cuba on September 17 in a path of mass destruction. It hit the Middle Gulf coast on September 20, passing over Berwick Bay, then moving inland by Baton Rouge and New Orleans. Winds reached speeds of 80 miles per hour; the speed of the hurricane after touching land was almost twice the rate during its approach in the Gulf of Mexico. The storm surge rose 15 feet, and the average barometric pressure was 29.6 inches.

New Orleans received the greatest rainfall in a given time period, measuring 1 inch in one hour, when the hurricane's center was 75 miles away. Mobile, Alabama, received 0.33 inch in a one-hour time period. Rain ended at all measuring stations in the three states simultaneously with the lowest barometer reading.

Property damage in Louisiana, Mississippi, and Alabama was approximately $5 million and included damage to public and private property, communication lines, roads and railroads, coal barges, and churches. Agriculture suffered as well; sugarcane and cotton were especially affected in southwest Louisiana, and rice crops in Crowley, Louisiana, were greatly harmed. Transportation was hindered; railroads were littered with debris, which caused delays, and many ships were washed ashore. Damages were estimated at $6 million. The hurricane moved north over the Great Lakes after ravaging the South.

Michelle C. K. McKowen

For Further Information:

Tannehill, Ivan Ray. *Hurricanes: Their Nature and History.* Princeton, N.J.: Princeton University Press, 1938.

1912: The Black River Hurricane

Date: November 18, 1912
Place: Jamaica
Classification: Category 3
Result: 100 dead

The year 1912 brought 8 tropical storms; 5 of these were hurricanes. This above-average storm activity included the Black River Hurricane of 1912, which was one of the area's most intense to date. It concentrated on Jamaica, losing intensity quickly after ravaging that country.

The hurricane developed over the southwestern Caribbean Sea, about 200 miles north of Panama, on November 11, 1912. It gained power over the course of the next few days. By the morning of November 16 the hurricane was 100 miles from Jamaica, where large waves began pounding the coasts of Savanna-la-Mar and Kingston.

Around 6 A.M. on November 18 the hurricane entered Negril Point, at the mouth of the Black River, about 70 miles west of Kingston. Its passage over the town of Black River consisted of torrential rains for two or more hours of raging destruction. Winds reached 120 miles per hour.

The hurricane's center moved northeast, wreaking havoc on town after town. In the town of Savanna-la-Mar, tides reached the highest points in a century; waves were reportedly 35 feet high. Warehouses close to the shore were broken open, toppling casks of Jamaican rum into the sea. Damage from wind and waves was substantial, sweeping away buildings and trees and killing over 100 people.

The hurricane receded from Jamaica during the morning of November 19. It quickly lost power but caused some flooding in Cuba's Guantanamo Bay.

Michelle C. K. McKowen

For Further Information:

Longshore, David. *Encyclopedia of Hurricanes, Typhoons, and Cyclones.* New York: Facts on File, 1998.

1915: Texas, Louisiana

Hurricane
Date: August 5-23, 1915
Place: Texas and Louisiana
Classification: Category 4
Result: 275 dead

On August 4, 1915, a huge hurricane was formed near the Cape Verde Islands. It moved south of the Greater Antilles and hit the Texas coast near Galveston on September 16. The hurricane's diameter was large; 12-foot waves pounded Galveston, and many residents escaped to the hills, remembering the monstrous Galveston Hurricane of 1900. Winds reached speeds of 120 miles per hour, and barometric pressure measured 27.91 inches. Beachfront properties were completely destroyed, and many important civic structures were damaged. A newly completed 8-mile seawall in Galveston was also damaged in several places, inundating the town's business center with 5 to 6 feet of water. At Virginia Point, a storm surge of 15.3 feet was observed, and 15-ton buoys at Trinity Shoals ended up 10 miles west of their usual location. In San Antonio, rain and wind ruined the season's cotton harvest.

The Weather Bureau warned residents of the possible severity of the hurricane twenty-four hours prior, but 275 people died in the storm. Various refuge sites protected citizens, including the Bolivar Point Lighthouse in Galveston, which lost its oil supply during the storm. Damages were estimated at about $50 million.

This hurricane was unusual in that it moved across the United States without crossing large mountain ranges, high-pressure areas, or other factors which would have affected the speed, winds, and precipitation levels of the hurricane. After raging through Texas and Louisiana it sped on through the Mississippi River Valley and Lake Erie, avoiding the Appalachian Plateau.

Michelle C. K. McKowen

For Further Information:

Cline, Isaac Monroe. *Tropical Cyclones.* New York: Macmillan, 1926.

1915: Louisiana

Hurricane
Date: September 29, 1915
Place: New Orleans, Louisiana
Classification: Category 4
Result: 275 dead

The second hurricane to hit the Gulf coast in 1915, this storm flooded New Orleans and caused Lake Pontchartrain to rise to overflow levels. It originated in the Caribbean Sea, moving past the Yucatán Channel and continuing northwest over the Gulf of Mexico, hitting land in southeastern Louisiana. The hurricane's center reached New Orleans about 8:00 on the evening of September 29, after moving about 40 miles in four hours. Barometric-pressure readings show that the storm had maintained intensity for twelve hours previous.

This hurricane broke the record for the highest tide on the Delta, and wind velocities were recorded at 140 miles per hour. The storm surge reached 16 feet, and barometric pressure reached 29.4 inches. The highest hourly precipitation was recorded in New Orleans, measuring 1.59 inches; this occurred seven hours before the center passed over the city. Lake Pontchartrain flooded, and winds carried structures along the lake into a mass of wreckage. The hurricane continued pounding New Orleans for about seven hours. In nearby Leeville, 99 out of 100 buildings were destroyed. The hurricane made the Orleans Levee District question the city's 10-foot high levees surrounding New Orleans; after the battering of two hurricanes in two months they suddenly seemed less than adequate.

Michelle C. K. McKowen

For Further Information:

Cline, Isaac Monroe. *Tropical Cyclones.* New York: Macmillan, 1926.

1919: Florida, Texas

Hurricane
Date: September 3, 1919-September 14, 1919
Place: Key West, Florida, and Corpus Christi, Texas
Speed: Estimated winds of 110 miles per hour in Key West
Result: Approximately 800 dead, $2 million in damage in Florida and $20 million in Texas

The great hurricane of September, 1919, formed as a tropical disturbance located south of Puerto Rico on September 3, 1919. As the storm moved east, it gained strength. By September 9, the hurricane was headed for the Florida Straits, passing about 35 miles south of Key West on the night of September 9-10. The steamship *Fred W. Weller,* near Dry Tortugas, Florida, recorded a barometric pressure of 27.37 inches, making it the third most intense hurricane to hit the United States until Hurricane Andrew in 1992 took its place. Key West itself reported about 300 fatalities during the night, as high winds, heavy rains, and a deadly storm surge lashed the community.

The hurricane moved slowly over the area around Key West, with gale-force winds blowing continuously from 7:00 A.M. on September 9 through 9:30 P.M. on September 10. The National Weather Bureau in Key West reported winds between 75 and 80 miles per hour until a strong gust blew off the anemometer cups atop the structure. The rain gauge, which had recorded 13 inches of precipitation, was also lost to the storm, and waves covered the entire island. Nearly all the buildings in the community suffered structural damage. The Weather Bureau's 85-foot-tall instrument tower collapsed onto the station's offices, which had been evacuated earlier. Afterward, the U.S. Weather Bureau announced, "In the terrific gusts that prevailed during the height of the storm, staunch brick structures had walls blown out, and large vessels which had been firmly secured, were torn from their moorings and blown on the banks."

After it moved into the Gulf of Mexico, weather forecasters lost track of the hurricane but predicted it would hit the mouth of the Mississippi River. Uncertainty in determining its destination meant storm warnings covered the entire Gulf coast region. On September 13, the storm unexpectedly veered away from Louisiana and headed for Texas. Corpus Christi received notice on Saturday, September 13, to prepare for its arrival. Despite warnings, hundreds of weekend visitors and local residents stayed in unprotected buildings constructed largely on beaches and low-lying areas, simply expecting to encounter large thunderstorms. As the hurricane made landfall, the barometer dropped to 28.67 inches, lower than in the Galveston Hurricane of 1900. Tides peaked at 10.5 feet, making them the highest tides the city had seen to that point, and destroyed hundreds of buildings. Along one stretch of beach, 900 homes vanished without a trace. As it proceeded inland, the system disintegrated. The storm killed at least 284 people in Texas.

Because the storm spent so much time at sea, at least 10 major ships and 25 smaller ones sank during the eight-day period from the storm's onset until it went ashore in Texas. The largest loss of life involved the Spanish steamship *Valbanera*, a 400-foot-long vessel. After passengers disembarked in Puerto Rico and Santiago, Cuba, including hundreds worried about the weather, the ship sailed for Havana with 488 passengers and crew. After the captain informed the dockmaster in Havana that the seas were too rough to risk an approach, the ship was lost on the night of September 9. Search and rescue operations uncovered the mast on September 19, about 40 miles west of Key West. Although divers found the ship undamaged by the storm and none of the lifeboats had been used, all the passengers and crew had perished. Locals dubbed the *Valbanera* the "Wreck of Whores," because the passengers allegedly included prostitutes bound for Havana.

James B. Seymour, Jr.

For Further Information:

Barnes, Jay. *Florida's Hurricane History.* Chapel Hill: University of North Carolina Press, 1998.

Corpus Christi: A Guide and History. American Guide series. Corpus Christi, Tex.: *Corpus Christi Caller-Times*, 1942.

Williams, John M., and Iver W. Duedall. *Florida Hurricanes and Tropical Storms.* Rev. ed. Gainesville: University Press of Florida, 1997.

1926: The Great Miami Hurricane

Date: September 15-22, 1926
Place: Miami, Florida
Classification: Category 4
Result: 243 dead, 2,000 injured

With winds approaching 138 miles per hour and a barometric pressure measured at a low 27.61 inches of mercury, the Great Miami Hurricane of 1926 is considered one of the most powerful storms to strike the U.S. mainland in the twentieth century. The hurricane began as a Cape Verde-type storm and initially was detected on September 11, 1926, as it moved nearly 1,000 miles east of the Leeward Islands. On September 16 it was located near the Turks Islands, where its winds were recorded at approximately 150 miles per hour. Passing north of Puerto Rico, the storm reached the Bahamas on the following day. Because no sophisticated tracking system was in existence at the time, residents of the Miami area were mostly unaware of the approaching storm. On the morning of September 17, the *Miami Herald* carried a small story on its front page noting the existence of the storm but indicating it was not expected to strike Florida. The U.S. Weather Bureau received its last report on the storm's location from Nassau in the Bahamas in the early afternoon of September 17, which prompted storm warnings to be issued for the Florida coast from Key West to Jupiter Inlet, 80 miles north of

Miami. That same afternoon the *Miami Daily News* published a front-page story alerting residents to a "tropical storm." The paper also reported a warning issued by the Weather Bureau's chief meteorologist that late-evening "destructive winds" could be expected in the area.

It was not until the late hours of September 17, as winds began to build, that citizens of Miami realized a major storm was about to pummel them. Until that point many of the area's residents, most of whom had recently settled in the region, either were unfamiliar with hurricanes or simply chose to ignore them. For the next eight hours, hurricane-force winds battered the Miami region. The average wind velocity during this period was approximately 76 miles per hour. Never, in recorded weather history, had a hurricane sustained its winds for such a long duration. The persistent storm dumped nearly 10 inches of rain on the city and generated a storm surge that exceeded 13 feet.

The deluge inundated Miami Beach and swept ocean waters across Biscayne Bay into the city of Miami. All types of watercraft, from schooners to dredges, were blown onto shores, sunk, or capsized, including a steam yacht that was once owned by William II of Germany. Thousands of homes and office buildings were destroyed or damaged. A major contributing factor to the destruction was the fact that many of the buildings were constructed at substandard levels as a consequence of nonexistent or inferior code restrictions in effect during the real-estate boom of the previous decade.

What was once considered the "playground" of America was left a scene of devastation as pleasure resorts were converted into temporary hospitals and morgues and office buildings into refugee centers. Water and debris were everywhere, transforming the appearance of an entire stretch of the Miami waterfront into something macabre. With roads washed out and causeways underwater, relief efforts were slowed considerably. Moreover, the persistent winds and absence of landing sites discouraged airplane pilots from attempting to enter the damaged areas. Instead, at least a dozen trains loaded with physicians, nurses, food, water, and other supplies descended on the city to help with the relief efforts.

Following its strike on the city, the storm moved on a northwesterly course toward the Lake Okeechobee area, where it proceeded to unleash its fury on the small community of Moore Haven, located on the southwestern side of the lake. In 1922 and 1924 heavy rains had raised the water level of the lake, which precipitated substantial flooding in the surrounding farm districts, though no lives were lost. As a result, the town's citizens decided to construct a muck dike to protect the region from future flooding, but local and state officials greatly underestimated the impact a major hurricane would have on the lake.

In due course the relentless winds drove the waters over and through the dike, inundating the area to a depth of up to 15 feet and taking a heavy toll in death and property. A lone watchman assigned to patrol the dike in order to give warning in the event of potential danger was on patrol when the dike succumbed to the rising water. Washed away by the initial overflow, he managed to escape and immediately attempted to alert others. However, his warnings either went unheard or were disregarded in the midst of the chaos. The rush of water drowned scores of residents and left the town without food, water, or power. Nearly every structure in Moore Haven was destroyed, except for a row of brick buildings in the town's central commercial district. Several homes were swept almost 2 miles from their foundations. At one point, 34 bodies were lying in the town's old post office building, which served as an emergency morgue. Rescuers attempting to reach the stricken city were met by an exodus of people fleeing the area in small boats to points where they could continue on foot to safe ground. Entire families, forced to carry all of their remaining possessions in bundles, were seen straggling along open roads.

In the aftermath many residents of the district launched an organized protest against government officials, whom they blamed for keeping the lake's water above reasonable levels prior to the storm. They pointed out that if the state had permitted the locks to be opened during the storm season and allowed the water level to remain near the specified minimum depth of 15 feet instead of 19 feet above sea level, the damage caused by the floodwaters would have been considerably less.

After striking Moore Haven, the storm continued on its northwesterly course, eventually dumping large amounts of rain on Pensacola before moving further inland, over interior Alabama and sections of Mississippi and Louisiana, before dissipating. All together, the storm left 243 people dead and nearly 2,000 injured in its wake.

William Hoffman

For Further Information:

Barnes, Jay. *Florida's Hurricane History.* Chapel Hill: University of North Carolina Press, 1998.

"Cities Built on Sand." *Weatherwise,* August/September, 1996, 20-27.

Reardon, L. F. *The Florida Hurricane and Disaster 1926.* Miami: Miami, 1926.

1926: Cuba

Hurricane

Date: October 16-22, 1926

Place: Havana, Matanzas, Piñar del Rio, and Santa Clara Provinces, Cuba; Bermuda

Speed: Highest winds estimated at 120-130 miles per hour

Result: About 650 dead, $100 million in damage

The second of two hurricanes in October, 1926, originated in the southwestern Caribbean on October 16. The storm reached Cuba on October 20 and ravaged the island for six hours. It came ashore at the Isle of Pines and spread its destruction before quickly veering out to sea. Waves 25 feet high surged over the sea wall in Havana harbor, flooding the downtown area with 2-6 feet of water. All structures sustained damage on their first floors as the tide reached nearly the second story.

The eye of the hurricane took thirty minutes to pass over Nueva Gerona, beginning at 10:30 A.M., before the storm left the island the same day. The hurricane bypassed Florida and headed out into the Atlantic Ocean, where it struck Bermuda on October 22. The eye took nearly an hour to pass over Bermuda, and sustained winds of 128 miles per hour and a barometric pressure of 28.43 inches. The storm then moved into the Atlantic and expired over colder waters.

High winds knocked over every tree in Havana's main park, and the Belen Observatory, founded in 1857, was demolished. The monument commemorating the American sailors lost aboard the battleship *Maine* collapsed during the storm. Two parallel marble columns crashed down, leaving only the 10-inch guns between them still intact. Most of the fatalities occurred in poorer neighborhoods, where inadequately constructed buildings collapsed on top of residents who tried to weather the storm surge and high winds. Thousands were left homeless in its aftermath. More affluent districts suffered less damage, with the Seville-Biltmore Hotel becoming a refugee center after the storm hit. Ships and boats provided more wreckage. Nearly 100 vessels, including 40 fishing boats and 2 Cuban naval vessels, sank in Havana harbor.

Areas outside Havana suffered extensive damage as well. In Batapano, with a population of just 2,000, at least 300 people died. The worst hit area was the Isle of Pines, where the storm landed. Major buildings, including a church that had stood for eighty years, collapsed under the wind and water. All the ships in the harbor at Isle of Pines sank. One witness reported that "[t]he harbor was filled with the protruding masts and funnels of small craft which had foundered, while the principal ferry slip was blocked by a fair-sized freighter which sank at its entrance." Seventeen Americans died in the town, along with hundreds of Cubans and other residents, with over 9,000 people left injured from the storm in this one community.

James B. Seymour, Jr.

For Further Information:

The New York Times, October 21-26, 1926.

Tannehill, Ivan Ray. *Hurricanes: Their Nature and History.* 1938. Reprint. Princeton, N.J.: Princeton University Press, 1956.

1928: San Felipe Hurricane

Also known as: Lake Okeechobee Hurricane
Date: September 10-16, 1928
Place: Florida and the Caribbean
Classification: Category 4
Result: 4,000 dead, 350,000 homeless

The San Felipe Hurricane, also known as the Lake Okeechobee Hurricane, was a ferocious Category 4 storm that claimed over 4,000 lives as it roared across the Caribbean islands of Guadeloupe, St. Kitts, and Montserrat; the Virgin Islands; and Puerto Rico before inflicting its full fury on Florida.

The Caribbean. The storm was spotted first by the crew of the ship SS *Cormack* in the Cape Verde Islands region in the eastern Atlantic in early September, 1928. By September 10, it had reached the mid-Atlantic, at which time it was classified as a Category 4 hurricane with winds of 135 miles per hour. The powerful storm crossed the islands of Guadeloupe, St. Kitts, and Montserrat on September 12. Its barometric pressure was recorded at 27.76 inches with winds between 160 and 170 miles per hour. The hurricane devastated the three islands. Buildings were destroyed, and roads were quickly inundated as 30-foot waves lashed against the shorelines. An estimated 520 people lost their lives, many of them in the flash floods spawned by the heavy rains accompanying the storm. The hurricane then proceeded south of St. Croix after dealing substantial damage to the Virgin Islands.

In the early morning hours of San Felipe Day on September 13, 1928 (the saint's commemoration day for which the storm received its name), the hurricane struck Puerto Rico near the port city of Arroyo, 32 miles southeast of San Juan, with the intensity of a Category 4 storm. Winds were registered at 135 miles per hour, with gusts up to 170 miles per hour, and blew steadily for four or five consecutive hours. In San Juan the wind reached its peak strength at about midafternoon. A short time earlier the Weather Bureau's anemometer registered 132 miles per hour, but the instrument was swept away by a gale.

The storm threw the city of San Juan into complete darkness and totally isolated it from the remainder of the island. All telegraph and telephone lines were destroyed, and all transportation was halted. Ships suffered extensive damage as a 19-foot storm surge swept ashore. The freight steamer *Helen* was ripped from its anchor during the peak of the storm, as were numerous smaller boats, and drifted onto rocks near the entrance of the harbor. The storm flattened the governor's palace and blew out its doors and windows, leaving it completely exposed to the torrential rains that soon flooded the building.

The hurricane wrought massive damage across the island. More than 19,000 buildings, representing 70 percent of the capital's homes and 40 percent of its businesses, were destroyed, leaving nearly 284,000 people without food or shelter. Trees by the thousands were uprooted, many of them smashing into homes or falling into streets.

Rainfall associated with the storm system was heavy and was a major contributing factor to the damage that occurred inland. Rain gauges recorded up to 30 inches of precipitation during the storm, which initiated mudslides and flash floods in the island's mountainous central regions. Whole villages were reported to have been destroyed by the onslaught. Altogether, over 1,400 people were killed in Puerto Rico during the storm that caused nearly $50 billion in damage to the island.

On September 15 the storm swept through the Bahamas, bringing heavy rains and 119-mile-per-hour winds to the eastern islands. Residents along Florida's east coast prepared to receive the full force of the approaching storm. On September 15 the Weather Bureau issued a warning that the hurricane was moving northwestward at a rate of 300 miles per day. Storm warnings were issued from Miami to Titusville, Florida.

Forecasters believed the storm could follow one of three paths: through the Florida Straits between Key West and Cuba and out into the Gulf of Mexico, to the north up along the East Coast, or straight ahead on a northwesterly direction that would take it to a point between Miami and Palm Beach.

Florida. On September 16, the hurricane approached to within 200 miles of Miami. Storm warnings were posted from Miami to Jacksonville, an indication that forecasters believed the storm would move in a northeasterly direction across the state once it made landfall. The Naval Radio Compass Station at Jupiter Inlet on the eastern coast, about 90 miles north of Miami, reported to the Navy Department that the storm was blowing with winds of more than 90 miles per hour and that the tide at Jupiter was more than 5 feet above normal. The compass station rode out the storm until early evening, when it reported that its radio tower had been blown down. It also sent a message informing the Navy Department that the barometric pressure had dropped to 28.79 inches and was still falling.

On the evening of September 16, the hurricane struck the coast near West Palm Beach, with winds estimated at over 100 miles per hour and a barometric pressure of 27.43 inches. An 11-foot storm surge, combined with over 10 inches of rain during the hurricane's passage, washed out numerous coastal roads. Many of the plush Palm Beach resorts and mansions perched along the shoreline received heavy damage. Close to 8,000 homes were either destroyed or damaged. Nearly 700 people were reported killed in Palm Beach County alone, many of them victims of the storm surge passing over the barrier island upon which the city is situated. The fashionable New Breakers Hotel was damaged severely when a tall chimney crashed through the roof, as was another elegant hotel, the Royal Poinciana, whose roof was torn.

From Boynton Beach to Lake Park, structures of all kinds were ripped from their foundations and carried for distances of hundreds of yards. Damage to the south in Miami was confined to broken windows and the scattered ruin of frail buildings, though some water destruction was also reported.

As predicted, the storm moved inland toward the Lake Okeechobee region. The storm that had brought devastation to the Palm Beach area was about to wield greater devastation.

Lake Okeechobee is the third largest freshwater lake within the United States. Located approximately 40 miles northwest of Palm Beach, it has a diameter of 40 miles and a maximum depth of 15 feet. Acting as a catch basin for the overflows produced by the rainy seasons, the lake served at the time as the chief water supply for central Florida. Dikes built around the lake were designed to restrain the overflows in order to protect the adjacent farming communities.

Almost totally unaware of the severity of the storm headed their way, residents of the tiny communities surrounding the lake, many of them migrant workers, carried on with their daily work routines. From the moment the storm struck, its exact path and the damage it was bringing were, for the most part, mysteries to inland inhabitants. There was no sophisticated communication system, so local residents had only rumors over the radio or unreliable wire communications to guide them.

As the storm moved across the lake's northern shore, driving all the water to one side of the lake, it caused the shallow waters to exceed the maximum height of 15 feet. In about thirty minutes the surge of water, combined with the heavy rainfall, overpowered the dikes protecting the lowlands at the lake's southern end. Hundreds of migrant workers were killed as a wall of water rushed through the region. Others clung to tops of trees, houses, or any other objects they could grab hold of to ride out the surge. Several hundred women and children who sought safety on barges survived the storm when the two boats carrying them were washed ashore by the surge at South Bay. Some people had to walk as much as 6 miles through water higher than their waists before they were able to reach safety. It was nearly midnight before the storm began to lose some of its fury.

Aftereffects. Relief was slow in coming to the isolated region, since the attention of the country was focused on the damage done to the state's eastern shore. However, as relief workers battled their way into West Palm Beach over water-covered roads, they quickly spread the word of the enormity of the destruction that had occurred inland. The hurricane leveled every building in the nearly 50-mile stretch between Clewiston and Canal Point, except for a hotel which was converted into a shelter for fleeing refugees from the nearby towns of Belle Glade, Ritta, Bayport, Miami Locks, and other farming and fishing villages. A section of State Road 25 that connects Palm Beach and Fort Myers was left several feet under water. The Ritta Islands, located in the lake itself, were swept nearly clean by the winds. No survivors could be found on the islands following the storm.

The devastation from the storm was total. An expanse of land that stretched from the lake south into the Everglades was left in ruin. Eyewitnesses reported wreckage and debris scattered in every direction and numerous bodies floating in canals. The Red Cross placed the death toll in the region at 1,836, though there was no way to know the exact toll for certain. It was impossible for relief workers to gather the remains of the dead, and the original idea of sending individual coffins to dry areas such as Sebring and West Palm Beach had to be abandoned. Instead, funeral pyres were arranged to dispose of the bodies.

Domesticated animals and wildlife also suffered. Much of the lake's abundant fish supply was destroyed when washed over the dikes and left to die as the water receded. The surge also wiped out some farmers' entire stocks of cattle, pigs, horses, and chickens.

Following its strike on Lake Okeechobee, the hurricane curved north-northeast and skirted the city of Jacksonville. Trees in the city were uprooted by winds of 50 to 60 miles per hour, and several small shacks were toppled, though the major business and prominent residential sections escaped with minor damage. A roller coaster in Jacksonville Beach, 18 miles away, was toppled by the winds, and a portion of a dancing pier collapsed.

There were indications the hurricane was diminishing in intensity on its trail north, but it still carried enough strength to destroy communication wires between Tampa and Jacksonville. At one stage in the course of the storm, an entire portion of the state located below a diagonal line running from Palm Beach northward to the town of Brooksville was cut off from the outside world. As the storm curved back toward Jacksonville, another large section of the central part of the state as well as a portion of the East Coast became isolated. The storm eventually moved up the Georgia and South Carolina coast toward Hatteras, North Carolina, where it passed back into the sea.

Despite losing much of its strength, tremendous amounts of rainfall accompanied the remnants of the storm on its way north. Savannah, Georgia, reported 11.42 inches of rain and winds of 50 miles per hour, while Charleston, South Carolina, registering 7.18 inches of precipitation and winds of 48 miles per hour, reported its shoreline strewn with the wreckage of small boats and piers. Both cities were nearly isolated by broken communication lines.

The Lake Okeechobee hurricane is considered the most catastrophic storm to hit the state of Florida in terms of lives lost. The enormity of the disaster led federal and state officials to develop a plan to rebuild the dikes that failed on the lake's southern shores so that a similar disaster would not occur in the future. In the three decades that followed, the U.S. Army Corps of Engineers built a 150-mile dike constructed from mud, sand, rock, and concrete. It is named for President Herbert Hoover.

William Hoffman

For Further Information:

Barnes, Jay. *Florida's Hurricane History.* Chapel Hill: University of North Carolina Press, 1998.

Longshore, David. *Encyclopedia of Hurricanes, Typhoons, and Cyclones.* New York: Facts on File, 1998.

1930: Dominican Republic

Hurricane

Date: September 3, 1930

Place: Santo Domingo, Dominican Republic

Result: 4,000 dead, 5,000 injured

On August 31, 1930, a storm was observed east of the Windward Islands. On September 1 it passed the island of Dominica at about 80 to 100 miles per hour, gaining wind speed as it reached Santo Domingo, capital of the Dominican Republic. On September 3 the hurricane's center passed through the capital, with top wind speeds clocked at 150 to 200 miles per hour.

The hurricane had a particularly small diameter, and because of this the barometer fell quickly and wind speeds increased dramatically. Property losses were estimated at $15 million, with high numbers of dead (4,000) and injured (5,000). The hurricane mainly affected Santo Domingo; outlying areas suffered minimal damage. This was one of the most severe hurricanes in Dominican history, demolishing nearly everything in its path, including trees, buildings, crops, and ships.

Michelle C. K. McKowen

For Further Information:

Tannehill, Ivan Ray. *Hurricanes: Their Nature and History.* Princeton, N.J.: Princeton University Press, 1938.

1931: The Great Belize Hurricane

Date: September 10, 1931

Place: Belize City, British Honduras (now Belize)

Speed: Highest recorded winds 132 miles per hour

Result: Estimated 1,000-3,000 dead, thousands left homeless, $7.5 million in damage

After more than a decade of fewer hurricanes than normal, the Caribbean Sea returned to full force in the 1930's, producing several major storms in September, 1931. On September 9, 1931, radio messages were received in Belize that a small but very powerful storm would reach hurricane force and make landfall on the 10th at or near Belize. Government officials at Belize and in several districts were advised; however, a decision was made not to inform the populace. It was the popular belief that Belize was immune from hurricanes; no person living at the time could remember a hurricane striking the city. It was also felt that announcement of the storm would incite panic among the city's inhabitants and among the many guests from the interior then in the city to celebrate the 138th anniversary of the Battle of St. George's Caye of 1798, a date widely celebrated as a national holiday.

Intermittent showers on the morning of the 10th did little to impede many groups from carrying out their annual marches. However, by 10 A.M. both wind and rain increased from the northeast, causing flooding on the north side of the city and canceling parades by school children. Winds reached hurricane force shortly after 2 P.M. and sustained a high of 132 miles per hour between 2:50 and 3 P.M. Much property damage was caused in this phase of the storm, but there was little loss of life. As the eye of the storm passed over the city, many residents, believing the storm to have passed, went about the area surveying the damage, particularly at the Jesuit college on the south side, which had collapsed, trapping several priests, teachers, and students.

At 3:44 the wind shifted to the southwest and quickly returned to hurricane force. Because the government anemometer then failed at winds of 80 miles per hour, speeds of the subsequent winds are uncertain. The winds brought with them a wave in excess of 9 feet, reaching 15 feet in some places. Because Belize lies at and below sea level, this was particularly devastating. Damage was most severe on the south side of Belize. Hardest hit were the Mesopotamia and Queen Charlotte Town areas. In Mesopota-

The wreckage caused by the Great Belize Hurricane. (AP/Wide World Photos)

mia, a recently reclaimed area, houses were so smashed as to render individual dwellings unrecognizable and the area impassable. In Queen Charlotte Town, an area of East Indian settlement, many families and all dwellings disappeared entirely. At about 5 P.M. the storm ceased.

Considerable damage was done to the central business district. Here the rising waters of the wave used the grounded boats and barges as battering rams to smash many buildings that had survived the earlier high winds. The harbor was choked with boats and rendered useless. Outside the city, the wave caused many deaths on the low-lying cayes or islets, particularly at St. George's Caye, a popular holiday retreat. Upriver from Belize there was little loss of life, but heavy rains, rising water, and high winds destroyed both crops and shelter.

September 11 was hot, dry, and sunny. The water receded quickly, leaving several feet of mud in the city. The government radio station had been destroyed, so there was some delay in reporting the disaster and requesting aid. Two U.S. warships responded immediately with supplies and doctors. A British ship arrived later, as did doctors from Mexico and Honduras. In general, the major work of clearing and disposal of the dead and debris was left to the local inhabitants.

The burial of so many dead posed a major concern, particularly in the tropical heat. Many were buried in trenches dug near the main cemetery. Most of the Mesopotamia area, given its inaccessibility, was set on fire, thereby cremating an estimated 1,000 bodies. Refugees were sent north to the town of Corozal and south to Stann Creek Town, but most returned to Belize within a few months.

The British government used the disaster to reassert tight fiscal control over the colony. Reconstruction loans were few and carried high interest rates. The extent of the damage to the city raised the issue of relocating the capital away from Belize. When, in 1961, Hurricane Hattie again devastated the area, the government began to build a new capital inland.

St. John Robinson

For Further Information:

Cain, Ernest E. *Cyclone! Being an Official Illustrated Record of a Hurricane and Tidal Wave Which Destroyed the City of Belize.* London: Stockwell, 1932.

Cavanaugh, Paul W. "The Hurricane at Belize." *Woodstock Letters* 61, no. 1 (February, 1932): 67-102.

Clarion (Belize), October 15, 1931.

McDonald, W. F. "Tropical Storms of September, 1931, in North American Waters." *Monthly Weather Review* 59 (September, 1931): 364-367.

Tannehill, Ivan R. *Hurricanes: Their Nature and History.* Princeton, N.J.: Princeton University Press, 1956.

1932: San Ciprian Hurricane

Date: September 26, 1932
Place: Puerto Rico
Result: 225 dead, 3,000 injured, $30 million in damage

The San Ciprian Hurricane followed closely on the heels of two other hurricanes. Because of this the pressure was very high over the eastern United States and the Atlantic. On September 26, 1932, at 10 P.M., the hurricane entered Puerto Rico at the town of Ceiba, passed through San Juan, and, as the pressure fell, traveled southward. Winds were estimated at about 120 miles per hour; exact measurements are not known because the measuring tower was destroyed.

High pressures to the north pushed the storm west into Mexico. Besides injured and dead victims, an estimated 75,000 to 250,000 persons were left homeless. Damages were estimated at $30 million, one of the most expensive disasters in the island's history.

Michelle C. K. McKowen

For Further Information:

Tannehill, Ivan Ray. *Hurricanes: Their Nature and History.* Princeton, N.J.: Princeton University Press, 1938.

1932: Cuba

Hurricane
Date: November 9, 1932
Place: Santa Cruz del Sur, Cuba
Result: 2,500 dead

On October 30, 1932, a hurricane formed 200 miles east of Guadeloupe. Before reaching Cuba it moved southwestward, then looped up slowly in the Caribbean Sea's center, and finally moved northeastward toward Cuba. It maintained its intensity throughout its life and at one point was one of the strongest tropical hurricanes ever recorded.

There is little data recorded about this hurricane; it was so strong upon entering the town of Santa Cruz del Sur that it destroyed all instruments and records and killed the scientist monitoring the storm. The winds reached a staggering 210 miles per hour, but the hurricane's destruction was caused mostly by ocean waves, which rose quickly and killed 2,500 in a town of 4,000.

Michelle C. K. McKowen

For Further Information:

Tannehill, Ivan Ray. *Hurricanes: Their Nature and History.* Princeton, N.J.: Princeton University Press, 1938.

1933: Mexico

Hurricane
Date: September 24, 1933
Place: Tampico, Mexico
Result: Hundreds dead

On September 16, 1933, a storm began southeast of Barbados. It continued until the 20th without a real center. Later this day the storm was proved to be a hurricane of small diameter and strong force by measurements on a ship that passed through the center of the storm. Barometric changes were especially large and rapid.

The hurricane moved northwest, entering the Yucatán Peninsula 40 miles south of the island of Cozumel. It continued through the southwestern Gulf of Mexico and moved inland on September 24, just south of Tampico. Tampico suffered much damage and hundreds of deaths.

Michelle C. K. McKowen

For Further Information:

Tannehill, Ivan Ray. *Hurricanes: Their Nature and History.* Princeton, N.J.: Princeton University Press, 1938.

1935: Florida

Also known as: Labor Day Hurricane
Hurricane
Date: September 2-5, 1935
Place: Florida Keys
Classification: Category 5
Result: Over 400 dead, $11 million in damage

On September 2, 1935, one of the most destructive hurricanes in American history struck the Florida Keys. The hurricane moved inland at Long Key and slowly progressed up the Matecumbe Keys during the late evening. After leaving the Keys, the storm, remembered as the Labor Day Hurricane, traveled up the West Coast of Florida near Tampa on September 3. It hit close to Cedar Key on the morning of September 4. The hurricane continued up the Gulf coast of Florida and crossed inland east of Tallahassee, where it lost strength. It moved across Georgia, the Carolinas, and Virginia, where it then moved out to the Atlantic Ocean.

The Labor Day Hurricane was small in size, with an eye that was only 8 miles wide and a forward speed averaging around 10 miles per hour. Winds accompanying the storm, however, were unbelievably strong, estimated at between 150 and 200 miles an hour. The barometric pressure dropped to below 27.00 inches, reaching as low as 26.55 at Upper Matecumbe Key, an unusually low reading. In fact, the barometric pressure during the Labor Day Hurricane was the lowest recorded in the Western Hemisphere until 1988. According to the National Oceanic and Atmospheric Administration (NOAA), the millibar reading, another measurement of atmospheric pressure, was 892, the lowest recorded in the twentieth century. The winds and extremely low barometric pressure worked together to create one of only two storms in the twentieth century to strike land in the United States at Category 5 on the Saffir-Simpson hurricane scale (the other being Hurricane Camille in 1969).

With such a tremendously powerful storm, it is not surprising that the 1935 hurricane resulted in widescale devastation. Yet it was not the wind but the resulting storm tides that led to the large number of deaths in the Florida Keys. It is estimated that the tides that swept across the middle Keys of Florida were approximately 18 to 20 feet above normal. A wall of water at least 17 feet high leveled homes, stores, and other structures in its path. It was reported that all but 1 of the 61 buildings in the Matecumbe Keys were destroyed. The storm surge killed over 400 people. There was no exact count of the dead because so many bodies were washed out to sea and never found.

The largest number of deaths resulting from the storm was at Upper Matecumbe Key. Many of the at least 408 who died were World War I veterans who had been hired by the Civilian Conservation Corps to help build a railroad across the Keys to Key West. The railroad was a dream of millionaire Henry Flagler. The veterans had been part of the Bonus Expeditionary Force, which had camped out in Washington, D.C., during the Great Depression to lobby for a veteran's bonus being debated in Congress. President Herbert Hoover ordered their camps destroyed, and later the new president, Franklin Delano Roosevelt, offered the veterans jobs in the Civilian Conservation Corps. The railroad-building camp was located at Upper Matecumbe Key and run by the Federal Emergency Relief Association. An estimated 252 veterans perished in the hurricane, while another 106 were injured.

When camp officials realized that the hurricane was growing in strength, they requested that a train be sent from Miami to carry veterans off the Keys. Unfortunately for the veterans and other Keys residents, the train was delayed through bureaucratic red tape and did not arrive until the evening the hurricane hit. The train itself was blown off the tracks at the town of Islamorada, and almost all the railroad workers died in the storm when a wall of water washed over the train.

While residents of the Keys had prepared for what forecasters had estimated would be a tropical storm, another drama was taking place in the Gulf of Mexico. The steamship *Dixie*, part of the Morgan Cruise Line, went aground on Carysfort Reef, 20 miles east of Key Largo, with 400 passengers and crew. The ship had been bound from New Orleans to New York when winds of more than 80 miles an hour caused it to run ashore. The coral reef on which the ship was grounded created a large hole in the ship, and the *Dixie* slowly began to take on water. Newspapers were filled with accounts of the rescue efforts throughout the Labor Day weekend. The rescue effort was delayed because the ship's officers had given an inaccurate position for the vessel. Eventually, four boats arrived in the area to help in the effort, but the high seas precluded an immediate off-loading of the passengers and crew. Two days and two nights passed be-

fore the first 165 passengers were rescued. The remainder of the passengers and crew were transferred to other ships throughout the third day. The survivors of the *Dixie* were taken by sea to Miami, where they boarded trains for New York City. They were much luckier than the veterans and other residents of the Florida Keys who suffered the most hardship throughout the storm.

The Labor Day Hurricane led to the fifth-highest number of deaths caused by hurricanes in the United States in the twentieth century. It had the highest estimated wind gusts in hurricane history. The storm signaled the end of Flagler's Miami-to-Key West railroad. Tracks and equipment were lost in the hurricane, and homes and businesses were flattened. It took years before the central Keys were rebuilt. Those who died in the Labor Day Hurricane are honored with a plaque in the city of Islamorada, a reminder of one of the worst natural disasters in American history.

Judith Boyce DeMark

For Further Information:

Barnes, Jay. *Florida's Hurricane History.* Chapel Hill: University of North Carolina Press, 1998.

Klinkenberg, Jeff. "Islamorada—the Big Wind." *St. Petersburg Times,* August 14, 1991.

The New York Times, September 2-8, 1935.

Parks, Pat. *The Railroad That Died at Sea.* Key West, Fla.: Langley Press, n.d.

1935: The Hairpin Hurricane

Date: October 22-25, 1935
Place: The Caribbean (Jamaica, Cuba, Haiti) and Central America (Honduras)
Result: 2,150 dead

The Hairpin Hurricane was one of the most disastrous hurricanes in West Indian history. It formed in the western Caribbean Sea sometime between October 17 and 19, 1935. It headed east past Jamaica, then to the southeast coast of Cuba, then southwest toward Honduras, where it eventually dissipated after causing much destruction.

The hurricane first crossed Navassa Island, between Haiti and Jamaica, on October 21. It neared the Cuban coast at Santiago on October 22. For the next couple of days, heavy rains and winds caused flooding in southwestern Haiti, Cuba, and Jamaica. On October 25 the hurricane hit Honduras at Cape Gracias, causing damage to banana plantations and other property.

Michelle C. K. McKowen

For Further Information:

Tannehill, Ivan Ray. *Hurricanes: Their Nature and History.* Princeton, N.J.: Princeton University Press, 1938.

1938: The Great New England Hurricane of 1938

Date: September 21, 1938
Place: Northeastern United States
Classification: Category 3
Result: About 680 dead, more than 1,700 injured, more than 19,000 requests for aid, $400 million in damage

Some analysts call the Great New England Hurricane of 1938 a triple storm: hurricane, flood, and tidal surge. Unusually heavy rains beginning September 18, 1938, caused rivers and streams to rise and flood low-lying areas, and the rain that accompanied the up to 100-mile-per-hour winds during the brief course of the hurricane added to these conditions. In shoreline areas and cities on tidal rivers additional flood conditions were caused by the tidal surges common to hurricanes, when the high winds drive the tide upon itself. Several towns and cities also suffered from fires that were started when electrical wires were short-circuited by water or by ships that were driven by high winds and the tide into buildings along the coast.

The Formation of the Storm. June of 1938 was the third-wettest June in New England weather records, followed by an abnormally wet and mild summer. It is suggested that a French meteorological observation at the Bilma Oasis in the Sahara Desert on September 4 noting a wind shift would, with modern radar tracking and satellite imagery not available then, have given the first hint of trouble. The shift resulted in an area of storminess off the west coast of Africa, entering the Atlantic in the Cape Verde region. On September 16 a storm of hurricane strength was reported northeast of Puerto Rico by a lightship and the Jacksonville office of the U.S. Weather Bureau. The bureau followed the storm's rapid progress westward, issuing a hurricane warning for southern Florida on September 19. The storm slowed and turned north, sparing Florida, and initially it was assumed to be heading out to sea.

This hurricane was abnormal in that it traveled northward at an average speed of 50 miles per hour rather than the more usual 20 to 30 miles per hour. In twelve hours it moved from a position off Cape Hatteras to southern Vermont and New Hampshire. More important from the standpoint of criticisms of inadequate warning by the Weather Bureau is the fact that less than six hours elapsed from its leaving the Florida area, traveling over water, until it hit Long Island, New York. Because of its rapid progress, the hurricane had destructive winds about 100 miles east of its center, while there was relatively little damage to property on the west side. Therefore, the worst of the destruction was concentrated on Long Island, Rhode Island, eastern Connecticut, central Massachusetts, and southern Vermont and New Hampshire. High winds lasted only about an hour and a half in any one area.

The Aftereffects. In spite of its brief tenure, the hurricane had tremendous temporary and some important lasting economic impact. Whole seaside communities along the Connecticut and Rhode Island coasts were wiped out by wind and tides, which ranged from 12 to 25 feet higher than normal. New beaches were cut, islands were formed as the water ran through strips of shore, and navigational charts of the time became worthless. Roads and railroad tracks along the shore were undermined, buckled, and tossed. Railroad service was interrupted from seven to fourteen days while crews removed trees, houses, and several good-sized boats from the tracks.

A storm surge causes giant waves to crash against a seawall during the Great New England Hurricane of 1938. (National Oceanic and Atmospheric Administration)

Inland, bridges were wiped out, roads buckled where undermined by usually small streams, and trees fell on roads and buildings. Winds blew roofs, walls, and often top stories off brick and wooden buildings. Dams were breached by the high waters. Apples ready for harvest were blown off the trees, and whole groves of maples were snapped, affecting the maple-syrup industry for years to come. It was a rare church whose steeple escaped being torn down, and village greens were permanently altered by the toppling of stately mature elms and oaks that had lined the streets. Most important, some mills upon which a town's economy depended were never rebuilt after the damage. In New England, all old mills were originally powered by water, so they were located on dammed rivers.

Although not as hard hit, portions of northern Vermont and New Hampshire also suffered from fallen trees and flooding. Maine was the least affected, escaping flooding and damaged only by diminishing, although still high, winds. Boats were driven ashore from Portland south, and train schedules were disrupted and road traffic affected by downed trees.

Examination of the Storm. The major New England rivers were already at flood stage before the hurricane struck. The wet summer meant that the heavy rains in the three days preceding the high winds did not soak into the ground but ran off into streams, which in turn fed the rivers. Tributaries most affected were the Farmington, Chicopee, Millers, Deerfield, and Ashuelot Rivers of the Connecticut; the Quinebaug and Shetucket of the Thames; and the Contoocock and Piscataquog of the Merrimack.

New England is not often subjected to serious floods or hurricanes and is even less affected by tornadoes. Accounts of the 1938 hurricane are compared to the Great Colonial Hurricane of August 14 or 15, 1635 (as recorded by Increase Mather in his *Remarkable Providences* of 1684); the Great September Gale of September 23, 1815, recorded by Noah Webster and others; the ice storm of 1921; and floods of 1927 and 1936, the latter providing benchmarks for high water two years later.

The 1938 storm was termed "unique," "unusual," and "most interesting" by meteorologists, and a "freak," the "worst in the history of the northeast" by Dr. Charles C. Clark, acting chief of the U.S. Weather Bureau. It was not a tropical hurricane in the strict sense of the word because before it reached the northeastern states it was transformed into an extra-tropical storm, with a definite frontal structure and two distinct air masses—tropical maritime and polar continental, a peculiar temperature and wind distribution in the upper atmosphere. Although winds of 60 miles per hour were common at the hurricane's worst, geographic conditions contributed to winds up to 100 miles per hour in some areas. At slightly higher elevations, weather devices recorded much higher velocities: 186 miles per hour at the Harvard Meteorological Observatory at the top of Blue Hill in Milton, Massachusetts, and 120 miles per hour at the top of the Empire State Building in New York City.

The Extent of the Destruction. Statistics, especially the count of dead and injured, vary considerably. An estimated 680 to 685 lost their lives. Estimates of those injured range from 700 to over 1,700. Nearly 20,000 applied for aid. There is no uncertainty, however, in the assessment that the $400 million in total damage was the highest for any storm to its date. One account lists 4,500 homes, summer cottages, and farm buildings destroyed; 2,605 boats lost and 3,369 damaged, with a total $2.6 million estimated in fishing boats, equipment, docks, and shore plants destroyed; 26,000 cars smashed; 275 million trees broken off or uprooted; nearly 20,000 miles of power and telephone lines down; and numerous farm animals killed. Some 10,000 railroad workers filled 1,000 washouts, replaced nearly 100 bridges, and removed buildings and 30 boats from the tracks. Bell System crews came from as far away as Virginia, Arkansas, and Nevada to help restore service. About half the estimated 5 million bushels of the apple crop was unharvested and destroyed.

On Fire Island, New York, the tide crossed from the ocean to the bay side over the land, sweeping everything from its path. In Westhampton, Long Island, only 26 of 179 beach houses remained, and most were uninhabitable. Every house in Watch Hill, Rhode Island's Napatree Point-Fort Road area was swept into Naragansett Bay, and only 15 of the 42 occupants in the 39 houses survived. Downtown Providence, Rhode Island, was flooded under 10 feet of water. New London, Connecticut, suffered $4 million in damage from water, 98-mile-per-hour winds, and the worst fire since General Benedict Arnold's troops burned the city in 1781. The fire was started by electrical wires short-circuited when a five-masted schooner was driven into a building. The small town of Peterborough in southern New Hampshire also suffered from fire as well as wind and water damage when wires were short-circuited by floodwater. In one instance along the Connecticut shore, a railroad engineer nudged a cabin cruiser and a house off the tracks, loaded all his passengers into the dining and first Pullman cars, disconnected the remainder of the train, and brought his riders to safety. In a number of towns and cities, including Ware and North Adams, Massachusetts, and Brandon, Vermont, rivers changed their courses and took over main streets. While portions of Springfield, Massachusetts, and Hartford, Connecticut, were flooded, these cities were not damaged as much as might have been expected because of dikes built after the 1936 flood and sandbag walls added by volunteers in 1938.

On September 23, two days after the storm had passed, the Connecticut River crested at 35.42 feet. This was 2 feet below the 1936 record, but nothing else approaching this had been recorded since 1854. A total of 17 inches of rain had fallen in the Connecticut Valley in four days. However, the amount of rain varied greatly from one area to another, as did the velocity of the wind.

Electrical, telephone, and railroad services were interrupted for up to two weeks, and other services and activities were disrupted as well. Flooding and wind damage to buildings in town and city centers made food and provisions hard to find for days. Roads were blocked as well while crews removed the trees that had fallen across them, interrupting school activity and preventing many from reaching their homes. Business and public buildings as well as churches and homes had to be repaired or rebuilt. The disruption to lives cannot be adequately reflected in any of these statistics.

Erika F. Pilver

For Further Information:

Allen, Everett S. *A Wind to Shake the World: The Story of the 1938 Hurricane.* Boston: Little, Brown, 1972. This is an autobiographical account by the author, who was in his first week as a reporter for the *Standard-Times* in New Bedford, Massachusetts. Filled with personal experiences and anecdotes, with some statistics in the last chapter.

Minsinger, William Elliott, ed. *The 1938 Hurricane: An Historical and Pictorial Summary.* Randolph Center, Vt.: Greenhills Books for Blue Hill Observatory, 1988. Contains technical as well as historical accounts and a large photo section. Some historical and technical accounts of the 1635 and

1815 storms as well as the 1938 hurricane.

Vallee, David R., and Richael P. Dion. *Southern New England Tropical Storms and Hurricanes: A Ninety-Eight-Year Summary (1909-1997)*. Taunton, Mass.: National Weather Service, 1998. Technical information on storms during the period listed.

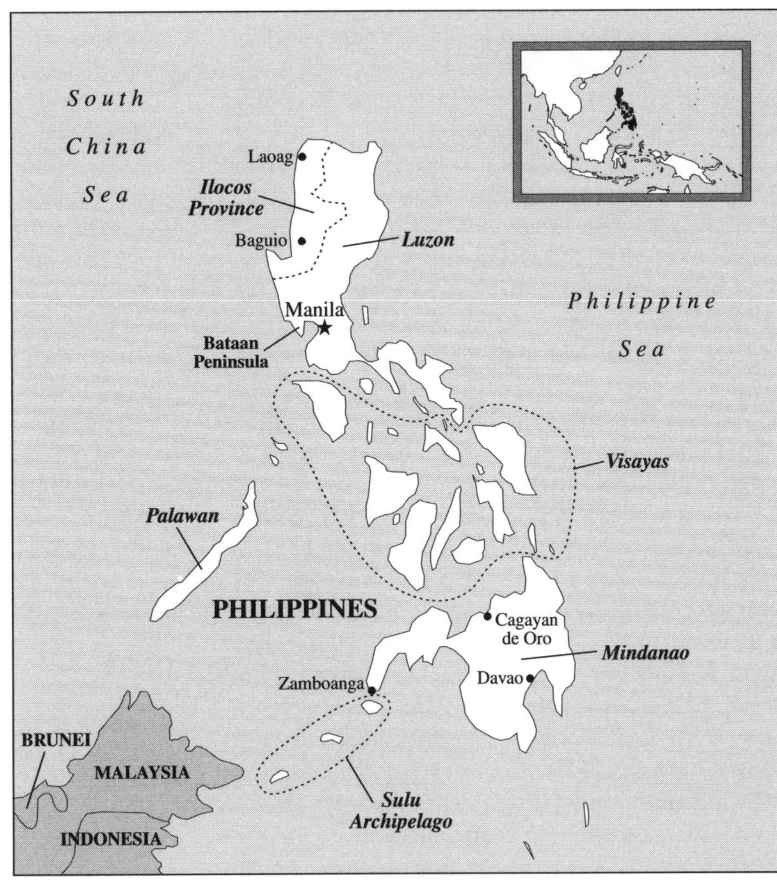

1944: Typhoon Cobra

Date: December 17-18, 1944
Place: Philippine Sea
Speed: 115-mile-per-hour wind gusts
Result: 790 dead, 3 destroyers lost, 146 planes destroyed

Each year between April and December, massive storms, which move in a westerly direction, originate in the warm waters of the northwestern Pacific. The area of the north Pacific Ocean between 10 and 30 degrees north latitudes is known as "Typhoon Alley." Most of the typhoons traversing this region affect the Philippines, particularly the Luzon Straits. The seven thousand islands and coral lagoons of the Philippines stretch over 1,200 miles between 5 and 22 degrees north latitude, the very path of the westerly typhoons. The country has the reputation of being the most storm-ridden country in the world. Ironically, given the death and destruction of typhoons, they also produce 40 percent of the rainfall needed for the lumber, rice, coconut, and sugar crops.

Many times during World War II, typhoons and hurricanes affected military operations. Meteorologists tracked these storms to ensure a minimum of interference with military operations in the Pacific. One such typhoon, Cobra, with 115-mile-per-hour winds and 70-foot seas, caused massive damage to the United States Third Fleet commanded by William Frederick Halsey, Jr. On December 18, 1944, 3 destroyers sank with a loss of 790 men, and a number of other ships were damaged in the Pacific, east of the Philippines.

In June, 1944, Halsey went to sea as commander of the Third Fleet and participated in the Battle of Leyte Gulf in the Philippines in late October, 1944. After resupplying in Ulithi, a United States supply island in the Pacific, he returned to Philippine waters on December 11, 1944, to protect General Douglas MacArthur's landing on the island of Mindoro. The task of the Third Fleet was to attack Japanese air bases on Luzon. Halsey's force included 86 ships, ranging from aircraft carriers to destroyers. In addition, 35 tankers, supply ships, and destroyers were responsible for the refueling of the task force.

On December 13 the combat fleet refueled without problems and continued air strikes against Japanese airfields on Luzon from a position 200 miles northeast of Manila. Because the high-speed operations consumed enormous quantities of fuel, Halsey scheduled refueling for the morning of December 17 in order to resume new operations by December 19. The rendezvous chosen for December 17 in the eastern Philippine Seas was beyond the Japanese fighter range, but unfortunately it was also in an area normally traversed by typhoons.

Because strong winds and rough seas produced by the approaching typhoon Cobra made refueling difficult, by noon on December 17, Halsey changed course and ordered refueling early on December 18. However, the fleet's weather expert, G. F. Kosco, did not recognize the approaching danger. He thought the storm, which had originated on December 15 north of Ulithi but was not yet recognized as a typhoon, was 450 miles east of the fleet. Actually, when Halsey changed course, the typhoon was only 120 miles southeast of the fleet.

To find calmer waters, Halsey changed the course again in the early afternoon of December 17. Unknown to the commander, he set a course parallel with the path of the typhoon, although the fleet was still moving west at 3 to 6 knots faster than the storm. At 10 P.M. on December 17, the barometer on the flag ship *New Jersey* fell to 29.76 and winds were 28 knots from north by east. Using the traditional naval method of locating the center of a storm by facing the wind and locating the center ten points to one's right, Kosco should have been able to locate the eye of the storm at that moment. Furthermore, he received little assistance from United States naval weather reports because there were not enough weather stations in the Pacific.

Halsey then made a crucial mistake in his search for calmer waters by ordering the fleet to sail south at midnight and then to continue northwest at 2 A.M. on December 18. This moved the fleet in the direct path of the typhoon. The weather turned more violent. By 5 A.M. on December 18, the center of the storm was only 90 miles from the flagship *New Jersey*. Only around noon on December 18, when the fleet was ordered to go southeast, was a route selected that would move the fleet away from the typhoon, whose eye was now only 37 miles away.

However, because the fleet was now spread out over 2,500 square miles of ocean, some ships suffered more from the typhoon than others. Depending on the position of the ship, the typhoon was most violent between 11 A.M. and 2 P.M. on that day. Finally, at 1:45 P.M. Halsey identified the storm as a typhoon. By this time 3 small destroyers, *Hull*, *Monaghan*, and *Spence*, commanded by young officers with no typhoon experience, had already disappeared underneath the ocean. Surprisingly, a number of sailors from these ships were rescued after the storm.

Despite the losses, Halsey attempted to resume military operations after finally refueling on December 19. However, he had to cancel his air strikes against Luzon when he ran into the tail of Typhoon Cobra near that island. Only after repairs at Ulithi did the Third Fleet resume action, on December 30. In June of 1945 Halsey was again surprised by a storm near Okinawa, when Typhoon Viper caused the death of 6 sailors and the loss of 80 planes. Official naval inquiries found Halsey responsible for failing to avoid the two typhoons because of "errors in judgment committed under stress of war operations." Still, many of the recommendations issued after December 26 to improve weather operations were adopted by the U.S. Navy. Weather stations were established on Guam and Leyte, and by May, 1945, three special weather ships were operating in the Philippine Seas.

Johnpeter Horst Grill

For Further Information:

Adamson, Hans Christian, and George Francis Kosco. *Halsey's Typhoon.* New York: Crown, 1967.

Baldwin, Hanson W. "When Third Fleet Met the Great Typhoon." *New York Times Sunday Magazine*, December 16, 1951.

Calhoun, C. Raymond. *Typhoon: The Other Enemy—The Third Fleet and the Pacific Storm of December, 1944.* Annapolis, Md.: Naval Institute, 1981.

Calhoun, C. Raymond, and John Hubble. "Typhoon." *Reader's Digest*, January, 1959, 46-50.

"Military Operations and Tropical Cyclones." In *Encyclopedia of Hurricanes, Typhoons, and Cyclones*, edited by David Longshore. New York: Facts on File, 1998.

Morison, Samuel Eliot. *History of the United States Naval Operations in World War II.* Vol. 13. Boston: Little, Brown, 1959.

1947: Florida, Gulf Coast

Hurricane
Date: September 4-21, 1947
Place: Florida and the Gulf coast
Classification: Category 4
Result: More than 50 dead

The most severe hurricane of 1947 developed off the North African coast in September and headed due west. It emerged from the Gulf of Mexico and struck the "Gold Coast" of Florida on September 17 as a Category 4 hurricane. Wind speeds at Hillsboro Light Station near Pompano Beach in Florida were clocked at a record-breaking 155 miles per hour, the highest recorded wind speeds in Florida at that time. Barometric pressure measured 27.75 inches. High tides were measured at Clewiston and Moore Haven, Florida, of 21.6 and 20.9 feet, respectively. In Florida, the hurricane reached from Cape Canaveral to Carysfort Reef Light Station (south of Miami), or a distance of roughly 240 miles.

The hurricane advanced to Mississippi and Louisiana, pounding their coastlines as a Category 3 storm. New Orleans, hit on the morning of September 19, experienced the utter calm of the eye of the storm but was also pounded with rain, including 7 feet of standing water at one time. Other cities surrounded by natural bodies of water, such as Bucktown, Slidell, and East Jefferson, were inundated, and people were forced to use boats or wade in hip-deep water. Along Lake Pontchartrain, a seawall and drainage system helped lessen damage, but water nonetheless flooded the surrounding areas. In Mississippi, National Guard troops reportedly lined the highways to prevent looting. Property damage reached about $100 million; 34 people were killed in Louisiana, and 26 were killed in Mississippi. Destruction included homes, businesses, roads, and tremendous damage to the dairy industries and wildlife. Cleanup efforts lasted a long time; in some places floodwater remained stagnant with no place to drain. This hurricane was the start of about twenty years of heavy storm activity; during these years seventeen hurricanes hit the United States, while only a handful struck from the late 1960's to the end of the century.

Michelle C. K. McKowen

For Further Information:

Persica, Dennis. "Blown Away." *New Orleans Times Picayune*, September 18, 1997, p. A1.

1951: Hurricane Charlie

Date: August 13-23, 1951
Place: Jamaica and Mexico
Classification: Category 3
Result: 280 dead, 2,000 injured, 50,000 homeless, $150 million in damage

A Cape Verde hurricane, Charlie was one of the last hurricanes named from the military phonetic alphabet. Intensifying as it approached the eastern Caribbean on August 13, 1951, Hurricane Charlie attained Category 3 status and was considered the worst hurricane to hit Jamaica at that time. The hurricane's 130-mile-per-hour winds and heavy rains devastated the southern coast of Jamaica. Waves as high as 30 feet washed a 10,000-ton freighter ashore. Uprooted palm trees dammed up water, and residents fled to rooftops in an effort to avoid drowning or electrocution from power lines. At Spanish Town, 9,000 buildings collapsed. Cars were swept into the ocean, and prisoners escaped from the jail in Kingston. Mudslides ruined sugar crops.

Authorities stated that 162 people were killed in Jamaica and another 2,000 were injured. Approximately 40,241 buildings were destroyed, and 50,000 people had no shelter. Charlie left Jamaica on August 18, passing the Cayman Islands and Cuba en route to the Yucatán. Charlie's winds reached 160 miles when the storm hit Cancún, where 3 people died. Moving into the Gulf of Mexico, Charlie weakened before striking Tampico, Mexico, on August 22. A dam burst, drowning 27 people. Another 88 were killed by debris. The name "Charlie" was retired the next year when the Weather Service stopped using the military system of naming storms.

Elizabeth D. Schafer

For Further Information:

"Disaster Piles up in Mexico Storms." *The New York Times*, August 26, 1951, p. 37.
"Storm in Caribbean Kills 50 in Jamaica." *The New York Times*, August 19, 1951, p. 1.
"27 Dead in Mexico as Dam Gives Way." *The New York Times*, August 24, 1951, p. 1.

1954: Hurricane Carol

Date: August 25-31, 1954
Place: North Carolina, the Atlantic seaboard, and New England

Speed: Sustained winds of 100 miles per hour and gusts up to 130 miles per hour
Result: 60 dead, 1,000 injured, $461 million in damage

Hurricane Carol formed east of the Bahamas in 1954 and began moving slowly in a northwesterly direction. On August 30, the tanker SS *Saconnett* reported winds of over 100 miles per hour with 30-foot waves. Storm warnings went up in North Carolina, the apparent target for the storm, as the hurricane moved forward gradually at a mere 4 miles per hour. The eye missed hitting Cape Hatteras on August 30, 1954, and left minimal damage in its wake. Carol knocked down power and phone lines and sent strong waves and tides into coastal communities, especially New Bern. The storm elevated tides only 3 to 5 feet above normal, and damages, mainly because of erosion, were kept low at $250,000. Then the hurricane became caught in a trough of low pressure, which rapidly drew the storm up the Atlantic coast as it topped 40 miles per hour in its forward motion.

After sparing North Carolina, Carol saved its might for New England, which was caught largely unprepared for the storm. Because it stretched 160 miles in diameter, forecasters predicted a slow movement north on August 30. When residents woke in Long Island on the morning of August 31, they discovered Carol had arrived ahead of schedule. Winds of 125 miles per hour stripped the paint off houses and cars and drew blood from exposed skin. Salt spray withered the leaves on trees, bringing an early autumn. Vacationers at Cape Cod and other resorts learned of the storm and fled inland, directly into the path of Carol. Many were caught in large traffic jams created by fleeing people, fallen trees, and downed power lines, and they experienced the brunt of the storm trapped in their vehicles.

Hurricane Carol hit Rhode Island the hardest. Tides in Narragansett Bay flooded southeastern Rhode Island and killed people attempting to flee in their cars. Waves ravaged the beaches, with one surge destroying 300 homes. Tides at Providence, the worst-hit community, ran 8 to 10 feet above normal, causing serious damage to the waterfront.

As the storm moved inland, destruction spread with it. Sustained winds clocked at 93 miles per hour knocked over the steeple of the Old North Church in Boston, which had given the signal to Paul Revere in the American Revolution. Not respecting the status of vacationers, the storm trapped Vice President Richard Nixon at a Maine cottage. As the storm moved over the hilly terrain of central New England, it rapidly lost power and had winds of only 46 miles per hour when it entered Quebec. Sixty people died in the storm, and about 1,000 were injured. Carol cost more than $461 million, with Rhode Island alone sustaining $201 million in damages, making the storm the most expensive hurricane in U.S. history up to that point.

James B. Seymour, Jr.

For Further Information:

Barnes, Jay. *North Carolina's Hurricane History*. Chapel Hill: University of North Carolina Press, 1995.

Bixby, William. *Hurricanes*. New York: David McKay, 1979.

Douglas, Marjory Stoneman. *Hurricanes*. New York: Rinehart, 1958.

The New York Times, September 1-4, 1954.

1954: Hurricane Hazel

Date: October 12-18, 1954
Place: From the Caribbean to Canada
Classification: Category 4
Speed: Up to 140 miles per hour
Result: 411 dead, $1 billion in damage

The hurricane season of 1954 was exceptional in the number of severe storms that it generated during a relatively short time span and in the number of these storms that menaced the East Coast of the United States. The season began in late August, when Hurricane Carol, a Category 2 storm, originated on August 25 east of the Bahamas and went on northward, skirting the eastern seaboard. Despite constantly threatening to move inland, Carol did not make landfall until it reached Connecticut and Rhode Island, causing fatalities and damage throughout New England and Canada.

Hurricane Dolly, which was active from August 31 to September 4, did give rise to some concern but proved in the end to have posed a very mild threat. Moving northeastward and parallel to the East Coast, Dolly never intensified beyond Category 1, nor did it venture any closer to land than 150 miles offshore.

Hurricane Edna, which flourished from Septem-

Hurricane Hazel batters homes along the shore of Morehead City, North Carolina. (AP/Wide World Photos)

ber 6 to 15, proved to be the most powerful of the three. Forming in the northeastern sector of the Caribbean, Edna traveled west to hit the Bahamas, then pivoted north to parallel the East Coast on a path similar to Carol's, before causing loss of life and wreaking havoc in New England, Nova Scotia, and New Brunswick.

The season's eighth tropical storm, Hazel, was to dwarf the others in intensity and destruction and to become the focus of folklore and nostalgia for decades thereafter. Hazel was to achieve some degree of uniqueness in refusing to conform to the general pattern of other storms by maintaining its high intensity level even after moving hundreds of miles over land.

Hazel formed off the southern portion of the Lesser Antilles on October 5. Slowly following a westerly trek off the coast of Venezuela, Hazel intensified to a Category 4 designation. The noted Miami weatherman Grady Norton, who pioneered meteorological techniques and the twenty-four-hour hurricane prediction, forecast on October 8 that Hazel would change its course to a northerly direction. On October 9 Hazel did turn north, initially toward the island of Jamaica.

Shuffling northwest, Hazel slammed western Haiti on October 12. Haiti's southern peninsula was the hardest hit area. Thousands of dwellings and other buildings were demolished. In Cayes, Haiti's third-largest urban area, some 700 families were left homeless. Wind gusts and flooding virtually destroyed the four villages of Marfranc, Bonbon Abricots, Anse D'Hainault, and Moton and heavily damaged the larger center of Jérémie. Even Puerto Rico—at the storm's edge—sustained 8 deaths, 2,000 newly homeless people, and $750,000 worth of damage to property.

Hazel then took an uncertain northeasterly course, gaining power and making landfall near Myrtle Beach, South Carolina, on October 15. The storm retained its greatest degree of intensity as it surged through South Carolina, North Carolina, Virginia, Maryland, Delaware, New Jersey, Pennsylvania, and New York. In terms of lives lost Hazel was one of the most lethal hurricanes occurring during the second half of the twentieth century; 411 are known to have died as a direct result of the storm.

North Carolina and Virginia, the states that bore the brunt of the wind force, saw traffic nearly immobilized, power lines downed, and a 150-mile-wide swath of uprooted and broken trees and severed branches. Beachfront property losses were reported at $20 million, with the overall damage to the eastern portion of North Carolina alone at $50 million.The traditional high tide of mid-October coincided with and was augmented by Hazel's winds and heavy rainfall and contributed to the widespread coastline destruction considered to have been the worst in North Carolina up to that time.

Wind gusts remained substantial as Hazel moved inland, with speeds being reported at 98 miles per hour in Wilmington, North Carolina; 90 miles per hour in Raleigh, North Carolina; 79 miles per hour in Richmond, Virginia; 70 miles per hour in Blackstone, Virginia; 50 miles per hour in Annapolis, Maryland; 60 miles per hour in Atlantic City, New Jersey; and 100 miles per hour in New York City. Security became a problem on the coastal fringes of North and South Carolina, and the governors of both states called out the National Guard to prevent potential looting of beachfront property.

At Grace Hospital in Richmond, during the height of the storm, a power failure caused doctors to complete the delivery of a baby girl by flashlight. In Wilmington, Delaware, a woman was caught up in a gale so fierce that it swept her over the street, and she died when it slammed her into a moving trolley car. In Brunswick County, Virginia, a housewife was crushed when Hazel's winds blew out the entire wall of a tobacco warehouse.

Though Hazel gradually abated in force on its path northward, many were killed by the floods triggered by its torrential rains. The hurricane's downpours swelled the Ohio River to flood stage, causing thousands of Ohio River Valley residents in Pennsylvania, West Virginia, and Ohio to be evacuated. At Pittsburgh the river crested at 5 feet above flood level, causing 4 deaths. At Wheeling, West Virginia, 2,000 families had to be relocated as the river climbed to 8.7 feet above flood level.

As Hazel closed in on the city of Toronto, Ontario, Canada, the weather service there issued only a storm advisory, and consequently most people were entirely unprepared for the horrific results of the hurricane. Dumping 7.2 inches of rain in its last major devastating blow, Hazel caused the Humber River to overflow its banks and to rapidly flood the city's western suburbs of Etobicoke, Bradford, Holland Marsh, Bridgeport, and Markham. Eighty-one residents died, including 35 on one particular street, Raymore Drive in Etobicoke. Hazel thereafter steadily deteriorated as it traveled across Ontario and western Quebec before petering out near Labrador.

Raymond Pierre Hylton

For Further Information:

Barnes, Jay. *North Carolina Hurricane History.* Chapel Hill: University of North Carolina Press, 1998.

Clark, Steve. "Is Hurricane Floyd Another Hazel?" *Richmond Times-Dispatch,* September 16, 1999.

Richmond Times-Dispatch, October 9-18, 1954.

1955: Hurricanes Connie and Diane

Date: August 4-19, 1955
Place: North Carolina, Virginia, Maryland, Pennsylvania, New York, New Jersey, Connecticut, Rhode Island, and Massachusetts
Classification: Category 3
Speed: Connie had maximum sustained winds of nearly 145 miles per hour; Diane had maximum sustained winds of 115 miles per hour
Result: More than 310 dead, over 6,000 injured, $1.5 billion in damage

When Hurricane Connie traveled north of Puerto Rico on August 6, 1955, it already had winds estimated at nearly 145 miles per hour and a barometric pressure of 27.88 inches. As it headed toward the U.S. shoreline, the Marines evacuated hundreds of aircraft from stations along the coast to bases as far away as Texas, and the U.S. Navy deployed 3 aircraft carriers and 87 other vessels to sea to ride out the storm.

The first fatalities attributed to Connie occurred when a Navy antisubmarine plane crashed while being evacuated, killing 2 crew members. Hundreds of vacationers along the shore traveled inland to escape the storm, and residents were told to prepare for the high winds and storm surges.

Taking an erratic path, Connie crossed over Cape Lookout, North Carolina, on August 12, and came ashore north of Morehead City, North Carolina. Once over land, it immediately began to lose its hurricane-force winds, dropping to only 72 miles per hour when passing near Wilmington, North Carolina, where it knocked down power lines and trees. Connie dissipated over Lake Huron on August 14, 1955. Although squall lines from Connie produced 5 tornadoes over South Carolina, the wind damage from the storm was minimal.

Rainfall and storm surge proved a different matter. Connie produced high tides that eroded North Carolina's beaches, and the storm dumped almost 12 inches of rain in some areas. The runoff from these downpours and the high tides inundated thousands of acres of farms in North Carolina, generating flooding as far north as New York. Corn and tobacco crops had been ready to be harvested before Connie's winds and rain destroyed them.

Most fatalities resulted from the flooding, although others died from traffic accidents caused by slick roads or by electrocution when entering flooded basements. In the worst episode, the *Levin J. Marvel*, a sixty-eight-year-old passenger schooner on a five-day cruise of the Chesapeake, capsized, killing 14 people, including an entire family from New York City on vacation. Spectators William McWilliams and George Kellum heroically pulled 6 people from the wreck. An investigation into the causes of this disaster was postponed when another hurricane threatened the same area within a matter of days.

The Fujiwara effect, in which one storm rotates around another, causing a mutual attraction between the storms, produced a dangerous situation for the Northeast. The same day Connie crossed into North Carolina, Diane reached hurricane status in the Caribbean and began to follow Connie's path. Aircraft that had just returned from bases in the Midwest were sent back, and coastal communities again were placed on alert. Although Diane produced maximum sustained winds of 115 miles per hour, the winds quickly dropped to 74 miles per hour as soon as the storm made landfall of August 17, 1955. The National Weather Service Bulletin fatefully warned that the only remaining danger would come from heavy rainfall and floods.

Coming just five days after Connie, Diane poured water on ground already saturated. Drawing on a warm, moist air mass from the Atlantic Ocean, Diane soaked the area, especially inland sections of the Northeast, with near-tropical rainfall. Places along the Blue Ridge Mountains were drenched by over 10 inches of rain, while eastern New York and southern New England had totals of over 12 inches, breaking long-standing records for rainfall amounts within a twenty-four-hour period. Boston recorded 15 inches of rain in a thirty-six-hour period, topping the previous record by 7 inches. By August 19, 1955, Diane traveled back out to sea, where it dissipated over the cold waters of the North Atlantic.

In Diane's wake, massive flash floods struck a six-state region. Pennsylvania, New York, New Jersey, Massachusetts, and Connecticut declared states of emergency by August 20, 1955. Highways closed, bridges washed out, and water and power supplies became unusable as the rains continued. Then the rivers rose. The Delaware River broke records when it crested and overflowed its banks. It flooded Trenton, New Jersey, while the legislature debated drought and water-conservation legislation. The Connecticut River rose over 19 feet when 13 inches of rain fell in twenty-four hours. In Seymour, Connecticut, the flood washed coffins out of a cemetery and sent them floating downstream, and in Putnam, Connecticut, floodwaters surged into a magnesium plant, causing burning barrels of magnesium to float in the streets, bursting into geysers of white hot flames.

In the worst incident, near Stroudsburg, Pennsylvania, a flash flood hit a summer camp, claiming 75 lives and leaving the entire community cut off from the outside world for several days. Because of the flooding, Operation "Kid Lift" evacuated thousands of children from summer camps in Pennsylvania, Connecticut, and New York. In Pennsylvania, Navy helicopters rescued 400 Boy Scouts from Camp Treasure Island on the Delaware River, and another 108 children were taken from Camp Pennington. Later, Army and National Guard helicopters saved 235 passengers stranded on a train in the Pocono Mountains. Anxious parents jammed phone lines trying to reach their children even while the airlift continued.

Because both storms arrived so close to each other and traveled over the same terrain, officials combined the damage from both. Most of Connie's damage was confined to North Carolina, while Diane inflicted the worst destruction on inland locations and New England. Diane became the worst natural disaster to hit Connecticut. The flooding from Connie and Diane represents the first billion-dollar hurricane pair in terms of damage in American history, with estimates ranging from $800 million to $1.5 billion.

James B. Seymour, Jr.

For Further Information:

Barnes, Jay. *North Carolina's Hurricane History.* Chapel Hill: University of North Carolina Press, 1995.

Douglas, Marjory Stoneman. *Hurricane.* New York: Rinehart, 1958.

The New York Times, August 9-September 7, 1955.

1955: Typhoon Iris

Date: August 20, 1955
Place: Fujian Province, China
Result: 2,334 dead in Fujian Province, 6 in Taiwan

Typhoon Iris was one of the most violent to strike China in the twentieth century. Had it occurred before the modern age, when there would have been minimal ability to give warning and protection, this storm could easily have resulted in tens of thousands of casualties. As it was, a total of 2,340 (including 6 in Taiwan) died, and twice that many were injured. More than 30,000 buildings were severely damaged or leveled.

Southeast China has a very long coast but lacks good harbors because of the twin problems of silting and inhospitable mountain-strewn shorelines. Fujian Province's Fuzhou and Xiamen are partial exceptions to this, but they cannot rival either Shanghai or Hong Kong as deep-water ports; a typhoon in Fujian takes relatively fewer lives as a result. Nonetheless, this area is fairly heavily populated, so the 1955 typhoon took many lives.

Richard L. Wilson

For Further Information:

Longshore, David. *Encyclopedia of Hurricanes, Typhoons, and Cyclones.* New York: Facts on File, 1998.

Samagalski, Alan, Robert Strauss, and Michael Buckley. *China.* South Yarra, Victoria, Australia: Lonely Planet, 1988.

1955: Hurricane Hilda

Date: September 19, 1955
Place: Mexico
Classification: Category 2
Result: 166 dead, 100 missing, thousands injured and homeless, thousands of buildings damaged

Forming in the Caribbean, the first hurricane named Hilda traveled past Louisiana before hitting Tampico, Mexico, on September 19, 1955. When Hurricane Hilda reached shore, it had a central pressure of 955 millibars and 108-mile-per-hour winds. Hurricane Hilda damaged Tampico's port and buildings, and hundreds of boats sank because of the storm's surges. Hilda's heavy rains caused extensive flooding, and the Pánuco River rose 6 feet. People sandbagged around homes and buildings. Approximately 166 people died during Hurricane Hilda, and another 100 were missing. At least 1,000 victims suffered hurricane-related injuries.

About 90 percent of Tampico's buildings were damaged, and 20,000 of the city's 110,000 population became homeless because of Hurricane Hilda. Pilots from the Mexican air force flew in relief supplies and food. Officials worried about epidemics developing because of refugees arriving from outside areas. The storm disrupted electricity and telegraph services, and generators were used to restore communications.

Hurricane Hilda dissipated over San Luis Potosi State in central Mexico. A second hurricane named Hilda hit Louisiana in 1964 and received more press coverage than its predecessor. After that storm, the name "Hilda" was retired.

Elizabeth D. Schafer

For Further Information:

"Hilda Rips Tampico in 'Worst Disaster.'" *The New York Times*, September 20, 1955, p. 1.

"Hurricane Tolls Continue to Rise." *The New York Times*, September 22, 1955, p. 23.

"20,000 Homeless in Tampico Storm." *The New York Times*, September 21, 1955, p. 28.

1955: Hurricane Janet

Date: September 21-29, 1955
Place: Windward Islands, Belize, and Mexico
Speed: About 150 miles per hour
Result: More than 700 deaths, over 250,000 homeless, over $100 million in damage

Hurricane Janet was the tenth tropical storm of a very productive 1955 season and set a number of records in its short but destructive life. Among these records were the unusual fact of its birth in the Atlantic going undetected; the extremely low barometric pressure recorded as the storm made landfall on the Belize-Mexico border, placing Janet among only 4 storms in the world to record pressure at or below 27.00 inches at the time of its occurrence; the unusual loss of a hurricane hunter airplane; and the record flooding in northern Mexico near the city of Tampico. Such was the unique character of this hurricane that the name "Janet" has been retired from the circulating names for hurricanes.

Meteorologists generally accept that tropical storms of the Atlantic Ocean cannot cross the New York-Cape Town shipping lanes without being detected. Yet no records of the tropical waves that produced Janet exist. The storm was first reported by pilots of Air France and Iberia airlines early on the morning of September 21, 1955, and had gained hurricane intensity when encountered by the SS *Mormacdale* in the evening of the same day.

Janet reached the island of Barbados between 11 P.M. and midnight on September 22-23 with sustained winds of 105 miles per hour, with gusts estimated between 110 and 125 miles per hour. On the very lightly forested hillsides of the island Janet dumped over 10 inches of rain. This combination of wind and rain severely damaged the sugarcane crop, destroyed many warehouses, and killed between 24 and 38 people. In the capital city of Bridgetown, most buildings, including stone structures, were badly damaged or destroyed as wind and rain were joined by a 7-foot storm surge, which swept away many houses. The surge also sent ashore numerous small craft, effectively blocking all inlets. Janet's toll of deaths and property damage made it the worst storm to strike Barbados since 1928.

Leaving Barbados, Janet passed between the islands of Grenada and Carriacou (the latter being the southernmost of the Grenadines) with sustained winds of 106 miles per hour early in the morning of September 23. Torrential rains preceded the storm, setting off mudslides and flash floods on the very steep island. The 106-mile-per-hour winds extended out for 50 miles, raking the northern edge of the island, dropping over 6 inches of rain and sending ashore a 9-foot storm surge at Levera Bay. During its passage by Grenada Janet ruined more than half of the island's commerce, severely damaging the nutmeg crop and the facilities for its storage. It is estimated that be-

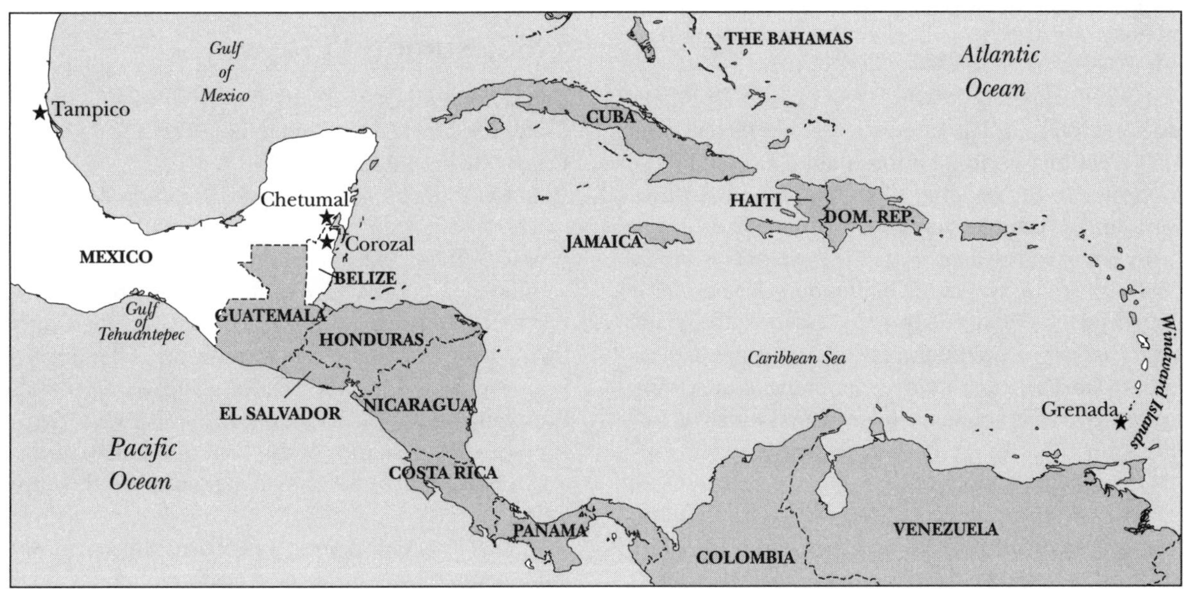

tween 125 and 200 people died in Grenada from drowning, building collapse, and mudslides. Over 100 were reported dead in the Grenadines.

On the morning of September 26, Janet produced another of those records which has set it apart, the destruction of a U.S. Navy hurricane reconnaissance plane. Because no part of the plane or its crew was ever found, reasons for the disappearance of the plane are still uncertain. However, it is generally believed that Janet's unusually low barometric pressure produced false readings on the plane's altimeter, causing the plane to fly into the sea while believing that it was considerably higher in the air. This incident, followed by three similar ones in the Pacific Ocean, led to the development of a radar-based altimeter.

By the time that Janet made landfall on the Belize-Mexico border, just before midnight on September 28, it had been classified as a Category 4 storm of extreme intensity. It brought with it sustained winds of 150 miles per hour, a 14- to 16-foot storm surge, and barometric pressure around 27.00 inches, among the lowest on record. The eyewall extended for 136 miles, extending the fury of the storm in all directions.

Chetumal, the capital of the then-territory of Quintana Roo, had all but 4 of its buildings destroyed, and these were badly damaged. Here the low pressure, reported by some survivors as resembling the explosion of aerial bombs, is believed to have contributed to the destruction. Despite evacuation measures, 120 bodies were found at Chetumal, and an unknown number are believed to have been swept out to sea.

Janet dropped over 9 inches of rain on Quintana Roo and left standing water to a height of 9 feet over 1,500 feet inland. In all, more than 500 people lost their lives to the storm in Quintana Roo, and property damage estimates exceeded $40 million.

By comparison, damage to the town of Corozal in northern Belize was light. While many houses were destroyed or damaged, the city escaped the giant wave that swept Chetumal. Particular to the experience of Corozal was the constant pelting of the city by flying debris thrown about by sustained winds of 146 miles per hour. Property damage in Belize was estimated at about $5 million.

Janet entered the Bay of Campeche in the early morning of September 28 and regained some of its force as it headed for the east coast of mainland Mexico, arriving at Tampico just after dawn on September 29. It brought winds of 129 miles per hour and dropped 11 inches of rain in the first few hours. Buildings were badly damaged, three-fourths of the city was flooded, and an estimated 20,000 people were left homeless, many of these stranded on the roofs of their former homes.

Janet's arrival with torrential rains coincided with the heavy rains recently produced by Hurricanes Gladys and Hilda. The results were catastrophic in two areas. First, this juncture of three hurricanes produced new records for precipitation in northeast Mexico. Janet thus spent the next week breaking up against the slopes of the Sierra Madre Oriental, creating flooding and mudslide conditions. The flooding of two rivers in particular, the Pánuco and the Tamesi, caused great numbers of poisonous snakes and snapping turtles to be washed into Tampico, where they attacked survivors of the storm. At least 30 people were believed to have been killed by snakebites.

St. John Robinson

For Further Information:

Dunn, Gordon E., Walter R. Davis, and Paul L. Morre. "Hurricanes of 1955." *Monthly Weather Review* 83 (December, 1955): 315-326.

"Janet, Hurricane." In *Encyclopedia of Hurricanes, Typhoons, and Cyclones*, edited by David Longshore. New York: Facts on File: 1998.

1956: Hurricane Flossy

Date: September 21-25, 1956
Place: Southeastern United States
Classification: Category 2
Result: 24 dead, millions of dollars in damage

A weak Category 2 hurricane, Flossy formed in the southwest Gulf of Mexico on the evening of September 21, 1956. Moving north-northwest over the Gulf's tepid water, Hurricane Flossy built up 107-mile-per-hour winds, which caused 6-foot surges along coastal Louisiana and Florida. Flossy's winds and waves damaged oil-drilling stands in the Gulf of Mexico, resulting in $2 million in damage to machinery and equipment.

With a low central pressure of 975 millibars, Flossy landed near New Orleans on September 23. The storm then moved back over the Gulf of Mexico before hitting shore on the night of September 24 at Laguna Beach in Florida. The hurricane weakened as it passed over southern Georgia, dropping more than 5 inches of rain. Because of the storm, 24 people died in Louisiana and Florida. Before satellites were first successfully orbited the next year, meteorologists tracking Flossy had limited hurricane detection and monitoring methods to observe the entire storm from birth to maturation to dissipation over large geographical areas. The name "Flossy" was retired from the hurricane list because of its severity.

Elizabeth D. Schafer

For Further Information:

"Gulf Hurricane Lashes Florida; Storm Abating, Moving to North." *The New York Times*, September 25, 1956, p. 1.

"Tropical Storm Moves into Gulf." *The New York Times*, September 23, 1956, p. 78.

1957: Hurricane Audrey

Date: June 27-30, 1957
Place: Louisiana and Texas
Classification: Category 4
Speed: Maximum wind unofficially 144 miles per hour, officially 105 miles per hour
Result: More than 500 dead, about $150 million in damage

Forecasts. On June 17, 1957, the U.S. Weather Bureau predicted the hurricane season that year would begin early. Only a week later, on Monday, June 24, the prediction came true, as a tropical depression developed west of the Yucatán Peninsula in the southernmost part of the Gulf of Mexico. At 10:30 that night, the Weather Bureau issued its first advisory about the storm; at noon on Tuesday, June 25, the wind having already reached hurricane speed, the Weather Bureau declared a hurricane watch for the coasts of Louisiana and Texas. By 4 P.M., Hurricane Audrey was moving north, its rotating wind increasing in speed.

On Wednesday, June 26, at 10 A.M., the Weather Bureau issued a hurricane warning, which said in part: "Tides are rising and will reach 5 to 8 feet along the Louisiana coast and over Mississippi Sound by late Thursday. All persons in low exposed places should move to higher ground." Although a revised warning, issued twelve hours later, mentioned tides of 9 feet, many people of Cameron Parish, in the marsh country of the southwest corner of Louisiana, thought they could safely spend Wednesday night in their homes. Furthermore, adults from Acadia and other families that had long lived in that part of Louisiana tended to think that their houses, built on sandy ridges called *chênières*, stood on the "higher ground" to which the Weather Bureau referred, because previous storms had not flooded the houses; newcomers to the parish, however, generally evacuated. When the families that had remained in or near the towns of Cameron, Creole, and Grand Chenier tried to leave at dawn on Thursday, June 27, rapidly rising water, combined with unexpectedly early hurricane wind and rain, made driving away virtually impossible, and the disaster began for them before 8 A.M., the hour when the eye of the hurricane reached the coast about halfway between the town of Cameron and the Texas state line.

Height of Water. Before Audrey arrived in Cameron Parish, its wind and the resultant waves of 45 or 50 feet in the Gulf of Mexico had already sunk a fishing boat and capsized an oil rig. On shore, or on what ordinarily would have been shore, it was not the wind directly, not even the several tornadoes generated by the hurricane, but the storm surge—the high tide with huge waves—that caused the most harm. For a shoreline at which normal tidal variation is small, the tides produced by Audrey were enormous, reaching 10.6 feet above mean sea level in Cameron itself, 12.1 feet on the beach due south of that town, 12.2 feet at Grand Chenier, 12.9 feet near Creole, and 13.9 feet midway between Creole and Grand Chenier. The onshore waves rose at times from 10 to 15 feet above the high-tide mark and smashed almost every building in their path.

Although no other area suffered as much as Cameron Parish did during Audrey, the hurricane brought flooding in Louisiana from the Texas border in the west to the Delta of the Mississippi River in the east. In western Louisiana, floodwaters reached as far north as Lake Charles. Even in east Texas, located west of where Audrey's eye met land and generally less damaged by Audrey than southwest Louisiana, significant water damage occurred.

Property Damage. In Port Arthur, Texas, storm rain accumulating on the roof of a nine-story build-

The fishing schooner Three Brothers *tossed onto a road in Louisiana by Hurricane Audrey.* (AP/Wide World Photos)

ing led to massive structural collapse. In Louisiana, a huge supply barge rammed into a storage tank on land. The fishing schooner *Three Brothers* washed ashore, as did many other vessels, including the shrimp boat *Audry.* At Grand Chenier, the hurricane totally destroyed about one-tenth of the houses; at Creole, it left only 1 building on its foundation; and in Cameron, where about 3,000 people had lived before June 27, only 2 buildings remained mostly intact—the parish courthouse, which served as a shelter during the storm, and an icehouse, which served briefly as a morgue in the storm's aftermath.

Death, Survival, and Heroism. Because Cameron Parish was rural, property damage was small in proportion to what it would have been had Audrey struck a low-lying urban area like metropolitan New Orleans. What made Audrey especially horrible was the toll in human lives. Not since the hurricane that destroyed Galveston, Texas, in 1900, had so many people in the western half of the U.S. Gulf coast died because of a tropical storm. Some people apparently died alone, like thirty-five-year-old Harry Melancon of Broussard, Louisiana, who happened to be driving an oil tanker truck in Cameron Parish when Audrey arrived and whose body was not found for five months. Others died after having taken what shelter they could with members of their family; eight-year-old Thelma Jo Gibbs, whose body was found in 1958, was one of those.

Some families lost only one member; others lost many. Eighteen members of one family died after they had taken shelter in the home of Robert Moore on the Front Ridge, southeast of Cameron. Ironically, some members of the family would have lived had they remained in the house of Susan Rose Moore, Robert Moore's mother, because it remained intact. Robert Moore's house, though newer, was swept off its foundation and broken apart by the storm surge.

Among the men in Robert Moore's house was Albert January, whose story suggests the struggle and terror common as hurricane victims fought for their own lives and those of their loved ones. When the house broke apart, January, his wife, their three children (ages eight, seven, and two years), and many other people held onto the roof while it floated away. Three times waves shoved Mrs. January and the children off, and three times Mr. January rescued them.

A fourth wave, however, proved deadly for Lucy LaSalle January and her children, Arthur Lee, Annie Lee, and John Randall, when Mr. January's rescue effort failed.

The story of Dr. Cecil Clark presents a similar sorrow but another kind of heroism. Thirty-three years old, Clark was the only physician in Cameron, where he had charge of the Cameron Medical Center. He and his wife, Sybil Baccigalopi Clark, a nurse-anesthetist, had five children: John (eight years), Joe (seven years), Elizabeth Dianne (three years), Celia Marie (eighteen months), and Jack Benjamin (three months). John and Joe had spent Wednesday night at the home of Dr. Clark's mother in Creole; they survived Audrey the next day by being tied to tree tops.

Meanwhile, early Thursday morning, to try to evacuate patients from the twelve-bed hospital at the medical center, Dr. and Mrs. Clark had left their three younger children at their presumably safe home in the care of Zulmae Dubois, their housekeeper. Their trip thwarted by rising water on the road, they returned, but Dr. Clark tried to go back again, this time without his wife but with a neighbor. Still unable to get through, Dr. Clark eventually had to ride out the storm in the concrete-block house of Mr. and Mrs. Philbert Richard, from which, after the storm had abated, he waded amid debris to the courthouse and began long hours of treating hundreds of sick or injured persons, among whom were the patients from the little hospital, whom nurses and deputy sheriffs with boats had evacuated in Dr. Clark's absence.

Not until Friday evening did Dr. Clark learn that his wife and their two older children had lived through the disaster. Although knocked unconscious momentarily, Mrs. Clark had swum and then drifted on wreckage until people in a little boat had rescued her from driftwood miles from where her house had stood. Late that night, during a short respite at a friend's home in Lake Charles, Dr. Clark learned of the deaths of his three younger children and Mrs. Dubois, who had all drowned when the waves destroyed the Clarks' house. Despite his own grief, he soon returned to Cameron to treat survivors. By late 1957, Dr. and Mrs. Clark had had the Cameron Medical Center rebuilt, and in December the American Medical Association awarded Dr. Clark a gold medal as "General Practitioner of the Year."

Not all of Audrey's more than 500 fatalities drowned. Some probably died of heart attacks under

Residents of Cameron, Louisiana, identify some of those killed by Hurricane Audrey. (AP/Wide World Photos)

the stress of the storm, although the exact number of heart-attack deaths will never be known because the great number of dead bodies made performing routine autopsies virtually impossible. Similarly, some people probably died from snakebites, although only one such case was confirmed. Seven-year-old Steve Broussard, Jr., of Pecan Island in Vermilion Parish, immediately east of Cameron Parish, survived the floodwaters that took the lives of his sisters Larissa, Veronica, and Estelle when their house floated into White Lake and then broke apart. In the dark of the morning of Friday, June 28, however, while he was floating on a part of the roof of his family's home, one of the thousands of water moccasins dislodged and infuriated by the hurricane crawled onto the wreckage and bit him on the ear. Hours later, after his father had braved hundreds of other snakes and fought off a maddened cow in an attempt to get help, the child died on his way to a hospital in Abbeville.

Aftermath. Lessening in intensity as it moved inland, Audrey nevertheless brought strong wind and much rain from the Gulf coast all the way up through the Ohio Valley states, New York, and New England and Canada. The storm damaged more property and caused more deaths, including 4 in Canada, before it ended.

In the United States, President Dwight D. Eisenhower declared the severely affected communities disaster areas. In southwest Louisiana, where the death toll was the worst, thousands of people joined in an effort to rescue and comfort survivors; to find, identify, and bury the dead; to retrieve sealed concrete tombs washed out of low-lying cemeteries; to clear away the big, innumerable piles of debris; to round up hungry and often hostile cattle and return them to their owners; to restore telephone service, electricity, gas, and safe drinking water; to rebuild homes and businesses; and to help victims resume something resembling ordinary life.

Amid heat, mosquitoes, and water moccasins, rescuers searched on foot and by boat for the living and the dead. Helicopters crisscrossed the sky. Military personnel, including members of the Coast Guard and the National Guard, were among the relief workers, as were men and women from the American Red Cross and the Salvation Army. Responding to reports that Audrey had impoverished some survivors, Governor Earl Long pressured insurance companies into paying great claims to Louisiana citizens for wind damage, despite the companies' contention that the insured had no flood coverage and that it was water that had caused most of the damage to homes and businesses.

Of the approximately 40,000 persons whom Audrey drove from their homes, about 22,000 went to Lake Charles, where many stayed at McNeese State College. In Lake Charles was the big, makeshift morgue that replaced the original one at the icehouse in Cameron and another one at a Lake Charles hospital. In shed 5 at the dockyard, hundreds of survivors walked calmly past the dead bodies cooled with blocks of ice and tried to identify those whom they had lost. The unidentified dead were eventually buried in special plots in several cemeteries.

Only slowly did some grieving people accept their loss. For a time after Audrey, one Cameron Parish resident reported, mothers would go to the border of the marsh, listen to the calls of the nutria (semiaquatic rodents), and hear in those mammalian sounds the cries of their missing babies, victims of the storm.

Victor Lindsey

For Further Information:

"Disasters: Audrey's Day of Horror." *Time*, July 8, 1957, 12.

Dunn, Gordon E., and Banner I. Miller. "The Hurricane Hazard by Regions." In *Atlantic Hurricanes*. Baton Rouge: Louisiana State University Press, 1960.

"G.P. in a Hurricane." *Time*, December 16, 1957, 39-40.

"In the Wake of Disaster." *Newsweek*, July 8, 1957, 22-24.

Ross, Nola Mae Wittler, and Susan McFillen Goodson. *Hurricane Audrey*. Sulphur, La.: Wise, 1997.

"Story of Hurricane Audrey—and the Warnings That Many Ignored." *U.S. News & World Report*, July 12, 1957, 62-63.

U.S. Army Corps of Engineers. "Descriptions of Hurricanes." In *History of Hurricane Occurrences along Coastal Louisiana*. Rev. ed. New Orleans: U.S. Army Engineer District, 1972.

1960: Hurricane Donna

Date: September 6-12, 1960
Place: From the Caribbean to New England

Classification: Category 4
Result: 168 dead, $1.8 billion in damage

The environmental damage inflicted by Hurricane Donna was significant. According to meteorologists, Donna retained the status of the most destructive Florida hurricane until Andrew hit in 1992. A Cape Verde hurricane that formed on September 1, 1960, Donna quickly moved to the Caribbean, where 120 people died, many because Cuban officials dismissed American storm warnings as a conspiracy to disrupt Cuba's economy through evacuations.

Donna's winds neared 200 miles per hour when they hit the Florida Keys on September 9. A 13-foot surge washed away part of the causeway between Key Largo and Key West. Returning to the Gulf of Mexico, Donna then moved ashore again near Fort Myers, Florida, skipping over to the Atlantic Ocean as it moved up the coast before striking Daytona Beach. In all, 13 people died in Florida. Donna also ruined the grapefruit, tangerine, and orange crops, and half of the world's largest mangrove-tree forest, and killed almost 40 percent of the planet's white herons. A monument in Everglades National Park documents Donna's ecological results.

Moving off the coast of Georgia, Donna gained energy and hit North Carolina's Outer Banks, then Virginia Beach, damaging dunes, before moving toward New England, causing damage as far north as Maine. Tides 11 feet high swept through New York harbor. Donna's final landfall occurred at New London, Connecticut. Apples and potatoes were damaged throughout that region. The name "Donna" was retired after the fury of the 1960 storm.

Elizabeth D. Schafer

For Further Information:

Barnes, Jay. *North Carolina's Hurricane History.* Chapel Hill: University of North Carolina, 1995.

Williams, John M., and Iver W. Duedall. *Florida Hurricanes and Tropical Storms.* Rev. ed. Gainesville: University Press of Florida, 1997.

1961: Hurricane Carla

Date: September 3-15, 1961
Place: Texas
Classification: Category 4
Result: 46 dead, $400 million in damage

Forming over the southwestern Caribbean near Nicaragua on September 3, 1961, Hurricane Carla was one of the largest and most powerful Gulf of Mexico storms recorded. Hurricane Carla's winds affected a 300-mile area stretching from Brownsville, Texas, to Louisiana. Hitting Port O'Connor, Texas, on September 11, Hurricane Carla's central pressure was 931 millibars, which was significant because the last Texas hurricane with such low pressure had been the one at Galveston in 1900. The storm surge peaked over 18 feet, and the town lost almost all of its buildings and shrimp boats.

Hurricane surges covered Follets Island near Galveston and washed 400 feet into the Matagorda Peninsula. The hurricane damaged piers at nearby Padre Island. Port Lavaca also sustained major hurricane damage to its causeway. Coastal tides of 22 feet flooded low-lying areas. Although 300,000 people had evacuated the Texas coast, 46 people died during the hurricane. Authorities calculated $400 million in property damage. Hurricane Carla dissipated over Kansas and Missouri, causing flash floods that resulted in $50 million of insurance claims. The name "Carla" was then retired from the hurricane list.

Elizabeth D. Schafer

For Further Information:

Hayes, Miles O. *Hurricanes as Geological Agents: Case Studies of Hurricanes Carla, 1961, and Cindy, 1963.* Austin: Bureau of Economic Geology, University of Texas, 1967.

Hogan, Warren L. *Hurricane Carla: A Tribute to the News Media.* Houston: Leaman-Hogan, 1961.

Treadwell, Mattie E. *Hurricane Carla, September 3-14, 1961.* Denton, Tex.: Department of Defense, 1962.

1961: Hurricane Hattie

Date: October 31-November 1, 1961
Place: British Honduras (now Belize)
Classification: Category 4
Result: More than 400 dead, thousands of buildings destroyed, millions of dollars in damage

The community of Stann Creek, British Honduras, after it was devastated by Hurricane Hattie in 1961. (AP/Wide World Photos)

Forming in the Caribbean, Hurricane Hattie struck British Honduras, now known as Belize, in Central America on October 31, 1961. Hattie was the country's most devastating hurricane. A Category 4 hurricane, Hattie's 140-mile-per-hour winds and torrential rains devastated Belize City as the storm landed at dawn. Winds gusted as high as 180 miles per hour, and the storm surge reached 12 feet, submerging barrier islands off the coast. Turneffe and Caulker Cays were covered with water. Many people drowned; despite efforts to evacuate tourists and residents, more than 400 people died. About 40 percent of the buildings in Belize City were destroyed.

Stann Creek, a fishing village west of the capital, suffered the loss of almost all of its structures and trees. The village's clay streets were covered with debris blown from houses by the hurricane, including a variety of kitchen appliances. Residents decided to restore their community, calling it Hattieville to memorialize the hurricane that was the catalyst for its transformation.

Elizabeth D. Schafer

For Further Information:

"Storm Hits British Honduras; Winds and Tides Batter Belize." *The New York Times*, November 1, 1961, p. 8.

"3 U.S. Ships Rush Aid in Hurricane." *The New York Times*, November 3, 1961, p. 22.

1963: Hurricane Flora

Date: September 28-October 9, 1963
Place: Haiti and Cuba

Classification: Category 4
Result: 6,000-8,000 dead, millions of dollars in damage

At the time it struck, Hurricane Flora was considered the second most deadly Atlantic hurricane. Unusual because it developed below 10 degrees north latitude, Hurricane Flora quickly gained energy from the warm equatorial ocean near its origin. By September 30, 1963, Flora was designated a Category 2 hurricane with 110-mile-per-hour winds. Pouring 6 inches of rain on Trinidad, Tobago, and Grenada that day, the hurricane started mudslides on the islands, which killed 36 people and hurt another 469.

Moving toward Haiti, Hurricane Flora achieved the Category 5 level with 170-mile-per-hour winds. Hitting Haiti on October 3, Flora's gusts caused 18-foot waves to sweep the shore. Approximately 5,000 people drowned when 11-foot surges inundated coastal Haitian villages. Another 100,000 people lost their shelter. Hurricane Flora devastated Haiti's coffee harvest, which was that country's primary source of economic stability.

As Flora traveled northwest from Haiti to Cuba, its pressure increased from 936 millibars to 970. Considered Cuba's deadliest hurricane at that time, Flora hit Santiago de Cuba with 107-mile-per-hour winds the morning of October 4 and remained over the island for three days because of a warm front. The towns of Oriente and Camagüey sustained extensive damage. Between 15 and 20 inches of rain caused flash floods on the Cauto and Contramestre Rivers, which broke levees. At least 90 percent of Cuba's sugar and coffee crops was ruined. Although thousands had been evacuated, 1,000 people died. Another 175,000 were impoverished by the storm.

Cuban leader Fidel Castro had ignored meteorological warnings from the United States but broadcasted radio messages criticizing the American trade embargo and Project Stormfury, an attempt to reduce storm intensity by seeding clouds with silver iodide crystals. Hurricane Flora dissipated over the Bahamas by October 9, and the name "Flora" was retired from the hurricane list.

Elizabeth D. Schafer

For Further Information:

"Haiti Storm Dead May Total 4,000; Cuba Is Hit Again." *The New York Times*, October 8, 1963, p. 1.
"Hurricane Sweeps North to Bahamas." *The New York Times*, October 9, 1963, p. 1.

Hurricane Flora strikes the coast of Cuba near the U.S. Naval Base at Guantanamo Bay in 1963. (AP/Wide World Photos)

1964: Hurricane Cleo

Date: August 21-27, 1964
Place: The Caribbean and Florida
Classification: Category 3
Result: 138 dead, $200 million in damage

A Cape Verde tropical storm, Cleo was considered one of the most devastating Category 3 hurricanes, wreaking havoc throughout the Caribbean and southern Florida. Attaining 110-mile-per-hour winds, Cleo first struck Guadeloupe on August 21, 1964, where 8-inch downpours started mudslides, killing 14 people and injuring 100 as houses were swept away from villages. Next, Cleo hit Haiti on August 24, with winds as high as 135 miles per hour, which sent 20-foot waves surging toward the island. Approximately 120 Haitians died, including drowning victims from Chardonnière, a fishing town that was covered with water.

Hurricane Cleo traveled northwest toward Cuba, striking the town of Condado on August 25. The hurricane caused damage to Taguasco and Chambas, located in the mountains. Although the Cuban government did not release casualty statistics, other reports indicated that 50 people had died in Cuba during the hurricane, which caused $70,000 in damage before it headed into the Florida Straits. Weakening, Cleo was reduced to a Category 2 hurricane.

Hurricane Cleo downed trees and caused this motorship to run aground in Miami. (AP/Wide World Photos)

The first hurricane to hit Miami since Hurricane King in 1950, Cleo caused $200 million in damage to Florida resorts, businesses, and agriculture on August 27. One day later, the new meteorological satellite Nimbus photographed Cleo. Moving through Georgia and the Carolinas, Hurricane Cleo passed over the Atlantic Ocean on September 1, temporarily losing hurricane status, until returning to shore the next day and moving northeast, dissipating in Nova Scotia.

Elizabeth D. Schafer

For Further Information:

Finney, John W. "A Weather Satellite Photographs Hurricane." *The New York Times*, August 29, 1964, p. 1.

"Miami Battered; Gale Winds Lash at Space Center." *The New York Times*, August 28, 1964, p. 1.

1965: Hurricane Betsy

Date: August 27-September 12, 1965
Place: Florida and Louisiana
Classification: Category 3
Result: 78 dead, thousands injured, $1.4 billion in damage

An extraordinarily powerful and unpredictable Category 3 hurricane, Betsy formed east of Barbados on August 27, 1965. Traveling 8 miles per hour, Betsy reached Guadeloupe the next day, where no fatalities were reported. Continuing northwest, Hurricane Betsy's pressure dropped to 990 millibars, and winds increased to 83 miles per hour. Affected by a high-pressure system, Betsy changed direction, heading northeast then gradually turning southeast on September 1.

By the next day, Hurricane Betsy had resumed its northwest path but had been displaced 500 miles west of its original location. With a central pressure of 942 millibars and 110-mile-per-hour winds, Betsy moved toward Turks and Caicos Islands, which sustained significant damage to property but no human deaths. Seemingly headed for the North Carolina coast, Betsy was again influenced by the high-pressure system and began moving southwest toward Cuba by September 6. Suddenly, the next day, the storm shifted west toward Florida and decreased its pressure to 957 millibars.

Betsy hit Biscayne Bay on September 8 with 135-mile-per-hour winds and surges as large as 9 feet. Because of Hurricane Betsy, 13 people died in Florida. The storm then continued across the Gulf of Mexico toward Louisiana, where devastation was great. Despite evacuations of over 300,000 people, 61 died in Louisiana, and 27,000 houses were leveled, in addition to other damage. Betsy weakened as it moved inland. Tornadoes produced by the dying hurricane killed 4 people in Arkansas. Total casualties tallied 78 dead, 17,500 hurt, and $1.4 billion in destruction, which was the first time a hurricane had achieved that monetary cost. The name "Betsy" was retired from the hurricane list.

Elizabeth D. Schafer

For Further Information:

"Death Toll May Reach 200 as Louisiana Cleans Up." *Montgomery Advertiser,* September 12, 1965, p. 1.

"President Tours Hurricane Area." *The New York Times,* September 11, 1965, p. 10.

Reed, Roy. "New Orleans Loss in Storm Heavy; 23 Dead in 3 States." *The New York Times,* September 11, 1965, p. 1.

1966: Hurricane Inez

Date: September 22-October 11, 1966

Place: The Caribbean, Florida, and Mexico

This church and house in Jadmal, Haiti, lost their roofs to the fury of Hurricane Inez. (AP/Wide World Photos)

Classification: Category 3
Result: 2,000 dead, tens of millions of dollars in damage

Hurricane Inez was one of the Caribbean's longest-duration hurricanes. Striking Guadeloupe as a tropical storm on September 24 and 25, 1966, Inez caused mudslides and floods that killed 23 people. More than $25 million of devastation occurred, including the ruination of the banana harvest. Hurricane Inez then moved toward Hispaniola, with winds intensifying to 140 miles per hour on the evening of September 28. The Dominican Republic suffered the almost complete obliteration of three towns: Duverge, Enriquillo, and Oviedo. In the latter location, only the town hall, sheltering many citizens, withstood the storm. Sugarcane fields were stripped of stalks.

Haiti suffered similar catastrophes. A foot of rainfall created rivers of water streaming down mountains and carrying people, animals, and property toward the Caribbean Sea. Haiti's beaches were covered with corpses. A weakened Inez crossed part of Cuba on September 30. With 81-mile-per-hour winds, Inez blew over some buildings and flattened sugarcane fields but caused no fatalities in Cuba. Over a two-day period, Inez changed direction and circled Cuba, returning to its starting point south of Florida.

Stagnating over the Bahamas because of a high-pressure air mass which influenced the hurricane's motion, Inez produced a tornado and rainstorms that caused 1 death on October 3. Moving west, Hurricane Inez intensified as it neared the Florida Keys, attaining Category 3 status with 125-mile-per-hour winds. Waves 12 feet high killed 1 surfer, and 4 additional people died in Florida. U.S. Highway 1 connecting the Keys was submerged. Inez struck north of Tampico, Mexico, eight days later on October 11. Hitting swampy and wooded areas, Inez caused no deaths and dissipated as it came into contact with thunderstorms over Mexican mountains.

Elizabeth D. Schafer

For Further Information:

"Hurricane Heads for Leeward Isles." *The New York Times*, September 27, 1966, p. 19.

"Hurricane Roars over Guadeloupe." *The New York Times*, September 28, 1966, p. 23.

"Winds of 150 Miles Per Hour Lashing Dominican Republic." *The New York Times*, September 29, 1966, p. 49.

1969: Hurricane Camille

Date: August 15-18, 1969
Place: Mississippi, Louisiana, Alabama, Virginia, and West Virginia
Classification: Category 5
Result: 258 dead, $1.5 billion in damage

Packing winds of nearly 200 miles per hour and a barometric pressure of 26.84 inches, Hurricane Camille was a storm of immense intensity and at the time only the second on record to strike the U.S. mainland with Category 5 force. From the time it was first designated a hurricane on August 15, 1969, as it moved from south of Cuba to its point of dissipation over the North Atlantic, Camille left a staggering amount of devastation, including 258 storm-related deaths and an estimated $1.5 billion in damage, much of it concentrated in the Gulf coast regions of Louisiana and Mississippi.

The Beginnings. For several days in its early stages, Camille moved at a leisurely pace across the Atlantic as a relatively disorganized tropical system. The storm was spawned on August 5 by a tropical wave moving off the coast of Africa. By August 9 it had reached tropical disturbance level, approaching the northern Leeward Islands, before passing through them on the following day. The same day a satellite photograph indicated it was no more than a weak cloud mass. On August 11 satellite imagery revealed the system had become an isolated block of clouds located between Puerto Rico and the Lesser Antilles and that it had broken into two circular air masses.

For a brief time officials at the U.S. Weather Service believed the tropical disturbance was unlikely to reach the status of a major storm. A hurricane hunter who flew into the tropical wave reported little organization in the cloud formation. However, after reaching the warm waters of the Caribbean, the disturbance rapidly intensified and was designated a tropical storm as it moved within 350 miles of Cuba. Camille's central pressure had dropped dramatically to 29.50 inches, and its sustained winds topped 65 miles per hour.

Coursing through the Caribbean, the storm continued its rapid intensification, with winds climbing to over 80 miles per hour and its barometric pressure falling to 28.67 inches. On August 15, the storm was upgraded to hurricane status, as it moved through the Yucatán Straits on its way northwest. Maximum winds were recorded at 115 miles per hour, with gales extending out 125 to 150 miles to the north of the storm's center and 50 miles to its south. Its forward movement was measured at 7 miles per hour.

Camille swept over the western tip of Cuba with 115-mile-per-hour winds, driving hundreds of residents to higher ground with its torrential rains. The weather station at Guane, center of a rich tobacco area, reported winds of 92 miles per hour. As the storm meandered toward the eastern Gulf of Mexico, it dumped nearly 10 inches of precipitation on the Isle of Pines, immediately south of the Cuban mainland. At the time, the U.S. Weather Bureau placed the storm's center about 250 miles south-southwest of Key West.

The region of Cuba struck by the storm is an area highly vulnerable to flooding owing to the runoff of rain that rushes down the mountainsides to the sea. The sugar crop and tobacco crop, both mainstays of the Cuban economy, suffered extensive damage during the storm's passage. In the central town of Puerto Cortes, 50 houses were destroyed. In many communities along the coast, power and telephone communications were cut off and large ranches and farms isolated by the flash floods.

Camille Continues to Intensify. Camille continued on a track that took it through the Yucatán Channel, and on August 16 its eye moved into the Gulf of Mexico. The storm's forward movement was measured at 12 miles per hour. It was located 400 miles south of the Florida panhandle and moving in a north-northwest direction. Camille's winds covered 80-mile-wide circles and buffeted across 200 miles of Gulf waters. Its barometric pressure tumbled to 27.13 inches.

Hurricane Camille not only continued to intensify but also surprised storm watchers by changing its course to a more northwesterly direction toward the

Hurricane Camille was one of the few storms to achieve Category 5 status. Its force was strong enough to hurl cars and rip apart buildings. (National Oceanic and Atmospheric Administration)

Louisiana-Mississippi-Alabama coastlines. On August 16 a hurricane watch was put into effect, stretching from Biloxi, Mississippi, to St. Marks, Florida. As the storm moved to within 250 miles of Mobile, Alabama, Camille's winds were estimated at 160 miles per hour and its speed at 12 miles per hour. The storm continued its on its track toward the mouth of the Mississippi River, prompting officials to extend the hurricane warning as far west as New Orleans.

Late in the evening on August 16, Camille's eye crossed into the Pass Christian, Mississippi, area with winds up to 200 miles per hour, accompanied by a monster tide 24 feet above normal. The hurricane skirted the mouth of the Mississippi River some 90 miles southeast of New Orleans in an area lined with small islands, bays, and harbors. On August 17, a final Air Force reconnaissance flight recorded a barometric pressure of 26.61 inches with maximum surface winds at more than 200 miles per hour. The barometric reading was second only to the 26.35 reading for the Labor Day Hurricane of 1935, the lowest ever recorded at the time. Later in the day, at 9 P.M., the National Hurricane Center issued a warning that Camille was "extremely dangerous" and was bringing 15- to 20-foot tides with it along the Mississippi-Alabama coast. Areas along the coast were advised to evacuate immediately.

Evacuation and Landfall. The main damage inflicted by the storm throughout the low coastal region was from the floods produced by the high tides and heavy rainfall. In Gulfport, Mississippi, all evacuation centers had run short of food and water even before Camille's arrival. The storm's track along the coastline was marked by a series of local communication and power failures. In a clear sign of the severity of the storm, the Mississippi River Bridge at New Orleans was closed to traffic, and the world's longest bridge, the 26-mile causeway that crosses Lake Pontchartrain, was shut down. Camille's winds lashed the causeway at more than 60 miles per hour and churned the lake's water into a caldron of violent waves.

Evacuations were ordered all the way from Grand Isle, Louisiana, to the Florida Panhandle. Over 100,000 people spent the night of August 17 in Red Cross shelters, in the area extending from New Orleans to Pensacola. Residents of the fishing villages of Louisiana's marshlands evacuated by the thousands. Nearly 90 percent of the population left their homes to take refuge. The Red Cross announced it had set up 394 evacuation centers in the Mississippi Delta area, with over 40,000 people reported in shelters as far away as Alexandria, Louisiana, 200 miles to the north, and Lafayette, located in the southwestern corner of the state. U.S. Coast Guard helicopters had to risk the storm's winds to rescue 30 men stranded on an oil rig in the Gulf of Mexico. Waves of 12 to 14 feet were reported at a rig located offshore from Timbalier Island, which is situated about 40 miles west of the mouth of the Mississippi River.

Following its swipe at southern Louisiana, Camille washed ashore near Gulfport just before midnight on August 17. Its barometric pressure stood at 26.84 inches, and its winds continued to whirl at 180 miles per hour. When ranked by size, Camille was a relatively small hurricane, with an eye less than 5 miles in diameter. Its hurricane-force winds reached out 45 miles in all directions, with gales extending out 150 miles. Mobile, located nearly 95 miles east of the storm's center, registered 44-mile-per-hour winds, while New Orleans, situated nearly 45 miles closer to the storm's core, received sustained winds of 52 miles per hour.

The Damage. Camille's lethal combination of high winds and high tides brought almost total destruction to the coastal areas from southeastern Louisiana to Biloxi. Because of the many shapes and sizes of the bays and inlets, surge heights varied at different locations. In several places in Louisiana, from the Empire Canal south to Buras, Boothville, and Venice, the surge poured over the levees on both the east and west banks of the Mississippi River, only to be trapped by the back levees, leaving the built-up areas between the embankments flooded with up to 16 feet of water. The east-bank levees were nearly destroyed as the wave action of the water severely eroded the land-side slope before reaching the back levees. The regions within the levees were almost totally destroyed. Few structures survived intact, and those that did ended up floating about until dumped between or on the levees.

The waves nearly wiped the small community of Buras off the map when the town was inundated with 15 feet of water in a matter of minutes. In one bizarre incident, a 200-foot barge loaded with combustible solvents was dumped by the waters in the middle of a highway running through the center of the town. As the storm surge swept over the river's east-bank levee, a swift influx of tidal waters disrupted the normal flow of the river, elevating its water level for a considerable distance upstream. Close to 66 percent of the total land area in Plaquemines Parish, representing about 414,000 acres of land, was flooded.

Along the coast, fires raged out of control, as firefighters were unable to reach them in the wake of the inundating tides. Buildings in Bay St. Louis, Mississippi, a scenic coastal town located 15 miles west of Gulfport near the Mississippi line, burned furiously. Its business district, comprising mainly a lumber mill and seafood packing center, was concentrated on a single street, half of which caved into the bay. An estimated 95 percent of the homes in the city were damaged.

Thousands of people in Louisiana, Mississippi, and Alabama were left homeless as the storm made its way across the coastline. The destruction wrought by Camille stretched along 50 miles of beach from Waveland, Mississippi, to Pascagoula, near the Alabama state line, and three or four blocks inland. The storm raised the Gulf of Mexico nearly 3 feet higher than normal as far as 125 miles east of Pass Christian, Mississippi, and 31 miles to the west. The U.S. Army Corps of Engineers later estimated that 100,000 tons of debris had to be cleared away in order to make passable nearly 530 miles of road. U.S. Highway 90, the main coastal road, was covered with sand in many sections; piled high with lumber, furniture, refrigerators, mattresses, and other debris in some stretches; and completely washed away in others. Nearly one-third of the Bay St. Louis Bridge and one-half of the Biloxi-Ocean Springs Bridge were damaged when the high tides shoved the spans off their supports. An estimated 50 percent of the resort properties in the Biloxi area were damaged and the other half destroyed. Fourteen counties in Mississippi suffered electrical power failures, some lasting for several days. Telephone service also was affected, as nearly 15 percent of telephones were put out of service, with the number jumping to 67 percent along the Gulf coast. Pascagoula faced a problem of another kind when it was invaded by hundreds of poisonous cottonmouth snakes seeking higher ground. One woman reported hundreds of black water moccasins and cottonmouths in her mother's backyard.

Homes and buildings that had withstood previous hurricane-level storms proved no match for Camille. Water stood 10-feet deep in the lobby of the plush Broadwater Beach Hotel. A wave of 22 feet inundated Pass Christian Isles, including the Richelieu apartment complex, where a decision by a group of people to ignore the warnings and ride out the storm with a "hurricane party" ended in tragedy when 23 of them died in the onslaught. Along with the storm surge, heavy precipitation, between 5 and 10 inches, moved inland with Camille. Rainfalls from 2 to 6 inches extended to portions of southeast Louisiana, central and northern Mississippi, and northwest Florida.

Stately oak trees that had also survived previous hurricane-force winds fell victim to Camille. Pine trees were blown down in forests nearly 70 miles inland. Roofs were torn from barracks at Camp Shelby, an Army base located more than 65 miles from the coast line.

Wind Speeds and Tides. Based on wind speeds measured at reconnaissance flight levels and measured surface pressure, maximum surface winds reached 201.5 miles per hour near the center of Camille on August 17. As the storm moved inland, many of the recording instruments were damaged or destroyed. The highest actual wind reading was taken on a drilling rig recorder, located about 15 miles from the storm's center, which registered a gust of 172 miles per hour. An Air National Guard Weather flight located at Gulfport Municipal Airport estimated sustained winds at over 100 miles per hour with gusts ranging between 150 to 200 miles per hour. Keesler Air Force Base in Biloxi measured winds at 81 miles per hour with gusts up to 129 miles per hour.

In Pascagoula, sustained winds of 81 miles per hour were recorded at a shipyard, while a local radio station reported winds at 104 miles per hour before it was knocked off the air. Winds west of Camille's center were lower than those extending east. Although Lakefront Airport reported sustained winds of 87 miles per hour with gusts of 109 miles per hour, winds at New Orleans generally ranged from 40 to 60 miles per hour with gusts up to 85 miles per hour. On the other hand, eastern portions of St. Tammany and Washington Parishes were raked by winds estimated at well over 100 miles per hour. As Camille moved ashore, sustained hurricane-force winds were generally confined to the storm's center, extending east of New Orleans to Pascagoula, with gusts reaching from New Orleans to Mobile Bay.

Enormous tidal surges marked Camille's arrival. The small towns of Pass Christian, Bay St. Louis, and Waveland were all but destroyed by a giant wave generated by the storm's backlash. Record-breaking tide levels were recorded from Waveland to Biloxi. Tides in some areas were measured up to 24 feet. Generally, they ran from about 15 to 22 feet above normal. The storm generated tides as high as 3 to 5 feet above normal as far away as Apalachicola, Florida. West of the storm's center, tides ranged from about 10 to 15 feet above normal but then dropped off substantially, running only 3 to 4 feet above normal west of the Mississippi. Grand Isle, located only 60 miles west of the hurricane, reported a tide of 3.6 feet.

The Death Toll and Aftereffects. Many of those who perished in the surge were found lashed together, usually family members or husbands and wives who were attempting to survive the rising waters. Every home in Pass Christian, a town of 4,000 people, was damaged. Nearly 100 bodies were discovered in the debris, including all 13 members of one family. At a local high school where residents had gathered, rescuers found a cluster of parents holding their children overhead to protect them from the raging floodwaters below. Generally, buildings located on hills of about 20 feet survived the high winds and storm surge, while structures situated around the 10-foot level were overwhelmed. As the winds diminished, National Guard troops in amphibious vehicles rushed in to rescue survivors clinging to trees and remnants of houses.

All together, 143 people were killed along the coast from Louisiana to Alabama. The storm also took a toll on fish and wildlife, especially in the estuary region lying east of the Mississippi River. Many deer and muskrats were killed. Only 40 to 50 of a deer herd of 500 roaming the area were believed to have survived. Millions of fish were killed, as were some shrimp, and oyster seedbeds located in the bays and inlets received considerable damage from debris deposited on them during the storm.

The storm caused little intrusion of saltwater into the lower reaches of the Mississippi River. Samples taken at the water supply intakes at New Orleans and Port Sulphur did not reveal any significant increases in salinity, though some locations along the eastern Louisiana coast did experience brief periods of additional salinity during Camille's passage.

Camille dealt a severe blow to the region's commercial shipping industry. A surveyor noted that 24 vessels, ranging from tugs to freighters, were found aground. Among the boats was the container ship *Mormacsun,* which only recently had been launched and was being outfitted at a shipyard when its mooring lines snapped, driving it aground. The storm caused the collision of 2 vessels set adrift in the waters, the 4,459-ton Greek freighter *Lion of Chaeronea* and the 10,648-ton U.S.-flagged *Windsor Victory.* Both ships suffered only minor damage. Three cargo ships in Gulfport harbor, the *Alamo Victory,* the *Hulda,* and the *Silver Hawk,* were severely damaged and washed ashore. A tug, the *Charleston,* in the process of towing the barge *City of Pensacola,* was in danger of sinking and had to be beached. Another victim, the 10,250-ton U.S.-flagged freighter *Venetia V,* docked in Mobile, was ripped from its moorings and set adrift.

The storm also inflicted severe damage on the area's petroleum industry, particularly in the offshore areas east of the Louisiana delta. Installations at South Pass, Main Pass, and Breton Sound were battered by the storm, as were facilities situated in the marshes and shallow bays, including Quarantine Bay, Cox Bay, and Black Bay. Two large oil slicks formed south of New Orleans, one a result of a leaking offshore well in Breton Sound, the other from a ruptured storage tank near the town of Venice in Plaquemines Parish. Because Venice was still under water from the high tides, the oil riding the top of the water lapped at the inundated houses and other buildings.

Facilities located west of the Mississippi River fared better, receiving only light damage. At least 4,000 oil wells, stretching from the Mississippi Delta to the St. Bernard Parish line, representing close to 10 percent of Louisiana's wells, were shut down and 3,000 employees evacuated prior to the storm's arrival. As a result of the precautionary measures, there were no reported injuries to petroleum industry personnel, despite direct hits on the facilities. Altogether, Camille destroyed 4 platforms, 3 drilling rigs, and 7 wells. In addition, 2 platforms, 7 drilling rigs, and a well suffered heavy damage.

An aerial survey by the U.S. Forest Service of 14 counties in southern Mississippi indicated that nearly 1.9 million acres of commercial forest land sustained damage. The storm completely defoliated some of the area's hardwood forests, with the pine forests suffering somewhat less damage. Agricultural and timber losses in Louisiana included 8,000 cattle and 150,000 orange trees in Plaquemines Parish, oyster beds in Plaquemines and St. Bernard Parishes, and over $40 million in damages to tung oil trees and timber in St. Tammany and Washington Parishes.

Camille Moves Inland. As Camille moved inland across Mississippi, its strength diminished, and on

August 18 it was downgraded to a tropical storm. By the time it reached the northern Mississippi border, it had been downgraded to a depression, though its rainy core remained surprisingly intact and its eye clearly visible on satellite photographs after more than a day over land. Its remnants finally merged with a moisture-filled air mass to produce record amounts of rainfall, in some cases more than 25 inches, throughout Tennessee, Kentucky, and Virginia. As it moved through West Virginia, the storm deposited nearly 5 inches of rain in the southern portions of the state.

The combination of weather factors produced rainfall amounts that rank with other record rainfalls throughout the world. Some amounts exceeded 25 inches, and totals in excess of 4 inches fell in an eight-hour period over a region 30 to 40 miles wide and 120 miles long. A U.S. Army Corps of Engineers' study later underscored the improbability of the rainfall amounts in Nelson County, Virginia, which totaled 27 inches within eight hours. The study concluded the probable maximum rainfall that was possible for the area was 28 inches in six hours and 31 inches in twelve hours. An unofficial 31-inch total that was recorded is believed by meteorologists to represent the probable maximum rainfall to be theoretically possible for Virginia during this period of the year.

As a measure of the storm's uniqueness, it is estimated that rainfalls of this magnitude occur only once every thousand years. Ironically, a severe drought had plagued Mississippi, Tennessee, and Kentucky for much of the summer before Camille's arrival, reducing soil moisture content far below normal levels. As a result, pasture conditions and crops were in poor shape, and though the rains alleviated some of the conditions, they were too late to overcome much of the drought damage.

Virginia experienced what many authorities considered was one of the worst natural disasters in the state's history. Thousands of families in the mountainous sections of west-central Virginia were left homeless by rains of 10 inches or more, as walls of water washed down mountain slopes and through countless homes, businesses, and industries located in valley communities. Many of the residents of the tiny mountain towns and hamlets were asleep when the floodwaters struck. The swollen streams and landslides precipitated by the torrential rains uprooted trees and hurled them down the mountainsides with enough force to smash houses and overturn automobiles. Entire families were swept away by the waters, while others climbed onto trees and roofs and waited until rescue helicopters could reach them.

In some areas whole sections of mountainside tumbled down like mudslides, dumping tons of silt on houses and their occupants. The entire downtown area of Glasgow, Virginia, was inundated by over 14 feet of water, which flooded nearly 75 percent of its homes. Among the hardest hit regions was Buena Vista, Virginia, located at the foot of the Blue Ridge Mountains, where some buildings stood 30 feet underwater. In Louisa County, an earthen dam broke, collapsing a 500-acre human-made lake.

Camille's remnants washed out close to 200 miles of primary and secondary roads and damaged or destroyed 133 bridges in Virginia, 92 of which were located in Nelson County. Route 29 between Amherst and Charlottesville suffered severe damage, with 5 major washouts and 30 landslides. At one point during the storm, only one highway crossing the state remained open for its entire length. The James River, a placid stream that normally runs 100 feet to a few hundred yards wide above Richmond, turned into a sprawling wet plain a mile wide in places. More than 80 bridges spanning major highways and secondary roads were washed away by the rampaging waters. Railroad routes throughout the state fared little better, as several railroad bridges were destroyed and long stretches of track put out of operation.

Camille regained tropical storm status when it crossed back into the North Atlantic but dissipated when it was absorbed by a cold front as it moved about 175 miles southeast of Cape Race, Newfoundland. Based on its path of destruction, Hurricane Camille ranks as one of the most devastating storms that struck the U.S. mainland in the twentieth century.

William Hoffman

For Further Information:

"Hurricane Camille." *Weatherwise*, July/August, 1999, 28-31.

Longshore, David. *Encyclopedia of Hurricanes, Typhoons, and Cyclones*. New York: Facts on File, 1998.

Report on Hurricane Camille 14-22 August 1969. New Orleans: U.S. Army Corps of Engineers, May, 1970.

U.S. Environmental Data Service. "Hurricane Camille." *Climatological Data: National Summary*, 1969, 451-475.

1970: East Pakistan

Cyclone
Date: November 12-13, 1970
Place: Ganges Delta and East Pakistan (now Bangladesh)
Speed: More than 100 miles per hour
Result: 300,000-500,000 dead, 600,000 homeless

On November 13, 1970, only minutes after midnight, after being tracked by satellite and radar from its birth a thousand miles to the south some two and a half days earlier, a massive cyclone struck the coastal region of East Pakistan (now Bangladesh). Laying waste to the delta formed by the Ganges and Brahmaputra Rivers, this cyclone wiped away entire villages, drowned an incalculable number of Bengalis, and compromised the agricultural production of the region. The response of the government of Pakistan, from its capital some 2,000 miles away, was perceived by the Bengalis of East Pakistan to be inadequate in substance and spirit. In addition to causing enormous physical damage, the cyclone and its aftermath contributed to the growing rift between the people of East Pakistan and the government that ruled them, thereby acting as a catalyst in the formation of the nation of Bangladesh the following year.

The Geography. The particular geography of this delta, where the Ganges and Brahmaputra Rivers meet and pour out into the Bay of Bengal after their long journeys from the Himalayas in the north, is both a blessing and a curse. The geography both makes the delta extremely productive and leaves it susceptible to destructive and all-too-frequent cyclones. This is the largest delta in the world, composed of a broad, low-lying, alluvial plain—interlaced with a network of smaller rivers, canals, swamps, and marshes—and, further downriver, a jumble of alluvial islands lying barely above sea level. The soils of this region are renewed every year during monsoon season, when the rivers, swollen with meltwater from the Himalayas and excess rainwater, overflow their banks and spread their nutrient-rich sediment over the plains and islands. This process makes the delta soils rich enough to support three harvests per year, providing a large percentage of the foodstuffs necessary to feed the country, one of the most densely populated on earth. As an area of low-lying islands and plains it is entirely defenseless, however, against flooding, especially that brought from the south by cyclone-driven storm surges.

The Ganges Delta is frequently visited by some of the most destructive cyclones on earth. In 1737, for example, a cyclone took the lives of at least 300,000 people. In 1991 another killed 200,000 people in Bangladesh. In numerous other years (there were eight cyclones in the 1960's) lesser cyclones have caused tens of thousands of fatalities. These cyclones are spawned every late spring and autumn north of the equator in the warm tropical waters of the Indian Ocean. The cyclones produced there are inherently no more powerful or intense than those produced in other regions of the world, but the geography of the Bay of Bengal in general, and of the Ganges Delta in particular, makes the cyclones especially destructive. The Bay of Bengal, shaped like a funnel, forces the cyclones, as they move north toward the Ganges Delta—which lies exactly at the northernmost point of the bay—into an increasingly narrower area, thereby concentrating the energy of the cyclone and the storm surge produced underneath.

The Cyclone. The cyclone that caused such havoc in East Pakistan in the autumn of 1970 was first identified by satellite at 9 A.M. on November 10 as a low-pressure area over the Indian Ocean, southeast of Madras, India, a coastal city on the western shores of the Bay of Bengal, and therefore some 1,000 miles to the south of East Pakistan. Moving northward, the low-pressure area evolved into a cyclonic storm with wind velocities of 55 miles per hour. The following morning the storm had reached a point some 650 miles south of Chittagong, East Pakistan's second-largest city and most important port, located just east of the Ganges Delta.

The storm progressed northward into the increasingly narrow, funnel-like Bay of Bengal, its winds now at hurricane force of 75 miles per hour. The accelerating winds and low-pressure area surrounding the eye of every cyclone tend to raise the water level of the ocean underneath by 1 or 2 feet, providing the basis of the storm surge associated with these storms. The approach of a cyclone to a coast forces the storm surge underneath into increasingly shallower water, thereby bringing it to ever-greater heights above normal sea level. This phenomenon is made worse at the top of the Bay of Bengal, where the coast nearly encircles the oncoming cyclone, concentrating, and hence raising, the storm surge even higher. Finally, as the cyclone strikes the very northern tip of the bay, its winds literally drive the storm surge into the extremely shallow water of the Ganges Delta and up and over its low-lying islands and plains.

As this particular hurricane made landfall just after midnight on November 13, 1970, it brought to the delta winds over 100 miles per hour and a storm surge with waves that measured up to 30 feet high. It did so at the worst possible moment: high tide, ensuring swift and sure destruction. The wind-driven storm surge literally flowed over the islands, removing everything in its path. Many islands were denuded of houses, crops, animals, and people. The storm surge, combined with the high tide and the quickly overflowing rivers—swollen with the torrents of rain delivered upriver by the cyclone—brought floodwaters up to 30 feet high in some places.

Fully half of the 242 square miles of Hatia Island remained under 20 feet of water for eight hours. In the trees, above the maximum floodwater line, clung many of the survivors, those delta residents fast enough and strong enough to latch onto trees and climb higher and higher as the waters continued to rise. Below them, at floodwater level, caught in the same trees, floated the corpses of drowned animals and individuals who did not reach safety.

The death toll of Bengalis was set officially at 300,000. Unofficially, it was thought to be much higher—500,000 or even 1 million. Observers attributed the higher death toll to three factors. Once the relief operations were underway, an untold number of corpses were cremated at the place and time they were found in order to lessen the possibility of epidemics. The cyclone struck at harvest time, when the population of this rich agricultural region swells with an influx of migrant workers helping to bring in the harvest. Uncounted and unknown, a large number of these people were assumed to be drowned. Finally, many of those who survived the immediate devastation died soon after of hunger, diseases, or injuries.

While the geographical characteristics and tidal circumstances made for an especially devastating cyclone, the particular socioeconomic characteristics of East Pakistan made it even worse. East Pakistan had one of the highest population densities in the world. At the time of the cyclone, it measured more than 1,300 people per square mile. Under the best of circumstances, evacuating such a large concentration of people under threat of imminent natural disaster would be enormously difficult. East Pakistan possessed, moreover, neither a transportation network nor, even more basic, a warning and evacuation system adequate to the task.

Soon after the disaster it was noted that while Calcutta Radio had reported from India about the cyclone and issued repeated emergency bulletins for hours before its arrival, Dhaka Radio—the only source of information for those living on the distant offshore islands of the Ganges Delta—had made only general reference to an arriving storm, failing to stress to its listeners the danger on the horizon. Having no radio at all, many other islands and villages received no news or warning whatsoever and were thus caught completely by surprise.

The Aftermath. For those who did survive the cyclone and its aftermath, daily life and long-term reconstruction alike would be enormously difficult. It was estimated that the cyclone and its storm surge destroyed the houses of 85 percent of the families in the affected region, leaving some 600,000 survivors homeless. The storm also seriously damaged the agricultural sector of the region, depleting food supplies throughout the country. Hundreds of fishing and transport vessels, including one freighter weighing over 150 tons, were washed inland or otherwise destroyed. Over 1 million head of livestock were drowned. At least 1.1 million acres of rice paddies, holding an estimated 800,000 tons of grain, were destroyed. The storm also incapacitated some 65 percent of East Pakistan's coastal fisheries, thereby seriously compromising the country's most important source of protein for years to come.

A disaster of this magnitude visited upon a poor region such as East Pakistan required enormous immediate and long-term relief, necessitating both international aid and the concerted efforts of the Pakistani government. Within less than a month some $50 million of relief supplies had been delivered to East Pakistan, contributed by foreign governments, international organizations, and private volunteer agencies. The League of Red Cross Societies expected, however, that East Pakistan would need direct foreign assistance at least until April of 1971.

The World Bank had also devised a long-term reconstruction plan to the amount of $185 million, to be administered by governmental authorities with the advice of World Bank specialists. The delivery and distribution of such aid, especially emergency relief, was not without problems. The floodwaters, teeming with decaying corpses and excrement, made perfect breeding grounds for typhoid and cholera, thereby hindering the establishment and staffing of distribution stations.

The real relief problems were human-made and contributed to problems between East Pakistan and the central Pakistani government in Karachi. Before the end of the month of November, East Pakistani political and social leaders began to accuse the governing authorities of "gross neglect, callous inattention, and utter indifference" to the suffering of the survivors of the cyclone; this criticism was not unwarranted. Two days before that announcement the League of Red Cross Societies had decided to postpone further delivery of aid because of the increasingly large stockpiles of relief supplies that remained in Dhaka, the capital of East Pakistan, awaiting final distribution. A team of Norwegian doctors and nurses reported that it had been idle for two days, still waiting for instructions from the governmental authorities.

The relief effort of the government of Pakistan itself, from its capital in Karachi, over 2,000 miles away on the other side of India, was perceived to be slow and insufficient. Only after the embarrassment of international pressure and publicity did the government of Pakistan respond to the plight of the East Pakistanis. Meanwhile, people continued to die of starvation and disease by the tens of thousands, and refugees continued to stream across the border into the already overcrowded Indian city of Calcutta.

Two days after the disaster, General Agha Mohammad Yahya Khan, the commander in chief of the armed forces and effective ruler of Pakistan, which at the time was under martial law, visited Dhaka briefly after a visit to Beijing. He left the next day: The people of East Pakistan and their political leaders perceived this as evidence of official indifference to their suffering. Sheikh Mujibur Rahman, the father of modern Bangladesh, commented from jail, "West Pakistan has a bumper wheat crop, but the first shipment of food grain to reach us is from abroad. . . . We have a large army, but it is left to the British Marines to bury our dead."

On December 7, 1970, less than a month after the cyclone struck the Ganges Delta, elections for the Pakistani National Assembly were held; for the first time East and West Pakistanis would elect their representatives directly. The results were telling; the Awami League, the political party calling for the independence of East Pakistan, won 160 out of 162 seats allotted to East Pakistan. In April of 1971, East Pakistan would rename itself Bangladesh and declare independence. By December, after civil war and the defeat of the Pakistani army in Bangladesh by the army of India, Bangladesh became recognized as an independent nation.

Rosa Alvarez Ulloa

For Further Information:

Cornell, James. "Cyclones: Hurricanes and Typhoons." *The Great International Disaster Book.* New York: Charles Scribner's Sons, 1976.

Frazier, Kendrick. "Hurricanes." In *The Violent Face of Nature: Severe Phenomena and Natural Disasters.* New York: William Morrow, 1979.

Heitzman, James, and Robert Worden. *Bangladesh: A Country Study.* 2d ed. Area Handbook Series DA Pam 550-175. Washington, D.C.: Government Printing Office, 1989.

Whittow, John. "High Winds." *Disasters: The Anatomy of Environmental Hazards.* Athens: University of Georgia Press, 1979.

1972: Hurricane Agnes

Date: June 21-23, 1972
Place: From Florida to New York
Classification: Category 1
Result: 122 dead, 116,000 homes destroyed, extensive flooding, $3 billion in damage

Although not a powerful storm, Hurricane Agnes inundated the Atlantic coast with torrential rains. Forming as a tropical depression over Mexico's Yucatán Peninsula, Agnes neared Cuba before turning north. Fueled by the warm Gulf of Mexico water, the tropical depression officially attained hurricane status by June 18, 1972. Agnes's low wind speeds resulted in a Category 1 hurricane rating, which it retained throughout its existence.

Hurricane Agnes went ashore near Apalachicola, Florida, causing $10 million in damage there. Creeping through Florida, Georgia, and the Carolinas, Agnes spawned at least 17 tornadoes. Several inches of rain soaked those southern states. In the Blue Ridge Mountains, Agnes's 10-inch rains triggered flash floods. Meteorologists estimate that Agnes dumped 28 trillion gallons of water on the mid-Atlantic region. During the storm, an anxious President Richard M. Nixon, recently notified of the Watergate break-in, could not fly to Washington, D.C., because of the weather.

From June 20 to 23, Agnes stagnated over Pennsylvania and New York, dumping more than 15 inches of rain, which overwhelmed dams on the Susquehanna and Genesee Rivers. Floodwaters swelled in nearby towns, submerging steel plants, houses, churches, and other structures. Displaced rats attacked people. Records indicate 122 people died because of Hurricane Agnes, and federal relief helped pay for some of the $3 billion damage.

Elizabeth D. Schafer

For Further Information:

Bailey, James F., J. L. Patterson, and J. L. H. Paulhus. *Hurricane Agnes Rainfall and Floods, June-July 1972.* Washington, D.C.: U.S. Government Printing Office, 1975.

U.S. Congress. *Aftermath of Hurricane Agnes: Field Hearing Before the Subcommittee on Policy Research and Insurance of the Committee on Banking, Finance, and Urban Affairs.* Washington, D.C.: U.S. Government Printing Office, 1990.

Ward, Kaari, ed. *Great Disasters: Dramatic True Stories of Nature's Awesome Powers.* Pleasantville, N.Y.: Reader's Digest, 1989.

1974: Hurricane Fifi

Date: September 14-22, 1974
Place: Honduras, Belize, Guatemala, and Mexico
Classification: Category 3
Result: 5,000 dead, 100,000 homeless, $500 million in damage

On September 14, 1974, a storm known as Tropical Depression Number 10 developed west of Guadeloupe. Officially declared a hurricane on September 17, Hurricane Fifi attained 74-mile-per-hour winds and 988-millibar pressure. Switching direction to east-southeast, Fifi prompted meteorologists to warn of strikes in Honduras and possibly Nicaragua, but no evacuations were implemented by those countries.

Gaining energy as it neared Central America, Hurricane Fifi's winds increased to 98 miles per hour, and a wall of rain descended from its clouds. Fifi struck the Honduran coast with 132-mile-per-hour winds and 971-millibar pressure on the early evening of September 18, flattening two towns, Trujillo and La Ceiba. Floodwaters and wind destroyed 182 villages and the country's banana crop. Many people died while escaping in buses that were washed into gorges. In twelve hours, almost 1,500 people were killed.

Fifi then gusted almost full-strength into Belize at noon on September 19, damaging several hundred buildings. At least 200 people drowned when Fifi passed through Guatemala. Rain from Fifi caused additional landslides in Honduras. Approximately 20 inches of rain caused mud to destroy Choloma, a town in northern Honduras, and 2,800 residents disappeared. Traveling to the Pacific Ocean on September 21, Fifi was renamed Tropical Storm Orlene, becoming the fourth North Atlantic hurricane to attain that status. Relief workers struggled to feed the 100,000 starving homeless and to bury or burn Fifi's dead to prevent epidemics, while government officials protested charges they had stolen aid sent by other countries.

Elizabeth D. Schafer

For Further Information:

"Honduras Hurricane Toll Reported to Reach 5,000; Floods Slow Relief Work." *The New York Times*, September 23, 1974, p. 1.

"Relief Is Slow in Reaching the Victims of Honduran Hurricane." *The New York Times*, September 25, 1974, p. 2.

Riding, Alan. "Choloma: Impoverished Little Town That Perished Under a Wall of Mud." *The New York Times*, September 23, 1974, p. 22.

1974: Cyclone Tracy

Date: December 24, 1974
Place: Darwin, Australia
Result: 50 dead, town destroyed

Cyclone Tracy formed on December 20, 1974, in the Arafura Sea, 435 miles (700 kilometers) northeast of Darwin, Australia. It struck Darwin on December 24 with gale-force winds and a radius of 33 miles (50 kilometers); winds were clocked at 186 miles per hour. The eye remained above the city's airport and northern suburbs for most of the duration.

Almost the entire city of Darwin was touched by the storm, resulting in 70 percent of the homes being destroyed or severely damaged. At least 49 deaths were reported as a result of the storm.

The threat of disease and the loss of all communication services caused mass evacuation of the population; about 25,000 people left the city soon after the storm. Rescue efforts commenced Christmas night, with defense forces assisting in the cleanup process. Between 1975 and 1979 more than 2,500 homes and buildings were reconstructed in Darwin.

Lauren Mitchell

For Further Information:

"Cyclone Tracy, Darwin." National Archives of Australia. http://www.naa.gov.au/RESEARCH/FACTSHET/FS176.html.

Marshall, Richard D. *Engineering Aspects of Cyclone Tracy, Darwin, Australia, 1974.* Washington, D.C.: U.S. Department of Commerce, National Bureau of Standards, 1976.

1976: Hurricane Belle

Date: August 8-10, 1976
Place: U.S. East Coast
Classification: Category 1
Result: 12 dead, $23.5 million in damage

Forming northeast of the Bahamas on August 8, 1976, Hurricane Belle turned toward the United States East Coast because of a high-pressure system. Strengthening to a Category 3 hurricane as it approached North Carolina, Belle attained 111-mile-per-hour winds and 964 millibars of pressure. Although Belle did not hit North Carolina's Outer Banks, the hurricane caused a 4-foot surge that created flash floods and eroded beaches.

Hurricane Belle alternated between moving north and moving northeast up the coast. Atlantic City, New Jersey, sustained $4.5 million in damage to its resorts and boardwalk from the hurricane. Three people died in car accidents caused by hurricane conditions, and 150,000 people in New Jersey temporarily lost electric power when the hurricane snapped poles and wires.

Losing power over the colder Atlantic Ocean water, Belle, at that time a Category 1 hurricane, struck Long Island on August 10. Belle's 90-mile-per-hour winds damaged cottages and buildings, and 1 man was killed when struck by a falling tree. Power service was interrupted to 275,000 Long Island residents; that island suffered $8 to $9 million in damage.

Hurricane Belle moved into New England during the evening of August 10, decimating 20 percent of Connecticut's apple harvest, worth $4 million. The hurricane caused $2.5 million in destruction in Vermont, harming especially its dairy and timber industries. Two people died in flash floods in that state.

Elizabeth D. Schafer

For Further Information:

"Long Island Evacuees Return to Their Homes After Hurricane as Cleanup Begins." *The New York Times*, August 11, 1976, p. 1.

Thomas, Robert, Jr. "Hurricane Sweeps Across L.I.,

Goes on to Pound Connecticut; Jersey Escapes Brunt of Storm." *The New York Times*, August 10, 1976, p. 1.

1979: Hurricane David

Date: August 30-September 7, 1979
Place: Dominican Republic, Puerto Rico, and the U.S. South
Classification: Category 4
Result: 2,068 dead, 60,000 homeless, hundreds of millions of dollars in damage

A Cape Verde hurricane, David began on August 28, 1979, almost 500 miles west of Senegal. Within two days, David was declared a hurricane that had 138-mile-per-hour winds and 945-millibar pressure when it struck Dominica. David destroyed the capital city of Roseau, and its 12-foot storm surge swept away coastal communities; 37 people died, and 60,000 lost their homes.

Returning to the Caribbean Sea late on August 30, David strengthened quickly, dropping to 933 millibars pressure and reaching 150-mile-per-hour winds. As a Category 4 hurricane, David headed northwest toward the Dominican Republic. American Civil Defense officials warned the Dominican Republic's government to initiate evacuation. Unfortunately, people were sheltered on hillsides, where they later died during mudslides. Before noon on August 31, Hurricane David hit the Dominican Republic. The Yaque del Norte River raced through a church in Padre Las Casas, where 438 refugees tied themselves together to attempt to find higher ground but were washed away by floodwaters when a dike broke.

By September 1, a weakened David passed over the Bahamas, causing flooding but no deaths. David hit Florida on September 3, causing $60 million in insurance claims. Returning to the ocean, the hurricane next landed near Charleston, South Carolina, and nearby resort areas. Dissipating into rainstorms from Virginia to New York, David caused power outages and flash flooding.

Elizabeth D. Schafer

For Further Information:

Grody, Norman C., and William C. Shen. *Observations of Hurricane David (1979) Using the Microwave Sounding Unit.* Washington, D.C.: National Oceanic and Atmospheric Administration, 1982.
McFadden, Robert D. "Dominicans Report 400 Killed by Hurricane and Flooding; Residents Flee Florida Keys." *The New York Times*, September 3, 1979, p. A1.
Raines, Howell. "Hurricane Batters the Florida Coast; Damage Widespread." *The New York Times*, September 4, 1979, p. A1.

1979: Hurricane Frederic

Date: September 7-14, 1979
Place: Alabama; also Mississippi and Florida
Classification: Category 3
Result: 8 dead, $1.7 billion in damage

One week after Hurricane David swept through the Caribbean, Hurricane Frederic formed over the Gulf of Mexico almost 50 miles north of Cuba on September 7, 1979. While Hurricane David inundated Florida and the Carolinas, Frederic became a tropical storm with 49-mile-per-hour winds and 1,000-millibar pressure. Within one day, Frederic matured into a Category 1 hurricane, attaining 77-mile-per-hour winds. By sunrise on September 12, Frederic had 145-mile-per-hour winds, qualifying it as a Category 4 hurricane. However, it was downgraded to Category 3 before it reached land.

Sweeping across Dauphin Island off the Alabama coast, Frederic moved into nearby Mobile Bay. At least 12,000 structures in Mobile were damaged, boats were washed aground, and shipyards in Mississippi suffered from wind and water. Frederic tore apart trees and caused power outages and cessation of telephone and water services to 250,000 residences. Approximately 8 inches of rain accompanied the hurricane, flooding parts of Mobile. Surges 20 feet high eroded a 100-mile area along the Alabama, Florida, and Mississippi coasts. In Alabama, 8 people died during Hurricane Frederic because of drowning, car wrecks, and collapsed buildings. Evacuation fortunately prevented higher death tolls. More than $1.7 billion worth of insurance claims were filed, making Frederic the most costly hurricane at that time.

Elizabeth D. Schafer

For Further Information:

Ellis, Margaret B. *A Wind Called Frederic: A Historical*

Photographic Documentation. Mobile, Ala.: M & A Studios, 1979.

McCoy, Lee. *Hurricane Frederic: September 12, 1979, an Uninvited Mobile Guest.* Mobile, Ala.: Lee McCoy, 1981.

Parker, Douglas W. *Hurricane Frederic: Post Disaster Report: 30 August-14 September 1979.* Mobile, Ala.: U.S. Army Corps of Engineers, Mobile District, 1981.

Winder, Jesse R., ed. *To Save an Island.* Foley, Ala.: Liberty Marketing, 1979. With aerial photography by John Hancock.

1980: Hurricane Allen

Date: August 1-11, 1980
Place: The Caribbean, Mexico, and Texas
Classification: Category 3-5
Result: 272 dead, $1 billion in damage

In August, 1980, meteorologists designated Hurricane Allen the second strongest Atlantic hurricane recorded in modern history at that time. A Labor Day 1935 hurricane that struck the Florida Keys was considered the most powerful hurricane to have originated in the Atlantic. Hurricane Allen replaced 1969's Hurricane Camille in the number-two position and wreaked such immense devastation that it served as a standard by which to compare other hurricane damage until Hurricane Gilbert surpassed Allen in 1988.

A Cape Verde storm, Hurricane Allen, the first hurricane of the season, began as a tropical disturbance on August 1, 1980, off the coast of North Africa. Allen quickly moved west, intensifying in strength and energy over the open sea. Allen's pressure continued to fall as it neared the Caribbean, where it became a tropical depression 200 miles east of Barbados. The tepid Caribbean Sea enabled the storm to attain Category 5 hurricane winds three times in cycles of strengthening and weakening during its trek toward Mexico. By the time it made landfall in the United States, however, Allen was a Category 3 hurricane.

On August 3, meteorologists flew a reconnaissance airplane into Hurricane Allen's eye and recorded its barometric pressure at 922 millibars. The scientists also projected that Hurricane Allen's winds could reach almost 200 miles per hour and warned that it might be the most severe hurricane of the twentieth century. Residents of Barbados, which had last endured a hurricane in 1955, began preparing for the storm. Lord Carrington, the British foreign secretary, left the island several hours before the hurricane arrived on August 4. As Hurricane Allen's 130-mile-per-hour winds pummeled the island, the government's radio station went off the air, and an 11-foot surge flooded resort beaches. Two hurricane-related deaths were reported.

The hurricane's eye moved north of Barbados and south of St. Lucia, where that island's banana plantations were demolished. More than 100 houses were destroyed. Waves swept boats to sea, and 160-mile-per-hour winds ripped the roof off the Victoria Hospital in the capital city of Castries. During the storm 16 people died in St. Lucia, and 30,000 of the island's 115,000 population evacuated to refugee centers. Allen caused an estimated $30 million of damage in St. Lucia.

Hurricane Allen passed south of Puerto Rico on August 4. Its pressure dropped to 911 millibars the next day as it approached Haiti, where 120-mile-per-hour winds capsized boats in Port au Prince harbor. Torrential rains flooded coffee fields and villages. Approximately 220 Haitians died in flash floods; many of the bodies were located later. The prevalence of mud and stick housing contributed to the high mortality rate.

Hurricane Allen hit Jamaica on August 6 with 100-mile-per-hour winds. Resort hotels at Port Maria were inundated with as much as 5 feet of water, and waves dragged people into the sea. Winds damaged citrus orchards. Floodwater washed out bridges, and several people were electrocuted by submerged power lines; 8 people died in Jamaica as a result of the hurricane. Three casualties were reported in the Dominican Republic and 1 in Guadeloupe.

At least 210,000 Cubans were evacuated from low elevations before the hurricane passed that island, causing deaths. Heading west over the Cayman Islands toward Mexico, Hurricane Allen strengthened over the Gulf of Mexico's warm water. On August 7, Allen's pressure was 899 millibars, just 7 millibars greater than the disastrous 1935 Florida hurricane. Mexican resorts evacuated tourists, but Hurricane Allen's winds caused the most damage in the uninhabited jungle of the Yucatán Peninsula.

Weakening and slowing as it moved northwest toward Texas, Hurricane Allen stalled, then struck

South Padre Island on August 9. Before Allen reached the Texas coast, meteorologists projected that it would affect the area stretching from Brownsville to Corpus Christi and urged evacuation of low-lying areas. Thirteen people died when a helicopter crashed while airlifting oil company personnel from a deep-sea drilling rig. Two people died and 2 were missing after a rig overturned while being towed to harbor from a Louisiana shipping channel. Texas officials approved delaying August elections in forty-nine counties, the first time such a state law was enacted because of a hurricane. Also, border guards stationed at Matamoros, Mexico, and Brownsville, Texas, relaxed regulations regarding the entry of Mexican nationals seeking refuge from Hurricane Allen.

Most intense along the southern Texas Gulf coast, Hurricane Allen's 185-mile-per-hour winds totaled $55 million damage in Texas. Two people drowned, and 2 others died of heart attacks because of the storm. The hurricane wiped out the fishing town of Port Mansfield, which had been completely evacuated, and the 4,000-foot-long seawall at Mustang Island was washed away. Brownsville was described as a ghost town after 200,000 people evacuated that city. High tides contaminated water supplies, causing freshwater shortages. At Corpus Christi, Allen's 160-mile-per-hour winds resulted in some minor destruction. The 10-foot surge was the highest recorded in fifty years. Two Liberian tankers carrying crude oil were grounded.

Hurricane Allen did not cause as much damage in Texas as forecasters had feared. Tornadoes and as much as 20 inches of rain soaked the Rio Grande Valley, ruining poorly built dwellings and citrus and cotton crops. Passing over vast open acreage such as the King Ranch, the remnants of Hurricane Allen disappeared during rainstorms in Mexico by August 11.

Hurricane Allen caused an estimated $1 billion worth of damage and 272 deaths in 8 countries. Meteorologists note Hurricane Allen's significance was its minimum recorded pressure. They used data collected from Hurricane Allen to model storm surges. The Texas coast did not experience another hurricane until Alicia hit three years later on August 13, 1983. Because Hurricane Allen was considered the most dangerous Caribbean hurricane at the time, "Allen" was retired from the list of hurricane names.

Elizabeth D. Schafer

For Further Information:

Crewdson, John M. "Storm Billed as a Tiger Turned out to Be a Pussycat." *The New York Times*, August 11, 1980, p. D8.

Ho, Francis P., and John F. Miller. *Pertinent Meteorological Data for Hurricane Allen of 1980.* Silver Spring, Md.: National Weather Service, 1983.

"Hurricane with 170-Miles per Hour Winds Heads for Jamaica." *The New York Times*, August 6, 1980, p. A8.

Stevens, William K. "Coast of Texas Is Whipped by Hurricane-Force Winds." *The New York Times*, August 10, 1980, p. A1.

1988: Hurricane Gilbert

Date: September 12-17, 1988
Place: Jamaica; Yucatán Peninsula, Tamaulipas, and Nuevo León, Mexico
Classification: Category 5
Speed: Maximum sustained winds of 175 miles per hour on the ground and 200 miles per hour in the air
Result: 260 dead, over $10 billion in damage

On September 10, 1988, located about 225 miles southeast of the Dominican Republic, Gilbert officially became a hurricane. At its peak, it had maximum sustained winds at ground level of 175 miles per hour and winds of 200 miles per hour in the atmosphere. With barometric pressure plunging to 26.13 inches, the lowest recorded at that time, Gilbert demonstrated the power of a Category 5 storm as it threatened the Caribbean and Gulf of Mexico. Narrowly missing Puerto Rico, the Dominican Republic, and Haiti, Gilbert headed directly for Jamaica.

Traveling over the island on September 12, 1988, Gilbert left 500,000 people out of a total population of 2.1 million homeless, and it damaged or destroyed 80 percent of the country's homes. In particular, high winds ripped the tin roofs off both shanties and mansions and left all the residents of the island without electricity. Gilbert's eye, at 40 miles wide, nearly covered the entire island, which is only 50 miles wide at its widest part. The destruction hit every part of Jamaica. At Machioneal beach, Gilbert deposited 6 houses. Five of them lacked walls, and the sixth was missing its roof. At the Princess Margaret Hospital,

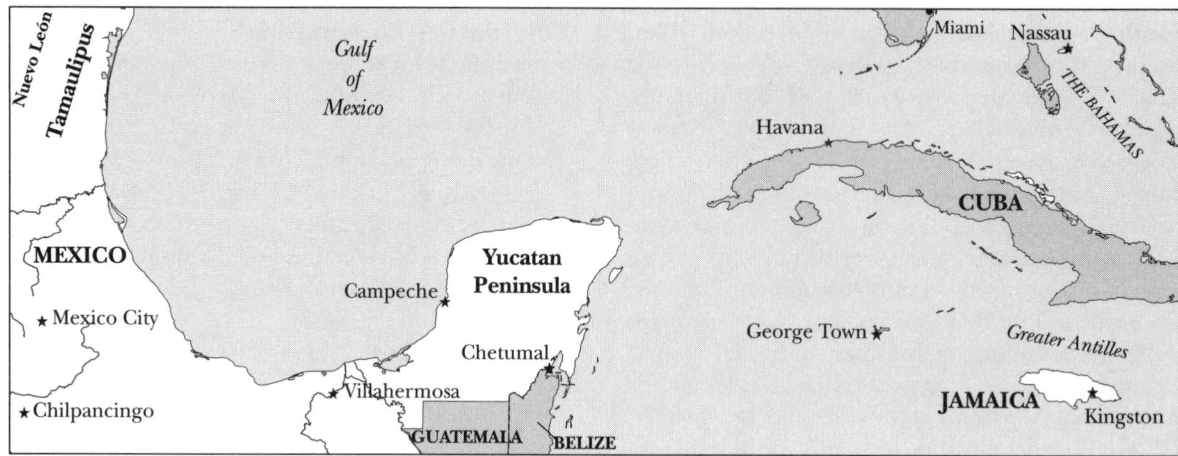

doctors, nurses, and orderlies evacuated patients from the third floor just minutes before its roof disappeared in the storm. Miraculously, no one was injured there.

When the storm moved away from Jamaica and into the warm waters of the Gulf of Mexico, it nearly doubled in strength to a Category 5 hurricane. Storm warnings went up from Biloxi, Mississippi, to Brownsville, Texas, and into Mexico. The entire Gulf coast region braced for Gilbert's next move. Offshore oil platforms halted operations when 5,000 workers were evacuated to safer locations. As the storm bore down on Mexico, centers of refuge in the Rio Grande Valley of Texas filled with people from both sides of the border seeking accommodations safe from the storm.

Hurricane Gilbert struck the Yucatán Peninsula at dawn on September 14, 1988, devastating the resort communities of Cancún and Cozumel. It destroyed the homes of 30,000 people in Yucatán State and another 10,000 in Campeche, on the west side of the peninsula, and ravaged the two major international airports at Cancún and Cozumel. Forty people died in the storm, and damage estimates began at $500 million. Half of the hotel rooms in the resorts in Cancún were ruined by Gilbert's winds and waters, and nearly half of the fishing fleet, the area's other major industry, was also obliterated.

In the worst single episode for the Yucatán Peninsula, winds seized a 300-foot-long Cuban freighter, called the *Portachernea-II*, 5 miles out in the Gulf of Mexico, and carried it into Cancún, where it met fishing boats riding at anchor to weather the storm. Gilbert hurled the vessel into the *Triunfador*, a 90-foot shrimp boat, and a string of other boats. The *Triunfador* capsized, killing 18 of the 28 people on board. Most of the people on the *Triunfador* had gone aboard the ship from smaller fishing vessels, hoping the larger one would be safer from the storm surge and hurricane-force winds. After smashing the *Triunfador*, the storm deposited the freighter alongside one of the resort hotels on the beach. Bodies from the wreck continued to wash ashore the following day.

As flooding and high tides swept across roads and bridges from Texas into Mexico, Gilbert's center struck 110 miles southwest of Brownsville, Texas, in a relatively unpopulated region in Tamaulipas and Nuevo León States, Mexico. Dropping more than 6 inches of rain, Gilbert flooded an area larger than the state of Colorado. Twenty tornadoes from Gilbert hit southern Texas, and 3 people in the United States died from the effects of the storm. Over 193,000 people in Mexico were left homeless. Flash floods from the high rainfall amounts stretched inland as the storm traveled northwest after entering Mexico, where the National Hurricane Center noted it would turn into an enormous rain system for the drought-ravaged farmlands of the American Midwest.

The worst of the flash floods took place in Monterrey, Tamaulipas, which is Mexico's third-largest city. After blocking other roads during an evacuation, police forced traffic from the main highway onto a river road alongside the normally dry Santa Catarina River. As rains poured onto the community, residents struggled to escape to higher ground. In what became known as the "detour of death," 4 buses full of refugees and several dozen cars were caught by a flash flood that swept along the banks of the Santa Catarina. Four members of the judical police drowned in a futile effort to save the almost 200 people carried away by the rampaging floodwaters. Jose Hinojosa Hernandez, a volunteer, died as he attempted to rescue people. Hernandez had earned a reputation as a Good Samaritan, appearing at other disaster sites and offering assistance to survivors. The flood claimed houses, bridges, and over 200 playgrounds and recreational areas that had filled the dry river banks prior to the torrential rainfall.

Jamaica had gone since 1951 without being struck by a powerful hurricane. Called the storm of the century, Gilbert was declared the worst natural disaster to hit Jamaican prime minister Edward P. G. Seaga's nation in the modern era. Seaga feared the effects of the hurricane would demolish the economic gains of the previous decade. Residents went without electricity, telephones, or running water, and property losses started at $500 million. Gilbert decimated the banana, citrus, coconut, coffee, sugar, marijuana, and winter vegetable crops, and widespread shortages of basic food led to severe inflation of prices. The tourist industry suffered as well, demonstrated when the island's largest hotel, the 558-room Holiday Inn at Rose Hall, closed for repairs.

Officially, 39 people died in Jamaica, not counting those shot for looting in the aftermath of the disaster. Mexico also witnessed horrible effects from Gilbert. The Santa Catarina flash flood produced the highest death toll, but people died as a result of flooding and storm surges in other areas. The tourist and fishing industries in the Yucatán were ravaged, while agriculture suffered the most in central Mexico.

James B. Seymour, Jr.

For Further Information:

Benesch, Susan. "Mexican Navy Heard SOS but Couldn't Save the Crew." *St. Petersburg Times*, September 20, 1988.

Branigin, William. "Death Toll in Mexico Reaches 136." *Washington Post*, September 20, 1988.

Layton, Leslie, et al. "Gulf Coast Gasps as Gilbert Gushes." *Engineering News-Record* 221, no. 12 (September 22, 1988): 13.

Moscoll, Philip. "Gilbert Gobbled Food of Future." *The Toronto Star*, September 23, 1988.

Oram, Roderick, and David Gardner. "Dissolving Gilbert Leaves Behind at Least 250 Dead." *Financial Times* (London), September 19, 1988.

Vick, Karl. "Jamaica Cleans up After Gilbert: Many Islanders Still Waiting for Hurricane Relief." *St. Petersburg Times*, September 21, 1988.

1989: Hurricane Hugo

Date: September 10-22, 1989

Place: The Caribbean, North Carolina, and South Carolina

Classification: Category 4-5

Speed: 136 miles per hour with gusts over 150 miles per hour

Result: At least 75 dead (41 in the United States), $10 billion in damage

Hurricane Hugo belongs to a class of major hurricanes called Cape Verde storms. These hurricanes usually originate from strong African disturbances that intensify as they move off the West African coast and produce a tropical depression as they pass close to the Cape Verde Islands. Other hurricanes that were Cape Verde storms include Hurricane Donna in 1960 and Hurricanes David and Frederic in 1979.

Hurricane Hugo began on September 9, 1989, as a cluster of thunderstorms off the coast of Africa. On September 10, 1989, it became a tropical depression when it was located approximately 125 miles south of the Cape Verde Islands. The depression continued on a due-west course over the eastern Atlantic Ocean for several days. By September 13 Hugo was located 1,200 miles east of the Leeward Islands and was moving westward at 20 miles per hour. The storm had gained sufficient strength and organization by this time to be classified as a hurricane by the National Hurricane Center, and its wind speeds were clocked in excess of 74 miles per hour. A day later, Hugo's winds had increased to 115 miles per hour. By September 15, sustained winds of 190 miles per hour were measured by reconnaissance aircraft at 1,500 feet. This made the hurricane a Category 5 storm on the Saffir-Simpson hurricane scale, the most intense category on the scale. Its central pressure was measured as low as 27.1 inches, which tied for the record minimum pressure in the Atlantic Ocean.

The Caribbean. Hurricane Hugo first reached land on September 16, when its eye passed over Guadeloupe. At that time its winds were estimated at

A sailboat that was washed ashore in Charleston, South Carolina, by Hurricane Hugo. (AP/Wide World Photos)

140 miles per hour. Its surface pressure was measured at 27.8 inches when its eye passed over the island. Approximately half of Pointe-à-Pitre, the capital city of Guadeloupe, was destroyed by the storm. In addition, 11 people were killed and 84 were injured. The neighboring island of Montserrat was also severely damaged. There, 10 people were killed and damages to property totaled $100 million.

Hurricane Hugo's next target was the Virgin Islands. On September 18, the eye of Hugo crossed the southwestern coastline of St. Croix. With maximum winds of 140 miles per hour the storm destroyed or damaged over 90 percent of the buildings on the island and left it without power, telephone service, or water. While the eye of the storm missed St. Thomas, the island still experienced extensive damage to buildings, utilities, and vegetation. Damage to the U.S. Virgin Islands totaled $500 million, while damage to the British Virgin Islands was estimated at another $200 million. Three people were killed by the storm, and another 7 died from storm-related causes. The damage was so extensive that in some areas of the Virgin Islands telephone service was not restored until March of 1990.

After hitting the Virgin Islands, Hurricane Hugo shifted slightly northward. It passed through Vieques Sound between the islands of Culebra and Vieques. The island of Culebra experienced sustained winds of 105 miles per hour and wind gusts of 150 miles per hour. Hurricane Hugo then moved over Puerto Rico on September 18. In the capital city of San Juan there were sustained winds of 77 miles per hour and peak gusts of 92 miles per hour. In Puerto Rico tens of thousands of people lost their homes, including 60 percent of the residents of Culebra. The most severe damage was to the electrical system, especially along the northeast coast of the island. All together, 35 municipalities were without power. A week after the storm an estimated 47,500 homes and businesses were still without power; as late as September 28, 10 days after the storm, electrical service was still only 40 percent restored.

Water service to the residents was also disrupted. One week after the storm, 25 percent of the island's residents were without water. In the first 10 days following the storm the U.S. Army Corps of Engineers distributed more than 2 million gallons of water from 33 tank trucks on the island. On Puerto Rico itself damage was estimated at $1 billion. In addition, there were 2 deaths directly caused by the storm and 22 hurricane-related deaths.

Other islands in the Carribean affected by Hurricane Hugo were St. Kitts-Nevis and Antigua and Barbuda. Together these islands reported 2 people killed and $160 million in damages. All together it is estimated that Hurricane Hugo did a total of $3 billion in damages before it targeted the southeastern coast of the United States.

The United States. Following its passage through the Caribbean, Hurricane Hugo weakened from a Category 4 to a Category 2 storm on the Saffir-Simpson hurricane scale. On the morning of September 19, the eye of the storm had become poorly defined, and its strongest sustained winds were 100 miles per hour. As Hugo moved toward the South Carolina coast it strengthened once again to a Category 4 storm. When it came ashore near Charleston, the Charleston navy shipyard recorded gusts as high as 137 miles per hour. After hitting land, Hugo's sustained surface winds were clocked at 87 miles per hour at the customs house in downtown Charleston. Further north, at Bull Bay, sustained winds were estimated to be as high as 121 miles per hour. When it hit the mainland, Hugo became the first Category 4 or higher storm to strike the United States coast since Hurricane Camille hit the Mississippi Gulf coast in 1969.

In South Carolina thousands of people voluntarily began moving inland more than twenty-four hours before Hugo made landfall. At 6 on the morning of September 21, South Carolina governor Carroll Campbell issued a mandatory evacuation order for the barrier islands and the coast of South Carolina. A subsequent mandatory evacuation of all one-story buildings in Charleston was issued by Mayor Joseph P. Riley, Jr., because of the fear of a tremendous storm surge. It was estimated that more than 186,000 people left their homes, from Myrtle Beach to Hilton Head, South Carolina. The early warnings and evacuations were credited with saving thousands of lives.

Hurricane Hugo struck the South Carolina coast on the night of September 21. The center of the storm passed over Sullivan's Island, just north of Charleston. Sullivan's Island had a storm surge of 13 feet above mean sea level. At Bull Bay the storm surge was 20 feet, the highest ever reported on the East Coast of the United States. The death and destruction caused by Hurricane Hugo along the immediate coast and inland were extensive. However, because of evacuations and because the right side of the eyewall crossed the coast in the one of the least populated reaches of South Carolina's coast, there were only 13 deaths in the state directly attributed to the storm. Of these, 6 deaths were from drowning and 7 were wind-related. Only 2 of the drowning deaths occurred in homes. Another 14 people died of storm-related causes.

The Damage. Property damage caused by Hugo was extensive. In Charleston an estimated 43 percent of the homes had at least $10,000 in damages. The roofs of Charleston city hall and the Charleston County courthouse were partially destroyed, causing significant damage to the contents of each. Several historical churches also lost their steeples. One week after Hugo only 25 percent of Charleston had electricity. The Charleston airport was closed to commercial traffic for a week due to damage to facilities and the lack of off-site power; full commercial service was not restored for eighteen days.

A survey by the Red Cross showed that 9,302 homes in the state were completely destroyed, over half of which were mobile homes. Another 26,772 homes suffered major damage, and 75,702 houses had minor damage. Major structural damage included loss of roofs, collapse of single-story masonry buildings, and complete destruction of mobile homes. The majority of inland wind damage was caused by falling trees, and along the coast major damage was caused by flooding. Approximately 65 percent of the houses on Sullivan's Island were structurally unsafe. On the barrier island to the north, the Isle of Palms, between 55 and 60 percent of the homes were deemed structurally unsafe. In addition, the Ben Sawyer Bridge, which provided the only access to the mainland from these islands, was blown out of position and tilted at a 30-degree angle. During this time the Red Cross served over 1 million meals to people. Between 1 and 1.5 million customers were without electrical power for two to three weeks; damage to power supply systems alone totaled more than $400 million.

Hurricane Hugo also caused extensive beach erosion and landward transport of sand from the beach. In some coastal areas Hugo did restore a more natural profile to beaches on which steep slopes had been artificially maintained. Beachfronts that lacked natural dune systems and natural vegetation were the most heavily damaged—residents in those areas suffered significant water damage.

In addition to damages to homes and government property, the timber, fishing, and tourism industries sustained heavy losses. For example, Hurricane Hugo destroyed more than 6 billion board feet of timber, more than three times the total lost in the Mount St. Helens volcanic eruption in 1980. The 150,000-acre Francis Marion National Forest, north of Charleston, had 70 percent of its trees damaged or destroyed. The value of the lost timber alone was estimated at over $1 billion. In North Carolina Hugo damaged more than 2.7 million acres of forest in twenty-six counties. Timber losses were valued at $250 million.

Hurricane Hugo had a faster forward movement than most storms. This resulted in higher-than-normal inland wind speeds. Columbia, South Carolina, which is over 100 miles from the coast, had sustained winds of 67 miles per hour, while Charlotte, North Carolina, recorded sustained winds of 60 miles per hour. As a result, Hugo caused destruction as far as 180 miles inland. In Charlotte, Hugo caused an estimated $366 million in damages. In the North Carolina counties of Mecklenburg, Gastonia, and Union, damage was estimated at $883 million. In North and South Carolina over 1.5 million people lost power because of the storm; Duke Power estimated that at least 700,000 of its customers lost service. In the weeks following Hugo, Duke Power had 9,000 workers replacing 8,800 poles, 700 miles of cable and wire, 6,300 transformers, and 1,700 electric meters. In some parts of North Carolina power was not restored for two weeks. Property losses in North Carolina totaled over $1 billion, while South Carolina had an estimated $4 billion loss. In addition, there was 1 death in North Carolina directly attributed to Hugo and 6 other storm-related deaths.

Additional death and destruction occurred as the remnants of Hurricane Hugo moved north. Virginia reported 6 storm-related deaths and damage estimated at $50 million, while 1 person died in New York.

At the time Hurricane Hugo struck in 1989, it was the most expensive hurricane in United States history. While figures vary, damages caused by the storm have been estimated as high as $7 billion in the United States, $2 billion in Puerto Rico, and $1 billion elsewhere. The total number of deaths linked to the storm, directly or storm-related, has been estimated at 75. Hugo remains one of the most destructive hurricanes to ever hit the Caribbean and the East Coast of the United States.

William V. Moore

For Further Information:

Barnes, Jay. *North Carolina's Hurricane History.* Rev. ed. Chapel Hill: University of North Carolina Press, 1998.

Committee on Natural Disaster Studies. *Hurricane Hugo: Puerto Rico, the Virgin Islands, and Charleston, South Carolina.* Vol. 6. Washington D.C.: National Academy of Science, 1994.

Fox, William Price. *Lunatic Wind: Surviving the Storm of the Century.* Chapel Hill, N.C.: Algonquin Books, 1992.

U.S. Department of Commerce, National Oceanic and Atmospheric Administration. *Natural Disaster Survey Report: Hurricane Hugo September 10-22, 1989.* Washington D.C.: U.S. Department of Commerce, 1990.

1991: Bangladesh

Cyclone
Date: April 30, 1991
Place: Southeastern Bangladesh
Result: 131,000 dead, at least 9 million homeless

On April 30, 1991, a cyclone originating in the Bay of Bengal struck southeastern Bangladesh. The storm was 185 miles in diameter, had winds of 145 miles per hour, and lasted eight hours. Storm surges created 20-foot-high waves that swamped at least 12 islands. Over 131,000 people were killed, and 9 million were left homeless. The death toll would have been higher if about 3 million people had not been evacuated to stone shelters on high ground, which were constructed after a 1985 cyclone that killed 10,000. About 80 percent of the residents' straw huts were blown away in the storm.

The effects of the cyclone were so extensive that thousands of those who survived the storm died later from hunger and water-borne diseases. Communications were severed for days after the event, and navy and other relief ships were called in to rescue those stranded on rooftops. The country's salt-manufacturing industry and shrimp farms were devastated by the storm. Bangladesh received at least $20 million in aid from other countries.

Lauren Mitchell

For Further Information:

Longshore, David. *Encyclopedia of Hurricanes, Typhoons, and Cyclones.* New York: Facts on File, 1998.

"Storm Toll Put at 25,000 in Bangladesh; Many Missing." *Los Angeles Times,* May 2, 1991, p. A1.

1991: Tropical Storm Thelma

Date: November 5, 1991
Place: Leyte, Philippines
Result: 3,000 dead

The eruption of Mount Pinatubo was not the only natural catastrophe to afflict the Philippines in 1991. The islands of Leyte, Samar, and Negros in the island nation were devastated by Tropical Storm Thelma in the fall of that year. On Tuesday, November 5, 1991, the Philippine weather bureau had announced Storm Signal Number 1 (the minimal alert level) to warn people of the impending storm. The people of the island of Leyte felt their atmosphere become drastically more humid in a matter of hours, though there was no overt sign of rainfall or thunderstorms. Tropical Storm Thelma (known in the Philippines by the regional name Uring) had arrived.

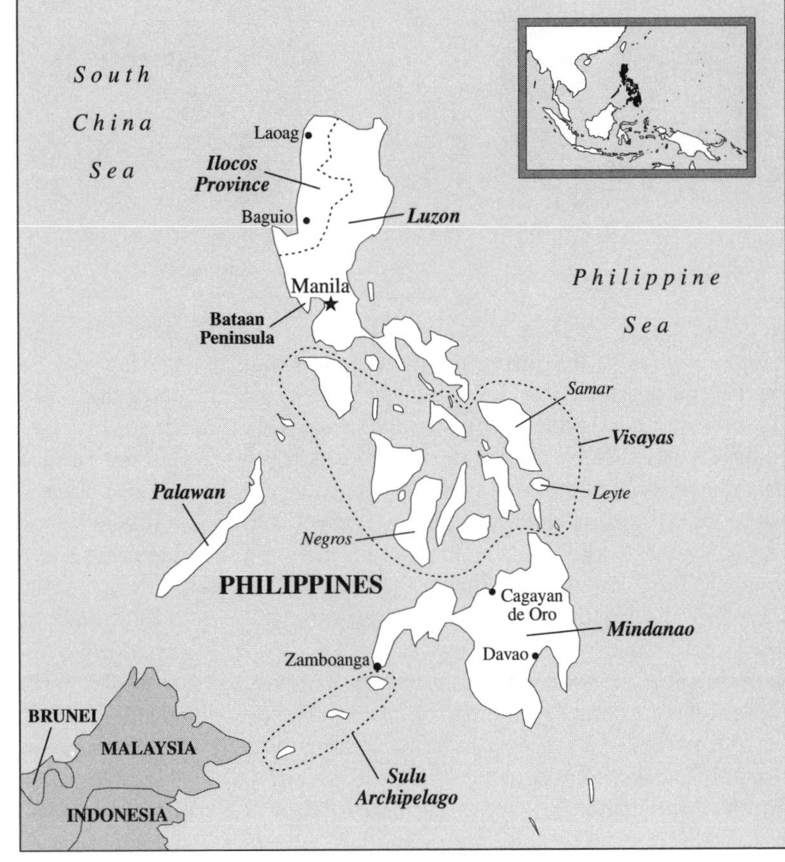

Fifty-three people were killed on the neighboring island of Negros. The blast concentrated its effects on Leyte, however, especially in the seaside city of Ormoc. Ominous crashes and peals of destruction resounded through the air as fences and utility poles were destroyed by rampaging winds. Vast amounts of rainfall cascaded down onto the city, destroying nearly everything and washing hundreds of people and thousands of animals into a sudden and watery death.

The damage caused by the heavy weather itself was merely the prelude to the more serious disaster. Flash flooding, brought on by the unexpectedly sudden rise in the water level, generated gigantic mudslides that hurtled over thousands of people, killing many instantly. The floodwaters reached a high of 10 feet (3 meters). Ormoc had never really been affected by floods before, so neither the town's buildings nor the people they contained were fully prepared for what faced them. Those who survived were covered in

Victims of Tropical Storm Thelma are loaded onto a truck in Ormoc, Leyte, Philippines. (AP/Wide World Photos)

mud and had to stumble around amid rubble and disrepair to try to find living family members and identify the dead.

Autos navigated around corpses, and other dead bodies lay arbitrarily stacked in piles. Some managed to preserve some of their belongings, but most were not so lucky. Cristina Guillotes, a thirty-four-year-old mother of three, said that she and her three young children clung to a small fragment of wood paneling from their house, but the small children were not able to hold on.

Ormoc's port was rendered completely useless, giving the community even more economic difficulties as it struggled to recover from the catastrophe. Urgently needed items began to trickle in, including chlorine, medicine, flashlights, canned food, and milk. It was not until the following Sunday, November 10, that roads were cleared sufficiently and artificial harbors imported to enable relief efforts to reach full power and for outside inspectors to survey the damage; these latter included the ambassadors of the United States and Japan. These nations were potential donors to the financing of the cleanup, but their ambassadors were also there because the actions of Japanese and American corporations were held partially liable for the damage done by the disaster.

Although natural in its immediate cause, the damage done by Tropical Storm Thelma was not wholly natural in its historical origins. A recent spate of illegal logging was widely blamed for the destruction, as it exacerbated the damage caused by the storm. Trees in a forest serve as containers of water; the tree's roots and the surrounding topsoil absorb precipitation, and each leaf and branch serves as a mini-cistern, taking in a few drops of water in an action that, when multiplied, serves to absorb a potentially large flow of liquid. After the loggers had cut down the trees, the brushwoods that surrounded them, if they had not already been uprooted by the loggers, withered as their accustomed distribution of the root system was disrupted. The brushwood was further disturbed by the conversion of much of the formerly forested land to sugarcane and coconut production. The brushwood may have seemed insignificant, but it had been the crucial element in stabilizing the topsoil that lay underneath. Without the trees and the brushwood to hold it down, the topsoil easily became mud in the aftermath of the typhoon. The consequent mudslides that rampaged through Ormoc glided down the slopes with relative ease, nothing standing in their way.

It was not just environmental groups that fastened the liability for the storm's extremity on the illegal logging. Many citizens' groups and government authorities joined in as well. Yet not everybody accepted this theory of the genesis of the catastrophe. Some scientists argued that the loggers had left hundreds of logs among the small streams that eventually coalesced to form the Ormoc River. These logs had contained the water, stemming its usual flow, and generating temporary human-made lakes that, when released by the typhoon, swept up the soil with unusual intensity.

This theory, like its counterpart, held the loggers accountable. Environmental awareness, and the exploitation of natural resources, were beginning to erase the line between natural and human-made disasters. The extensive stripping of Leyte's forests had been recognized before, but the typhoon brought home the urgency of stanching the denudation's ravages. The debate that had previously existed on whether to impose a partial or total logging ban gave way to an almost total public consensus in Leyte that demanded a strictly enforced total logging ban. Mayor Maria Victoria Locsin spoke eloquently on behalf of the town's grievances. Billboards around Ormoc proclaimed, "When Nature Is Disturbed, She Reacts Violently."

Scientists also urged hydrological studies to advance flood preparedness and stricter requirements for building construction. Preventive measures were ordered to ensure against future floods, including dredging some of the local rivers and moving inhabitants to higher ground. However, the most viable remedy, reforestation, was something that would not happen overnight. In 1998, President Joseph Estrada of the Philippines declared the anniversary of November 5 a special holiday to commemorate the loss of life in the dreadful typhoon.

Nicholas Birns

For Further Information:

Brillantes, Alex. B., Jr., "The Philippines in 1991: Disasters and Decisions." *Asian Survey* 32, no. 2 (February, 1992): 340-346.

Filipino Reporter, July 2, 1998.

Mydans, Seth. "In Filipino Town, Bodies Uncounted." *The New York Times*, November 8, 1991, p. 3.

________. "More than 2,000 Die as Floods Swamp Towns in Philippines." *The New York Times*, November 7, 1991, p. 1.

Virug, Mantes Danguilan. *Power from the Forest: The Politics of Logging*. Quezon City, Philippines: Philippine Center for Investigative Journalism, 1993.

1992: Hurricane Andrew

Date: August 22-26, 1992
Place: Florida, Louisiana, and the Bahamas
Classification: Category 4
Result: 50 dead, $26 billion in damage

Although relatively small in size, Hurricane Andrew was a storm of enormous intensity that left a mammoth trail of destruction along its path across the Bahamas, south Florida, and Louisiana. Its final toll was an estimated $26 billion in damage in the United States alone, ranking it at the time as the most expensive natural disaster in the nation's history.

Andrew's Beginnings. Hurricane Andrew began as a tropical wave off the west coast of Africa and passed south of the Cape Verde Islands on August 15, 1992, at a speed of 18 miles per hour. As it continued its west-northwest movement, the storm picked up its pace to 23 miles per hour, nearly twice the speed of an average hurricane. Over the next few days, the storm passed to the south of a high-pressure system as steering winds began to move it closer to a strong upper-level, low-pressure system located near Bermuda. The currents gradually changed, and Andrew turned slowly to a northwesterly course. On August 20, the storm weakened to the point of almost disintegrating. The lower section of the storm was moving to the northwest, while the upper part of it was steered by strong upper-level winds to the northeast.

However, significant changes in the overall weather environment began to occur the following day. Satellite imagery indicated the upper-level, low-pressure system near Bermuda had broken up, which decreased the wind-shear effect on Andrew. It enabled the storm to gather its pieces together, regain strength, and resume its movement. As it migrated further into the Atlantic, the storm increased in intensity and was designated the first tropical storm of the 1992 hurricane season. Simultaneously, a strong high-pressure system began to build along the U.S. southeast coast, which helped steer the storm directly west into warm tropical waters.

With winds measuring over 75 miles per hour, Andrew reached hurricane status at a point 800 miles east of Miami on August 22 and rapidly strengthened to a Category 4 storm. As it approached a point approximately 330 miles east of the Florida coast, a hurricane watch was posted from Titusville south to Vero Beach, south through the Florida Keys and over to the West Coast to Fort Myers.

Andrew maintained a due-west course and crossed Eleuthera Island and the southern Berry Islands in the Bahamas on August 23. Eleuthera Island suffered extensive damage when a 23-foot storm surge, one of the largest on record, washed ashore, leaving coastal areas in ruin. Government Harbour, Hatchet Bay, and Upper and Lower Bogue were among the communities severely damaged. Nearly every house on Current Island was destroyed.

Andrew weakened somewhat following its passage over the Bahamas but quickly regained its strength as it moved through the Florida Straits. At this stage

The devastation wreaked by Hurricane Andrew on Florida City, Florida. (AP/Wide World Photos)

weather forecasters noted a decreasing diameter and corresponding strengthening of the storm's "eyewall" convection. Measurements indicated a more vigorous counterclockwise rotation with the radius of maximum wind in the eyewall reaching 12 miles. Meteorologists believed the storm was undergoing a phenomenon called "eyewall replacement," in which the inner wall disintegrates and is replaced by the outer wall. During the replacement cycle, the storm would weaken, then immediately regain its strength as the new outer wall replaced the older inner one.

As the storm churned in the direction of Florida's east coast, Governor Lawton Chiles declared a state of emergency and alerted the National Guard for duty. Nearly 1 million people were ordered to evacuate the coastal areas of Broward County, Dade County, and the northern Florida Keys in Monroe County. Because Andrew had a smaller diameter than most hurricanes, the stronger winds did not become apparent to residents until the storm was almost on top of land. This served to hamper evacuation efforts, as many boaters waited until the final hours to move their craft inland, creating delays for land traffic as drawbridges were raised to allow the boats entrance to safer waters.

The potential for a natural disaster of epic proportions was apparent to officials, given the lay of the land in south Florida. The highest natural land elevation in the entire state is only 345 feet above sea level, and elevations in the southern portion of the state are even lower, with few rising above 20 feet. In addition, the state's coastal regions are low and flat and marked by numerous small bays, inlets, and a continuous series of barrier islands.

Throughout southern Florida residents made preparations for Andrew's arrival. Merchants and homeowners boarded up their properties and stocked up on water, groceries, gasoline, batteries, and candles in the event of a blackout or shortage. The rapid intensification of the storm came unexpectedly to local officials. In an advisory issued on Saturday, August 22, the National Hurricane Center (NHC) forecast that tropical storm winds would arrive in Miami at about 9 P.M. Monday. In its next advisory, issued six hours later, the NHC warned residents that the tropical storm winds would arrive around 5 A.M. Monday.

Hurricane Andrew slammed into south Florida around 5:05 A.M. on August 24, 1992, near Florida City, about 19 miles south of downtown Miami, and was accompanied by sustained winds estimated at 140 miles per hour with gusts up to 175 miles per hour and a storm surge of close to 16 feet. The surge pushed the waters of Biscayne Bay inland for several hundred yards. Due to the eyewall's contraction, hurricane-force winds extended out only about 30 miles around the wall. Officials considered it fortunate that the storm did not carry the heavy amounts of precipitation normally associated with a hurricane of Andrew's size.

The Damage. Immediately after its rapid passage over south Florida, the extent of damage and casualties could not be readily determined. National media reports initially indicated it was not as severe as expected and that downtown Miami and Miami Beach were relatively intact. As additional information began to filter in, the complete magnitude of the storm's impact became apparent.

The worst damage inflicted by Andrew was in southern Dade County, from the Miami suburb of Kendall, south through Homestead and Florida City, to the Florida Keys. Scores of neighborhoods lost all of their trees, with many crashing into homes and parked cars. Few homes were left standing as the gusting winds reached sufficient strength to strip the paint and roofs off houses and topple telephone and power lines, leaving nearly all of Dade County without electricity. The powerful winds were able to hurl concrete beams more than 150 feet, lift large trucks into the air, and disintegrate mobile homes. Air-conditioning units were torn from roofs, leaving gaping holes for the torrential rains to pour through, flooding floors below. In some areas the sustained winds unofficially reached 175 miles per hour, with some gusts reaching as high as 212 miles per hour. Barometric pressure registered a low at 27.23 inches.

Andrew heavily damaged offshore structures, including the artificial reef system off the southeast coast. One measure of its strength was its impact on the *Belzona Barge*, a 350-ton barge that prior to the hurricane was sitting in 68 feet of water on the ocean floor. A thousand tons of concrete from an old bridge lay on its deck. Andrew shoved the barge 700 feet to the west and stripped it of several large sections of steel-plate siding. Only 50 to 100 tons of concrete remained on the barge's deck. Another ship, the 210-ton freighter *Seaward Explorer*, moored off Elliot Key, was separated from its anchor by the surge and carried over the submerged key and across Biscayne Bay, where it finally was washed ashore.

This Hurricane Andrew survivor sits in front of the remains of his house. (AP/Wide World Photos)

Wind Speeds. According to a report issued by the National Ocean and Atmospheric Administration, measuring the storm's sustained wind speeds became problematic once it reached land. Weather experts noted that the estimates were for those winds occurring primarily within the northern eyewall over an open environment, such as at an airport and at a standard 33-foot (10-meter) height. The winds occurring at other locations were subject to their complex interactions with buildings, trees, and other obstacles in their path. Such obstructions generate a drag that generally reduces the wind speeds. However, they are also capable of producing brief accelerations of winds in areas approximate to the structures. As a result, the wind gusts experienced at a given location, such as a building situated in the core region of the hurricane, can vary significantly and cannot be precisely measured.

The National Hurricane Center in Coral Gables noted the unfortunate circumstance of not having official measurements of surface winds near the area of landfall where maximum winds were likely to have occurred. The strongest sustained wind, registered at 141 miles per hour with a gust up to 169 miles per hour, occurred close to 1 nautical mile east of the shoreline. Many transmissions of wind speeds were interrupted when instruments presumably were disabled by the storm. A subsequent inspection revealed that one anemometer situated near the eye's path was bent 90 degrees from its normal vertical position. Wind measurements taken by aircraft at about 10,000 feet, when adjusted, support the estimate of sustained surface winds of 145 miles per hour.

There were no confirmed reports of tornadoes associated with Andrew as it passed over the Bahamas or Florida. A few unconfirmed funnel sightings were reported over the Florida counties of Glades, Collier, and Highlands. A number of weather observers did note the similarities in damage patterns between Hurricane Andrew and a tornado. While countless houses deep inland were leveled by Andrew, low-lying beachfront condominiums went unscathed. In Naranja Lakes, a south Dade County suburb, buildings whose tops were blown off stood across from others that were left undamaged. Scientists believe the random pattern of damage caused by Andrew was the result of small thunderstorms packed within the hurricane. The storms created vertical columns of air that opened vents in the eye's wall of clouds, which allowed the hurricane's most powerful winds to rush to the ground nearly 2,000 feet below with the concentrated fury of a tornado. Traveling west at 20 miles per hour the storm cut a swath of destruction that was easily discernible and unique to hurricane activity.

Further Damage. Throughout the region power lines and traffic lights dangled to windshield levels. Shredded shrubs and downed trees made driving through streets a hazardous chore. Numerous side streets were rendered impassable because of the debris. In addition, close to 3,000 water mains were damaged, along with 1,900 traffic lights, 100,000 traffic signs, and 2,200 street lights. Damage was also inflicted on 59 hospitals and health facilities, 7 post offices, 278 schools, Florida International University, Dade Community College, and the University of Miami.

In the fashionable seaside community of Coconut Grove, dozens of recreational boats were washed up into the streets and parking lots. At suburban airports, hangars were ripped apart and small planes piled atop one another. Homestead Air Force Base, located at the southern tip of the state between Everglades National Park and Miami, took a direct hit. Most of the air base's 200 buildings, including hangars, communication equipment, offices, housing, and other facilities, received damage. Nearly all of Homestead's 70 aircraft and 5,000 active-duty personnel had been evacuated; however, 2 F-16 fighters that remained were destroyed when a hangar door swung onto them. The base was home to two F-16 fighter wings and a U.S. Customs Service antidrug operation.

One of the hardest hit areas was Coral Gables in south Miami, where the National Hurricane Center is located and where gusts of wind up to 164 miles per hour were recorded. The storm blew the radar off the center's roof and shattered the building's windows. On the other hand, Miami Beach's Art Deco district escaped the brunt of the storm, though the plush Fontainebleau Hilton hotel was left with several feet of water in its lobby.

Nearly 90 percent of Florida City's 1,900 homes were either destroyed, severely damaged, or marginally damaged, including 1,475 mobile homes, 1,041 single-family homes, and 470 apartment units. In addition, a majority of its businesses fell victim to the storm, leaving residents both homeless and jobless. The city's entire infrastructure was also crippled severely. The city hall, police station, water and sewer system, and all of the city's parks were damaged, along with an elementary school, 9 churches, a museum, a community center, and a football field.

The story was similar in Homestead, where 85 to 90 percent of the housing units were destroyed or damaged. Among them were 1,167 manufactured housing units, 9,059 single-family dwelling units, and 7,580 multifamily units. Eight public schools and 22 parks in the city received severe damage, as did the Homestead branch of Metro Dade Community College.

The personal testimony of many residents reflects the fury of Andrew. Many recalled how their ears popped and sinuses ached as the barometric pressure plunged. Some heard the popping of automobiles while other claimed that the water was sucked from their toilets. Above all, it was the sound of the winds, described as akin to the blast of jet engines or the roar of a freight train, that many found most terrifying.

All together, nearly 25,000 homes were destroyed and close to 100,000 others were damaged in the region. Also destroyed or damaged were an estimated 8,000 businesses, putting over 80,000 people out of work. The National Guard provided tent cities for the homeless, but many chose to stay in what remained of their homes to protect them from looters. Nearly 43 deaths in Dade County alone were attributed directly or indirectly to the storm. Law enforcement officials, using police dogs, conducted searches immediately after the storm through the remnants of mobile-home parks. With communication outlets severely crippled, some local jurisdictions took to dropping leaflets from helicopters and sending automobiles mounted with loudspeakers through the most devastated areas to announce the latest information. In Miami authorities declared a curfew from 7 P.M. to

7 A.M., and police cordoned off many sections of the town.

As the wind diminished and the water receded, U.S. Army combat troops joined National Guard forces and police in setting up barricades around the major commercial centers in downtown Miami and Coconut Grove to prevent looting.

Andrew also took a heavy toll on animals. Hundreds of horses were killed and many other injured by flying debris. Thousands of pets roamed free as their confines collapsed around them. Although few, if any, animals escaped from local zoos, hundreds of monkeys and baboons fled from area research facilities, and countless numbers of exotic birds were reported missing. Agricultural damage in Dade County exceeded $1 billion, including an approximate $128 million loss in tropical orchards, a $349 million loss in crop production, and a $12.5 million loss in aqua culture and livestock.

An estimated 15,000 pleasure boats were victimized by Andrew's winds. The boat damage for the entire region approached $20 million. Only a handful of deaths were attributed to boaters who elected to ride out the storm in their boats, an unusually low death count for a storm of Andrew's magnitude.

Though the storm roiled the shallow waters of Biscayne Bay, 8 miles wide and only 12 feet deep, its major sediment deposits and grass beds were left relatively intact. The shallow waters had the effect of amplifying the storm surge so that the tide rose an estimated 12 to 16 feet above normal by the time it reached the western shore. The waters in the western portion of the bay were noticeably brackish following the storm. Freshwater extended out several hundred yards from the shoreline, and salinity was measured at 11 parts per 1,000 compared with the normal 34 parts per 1,000 up to a mile and a half out. Much of this effect was attributed to the decision of the state's water-management agencies to lower the level of Lake Okeechobee in anticipation of the storm to prevent excessive overflows.

The highest recorded high-water mark was 16.88 feet, at the Burger King Corporate Headquarters in south Dade County. High-water marks diminished from this point north to Broad Causeway, where they reached to 5.17 feet, and south to Key Largo, where they reached up to 5.49 feet. On the west coast of Florida, high-water marks ranged from 4.38 feet at Everglades City to 6.85 feet at West Goodland. The farthest the tidal surge extended inland was an estimated 3 miles from the eastern coastline. The surge's north-south range extended nearly 33 miles along the eastern coast.

Despite the massive devastation, civil defense officials estimated the damage could have been far worse if the hurricane had crossed the Florida peninsula a few miles farther north, through more densely populated regions. The relatively small diameter of the storm had the effect of reducing its exposure to more vulnerable coastal communities and thus was a major contributing factor in limiting overall damage and loss of life. According to officials, an additional factor in reducing fatalities was the evacuation and hurricane preparedness programs that were in force prior to the storm's arrival.

Florida's substantial natural resource base felt the full fury of Andrew. The storm's eye crossed 3 National Park Service sites: Biscayne National Park, Everglades National Park, and Big Cypress National Preserve. Artificial reefs along the coastline were severely damaged, as were thousands of acres of mangrove forest. Shorelines were littered with tons of marine debris as the strong currents tore away sea fans, sponges, and coral in areas of Biscayne Bay. The fragile Everglades region was damaged as entire groves of trees were flattened and exotic plants and wildlife habitats were destroyed. Virtually all large trees located in islands of dense undergrowth were defoliated. However, the storm had little effect on the interior freshwater lands of the Everglades, which are composed mainly of sawgrass. Samplings by the South Florida Water Management District following the storm indicate nearly all poststorm water-quality properties, including turbidity, color, ammonia, and dissolved phosphate, were within the range of prestorm values.

The most prominent inhabitants of the marshlands, the alligators, appeared to have weathered the storm, though some of their nests were destroyed. All the radio-tagged Florida panthers, radio-tagged black bears, and white-tailed deer survived the hurricane. Egrets, herons, and ibis also came through the storm relatively unscathed. The largest concentration of dead birds discovered was at a roost in Biscayne Bay, where the corpses of approximately 200 white ibis were found.

One of the reasons for the relatively small damage to animals and plants was the nature of the storm. Unlike previous hurricane storm surges that inundated large areas of the marshlands with saltwater,

Andrew's was unable to push deep inland owing to its direct westerly path that took it over Florida's relatively high east coast. In retrospect, the fact that Hurricane Andrew was a rapidly moving, compact, relatively dry storm rather than a larger, slower, or wetter system spared Florida an even greater natural disaster.

Moving On. Andrew moved quickly in an almost direct line across the extreme southern section of Florida in about four hours, entering the Gulf of Mexico south of Marco Island in a somewhat weakened state but with its eye still intact. As it plowed across the southern peninsula, it left a swath of destruction 25 miles wide and 60 miles long, though the impact of its storm surge on the southwest coast of the state was minimal.

Once again over warm waters, the storm began to intensify as it turned northwest toward the Louisiana coast. As it churned through the Gulf waters, Andrew continued to wreak damage estimated at a half billion dollars. Its winds toppled platforms, blew 5 drilling wells off location, caused 2 fires, and created 7 incidents of pollution.

Fearing a repeat of the scenes of devastation in southern Florida, officials and residents launched a massive evacuation effort along the Mississippi Delta region. An estimated 1.25 million people were evacuated from parishes in southeastern and south-central Louisiana. The eye of the storm skirted the Louisiana coast about 85 miles southwest of New Orleans. It finally made landfall approximately 20 miles west-southwest of Morgan City on the morning of August 26, leaving Grand Isle, the state's only inhabited barrier island, completely underwater. The storm struck with a Category 3 force as sustained winds of 140 miles per hour buffeted the sparsely populated marshlands.

Louisiana is known for its many bayous and waterways, which constitute much of the state's topography. Numerous barrier islands dot the coastline but generally are used as game preserves. A large portion of the southeastern section of the state rests at or below sea level and is not conducive to rapid runoff, thus making overflows potentially protracted and severe.

As it slid along the Louisiana coast, Andrew dealt a severe blow to the state's fishing industry, inflicting nearly $160 million in damage to freshwater fisheries. The state did fare much better than Florida in damage to boats, as Andrew missed the major shipping areas north and east of New Orleans. Many boat owners had enough advance warning to move their vessels into one of the numerous bayous, where they had more protection from the storm.

The storm continued to move west across southern Louisiana toward the cities of Lafayette and New Iberia. It spawned numerous tornadoes that caused widespread damage in several Mississippi, Alabama, and Georgia communities. One tornado occurred in the city of Laplace, Louisiana, killing 2 people and injuring 32 others. Tornadoes also were reported in the parishes of Ascension, Iberville, Baton Rouge, Pointe Coupe, and Avoyelles, though no casualties were reported.

Numerous reports of funnel clouds were received by officials in Mississippi and were believed to have caused damage in several of the state's counties. In Alabama, two tornadoes struck the mainland, while another hit Dauphin Island. Several destructive tornadoes that roared through Georgia were attributed to Andrew. Although rainfall was heavy throughout the region, it resulted in little significant flooding because of the dry conditions along the coast. Rivers were at midsummer stages, and soils were parched from lack of rain. An estimated 25 percent or less of the rain generated by Andrew ended up in the rivers as runoff. The remaining portion either was absorbed by the soils and plants or evaporated.

On August 26, Andrew was downgraded to a tropical storm as it moved northeast through Mississippi. The remnants of Andrew continued to produce heavy downpours that often exceeded 10 inches. On August 28, Andrew merged with a frontal system over the mid-Atlantic states, ending its trail of destruction.

William Hoffman

For Further Information:

Barnes, Jay. *Florida's Hurricane History.* Chapel Hill: University of North Carolina Press, 1998.

Fyerdam, Rick. *When Natural Disaster Strikes: Lessons from Hurricane Andrew.* Miami Beach, Fla.: Hospice Foundation of America, 1994.

Pielke, Jr., Roger A., and Roger A. Pielke, Sr. *Hurricanes: Their Nature and Impacts on Society.* New York: John Wiley & Sons, 1997.

Pimm, Stuart L., Gary E. Davis, and Lloyd L. Loope. "Hurricane Andrew." *Bioscience,* April, 1994, 224-229.

Rappaport, Ed. "Hurricane Andrew—A Preliminary Look." *Mariners Weather Log,* Fall, 1992, 16-25.

1994: Tropical Storm Gordon

Date: November 8-21, 1994
Place: The Caribbean and Florida
Classification: Category 1
Result: Several hundred to 1,000 dead, millions of dollars in damage

Having a longer duration as a tropical storm than as a hurricane, Gordon caused extensive damage throughout the Caribbean and Florida. Forming as Tropical Storm Number 12 east of Costa Rica on November 8, 1994, Gordon existed primarily as thunderstorms. Gordon's rainfall triggered flash floods and mudslides in Costa Rica and Nicaragua.

Striking southeast Jamaica on November 13, Gordon's 44-mile-per-hour winds and heavy rains caused 2 deaths and $50 million in damages. Gordon caused mudslides from flash flooding that killed at least 380 Haitians. American occupation troops in Haiti estimated 1,000 people had died.

Tropical Storm Gordon then headed toward Florida. Gordon's inclement weather forced the space shuttle *Atlantis* to land in California instead of at Cape Canaveral. Almost 500,000 Floridians were without electricity, and hundreds of houses were damaged, as were winter cucumber and strawberry crops.

Returning to the Atlantic Ocean near Vero Beach, Gordon became a Category 1 hurricane on November 17. With 980-millibar pressure and 85-mile-per-hour winds, Gordon created 16-foot surges on the Outer Banks, causing $2 million worth of destruction. Changing direction, Gordon lost energy because of wind shear and was a tropical depression when it returned to Florida on November 21, producing heavy rain and 13-foot waves that drowned 2 fishermen.

Elizabeth D. Schafer

For Further Information:

Longshore, David. *Encyclopedia of Hurricanes, Typhoons, and Cyclones.* New York: Facts on File, 1998.

1995: Hurricane Luis

Date: August 31-September 6, 1995
Place: The Caribbean
Classification: Category 4
Result: 16 dead, $2.5 billion in damage

During the last week of August of 1995, four tropical storms, including Luis, formed concurrently in the Atlantic, traveling toward the Caribbean. On August 31, Luis attained 140-mile-per-hour winds and was named a Category 4 hurricane. Moving several hundred miles east of the Leeward Islands, Luis passed between Guadeloupe and Antigua on September 5. Heading northwest, the hurricane moved through the northern islands of this chain, 6 of which suffered from Luis's winds and associated surges. Anguilla, Antigua, and Barbuda, in addition to Saint-Barthélemy, St. Kitts, and St. Martin, were directly in the storm's path and were devastated. The British Virgin Islands also endured the hurricane's impact.

Heading northwest, Hurricane Luis did not directly hit Puerto Rico or the U.S. Virgin Islands, despite warnings that it might. Those islands, however, were battered by powerful waves as Luis turned toward the open sea. Similar surges washed against American beaches, resulting in erosion and flooding. By September 9, Luis had lost its strength and became a Category 2 hurricane, moving several hundred miles west past Bermuda, which endured gusts and torrential downpours. Hurricane Luis caused 16 deaths and approximately $2.5 billion in damage.

Elizabeth D. Schafer

For Further Information:

Sack, Kevin. "Hurricane Leaves Trail of Destruction in Caribbean Isles." *The New York Times*, September 7, 1995, p. A12.

"St. Maarten Is Left Smashed and Looted After Luis." *The New York Times*, September 8, 1995, p. A3.

1995: Hurricane Marilyn

Date: September 15-16, 1995
Place: The U.S. Virgin Islands
Classification: Category 2
Result: 11 dead, $1.5 billion in damage

Originating near the African coast on September 7, 1995, Marilyn became a hurricane one week later, east of Barbados. Passing over Dominica with 80-mile-per-hour winds that afternoon, Marilyn fol-

Hurricane Marilyn tossed boats from the sea onto the shore in the U.S. Virgin Islands. (AP/Wide World Photos)

lowed a northern path through the Caribbean slightly southwest of where Luis had traveled the previous week. On September 15, Hurricane Marilyn hit the U.S. Virgin Islands. Considered a Category 2 hurricane, Marilyn's pressure decreased from 985 to 972 millibars over a twelve-hour period, and its winds increased to 100 miles per hour.

Hurricane Marilyn inflicted severe damage to St. Thomas and St. John in the U.S. Virgin Islands that day. Although Puerto Rico was not directly hit by Marilyn, the nearby islands Culebra and Vieques were. The British Virgin Islands sustained some damage, but it was not comparable to that caused by Hurricane Luis a week before Marilyn struck.

With 115-mile-per-hour wind speeds, Hurricane Marilyn was designated a Category 3 hurricane as it moved over Caribbean waters on September 16. Marilyn dropped to its lowest pressure, 949 millibars, producing large waves that battered Puerto Rico and the Virgin Islands. Moving west of Bermuda on September 19, Marilyn traveled nearer that island than Luis had, causing damage from wind gusts. Hurricane Marilyn created a surge along the Atlantic coast but did not move inland.

Elizabeth D. Schafer

For Further Information:

"Hurricane Batters Virgin Islands with Nearly 100 Miles Per Hour Winds." *The New York Times*, September 16, 1995, p. 7.

Navarro, Mireya. "An Island Paradise Lost as Storm Leaves Ruins." *The New York Times*, September 19, 1995, p. B7.

U.S. National Weather Service. *Hurricane Marilyn, September 15-16, 1995*. Silver Spring, Md.: Author, 1996.

1995: Hurricane Opal

Date: October 4, 1995
Place: Florida, North Carolina, Georgia, and Alabama
Classification: Category 3
Result: 63 dead, $3 billion in damage

Opal was the first hurricane to receive a name beginning with the letter *O*. Hurricane Opal began as a tropical depression on September 27, 1995, east of the Yucatán Peninsula. The storm gained strength from the warm water near the Bay of Campeche. On October 3, Opal traveled northeast toward the Florida panhandle with winds attaining 115 miles per hour. Opal's pressure was 940 millibars, and winds were 125 miles per hour when the hurricane hit Pensacola, Florida, late the next day. Satellite images revealed that Opal was asymmetrical with the most powerful winds moving to the east. The Florida coast suffered wind damage to buildings and beaches as well as destruction by 15-foot surges.

While Opal's wind speed weakened, the hurricane accelerated inland, causing damage throughout Alabama and Georgia. Spawning tornadoes, Opal devastated the region's pine trees, and newscasters described the landscape as a forest on its side. Interstates were covered by trees, which emergency crews chopped off at the edge of pavement to open roads. Houses and cars were destroyed, and many residents went without power for almost two weeks. At least 13 people died in the United States, and 50 deaths from flooding in Guatemala and Mexico were credited to Opal. Damages totaled $3 billion.

Elizabeth D. Schafer

For Further Information:

Smothers, Ronald. "Deadly Hurricane Opal Loses Power as It Races North." *The New York Times*, October 6, 1995, p. A24.

_______. "Hurricane Slams into Florida with Winds of 145 M.p.h." *The New York Times*, October 5, 1995, p. B16.

1996: Hurricane Bertha

Date: July 5-15, 1996
Place: Puerto Rico, U.S. Virgin Islands, and the U.S. East Coast
Classification: Category 2
Result: 4 dead, almost 8,000 houses damaged, $194 million in damage

Considered the strongest hurricane ever to hit North Carolina during the month of July, Hurricane Bertha struck Wrightsville Beach during the height of tourist season on the afternoon of July 12, 1996. A Category 2 hurricane, Bertha sported winds measured at 105 miles per hour, and its pressure was 966 millibars. Bertha caused 15-foot waves that damaged piers, stores, and cottages along beaches. A ferris wheel was pushed off its stand at an amusement park. Part of Topsail Island was submerged, and the bridge to shore was swept away, trapping people who had not evacuated and who waited on rooftops for Coast Guard helicopters to rescue them.

Traveling north from the Wilmington, North Carolina, area, Bertha wreaked destruction at Camp Lajeune before proceeding to New Bern. At the Croatan National Forest, pine trees were stripped of branches. By midnight, Bertha had moved across rural fields. Agricultural losses totaled $155 million after thousands of acres of corn, cotton, and tobacco were destroyed. The hurricane's 75-mile-per-hour winds tore power lines, resulting in at least 400,000 North Carolinians losing electricity.

Hurricane Bertha moved into Virginia the next morning. The hurricane brought high winds and rain to New England, where beaches were closed. Four people died because of Hurricane Bertha, and 5,800 houses were damaged, with another 1,000 considered unsafe for occupancy. Total damages totaled $194 million.

Elizabeth D. Schafer

For Further Information:

Parker, Bobby, ed. *The Savage Season: Hurricanes Bertha and Fran, Summer of 1996.* Wilmington, N.C.: Wilmington Star-News, 1996.

1996: Hurricane Fran

Date: September 1-8, 1996
Place: North Carolina, South Carolina, Virginia, and West Virginia
Classification: Category 3
Result: 38 dead, $6.57 billion in damage

Wilmington, North Carolina, was recovering from Hurricane Bertha when Hurricane Fran arrived eight weeks later. Mimicking Bertha's travels, Fran moved through North Carolina's "Hurricane Alley" to inflict another round of damage. Attaining Category 3 status with 115-mile-per-hour winds, Hurricane Fran struck the coast at 8:45 P.M. on September 5, 1996, near the mouth of the Cape Fear River, damaging beaches, boats, and marinas.

Fran weakened to a tropical storm and reached Virginia in the early morning on September 6. The storm flooded the southwestern part of that state. Moving northwest over the Blue Ridge Mountains, Fran's rainfall contributed to the flooding of rivers throughout the region. The Potomac River reached 5 feet above flood stage and filled the streets of Washington, D.C., and it suburbs with water. Floodwaters damaged the restored C&O Canal. Fran's flooding was compared to that caused by Hurricane Agnes in 1972.

Hurricane Fran inflicted $6.57 billion worth of destruction, killing 38 people and damaging 30,000 homes and 900 businesses. Hurricane-related damage was reported as far inland as Raleigh, with 51 North Carolina counties declared disaster areas. Hurricanes Fran and Bertha heightened debate about whether federal aid should be distributed to rebuild beachfront property along "Hurricane Alley."

Elizabeth D. Schafer

FOR FURTHER INFORMATION:

Parker, Bobby, ed. *The Savage Season: Hurricanes Bertha and Fran, Summer of 1996.* Wilmington, N.C.: Wilmington Star-News, 1996.

In Surf City, North Carolina, the remains of a home battered by Hurricane Fran. (AP/Wide World Photos)

U.S. Congress. *Federal Response to Hurricane Fran.* Washington, D.C.: U.S. Government Printing Office, 1997.

"Puerto Rico Asks for U.S. Aid to Recover from Hurricane." *The New York Times,* September 18, 1996, p. B10.

1996: Hurricane Hortense

Date: September 10-14, 1996
Place: Puerto Rico and the Dominican Republic
Classification: Category 1
Result: 22 dead, millions of dollars in damage

Puerto Rico residents were not prepared for Hurricane Hortense because meteorologists were unsure whether the tropical storm would intensify into a hurricane. Tropical Storm Hortense attained 80-mile-per-hour winds and was designated a Category 1 hurricane. On September 10, 1996, Hortense showered eastern Puerto Rico with 18 inches of rain that caused deadly flooding and mudslides. Rivers such as the Rio Grande de Loiza covered low-lying areas. Highways disappeared under water. Governor Pedro J. Rossello tried to convince some reluctant residents to evacuate from vulnerable areas. About 8,000 families moved to 250 schools that served as temporary shelters. These precautions significantly lowered the number of casualties to 22 in Puerto Rico and the nearby Dominican Republic.

At least 85 percent of Puerto Rico's 3.8 million population had no electricity because of Hurricane Hortense. Water service was interrupted for 93 percent of Puerto Ricans. Governor Rossello conducted a helicopter tour of Puerto Rico, viewing the 8,500 damaged homes. The island lost an estimated $127 million worth of coffee and plantain crops, as compared to $100 million in losses wreaked by Hurricane Hugo in 1989. The airport and port of San Juan remained open during Hurricane Hortense because tourism and the cruise-ship industry were vital for Puerto Rico's economy.

Elizabeth D. Schafer

For Further Information:

"Hurricane Hortense Bypasses Bahamas." *The New York Times,* September 13, 1996, p. A14.

"Hurricane Slams into Puerto Rico." *The New York Times,* September 11, 1996, p. A1.

1996: Hurricane Lili

Date: October 14-29, 1996
Place: Costa Rica, Cuba, Honduras, Nicaragua, and Great Britain
Classification: Category 1
Result: 19 dead, millions of dollars in damage

Forming in the southwest Caribbean on October 14, 1996, Hurricane Lili attained Category 1 level winds that caused large waves to crash against the coasts of Costa Rica, Nicaragua, and Honduras. Hurricane Lili then moved north toward Cuba, where 247,000 people were evacuated. On October 18, Lili landed on Cuba's southwestern coast at Cienfuegos. Still a Category 1 hurricane, Lili's 90-mile-per-hour winds stripped 16,000 tons of oranges and grapefruits from orchards. The hurricane caused 22-foot waves to erode Cuban beaches and flood villages. Approximately 2,300 buildings and 1 bridge were ruined, and 47,000 structures were harmed, including a resort, sugar refinery, and historic sites in Old Havana. No fatalities were reported in Cuba.

Hurricane Lili was unique because it traveled 4,400 miles across the Atlantic Ocean and hit Great Britain on October 28. Lili sustained its 90-mile-per-hour winds to cause surges against the coast of Wales, 15-foot waves in the Bristol Channel, and 4-foot tides in the Thames River. Hurricane Lili destroyed 500 vacation cottages with wind and flood damage. The storm also broke the line connecting an American oil-drilling platform with a 69-member crew aboard a towboat and washed a large sailboat ashore. Five people died in Great Britain because of Hurricane Lili, and thousands temporarily lost electricity. Great Britain suffered an equivalent of $300 million in damage.

Elizabeth D. Schafer

For Further Information:

Longshore, David. *Encyclopedia of Hurricanes, Typhoons, and Cyclones.* New York: Facts on File, 1998.

1997: Hurricane Nora

Date: September 18-26, 1997
Place: Baja California, Mexico; California; and Arizona
Classification: Category 2
Result: 2 dead, millions of dollars in damage

In late September, Hurricane Nora formed over the Pacific Ocean and moved east toward Baja California. According to meteorologists, the weather phenomenon El Niño did not produce Nora but did influence the hurricane's intensity and push it toward land. On September 24, 1997, Nora attained wind speeds of 109 miles, and residents of Baja California, Southern California, and southwestern Arizona prepared for the storm to hit land that night.

Nora's counterclockwise winds prevented sea breezes from cooling Southern California. A record temperature of 99 degrees Fahrenheit set in 1978 was matched. Nora's winds caused 20-foot breakers to flood houses on Seal Beach; 3 homes were seriously damaged, and 45 others received lesser injuries. About 2 inches of rain poured in Imperial Valley, and 4 inches fell in nearby mountains. Los Angeles received almost half an inch of rain, the first rain in 219 days. At Yuma, Arizona, where the annual rainfall averages 3.6 inches, Nora produced 2.3 inches of rain.

Rainfall caused traffic accidents as moistened grease and oil stains made streets slick. A total of 230 accidents, 2 of them fatal, were reported. Also, 125,000 homes lost electrical power. Approximately, $4 million of crop damage was reported, and officials warned that rainwaters would wash pollutants into the ocean. Hurricane Nora dissipated over Arizona on September 26.

Elizabeth D. Schafer

For Further Information:

"Arizonans Are Spared as Storm Pulls Its Punch." *The New York Times,* September 26, 1997, p. A16.

Malnic, Eric. "Nora Batters Inland Areas as Flooding Closes Roads." *Los Angeles Times,* September 25, 1997, p. A3.

Malnic, Eric, and Tony Perry. "Nora Sweeps by, Bringing Rain and Floods." *Los Angeles Times,* September 26, 1997, p. A1.

1997: Hurricane Pauline

Date: October 6-10, 1997
Place: Oaxaca and Guerrero, Mexico
Speed: Winds of 120 miles per hour
Result: At least 230 dead, 50,000 homeless

Hurricane Pauline began as a tropical wave from Africa that crossed South America and entered the Pacific Ocean. The wave became a tropical depression on October 5, 1997, and reached hurricane status on October 6. It turned northwest as it intensified, drifting along the Mexican coastline. Warnings, sent the day before the hurricane struck, failed to predict what it would do or how powerful it would be. Category 4 hurricanes, such as Pauline became, were largely unknown along the Pacific coast of Mexico. Meteorologists blamed the effects of El Niño for the unexpected severity of the storm.

Pauline struck the Mexican resort community of Acapulco hardest, dropping large amounts of rainfall on the area. Wind caused little damage; instead, heavy downpours touched off massive mudslides in the hillsides surrounding Acapulco. The tourist hotels, built on sturdy ground of good materials, withstood the hurricane with minimal damage. None of the tourists were affected by the storm, and most slept through the worst of it.

The shantytowns along the hills of Acapulco, where the hotel workers lived, suffered a different experience. The structures, made of insubstantial, scavenged material, were built illegally in canyons and along dried riverbeds, which became conduits for the mud and water the storm produced. Many residents were washed away, and over 50,000 people were left homeless. Official Mexican state figures placed the death toll at 230 people, while the Mexican Red Cross claimed over 400 lives had been lost. Hurricane Pauline dissipated on October 10 near Tuxpan in the state of Jalisco.

James B. Seymour, Jr.

For Further Information:

Lawrence, Miles B. "Eastern North Pacific Hurricane Season of 1997." *Monthly Weather Review* 127, no. 10 (October, 1999): 2440.

"The Lessons of Hurricane Pauline." *The Economist,* October 18, 1997.

Wall Street Journal, October 13, 1997.

1998: Hurricane Georges

Date: September 16-29, 1998
Place: The Caribbean and the U.S. South
Classification: Category 2-4
Speed: Sustained winds of 75-110 miles per hour
Result: Approximately 400 dead, 81,000 homes damaged or destroyed

The seventh tropical storm of the 1998 storm season was identified by the National Hurricane Center on September 16 and given the name "Georges." At that point, the storm was about 1,800 miles east of the Leeward Islands and moving nearly due west at 20 miles per hour. The U.S. National Weather service started issuing coastal flooding advisories for Florida and Louisiana, even though the bulk of the storm was still approximately four days from landfall.

As Georges moved west it picked up strength and reached hurricane status on September 18. The Federal Emergency Management Agency (FEMA) began preparations in the U.S. territories along the storm path, and other governments along Georges's path were informed of the potential threat. An emergency response team was dispatched to St. Thomas in anticipation that the storm would strike there. By the time Georges struck, emergency medical and search and rescue teams were ready for rapid deployment.

Hurricane Georges rolled over the Virgin Islands and Puerto Rico on September 21, doing moderate damage to the former and more extensive damage to the latter. The island of St. Kitts lost 85 percent of its homes and suffered 5 deaths. Three deaths in Puerto Rico were attributed directly to the storm, as was $2 billion in damage. FEMA preparations appear to have greatly reduced casualties in these locations, however. While damage was extensive, repair and recovery operations began immediately after the storm's departure. Advanced preparations and quick

A Puerto Rican family stands among their destroyed belongings in what was their home before the fury of Hurricane Georges. (FEMA)

response greatly reduced the lingering effects of the storm, and some semblance of order was rapidly achieved.

Next in the path of the storm were Hispaniola, home to the Dominican Republic and Haiti, and Cuba. Here the preparations were not as extensive, as local governments did not have the necessary resources or chose to ignore warnings about the potential threat. This lack of preparation showed, as at least 288 people died in the Dominican Republic and 59 more were officially listed as missing. Most residents of the hardest hit regions believe that the official count is extremely low.

Striking on September 22, the storm caused extensive flooding and mudslides in the Dominican Republic, and the final death toll may never be known because of this. The Sabaneta Dam overflowed, causing the San Juan River to speed downstream at 100 times the normal flow rate. Several villages in its path were destroyed. In the single, worst incident, the flooded Nizao River swallowed a San Cristobal schoolhouse, claiming more than 30 people who were sheltered there. More casualties can be attributed to flooding caused by the heavy rains than to the high winds and water surge of the storm itself.

After crossing the Dominican Republic, the weakened storm struck Haiti. There, flooding destroyed large portions of Port-au-Prince and Cap Haitien, killing 87 people. There was also significant damage to other areas of the country. In addition to the water, high winds caused extensive damage to crops and weaker buildings.

The storm picked up strength as it crossed the open water on the way to Cuba. Many of the key agricultural crops were destroyed or severely damaged when the storm hit. Cuba was better prepared for the strike, and Hurricane Georges claimed only 4 lives before passing by the island and moving on toward Florida.

By September 23, Georges was located about 650 miles east-southeast of Key West, Florida, moving toward the Florida coast at 15 miles per hour. On September 25, the storm reached Category 2 strength, with winds topping 100 miles per hour as it moved toward the Florida Keys. Even though it was still 85 miles from the coast, Florida was already being hit with rain and tropical-storm-strength winds. Florida officials ordered a mandatory evacuation affecting 1.9 million people, the largest such evacuation in history.

Crossing through the Keys during the night of September 25-26, Georges headed for landfall on the Mississippi Gulf coast. As the storm advanced through the Gulf, hurricane-force winds extended across a 230-mile-wide swath. These winds produced a storm surge of some 15 feet above normal tide and very heavy rains.

Hurricane Georges made landfall near Biloxi, Mississippi, early on September 28, with maximum sustained winds of 105 miles per hour and gusts up to 125 miles per hour. About 15 inches of rain accompanied the storm in some areas. After reaching the mainland, Georges began to lose strength and stall. By late evening on September 28, the storm was downgraded from a hurricane to a tropical storm, and by midday on September 29, it was again downgraded, this time to tropical depression. This stall, however, led to some locations receiving over 2 feet of rain in a twenty-four-hour period, causing flooding in many places. In the end, though, fewer than 1,000 homes in the continental United States were totally destroyed by the storm.

While damage to the continental United States was extensive, advanced preparations by FEMA and state officials led to no deaths directly attributed to the storm. This was a significant accomplishment, considering the magnitude of the storm and the history of hurricanes hitting the United States.

Jacob P. Kovel

For Further Information:

Federal Emergency Management Agency. "Hurricane Georges Updates." *Storm Watch*, www.fema.gov, September, 1998.

Larmer, Brook. "Natural Disaster?" *Newsweek*, October 26, 1998.

Larmer, Brook, and Susan H. Greenberg. "Fury of Georges." *Newsweek*, October 5, 1998.

Pedersen, Daniel. "A Deadly Spree for Georges." *Newsweek*, October 5, 1998.

Van Dijken, Gert, moderator. "Georges—Updates from the Islands." *The Caribbean Hurricane Page*, www.gobeach.com/hurr.htm, September, 1998.

1998: Hurricane Mitch

Date: October 27, 1998
Place: Central America

Classification: Category 5
Result: More than 11,000 dead, 1 million homeless, $4 billion in damage

Topography. Central America is an isthmus over 1,200 miles in length, connecting the continents of North and South America. It runs from Mexico's southern state of Chiapas to Colombia's western border. Mountainous throughout its entire length, the isthmus is also home to at least twenty-one active volcanoes as well as a number that are dormant. To the east lies the Caribbean Sea, and on the west coast the isthmus is bordered by the Pacific Ocean. Because of the existence of the volcanoes the soil in most of the area is quite fertile, providing excellent sites for plantation crops such as coffee and bananas.

Extensive lowlands exist on both flanks of the isthmus, and deep-water ports are located on both coasts. The plains provide areas for the cultivation of bananas, corn, cotton, and sugarcane. Guatemala, Honduras, Nicaragua, and Costa Rica are homes to some of the world's largest exporters of bananas. The United Fruit Company produces most of its bananas in Guatemala.

The mountain chain that runs through the center of Central America complicates communication and transportation between the east and west coasts. The ports are adequate for coastal ship traffic, but serviceable berths for large ocean-going vessels are limited throughout the area. The history of the area is replete with extensive damage to property and loss of life caused by both frequent volcanic eruptions and earthquakes. All of the isthmus's countries have experienced these disasters from time to time.

Climatology. Considerable diversity of climate exists within the region, given the extremes in eleva-

tion. On the Caribbean coast spacious lowlands and tropical forests extend inland for up to 50 miles. In those areas the weather is generally humid, frequently plagued with excessive rainfall. The lowlands are often referred to as the *tierra caliente*, or hot zone. As one moves toward the center of the isthmus and into the foothills, the weather changes. The area becomes cooler, and the rainfall diminishes as the elevation increases. Coffee plantations thrive in what is referred to as the *tierra templada*, or temperate zone.

The highest elevations in the mountains, *tierra fría*, or the cold zone, provide for distinct seasons. The rainy period lasts from May to October, and sunshine during these months is scarce. The availability of water is sometimes restricted on the western slopes of the mountain ranges. The water-bearing cloud formations are sometimes blocked off by the mountains themselves. The western slopes on the Pacific side are home to both coffee and banana cultivation. Some of the isthmus's most fertile soils are found in these areas. The same rainy season, from May to October, also applies to this region.

The Pacific plains between the mountains and the sea are much more narrow than those on the Caribbean side, and the descent from the highlands is much more abrupt. Water supply can be a problem in the Pacific lowlands as well, with periods of drought not uncommon. Occasionally, heavy rains in the mountains cause severe flooding in the Pacific plains. This proved to be the case when Hurricane Mitch struck the isthmus. El Salvador, especially, suffered substantial damage as a result of the runoff.

Central America is dotted with lakes and contains a number of rivers, most of the which are not navigable. Some of the rivers are dammed and provide hydroelectric power to areas throughout Central America. Many of the lakes contain fresh fish, but transportation problems limit the degree to which this resource can be exploited commercially.

Politics. Central America contains 7 separate independent countries. The 5 original members of the Central America Republic, formed after locals secured their independence from Spain, are Guatemala, El Salvador, Honduras, Nicaragua, and Costa Rica. The sixth, Panama, came into being as a result of the politics involved in building the Panama Canal. It declared its independence in 1903. The seventh, Belize, is a former colony of Great Britain, and used to be called British Honduras. Despite protests from Guatemala, which laid claim to Belize as part of its own territory, the country become independent from Great Britain in 1981.

In the nineteenth century, following their declaration of independence from Spain, the countries of the isthmus became involved in a scene of political chaos. The original group of five members of a hastily constructed federal republic became participants in a series of fratricidal wars in which one after the other sought to dominate the group. Outside economic and political interests also sought to exploit this divisiveness for selfish gains. As late as 1968 Honduras and El Salvador engaged in a brief skirmish called the Soccer War. In the 1980's both El Salvador and Nicaragua experienced civil wars within their borders. General elections in both countries, closely monitored by outsiders, brought an end to these disturbances. Since that time, the countries in the region have attempted to address their internal and external political problems in a more peaceful and cooperative manner.

People. Each of Central America's countries has a different racial and cultural profile. Guatemala, for example, has primarily a Native American population. A strong tribal identification on the part of many people still persists. The indigenous peoples continue to speak their own languages; Spanish is a second language in most of the Indian enclaves. Costa Rica, on the other hand, had few Indians that survived the Spanish conquest and today claims to be the most European of the group, calling itself "the Switzerland of Central America." It does, however, have a substantial black minority on its eastern shore.

Panama has the largest black population on the isthmus, owing to the influx of Caribbean workers into the country at the time the canal was being constructed, early in the twentieth century. El Salvador, the small country on Central America's west coast with no exposure to the Caribbean, is home to few blacks. Its Indian population, for the most part, has been Europeanized owing, in no small degree, to the massacre of a large number of the indigenous population during an internal conflict in 1930.

Belize has a largely black population that immigrated into its boundaries during British colonial rule. Unlike its Central American neighbors, Belize's official language is English. Eastern Nicaragua is more Caribbean in many respects than Hispanic, reflecting its exposure to Caribbean influences. The indigenous inhabitants of its Miskito coastal area speak

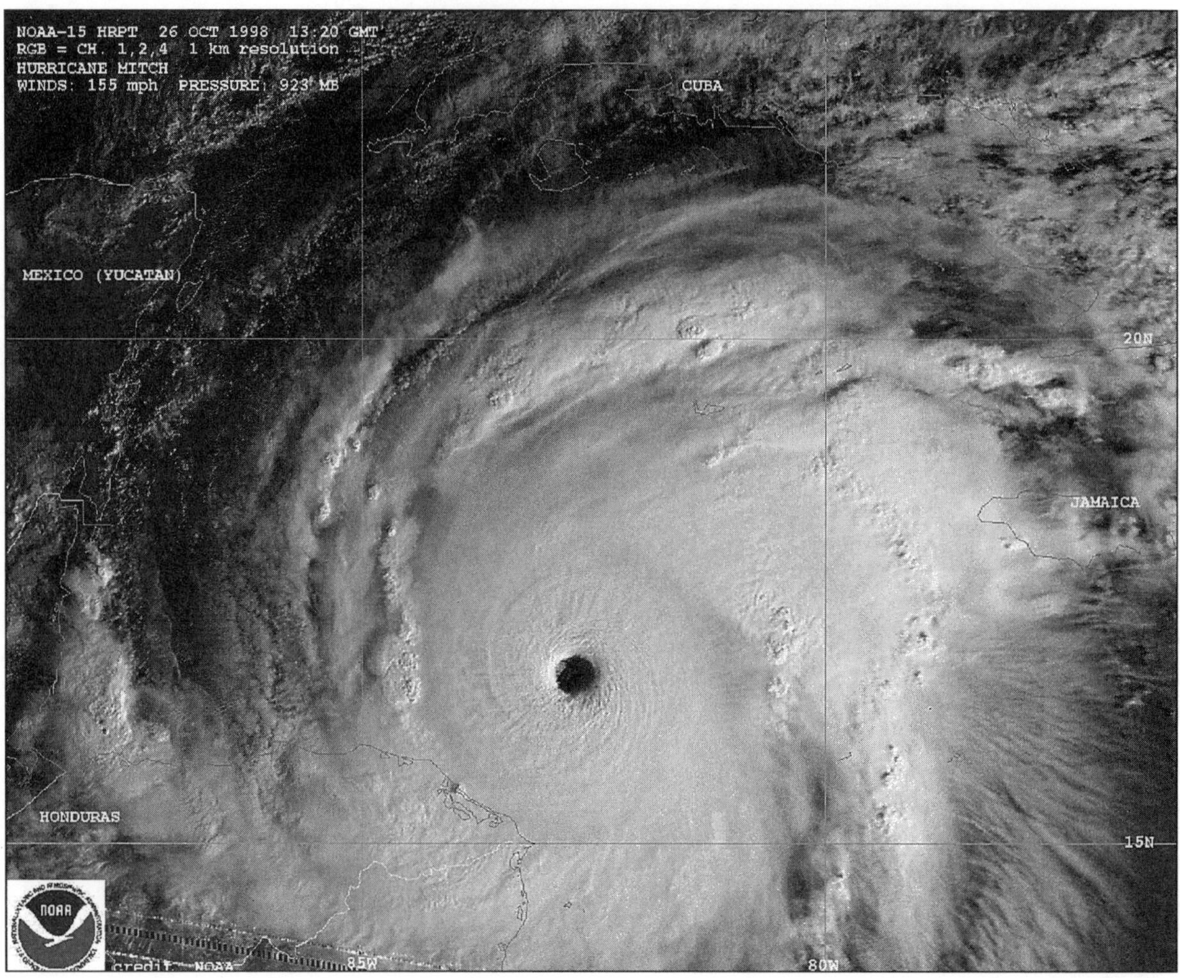

A satellite photo of Hurricane Mitch on October 26, 1998, over the Caribbean Sea on its approach to Central America. (AP/Wide World Photos)

either their own language or English in preference to Spanish. In addition to the Miskitos, some 20,000 English-speaking blacks, descendants of West Indians, make their home in the area. The population of Honduras also reflects the influences of a West Indian immigration, although the majority of its inhabitants are either American Indian or mestizo.

Hurricane Mitch. Hurricane Mitch began as a tropical wave that moved across West Africa beginning on October 8, 1998. For the next seven days it moved over the tropical Atlantic to the Caribbean Sea, entering that body of water on the 18th and 19th. Showers and thunderstorms developed at that time, coming to the attention of a United States Air Force Reserve reconnaissance plane patrolling the area. On October 22, the plane reported that the storm had become a tropical depression, a harbinger of the troublesome weather conditions ahead.

Mitch achieved hurricane strength on October 24, developing heavy winds and dumping enormous quantities of rain on Jamaica and the Cayman Islands. Damage to the Caribbean islands proved to be slight compared to what followed as the storm moved further west. Mitch reached the Central American coast on October 27. The hurricane turned out to be one of the most powerful Atlantic storms on record, with winds exceeding 180 miles per hour. As a result, Central America and southern Mexico experienced torrential rainfall for several days in a row, inundating some principal cities and much of the countryside as well. The U.S. National Hurricane Center classified Mitch as a Category 5 hurricane.

As it moved toward the mainland, the direction of the storm in its earliest stages proved to be unpredictable. Not knowing what to expect, most of the population of Belize City, estimated at 75,000 persons, fled inland. The refugees utilized both private transportation and government-commandeered buses. Mexico's southern state of Quintana Roo evacuated all of its villages in a 165-mile swath south of the city of Playa del Carmen. The tens of thousands of tourists staying in the resort cities of Cancún and Cozumel stood in long lines at airports seeking flights inland to any destination available that was considered outside the danger zone. Cancún had been hit in 1988 by Hurricane Gilbert, during which some 300 people were killed.

After moving briefly through the Caribbean on October 25, Mitch arrived off the coast of Honduras two days later, making landfall on the morning of the 29th. Because of the slow progress of the storm, the rainfall from it reached tremendous proportions, estimated at up to 35 inches initially, primarily in Honduras and Nicaragua. The resulting flash floods and mudslides pouring down from the isthmus's central mountain range killed thousands of people.

The Damage. The damage suffered by the areas reached by Mitch resulted primarily from the rainfall rather than the direct loss caused by the heavy winds themselves. Before it ended, the hurricane dumped a peak load of 50 inches of rain in some areas. The high waters that followed carved paths of destruction that destroyed entire neighborhoods, especially the low-lying communities exposed to raging rivers that had been only small streams prior to the hurricane.

The storm not only destroyed homes but also wiped out roads, schools, and bridges, impeding any attempts to furnish aid to its victims. In addition to the destruction of the isthmus's commercial agriculture, many poor families lost the small plots of land from which they drew much of their basic diet, consisting of corn, beans, rice, and other vegetables. Fertile topsoil washed away in the heavy inundation. Chickens, pigs, and cattle also disappeared under the rising floodwaters. Military mines, souvenirs of the civil wars of the previous decade, washed down from the mountains, ending up in areas where survivors sought to start replanting. A number of deaths and serious injuries occurred after the storm was over as a result of this further threat to life and property.

Substantial damage to the commercial banana plantations along the Central American east coast also meant the loss of livelihood for hundreds of workers. Until the banana area could be replanted, estimated to take a full year at least, no work existed for the majority of the employees of such large concerns as the United Fruit Company and its numerous subsidiaries.

The contamination of local drinking water gave rise to the threat of dysentery and other waterborne communicable diseases for the survivors. Little children were exposed to respiratory illnesses. Wells caved in, debris clogged streams, and rotting garbage contaminated neighborhood cisterns. The authorities advised citizens that water had to be boiled before it could be used for either drinking or cooking. A large number of schools also fell victim to the storm, depriving the children in many areas of the opportunity to continue pursuing their education.

Once the storm hit the Central American mainland, it soon became apparent that the neighboring countries of Honduras and Nicaragua would sustain the most damage, with lesser problems arising in El Salvador and Guatemala. Mitch largely spared Belize, southern Mexico, and Costa Rica.

Nicaragua's most deadly loss occurred when a mudslide, triggered by the collapse of a wall of the volcano Casitas, wiped out whole villages. The onrushing mud and rain reached to the rooftops of the tiny pueblo of El Porvenir, close to the volcano, and buried many of its inhabitants before they had the opportunity to evacuate. Posoltega, another nearby village, met an equally horrendous fate. Only a few hundred of its 2,000 inhabitants survived the sea of mud that tore through the small hamlet.

In its initial assessment, the Honduran government estimated that the final death count in the country could reach 5,000. Honduras's president, Carlos Roberto Flores Facusse, said that the floods and landslides had wiped out many villages as well as whole neighborhoods in the larger cities. Two large rivers, the Ulúa and Chameleon, rose so high as to isolate Honduras's second major city, San Pedro Sula, and convert the valley surrounding it into a lake. The Choluteca River near the country's capital, Tegucigalpa, also flooded over its banks, pouring into the city at such a rapid rate that the water reached the second story of Tegucigalpa's major commercial buildings. The president estimated that the storm had destroyed over 70 percent of the nation's crops, the economic mainstay of this nation of 6 million people. The dollar crop loss amounted to $6 billion for the impoverished country. One million homes needed to be replaced.

El Salvador, on Central America's west coast, suffered mostly from the heavy runoff of rain from the mountains of its eastern highlands. The water poured into the country's principal river, the Lempa, so quickly that it destroyed a number of villages on its banks. Remote villages, such as Chicuma, El Salitre, Las Marías, and Hacienda Vieja, lost all of their subsistence crops.

While Guatemala did not experience the same degree of damage as did neighboring Honduras and Nicaragua, the Polochic River Valley and the southern coast lost over $1 million in vital food supplies as well as a substantial amount of housing and potable water. A plane carrying religious missionaries seeking to do relief work crashed, killing 10 passengers and injuring 7 others. The plane had sought to fly into San Andreas Xecul, 60 miles west of Guatemala City, during the downpour.

Relief Efforts. For Nicaragua and Honduras, the poorest of the Central American republics, Mitch created an economic disaster. Neither country possessed the resources to meet their immediate emergency requirements, much less the long-term essentials needed restore the countries to their pre-hurricane conditions. Their governments pleaded for outside assistance.

The destruction of the roads and bridges throughout Central America precluded any rapid response by surface vehicles to much of the damaged countryside. As a result, both foreign governments and private groups began massive airlifts, utilizing light planes and helicopters to ship emergency food and medical supplies into the more remote areas of both countries.

President Bill Clinton of the United States pledged $80 million for immediate emergency aid, then raised the total dollar commitment to $300 million by March of 1999. The U.S. Congress had an additional total increase to over $1 billion under advisement. Former U.S. president Jimmy Carter urged that the $16 billion in foreign debt owed by Honduras and Nicaragua be forgiven by their first-world creditors. Scores of nongovernmental organizations throughout Europe, including those from such small countries as Ireland, Finland, and Denmark, joined in the major effort. Mitch had set the economic development of Central America back by twenty years.

The United States government sent in Army engineers to reconstruct the key roads necessary to open the badly damaged backlands. The engineers built four pontoon bridges at critical junctures to replace key destroyed structures. These so-called temporary replacements were designed to be strong enough to support all but the heaviest of trucks, supplies, and equipment. Military helicopters from a number of countries continued to push far into the hinterland to deliver food and medical supplies and to establish bases from which the rescuers could operate. Medical teams from the U.S. Army, Navy, and Air Force, the reserves from all three, and the National Guard sent in medical teams to cope with respiratory and gastrointestinal diseases and cholera.

A major problem developed with the indiscriminate influx of various types of medicinal supplies into the beleaguered countries. Initially, the affected countries provided little direction for their transmittal. Finally, the Pan American Health Organization took over and established a priority list of critical medicines that the personnel on site felt were needed, seeking to end the shipment of unwanted or inappropriate drugs.

The response to requests for aid by Central Americans living abroad proved to be overwhelming. Southern California, home to many Central American immigrant families, responded with tons of medicines, food, and clothing. The American Red Cross alone received over 100,000 inquiries during the first five days following the commencement of the storm. Directed to deliver their contributions to the consulates representing Honduras and Nicaragua, those anxious to help found that these officials could not cope with the influx of aid packages. The sorting, boxing, and storage of the goods and their transportation to Central America were beyond the physical and financial capabilities of these small offices.

Confusion reigned when the goods arrived at their Central American destinations as well. Neither Honduras nor Nicaragua had organized distribution centers to process the materials received from various overseas sources. At the Honduran port of Puerto Cortés, by early January, over 1,000 huge containers of relief supplies lay unclaimed at the docks. Ships seeking to unload more supplies had a difficult time finding any adequate space ashore for their cargos.

In the case of Nicaragua, the Catholic Church had been designated initially to fulfill the distribution function. A change in government plans resulted when President Arnoldo Alemán assigned his Liberal Party to the task, seeking to take political advantage of the catastrophe. Not only did many of the contributions end up in hands for which they were not originally intended, but also a great deal of the material continued to remain stranded at the airport and seaport sites where it had been unloaded. Alemán, in a further gesture of defiance to the international community, refused to allow President Fidel Castro's Cuban medical teams and supplies to enter the country, despite the great shortage throughout the devastated areas of Nicaragua.

Faced with the backup of supplies, relief agencies asked the public to donate cash rather than goods. Unfortunately, those wishing to help preferred to collect canned goods and clothing in their own communities regardless of how appropriate such collected goods were. They continued to ship the accumulated commodities to the already-crowded port facilities. Once there, local relief organizations, hamstrung by local government red tape, quite often lacked the funds to pay for shipment of the goods into the interior.

Moreover, the fact that the major commercial fruit companies had to devise a recovery program before they could start producing for the export market exacerbated the problems for both Honduras and Nicaragua further. The two countries characteristically suffer a high employment rate, but Mitch wiped out most of the jobs held by those agricultural workers with the big fruit producers. The number of laborers heading north to the United States to find work increased substantially. Often they were accompanied by young boys and girls of school age who could not continue their education because of the heavy destruction of the school plants throughout the isthmus. Moreover, rumors began to circulate among the unemployed that the U.S. government had approved the entry of immigrants into the country because of Mitch's damage. Such was not the case. The government had agreed only to suspend temporarily the deportation of illegals already residing in the United States. The new wave of illegal immigrants, when apprehended, were turned back by the American border patrol.

Conclusion. Hurricane Mitch precipitated a series of unmitigated disasters in Central America. Thousands of residents of the isthmus either died, suffered debilitating injuries, or simply disappeared as a result of the storm's ferocity. The infrastructure to all the countries in the area experienced extensive damage. Mitch destroyed roads, bridges, communications lines, and key public buildings, such as hospitals and schools. Critical crops and livestock were lost in the ensuing deluge. Long after the storm was over, corpses littered the paths of the torrents of water that had passed through inhabited areas.

Within a few days of the storm's inception it became apparent that both Honduras and Nicaragua would sustain the greatest long-term damage. Whole communities in both countries had disappeared under the heavy inundations that accompanied the fierce winds. The governments of the two nations could not cope with the immensity of the tragedy. The rest of the world community would have to respond to the emergency created by the hurricane.

During the decade prior to the 1998 debacle, the U.S. government gradually had reduced the aid it had provided to the fledgling democracies of the area. Having determined that Central America would not fall under the influence of the former Soviet Union and Cuba, the interests of American foreign policy turned elsewhere. U.S. aid had amounted to hundreds of millions of dollars to rightist elements in conflict with leftist governments and insurrections, but the American government stopped paying. By 1998, aid to El Salvador had diminished from $500 million annually to a mere $35 million. At one time in the 1980's the American government had spent over $300 million a year supporting Nicaragua's Contra movement. In 1998 the U.S. commitment to that country had dropped to $24 million.

Nevertheless, when Mitch hit the isthmus the United States quickly furnished emergency aid. Other countries, large and small, forwarded money and relief supplies as well. The World Bank provided emergency loans for the reconstruction of both housing and commercial buildings. Nongovernmental organizations, such as the American Red Cross, Cooperative for American Relief to Everywhere (CARE), and United Nations children's fund (UNICEF), responded promptly with goods and aid workers.

The work of the rehabilitation of Central America would continue for a long time, taking years for the area to recover from the effects of the storm. The vast majority of the region's poor were still living below the poverty level in 2000. It has been argued that the United States could do some things to alleviate some of Central America's economic and social problems: canceling the outstanding debt owed to the United States by Honduras and Nicaragua, offering the same trade agreements to Central America as are presently enjoyed by Mexico and Canada under the North American Free Trade Agreement (NAFTA) treaty, and giving Central American immigrants currently residing and working in the United States at least temporary protection from deportation until the economic emergencies in their home countries are brought under control.

Suggested measures for improving the Central American economy from within included the affected governments launching social programs designed to alleviate the economic hardship facing the poorest segments of their societies. Restoration of the economies cannot be left to market conditions or to chance. Also, a common emergency policy in the region would ensure a cooperative effort to meet the threat of natural disasters such as Hurricane Mitch, which are likely to threaten Central America again in the future.

Carl Henry Marcoux

For Further Information:

Bulmer-Thomas, Victor. *The Political Economy of Central America Since 1920.* Cambridge, England: Cambridge University Press, 1987.

Granby, Phil. "Hurricane Mitch Aftermath." *Journal of the American Medical Association,* April 7, 1999, 1162.

LeoGrande, William M. "Central America's Agony." *The Nation,* January 25, 1999, 21.

MacEoin, Gary. "Corruption Hinders Hurricane Recovery." *National Catholic Reporter,* April 30, 1999, 6.

_______. "Disaster Aid Likely to Benefit Nicaragua's Wealthy." *National Catholic Reporter,* March 26, 1999, 6.

Morris, Kelly. "Illness from Hurricane Mitch Starts to Rise." *Lancet,* November 28, 1998, 1766.

Padgett, Tim. "The Catastrophe of Hurricane Mitch." *Time International,* November 16, 1998.

Ramsay, Sarah. "Local and International Aid Mobilised in the Wake of Hurricane Mitch." *Lancet,* November 14, 1998, 1608.

Rodriguez, Mario. *Central America.* Englewood Cliffs, N.J.: Prentice-Hall, 1965.

Woodward, Ralph Lee, Jr. *Central America: A Nation Divided.* 2d ed. New York: Oxford University Press, 1985.

Zarembo, Alan. "Helping Honduras." *U.S. News and World Report,* December 21, 1998.

_______. "A Hurricane's Orphans." *Newsweek,* March 15, 1999, 43.

1999: Hurricane Floyd

Date: September 14-17, 1999
Place: From the Bahamas to the U.S. East Coast, especially North Carolina
Classification: Category 4
Speed: 155 miles per hour on September 14, 1999
Result: 68 dead, more than 3 million people evacuated

When it was officially announced on September 14, 1999, that Hurricane Floyd, then approximately 360 miles east-southeast of Miami, Florida, and bearing down on the Bahamas and the Florida coast, was estimated to have attained wind speeds of nearly 155 miles per hour, it triggered the most massive evacuation and storm-preparation efforts in the history of the United States. Floyd was even feared to be the long-anticipated "Hurricane X"—a megastorm or series of such storms brought about by new conditions set in motion by global warming. Under altered climatic conditions it was thought possible that hurricane wind speeds exceeding 200 miles per hour might regularly occur. As it was, Floyd became a very high Category 4 storm; only a shade below the Category 5 range, which had last occurred during the devastating visitation of Hurricane Camille in 1969. Adding to the level of anxiety was the altered demographics of the southeastern United States, the area that had experienced the greatest population growth since the time of Camille.

Floyd was given the designation of a tropical storm on September 8,1999, and as it traveled west-northwest toward the Caribbean it was able to gain enormous strength from an exceptionally large stretch of warm water in its path, as well as the lack of westerly winds that might have served to impede its surge of power. By September 10, it was upgraded to a Category 1 hurricane. On September 12, it skirted the Leeward and Virgin Islands and Puerto Rico, and the following day it had risen dramatically in intensity to Category 4, at 140 miles per hour. At that stage, the

Bahamas was put under warning, and the Florida Coast from West Palm Beach to Cocoa Beach was placed under hurricane watch.

On September 14, Floyd had been measured at close to the Category 5 level and was being compared to both Camille and the Labor Day Hurricane of 1935. The watch was extended from Florida City, Florida, to Savannah, Georgia. An evacuation was ordered for coastal residents of Florida, Georgia, and—as it appeared probable that Floyd might veer to the north—South and North Carolina. The evacuation proved to be chaotic, creating massive traffic jams along clogged interstates and secondary roads into southeastern tidewater Virginia and spawning numerous traffic accidents. Walt Disney World at Orlando, Florida, closed for the first time ever, NASA abandoned Cape Canaveral, and the Kennedy Space Center was stripped of all personnel apart from a skeleton staff of 102 technicians. President Bill Clinton cut short diplomatic meetings in New Zealand and, preemptively declaring Florida, Georgia, South Carolina, and North Carolina disaster areas, returned to Washington, D.C., on September 16.

Floyd entered the Bahamas on September 15, downing power lines, felling trees, disabling airport runways, and flooding the coast. Abaco, Eleuthera, Cat, and San Salvador Islands received the brunt of the storm s force, but the evacuation of much of the population to shelters in inland areas is credited with minimizing casualties. Only 1 individual perished, a Freeport man who was washed out to sea.

As Floyd approached the mainland, the storm began to weaken in intensity. First, Hurricane Dennis, which had traveled through the same area only days previously, had left a residue of cold ocean water that worked to dissipate Floyd s power. Then, a cold westerly air flow began to work on Floyd s top layers, beginning, in effect, a process of "decapitation." While slowing the hurricane's gusts, the wester also brought about greater precipitation. As predicted, Floyd

Rows of houses in Greenville, North Carolina, are flooded after Hurricane Floyd dumped as much as 20 inches of rain on the coast. (FEMA)

turned to the north and made landfall near Cape Fear, North Carolina, though much diminished in power, becoming a Category 2 hurricane with winds around 100 miles per hour.

The eye of the hurricane passed through eastern North Carolina and Virginia and along the coast as far as New York and Connecticut. While the wind damage was minimized, the flooding from torrential rains accounted for much of the damage to human beings and to property. States of emergency were declared in both New Jersey and New York, where the scheduled United Nations meeting was postponed.

Although 11 states—Florida, Georgia, South Carolina, North Carolina, Virginia, Maryland, Delaware, New Jersey, Pennsylvania, New York, and Connecticut—qualified for damage relief, North Carolina's coastal plain sustained the greatest devastation. There, 15 to 20 inches of rain fell, there were 56 deaths by drowning and in traffic accidents, some 6,000 houses were destroyed, and 12,000 buildings sustained severe damage. Damage estimates three months later stood at over $6 billion at the least. Rescue operations by scuba divers and by helicopter crews, who retrieved people marooned on the rooftops of their own homes, kept down the death toll.

In North Carolina and, to a lesser extent, southeastern Virginia, the problem was compounded by the rainfall that had been dumped by Hurricane Dennis, which had already saturated the ground and waterways. The overflow of the Tar, Cape Fear, Neuse, and Waccamaw Rivers inundated over 6,000 square miles. A potentially serious health problem developed when the carcasses of some 100,000 drowned hogs and 50,000 cattle, as well as organic waste material, began to decompose and fouled the surrounding waters. Thirty cities were flooded, 2,000 residents of the small town of Tarboro, North Carolina, were forced to seek refuge in emergency shelters, and over 300 roads were rendered impassable, making rescue and relief efforts more difficult. The deterioration of Hurricane Floyd only continued further speculation as to when the real "Hurricane X" would strike, speculation that was only heightened by the revelation that the hurricane season of 1999 had seen, for the first time, 5 storms of Category 4 intensity: Bret, Cindy, Floyd, Gert, and Lenny.

Raymond Pierre Hylton

For Further Information:

Beals, Gregory, and Evan Thomas. "The Path of an Imperfect Storm." *Newsweek*, September 27, 1999, 23-25.

Begley, Sharon, and Thomas Hayden. "Floyd's Watery Wrath." *Newsweek*, September 27, 1999, 19-21.

Lemonick, Michael D. "A Very Close Call." *Time*, September 27, 1999, 35-37.

Marcus, David L., and David Whitman. "More Sound than Fury." *U.S. News and World Report*, September 27, 1999, 16-22.

Nash, J. Madeleine. "Wait Till Next Time." *Time*, September 27, 1999, 39-40.

Richmond Times-Dispatch, September 12-17, 1999.

Natural Disasters

Time Line

c. 65,000,000 B.C.E.: Atlantic Ocean meteorite
c. 48,000-13,000 B.C.E.: Arizona meteorite
c. 5000 B.C.E.: Mazama eruption, Oregon
2400 B.C.E.: The Great Flood, worldwide
c. 1470 B.C.E.: Thera eruption, Aegean Sea
464 B.C.E.: Sparta earthquake
430 B.C.E.: The Plague of Athens
373 B.C.E.: Greece earthquake
218 B.C.E.: Alps avalanche, Italy
217 B.C.E.: North Africa earthquake
64 C.E.: The Great Fire of Rome
79: Vesuvius eruption, Italy
c. 186: Taupo eruption, New Zealand
365: Egypt earthquake
365: Egypt tsunami
526: Syria earthquake
541: The Plague of Justinian, Constantinople and the Mediterranean
1064: Egypt famine
1169: Etna eruption, Sicily
1200: Egypt famine
1228: Netherlands flood
1281: Japan typhoon
1290: China earthquake
1320: The Black Death epidemic, Europe
1360: France hailstorm
1362: Öræfajökull eruption, Iceland
1421: Netherlands flood
1490: Europe syphilis epidemic
1502: Dominican Republic hurricane
1520: Aztec Empire smallpox epidemic
1556: China earthquake
1559: Florida hurricane
1570: Netherlands flood
1574: The Flood of Leiden, Netherlands
1586: Kelut eruption, Indonesia
1591: Taal eruption, Philippines
1596: Japan tsunami
1601: Russia famine
1622: Cuba hurricane
1631: Vesuvius eruption, Italy
1638: England tornado
1640: Japan tsunami
1642: China flood
1657: The Meireki Fire, Japan
1665: The Great Plague of London
1666: West Indies hurricane
1666: The Great Fire of London
1669: Etna eruption, Sicily
1683: Timor eruption, Indonesia
1692: Jamaica earthquakes
1703: England hurricane
1703: Japan earthquake
1713: North Carolina hurricane
1715: Florida hurricane
1718: Switzerland avalanche
1722: Russia ergotism epidemic
1722: Jamaica hurricane
1735: New England diphtheria epidemic
1737: Bay of Bengal cyclone
1737: India cyclone
1740: Ireland famine
1741: Cotopaxi eruption, Ecuador
1741: Japan tsunami
1755: Lisbon earthquake, Portugal
1759: Jorullo eruption, Mexico
1766: Mayon eruption, Philippines
1769: India famine
1769: Italy lightning strike
1772: Papandayan eruption, Indonesia
1775: The Hurricane of Independence, U.S. East Coast
1779: Sakurajima eruption, Japan
1780: The Great Hurricane of 1780, Caribbean
1783: Asama eruption, Japan
1783: Italy earthquake
1783: Laki eruption, Iceland
1784: South Carolina hailstorm
1788: Jamaica famine
1790: Kilauea eruption, Hawaii
1790: Skull Famine, India
1792: Unzen eruption, Japan
1793: Philadelphia yellow fever epidemic
1794: Tunquraohua eruption, Ecuador
1795: Denmark fire
1797: Ecuador earthquake
1798: New England blizzard

1799: Spain and North Africa yellow fever epidemic
1806: Guadeloupe hurricane
1807: Luxembourg lightning strike
1811: New Madrid earthquakes, Missouri
1812: Venezuela earthquake
1812: La Soufrière eruption, St. Vincent
1814: Mayon eruption, Philippines
1815: Tambora eruption, Indonesia
1815: Year Without a Summer famine, United States and Europe
1819: Gulf Coast hurricane
1822: Galung Gung eruption, Indonesia
1822: Chile earthquake
1824: Neva River flood, Russia
1825: Puerto Rico hurricane
1825: Canada fire
1829: Europe cholera or Asiatic cholera epidemic
1831: Caribbean and Gulf Coast hurricane
1832: New York City cholera epidemic
1832: New Orleans cholera epidemic
1833: India famine
1835: Cosigüina eruption, Nicaragua
1835: Chile earthquake
1835: Florida hurricane
1837: West Indies hurricane
1840: Worldwide cholera epidemic
1840: Mississippi tornado
1841: The October Gale, Massachusetts (hurricane)
1842: Germany fire
1844: Mexico hurricane
1845: Nevado del Ruiz eruption, Colombia
1845: The Great Irish Famine
1846: Florida hurricane
1846: The Donner Party famine, California
1848: New York City cholera epidemic
1848: Turkey fire
1851: San Francisco fire
1853: India hailstorm
1853: Niuafo'ou eruption, Tonga
1853: New Orleans yellow fever epidemic
1856: Greece lightning strike
1856: Louisiana hurricane
1857: Fort Tejon earthquake, California
1859: Ecuador earthquake
1860: Iowa tornado
1862: Massachusetts hurricane
1862: China typhoon
1863: Philippines earthquake
1866: Georgia hurricane
1866: Canada fire
1867: New Orleans yellow fever epidemic
1867: San Narciso Hurricane, Puerto Rico and Virgin Islands
1868: South America earthquake
1868: California earthquake
1869: Sexby's Gale, Massachusetts (hurricane)
1870: Turkey fire
1871: Wisconsin fire
1871: The Great Chicago Fire
1872: Owens Valley earthquake, California
1872: Zanzibar hurricane
1872: Vesuvius eruption, Italy
1872: The Great Boston Fire
1873: The Great Nova Scotia Hurricane
1876: India famine
1876: China famine
1877: Cotopaxi eruption, Ecuador
1878: Mississippi Valley yellow fever epidemic
1879: Scotland bridge collapse (wind gusts)
1880: Missouri tornado
1880: England mine explosion
1881: Turkey earthquake
1882: Iowa tornado
1883: North Sea ship collision (fog)
1883: Krakatau eruption, Indonesia
1883: North Atlantic ship collision (fog)
1884: U.S. South tornadoes
1884: Colorado mine explosion
1884: Virginia mine explosion
1885: India earthquake
1886: U.S. Midwest blizzard
1886: Minnesota tornado
1886: Texas hurricane
1886: Charleston earthquake, South Carolina
1887: Riviera earthquakes
1887: Switzerland flood
1887: Yellow River flood, China
1887: English Channel ship collision (fog)
1888: The Great Blizzard of 1888, U.S. Northeast
1888: India hailstorm
1888: Bandai eruption, Japan
1889: The Johnstown Flood, Pennsylvania
1890: Mississippi River flood
1890: Kentucky tornado
1890: English Channel shipwreck (fog)
1891: U.S. Midwest blizzard

1891: Japan earthquake
1892: Worldwide cholera epidemic
1892: Worldwide bubonic plague epidemic
1892: Oklahoma mine explosion
1892: Switzerland avalanche
1893: The Sea Islands Hurricane, Georgia and the Carolinas
1893: U.S. South hurricane
1894: Minnesota fire
1896: Texas tornado
1896: St. Louis tornado
1896: Japan tsunami
1897: India earthquake
1897: Mayon eruption, Philippines
1898: U.S. Northeast blizzard
1899: Wisconsin tornado
1899: San Ciriaco Hurricane, Puerto Rico
1899: Alaska earthquake
1900: Galveston Hurricane, Texas
1900: Uganda African sleeping sickness epidemic
1900: New York State typhoid epidemic
1900: New Jersey fire
1902: Russia earthquake
1902: Guatemala earthquake
1902: La Soufrière eruption, St. Vincent
1902: Pelée eruption, Martinique
1902: Texas tornado
1902: Pennsylvania mine explosion
1902: Santa María eruption, Guatemala
1902: Turkestan earthquake
1903: South Pacific tsunami
1903: Canada rockslide
1903: Armenia earthquake
1903: Kansas and Missouri Rivers flood
1903: Georgia tornado
1903: Willow Creek flood, Oregon
1903: Wyoming mine explosion
1904: Maryland fire
1904: Arkansas River flood, Colorado
1905: India earthquake
1905: Oklahoma tornado
1905: Vesuvius eruption, Italy
1905: Italy earthquake
1906: Masaya eruption, Nicaragua
1906: Colombia and Ecuador earthquakes
1906: Taiwan earthquake
1906: San Francisco earthquake
1906: Chile earthquake
1906: Florida hurricane
1907: Jamaica earthquake
1907: West Virginia mine explosion
1907: Pennsylvania mine explosion
1908: Massachusetts fire
1908: U.S. South tornadoes
1908: Siberia comet or meteorite
1908: Pennsylvania mine explosion
1908: Italy earthquake
1909: Caribbean and Mexico hurricane
1909: U.S. South hurricane
1909: Illinois fire
1910: Washington State avalanche
1911: Taal eruption, Philippines
1911: New York and Pennsylvania heat wave
1911: Yangtze River flood, China
1912: Mississippi River flood
1912: The Sinking of *Titanic* (iceberg)
1912: Katmai eruption, Alaska
1912: The Black River Hurricane, Jamaica
1913: Nebraska tornadoes
1913: Ohio, Indiana, and Illinois flood
1913: New Mexico mine explosion
1914: West Virginia mine explosion
1914: Canada ship collision (fog)
1915: Italy earthquake
1915: British Columbia avalanche
1915: Zhu River flood, China
1915: Texas and Louisiana hurricane
1915: Louisiana hurricane
1916: Netherlands flood
1916: Southern California flood
1916: Chicago heat wave
1916: United States polio epidemic
1916: Alps avalanche, Italy
1917: English Channel ship collision (fog)
1917: Colorado mine explosion
1917: Illinois tornadoes
1917: Boquerón eruption, El Salvador
1917: New York City heat wave
1917: Nova Scotia ship explosion
1918: Worldwide influenza epidemic
1918: Minnesota fire
1919: Kelut eruption, Indonesia
1919: Minnesota tornado
1919: Florida and Texas hurricane
1920: Chicago tornado
1920: U.S. South tornado
1920: The Great Russian Famine
1920: China earthquake
1921: Arkansas River flood, Colorado

1921: San Antonio River flood, Texas
1922: U.S. East Coast blizzard
1923: Wyoming mine explosion
1923: The Great Kwanto Earthquake, Japan
1923: Northern California fire
1924: West Virginia mine explosion
1924: U.S. South tornado
1924: Ohio tornado
1925: The Great Tri-State Tornado, Missouri, Illinois, and Indiana
1925: Ohio airship crash (wind gusts)
1926: Mauna Loa eruption, Hawaii
1926: New Jersey lightning strike
1926: The Great Miami Hurricane
1926: Cuba hurricane
1926: Colombia landslide
1927: Texas tornado
1927: Mississippi River flood
1927: U.S. Midwest tornado
1927: China earthquake
1927: Kentucky River flood
1927: St. Louis tornado
1927: New England flood
1927: Pittsburgh factory explosion
1928: St. Francis Dam Collapse, Southern California (flood)
1928: Pennsylvania mine explosion
1928: Rokatenda eruption, Indonesia
1928: San Felipe Hurricane, Florida and Caribbean
1929: Pennsylvania mine explosion
1930: Dominican Republic hurricane
1931: Ecuador landslide
1931: Italy avalanche
1931: New Zealand earthquake
1931: China mine explosion
1931: United States heat wave
1931: Yangtze River flood, China
1931: The Great Belize Hurricane
1931: Merapi eruption, Indonesia
1932: U.S. South tornadoes
1932: Dust Bowl, Great Plains (dust storms)
1932: France mudslides
1932: California airship unmooring (wind gusts)
1932: San Ciprian Hurricane, Puerto Rico
1932: Cuba hurricane
1933: Japan tsunami
1933: Long Beach earthquake
1933: Mexico hurricane
1933: France train collision (fog)
1934: India earthquake
1934: Japan fire
1935: Florida hurricane
1935: The Hairpin Hurricane, Caribbean and Central America
1936: U.S. South tornadoes
1937: Ohio River flood, U.S. Midwest
1937: Texas school explosion
1937: The *Hindenburg* Disaster, New Jersey (explosion)
1938: Custer Creek flood, Montana
1938: The Great New England Hurricane of 1938
1939: Chile earthquake
1939: Yellow River flood, China
1939: Japan blizzard
1939: Turkey earthquake
1940: Washington State bridge collapse (wind gusts)
1940: U.S. Midwest blizzard
1941: China freeze
1941: U.S. Midwest blizzard
1941: Peru mudslide
1942: Mississippi tornadoes
1943: Paricutín eruption, Mexico
1943: Montana mine explosion
1943: Black Wednesday smog, Los Angeles
1944: India ship explosion
1944: West Virginia, Pennsylvania, and Maryland tornado
1944: Cleveland gas tanks explosion
1944: Typhoon Cobra, Philippines
1945: U.S. Midwest tornadoes
1945: New York City plane crash (fog)
1946: Hawaii tsunami
1946: Japan tsunami
1947: Western Europe freeze
1947: Texas, Oklahoma, and Kansas tornadoes
1947: Texas ship explosion
1947: Florida and Gulf Coast hurricane
1948: U.S. South freeze
1948: U.S. Midwest and East freeze
1948: Columbia River flood, U.S. Northwest
1948: Japan earthquake
1948: New York City heat wave
1948: Pennsylvania smog
1949: Missouri tornado
1949: Ecuador earthquake

1949: China fire
1950: India earthquake
1950: Nebraska flood
1950: Huai and Yangtze Rivers flood, China
1951: Lamington eruption, New Guinea
1951: Alps avalanche
1951: Kansas and Missouri Rivers flood
1951: Texas heat wave
1951: Hurricane Charlie, Jamaica and Mexico
1951: Po River flood, Italy
1951: Hibok-Hibok eruption, Philippines
1951: Illinois mine explosion
1952: Sierra Nevada blizzard
1952: Austria avalanches
1952: U.S. South tornadoes
1952: Kern County earthquake, California
1952: The Great London Fog (smog)
1952: Austria avalanche
1953: North Sea flood, Netherlands, Great Britain, and Belgium
1953: Texas tornado
1953: The Flint-Beecher Tornado, Michigan and Ohio
1953: Massachusetts tornado
1954: Alps avalanche, Austria, Italy, Germany, Switzerland
1954: Rio Grande flood, Texas and Mexico
1954: Tibet flood
1954: Iran flood
1954: Hurricane Carol, U.S. East Coast
1954: Algeria earthquake
1954: Hurricane Hazel, Caribbean, U.S. East Coast, Canada
1954: Haiti landslide
1955: Kansas and Oklahoma tornadoes
1955: Hurricanes Connie and Diane, U.S. East Coast
1955: Typhoon Iris, China
1955: California heat wave
1955: Hurricane Hilda, Mexico
1955: Hurricane Janet, Windward Islands, Belize, and Mexico
1955: Mexico landslide
1955: Northern California flood
1956: Europe blizzard
1956: New England ice storm
1956: North Atlantic ship collision (fog)
1956: Hurricane Flossy, southeastern United States
1956: Cleveland National Forest fire
1957: Virginia mine explosion
1957: Missouri tornado
1957: Hurricane Audrey, Louisiana and Texas
1957: Western Europe heat wave
1957: Iran earthquake
1957: Finland lightning strike
1957: Iraq hailstorm
1957: England train collision (fog)
1958: U.S. East Coast and Midwest blizzard
1958: Saudi Arabia heat wave
1958: Nova Scotia rockslide
1959: The Great Leap Forward Famine, China
1959: North Sea ship collision (iceberg)
1959: St. Louis tornado
1959: Malpasset Dam Collapse, France (flood)
1960: South Africa rockslide
1960: Philippines rockslide
1960: Morocco earthquakes
1960: Chile earthquake
1960: Hawaii tsunami
1960: India heat wave
1960: Hurricane Donna, Caribbean, U.S. East Coast
1960: New York City plane collision (fog)
1961: Ukraine mudslide
1961: Japan landslides and mudslides
1961: Hurricane Carla, Texas
1961: Hurricane Hattie, Belize
1962: Peru avalanche
1962: Germany mine explosion
1962: Germany flood
1962: Peru mudslide
1962: Iran earthquake
1962: Spain flood
1962: London smog
1962: Pennsylvania mine explosion
1963: Agung eruption, Indonesia
1963: Yugoslavia earthquake
1963: Hurricane Flora, Haiti and Cuba
1963: The Vaiont Dam Disaster, Italy (rockslide)
1963: Surtsey Island eruption, Iceland
1963: Japan mine explosion
1963: Maryland lightning strike
1964: The Great Alaska Earthquake
1964: Hurricane Cleo, Caribbean and Florida
1965: British Columbia avalanche
1965: Chile earthquake
1965: U.S. Midwest tornadoes
1965: India mine explosion

1965: Japan mine explosion
1965: India heat wave
1965: Arkansas and South Platte Rivers flood, Great Plains
1965: Hurricane Betsy, Florida and Louisiana
1965: Taal eruption, Philippines
1965: Brazil heat wave
1966: Brazil flood
1966: Rio de Janeiro landslides, mudslides, and rockslides
1966: India heat wave
1966: New York City heat wave
1966: Turkey earthquake
1966: Hurricane Inez, Caribbean, Florida, and Mexico
1966: The Aberfan Disaster, Wales (landslide)
1966: Italy flood
1967: Brazil flood
1967: Rio de Janeiro landslides, mudslides, and rockslides
1967: Mexico heat wave
1967: Portugal flood
1967: U.S. Southwest blizzard
1968: Democratic Republic of Congo mudslide
1968: Mexico heat wave
1968: Arenal eruption, Costa Rica
1968: India flood
1968: Japan heat wave
1968: North Africa drought
1968: Iran earthquake
1969: Southern California mudslides
1969: Hurricane Camille, U.S. South
1969: Tunisia flood
1969: Rio de Janeiro heat wave
1970: France avalanche
1970: Texas tornado
1970: Peru earthquake
1970: East Pakistan cyclone
1971: Sylmar earthquake, Southern California
1971: Mississippi Delta tornadoes
1971: Peru avalanche
1971: Afghanistan landslide
1972: Argentina heat wave
1972: Iran blizzard
1972: Buffalo Creek flood, West Virginia
1972: Bangladesh tornado
1972: Iran earthquake
1972: India heat wave
1972: Rhodesia mine explosion
1972: Rapid Creek flood, South Dakota
1972: Hong Kong landslides
1972: Hurricane Agnes, U.S. East Coast
1972: Philippines flood
1972: Africa, Asia famine
1972: Nicaragua earthquakes
1973: Heimaey Island eruption, Iceland
1973: Mississippi River flood
1973: Mexico earthquake
1974: Australia flood
1974: Tubarão River flood, Brazil
1974: The Jumbo Tornado Outbreak, U.S. South, Midwest, and Canada
1974: Bangladesh flood
1974: Hurricane Fifi, Mexico, Central America
1974: Cyclone Tracy, Australia
1974: Pakistan earthquake
1975: China earthquake
1975: Turkey earthquake
1975: Rhodesia lightning strike
1975: India mine explosion
1976: Guatemala earthquake
1976: Italy earthquake
1976: Teton Dam Collapse, Idaho (flood)
1976: Zaire, Sudan Ebola virus epidemic
1976: Philadelphia Legionnaires' disease epidemic
1976: China earthquake
1976: Big Thompson River flood, Colorado
1976: Hurricane Belle, U.S. East Coast
1976: Philippines earthquake
1976: Turkey earthquake
1977: Nyiragongo eruption, Zaire
1977: Romania earthquake
1977: Tenerife plane collision, Canary Islands (fog)
1978: Scotland blizzard
1978: Yamuna and Ganges Rivers flood, India
1978: Iran earthquake
1979: Soviet Union anthrax epidemic
1979: Texas and Oklahoma tornadoes
1979: Hurricane David, Dominican Republic, Puerto Rico, and the U.S. South
1979: Hurricane Frederic, Alabama and Mississippi
1980: Worldwide AIDS epidemic
1980: Mount St. Helens eruption, Washington

1980: United States heat wave
1980: Hurricane Allen, Caribbean, Mexico, and Texas
1980: Algeria earthquake
1980: Italy earthquake
1981: Africa drought
1981: Yellow River flood, China
1982: San Francisco landslides and mudslides
1982: Austria avalanche
1982: Alps avalanches, France
1982: El Chichón eruption, Mexico
1982: Nicaragua and Honduras flood
1982: Pacific Ocean El Niño
1982: Ganges River flood, India
1982: North Yemen earthquake
1983: Australia fire
1983: Ganges and Brahmaputra Rivers flood, Bangladesh
1984: Africa famine
1984: The Carolinas tornadoes
1985: Canada, Ohio, and Pennsylvania tornadoes
1985: Italy flood
1985: Texas plane crash (wind gusts)
1985: Mexico City earthquake
1985: Nevado del Ruiz eruption, Colombia
1986: Lake Nyos eruption, Cameroon
1986: California drought
1987: Ecuador earthquake
1987: China fire
1987: Texas tornado
1987: Whittier earthquake, Southern California
1988: Bangladesh flood
1988: Yellowstone National Park fire
1988: Hurricane Gilbert, Jamaica and Mexico
1988: Armenia earthquakes
1989: Soviet Union pipeline explosion
1989: Hurricane Hugo, Caribbean and the Carolinas
1989: Loma Prieta earthquake, Northern California
1989: Alabama tornado
1990: Iran earthquake
1990: Philippines earthquake
1991: Italy ship collision (fog)
1991: Kansas tornado
1991: Bangladesh cyclone
1991: Pinatubo eruption, Philippines
1991: Yangtze River flood, China
1991: The Oakland Hills Fire, Northern California
1991: Tropical Storm Thelma, Philippines
1991: California dust storm
1992: Turkey earthquakes
1992: Mexico sewer explosion
1992: Landers and Big Bear earthquakes, Southern California
1992: Hurricane Andrew, Florida, Louisiana, and the Bahamas
1992: Indonesia earthquake
1993: U.S. East Coast blizzard
1993: The Great Mississippi River Flood of 1993
1993: India earthquakes
1993: Southern California fire
1994: Northridge earthquake, Southern California
1994: U.S. South tornado
1994: Bolivia earthquake
1994: Tropical Storm Gordon, Caribbean and Florida
1994: Merapi eruption, Indonesia
1995: California flood
1995: Northern Europe flood
1995: Kobe earthquake, Japan
1995: India avalanche
1995: Zaire Ebola virus epidemic
1995: Arizona dust storm
1995: Texas hailstorm
1995: Russia earthquake
1995: Honduras lightning strike
1995: India heat wave
1995: U.S. Midwest and Northwest heat wave
1995: Hurricane Luis, Caribbean
1995: Hurricane Marilyn, U.S. Virgin Islands
1995: Hurricane Opal, U.S. South
1995: Iceland avalanche
1996: The Blizzard of '96, U.S. East Coast
1996: India avalanches
1996: Sudan sandstorm
1996: Nepal blizzard
1996: Pakistan heat wave
1996: Oklahoma and Texas heat wave
1996: Hurricane Bertha, Puerto Rico, Virgin Islands, U.S. East Coast
1996: Yosemite National Park rockslide
1996: Spain flood
1996: India blizzard
1996: Hurricane Fran, U.S. East Coast

1996: Hurricane Hortense, Dominican Republic and Puerto Rico
1996: Iceland flooding (glacier)
1996: Hurricane Lili, Central America, Cuba, and Great Britain
1996: Oregon mudslides
1996: Europe freeze
1996: U.S. West Coast flood
1997: Pacific Ocean El Niño
1997: Iran earthquakes (northwest)
1997: Pakistan earthquake
1997: Red River flood, North Dakota and Minnesota
1997: Egypt sandstorm
1997: Iran earthquake (northeast)
1997: Hong Kong avian influenza epidemic
1997: Texas tornado
1997: Soufrière Hills eruption, Montserrat
1997: Rhine and Oder Rivers flood, Central Europe
1997: Michigan tornado
1997: Australia landslide
1997: Colorado River flood, Arizona
1997: Hurricane Nora, Mexico, California, and Arizona
1997: Indonesia fire
1997: Italy earthquakes
1997: Hurricane Pauline, Mexico
1998: Canada ice storm
1998: U.S. Northeast ice storm
1998: Afghanistan earthquake
1998: Mississippi, Alabama, and Georgia tornado
1998: U.S. South heat wave
1998: U.S. East Coast and Midwest drought
1998: Papua New Guinea tsunami
1998: Yangtze River flood, China
1998: Hurricane Georges, Caribbean and U.S. South
1998: Texas flood
1998: Nigeria pipeline explosion
1998: Democratic Republic of Congo lightning strike
1998: Hurricane Mitch, Central America
1999: The Blizzard of '99, U.S. Midwest and East Coast
1999: Colombia earthquake
1999: France avalanche
1999: Washington State avalanche
1999: Switzerland avalanche
1999: Austria avalanches
1999: Alaska avalanche
1999: Oklahoma and Kansas tornado
1999: U.S. Midwest and East Coast heat wave
1999: New York encephalitis epidemic
1999: Utah tornado
1999: Turkey earthquake
1999: Mexico flood
1999: Hurricane Floyd, Bahamas, U.S. East Coast
1999: Taiwan earthquake
1999: Venezuela flood
2000: Georgia tornadoes
2000: Mozambique flood
2000: New Mexico fire

Geographical List

AFGHANISTAN
1971: Afghanistan landslide
1998: Afghanistan earthquake

AFRICA. *See also individual countries*
217 B.C.E.: North Africa earthquake
1799: Spain and North Africa yellow fever epidemic
1968: North Africa drought
1972: Africa, Asia famine
1981: Africa drought
1984: Africa famine

ALABAMA
1979: Hurricane Frederic, Alabama and Mississippi
1989: Alabama tornado
1995: Hurricane Opal, U.S. South

ALASKA
1899: Alaska earthquake
1912: Katmai eruption, Alaska
1964: The Great Alaska Earthquake
1999: Alaska avalanche

ALGERIA
1954: Algeria earthquake
1980: Algeria earthquake

ALPS
218 B.C.E.: Alps avalanche, Italy
1916: Alps avalanche, Italy
1951: Alps avalanche
1954: Alps avalanche, Austria, Italy, Germany, Switzerland
1982: Alps avalanches, France

ARGENTINA
1972: Argentina heat wave

ARIZONA
c. 48,000-13,000 B.C.E.: Arizona meteorite
1995: Arizona dust storm
1997: Colorado River flood, Arizona
1997: Hurricane Nora, Mexico, California, and Arizona

ARMENIA
1903: Armenia earthquake
1988: Armenia earthquakes

ASIA. *See also individual countries*
1972: Africa, Asia famine

ATLANTIC OCEAN
c. 65,000,000 B.C.E.: Atlantic Ocean meteorite
1883: North Sea ship collision (fog)
1883: North Atlantic ship collision (fog)
1887: English Channel ship collision (fog)
1890: English Channel shipwreck (fog)
1912: The Sinking of *Titanic* (iceberg)
1917: English Channel ship collision (fog)
1953: North Sea flood, Netherlands, Great Britain, and Belgium
1956: North Atlantic ship collision (fog)
1959: North Sea ship collision (iceberg)
1977: Tenerife plane collision, Canary Islands (fog)

AUSTRALIA
1974: Australia flood
1974: Cyclone Tracy, Australia
1983: Australia fire
1997: Australia landslide

AUSTRIA
1952: Austria avalanches
1952: Austria avalanche
1954: Alps avalanche, Austria, Italy, Germany, Switzerland
1982: Austria avalanche
1999: Austria avalanches

BAHAMAS
1992: Hurricane Andrew, Florida, Louisiana, and the Bahamas
1999: Hurricane Floyd, Bahamas, U.S. East Coast

BANGLADESH. *See also* EAST PAKISTAN
1972: Bangladesh tornado
1974: Bangladesh flood
1983: Ganges and Brahmaputra Rivers flood, Bangladesh

1988: Bangladesh flood
1991: Bangladesh cyclone

BELGIUM
1953: North Sea flood, Netherlands, Great Britain, and Belgium

BELIZE
1931: The Great Belize Hurricane
1955: Hurricane Janet, Windward Islands, Belize, and Mexico
1961: Hurricane Hattie, Belize
1974: Hurricane Fifi, Mexico, Central America

BOLIVIA
1994: Bolivia earthquake

BRAZIL
1965: Brazil heat wave
1966: Rio de Janeiro landslides, mudslides, and rockslides
1966: Brazil flood
1967: Brazil flood
1967: Rio de Janeiro landslides, mudslides, and rockslides
1969: Rio de Janeiro heat wave
1974: Tubarão River flood, Brazil

BRITISH COLUMBIA
1915: British Columbia avalanche
1965: British Columbia avalanche

CALIFORNIA
1846: The Donner Party famine, California
1851: San Francisco fire
1857: Fort Tejon earthquake, California
1868: California earthquake
1872: Owens Valley earthquake, California
1906: San Francisco earthquake
1916: Southern California flood
1923: Northern California fire
1928: St. Francis Dam Collapse, Southern California (flood)
1932: California airship unmooring (wind gusts)
1933: Long Beach earthquake
1943: Black Wednesday smog, Los Angeles
1952: Sierra Nevada blizzard
1952: Kern County earthquake, California
1955: California heat wave
1955: Northern California flood
1956: Cleveland National Forest fire
1969: Southern California mudslides
1971: Sylmar earthquake, Southern California
1982: San Francisco landslides and mudslides
1986: California drought
1987: Whittier earthquake, Southern California
1989: Loma Prieta earthquake, Northern California
1991: The Oakland Hills Fire, Northern California
1991: California dust storm
1992: Landers and Big Bear earthquakes, Southern California
1993: Southern California fire
1994: Northridge earthquake, Southern California
1995: California flood
1996: Yosemite National Park rockslide
1997: Hurricane Nora, Mexico, California, and Arizona

CAMEROON
1986: Lake Nyos eruption, Cameroon

CANADA
1825: Canada fire
1866: Canada fire
1873: The Great Nova Scotia Hurricane
1903: Canada rockslide
1914: Canada ship collision (fog)
1915: British Columbia avalanche
1917: Nova Scotia ship explosion
1954: Hurricane Hazel, Caribbean, U.S. East Coast, Canada
1958: Nova Scotia rockslide
1965: British Columbia avalanche
1985: Canada, Ohio, and Pennsylvania tornadoes
1998: Canada ice storm

CANARY ISLANDS
1977: Tenerife plane collision, Canary Islands (fog)

CARIBBEAN
1502: Dominican Republic hurricane
1622: Cuba hurricane
1666: West Indies hurricane
1692: Jamaica earthquakes
1722: Jamaica hurricane
1780: The Great Hurricane of 1780, Caribbean
1788: Jamaica famine
1806: Guadeloupe hurricane

1812: La Soufrière eruption, St. Vincent
1825: Puerto Rico hurricane
1831: Caribbean and Gulf Coast hurricane
1837: West Indies hurricane
1867: San Narciso Hurricane, Puerto Rico and Virgin Islands
1899: San Ciriaco Hurricane, Puerto Rico
1902: La Soufrière eruption, St. Vincent
1902: Pelée eruption, Martinique
1907: Jamaica earthquake
1909: Caribbean and Mexico hurricane
1912: The Black River Hurricane, Jamaica
1926: Cuba hurricane
1928: San Felipe Hurricane, Florida and Caribbean
1930: Dominican Republic hurricane
1932: San Ciprian Hurricane, Puerto Rico
1932: Cuba hurricane
1935: The Hairpin Hurricane, Caribbean and Central America
1951: Hurricane Charlie, Jamaica and Mexico
1954: Hurricane Hazel, Caribbean, U.S. East Coast, Canada
1954: Haiti landslide
1955: Hurricane Janet, Windward Islands, Belize, and Mexico
1960: Hurricane Donna, Caribbean, U.S. East Coast
1963: Hurricane Flora, Haiti and Cuba
1964: Hurricane Cleo, Caribbean and Florida
1966: Hurricane Inez, Caribbean, Florida, and Mexico
1979: Hurricane David, Dominican Republic, Puerto Rico, and the U.S. South
1980: Hurricane Allen, Caribbean, Mexico, and Texas
1988: Hurricane Gilbert, Jamaica and Mexico
1989: Hurricane Hugo, Caribbean and the Carolinas
1992: Hurricane Andrew, Florida, Louisiana, and the Bahamas
1994: Tropical Storm Gordon, Caribbean and Florida
1995: Hurricane Luis, Caribbean
1995: Hurricane Marilyn, U.S. Virgin Islands and Puerto Rico
1996: Hurricane Bertha, Puerto Rico, Virgin Islands, U.S. East Coast
1996: Hurricane Hortense, Dominican Republic and Puerto Rico
1996: Hurricane Lili, Central America, Cuba, and Great Britain
1997: Soufrière Hills eruption, Montserrat
1998: Hurricane Georges, Caribbean and U.S. South
1999: Hurricane Floyd, Bahamas, U.S. East Coast

CENTRAL AMERICA. *See also individual countries*
1935: The Hairpin Hurricane, Caribbean and Central America
1998: Hurricane Mitch, Central America

CHILE
1822: Chile earthquake
1835: Chile earthquake
1906: Chile earthquake
1939: Chile earthquake
1960: Chile earthquake
1965: Chile earthquake

CHINA
1290: China earthquake
1556: China earthquake
1642: China flood
1862: China typhoon
1876: China famine
1887: Yellow River flood, China
1911: Yangtze River flood, China
1915: Zhu River flood, China
1920: China earthquake
1927: China earthquake
1931: China mine explosion
1931: Yangtze River flood, China
1939: Yellow River flood, China
1941: China freeze
1949: China fire
1950: Huai and Yangtze Rivers flood, China
1955: Typhoon Iris, China
1959: The Great Leap Forward Famine, China
1975: China earthquake
1976: China earthquake
1981: Yellow River flood, China
1987: China fire
1991: Yangtze River flood, China
1998: Yangtze River flood, China

COLOMBIA
1845: Nevado del Ruiz eruption, Colombia
1906: Colombia and Ecuador earthquakes

EUROPE. *See also individual countries*
1320: The Black Death (epidemic)
1490: Europe syphilis epidemic
1815: Year Without a Summer, United States and Europe (famine)
1829: Europe cholera or Asiatic cholera epidemic
1947: Western Europe freeze
1956: Europe blizzard
1957: Western Europe heat wave
1995: Northern Europe flood
1996: Europe freeze
1997: Rhine and Oder Rivers flood, Central Europe

FINLAND
1957: Finland lightning strike

FLORIDA
1559: Florida hurricane
1715: Florida hurricane
1835: Florida hurricane
1846: Florida hurricane
1906: Florida hurricane
1919: Florida and Texas hurricane
1926: The Great Miami Hurricane
1928: San Felipe Hurricane, Florida and Caribbean
1935: Florida hurricane
1947: Florida and Gulf Coast hurricane
1964: Hurricane Cleo, Caribbean and Florida
1965: Hurricane Betsy, Florida and Louisiana
1966: Hurricane Inez, Caribbean, Florida, and Mexico
1992: Hurricane Andrew, Florida, Louisiana, and the Bahamas
1994: Tropical Storm Gordon, Caribbean and Florida
1995: Hurricane Opal, U.S. South

FRANCE
1360: France hailstorm
1887: Riviera earthquakes
1932: France mudslides
1933: France train collision (fog)
1959: Malpasset Dam Collapse, France (flood)
1970: France avalanche
1982: Alps avalanches, France
1999: France avalanche

GEORGIA
1866: Georgia hurricane
1893: The Sea Islands Hurricane, Georgia and the Carolinas
1903: Georgia tornado
1995: Hurricane Opal, U.S. South
2000: Georgia tornadoes

GERMANY
1842: Germany fire
1954: Alps avalanche, Austria, Italy, Germany, Switzerland
1962: Germany mine explosion
1962: Germany flood

GREAT BRITAIN. *See also* ENGLAND; IRELAND; SCOTLAND; WALES
1953: North Sea flood, Netherlands, Great Britain, and Belgium
1996: Hurricane Lili, Central America, Cuba, and Great Britain

GREAT PLAINS
1932: Dust Bowl, Great Plains (dust storms)
1965: Arkansas and South Platte Rivers flood, Great Plains

GREECE
464 B.C.E.: Sparta earthquake
430 B.C.E.: The Plague of Athens
373 B.C.E.: Greece earthquake
1856: Greece lightning strike

GUADELOUPE
1806: Guadeloupe hurricane

GUATEMALA
1902: Guatemala earthquake
1902: Santa María eruption, Guatemala
1974: Hurricane Fifi, Mexico, Central America
1976: Guatemala earthquake

GULF COAST
1819: Gulf Coast hurricane
1947: Florida and Gulf Coast hurricane

HAITI
1954: Haiti landslide
1963: Hurricane Flora, Haiti and Cuba

HAWAII
1790: Kilauea eruption, Hawaii
1926: Mauna Loa eruption, Hawaii
1946: Hawaii tsunami
1960: Hawaii tsunami

HONDURAS
1974: Hurricane Fifi, Mexico, Central America
1995: Honduras lightning strike
1996: Hurricane Lili, Central America, Cuba, and Great Britain

HONG KONG
1972: Hong Kong landslides
1997: Hong Kong avian influenza epidemic

ICELAND
1362: Öræfajökull eruption, Iceland
1783: Laki eruption, Iceland
1963: Surtsey Island eruption, Iceland
1973: Heimaey Island eruption, Iceland
1995: Iceland avalanche
1996: Iceland flooding (glacier)

IDAHO
1976: Teton Dam Collapse, Idaho (flood)
1988: Yellowstone National Park fire

ILLINOIS
1871: The Great Chicago Fire
1909: Illinois fire
1916: Chicago heat wave
1917: Illinois tornadoes
1920: Chicago tornado
1925: The Great Tri-State Tornado, Missouri, Illinois, and Indiana
1951: Illinois mine explosion

INDIA
1737: Bay of Bengal cyclone
1769: India famine
1790: Skull Famine, India
1833: India famine
1853: India hailstorm
1876: India famine
1885: India earthquake
1888: India hailstorm
1897: India earthquake
1905: India earthquake
1934: India earthquake
1944: India ship explosion
1950: India earthquake
1960: India heat wave
1965: India mine explosion
1965: India heat wave
1966: India heat wave
1968: India flood
1972: India heat wave
1975: India mine explosion
1978: Yamuna and Ganges Rivers flood, India
1982: Ganges River flood, India
1993: India earthquakes
1995: India avalanche
1995: India heat wave
1996: India avalanches
1996: India blizzard

INDIANA
1925: The Great Tri-State Tornado, Missouri, Illinois, and Indiana

INDONESIA
1586: Kelut eruption, Indonesia
1683: Timor eruption, Indonesia
1772: Papandayan eruption, Indonesia
1815: Tambora eruption, Indonesia
1822: Galung Gung eruption, Indonesia
1883: Krakatau eruption, Indonesia
1919: Kelut eruption, Indonesia
1928: Rokatenda eruption, Indonesia
1931: Merapi eruption, Indonesia
1963: Agung eruption, Indonesia
1992: Indonesia earthquake
1994: Merapi eruption, Indonesia
1997: Indonesia fire

IOWA
1860: Iowa tornado
1882: Iowa tornado

IRAN
1954: Iran flood
1957: Iran earthquake
1962: Iran earthquake
1968: Iran earthquake
1972: Iran blizzard
1972: Iran earthquake
1978: Iran earthquake

1990: Iran earthquake
1997: Iran earthquakes (northwest)
1997: Iran earthquake (northeast)

IRAQ
1957: Iraq hailstorm

IRELAND
1740: Ireland famine
1845: The Great Irish Famine

ITALY
218 B.C.E.: Alps avalanche, Italy
64 C.E.: The Great Fire of Rome
79: Vesuvius eruption, Italy
1169: Etna eruption, Sicily
1631: Vesuvius eruption, Italy
1669: Etna eruption, Sicily
1769: Italy lightning strike
1783: Italy earthquake
1872: Vesuvius eruption, Italy
1887: Riviera earthquakes
1905: Vesuvius eruption, Italy
1905: Italy earthquake
1908: Italy earthquake
1915: Italy earthquake
1916: Alps avalanche, Italy
1931: Italy avalanche
1951: Po River flood, Italy
1954: Alps avalanche, Austria, Italy, Germany, Switzerland
1963: The Vaiont Dam Disaster, Italy (rockslide)
1966: Italy flood
1976: Italy earthquake
1980: Italy earthquake
1985: Italy flood
1991: Italy ship collision (fog)
1997: Italy earthquakes

JAMAICA
1692: Jamaica earthquakes
1722: Jamaica hurricane
1788: Jamaica famine
1907: Jamaica earthquake
1912: The Black River Hurricane, Jamaica
1951: Hurricane Charlie, Jamaica and Mexico
1988: Hurricane Gilbert, Jamaica and Mexico

JAPAN
1281: Japan typhoon
1596: Japan tsunami
1640: Japan tsunami
1657: The Meireki Fire, Japan
1703: Japan earthquake
1741: Japan tsunami
1779: Sakurajima eruption, Japan
1783: Asama eruption, Japan
1792: Unzen eruption, Japan
1888: Bandai eruption, Japan
1891: Japan earthquake
1896: Japan tsunami
1923: The Great Kwanto Earthquake, Japan
1933: Japan tsunami
1934: Japan fire
1939: Japan blizzard
1946: Japan tsunami
1948: Japan earthquake
1961: Japan landslides and mudslides
1963: Japan mine explosion
1965: Japan mine explosion
1968: Japan heat wave
1995: Kobe earthquake, Japan

KANSAS
1903: Kansas and Missouri Rivers flood
1947: Texas, Oklahoma, and Kansas tornadoes
1951: Kansas and Missouri Rivers flood
1955: Kansas and Oklahoma tornadoes
1991: Kansas tornado

KENTUCKY
1890: Kentucky tornado
1927: Kentucky River flood

LOUISIANA
1832: New Orleans cholera epidemic
1853: New Orleans yellow fever epidemic
1856: Louisiana hurricane
1867: New Orleans yellow fever epidemic
1915: Texas and Louisiana hurricane
1915: Louisiana hurricane
1957: Hurricane Audrey, Louisiana and Texas
1965: Hurricane Betsy, Florida and Louisiana
1971: Mississippi Delta tornadoes
1992: Hurricane Andrew, Florida, Louisiana, and the Bahamas

LUXEMBOURG
1807: Luxembourg lightning strike

MARTINIQUE
1902: Pelée eruption, Martinique

MARYLAND
1904: Maryland fire
1944: West Virginia, Pennsylvania, and Maryland tornado
1963: Maryland lightning strike

MASSACHUSETTS
1841: The October Gale, Massachusetts (hurricane)
1862: Massachusetts hurricane
1869: Sexby's Gale, Massachusetts (hurricane)
1872: The Great Boston Fire
1908: Massachusetts fire
1953: Massachusetts tornado

MEDITERRANEAN
c. 1470 B.C.E.: Thera eruption, Aegean Sea
541: The Plague of Justinian, Constantinople and the Mediterranean
1169: Etna eruption, Sicily
1669: Etna eruption, Sicily
1887: Riviera earthquakes

MEXICO
1520: Aztec Empire smallpox epidemic
1759: Jorullo eruption, Mexico
1844: Mexico hurricane
1909: Caribbean and Mexico hurricane
1933: Mexico hurricane
1943: Paricutín eruption, Mexico
1951: Hurricane Charlie, Jamaica and Mexico
1954: Rio Grande flood, Texas and Mexico
1955: Hurricane Hilda, Mexico
1955: Hurricane Janet, Windward Islands, Belize, and Mexico
1955: Mexico landslide
1966: Hurricane Inez, Caribbean, Florida, and Mexico
1967: Mexico heat wave
1968: Mexico heat wave
1973: Mexico earthquake
1974: Hurricane Fifi, Mexico, Central America
1980: Hurricane Allen, Caribbean, Mexico, and Texas
1982: El Chichón eruption, Mexico
1985: Mexico City earthquake
1988: Hurricane Gilbert, Jamaica and Mexico
1992: Mexico sewer explosion
1997: Hurricane Nora, Mexico, California, and Arizona
1997: Hurricane Pauline, Mexico
1999: Mexico flood

MICHIGAN
1953: The Flint-Beecher Tornado, Michigan and Ohio
1997: Michigan tornadoes

MIDWEST, U.S.
1886: Midwest blizzard
1891: Midwest blizzard
1927: Midwest tornado
1937: Ohio River flood, Midwest
1940: Midwest blizzard
1941: Midwest blizzard
1945: Midwest tornadoes
1948: Midwest and East freeze
1958: East Coast and Midwest blizzard
1965: Midwest tornadoes
1974: The Jumbo Tornado Outbreak, South, Midwest, and Canada
1995: Midwest and Northwest heat wave
1998: East Coast and Midwest drought
1999: The Blizzard of '99, Midwest and East Coast
1999: Midwest and East Coast heat wave

MINNESOTA
1886: Minnesota tornado
1894: Minnesota fire
1918: Minnesota fire
1919: Minnesota tornado
1997: Red River flood, North Dakota and Minnesota

MISSISSIPPI
1840: Mississippi tornado
1878: Mississippi Valley yellow fever epidemic
1942: Mississippi tornadoes
1971: Mississippi Delta tornadoes
1979: Hurricane Frederic, Alabama and Mississippi
1998: Mississippi, Alabama, and Georgia tornado

MISSISSIPPI RIVER
1890: Mississippi River flood
1912: Mississippi River flood
1927: Mississippi River flood
1973: Mississippi River flood
1993: The Great Mississippi River Flood of 1993

MISSOURI
1811: New Madrid earthquakes, Missouri
1880: Missouri tornado
1896: St. Louis tornado
1903: Kansas and Missouri Rivers flood
1925: The Great Tri-State Tornado, Missouri, Illinois, and Indiana
1927: St. Louis tornado
1949: Missouri tornado
1951: Kansas and Missouri Rivers flood
1957: Missouri tornado
1959: St. Louis tornado

MONTANA
1938: Custer Creek flood, Montana
1943: Montana mine explosion
1988: Yellowstone National Park fire

MONTSERRAT
1997: Soufrière Hills eruption, Montserrat

MOROCCO
1960: Morocco earthquakes

MOZAMBIQUE
2000: Mozambique flood

NEBRASKA
1913: Nebraska tornadoes
1950: Nebraska flood

NEPAL
1996: Nepal blizzard

NETHERLANDS
1228: Netherlands flood
1421: Netherlands flood
1570: Netherlands flood
1574: The Flood of Leiden, Netherlands
1916: Netherlands flood
1953: North Sea flood, Netherlands, Great Britain, and Belgium

NEW ENGLAND
1735: New England diphtheria epidemic
1798: New England blizzard
1927: New England flood
1938: The Great New England Hurricane of 1938
1954: Hurricane Carol, U.S. East Coast
1956: New England ice storm
1960: Hurricane Donna, Caribbean, U.S. East Coast

NEW GUINEA
1951: Lamington eruption, New Guinea

NEW JERSEY
1900: New Jersey fire
1926: New Jersey lightning strike
1937: The *Hindenburg* Disaster, New Jersey (explosion)

NEW MEXICO
1913: New Mexico mine explosion
2000: New Mexico fire

NEW YORK
1832: New York City cholera epidemic
1848: New York City cholera epidemic
1900: New York State typhoid epidemic
1911: New York and Pennsylvania heat wave
1917: New York City heat wave
1945: New York City plane crash (fog)
1948: New York City heat wave
1960: New York City plane collision (fog)
1966: New York City heat wave
1999: New York encephalitis epidemic

NEW ZEALAND
c. 186: Taupo eruption, New Zealand
1931: New Zealand earthquake

NICARAGUA
1835: Cosigüina eruption, Nicaragua
1906: Masaya eruption, Nicaragua
1972: Nicaragua earthquakes
1982: Nicaragua and Honduras flood
1996: Hurricane Lili, Central America, Cuba, and Great Britain

NIGERIA
1998: Nigeria pipeline explosion

NORTH CAROLINA
1713: North Carolina hurricane
1893: The Sea Islands Hurricane, Georgia and the Carolinas
1954: Hurricane Carol, U.S. East Coast
1984: The Carolinas tornadoes
1989: Hurricane Hugo, Caribbean and the Carolinas
1995: Hurricane Opal, U.S. South
1996: Hurricane Fran, U.S. East Coast
1999: Hurricane Floyd, Bahamas, U.S. East Coast

NORTH DAKOTA
1997: Red River flood, North Dakota and Minnesota

NORTH SEA
1883: North Sea ship collision (fog)
1953: North Sea flood, Netherlands, Great Britain, and Belgium
1959: North Sea ship collision (iceberg)

NORTH YEMEN
1982: North Yemen earthquake

NOVA SCOTIA
1873: The Great Nova Scotia Hurricane
1917: Nova Scotia ship explosion
1958: Nova Scotia rockslide

OHIO
1913: Ohio, Indiana, and Illinois flood
1924: Ohio tornado
1925: Ohio airship crash (wind gusts)
1944: Cleveland gas tanks explosion
1953: The Flint-Beecher Tornado, Michigan and Ohio

OKLAHOMA
1892: Oklahoma mine explosion
1905: Oklahoma tornado
1947: Texas, Oklahoma, and Kansas tornadoes
1979: Texas and Oklahoma tornadoes
1996: Oklahoma and Texas heat wave
1999: Oklahoma and Kansas tornado

OREGON
c. 5000 B.C.E.: Mazama eruption, Oregon
1903: Willow Creek flood, Oregon
1996: Oregon mudslides

PACIFIC OCEAN
1853: Niuafo'ou eruption, Tonga
1903: South Pacific tsunami
1951: Lamington eruption, New Guinea
1982: Pacific Ocean El Niño
1997: Pacific Ocean El Niño

PAKISTAN
1974: Pakistan earthquake
1996: Pakistan heat wave
1997: Pakistan earthquake

PAPUA NEW GUINEA
1951: Lamington eruption, New Guinea
1998: Papua New Guinea tsunami

PENNSYLVANIA
1793: Philadelphia yellow fever epidemic
1889: The Johnstown Flood, Pennsylvania
1902: Pennsylvania mine explosion
1907: Pennsylvania mine explosion
1908: Pennsylvania mine explosion
1927: Pittsburgh factory explosion
1928: Pennsylvania mine explosion
1929: Pennsylvania mine explosion
1944: West Virginia, Pennsylvania, and Maryland tornado
1948: Pennsylvania smog
1962: Pennsylvania mine explosion
1976: Philadelphia Legionnaires' disease epidemic

PERU
1941: Peru mudslide
1962: Peru avalanche
1962: Peru mudslide
1970: Peru earthquake
1971: Peru avalanche

PHILIPPINES
1591: Taal eruption, Philippines
1766: Mayon eruption, Philippines
1814: Mayon eruption, Philippines
1863: Philippines earthquake
1897: Mayon eruption, Philippines
1911: Taal eruption, Philippines
1944: Typhoon Cobra, Philippines
1951: Hibok-Hibok eruption, Philippines
1960: Philippines rockslide

1965: Taal eruption, Philippines
1972: Philippines flood
1976: Philippines earthquake
1990: Philippines earthquake
1991: Pinatubo eruption, Philippines
1991: Tropical Storm Thelma, Philippines

PORTUGAL
1755: Lisbon earthquake, Portugal
1967: Portugal flood

PUERTO RICO
1825: Puerto Rico hurricane
1867: San Narciso Hurricane, Puerto Rico and Virgin Islands
1899: San Ciriaco Hurricane, Puerto Rico
1932: San Ciprian Hurricane, Puerto Rico
1979: Hurricane David, Dominican Republic, Puerto Rico, and the U.S. South
1995: Hurricane Marilyn, U.S. Virgin Islands and Puerto Rico
1996: Hurricane Bertha, Puerto Rico, Virgin Islands, U.S. East Coast
1996: Hurricane Hortense, Dominican Republic and Puerto Rico

RHODESIA
1972: Rhodesia mine explosion
1975: Rhodesia lightning strike

ROMANIA
1977: Romania earthquake

RUSSIA. *See also* SOVIET UNION
1601: Russia famine
1722: Russia ergotism epidemic
1824: Neva River flood, Russia
1902: Russia earthquake
1908: Siberia comet or meteorite
1920: The Great Russian Famine
1995: Russia earthquake

ST. VINCENT
1812: La Soufrière eruption, St. Vincent
1902: La Soufrière eruption, St. Vincent

SAUDI ARABIA
1958: Saudi Arabia heat wave

SCOTLAND
1879: Scotland bridge collapse (wind gusts)
1978: Scotland blizzard

SIBERIA
1908: Siberia comet or meteorite

SOUTH, U.S.
1884: South tornadoes
1893: South hurricane
1908: South tornadoes
1909: South hurricane
1920: South tornado
1924: South tornado
1932: South tornadoes
1936: South tornadoes
1948: South freeze
1952: South tornadoes
1969: Hurricane Camille, U.S. South
1979: Hurricane David, Dominican Republic, Puerto Rico, and the South
1994: South tornado
1998: South heat wave
1998: Hurricane Georges, Caribbean and South

SOUTH AFRICA
1960: South Africa rockslide

SOUTH CAROLINA
1784: South Carolina hailstorm
1886: Charleston earthquake, South Carolina
1893: The Sea Islands Hurricane, Georgia and the Carolinas
1984: The Carolinas tornadoes
1989: Hurricane Hugo, Caribbean and the Carolinas
1996: Hurricane Fran, U.S. East Coast

SOUTH DAKOTA
1972: Rapid Creek flood, South Dakota

SOVIET UNION. *See also* RUSSIA
1961: Ukraine mudslide
1979: Soviet Union anthrax epidemic
1989: Soviet Union pipeline explosion

SPAIN
1799: Spain and North Africa yellow fever epidemic
1962: Spain flood

1977: Tenerife plane collision, Canary Islands (fog)
1996: Spain flood

SUDAN
1976: Zaire, Sudan Ebola virus epidemic
1996: Sudan sandstorm

SWITZERLAND
1718: Switzerland avalanche
1887: Switzerland flood
1892: Switzerland avalanche
1954: Alps avalanche, Austria, Italy, Germany, Switzerland
1999: Switzerland avalanche

SYRIA
526: Syria earthquake

TAIWAN
1906: Taiwan earthquake
1999: Taiwan earthquake

TENERIFE
1977: Tenerife plane collision, Canary Islands (fog)

TENNESSEE
1971: Mississippi Delta tornadoes

TEXAS
1886: Texas hurricane
1896: Texas tornado
1900: Galveston Hurricane, Texas
1902: Texas tornado
1915: Texas and Louisiana hurricane
1919: Florida and Texas hurricane
1921: San Antonio River flood, Texas
1927: Texas tornado
1937: Texas school explosion
1947: Texas, Oklahoma, and Kansas tornadoes
1947: Texas ship explosion
1951: Texas heat wave
1953: Texas tornado
1954: Rio Grande flood, Texas and Mexico
1957: Hurricane Audrey, Louisiana and Texas
1961: Hurricane Carla, Texas
1970: Texas tornado
1979: Texas and Oklahoma tornadoes
1980: Hurricane Allen, Caribbean, Mexico, and Texas
1985: Texas plane crash (wind gusts)
1987: Texas tornado
1995: Texas hailstorm
1997: Texas tornado
1998: Texas flood

TIBET
1954: Tibet flood

TONGA
1853: Niuafo'ou eruption, Tonga

TUNISIA
1969: Tunisia flood

TURKESTAN
1902: Turkestan earthquake

TURKEY
541: The Plague of Justinian, Constantinople and the Mediterranean
1848: Turkey fire
1870: Turkey fire
1881: Turkey earthquake
1939: Turkey earthquake
1966: Turkey earthquake
1975: Turkey earthquake
1976: Turkey earthquake
1992: Turkey earthquakes
1999: Turkey earthquake

UGANDA
1900: Uganda African sleeping sickness epidemic

UKRAINE
1961: Ukraine mudslide

UNITED STATES. *See also individual states and regions*
1735: New England diphtheria epidemic
1775: The Hurricane of Independence, East Coast
1798: New England blizzard
1815: Year Without a Summer, United States and Europe
1884: South tornadoes
1886: Midwest blizzard
1888: The Great Blizzard of 1888, Northeast
1891: Midwest blizzard
1893: South hurricane